THE
GHOST DANCE

THE
GHOST DANCE

James Mooney

Published in the U.S.A. 1996 by JG Press
Distributed by World Publications, Inc.

The JG Press imprint is a trademark of JG Press, Inc.,
455 Somerset Avenue, North Dighton, MA 02764.

This edition published by special arrangement
with W.S. Konecky Associates, Inc.

ISBN: 1-57215-201-X

T   100663

Say, shall not I at last attain
  Some height, from whence the Past is clear,
  In whose immortal atmosphere
I shall behold my dead again?
                    Bayard Taylor.

For the fires grow cold and the dances fail,
  And the songs in their echoes die;
And what have we left but the graves beneath,
  And, above, the waiting sky?
                    The Song of the Ancient People.

My Father, have pity on me!
I have nothing to eat,
I am dying of thirst—
Everything is gone!
                    Arapaho Ghost Song.

Publisher's Note

This edition of James Mooney's Ghost Dance is a reprint of Part 2 of the Fourteenth Annual Report of the Bureau of Ethnology to the Secretary of the Smithsonian Institution. Part 1 of this report contains various papers on other subjects unrelated to the Ghost Dance written by other authors. As a result of this arrangement plate and figures numbers have been continued from part 1. Thus the first plate in this volume is numbered LXXXVI. The first figure is number 56. Because these figures and plates are referred to throughout the text by these numbers, we have retained this system of numbering in the present edition.

CONTENTS

	Page
Introduction	15
The narrative	19
Chapter I—Paradise lost	19
II—The Delaware prophet and Pontiac	24
III—Tenskwatawa the Shawano prophet	32
IV—Tecumtha and Tippecanoe	43
V—Känakûk and minor prophets	54
Känakûk	54
Pa'thĕskĕ	62
Tä'vibo	63
Nakai-doklĭ'ni	66
The Potawatomi prophet	67
Cheez-tah-paezh the Sword-bearer	68
VI—The Smohalla religion of the Columbia region	70
Smohalla	70
Joseph and the Nez Percé war	73
VII—Smohalla and his doctrine	78
VIII—The Shakers of Puget sound	108
IX—Wovoka the messiah	126
X—The doctrine of the Ghost dance	139
Appendix:	
The Mormons and the Indians	154
Porcupine's account of the messiah	155
The Ghost dance among the Sioux	158
Selwyn's interview with Kuwapi	160
XI—The Ghost dance west of the Rockies	164
XII—The Ghost dance east of the Rockies.—among the Sioux	178
Appendix: Causes of the outbreak	191
Commissioner Morgan's statement	191
Ex-Agent McGillycuddy's statement	193
Statement of General Miles	195
Report of Captain Hurst	198
Statement of American Horse	201
Statement of Bishop Hare	202
XIII—The Sioux outbreak—Sitting Bull and Wounded Knee	205
Appendix: The Indian story of Wounded Knee	246
XIV—Close of the outbreak—The Ghost dance in the south	249
XV—The ceremony of the Ghost dance	277
Among the northern Cheyenne	277
Among the Sioux	277
Song rehearsals	280
Preparations for the dance	280
Giving the feather	281
The painting of the dancers	281

The narrative—Continued   Page
    Chapter XV—The ceremony of the Ghost dance—Continued
        The ceremony 282
        The crow dance.. 283
        The hypnotic process 284
        The area covered by the dance................................. 288
        Present condition of the dance................................ 289
    XVI—Parallels in other systems.................................... 290
        The Biblical period 290
        Mohammedanism 292
        Joan of Arc 294
        Dance of Saint John... 297
        The Flagellants 297
        Ranters, Quakers, and Fifth-Monarchy men............... 298
        French prophets... 300
        Jumpers 301
        Methodists 301
        Shakers 303
        Kentucky revival... 304
        Adventists 306
        Other parallels 307
            Beekmanites 307
            Patterson and Brown's mission...................... 308
            Wilderness worshipers............................... 308
            Heavenly recruits 309
        Appendix: Hypnotism and the dance among the Der-
            vishes 310
The songs 315
    Introductory.. 315
    The Arapaho.. 315
        Tribal synonymy 315
        Tribal signs 316
        Sketch of the tribe 316
        Songs of the Arapaho... 320
        1. Opening song: *Eyehe'! nä'nisa'na*—O, my children!.......... 320
        2. *Sĕ'icha' heita'wuni'na*—The sacred pipe tells me.............. 321
        3. *Ate'bĕ tiäwu'nänu'*—When at first I liked the whites.......... 323
        4. *A'bä'ni'hi'*—My partner 324
        5. *A'-nisûna'a'hu*—My father 324
        6. *E'yehe'! Wû'nayu'uhu'*—*E'yehe'!* They are new 325
        7. *Hi'sähi'hi*—My partner! My partner 326
        8. *Ä'-nani'ni'bi'nä'si waku'na*—The wind makes the head-feathers
           sing 327
        9. *He'! Näne'th bishiqa'wă*—When I met him approaching....... 327
      10. *Häna'na'wunănu*—I take pity on those 328
      11. *A-ni'qu wa'wanä'nibä'tia'*—Father, now I am singing it........ 328
      12. *Ha'yana'-usi'ya'*—How bright is the moonlight!.............. 328
      13. *Ha'ti ni'bät*—The cottonwood song......................... 329
      14. *Eyehe'! A'nie'sa'na'*—The young Thunderbirds................ 330
      15. *A'he'sûna'nini năya'qûti'hi*—Our father, the Whirlwind....... 332
      16. *A'he'sûna'nini năya'qûti'*—Our father, the Whirlwind 332
      17. *Ninaä'niahu'na*—I circle around 332
      18. *Ha'nahawu'nĕn bĕni'ni'na*—The *Hanahawunĕn* gave it to me ... 333
      19. *Ate'be' tana'-ise'ti*—When first our father came.............. 333
      20. *A-ni'änĕ'thăhi'nani'na*—My father did not recognize me...... .. 334

The songs—Continued   Page
  The Arapaho—Continued
    Songs of the Arapaho—Continued
       21. *Ni'-athu'-a-u' ä'hakä'nith'ü*—The whites are crazy 334
       22. *Na'ha'ta bi'taa'wu*—The earth is about to move 335
       23. *Ahe'sûna'nini ächiqa'hä'wa-ŭ'*—I am looking at my father 335
       24. *Ha'änake'i*—The rock 335
       25. *Wa'wa'na'danä'diä'*—I am about to hum 336
       26. *A-te'bĕ dii'nĕtita'niĕg*—At the beginning of existence.......... 337
       27. *Tahu'na'änä'nia'huna*—It is I who make the thunder 338
       28. *Ani'qu ne'chawu'nani*—Father, have pity on me.............. 339
       29. *A-ni'niha'niahu'na*—I fly around yellow...................... 339
       30. *Niha'nata'yeche'ti*—The yellow hide......................... 340
       31. *A-bää'thina'hu*—The cedar tree 340
       32. *Wa'wa nû'nanû'naku'ti*—Now I am waving an eagle feather... 341
       33. *A-ni'qana'ga*—There is a solitary bull...................... 342
       34. *A-nĕä'thibiwä'hanä*—The place where crying begins 343
       35. *Thi'äya' he'nää'awä*—When I see the *thi'äya*................... 343
       36. *A-hu'hu ha'geni'sti'ti*—The crow is making a road 344
       37. *Bi'taa'wu hu'hu'*—The crow brought the earth................ 345
       38. *Ni'nini'tubi'na hu'hu'* (I)—The crow has called me........... 345
       39. *Nû'nanû'naa'tăni'na hu'hu'* (I)—The crow is circling above me. 346
       40. *Iyu hä'thäbĕ'nawa'*—Here it is, I hand it to you 346
       41. *Hanaĕ'hi ya'ga'ahi'na*—Little boy, the coyote gun............... 346
       42. *He'sûna' na'nahatha'hi*—The father showed me 347
       43. *Nänisa'tăqu'thi Chïnachi'chibä'iha'*—The seven venerable priests. 348
       44. *Nä'nisa'tăqi Chï'năchi'chibä'iha'*—The seven venerable priests . 352
       45. *Nû'nanû'naa'tani'na hu'hu'* (II)............................... 352
       46. *Na'tănu'ya chĕ'bi'nh*—The pemmican that I am using......... 353
       47. *Häï'nawa' hä'ni'ta'quna'ni*—I know, in the pitfall 353
       48. *Bä'hinä'nina'tä ni'tabä'na*—I hear everything............... 355
       49. *A-bä'qati' hä'nichä'bi'hinä'na*—With the wheel I am gambling. 356
       50. *Ani'äsa'kua'na*—I am watching................................ 357
       51. *Ni'çhi'ä i'theti'hi*—(There) is a good river 357
       52. *Ni'nini'tubi'na hu'hu'* (II) 358
       53. *Anihä'ya atani'tă'nu'nawa'*—I use the yellow (paint).......... 359
       54. *Ni'naä'niahu'tawa bi'taa'wu*—I am flying about the earth 359
       55. *I'nita'ta'-usä'na*—Stand ready................................ 360
       56. *Wa'wäthä'bi*—I have given you magpie feathers 360
       57. *Ani'qa hĕ'tabi'nuhu'ni'na*—My father, I am poor 361
       58. *Nä'nisa'taqu'thi hu'na*—The seven crows...................... 361
       59. *Ahu'nä he'sûna'nïn*—There is our father 362
       60. *Ga'awa'hu*—The ball, the ball 362
       61. *Ahu' ni'higa'hu*—The Crow is running 362
       62. *Ya'thä-yû'na*—He put me in five places 363
       63. *Ni'naä'qa'wa chibä'ti*—I am going around the sweat-house.... 363
       64. *Hise'hi*—My comrade.. 364
       65. *Na'tu'wani'sa*—My top, my top 367
       66. *He'na'ga'nawa'nen*—When we dance until daylight 368
       67. *Ni'nä'nina'ti'naku'ni'na*—I wear the morning star 368
       68. *A-ne'na' tabi'ni'na*—My mother gave it to me................. 369
       69. *Yi'hä'ä'ä'hi'hï'*—Gambling song (Paiute gambling songs)..... 370
       70. *Ni'qa-hu'hu'*—My father, my father 372
       71. *A'hu'nawu'hu'*—With red paint.............................. 372
       72. *Ani'qa naga'qu*—Father, the Morning Star 372
       73. *Ahu'yu häthi'na*—Closing song............................... 373
  Arapaho glossary 374

The songs—Continued   Page
    The Cheyenne... 385
        Tribal synonymy.. 385
        Tribal sign.. 386
        Sketch of the tribe... 386
        Songs of the Cheyenne... 390
            1. *O'tä nä'nisĭ'näsists*—Well, my children........................ 390
            2. *Ehä'n esho'ini'*—Our father has come.......................... 390
            3. *Nä'niso'näsĭ'stsihi'*—My children............................. 391
            4. *Nä'see'nehe' ehe'yowo'mi*—I waded into the yellow river....... 392
            5. *Wosi'vä-ă'ă'*—The mountain is circling........................ 392
            6. *Ni'ha-i'hi'hi'*—My father, I come............................. 393
            7. *Hi'awu'hi*—We have put the devil aside........................ 393
            8. *Ni'ha e'yehe'!*—My father, my father.......................... 393
            9. *Ä'minŭ'qi*—My comrade... 394
            10. *He'stutu'ai*—The buffalo head................................ 394
            11. *Nä'mio'ts*—I am coming in sight.............................. 396
            12. *A'gachi'hi*—The crow is circling............................. 396
            13. *Nä'nise'näsĕ'stse*—My children, I am now humming............. 396
            14. *Ogo'ch ehe'eye'!*—The crow, the crow........................ 397
            15. *Tsĭso'soyo'tsĭto'ho*—While I was going about................. 397
            16. *Ni'ha e'yehe'e'yeye'!*—My father, my father.................. 398
            17. *A'ga'ch ehe'e'ye'!*—The crow, the crow....................... 399
            18. *Nä'niso'näsĭ'stsi he'e'ye'!*—My children, my children........ 399
            19. *Agu'ga'-ihi*—The crow woman.................................. 400
        Cheyenne glossary... 401
    The Comanche.. 405
        Tribal synonymy... 405
        Tribal sign... 405
        Sketch of the tribe... 405
        Songs of the Comanche... 408
            1. *Heyo'hänä häe'yo*... 408
            2. *Ya'hi'yŭ'niva'hu*.. 409
            3. *Yani'tsini'hawa'na*.. 409
            4. *Ni'nini'tuwi'na*... 409
    The Paiute, Washo, and Pit River tribes..................................... 410
        Paiute tribal synonymy.. 410
        Sketch of the Paiute.. 410
            Characteristics... 410
            Genesis myth.. 412
        The Washo... 413
        The Pit River Indians... 414
        Songs of the Paiute... 414
            1. *Nüvä ka ro'räni*—The snow lies there......................... 414
            2. *Dĕna' gayo'n*—A slender antelope............................. 415
            3. *Do tĭ'mbi*—The black rock.................................... 415
            4. *Päsü' wĭ'noghän*—The wind stirs the willows.................. 415
            5. *Pägü'nävä'*—Fog! Fog!.. 416
            6. *Wŭmbĭ'ndomä'n*—The whirlwind................................. 416
            7. *Kosi' wŭmbi'ndomä'*—There is dust from the whirlwind......... 416
            8. *Dombi'na so'wina'*—The rocks are ringing..................... 417
            9. *Sŭ'ng-ä ro'yonji'*—The cottonwoods are growing tall.......... 417
        Paiute glossary... 418
    The Sioux... 419
        Tribal synonymy... 419
        Tribal sign... 419

The songs—Continued   Page
  The Sioux—Continued
    Sketch of the tribe...... 420
    Songs of the Sioux 423
      1. Opening song: *A'te he'ye e'yayo*—The father says so 423
      2. *Michi'nkshi nañpe*—My son, let me grasp your hand 423
      3. *He tuwe'cha he*—Who think you comes there? 426
      4. *Wana'yañ ma'niye*—Now he is walking 426
      5. *Lechel miyo'qañ-kte*—This is to be my work 427
      6. *Michinkshi'yi tewa'qila che*—I love my children 427
      7. *Mila kiñ hiyu'michi'chiyana*—Give me my knife 427
      8. *Le he'yahe'*—This one says 430
      9. *Niya'te-ye' he'u'we*—It is your father coming 430
      10. *Miyo'qañ kiñ wañla'ki*—You see what I can do 430
      11. *Michĭnkshi mita'waye*—It is my own child 431
      12. *A'te he' u-we*—There is the father coming 431
      13. *Wa'sna wa'tiñ-kta*—I shall eat pemmican 431
      14. *A'te lena ma'qu-we*—The father gave us these 431
      15. *Ina' he'kuwo'*—Mother, come home 432
      16. *Wa'na wanasa'pi-kta*—Now they are about to chase the buffalo 432
      17. *He! Kii'ñyañka a'gali'-ye*—He! They have come back racing 433
      18. *Mi'ye wañma'yañka-yo!*—Look at me! 433
      19. *Maka' sito'maniyañ*—The whole world is coming 434
      20. *Le'na wa'kañ*—These sacred things 434
      21. *Miyo'qañ kiñ chichu'-che*—I have given you my strength 434
      22. *Michi'nkshi tahe'na*—My child, come this way 435
      23. *Wana wichĕ'shka*—Now set up the tipi 435
      24. *A'te mi'chuye*—Father, give them to me 436
      25. *Hañpa wecha'ghe*—I made moccasins for him 436
      26. *Waka'ñyañ iñya'ñkiñ-kte*—The holy (hoop) shall run 437
    Sioux glossary 437
  The Kiowa and Kiowa Apache 440
    Kiowa tribal synonymy 440
    Kiowa tribal sign 440
    Sketch of the Kiowa 440
    The Kiowa Apache 443
    Songs of the Kiowa 443
      1. *Da'ta-i so'da'te*—The father will descend 443
      2. *Da'k'iñ'ago (ĭm) zä'nteähe'dal*—The spirit army is approaching 444
      3. *Gu'ato ädâ'ga*—I scream because I am a bird 445
      4. *Da'ta-i nyä'hoänga'mo*—The father shows me the road 446
      5. *Dak'iñ'a bate'yä*—The spirit (God) is approaching 446
      6. *Na'da'g äka'na*—Because I am poor 447
      7. *Ze'bät-gâ'ga igu'änpa'-ima'*—He makes me dance with arrows 447
      8. *Be'ta! To'ngyä-gu'adäl*—Red Tail has been sent 448
      9. *Da'ta-i änka'ñgo'na*—My father has much pity for us 448
      10. *Da'ta-i iñka'ñtähe'dal*—My father has had pity on me 448
      11. *Dak'iñ'ago äho'ähe'dal*—The spirit host is advancing 449
      12. *E'hyuñ'i degiä'ta*—I am mashing the berries 450
      13. *Go'mgyä-da'ga*—That wind shakes my tipi 450
      14. *Dak'iñ'a dakañ'tähe'dal*—God has had pity on us 450
      15. *Anso' gyätä'to*—I shall cut off his feet 451
    Kiowa glossary 451
  The Caddo and associated tribes 454
    Caddo tribal synonymy 454
    Caddo tribal sign 454

The songs—Continued   Page
    The Caddo and associated tribes—Continued
        Sketch of the Caddo 454
        The Wichita, Kichai, and Delaware 457
        Songs of the Caddo 458
            1. *Ha'yo ta'ia' ä'ä'* — Our father dwells above 458
            2. *Wû'nti ha'yano' di'witi'a* —All our people are going up......... 458
            3. *Núna ĭ'tsiya'* —I have come............................ 459
            4. *Na'tsiwa'ya* —I am coming.. 459
            5. *Na'-iye' ino' ga'nio'sït* —My sister above 459
            6. *Na'a ha'yo ha'wano* —Our father above (has) paint............ 460
            7. *Wû'nti ha'yano ka'ka'na'* —All the people cried................ 460
            8. *Na'wi i'na* —We have our mother below 460
            9. *Ni' ika' na'a* —Our grandmother and our father above........ 461
          10. *Hi'na ha'natobi'na* —The eagle feather headdress.............. 461
          11. *Na' aa' o'wi'ta'* —The father comes from above................. 461
          12. *Na' iwi' o'wi'ta'* —See! the eagle comes....................... 462
          13. *A'nana' hana'nito'* —The feather has come back.............. 463
          14. *Na' iwi' ha'naa'* —There is an eagle above.................... 463
          15. *Wi'tä' Ha'sini'* —Come on, Caddo............................ 463
    Caddo glossary 464
Authorities cited... 466

ILLUSTRATIONS

Facing Page

LXXXVI. The prayer-stick 60
LXXXVII. Chief Joseph 74
LXXXVIII. Map showing the distribution of the tribes of the upper
Columbia 78
LXXXIX. Smohalla and his priests 82
XC. Smohalla church on Yakima reservation 84
XCI. Interior of Smohalla church 88
XCII. Winter view in Mason valley showing snow-covered sage-
brush 130
XCIII. Sioux ghost shirts from Wounded Knee battlefield 150
XCIV. Sioux sweat-house and sacrifice pole 184
XCV. Map of the country embraced in the campaign against the
Sioux 212
XCVI. Map of Standing Rock agency and vicinity 216
XCVII. Map of Wounded Knee battlefield 230
XCVIII. After the battle 234
XCIX. Battlefield of Wounded Knee 236
C. Burying the dead 238
CI. Grave of the dead at Wounded Knee 240
CII. Battlefield after the blizzard 242
CIII. Arapaho ghost shirt, showing coloring 256
CIV. Arapaho ghost shirt—reverse 258
CV. Black Coyote 260
CVI. Biäñki, the Kiowa dreamer 270
CVII. Biäñki's vision 272
CVIII. Kiowa summer shelter 274
CIX. The Ghost dance (buckskin painting) 276
CX. Sacred objects from the Sioux Ghost dance 278
CXI. Sacred objects from the Sioux Ghost dance 280
CXII. The Ghost dance—small circle 282
CXIII. The Ghost dance—larger circle 284
CXIV. The Ghost dance—large circle 286
CXV. The Ghost dance—praying 288
CXVI. The Ghost dance—inspiration 290
CXVII. The Ghost dance—rigid 292
CXVIII. The Ghost dance—unconscious 294
CXIX. The crow dance 296
CXX. Arapaho bed 324
CXXI. The sweat-lodge: Kiowa camp on the Washita 342
CXXII. Dog-soldier insignia 350

FIGURE 56. Tenskwatawa the Shawano prophet, 1808 and 1831 32
57. Greenville treaty medal 33
58. Tecumtha 44
59. Harrison treaty pipe 50
60. Känakûk the Kickapoo prophet 55

Page

FIGURE 61. Känakûk's heaven.. 56
62. Onsawkie 60
63. Nakai'-doklī'ni's dance wheel...................................... 66
64. Smohalla's flag... 88
65. Charles Ike, Smohalla interpreter.................................. 90
66. Diagram showing arrangement of worshipers at Smohalla service.. 91
67. John Slocum and Louis Yowaluch.................................... 108
68. Shaker church at Mud bay 120
69. Wovoka 126
70. Navaho Indians... 172
71. Vista in the Hopi pueblo of Walpi................................. 174
72. A Sioux warrior—Weasel Bear....................................... 206
73. Red Cloud 208
74. Short Bull 213
75. Kicking Bear 215
76. Red Tomahawk 218
77. Sitting Bull the Sioux medicine-man............................... 220
78. Sketch of the country of the Sitting Bull fight, December 15, 1890. 221
79. Survivors of Wounded Knee—Blue Whirlwind and children...... 239
80. Survivors of Wounded Knee—Marguerite Zıtkala-noni............ 240
81. Survivors of Wounded Knee—Jennie Sword 241
82. Survivors of Wounded Knee—Herbert Zitkalazi 242
83. Sitting Bull the Arapaho apostle.................................... 258
84. Two Kiowa prophecies (from a Kiowa calendar)................... 269
85. Poor Buffalo 270
86. Sitting Bull comes down (from a Kiowa calendar)................. 271
87. Ä'piatañ 274
88. Arapaho tipi and windbreak 319
89. Bea of the prairie tribes.. 325
90. Shinny stick and ball 326
91. Wakuna or head-feathers.. 326
92. The Thunderbird.. 331
93. Hummer and bullroarer 336
94. Dog-soldier insignia—rattle and quirt 349
95. Diagram of awl game... 364
96. Sticks used in awl game... 365
97. Trump sticks used in awl game..... 365
98. Baskets used in dice game... 366
99. Dice used in dice game... 367
100. Cheyenne camping circle 388
101. Paiute wikiup.. 411
102. Native drawings of Ghost dance—A, Comanche; B, Sioux 422
103. Jerking beef 428
104. Kiowa camping circle 442

THE GHOST-DANCE RELIGION

By James Mooney

INTRODUCTION

In the fall of 1890 the author was preparing to go to Indian Territory, under the auspices of the Bureau of Ethnology, to continue
researches among the Cherokee, when the Ghost dance began to attract
attention, and permission was asked and received to investigate that
subject also among the wilder tribes in the western part of the territory. Proceeding directly to the Cheyenne and Arapaho, it soon
became evident that there was more in the Ghost dance than had
been suspected, with the result that the investigation, to which it
had been intended to devote only a few weeks, has extended over a
period of more than three years, and might be continued indefinitely,
as the dance still exists (in 1896) and is developing new features at
every performance. The uprising among the Sioux in the meantime
made necessary also the examination of a mass of documentary material
in the files of the Indian Office and the War Department bearing on
the outbreak, in addition to the study in the field of the strictly religious features of the dance.

The first visit of about four months (December, 1890–April, 1891)
was made to the Arapaho, Cheyenne, Kiowa, Comanche, Apache, Caddo,
and Wichita, all living near together in the western part of what was
then Indian Territory, but is now Oklahoma. These tribes were all
more or less under the influence of the new religion. The principal
study was made among the Arapaho, who were the most active propa-
gators of the "Messiah" doctrine among the southern tribes and are
especially friendly and cordial in disposition.

On returning to Washington, the author received a commission to
make an ethnologic collection for the World's Columbian Exposition,
and, selecting the Kiowa for that purpose as a representative prairie
tribe, started out again almost immediately to the same field. This
trip, lasting three months, gave further opportunity for study of the
Ghost dance among the same tribes. After returning and attending
to the labeling and arranging of the collection, a study was made of all
documents bearing on the subject in possession of the Indian Office and

the War Department.   Another trip was then made to the field for the purpose of investigating the dance among the Sioux, where it had attracted most attention, and among the Paiute, where it originated. On this journey the author visited the Omaha, Winnebago, Sioux of Pine Ridge, Paiute, Cheyenne, and Arapaho; met and talked with the messiah himself, and afterward, on the strength of this fact, obtained from the Cheyenne the original letter containing his message and instructions to the southern tribes.   This trip occupied about three months.

A few months later, in the summer of 1892, another journey was made to the West, in the course of which the southern tribes and the Sioux were revisited, and some time was spent in Wyoming with the Shoshoni and northern Arapaho, the latter of whom were perhaps the most earnest followers of the messiah in the north.   This trip consumed four months.   After some time spent in Washington in elaborating notes already obtained, a winter trip (1892–93) was made under another commission from the World's Fair to the Navaho and the Hopi or Moki, of New Mexico and Arizona.   Although these tribes were not directly concerned in the Ghost dance, they had been visited by apostles of the new doctrine, and were able to give some account of the ceremony as it existed among the Havasupai or Cohonino and others farther to the west.   On the return journey another short stay was made among the Kiowa and Arapaho.   In the summer of 1893 a final visit, covering a period of five months, was made to the western tribes of Oklahoma, bringing the personal observation and study of the Ghost dance down to the beginning of 1894.

The field investigation therefore occupied twenty-two months, involving nearly 32,000 miles of travel and more or less time spent with about twenty tribes.   To obtain exact knowledge of the ceremony, the author took part in the dance among the Arapaho and Cheyenne.   He also carried a kodak and a tripod camera, with which he made photographs of the dance and the trance both without and within the circle.   Several months were spent in consulting manuscript documents and printed sources of information in the departments and libraries at Washington, and correspondence was carried on with persons in various parts of the country who might be able to give additional facts.   From the beginning every effort was made to get a correct statement of the subject. Beyond this, the work must speak for itself.

As the Ghost dance doctrine is only the latest of a series of Indian religious revivals, and as the idea on which it is founded is a hope common to all humanity, considerable space has been given to a discussion of the primitive messiah belief and of the teachings of the various Indian prophets who have preceded Wovoka, together with brief sketches of several Indian wars belonging to the same periods.

In the songs the effort has been to give the spirit and exact rendering, without going into analytic details.   The main purpose of the work is not linguistic, and as nearly every tribe concerned speaks a different language from all the others, any close linguistic study must be left to the philologist who can afford to devote a year or more to an individual tribe. The only one of these tribes of which the author claims intimate knowledge is the Kiowa.

Acknowledgments are due the officers and members of the Office of Indian Affairs and the War Department for courteous assistance in obtaining documentary information and in replying to letters of inquiry; to Mr De Lancey W. Gill and Mr J. K. Hillers and their assistants of the art and photographic divisions of the United States Geological Survey; to Mr A. R. Spofford, Librarian of Congress; to Mr F. V. Coville, botanist, Agricultural Department; Honorable T. J. Morgan, former Commissioner of Indian Affairs; Major J. W. Mac-Murray, first artillery, United States Army; Dr Washington Matthews, surgeon, United States Army; Captain H. L. Scott, seventh cavalry, United States Army; Captain J. M. Lee, ninth infantry, United States Army; Captain E. L. Huggins, second cavalry, United States Army, of the staff of General Miles; the late Captain J. G. Bourke, third cavalry, United States Army; Captain H. G. Browne, twelfth infantry, United States Army; Judge James Wickersham, Tacoma, Washington; Dr George Bird Grinnell, editor of "Forest and Stream," New York city; Mr Thomas V. Keam and the late A. M. Stephen, Keams Canyon, Arizona; Rev. H. R. Voth, Oraibi, Arizona; General L. W. Colby, Washington, District of Columbia; Mr D. B. Dyer, Augusta, Georgia; Rev. Myron Eells, Tacoma, Washington; Mr Emile Berliner and the Berliner Gramophone Company, for recording, and Professors John Philip Sousa and F. W. V. Gaisberg, for arranging the Indian music; W. S. Godbe, Bullionville, Nevada; Miss L. McLain, Washington City; Addison Cooper, Nashville, Tennessee; Miss Emma C. Sickels, Chicago; Professor A. H. Thompson, United States Geological Survey, Washington; Mrs L. B. Arnold, Standing Rock, North Dakota; Mr C. H. Bartlett, South Bend, Indiana; Dr T. P. Martin, Taos, New Mexico, and to the following Indian informants and interpreters: Philip Wells, Louis Menard, Ellis Standing Bear, American Horse, George Sword, and Fire Thunder, of Pine Ridge, South Dakota; Henry Reid, Rev. Sherman Coolidge, Norcok, Sage, and Sharp Nose, of Fort Washakie, Wyoming; Charley Sheep of Walker river, Nevada; Black Coyote, Sitting Bull, Black Short Nose, George Bent, Paul Boynton, Robert Burns, Jesse Bent, Clever Warden, Grant Left-hand, and the Arapaho police at Darlington, Oklahoma; Andres Martinez, Belo Cozad, Paul Setkopti, Henry Poloi, Little Bow, William Tivis, George Parton, Towakoni Jim, Robert Dunlap, Kichai, John Wilson, Tama, Igiagyahona, Deoñ, Mary Zotom, and Eliza Parton of Anadarko, Oklahoma.

THE NARRATIVE

CHAPTER I

PARADISE LOST

There are hours long departed which memory brings
Like blossoms of Eden to twine round the heart.
Moore.

The wise men tell us that the world is growing happier—that we live longer than did our fathers, have more of comfort and less of toil, fewer wars and discords, and higher hopes and aspirations. So say the wise men; but deep in our own hearts we know they are wrong. For were not we, too, born in Arcadia, and have we not—each one of us—in that May of life when the world was young, started out lightly and airily along the path that led through green meadows to the blue mountains on the distant horizon, beyond which lay the great world we were to conquer? And though others dropped behind, have we not gone on through morning brightness and noonday heat, with eyes always steadily forward, until the fresh grass began to be parched and withered, and the way grew hard and stony, and the blue mountains resolved into gray rocks and thorny cliffs? And when at last we reached the toilsome summits, we found the glory that had lured us onward was only the sunset glow that fades into darkness while we look, and leaves us at the very goal to sink down, tired in body and sick at heart, with strength and courage gone, to close our eyes and dream again, not of the fame and fortune that were to be ours, but only of the old-time happiness that we have left so far behind.

As with men, so is it with nations. The lost paradise is the world's dreamland of youth. What tribe or people has not had its golden age, before Pandora's box was loosed, when women were nymphs and dryads and men were gods and heroes? And when the race lies crushed and groaning beneath an alien yoke, how natural is the dream of a redeemer, an Arthur, who shall return from exile or awake from some long sleep to drive out the usurper and win back for his people what they have lost. The hope becomes a faith and the faith becomes the creed of priests and prophets, until the hero is a god and the dream a religion, looking to some great miracle of nature for its culmination and accomplishment. The doctrines of the Hindu avatar, the Hebrew Messiah, the Christian millennium, and the Hesûnanin of the Indian Ghost dance are essentially the same, and have their origin in a hope and longing common to all humanity.

Probably every Indian tribe, north and south, had its early hero god, the great doer or teacher of all first things, from the Iuskeha and Manabozho of the rude Iroquoian and Algonquian to the Quetzalcoatl, the Bochica, and the Viracocha of the more cultivated Aztecs, Muyscas, and Quichuas of the milder southland. Among the roving tribes of the north this hero is hardly more than an expert magician, frequently degraded to the level of a common trickster, who, after ridding the world of giants and monsters, and teaching his people a few simple arts, retires to the upper world to rest and smoke until some urgent necessity again requires his presence below. Under softer southern skies the myth takes more poetic form and the hero becomes a person of dignified presence, a father and teacher of his children, a very Christ, worthy of all love and reverence, who gathers together the wandering nomads and leads them to their destined country, where he instructs them in agriculture, house building, and the art of government, regulates authority, and inculcates peaceful modes of life. "Under him, the earth teemed with fruits and flowers without the pains of culture. An ear of Indian corn was as much as a single man could carry. The cotton, as it grew, took of its own accord the rich dyes of human art. The air was filled with intoxicating perfumes and the sweet melody of birds. In short, these were the halcyon days, which find a place in the mythic systems of so many nations in the Old World. It was the golden age of Anahuac." (*Prescott, 1.*)[1] When at last his work is well accomplished, he bids farewell to his sorrowing subjects, whom he consoles with the sacred promise that he will one day return and resume his kingdom, steps into his magic boat by the seashore, and sails away out of their sight to the distant land of sunrise.

Such was Quetzalcoatl of the Aztecs, and such in all essential respects was the culture god of the more southern semicivilized races. Curiously enough, this god, at once a Moses and a messiah, is usually described as a white man with flowing beard. From this and other circumstances it has been argued that the whole story is only another form of the dawn myth, but whether the Indian god be an ancient deified lawgiver of their own race, or some nameless missionary who found his way across the trackless ocean in the early ages of Christianity, or whether we have here only a veiled parable of the morning light bringing life and joy to the world and then vanishing to return again from the east with the dawn, it is sufficient to our purpose that the belief in the coming of a messiah, who should restore them to their original happy condition, was well nigh universal among the American tribes.

This faith in the return of a white deliverer from the east opened the gate to the Spaniards at their first coming alike in Haiti, Mexico, Yucatan, and Peru. (*Brinton, 1.*) The simple native welcomed the white strangers as the children or kindred of their long-lost benefactor,

---

[1] Parenthetic references throughout the memoir are to bibliographic notes following The Songs.

immortal beings whose near advent had been foretold by oracles and omens, whose faces borrowed from the brightness of the dawn, whose glistening armor seemed woven from the rays of sunlight, and whose god-like weapons were the lightning and the thunderbolt. Their first overbearing demands awakened no resentment; for may not the gods claim their own, and is not resistance to the divine will a crime? Not until their most sacred things were trampled under foot, and the streets of the holy city itself ran red with the blood of their slaughtered princes, did they read aright the awful prophecy by the light of their blazing temples, and know that instead of the children of an incarnate god they had welcomed a horde of incarnate devils. "The light of civilization would be poured on their land. But it would be the light of a consuming fire, before which their barbaric glory, their institutions, their very existence and name as a nation, would wither and become extinct. Their doom was sealed when the white man had set his foot on their soil." (*Prescott, 2.*)

The great revolt of the Pueblo Indians in August, 1680, was one of the first determined efforts made by the natives on the northern continent to throw off the yoke of a foreign oppressor. The Pueblo tribes along the Rio Grande and farther to the west, a gentle, peaceful race, had early welcomed the coming of the Spaniards, with their soldiers and priests, as friends who would protect them against the wild marauding tribes about them and teach them the mysteries of a greater "medicine" than belonged to their own kachinas. The hope soon faded into bitter disappointment. The soldiers, while rough and overbearing toward their brown-skin allies, were yet unable to protect them from the inroads of their enemies. The priests prohibited their dances and simple amusements, yet all their ringing of bells and chanting of hymns availed not to bring more rain on the crops or to turn aside the vengeful Apache. "What have we gained by all this?" said the Pueblos one to another; "not peace and not happiness, for these new rulers will not protect us from our enemies, and take from us all the enjoyments we once knew."

The pear was ripe. Popé, a medicine-man of the Tewa, had come back from a pilgrimage to the far north, where he claimed to have visited the magic lagoon of Shipapu, whence his people traced their origin and to which the souls of their dead returned after leaving this life. By these ancestral spirits he had been endowed with occult powers and commanded to go back and rouse the Pueblos to concerted effort for deliverance from the foreign yoke of the strangers.

Wonderful beings were these spirit messengers. Swift as light and impalpable as thought, they passed under the earth from the magic lake to the secret subterranean chamber of the oracle and stood before him as shapes of fire, and spoke, telling him to prepare the strings of yucca knots and send them with the message to all the Pueblos far and near, so that in every village the chiefs might untie one knot from the string each day, and know when they came to the last knot that then was the time to strike.

From the Pecos, across the Rio Grande to Zuñi and the far-distant Hopi mesas, every Pueblo village accepted the yucca string and began secret preparation for the rising. The time chosen was the new moon of August, 1680, but, through a partial discovery of the plot, the explosion was precipitated on the 10th. So sudden and complete was the surprise that many Spaniards in the Pueblo country, priests, soldiers, and civilians, were killed, and the survivors, after holding out for a time under Governor Otermin at Santa Fé, fled to El Paso, and in October there remained not a single Spaniard in all New Mexico. (*Bandelier, 1 a, 1 b.*)

Despite their bitter disappointment, the southern nations continued to cherish the hope of a coming redeemer, who now assumed the character of a terrible avenger of their wrongs, and the white-skin conqueror has had bloody occasion to remember that his silent peon, as he toils by blue Chapala or sits amid the ruins of his former grandeur in the dark forests of Yucatan, yet waits ever and always the coming of the day which shall break the power of the alien Spaniard and restore to their inheritance the children of Anahuac and Mayapan. In Peru the natives refused to believe that the last of the Incas had perished a wanderer in the forests of the eastern Cordilleras. For more than two centuries they cherished the tradition that he had only retired to another kingdom beyond the mountains, from which he would return in his own good time to sweep their haughty oppressors from the land. In 1781 the slumbering hope found expression in a terrible insurrection under the leadership of the mestizo Condorcanqui, a descendant of the ancient royal family, who boldly proclaimed himself the long lost Tupac Amaru, child of the sun and Inca of Peru. With mad enthusiasm the Quichua highlanders hailed him as their destined deliverer and rightful sovereign, and binding around his forehead the imperial fillet of the Incas, he advanced at the head of an immense army to the walls of Cuzco, declaring his purpose to blot out the very memory of the white man and reestablish the Indian empire in the City of the Sun. Inspired by the hope of vengeance on the conqueror, even boys became leaders of their people, and it was only after a bloody struggle of two years' duration that the Spaniards were able to regain the mastery and consigned the captive Inca, with all his family, to an ignominious and barbarous death. Even then so great was the feeling of veneration which he had inspired in the breasts of the Indians that "notwithstanding their fear of the Spaniards, and though they were surrounded by soldiers of the victorious army, they prostrated themselves at the sight of the last of the children of the sun, as he passed along the streets to the place of execution." (*Humboldt, 1.*)

In the New World, as in the Old, the advent of the deliverer was to be heralded by signs and wonders. Thus in Mexico, a mysterious rising of the waters of Lake Tezcuco, three comets blazing in the sky, and a strange light in the east, prepared the minds of the people for the near coming of the Spaniards. (*Prescott, 3.*) In this connection, also, there was usually a belief in a series of previous destructions by flood, fire, famine, or pestilence, followed by a regeneration through the omnipotent might of the savior. The doctrine that the world is old and worn out, and that the time for its renewal is near at hand, is an essential part of the teaching of the Ghost dance. The number of these cycles of destruction was variously stated among different tribes, but perhaps the most sadly prophetic form of the myth was found among the Winnebago, who forty years ago held that the tenth generation of their people was near its close, and that at the end of the thirteenth the red race would be destroyed. By prayers and ceremonies they were then endeavoring to placate their angry gods and put farther away the doom that now seems rapidly closing in on them. (*Schoolcraft, Ind. Tribes, 1.*)

CHAPTER II

THE DELAWARE PROPHET AND PONTIAC

Hear what the Great Spirit has ordered me to tell you: Put off entirely the customs which you have adopted since the white people came among us.—*The Delaware Prophet.*

This is our land, and not yours.—*The Confederate Tribes, 1752.*

The English advances were slow and halting, for a long period almost imperceptible, while the establishment of a few small garrisons and isolated trading stations by the French hardly deserved to be called an occupancy of the country. As a consequence, the warlike northern tribes were slow to realize that an empire was slipping from their grasp, and it was not until the two great nations prepared for the final struggle in the New World that the native proprietors began to read the stars aright. Then it was, in 1752, that the Lenape chiefs sent to the British agent the pointed interrogatory: "The English claim all on one side of the river, the French claim all on the other—where is the land of the Indians?" (*Bancroft, 1.*) Then, as they saw the French strengthening themselves along the lakes, there came a stronger protest from the council ground of the confederate tribes of the west: "This is our land and not yours. Fathers, both you and the English are white; the land belongs to neither the one nor the other of you, but the Great Being above allotted it to be a dwelling place for us; so, fathers, I desire you to withdraw, as I have desired our brothers, the English." A wampum belt gave weight to the words. (*Bancroft, 2.*) The French commander's reply was blunt, but more practiced diplomats assured the red men that all belonged to the Indian, and that the great king of the French desired only to set up a boundary against the further encroachments of the English, who would otherwise sweep the red tribes from the Ohio as they had already driven them from the Atlantic. The argument was plausible. In every tribe were French missionaries, whose fearless courage and devotion had won the admiration and love of the savage; in every village was domiciliated a hardy voyageur, with his Indian wife and family of children, in whose veins commingled the blood of the two races and whose ears were attuned alike to the wild songs of the forest and the rondeaus of Normandy or Provence. It was no common tie that bound together the Indians and the French, and when a governor of Canada and the general of his army stepped into the circle of braves to dance the war dance and sing the war song with their red allies, thirty-three wild tribes declared on the wampum belt, "The French are our brothers and their king is our father. We will try his hatchet upon the English" (*Bancroft, 3*), and through seven years of blood and death the lily and the totem were borne abreast until the flag of France went down forever on the heights of Quebec.

For some time after the surrender the unrest of the native tribes was soothed into a semblance of quiet by the belief, artfully inculcated by their old allies, that the king of France, wearied by his great exertions, had fallen asleep for a little while, but would soon awake to take vengeance on the English for the wrongs they had inflicted on his red children. Then, as they saw English garrisons occupying the abandoned posts and English traders passing up the lakes even to the sacred island of the Great Turtle, the despairing warriors said to one another, "We have been deceived. English and French alike are white men and liars. We must turn from both and seek help from our Indian gods."

In 1762 a prophet appeared among the Delawares, at Tuscarawas, on the Muskingum, who preached a union of all the red tribes and a return to the old Indian life, which he declared to be the divine command, as revealed to himself in a wonderful vision. From an old French manuscript, written by an anonymous eyewitness of the scene which he describes, we have the details of this vision, as related by Pontiac to his savage auditors at the great council of the tribes held near Detroit in April, 1763. Parkman gives the story on the authority of this manuscript, which he refers to as the "Pontiac manuscript," and states that it was long preserved in a Canadian family at Detroit, and afterward deposited with the Historical Society of Michigan. It bears internal evidence of genuineness, and is supposed to have been written by a French priest. (*Parkman, 1.*) The vision, from the same manuscript, is related at length in Schoolcraft's Algic Researches.

According to the prophet's story, being anxious to know the "Master of Life," he determined, without mentioning his desire to anyone, to undertake a journey to the spirit world. Ignorant of the way, and not knowing any person who, having been there, could direct him, he performed a mystic rite in the hope of receiving some light as to the course he should pursue. He then fell into a deep sleep, in which he dreamed that it was only necessary to begin his journey and that by continuing to walk forward he would at last arrive at his destination.

Early the next morning, taking his gun, ammunition, and kettle, he started off, firmly convinced that by pressing onward without discouragement he should accomplish his object. Day after day he proceeded without incident, until at sunset of the eighth day, while preparing to encamp for the night by the side of a small stream in a little opening in the forest, he noticed, running out from the edge of the prairie, three wide and well-trodden paths. Wondering somewhat that they should be there, he finished his temporary lodging and, lighting a fire, began to prepare his supper. While thus engaged, he observed with astonishment that the paths became more distinct as the night grew darker.

Alarmed at the strange appearance, he was about to abandon his encampment and seek another at a safer distance, when he remembered his dream and the purpose of his journey. It seemed to him that one of these roads must lead to the place of which he was in search, and he determined, therefore, to remain where he was until morning, and then take one of the three and follow it to the end. Accordingly, the next morning, after a hasty meal, he left his encampment, and, burning with the ardor of discovery, took the widest path, which he followed until noon, when he suddenly saw a large fire issuing apparently from the earth. His curiosity being aroused, he went toward it, but the fire increased to such a degree that he became frightened and turned back.

He now took the next widest of the three paths, which he followed as before until noon, when a similar fire again drove him back and compelled him to take the third road, which he kept a whole day without meeting anything unusual, when suddenly he saw a precipitous mountain of dazzling brightness directly in his path. Recovering from his wonder, he drew near and examined it, but could see no sign of a road to the summit. He was about to give way to disappointment, when, looking up, he saw seated a short distance up the mountain a woman of bright beauty and clad in snow-white garments, who addressed him in his own language, telling him that on the summit of the mountain was the abode of the Master of Life, whom he had journeyed so far to meet. "But to reach it," said she, "you must leave all your cumbersome dress and equipments at the foot, then go and wash in the river which I show you, and afterward ascend the mountain."

He obeyed her instructions, and on asking how he could hope to climb the mountain, which was steep and slippery as glass, she replied that in order to mount he must use only his left hand and foot. This seemed to him almost impossible, but, encouraged by the woman, he began to climb, and at length, after much difficulty, reached the top. Here the woman suddenly vanished, and he found himself alone without a guide. On looking about, he saw before him a plain, in the midst of which were three villages, with well-built houses disposed in orderly arrangement. He bent his steps toward the principal one, but after going a short distance he remembered that he was naked, and was about to turn back when a voice told him that as he had washed himself in the river he might go on without fear. Thus bidden, he advanced without hesitation to the gate of the village, where he was admitted and saw approaching a handsome man in white garments, who offered to lead him into the presence of the Master of Life. Admiring the beauty of everything about him, he was then conducted to the Master of Life, who took him by the hand and gave him for a seat a hat bordered with gold. Afraid of spoiling the hat, he hesitated to sit down until again told to do so, when he obeyed, and the Master of Life thus addressed him:

I am the Master of Life, whom you wish to see and with whom you wish to speak. Listen to what I shall tell you for yourself and for all the Indians.

He then commanded him to exhort his people to cease from drunkenness, wars, polygamy, and the medicine song, and continued:

The land on which you are, I have made for you, not for others. Wherefore do you
suffer the whites to dwell upon your lands? Can you not do without them? I know
that those whom you call the children of your Great Father [the King of France]
supply your wants; but were you not wicked as you are you would not need them.
You might live as you did before you knew them. Before those whom you call your
brothers [the French] had arrived, did not your bow and arrow maintain you? You
needed neither gun, powder, nor any other object. The flesh of animals was your
food; their skins your raiment. But when I saw you inclined to evil, I removed the
animals into the depths of the forest that you might depend on your brothers for
your necessaries, for your clothing. Again become good and do my will and I will
send animals for your sustenance. I do not, however, forbid suffering among you your
Father's children. I love them; they know me; they pray to me. I supply their
own wants, and give them that which they bring to you. Not so with those who
are come to trouble your possessions [the English]. Drive them away; wage war
against them; I love them not; they know me not; they are my enemies; they are
your brothers' enemies. Send them back to the lands I have made for them. Let
them remain there. (*Schoolcraft, Alg. Res., 1.*)

The Master of Life then gave him a prayer, carved in Indian hieroglyphics upon a wooden stick, which he was told to deliver to his chief
on returning to earth. (*Parkman, 2.*)   His instructor continued:

Learn it by heart, and teach it to all the Indians and children. It must be repeated
morning and evening. Do all that I have told thee, and announce it to all the
Indians as coming from the Master of Life. Let them drink but one draught, or two
at most, in one day. Let them have but one wife, and discontinue running after
other people's wives and daughters. Let them not fight one another. Let them
not sing the medicine song, for in singing the medicine song they speak to the evil
spirit. Drive from your lands those dogs in red clothing; they are only an injury to
you. When you want anything, apply to me, as your brothers do, and I will give to
both. Do not sell to your brothers that which I have placed on the earth as food. In
short, become good, and you shall want nothing. When you meet one another, bow
and give one another the [left] hand of the heart. Above all, I command thee to
repeat morning and evening the prayer which I have given thee.

The Indian received the prayer, promising to do as he had been
commanded and to recommend the same course to others. His former
conductor then came and, leading him to the foot of the mountain, bid
him resume his garments and go back to his village. His return
excited much surprise among his friends, who had supposed him lost.
They asked him where he had been, but as he had been commanded
to speak to no one until he had seen the chief, he motioned with his
hand to signify that he had come from above. On entering the village
he went at once to the wigwam of the chief, to whom he delivered the
prayer and the message which he had received from the Master of Life.
(*Schoolcraft, Alg. Res., 2.*)

Although the story as here given bears plain impress of the white
man's ideas, it is essentially aboriginal. While the discrimination
expressed by the Master of Life in favor of the French and against
the English may have been due to the fact that the author of the

manuscript was a Frenchman, it is more probable that we have here set forth only the well-known preference of the wild tribes. The occupancy of a region by the English always meant the speedy expulsion of the natives. The French, on the contrary, lived side by side with the red men, joining in their dances and simple amusements, and entering with fullest sympathy into their wild life, so that they were regarded rather as brethren of an allied tribe than as intruders of an alien race. This feeling is well indicated in the prophet's narrative, where the Indians, while urged to discard everything that they have adopted from the whites, are yet to allow the French to remain among them, though exhorted to relentless war on the English. The difference received tragic exemplification at Michilimackinac a year later, when a handful of French traders looked on unarmed and unhurt while a crew of maddened savages were butchering, scalping, and drinking the blood of British soldiers. The introduction of the trivial incident of the hat is characteristically Indian, and the confounding of dreams and visions with actual happenings is a frequent result of mental exaltation of common occurrence in the history of religious enthusiasts. The Delaware prophet regards the whole experience as an actual fact instead of a distempered vision induced by long fasts and vigils, and the hieroglyphic prayer—undoubtedly graven by himself while under the ecstasy—is to him a real gift from heaven. The whole story is a striking parallel of the miraculous experiences recounted by the modern apostles of the Ghost dance. The prayer-stick also and the heavenly map, later described and illustrated, reappear in the account of Känakûk, the Kickapoo prophet, seventy years afterward, showing in a striking manner the continuity of aboriginal ideas and methods.

The celebrated missionary, Heckewelder, who spent fifty years among the Delawares, was personally acquainted with this prophet and gives a detailed account of his teachings and of his symbolic parchments. He says:

In the year 1762 there was a famous preacher of the Delaware nation, who resided at Cayahaga, near Lake Erie, and travelled about the country, among the Indians, endeavouring to persuade them that he had been appointed by the Great Spirit to instruct them in those things that were agreeable to him, and point out to them the offences by which they had drawn his displeasure on themselves, and the means by which they might recover his favour for the future. He had drawn, as he pretended, by the direction of the Great Spirit, a kind of map on a piece of deerskin, somewhat dressed like parchment, which he called "the great Book or Writing." This, he said, he had been ordered to shew to the Indians, that they might see the situation in which the Mannitto had originally placed them, the misery which they had brought upon themselves by neglecting their duty, and the only way that was now left them to regain what they had lost. This map he held before him while preaching, frequently pointing to particular marks and spots upon it, and giving explanations as he went along.

The size of this map was about fifteen inches square, or, perhaps, something more. An inside square was formed by lines drawn within it, of about eight inches each way; two of these lines, however, were not closed by about half an inch at the corners.

Across these inside lines, others of about an inch in length were drawn with sundry other lines and marks, all which was intended to represent a strong inaccessible barrier, to prevent those without from entering the space within, otherwise than at the place appointed for that purpose. When the map was held as he directed, the corners which were not closed lay at the left-hand side, directly opposite to each other, the one being at the southeast by south, and the nearest at the northeast by north. In explaining or describing the particular points on this map, with his fingers always pointing to the place he was describing, he called the space within the inside lines "the heavenly regions," or the place destined by the Great Spirit for the habitation of the Indians in future life. The space left open at the southeast corner he called the "avenue," which had been intended for the Indians to enter into this heaven, but which was now in the possession of the white people; wherefore the Great Spirit had since caused another "avenue" to be made on the opposite side, at which, however, it was both difficult and dangerous for them to enter, there being many impediments in their way, besides a large ditch leading to a gulf below, over which they had to leap; but the evil spirit kept at this very spot a continual watch for Indians, and whoever he laid hold of never could get away from him again, but was carried to his regions, where there was nothing but extreme poverty; where the ground was parched up by the heat for want of rain, no fruit came to perfection, the game was almost starved for want of pasture, and where the evil spirit, at his pleasure, transformed men into horses and dogs, to be ridden by him and follow him in his hunts and wherever he went.

The space on the outside of this interior square was intended to represent the country given to the Indians to hunt, fish, and dwell in while in this world; the east side of it was called the ocean or "great salt-water lake." Then the preacher, drawing the attention of his hearers particularly to the southeast avenue, would say to them, "Look here! See what we have lost by neglect and disobedience; by being remiss in the expression of our gratitude to the Great Spirit for what he has bestowed upon us; by neglecting to make to him sufficient sacrifices; by looking upon a people of a different colour from our own, who had come across a great lake, as if they were a part of ourselves; by suffering them to sit down by our side, and looking at them with indifference, while they were not only taking our country from us, but this (pointing to the spot), this, our own avenue, leading into those beautiful regions which were destined for us. Such is the sad condition to which we are reduced. What is now to be done, and what remedy is to be applied? I will tell you, my friends. Hear what the Great Spirit has ordered me to tell you! You are to make sacrifices, in the manner that I shall direct; to put off entirely from yourselves the customs which you have adopted since the white people came among us. You are to return to that former happy state, in which we lived in peace and plenty, before these strangers came to disturb us; and, above all, you must abstain from drinking their deadly *beson*, which they have forced upon us, for the sake of increasing their gains and diminishing our numbers. Then will the Great Spirit give success to our arms; then he will give us strength to conquer our enemies, to drive them from hence, and recover the passage to the heavenly regions which they have taken from us."

Such was in general the substance of his discourses. After having dilated more or less on the various topics which I have mentioned, he commonly concluded in this manner: "And now, my friends, in order that what I have told you may remain firmly impressed on your minds, and to refresh your memories from time to time, I advise you to preserve, in every family at least, such a book or writing as this, which I will finish off for you, provided you bring me the price, which is only one buckskin or two doeskins apiece." The price was of course bought (*sic*), and the book purchased. In some of those maps, the figure of a deer or turkey, or both, was placed in the heavenly regions, and also in the dreary region of the evil spirit. The former, however, appeared fat and plump, while the latter seemed to have nothing but skin and bones. (*Heckewelder, 1.*)

From the narrative of John McCullough, who had been taken by the Indians when a child of 8 years, and lived for some years as an adopted son in a Delaware family in northeastern Ohio, we gather some additional particulars concerning this prophet, whose name seems to be lost to history. McCullough himself, who was then but a boy, never met the prophet, but obtained his information from others who had, especially from his Indian brother, who went to Tuscarawas (or Tuscalaways) to see and hear the new apostle on his first appearance.

It was said by those who went to see him that he had certain hieroglyphics marked on a piece of parchment, denoting the probation that human beings were subjected to whilst they were living on earth, and also denoting something of a future state. They informed me that he was almost constantly crying whilst he was exhorting them. I saw a copy of his hieroglyphics, as numbers of them had got them copied and undertook to preach or instruct others. The first or principal doctrine they taught them was to purify themselves from sin, which they taught they could do by the use of emetics and abstinence from carnal knowledge of the different sexes; to quit the use of firearms, and to live entirely in the original state that they were in before the white people found out their country. Nay, they taught that that fire was not pure that was made by steel and flint, but that they should make it by rubbing two sticks together. . . . It was said that their prophet taught them, or made them believe, that he had his instructions immediately from *Keesh-she-la-mil-lang-up*, or a being that *thought* us into being, and that by following his instructions they would, in a few years, be able to drive the white people out of their country.

I knew a company of them who had secluded themselves for the purpose of purifying from sin, as they thought they could do. I believe they made no use of firearms. They had been out more than two years before I left them. . . . It was said that they made use of no other weapons than their bows and arrows. They also taught, in shaking hands, to give the left hand in token of friendship, as it denoted that they gave the heart along with the hand. (*Pritts, 1.*)

The religious ferment produced by the exhortations of the Delaware prophet spread rapidly from tribe to tribe, until, under the guidance of the master mind of the celebrated chief, Pontiac, it took shape in a grand confederacy of all the northwestern tribes to oppose the further progress of the English. The coast lands were lost to the Indians. The Ohio and the lakes were still theirs, and the Alleghanies marked a natural boundary between the two sections. Behind this mountain barrier Pontiac determined to make his stand. Though the prospect of a restoration of the French power might enable him to rally a following, he himself knew he could expect no aid from the French, for their armies had been defeated and their garrisons were already withdrawn; but, relying on the patriotism of his own red warriors, when told that the English were on their way to take possession of the abandoned posts, he sent back the haughty challenge, "I stand in the path."

To Pontiac must be ascribed the highest position among the leaders of the Algonquian race. Born the son of a chief, he became in turn the chief of his own people, the Ottawa, whom it is said he commanded on the occasion of Braddock's defeat. For this or other services in behalf of the French he had received marks of distinguished consideration from

Montcalm himself. By reason of his natural ability, his influence was felt and respected wherever the name of his tribe was spoken, while to his dignity as chief he added the sacred character of high priest of the powerful secret order of the Midé. (*Parkman, 3.*) Now, in the prime of manhood, he originated and formulated the policy of a confederation of all the tribes, an idea afterward taken up and carried almost to a successful accomplishment by the great Tecumtha. As principal chief of the lake tribes, he summoned them to the great council near Detroit, in April, 1763, and, as high priest and keeper of the faith, he there announced to them the will of the Master of Life, as revealed to the Delaware prophet, and called on them to unite for the recovery of their ancient territories and the preservation of their national life. Under the spell of his burning words the chiefs listened as to an oracle, and cried out that he had only to declare his will to be obeyed. (*Parkman, 4.*) His project being unanimously approved, runners were sent out to secure the cooperation of the more remote nations, and in a short time the confederation embraced every important tribe of Algonquian lineage, together with the Wyandot, Seneca, Winnebago, and some of those to the southward. (*Parkman, 5.*)

Only the genius of a Pontiac could have molded into a working unit such an aggregation of diverse elements of savagery. His executive ability is sufficiently proven by his creation of a regular commissary department based on promissory notes—hieroglyphics graven on birch-bark and signed with the otter, the totem of his tribe; his diplomatic bent appeared in his employment of two secretaries to attend to this unique correspondence, each of whom he managed to keep in ignorance of the business transacted by the other (*Parkman, 6*); while his military capacity was soon to be evinced in the carefully laid plan which enabled his warriors to strike simultaneously a crushing blow at every British post scattered throughout the 500 miles of wilderness from Pittsburg to the straits of Mackinaw.

The history of this war, so eloquently told by Parkman, reads like some old knightly romance. The warning of the Indian girl; the concerted attack on the garrisons; the ball play at Mackinac on the king's birthday, and the massacre that followed; the siege of Fort Pitt and the heroic defense of Detroit; the bloody battle of Bushy run, where the painted savage recoiled before the kilted Highlander, as brave and almost as wild; Bouquet's march into the forests of the Ohio, and the submission of the vanquished tribes—all these things must be passed over here. They have already been told by a master of language. But the contest of savagery against civilization has but one ending, and the scene closes with the death of Pontiac, a broken-spirited wanderer, cut down at last by a hired assassin of his own race, for whose crime the blood of whole tribes was poured out in atonement. (*Parkman, 7.*)

Chapter III

TENSKWATAWA THE SHAWANO PROPHET

I told all the redskins that the way they were in was not good, and that they
ought to abandon it.—*Tenskwatawa*.

A very shrewd and influential man, but circumstances have destroyed him.—
Catlin.

Forty years had passed away and changes had come to the western
territory. The cross of Saint George, erected in the place of the lilies
of France, had been supplanted by the flag of the young republic,
which in one generation had extended its sway from the lakes to the

Fig. 56—Tenskwatawa the Shawano prophet, 1808 and 1831.

gulf and from the Atlantic to the Rocky mountains. By treaties made
in 1768 with the Iroquois and Cherokee, the two leading Indian con-
federacies in the east, the Ohio and the Kanawha had been fixed as the
boundary between the two races, the Indians renouncing forever their
claims to the seaboard, the Delaware, and the Susquehanna, while they
were confirmed in their possession of the Alleghany, the Ohio, and the
great northwest. But the restless borderer would not be limited, and
encroachments on the native domain were constantly being made,
resulting in a chronic warfare which kept alive the spirit of resentment.
The consequence was that in the final struggle of the Revolution the

Indian tribes ranged themselves on the British side. When the war ended and a treaty of peace was made between the new government and the old, no provision was made for the red allies of the king, and they were left to continue the struggle single-handed. The Indians claimed the Ohio country as theirs by virtue of the most solemn treaties, but pioneers had already occupied western Pennsylvania, western Virginia, and Kentucky, and were listening with eager attention to the reports brought back by adventurous hunters from the fertile lands of the Muskingum and the Scioto. They refused to be bound by the treaties of a government they had repudiated, and the tribes of the northwest were obliged to fight to defend their territories. Under the able

FIG. 57—Greenville treaty medal, obverse and reverse.

leadership of Little Turtle they twice rolled back the tide of white invasion, defeating two of the finest armies ever sent into the western country, until, worn out by twenty years of unceasing warfare, and crushed and broken by the decisive victory of Wayne at the Fallen Timbers, their villages in ashes and their cornfields cut down, the dispirited chiefs met their conqueror at Greenville in 1795 and signed away the rights for which they had so long contended.

By this treaty, which marks the beginning of the end with the eastern tribes, the Indians renounced their claims to all territory east of a line running in a general way from the mouth of the Cuyahoga on Lake Erie to the mouth of the Kentucky on the Ohio, leaving to the whites the better portion of Ohio valley, including their favorite hunting ground of Kentucky. The Delaware, the Wyandot, and the Shawano, three of the leading tribes, were almost completely shorn of their ancient inheritance and driven back as refugees among the Miami.

The Canadian boundary had been established along the lakes; the Ohio was lost to the Indians; for them there was left only extermination or removal to the west. Their bravest warriors were slain. Their ablest chieftain, who had led them to victory against St Clair, had bowed to the inevitable, and was now regarded as one with a white man's heart and a traitor to his race. A brooding dissatisfaction settled down on the tribes. Who shall deliver them from the desolation that has come on them?

Now arose among the Shawano another prophet to point out to his people the "open door" leading to happiness. In November, 1805, a young man named Laulewasikaw (Lalawé'thika, a rattle or similar instrument—*Gatschet*), then hardly more than 30 years of age, called around him his tribesmen and their allies at their ancient capital of Wapakoneta, within the present limits of Ohio, and there announced himself as the bearer of a new revelation from the Master of Life, who had taken pity on his red children and wished to save them from the threatened destruction. He declared that he had been taken up to the spirit world and had been permitted to lift the veil of the past and the future—had seen the misery of evil doers and learned the happiness that awaited those who followed the precepts of the Indian god. He then began an earnest exhortation, denouncing the witchcraft practices and medicine juggleries of the tribe, and solemnly warning his hearers that none who had part in such things would ever taste of the future happiness. The firewater of the whites was poison and accursed; and those who continued its use would after death be tormented with all the pains of fire, while flames would continually issue from their mouths. This idea may have been derived from some white man's teaching or from the Indian practice of torture by fire. The young must cherish and respect the aged and infirm. All property must be in common, according to the ancient law of their ancestors. Indian women must cease to intermarry with white men; the two races were distinct and must remain so. The white man's dress, with his flint-and-steel, must be discarded for the old time buckskin and the firestick. More than this, every tool and every custom derived from the whites must be put away, and they must return to the methods which the Master of Life had taught them. When they should do all this, he promised that they would again be taken into the divine favor, and find the happiness which their fathers had known before the coming of the whites. Finally, in proof of his divine mission, he announced that he had received power to cure all diseases and to arrest the hand of death in sickness or on the battlefield. (*Drake, Tecumseh, 1.* To avoid repetition, it may be stated that, except when otherwise noted, the principal facts concerning Tecumtha and the prophet are taken from Drake's work, the most valuable published on the subject. The prophet and his doctrines are also spoken of at some length by Tanner, Kendall, Warren, and Catlin, as hereafter quoted, while the history of Tecumtha is a part of the history of Ohio valley, to be found in any work treating of that section and period)

In an account quoted by Drake, probably from an English writer, it is stated that the prophet was noted for his stupidity and intoxication until his fiftieth (?) year, when one day, while lighting his pipe in his cabin, he suddenly fell back apparently lifeless and remained in that condition until his friends had assembled for the funeral, when he revived from his trance, and after quieting their alarm, announced that he had been to the spirit world and commanded them to call the people together that he might tell them what he had seen. When they had assembled, he declared that he had been conducted to the border of the spirit world by two young men, who had permitted him to look in upon its pleasures, but not to enter, and who, after charging him with the message to his people already noted, had left him, promising to visit him again at a future time. (*Drake, Ab. Races, 1.*)

Although the language of this account is somewhat overdrawn, the main statements are probably correct, as it is in complete accordance with the Indian system by which all truth has been revealed in dreams and trances from the first dawn of tradition down to Smohalla and the messiah of the Ghost dance.

His words aroused an intense excitement among his hearers, and the impression deepened as the tidings of the new gospel were carried from camp to camp. Those who were addicted to drunkenness—the besetting sin of the Indians since their acquaintance with the whites—were so thoroughly alarmed at the prospect of a fiery punishment in the spirit world that for a long time intoxication became practically unknown among the western tribes. Their zeal led also to the inauguration of a crusade against all who were suspected of dealing in witchcraft or magic arts; but here the prophet took advantage of this feeling to effectually rid himself of all who opposed his sacred claims. It was only necessary for him to denounce such a person as a witch to have him pay the forfeit with reputation, if not with life.

Among the first of his victims were several Delawares—Tatepocoshe (more generally known as Teteboxti), Patterson, his nephew, Coltos, an old woman, and an aged man called Joshua. These were successively marked by the prophet, and doomed to be burnt alive. The tragedy was commenced with the old woman. The Indians roasted her slowly over a fire for four days, calling upon her frequently to deliver up her charm and medicine bag. Just as she was dying, she exclaimed that her grandson, who was then out hunting, had it in his possession. Messengers were sent in pursuit of him, and when found he was tied and brought into camp. He acknowledged that on one occasion he had borrowed the charm of his grandmother, by means of which he had flown through the air over Kentucky, to the banks of the Mississippi, and back again, between twilight and bedtime; but he insisted that he had returned the charm to its owner, and, after some consultation, he was set at liberty. The following day a council was held over the case of the venerable chief

Tatepocoshe, he being present. His death was decided upon after full deliberation; and, arrayed in his finest apparel, he calmly assisted in building his own funeral pile, fully aware that there was no escape from the judgment that had been passed upon him. The respect due to his whitened locks induced his executioners to treat him with mercy. He was deliberately tomahawked by a young man, and his body was then placed upon the blazing fagots and consumed. The next day the old preacher Joshua met a similar fate. The wife of Tatepocoshe and his nephew Billy Patterson were then brought into the council house and seated side by side. The latter had led an irreproachable life, and died like a Christian, singing and pray-ing amid the flames which destroyed his body. While preparations were making for the immolation of Tatecoposhe's wife, her brother, a youth of 20 years of age, suddenly started up, took her by the hand, and, to the amazement of the council, led her out of the house. He soon returned, and exclaiming, "The devil has come among us (alluding to the prophet), and we are killing each other," he reseated himself in the midst of the crowd. This bold step checked the wild frenzy of the Indians, put an end to these cruel scenes, and for a time greatly impaired the impostor's influence among the Delawares. (*Drake, Tecumseh, 2.*)

The prophet now changed his name to Tenskwatawa, "The Open Door" (from *skwa'te,* a door, and *the'nui,* to be open; frequently spelled Elskwatawa), significant of the new mode of life which he had come to point out to his people, and fixed his headquarters at Greenville, Ohio, where representatives from the various scattered tribes of the northwest gathered about him to learn the new doctrines. Some, especially the Kickapoo, entered fervently into his spirit, while others were disposed to oppose him. The Miami, who regarded the Shawano as intruders, were jealous of his influence, and the chiefs of his own tribe were somewhat inclined to consider him in the light of a rival. To estab-lish his sacred character and to dispel the doubts of the unbelievers, he continued to dream dreams and announce wonderful revelations from time to time, when an event occurred which effectually silenced opposi-tion and stamped him as one inspired.

By some means he had learned that an eclipse of the sun was to take place in the summer of 1806. As the time drew near, he called about him the scoffers and boldly announced that on a certain day he would prove to them his supernatural authority by causing the sun to become dark. When the day and hour arrived and the earth at mid-day was enveloped in the gloom of twilight, Tenskwatawa, standing in the midst of the terrified Indians, pointed to the sky and cried, "Did I not speak truth? See, the sun is dark!" There were no more doubters now. All proclaimed him a true prophet and the messenger of the Master of Life. His fame spread abroad and apostles began to carry his revelations to the remotest tribes.

We get but fragmentary light in regard to the details of the doctrine and ceremonies of this religious revival, as well as of that which pre-ceded it. There were then no railroads, no newspaper correspondents to gather each day's proceedings, and no telegraph to flash the news across the continent before nightfall; no reservation system, with its attendant army of employees, everyone a spy when an emergency arose; and no investigators to go among the tribes and study the matter from an ethnologic point of view. Our information is derived chiefly from military officers, who knew these things only as vague rumors of Indian unrest fomented by British agents; from the statements of a few illiterate interpreters or captives among the savages, and from the misty recollections of old men long after the excitement had passed away. Of the dances which are a part of every important Indian ceremony, the songs which they chanted, the peculiar dress or adornments which probably distinguished the believers—of all these we know nothing; but we may well surmise that the whole elaborate system of Indian mythology and ceremonial was brought into play to give weight to the words of the prophet, and enough is known to show that in its leading features the movement closely resembled the modern Ghost dance.

It is impossible to know how far the prophet was responsible for the final shaping of the doctrine. Like all such movements, it undoubtedly grew and took more definite form under the hands of the apostles who went out from the presence of its originator to preach to the various tribes. A religion which found adherents alike in the everglades of Florida and on the plains of the Saskatchewan must necessarily have undergone local modifications. From a comparison of the various accounts we can arrive at a general statement of the belief.

The prophet was held to be an incarnation of Manabozho, the great "first doer" of the Algonquian system. His words were believed to be the direct utterances of a deity. Manabozho had taught his people certain modes of living best suited to their condition and capacity. A new race had come upon them, and the Indians had thrown aside their primitive purity of life and adopted the innovations of the whites, which had now brought them to degradation and misery and threatened them with swift and entire destruction. To punish them for their disobedience and bring them to a sense of their duty, Manabozho had called the game from the forests and shut it up under the earth, so that the tribes were now on the verge of starvation and obliged to eat the flesh of filthy hogs. They had also lost their old love for one another and become addicted to the secret practices of the poisoner and the wizard, together with the abominable ceremonies of the calumet dance. They must now put aside all these things, throw away the weapons and the dress of the white man, pluck out their hair as in ancient times, wear the eagle feather on their heads, and clothe themselves again with the breechcloth and the skins of animals slain with the bows and arrows which Manabozho had given them. (*Kendall, 1.*) They must have done with the white man's flint-and-steel, and cook their food over a fire made by rubbing together two sticks, and this fire must always be kept burning in their lodges, as it was a symbol of the eternal life, and their care for it was an evidence of their heed to the divine commands. The firewater must forever be put away, together with the medicine bags and poisons and the wicked juggleries which had corrupted the ancient purity of the Midé rites. Instead of these the prophet gave them new songs and new medicines. Their women must cease from any connection with white men. They were to love one another and make an end of their constant wars, to be kind to their children, to keep but one dog in a family, and to abstain from lying and stealing. If they would listen to his voice and follow his instructions, the incarnate Manabozho promised that at the end of four years (i. e., in 1811) he would bring on two days of darkness, during which he would travel invisibly throughout the land, and cause the animals which he had created to come forth again out of the earth. (*Kendall, 2.*) They were also promised that their dead friends would be restored to them.

The ideas as to the catastrophe that was to usher in the new era seem to have varied according to the interpreter of the belief. Among the Ottawa, and perhaps among the lake tribes generally, there was to be a period of darkness, as already stated. Among the Cherokee, and probably also among the Creek, it was believed that there would be a terrible hailstorm, which would overwhelm with destruction both the whites and the unbelievers of the red race, while the elect would be warned in time to save themselves by fleeing to the high mountain tops. The idea of any hostile combination against the white race seems to have been no part of the doctrine. In the north, however, there is always a plain discrimination against the Americans. The Great Father, through his prophet, is represented as declaring himself to be the common parent alike of Indians, English, French, and Spaniards; while the Americans, on the contrary, "are not my children, but the children of the evil spirit. They grew from the scum of the great water, when it was troubled by an evil spirit and the froth was driven into the woods by a strong east wind. They are numerous, but I hate them. They are unjust; they have taken away your lands, which were not made for them." (*Kendall, 3.*)

From the venerable James Wafford, of the Cherokee nation, the author in 1891 obtained some interesting details in regard to the excitement among the Cherokee. According to his statement, the doctrine first came to them through the Creek about 1812 or 1813. It was probably given to the Creek by Tecumtha and his party on their visit to that tribe in the fall of 1811, as will be related hereafter. The Creek were taught by their prophets that the old Indian life was soon to return, when "instead of beef and bacon they would have venison, and instead of chickens they would have turkeys." Great sacred dances were inaugurated, and the people were exhorted to be ready for what was to come. From the south the movement spread to the Cherokee, and one of their priests, living in what is now upper Georgia, began to preach that on a day near at hand there would be a terrible storm, with a mighty wind and hailstones as large as hominy mortars, which would destroy from the face of the earth all but the true believers who had previously taken refuge on the highest summits of the Great Smoky mountains. Full of this belief, numbers of the tribe in Alabama and Georgia abandoned their bees, their orchards, their slaves, and everything else that might have come to them through the white man, and, in spite of the entreaties and remonstrances of friends who put no faith in the prediction, took up their toilsome march for the mountains of Carolina. Wafford, who was then about 10 years of age, lived with his mother and stepfather on Valley river, and vividly remembers the troops of pilgrims, with their packs on their backs, fleeing from the lower country to escape from the wrath to come. Many of them stopped at the house of his stepfather, who, being a white man, was somewhat better prepared than his neighbors to entertain travelers, and who took the opportunity to endeavor to persuade them to turn back, telling them that their hopes and fears alike were groundless. Some listened to him and returned to their homes, but others went on and climbed the mountain, where they waited until the appointed day arrived, only to find themselves disappointed. Slowly and sadly then they took up their packs once more and turned their faces homeward, dreading the ridicule they were sure to meet there, but yet believing in their hearts that the glorious coming was only postponed for a time. This excitement among the Cherokee is noted at some length in the Cherokee Advocate of November 16, 1844, published at Tahlequah, Cherokee Nation. Among the Creek the excitement, intensified by reports of the struggle now going on in the north, and fostered and encouraged by the emissaries of Spain and England, grew and spread until it culminated in the summer of 1813 in the terrible Creek war.

Enough is known of the ceremonial of this religion to show that it must have had an elaborate ritual. We learn from Warren that the adherents of the prophet were accustomed to perform certain ceremonies in solemn councils, and that, after he had prohibited the corrupt secret rites, he introduced instead new medicines and songs, and that at the ancient capital of the Ojibwa on Lake Superior the Indians collected in great numbers and performed these dances and ceremonies day and night. (*Warren, 1.*) They were also instructed to dance naked, with their bodies painted and with the warclub in their hands. (*Kendall, 4.*) The solemn rite of confirmation, known as "shaking hands with the prophet," was particularly impressive. From the narrative of John Tanner, a white man captured when a child from his home in Kentucky and brought up among the wild Ojibwa, we get the best contemporary account of the advent of the new doctrine in the north and its effect on the lake tribes. He says:

It was while I was living here at Great Wood river that news came of a great man among the Shawneese, who had been favoured by a revelation of the mind and will of the Great Spirit. I was hunting in the prairie, at a great distance from my lodge, when I saw a stranger approaching. At first I was apprehensive of an enemy, but as he drew nearer, his dress showed him to be an Ojibbeway; but when he came up, there was something very strange and peculiar in his manner. He signified to me that I must go home, but gave no explanation of the cause. He refused to look at me or enter into any kind of conversation. I thought he must be crazy, but nevertheless accompanied him to my lodge. When we had smoked, he remained a long time silent, but at last began to tell me he had come with a message from the prophet of the Shawneese. "Henceforth," said he, "the fire must never be suffered to go out in your lodge. Summer and winter, day and night, in the storm, or when it is calm, you must remember that the life in your body and the fire in your lodge are the same and of the same date. If you suffer your fire to be extinguished, at that moment your life will be at its end. You must not suffer a dog to live; you must never strike either a man, a woman, a child, or a dog. The prophet himself is coming to shake hands with you; but I have come before, that you may know what is the will of the Great Spirit, communicated to us by him, and to inform you that the preservation of your life, for a single moment, depends on your entire obedience. From this time forward we are neither to be drunk, to steal, to lie, or to go against our enemies. While we yield an entire obedience to these commands of the Great Spirit, the Sioux, even if they come to our country, will not be able to see us; we shall be protected and made happy." I listened to all he had to say, but told him, in answer, that I could not believe we should all die in case our fire went out; in many instances, also, it would be difficult to avoid punishing our children; our dogs were useful in aiding us to hunt and take animals, so that I could not believe the Great Spirit had any wish to take them from us. He continued talking to us until late at night; then he lay down to sleep in my lodge. I happened to wake first in the morning, and, perceiving the fire had gone out, I called him to get up and see how many of us were living and how many dead. He was prepared for the ridicule I attempted to throw upon his doctrine, and told me that I had not yet shaken hands with the prophet. His visit had been to prepare me for this important event, and to make me aware of the obligations and risks I should incur, by entering into the engagement implied in taking in my hand the message of the prophet. I did not rest entirely easy in my unbelief. The Indians, generally, received the doctrine of this man with great humility and fear. Distress and anxiety was visible in every countenance. Many killed their dogs, and endeavored to practice obedience to all the commands of this new preacher, who still remained among us. But, as was usual with me, in any emergency of this kind, I went to the traders, firmly believing that if the Deity had any communications to make to men, they would be given, in the first instance, to white men. The traders ridiculed and despised the idea of a new revelation of the Divine will, and the thought that it should be given to a poor Shawnee. Thus was I confirmed in my infidelity. Nevertheless, I did not openly avow my unbelief to the Indians, only I refused to kill my dogs, and showed no great degree of anxiety to comply with his other requirements. As long as I remained among the Indians, I made it my business to conform, as far as appeared consistent with my immediate convenience and comfort, with all their customs. Many of their ideas I have adopted, but I always found among them opinions which I could not hold. The Ojibbeway whom I have mentioned remained some time among the Indians in my neighborhood, and gained the attention of the principal men so effectually that a time was appointed and a lodge prepared for the solemn and public espousing of the doctrines of the prophet. When the people, and I among them, were brought into the long lodge, prepared for this solemnity, we saw something carefully concealed under a blanket, in figure and dimensions bearing some resemblance to the form of a man. This was accompanied by two young men, who, it was understood, attended constantly upon it, made its bed at night, as for a man, and slept near it. But while we remained no one went near it or raised the blanket which was spread over its unknown contents. Four strings of mouldy and discoloured beans were all the remaining visible insignia of this important mission. After a long harangue, in which the prominent features of the new revelation were stated and urged upon the attention of all, the four strings of beans, which we were told were made of the flesh itself of the prophet, were carried with much solemnity to each man in the lodge, and he was expected to take hold of each string at the top, and draw them gently through his hand. This was called shaking hands with the prophet, and was considered as solemnly engaging to obey his injunctions, and accept his mission as from the Supreme. All the Indians who touched the beans had previously killed their dogs; they gave up their medicine bags, and showed a disposition to comply with all that should be required of them.

We had now been for some time assembled in considerable numbers. Much agitation and terror had prevailed among us, and now famine began to be felt. The faces of men wore an aspect of unusual gloominess; the active became indolent, and the spirits of the bravest seemed to be subdued. I started to hunt with my dogs, which I had constantly refused to kill or suffer to be killed. By their assistance, I found and killed a bear. On returning home, I said to some of the Indians, "Has not the Great Spirit given us our dogs to aid us in procuring what is needful for the support of our life, and can you believe he wishes now to deprive us of their services? The prophet, we are told, has forbid us to suffer our fire to be extinguished in our lodges, and when we travel or hunt, he will not allow us to use a flint and steel, and we are told he requires that no man should give fire to another. Can it please the Great Spirit that we should lie in our hunting camps without fire, or is it more agreeable to him that we should make fire by rubbing together two sticks than with a flint and a piece of steel?" But they would not listen to me; and the serious enthusiasm which prevailed among them so far affected me that I threw away my flint and steel, laid aside my medicine bag, and, in many particulars, complied with the new doctrines; but I would not kill my dogs. I soon learned to kindle a fire by rubbing some dry cedar, which I was careful to carry always about me, but the discontinuance of the use of flint and steel subjected many of the Indians to much inconvenience and suffering. The influence of the Shawnee prophet was very sensibly and painfully felt by the remotest Ojibbeways of whom I had any knowledge, but it was not the common impression among them that his doctrines had any tendency to unite them in the accomplishment of any human purpose. For two or three years drunkenness was much less frequent than formerly, war was less thought of, and the entire aspect of affairs among them was somewhat changed by the influence of one man. But gradually the impression was obliterated; medicine bags, flints, and steels were resumed; dogs were raised, women and children were beaten as before, and the Shawnee prophet was despised. At this day he is looked upon by the Indians as an impostor and a bad man. (*Tanner, 1.*)

Tanner's account is confirmed by Warren, from the statements of old men among the Ojibwa who had taken part in the revival. According to their story the ambassadors of the new revelation appeared at the different villages, acting strangely and with their faces painted black — perhaps to signify their character as messengers from the world of shades. They told the people that they must light a fire with two dry sticks in each of their principal settlements, and that this fire must always be kept sacred and burning. They predicted the speedy return of the old Indian life, and asserted that the prophet would cause the dead to rise from the grave. The new belief took sudden and complete possession of the minds of the Ojibwa and spread "like wildfire" from end to end of their widely extended territory, and even to the remote northern tribes in alliance with the Cree and Asiniboin. The strongest evidence of their implicit obedience to the new revelation was given by their attention to the command to throw away their medicine bags, the one thing which every Indian holds most sacred. It is said that the shores of Lake Superior, in the vicinity of the great village of Shagawaumikong (Bayfield, Wisconsin), were strewn with these medicine bags, which had been cast into the water. At this ancient capital of the tribe the Ojibwa gathered in great numbers, to dance the dances and sing the songs of the new ritual, until a message was received from the prophet inviting them to come to him at Detroit, where he would explain in person the will of the Master of Life. This was in 1808. The excitement was now at fever heat, and it was determined to go in a body to Detroit. It is said that 150 canoe loads of Ojibwa actually started on this pilgrimage, and one family even brought with them a dead child to be restored to life by the prophet. They had proceeded a considerable distance when they were met by an influential French trader, who reported, on the word of some who had already visited the prophet's camp and returned, that the devotees there were on the brink of starvation — which was true, as the great multitude had consumed their entire supply of provisions, and had been so occupied with religious ceremonies that they had neglected to plant their corn. It was also asserted that during the prophet's frequent periods of absence from the camp, when he would disappear for several days, claiming on his return that he had been to the spirit world in converse with the Master of Life, that he was really concealed in a hollow log in the woods. This is quite probable, and entirely consistent with the Indian theory of trances and soul pilgrimages while the body remains unconscious in one spot. These reports, however, put such a damper on the ardor of the Ojibwa that they returned to their homes and gradually ceased to think about the new revelation. As time went on a reaction set in, and those who had been most active evangelists of the doctrine among the tribe became most anxious to efface the remembrance of it. One good, however, resulted to the Ojibwa from the throwing away of the poisonous compounds formerly in common use by the lower order of doctors, and secret poisoning became almost unknown. (*Warren, 2.*)

When the celebrated traveler Catlin went among the prairie tribes some thirty years later, he found that the prophet's emissaries—he says the prophet himself, which is certainly a mistake—had carried the living fire, the sacred image, and the mystic strings (see portrait and description) even to the Blackfeet on the plains of the Saskatchewan, going without hindrance among warring tribes where the name of the Shawano had never been spoken, protected only by the reverence that attached to their priestly character. There seems no doubt that by this time they had developed the plan of a confederacy for driving back the whites, and Catlin asserts that thousands of warriors among those remote tribes had pledged themselves to fight under the lead of Tecumtha at the proper time. His account of the prophet's methods in the extreme northwest agrees with what Tanner has reported from the Ojibwa country. (*Catlin, 1.*) But disaster followed him like a shadow. Rivals, jealous of his success, came after him to denounce his plans as visionary and himself as an impostor. The ambassadors were obliged to turn back to save their lives and retrace their way in haste to the far distant Wabash, where the fatal battle of Tippecanoe and the death of his great brother, Tecumtha, put an end to all his splendid dreams.

CHAPTER IV

TECUMTHA AND TIPPECANOE

These lands are ours. No one has a right to remove us, because we were the first owners.—*Tecumtha to Wells, 1807.*

The Great Spirit gave this great island to his red children. He placed the whites on the other side of the big water. They were not contented with their own, but came to take ours from us. They have driven us from the sea to the lakes—we can go no farther.—*Tecumtha, 1810.*

The President may sit still in his town and drink his wine, while you and I will have to fight it out.—*Tecumtha to Harrison, 1810.*

And now we begin to hear of the prophet's brother, Tecumtha, the most heroic character in Indian history. Tecumtha, "The Meteor," was the son of a chief and the worthy scion of a warrior race. His tribe, the Shawano, made it their proud boast that they of all tribes had opposed the most determined resistance to the encroachments of the whites. His father had fallen under the bullets of the Virginians while leading his warriors at the bloody battle of Point Pleasant, in 1774. His eldest and dearest brother had lost his life in an attack on a southern frontier post, and another had been killed fighting by his side at Wayne's victory in 1794. What wonder that the young Tecumtha declared that his flesh crept at the sight of a white man!

But his was no mean spirit of personal revenge; his mind was too noble for that. He hated the whites as the destroyers of his race, but prisoners and the defenseless knew well that they could rely on his honor and humanity and were safe under his protection. When only a boy—for his military career began in childhood—he had witnessed the burning of a prisoner, and the spectacle was so abhorrent to his feelings that by an earnest and eloquent harangue he induced the party to give up the practice forever. In later years his name was accepted by helpless women and children as a guaranty of protection even in the midst of hostile Indians. Of commanding figure, nearly six feet in height and compactly built; of dignified bearing and piercing eye, before whose lightning even a British general quailed; with the fiery eloquence of a Clay and the clear-cut logic of a Webster; abstemious in habit, charitable in thought and action, brave as a lion, but humane and generous withal—in a word, an aboriginal American knight—his life was given to his people, and he fell at last, like his father and his brothers before him, in battle with the destroyers of his nation, the champion of a lost cause and a dying race.

His name has been rendered "The Shooting Star" and "The Panther Crouching, or Lying in Wait." From a reply to a letter of inquiry addressed to Professor A. S. Gatschet, the well-known philologist, I extract the following, which throws valuable light on the name system and mythology of the Shawano, and shows also that the two renderings, apparently so dissimilar, have a common origin:

Shawano personal names are nearly all clan names, and by their interpretation the clan to which the individual or his father or mother belongs may be discovered. Thus, when a man is called "tight fitting" or "good fit," he is of the *Rabbit* clan, because the fur fits the rabbit very tightly and closely. The name of Tecumtha is

Fig. 58—Tecumtha.

One of the finest looking men I ever saw—about 6 feet high, straight, with large, fine features, and altogether a daring, bold-looking fellow.—*Captain Floyd, 1810.*

One of those uncommon geniuses which spring up occasionally to produce revolutions and overturn the established order of things.—*Governor Harrison.*

derived from *nila ni tka'mthka*, "I cross the path or way of somebody, or of an animal." This indicates that the one so named belongs to the clan of the round-foot or claw-foot animals, as panther, lion, or even raccoon. Tecumtha and his brother belonged to the clan of the *manetuwi msipessi* or "miraculous panther" (*msi*, great, big; *pishiwi*, abbreviated *pessi*, cat, both combined meaning the American lion). So the translations "panther lying in wait," or "crouching lion," give only the sense of the name, and no animal is named in it. But the *msi-pessi*, when the epithet miraculous (*manetuwi*) is added to it, means a "celestial tiger," i. e., a meteor or shooting star. The *manetuwi msi-pessi* lives in water only and is visible not as an animal, but as a shooting star, and exceeding in size other shooting stars. This monster gave name to a Shawano clan, and this clan, to which Tecumtha belonged, was classed among the claw-foot animals also. The quick motion of the shooting star was correctly likened to that of a tiger or wildcat rushing upon his prey. Shooting stars are supposed to be souls of great men all over America. The home of the dead is always in the west, where the celestial bodies set, and since meteors travel westward they were supposed to return to their western home.

Tecumtha was now in the prime of manhood, being about 40 years of age, and had already thought out his scheme of uniting all the tribes in one grand confederation to resist the further encroachments of the whites, on the principle that the Indians had common interests, and that what concerned one tribe concerned all. As the tribes were constantly shifting about, following the game in its migrations, he held that no one tribe had any more than a possessory right to the land while in actual occupancy, and that any sale of lands, to be valid, must be sanctioned by all the tribes concerned. His claim was certainly founded in justice, but the government refused to admit the principle in theory, although repeatedly acting on it in practice, for every important treaty afterward made in Mississippi valley was a joint treaty, as it was found impossible to assign the ownership of any considerable section to any one particular tribe. The Shawano themselves hunted from the Cumberland to the Susquehanna. As a basal proposition, Tecumtha claimed that the Greenville treaty, having been forced on the Indians, was invalid; that the only true boundary was the Ohio, as established in 1768, and that all future cessions must have the sanction of all the tribes claiming rights in that region.

By this time there were assembled at Greenville to listen to the teachings of the prophet hundreds of savages, representing all the widely extended tribes of the lake region and the great northwest, all wrought up to the highest pitch of excitement over the prospect of a revival of the old Indian life and the perpetuation of aboriginal sovereignty. This was Tecumtha's opportunity, and he was quick to improve it. Even those who doubted the spiritual revelations could see that they were in danger from the continued advances of the whites, and were easily convinced that safety required that they should unite as one people for the preservation of a common boundary. The pilgrims carried back these ideas to their several tribes, and thus what was at first a simple religious revival soon became a political agitation. They were equally patriotic from the Indian point of view, and under the circumstances one was almost the natural complement of the other. All the evidence goes to show that the movement in its inception was purely religious and peaceable; but the military spirit of Tecumtha afterward gave to it a warlike and even aggressive character, and henceforth the apostles of the prophet became also recruiting agents for his brother. Tecumtha himself was too sensible to think that the whites would be destroyed by any interposition of heaven, or that they could be driven out by any combination of the Indians, but he did believe it possible that the westward advance of the Americans could be stopped at the Ohio, leaving his people in undisturbed possession of what lay beyond. In this hope he was encouraged by the British officials in Canada, and it is doubtful if the movement would ever have become formidable if it had not been incited and assisted from across the line.

In the spring of 1807 it was estimated that at Fort Wayne fifteen hundred Indians had recently passed that post on their way to visit the prophet, while councils were constantly being held and runners were going from tribe to tribe with pipes and belts of wampum. It was plain that some uncommon movement was going on among them, and it also was evident that the British agents had a hand in keeping up the excitement. The government became alarmed, and the crisis came when an order was sent from the President to Tecumtha at Greenville to remove his party beyond the boundary of 1795 (the Greenville treaty). Trembling with excitement, Tecumtha rose and addressed his followers in a passionate speech, dwelling on the wrongs of the Indians and the continued encroachments of the whites. Then, turning to the messenger, he said, "These lands are ours. No one has a right to remove us, because we were the first owners The Great Spirit above has appointed this place for us, on which to light our fires, and here we will remain. As to boundaries, the Great Spirit above knows no boundaries nor will his red children acknowledge any." (*Drake, Tecumseh, 3.*) From this time it was understood that the Indians were preparing to make a final stand for the valley of the Ohio. The prophet continued to arouse their enthusiasm by his inspired utterances, while Tecumtha became the general and active organizer of the warriors. At a conference with the governor of Ohio in the autumn of 1807 he fearlessly denied the validity of the former treaties, and declared his intention to resist the further extension of the white settlements on Indian lands.

The next spring great numbers of Indians came down from the lakes to visit Tecumtha and his brother, who, finding their following increasing so rapidly, accepted an invitation from the Potawatomi and Kickapoo, and removed their headquarters to a more central location on the Wabash. The Delaware and Miami, who claimed precedence in that region and who had all along opposed the prophet and Tecumtha, protested against this move, but without effect. The new settlement, which was on the western bank of the river, just below the mouth of the Tippecanoe, was known to the Indians as Kehtipaquononk, "the great clearing," and was an old and favorite location with them. It had been the site of a large Shawano village which had been destroyed by the Americans in 1791, and some years later the Potawatomi had rebuilt upon the same place, to which they now invited the disciples of the new religion. The whites had corrupted the name to Tippecanoe, and it now generally became known as the Prophet's town.

Nothing else of moment occurred during this year, but it was learned that Tecumtha contemplated visiting the southern tribes in the near future to enlist them also in his confederacy.   In 1809, however, rumors of an approaching outbreak began to fill the air, and it was evident that the British were instigating the Indians to mischief in anticipation of a war between England and the United States.   Just at this juncture the anger of Tecumtha's party was still further inflamed by the negotiation of treaties with four tribes by which additional large tracts were ceded in Indiana and Illinois.   The Indians now refused to buy ammunition from the American traders, saying that they could obtain all they wanted for nothing in another quarter.   In view of the signs of increasing hostility, Governor Harrison was authorized to take such steps as might be necessary to protect the frontier.   Tecumtha had now gained over the Wyandot, the most influential tribe of the Ohio region, the keepers of the great wampum belt of union and the lighters of the council fire of the allied tribes.   Their example was speedily followed by the Miami, whose adhesion made the tribes of the Ohio and the lakes practically unanimous.   The prophet now declared that he would follow in the steps of Pontiac, and called on the remote tribes to assist those on the border to roll back the tide which would otherwise overwhelm them all.   In return, the Sauk and Fox sent word that they were ready whenever he should say the word.

In the summer of 1810, according to a previous arrangement, Tecumtha, attended by several hundred warriors, descended the river to Vincennes to confer with Governor Harrison on the situation.   The conference began on the 15th of August and lasted three days.   Tecumtha reiterated his former claims, saying that in uniting the tribes he was endeavoring to dam the mighty water that was ready to overflow his people.   The Americans had driven the Indians from the sea and threatened to push them into the lakes; and, although he disclaimed any intention of making war against the United States, he declared his fixed resolution to insist on the old boundary and to oppose the further intrusion of the whites on the lands of the Indians, and to resist the survey of the lands recently ceded.   He was followed by chiefs of five different tribes, each of whom in turn declared that he would support the principles of Tecumtha.   Harrison replied that the government would never admit that any section belonged to all the Indians in common, and that, having bought the ceded lands from the tribes who were first found in possession of them, it would defend its title by arms.   To this Tecumtha said that he preferred to be on the side of the Americans, and that if his terms were conceded he would bring his forces to the aid of the United States in the war which he knew was soon to break out with England, but that otherwise he would be compelled to join the British.   The governor replied that he would state the case to the President, but that it was altogether unlikely that he would consent to the conditions.   Recognizing the inevitable, Tecumtha expressed the hope that, as the President was to determine the matter, the Great Spirit would put sense into his head to induce him to give up the lands, adding,

"It is true, he is so far off he will not be injured by the war. He may sit still in his town and drink his wine, while you and I will have to fight it out." The governor then requested that in the event of an Indian war Tecumtha would use his influence to prevent the practice of cruelties on women and children and defenseless prisoners. To this he readily agreed, and the promise was faithfully kept. (*Drake, Tecumseh, 4.*)

The conference had ended with a tacit understanding that war must come, and both sides began to prepare for the struggle. Soon after it was learned that the prophet had sent belts to the tribes west of the Mississippi, inviting them to join in a war against the United States. Outrages on the Indians by settlers intensified the hostile feeling, and the Delawares refused to deliver up a murderer until some of the whites who had killed their people were first punished. Harrison himself states that the Indians could rarely obtain satisfaction for the most unprovoked wrongs. In another letter he says that Tecumtha "has taken for his model the celebrated Pontiac, and I am persuaded he will bear a favorable comparison in every respect with that far-famed warrior."

In July, 1811, Tecumtha again visited Harrison at Vincennes. In the course of his talk he said that the whites were unnecessarily alarmed, as the Indians were only following the example set them by the colonies in uniting for the furtherance of common interests. He added that he was now on his way to the southern tribes to obtain their adhesion also to the league, and that on his return in the spring he intended to visit the President to explain his purposes fully and to clear away all difficulties. In the meantime he expected that a large number of Indians would join his colony on the Wabash during the winter, and to avoid any danger of collision between them and the whites, he requested that no settlements should be made on the disputed lands until he should have an opportunity to see the President. To this Harrison replied that the President would never give up a country which he had bought from its rightful owners, nor would he suffer his people to be injured with impunity. This closed the interview, and the next day Tecumtha started with his party for the south to visit the Creek and Choctaw. About the same time it was learned that the British had sent a message to the prophet, telling him that the time had now come for him to take up the hatchet, and inviting him to send a party to their headquarters at Malden (now Amherstburg, Ontario) to receive the necessary supplies. In view of these things Harrison suggested to the War Department that opportunity be taken of Tecumtha's absence in the south to strike a blow against his confederacy. Continuing in the same letter, he says of the great Indian leader:

The implicit obedience and respect which the followers of Tecumseh pay to him is really astonishing, and more than any other circumstance bespeaks him one of those uncommon geniuses which spring up occasionally to produce revolutions and overturn the established order of things. If it were not for the vicinity of the United States, he would perhaps be the founder of an empire that would rival in glory Mexico or Peru. No difficulties deter him. For four years he has been in constant motion. You see him to-day on the Wabash, and in a short time hear of him on the shores of Lake Erie or Michigan or on the banks of the Mississippi, and wherever he goes he makes an impression favorable to his purposes. He is now upon the last round, to put a finishing stroke to his work. I hope, however, before his return that that part of the fabric which he considered complete will be demolished, and even its foundations rooted up. (*Drake, Tecumseh, 5.*)

On this trip Tecumtha went as far as Florida and engaged the Seminole for his confederacy. Then, retracing his steps into Alabama, he came to the ancient Creek town of Tukabachi, on the Tallapoosa, near the present site of Montgomery. What happened here is best told in the words of McKenney and Hall, who derived their information from Indians at the same town a few years later:

He made his way to the lodge of the chief called the Big Warrior. He explained his object, delivered his war talk, presented a bundle of sticks, gave a piece of wampum and a war hatchet—all which the Big Warrior took—when Tecumthé, reading the spirit and intentions of the Big Warrior, looked him in the eye, and, pointing his finger toward his face, said: "Your blood is white. You have taken my talk, and the sticks, and the wampum, and the hatchet, but you do not mean to fight. I know the reason. You do not believe the Great Spirit has sent me. You shall know. I leave Tuckhabatchee directly, and shall go straight to Detroit. When I arrive there, I will stamp on the ground with my foot and shake down every house in Tuckhabatchee." So saying, he turned and left the Big Warrior in utter amazement at both his manner and his threat, and pursued his journey. The Indians were struck no less with his conduct than was the Big Warrior, and began to dread the arrival of the day when the threatened calamity would befall them. They met often and talked over this matter, and counted the days carefully to know the day when Tecumthé would reach Detroit. The morning they had fixed upon as the day of his arrival at last came. A mighty rumbling was heard—the Indians all ran out of their houses—the earth began to shake; when at last, sure enough, every house in Tuckhabatchee was shaken down. The exclamation was in every mouth, "Tecumthé has got to Detroit!" The effect was electric. The message he had delivered to the Big Warrior was believed, and many of the Indians took their rifles and prepared for the war. The reader will not be surprised to learn that an earthquake had produced all this; but he will be, doubtless, that it should happen on the very day on which Tecumthé arrived at Detroit, and in exact fulfillment of his threat. It was the famous earthquake of New Madrid on the Mississippi. (*McKenney and Hall, 1.*)

The fire thus kindled among the Creek by Tecumtha was fanned into a blaze by the British and Spanish traders until the opening of the war of 1812 gave the opportunity for the terrible outbreak known in history as the Creek war.

While Tecumtha was absent in the south, affairs were rapidly approaching a crisis on the Wabash. The border settlers demanded the removal of the prophet's followers, stating in their memorial to the President that they were "fully convinced that the formation of this combination headed by the Shawano prophet was a British scheme, and that the agents of that power were constantly exciting the Indians to hostility against the United States." Governor Harrison now sent messages to the different tribes earnestly warning them of the consequences of a hostile outbreak, but about the same time the prophet himself announced that he had now taken up the tomahawk against the United States, and would only lay it down with his life, unless the wrongs of the Indians were redressed. It was known also that he was arousing his followers to a feverish pitch of excitement by the daily practice of mystic rites.

Harrison now determined to break up the prophet's camp. Accordingly, at the head of about 900 men, including about 250 regulars, he marched from Vincennes, and on the 5th of November, 1811, encamped within a few miles of the prophet's town. The Indians had fortified the place with great care and labor. It was sacred to them as the spot where the rites of the new religion had been so long enacted, and by these rites they believed it had been rendered impregnable to the attacks of the white man. The next day he approached still nearer, and was met by messengers from the town, who stated that the prophet was anxious to avoid hostilities and had already sent a pacific message by several chiefs, who had unfortunately gone down on the other side of the river and thus had failed to find the general. A truce was accordingly agreed on until the next day, when terms of peace were to be arranged between the governor and the chiefs. The army encamped on a spot pointed out by the Indians, an elevated piece of ground rising out of a marshy prairie, within a mile of the town. Although Harrison did not believe that the Indians would make a night attack, yet as a precaution he had the troops sleep on their arms in order of battle.

At 4 o'clock in the morning of the 7th, Governor Harrison, according to his practice, had risen preparatory to the calling up the troops, and was engaged, while drawing on his boots by the fire, in conversation with General Wells, Colonel Owen, and Majors Taylor and Hurst. The orderly drum had been roused for the purpose of giving the signal for the troops to turn out, when the attack of the Indians suddenly commenced upon the left flank of the camp. The whole army was instantly on its feet, the camp fires were extinguished, the governor mounted his horse and proceeded to the point of attack. Several of the companies had taken their places in the line within forty seconds from the report of the first gun, and the whole of the troops were prepared for action in the course

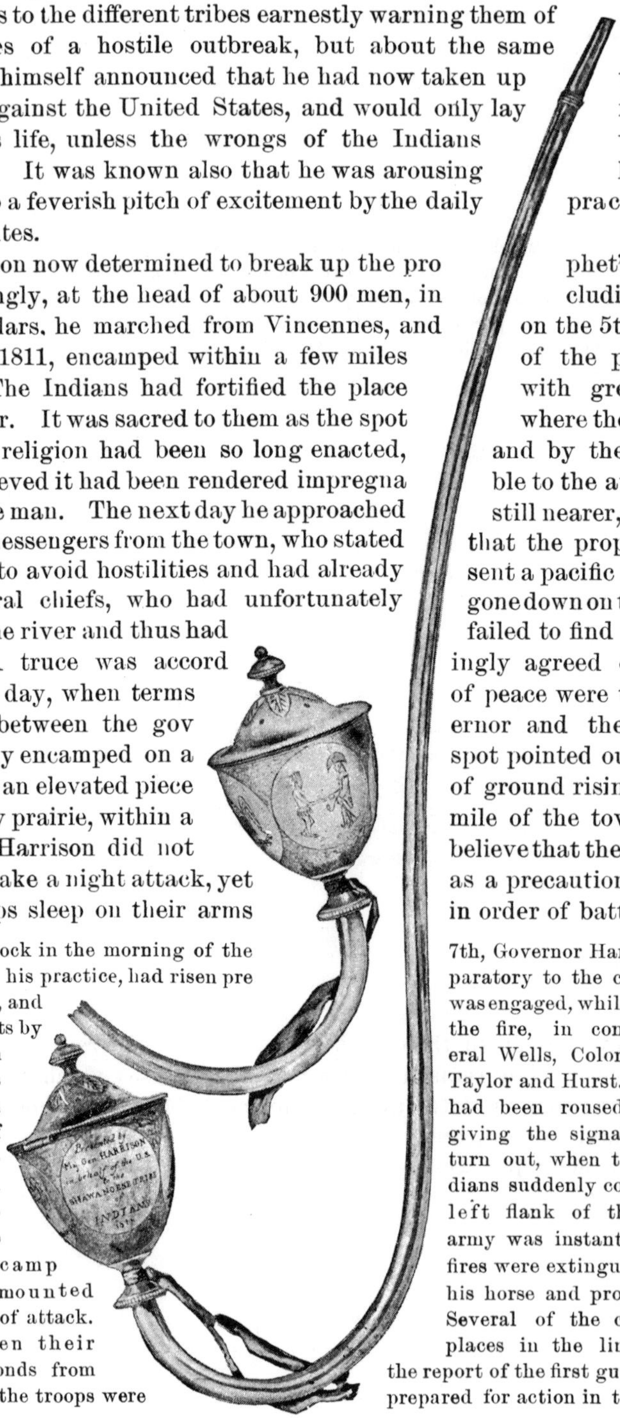

FIG. 59—Harrison treaty pipe.

of two minutes, a fact as creditable to their own activity and bravery as to the skill and bravery of their officers. The battle soon became general, and was maintained on both sides with signal and even desperate valor. The Indians advanced and retreated by the aid of a rattling noise, made with deer hoofs, and persevered in their treacherous attack with an apparent determination to conquer or die upon the spot. The battle raged with unabated fury and mutual slaughter until daylight, when a gallant and successful charge by our troops drove the enemy into the swamp and put an end to the conflict.

Prior to the assault the prophet had given assurances to his followers that in the coming contest the Great Spirit would render the arms of the Americans unavailing; that their bullets would fall harmless at the feet of the Indians; that the latter should have light in abundance, while the former would be involved in thick darkness. Availing himself of the privilege conferred by his peculiar office, and perhaps unwilling in his own person to attest at once the rival powers of a sham prophecy and a real American bullet, he prudently took a position on an adjacent eminence, and when the action began, he entered upon the performance of certain mystic rites, at the same time singing a war song. In the course of the engagement he was informed that his men were falling. He told them to fight on—it would soon be as he had predicted. And then, in louder and wilder strains, his inspiring battle song was heard commingling with the sharp crack of the rifle and the shrill war whoop of his brave but deluded followers. (*Drake, Tecumseh, 6.*)

Drake estimates the whole number of Indians engaged in the battle at between 800 and 1,000, representing all the principal tribes of the region, and puts the killed at probably not less than 50, with an unusually large proportion of wounded. Harrison's estimate would seem to put the numbers much higher. The Americans lost 60 killed or mortally wounded, and 188 in all. (*Drake, Tecumseh, 7.*) In their hurried retreat the Indians left a large number of dead on the field. Believing on the word of the prophet that they would receive supernatural aid from above, they had fought with desperate bravery, and their defeat completely disheartened them. They at once abandoned their town and dispersed, each to his own tribe. Tecumtha's great fabric was indeed demolished, and even its foundations rooted up.

The night before the engagement the prophet had performed some medicine rites by virtue of which he had assured his followers that half of the soldiers were already dead and the other half bereft of their senses, so that the Indians would have little to do but rush into their camp and finish them with the hatchet. The result infuriated the savages. They refused to listen to the excuses which are always ready to the tongue of the unsuccessful medicine-man, denounced him as a liar, and even threatened him with death. Deserted by all but a few of his own tribe, warned away from several villages toward which he turned his steps, he found refuge at last among a small band of Wyandot; but his influence and his sacred prestige were gone forever, and he lived out his remaining days in the gloom of obscurity.

From the south Tecumtha returned through Missouri, Iowa, and Illinois, everywhere making accessions to his cause, but reached the Wabash at last, just a few days after the battle, only to find his followers scattered to the four winds, his brother a refugee, and the great object of his life—a confederation of all the tribes—brought to nothing. His grief and disappointment were bitter. He reproached his brother in unmeasured terms for disobeying his instructions to preserve peace in his absence, and when the prophet attempted to reply, it is said that Tecumtha so far forgot his dignity as to seize his brother by the hair and give him a violent shaking, threatening to take his life.

Early in 1812 Tecumtha sent a message to Governor Harrison, informing him of his return from the south, and stating that he was now ready to make the proposed visit to the President. To this Harrison replied, giving his permission, but refusing to allow any party to accompany him. This stipulation did not please the great leader, who had been accustomed to the attendance of a retinue of warriors wherever he went. He declined the terms, and thus terminated his intercourse with the governor. In June, 1812, he visited the agent at Fort Wayne, and there reiterated the justice of his position in regard to the ownership of the Indian lands, again disclaimed having had any intention of making war against the United States, and reproached Harrison for marching against his people in his absence. In return, the agent endeavored to persuade him now to join forces with the United States in the approaching conflict with England. "Tecumtha listened with frigid indifference, made a few general remarks in reply, and then with a haughty air left the council house and took his departure for Malden, where he joined the British standard." (*Drake, Tecumseh, 8.*) His subsequent career is a part of the history of the war of 1812.

Formal declaration of war against Great Britain was made by the United States on June 18, 1812. Tecumtha was already at Malden, the British headquarters on the Canadian side, and when invited by some friendly Indians to attend a council near Detroit in order to make arrangements for remaining neutral, he sent back word that he had taken sides with the king, and that his bones would bleach on the Canadian shore before he would recross the river to join in any council of neutrality. A few days later he led his Indians into battle on the British side. For his services at Maguaga he was soon afterward regularly commissioned a brigadier general in the British army.

We pass over the numerous events of this war—Maguaga, the Raisin, Fort Meigs, Perry's victory—as being outside the scope of our narrative, and come to the battle of the Thames, October 5, 1813, the last ever fought by Tecumtha. After Perry's decisive victory on the lake, Proctor hastily prepared to retreat into the interior, despite the earnest protests of Tecumtha, who charged him with cowardice, an imputation which the British general did not dare to resent. The retreat was begun with Harrison in close pursuit, until the British and Indians reached a spot on the north bank of the Thames, in the vicinity of the present Chatham, Ontario. Here, finding the ground favorable for defense, Tecumtha resolved to retreat no farther, and practically compelled Proctor to make a stand. The Indian leader had no hope of triumph in the issue. His sun had gone down, and he felt himself already standing in the shadow of death. He was done with life and desired only to close it, as became a warrior, striking a last blow against the hereditary enemy of his race. When he had posted his men, he called his chiefs about him and calmly said, "Brother warriors, we are now about to enter into an engagement from which I shall never come out—my body will remain on the field of battle." He then unbuckled his sword, and, placing it in the hands of one of them, said, "When my son becomes a noted warrior and able to wield a sword, give this to him." He then laid aside his British military dress and took his place in the line, clothed only in the ordinary deerskin hunting shirt. (*Drake, Tecumseh, 9.*) When the battle began, his voice was heard encouraging his men until he fell under the cavalry charge of the Americans, who had already broken the ranks of the British regulars and forced them to surrender. Deprived of their leader and deserted by their white allies, the Indians gave up the unequal contest and fled from the field. Tecumtha died in his forty-fourth year.

After the close of the war the prophet returned from Canada by permission of this government and rejoined his tribe in Ohio, with whom he removed to the west in 1827. (*Schoolcraft, Ind. Tribes, 2.*) Catlin, who met and talked with him in 1832, thus speaks of him:

This, no doubt, has been a very shrewd and influential man, but circumstances have destroyed him, as they have many other great men before him, and he now lives respected, but silent and melancholy, in his tribe. I conversed with him a great deal about his brother Tecumseh, of whom he spoke frankly, and seemingly with great pleasure; but of himself and his own great schemes he would say nothing. He told me that Tecumseh's plans were to embody all the Indian tribes in a grand confederacy, from the province of Mexico to the Great Lakes, to unite their forces in an army that would be able to meet and drive back the white people, who were continually advancing on the Indian tribes and forcing them from their lands toward the Rocky mountains; that Tecumseh was a great general, and that nothing but his premature death defeated his grand plan. (*Catlin, 2.*)

CHAPTER V

KÄNAKÛK AND MINOR PROPHETS

KÄNAKÛK

My father, the Great Spirit holds all the world in his hands. I pray to him that we may not be removed from our lands. . . . Take pity on us and let us remain where we are.—*Känakûk.*

I was singularly struck with the noble efforts of this champion of the mere remnant of a poisoned race, so strenuously laboring to rescue the remainder of his people from the deadly bane that has been brought amongst them by enlightened Christians.—*Catlin.*

The scene now shifts to the west of the Mississippi. With the death of Tecumtha the confederacy of the northwestern tribes fell to pieces, and on the closin of the war of 1812 the government inaugurated a series of treaties resulting, within twenty years, in the removal of almost every tribe beyond the Mississippi and the appropriation of their former country by the whites. Among others the Kickapoo, by the treaty of Edwardsville in 1819, had ceded the whole of their ancient territory in Illinois, comprising nearly one-half the area of the state, in exchange for a much smaller tract on Osage river in Missouri and $3,000 in goods. (*Treaties, 1.*) The government also agreed to furnish two boats to take them up the river to their new home, where "the United States promise to guarantee to the said tribe the peaceable possession of the tract of land hereby ceded to them, and to restrain and prevent all white persons from hunting, settling, or otherwise intruding upon it."

For some reason, however, the Kickapoo manifested no overwhelming desire to remove from their villages and cornfields on the broad prairies of Illinois to the rugged hills of Missouri. This may have been due to the innate perversity of the savage, or possibly to the fact that the new country guaranteed to them was already occupied by their hereditary enemies, the Osage, who outnumbered the Kickapoo three to one. To be sure, these aboriginal proprietors had agreed to surrender the territory to the United States, but they were still at home to all visitors, as the immigrant Cherokee had learned to their cost. Be that as it may, several years passed and it began to be suspected that the Kickapoo were not anxious to go west and grow up with the country Investigation disclosed the fact that, instead of removing to the reservation on Osage river, one-half of the tribe had gone southward·in a body and crossed over to the Spanish side of Red river (now Texas), where they might reasonably hope to be secure from the further advance of the Americans. Others were preparing to follow, and the govern-

ment agents were instructed to make a strong effort to effect the immediate removal of the tribe to Missouri and to prevent the emigration
of any more to the south.

It now appeared that they were encouraged to hold their ground by a
new prophet who had sprung up among them, named Känakûk. The

FIG. 60—Känakûk the Kickapoo prophet.

name (also spelled Kee-an-ne kuk and Kanacuk), refers to putting the
foot upon a fallen object, and does not denote " the foremost man," as
rendered by Catlin. In a letter written to General Clark, in February,
1827—a few days after the prophet himself had visited General Clark—
the agent, Mr Graham, after reporting his failure to induce the tribe to

remove, states that the prophet "had no idea of giving up his lands," and continues:

This man has acquired an influence over his people through supposed revelations from God, which he urges on them with an eloquence, mildness, and firmness of manner that carries to their credulous ears conviction of his communications with God.

To give a favorable turn to his mind, I apparently gave credence to his statements of these revelations, and attempted to put a construction on them for him. He listened to me with great attention, and, after I had finished, said I might be right; that God would talk to him again and he would let me know what he said. In the meantime he would use his influence to get his people to move, but that he could not himself come over until all had removed; that there were many bad men yet among them, whom he hoped to convert to the ways of God, and then all would come over. He would preach to his men and warn them from taking away or injuring the property of the white people, and if any white man struck them—to use his own expression—he would bow his head and not complain; he would stop any attempt to take revenge. He seems to have a wonderful influence over those Indians who accompanied him. They neither drank nor painted, were serious, though not gloomy. (*Ind. Off., 1.*)

In the same month Känakûk himself visited General Clark at Saint Louis, and in the course of a long talk explained the origin of his divine mission and the nature of his doctrine, illustrating the subject by means

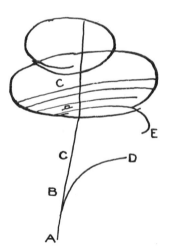

FIG. 61—Känakûk's heaven.

of a peculiar diagram (figure 61), and closing with an earnest appeal in behalf of his people that they should be allowed to remain undisturbed. Although it was said by the traders that he had stolen his inspiration from a Methodist preacher, it is plain from an examination of his doctrine that he was the direct spiritual successor of Tenskwatawa and the Delaware prophet, who in their generation had preached to the same tribe. Like his predecessors, also, he condemned the use of "medicine bags" and medicine songs, which, although universal among the tribes, seem to have been regarded by the better class of Indians as witchcraft was in former days among the whites.

After the usual preliminary expressions of mutual friendship and good will, Känakûk stated that all his people were united in sentiment, and then proceeded to explain his religious views as follows:

My father, the Great Spirit has placed us all on this earth; he has given to our nation a piece of land. Why do you want to take it away and give us so much trouble? We ought to live in peace and happiness among ourselves and with you. We have heard of some trouble about our land. I have come down to see you and have all explained.

*   *   *   *   *   *   *

My father, the Great Spirit appeared to me; he saw my heart was in sorrow about our land; he told me not to give up the business, but go to my Great Father and he would listen to me. My father, when I talked to the Great Spirit, I saw the chiefs holding the land fast. He told me the life of our children was short and that the earth would sink.

My father, I will explain to you what the Great Spirit said to me—to do so, I must make some marks. The Great Spirit says: My father, we started from this point (A, figure 61). We are here now (B). When we get here (C), the Great Spirit will appear to me again. Here (B) the Great Spirit gave his blessings to the Indians and told them to tell his people to throw away their medicine bags and not to steal, not to tell lies, not to murder, not to quarrel, and to burn their medicine bags. If they did not, they could not get on the straight way, but would have to go the crooked path of the bad here (D); that when we got to this place (the curved line, E), we would not be able to cross it unless we were all good. It was fire. That we should go to this place (E), where there would be collected all the red chiefs and there would be a great preaching. That if we had not thrown away all our bad doings, these two points would meet (D and E), and then the Great Spirit would destroy everything and the world would be turned over. That if we would be good and throw away all our bad doings, we would cross this fire, when we would [come] to water (second line), which we would cross. There we would come to a country where there was nothing but a prairie and nothing grew upon it. There the sun would be hid from us by four black clouds. When we get here (C), the Great Spirit will explain these round marks.

My father, I have now explained as well as I can, with much pains, our situation. I wish you to tell me the truth and hide nothing from me. I have heard that some of your warriors are going to take up the tomahawk. I explained to you last fall our situation. We are now here (B), where we are in great trouble. I told you of all our troubles. I asked you to reflect on our situation and that we would come back to see you.

     *   *   *   *   *   *

My father, you call all the redskins 'your children. When we have children, we treat them well. That is the reason I make this long talk to get you to take pity on us and let us remain where we are.

My father, I wish after my talk is over you would write to my Great Father, the president, that we have a desire to remain a little longer where we now are. I have explained to you that we have thrown all our badness away and keep the good path. I wish our Great Father could hear that. I will now talk to my Great Father, the president.

My Great Father, I don't know if you are the right chief, because I have heard some things go wrong. I wish you to reflect on our situation and let me know. I want to talk to you mildly and in peace, so that we may understand each other. When I saw the Great Spirit, he told me to throw all our bad acts away. We did so. Some of our chiefs said the land belonged to us, the Kickapoos; but this is not what the Great Spirit told me—the lands belong to him. The Great Spirit told me that no people owned the lands—that all was his, and not to forget to tell the white people that when we went into council. When I saw the Great Spirit, he told me, Mention all this to your Great Father. He will take pity on your situation and let you remain on the lands where you are for some years, when you will be able to get through all the bad places (the marks in the figure), and where you will get to a clear piece of land where you will all live happy. When I talked to the Great Spirit, he told me to make my warriors throw their tomahawks in the bad place. I did so, and every night and morning I raise my hands to the Great Spirit and pray to him to give us success. I expect, my father, that God has put me in a good way—that our children shall see their sisters and brothers and our women see their children. They will grow up and travel and see their totems. The Great Spirit told me, " Our old men had totems. They were good and had many totems. Now you have scarcely any. If you follow my advice, you will soon have totems again." Say this to my Great Father for me.[1]

    *   *   *   *   *   *   *

My father, since I talked with the Great Spirit, our women and children and ourselves, we have not such good clothes, but we don't mind that. We think of praying every day to the Great Spirit to get us safe to the good lands, where all will be peace and happiness.

My father, the Great Spirit holds all the world in his hands. I pray to him that we may not be removed from our land until we can see and talk to all our totems. . . .

My father, when I left my women and children, they told me, "As you are going to see our Great Father, tell him to let us alone and let us eat our victuals with a good heart."

    *   *   *   *   *   *   *

My father, since my talk with the Great Spirit we have nothing cooked until the middle of the day. The children get nothing in the morning to eat. We collect them all to pray to the Great Spirit to make our hearts pure, and then eat. We bring our children up to be good.

My father, I will tell you all I know. I will put nothing on my back. God told me, Whenever you make a talk, tell everything true. Keep nothing behind, and then you will find everything go right.

    *   *   *   *   *   *   *

My father, when I talked with the Great Spirit, he did not tell me to sell my lands, because I did not know how much was a dollar's worth, or the game that run on it. If he told me so, I would tell you to-day.

My father, you have heard what I have said. I have represented to you our situation, and ask you to take pity on us and let us remain where we are. . . .

My father, I have shown you in the lines I have made the bad places. Our warriors even are afraid of those dark places you see there. That is the reason they threw their tomahawks aside and put up their hands to the Great Spirit.

    *   *   *   *   *   *   *

My father, every time we eat we raise our hands to the Great Spirit to give us success.

My father, we are sitting by each other here to tell the truth. If you write anything wrong, the Great Spirit will know it. If I say anything not true, the Great Spirit will hear it.

My father, you know how to write and can take down what is said for your satisfaction. I can not; all I do is through the Great Spirit for the benefit of my women and children.

My father, everything belongs to the Great Spirit. If he chooses to make the earth shake, or turn it over, all the skins, white and red, can not stop it. I have done. I trust to the Great Spirit. (*Ind. Off., 2.*)

A few years later, in 1831, Catlin visited Känakûk, who was still living with the remnant of his people in Illinois, and was then regarded as their chief. He still preached the same doctrine, which the artist incorrectly supposed was the Christian religion — probably from the fact that the meetings were held on Sunday in imitation of the whites — and especially was constantly and earnestly exhorting his tribesmen to cease from drinking whisky, which threatened to destroy their race. His influence had extended into Michigan, and many of the Potawatomi

---

[1] The totem is the badge of a clan or gens of a tribe. The meaning is that by disease and death many of their gentes had become entirely extinct, but that by heeding the prophet's advice they would again become a numerous people.

were counted among his disciples. Catlin, who painted his portrait (of which figure 60 is a reproduction), heard him preach, and expressed surprise and admiration at the ease and grace of his manner and his evident eloquent command of language. The traveler continues:

I was singularly struck with the noble efforts of this champion of the mere remnant of a poisoned race so strenuously laboring to rescue the remainder of his people from the deadly bane that has been brought amongst them by enlightened Christians. How far the efforts of this zealous man have succeeded in Christianizing, I can not tell, but it is quite certain that his exemplary and constant endeavors have completely abolished the practice of drinking whisky in his tribe, which alone is a very praiseworthy achievement, and the first and indispensable step toward all other improvements. I was some time amongst those people, and was exceedingly pleased and surprised also to witness their sobriety and their peaceable conduct, not having seen an instance of drunkenness, or seen or heard of any use made of spirituous liquors whilst I was amongst the tribe. (*Catlin, 3.*)

After mentioning, although apparently not crediting the assertion of the traders, that the prophet had borrowed his doctrines from a white man, Catlin goes on to describe a peculiar prayer-stick which Känakûk had given to his followers, and which reminds us at once of the similar device of the Delaware prophet of 1764, and is in line with the whole system of birchbark pictographs among the northern tribes. These sticks were of maple, graven with hieroglyphic prayers and other religious symbols. They were carved by the prophet himself, who distributed them to every family in the tribe, deriving quite a revenue from their sale, and in this way increasing his influence both as a priest and as a man of property. Apparently every man, woman, and child in the tribe was at this time in the habit of reciting the prayers from these sticks on rising in the morning and before retiring for the night. This was done by placing the right index finger first under the upper character while repeating a short prayer which it suggested, then under the next, and the next, and so on to the bottom, the whole prayer, which was sung as a sort of chant, occupying about ten minutes.

Without undertaking to pass judgment on the purity of the prophet's motives, Catlin strongly asserts that his influence and example were good and had effectually turned his people from vice and dissipation to temperance and industry, notwithstanding the debasing tendency of association with a frontier white population.

The veteran missionary, Allis, also notes the use of this prayer-stick as he observed it in 1834 among the Kickapoo, then living near Fort Leavenworth, in Kansas. The prophet's followers were accustomed to meet for worship on Sunday, when Känakûk delivered an exhortation in their own language, after which they formed in line and marched around several times in single file, reciting the chant from their prayer-sticks and shaking hands with the bystanders as they passed. As they departed they continued to chant until they arrived at the "father's house" or heaven, indicated by the figure of a horn at the top of the prayer-stick. The worshipers met also on Fridays and made confession of their sins, after which certain persons appointed for the purpose gave each penitent several strokes with a rod of hickory, according to the gravity of his offense. (*Allis, 1.*)

Through the kindness of Mr C. H. Bartlett, of South Bend, Indiana, the United States National Museum has recently come into possession

FIG. 62—Onsawkie.

of one of these prayer-sticks. The stick, of which plate LXXXVI gives a good idea, is of maple, a little more than 12 inches in length, $2\frac{9}{16}$ inches in its greatest width, and three-eighths of an inch thick. It is said to have been painted a bright red on one side and a vivid green on the other. The paint has now disappeared, however, leaving bare

THE PRAYER-STICK

the surface of the wood, polished from long use. One side is carved with the symbolic figures already mentioned, while the other is smooth. In all its details it is a neat specimen of Indian workmanship. According to the tradition of the Armstrong family, its former owners, the small square in the lower left-hand corner represents hell or the final abode of the wicked, while the house with the four pine (?) trees, at the top, symbolizes the spiritual home of the devout followers of the prophet. As is well known, four is the sacred number of many Indian tribes. The significance of several other lines above and below is unknown. Along the shaft of the stick from bottom to top are the prayer characters, arranged in three groups of five each, one group being near the bottom, while the others are along the upper portion of the shaft and are separated one from the other by a small circle. The characters bear some resemblance to the old black-letter type of a missal, while the peculiar arrangement is strongly suggestive of the Catholic rosary with its fifteen "mysteries" in three groups of five each. It will be remembered that the earliest and most constant missionaries among the Kickapoo and other lake tribes were Catholic, and we may readily see that their teachings and ceremonies influenced this native religion, as was afterward the case with the religions of Smohalla and the Ghost dance. Neither three nor five are commonly known as sacred numbers among the Indians, while three is distinctly Christian in its symbolism. It is perhaps superfluous to state that the ideas of heaven and hell are not aboriginal, but were among the first incorporated from the teachings of the white missionaries. The characters resembling letters may be from the alphabetic system of sixteen characters which it is said the Ojibwa invented for recording their own language, and taught to the Kickapoo and Sauk, and which resembled somewhat the letters of the Roman alphabet, from which they apparently were derived. (*Hamilton, 1.*)

This prayer-stick or "bible," as it has been called, was obtained by Mr Bartlett from Mr R. V. Armstrong, of Mill Creek, Indiana, who stated that it was the only remaining one of a large number which had been in possession of the family for many years. The story of the manner in which it was originally obtained, as told by Mr Armstrong, is interesting. "His father, Reverend James Armstrong, was a Methodist minister and missionary who had been sent to northern Indiana in the early part of this century. In 1830, while living on Shawnee prairie, 3 miles from the present site of Attica, Indiana, a large band of Kickapoo Indians came to his house to visit the missionary, and apparently regarded the interview as of great importance to themselves. They declared that they were from beyond the Mississippi river, that they had heard of Mr Armstrong and his missionary labors, and that they believed him to be the one for whom their people had long been looking. Each Indian held in his hand one of these wooden crosses, and as they knelt on the grass in front of the missionary's house, they went through their devotions in their own tongue, moving their fingers over the inscription that ascends the shaft of the cross. The missionary understood them to state that this cross was their "bible," that they knew that it was not the true bible, but that they had been told to use it until one should come who would give them in exchange the genuine word of God. Thereupon the missionary gathered up their crosses—and there were more than a large basketful of them—and gave in exchange to each a copy of the New Testament. The Indians received the books with profuse expressions of gratitude and apparently viewed them at once as sacred possessions. These wise men from the west then went away to their far country."

Känakûk died of smallpox in 1852, in Kansas, where his people had been removed in spite of his eloquent appeals in their behalf. For many years he had been recognized as the chief of his tribe, and as such exerted a most beneficial influence over the Kickapoo in restraining the introduction and use of liquor among them. At the same time he stanchly upheld the old Indian idea and resisted every advance of the missionaries and civilization to the last. He was regarded as possessed of supernatural powers, and in his last illness asserted that he would arise again three days after death. In expectation of the fulfillment of the prophecy, a number of his followers remained watching near the corpse until they too contracted the contagion and died likewise. (*Comr.*, *1*.) After his death, the decline of his tribe was rapid and without check. In 1894 there remained only 514, about equally divided between Kansas and Oklahoma. These few survivors of a large tribe still hold in loving reverence the name of their chief and prophet.

PA'THĔSKĔ

Recent personal investigation among the Winnebago failed to develop any knowledge of a former doctrine of an approaching destruction of the world, as mentioned in a statement already quoted (see page 661). It appeared, however, that at the time indicated, about 1852 or 1853, while the tribe was still living on Turkey river, Iowa, a prophet known as Pa'thĕskĕ, or Long Nose, announced that he had been instructed in a vision to teach his people a new dance, which he called the friendship dance (chû'koraki'). This they were to perform at intervals for one whole year, at the end of which time, in the spring, they must take the warpath against their hereditary enemy, the Sioux, and would then reap a rich harvest of scalps. The dance, as he taught it to them, he claimed to have seen performed by a band of spirits in the other world, whither he had been taken after a ceremonial fast of several days' duration. It differed from their other dances, and, although warlike in its ultimate purpose, was not a war dance. It was performed by the men alone, circling around a fire within the lodge. He also designated a young man named Sara'minûka, or "Indistinct," as the proper one to lead the expedition at the appointed time.

The friendship dance went on all through the summer and winter until spring, when the prophet announced that he had received a new revelation forbidding the proposed expedition. His digusted followers at once denounced him as an impostor and abandoned the dance. Sara'minûka was soon afterward killed by an accident, which was considered by the Indians a direct retribution for his failure to carry out his part of the program. The prophet died a few years later while on a visit to Washington with a delegation of his tribe.

Although the old men consulted on the subject seemed to know nothing of any predicted destruction of the world in this connection, it is probable that the statement given by Agent Fletcher at the time was correct, as such cycle myths are very general among the Indian and other primitive tribes. The Arapaho informed the author that we are now living in the sixth cycle, and that the final catastrophe will take place at the close of the seventh.

TÄ'VIBO

About 1870 another prophet arose among the Paiute in Nevada. As most Indian movements are unknown to the whites at their inception, the date is variously put from 1869 to 1872. He is said to have been the father of the present "messiah," who has unquestionably derived many of his ideas from him, and lived, as does his son, in Mason valley, about 60 miles south of Virginia City, not far from Walker River reservation. In talking with his son, he said that his father's name was Tä'vibo or "White man," and that he was a *capita* (Spanish, *capitan*) or petty chief, but not a prophet or preacher, although he used to have visions and was invulnerable. From concurrent testimony of Indians and white men, however, there seems to be no doubt that he did preach and prophesy and introduce a new religious dance among his people, and that the doctrine which he promulgated and the hopes which he held out twenty years ago were the foundation on which his son has built the structure of the present messiah religion. He was visited by Indians from Oregon and Idaho, and his teachings made their influence felt among the Bannock and Shoshoni, as well as among all the scattered bands of the Paiute, to whom he continued to preach until his death a year or two later. (*G. D., 1 and 2; A. G. O., 1; Phister, 1.*)

Captain J. M. Lee, Ninth infantry, formerly on the staff of General Miles, was on duty in that neighborhood at the time and gives the following account of the prophet and his doctrines in a personal letter to the author:

I was on Indian duty in Nevada in 1869, 1870, and 1871. When visiting Walker Lake reservation in 1869–70, I became acquainted with several superstitious beliefs then prevailing among the Paiute Indians. It was a rough, mountainous region roundabout, and mysterious happenings, according to tradition, always occurred when the prophet or medicine-men went up into the mountains and there received their revelations from the divine spirits. In the earlier part of the sixties the whites began to come in and appropriate much of the Indian country in Nevada, and in the usual course it turned out that the medicine-men or prophets were looked to for relief. The most influential went up alone into the mountain and there met the Great Spirit. He brought back with him no tablets of stone, but he was a messenger of good tidings to the effect that within a few moons there was to be a great upheaval or earthquake. All the improvements of the whites—all their houses, their goods, stores, etc.—would remain, but the whites would be swallowed up, while the Indians would be saved and permitted to enjoy the earth and all the fullness thereof, including anything left by the wicked whites. This revelation was duly proclaimed by the prophet, and attracted a few believers, but the doubting skeptics were too many, and they ridiculed the idea that the white men would fall into the holes and be swallowed up while the Indians would not. As the prophet could not enforce his belief, he went up into the mountain again and came back with a second revelation, which was that when the great disaster came, all, both Indians and whites, would be swallowed up or overwhelmed, but that at the end of three days (or a few days) the Indians would be resurrected in the flesh, and would live forever to enjoy the earth, with plenty of game, fish, and pine nuts, while their enemies, the whites, would be destroyed forever. There would thus be a final and eternal separation between Indians and whites.

This revelation, which seemed more reasonable, was rather popular for awhile, but as time wore along faith seemed to weaken and the prophet was without honor even in his own country. After much fasting and prayer, he made a third trip to the mountain, where he secured a final revelation or message to the people. The divine spirit had become so much incensed at the lack of faith in the prophecies, that it was revealed to his chosen one that those Indians who believed in the prophecy would be resurrected and be happy, but those who did not believe in it would stay in the ground and be damned forever with the whites.

It was not long after this that the prophet died, and the poor miserable Indians worried along for nearly two decades, eating grasshoppers, lizards, and fish, and trying to be civilized until the appearance of this new prophet Quoit-tsow, who is said to be the son, either actual or spiritual, of the first one.

Additional details are given in the following interesting extract from a letter addressed to the Commissioner of Indian Affairs, under date of November 19, 1890, by Mr Frank Campbell, who has an intimate acquaintance with the tribe and was employed in an official capacity on the reservation at the time when Tävibo first announced the new revelation. It would appear from Mr Campbell's statement that under the new dispensation both races were to meet on a common level, and, as this agrees with what Professor Thompson, referred to later on, afterward found among the eastern Paiute, it is probable that the original doctrine had been very considerably modified since its first promulgation a few years before.

Eighteen years ago I was resident farmer on Walker Lake Indian reserve, Nevada. I had previously been connected with the Indian service at the reserve for ten years, was familiar with the Paiute customs, and personally acquainted with all the Indians in that region. In 1872 an Indian commenced preaching a new religion at that reserve that caused a profound sensation among the Paiute. For several months I was kept in ignorance of the cause of the excitement—which was remarkable, considering the confidence they had always reposed in me. They no doubt expected me to ridicule the sayings of the new messiah, as I had always labored among them to break down their superstitious beliefs. When finally I was made acquainted with the true facts of the case, I told them the preachings of Waugh-zee-waugh-ber were good and no harm could come from it. Indian emissaries visited the reserve from Idaho, Oregon, and other places, to investigate the new religion. I visited the Indian camp while the prophet was in a trance and remained until he came to. In accordance with instructions, the Indians gathered around him and joined in a song that was to guide the spirit back to the body. Upon reanimation he gave a long account of his visit in the spirit to the Supreme Ruler, who was then on the way with all the spirits of the departed dead to again reside upon this earth and change it into a paradise. Life was to be eternal, and no distinction was to exist between races.

This morning's press dispatches contain an account of Porcupine's visit to Walker lake . . . that proves to me that the religion started at Walker lake eighteen years ago is the same that is now agitating the Indian world. There is nothing in it to cause trouble between whites and Indians unless the new Messiah is misquoted and his doctrine misconstrued. I left Walker Lake reserve in June, 1873, and at the time supposed this craze would die out, but have several times since been reminded by Nevada papers and letters that it was gradually spreading. (*G. D., 3.*)

The name given by Campbell certainly does not much resemble Tävibo, but it is quite possible that the father, like the son, had more than one name. It is also possible that "Waughzeewaughber" was not the prophet described by Captain Lee, but one of his disciples who had taken up and modified the original doctrine. The name Tävibo refers to the east (*tävänagwat*) or place where the sun (*täbi*) rises. By the cognate Shoshoni and Comanche the whites are called *Taivo*.

From oral information of Professor A. H. Thompson, of the United States Geological Survey, I learn some particulars of the advent of the new doctrine among the Paiute of southwestern Utah. While his party was engaged in that section in the spring of 1875, a great excitement was caused among the Indians by the report that two mysterious beings with white skins (it will be remembered that the father of Wovoka was named Tävibo or "white man") had appeared among the Paiute far to the west and announced a speedy resurrection of all the dead Indians, the restoration of the game, and the return of the old-time primitive life. Under the new order of things, moreover, both races alike were to be white. A number of Indians from Utah went over into Nevada, where they met others who claimed to have seen these mysterious visitors farther in the west. On their return to Utah they brought back with them the ceremonial of the new belief, the chief part of the ritual being a dance performed at night in a circle, with no fire in the center, very much as in the modern Ghost dance.

It is said that the Mormons, who hold the theory that the Indians are the descendants of the supposititious "ten lost tribes," cherish, as a part of their faith, the tradition that some of the lost Hebrew emigrants are still ice-bound in the frozen north, whence they will one day emerge to rejoin their brethren in the south. When the news of this Indian revelation came to their ears, the Mormon priests accepted it as a prophecy of speedy fulfillment of their own traditions, and Orson Pratt, one of the most prominent leaders, preached a sermon, which was extensively copied and commented on at the time, urging the faithful to arrange their affairs and put their houses in order to receive the long-awaited wanderers.

According to the statement of the agent then in charge at Fort Hall, in Idaho, the Mormons at the same time—the early spring of 1875— sent emissaries to the Bannock, urging them to go to Salt Lake City to be baptized into the Mormon religion. A large number accepted the invitation without the knowledge of the agent, went down to Utah, and were there baptized, and then returned to work as missionaries of the new faith among their tribes. As an additional inducement, free rations were furnished by the Mormons to all who would come and be baptized, and "they were told that by being baptized and going to church the old men would all become young, the young men would never be sick, that the Lord had a work for them to do, and that they were the chosen people of God to establish his kingdom upon the earth," etc. It is also asserted that they were encouraged to resist the authority of the government. (*Comr., 2.*) However much of truth there may be in these reports, and we must make considerable allowance for local prejudice, it is sufficiently evident that the Mormons took an active interest in the religious ferment then existing among the neighboring tribes and helped to give shape to the doctrine which crystallized some years later in the Ghost dance.

NAKAI'-DOKLĬ'NI

Various other prophets of more or less local celebrity have arisen from time to time among the tribes, and the resurrection of the dead and the return of the olden things have usually figured prominently in their prophecies. In fact, this idea has probably been the day-dream of every Indian medicine-man since the whites first landed in America. Most of these, however, have been unknown to fame outside of their own narrow circles, except where chance or deliberate purpose has given a warlike meaning to their teachings and thus made them the subjects of official notice.

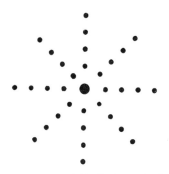

Fig. 63—Nakaí'-doklĭ'ni's dance-wheel.

Among these may be mentioned the Apache medicine-man Nakai'-doklĭ'ni, who attracted some attention for a time in southern Arizona in 1881. (*Bourke, 1.*) In the early part of this year he began to advertise his supernatural powers, claiming to be able to raise the dead and commune with spirits, and predicting that the whites would soon be driven from the land. He taught his followers a new and peculiar dance, in which the performers were ranged like the spokes of a wheel, all facing inward, while he, standing in the center, sprinkled them with the sacred *hoddentin*[1] as they circled around him.

In June of 1881 he announced to his people, the White Mountain band of Apache on San Carlos reservation, that on condition of receiving a sufficient number of horses and blankets for his trouble he would bring back from the dead two chiefs who had been killed a few months before. The proposition naturally aroused great excitement among the Indians. Eager to have once more with them their beloved chiefs, they willingly produced the required ponies, and when remonstrated with by the agent, replied that they would wait until the specified time for the fulfillment of the prediction, when, if the dead chiefs failed to materialize, they would demand the restoration of the property. (*Comr., 3.*)

Accordingly Nakai'-doklĭ'ni began his prayers and ceremonies, and the dance was kept up regularly at his camp on Cibicu creek until August, when it was reported to Colonel E. A. Carr, commanding at Fort Apache, that the medicine-man had announced that the dead chiefs refused to return because of the presence of the whites, but that when the whites left, the dead would return, and that the whites would be out of the country when the corn was ripe.

As matters seemed to be getting serious, the agent now called on the commanding officer to "arrest or kill him, or both." The officer prepared to make the arrest when Nakai'-doklĭ'ni should come down to the post to lead the dance which had been arranged to take place in a few days. The prophet failed to put in an appearance, however, and messengers were sent to his camp to ask him to come to the fort the next Sunday. To this message he returned an evasive reply, whereon Colonel Carr, with 85 white troops and 23 Apache scouts, started for his camp in Cibicu canyon to put him under arrest. They arrived at the village on August 30. Nakai'-doklĭ'ni submitted quietly to arrest, but as the troops were making camp for the night, their own scouts, joined by others of the Indians, opened fire on them. A sharp skirmish ensued, in which several soldiers were killed or wounded, but the Indians were repulsed with considerable loss, including the prophet himself, who was killed at the first fire. The result was another in the long series of Apache outbreaks. (*Comr., 4; Sec. War, 1; A. G. O., 2.*)

THE POTAWATOMI PROPHET

In 1883 a new religion was introduced among the Potawatomi and Kickapoo, of the Pottawotomie and Great Nemaha agency in north-

---

[1] *Hadn-tin* or *hoddentin*, in Navaho *tadatin*, is a sacred yellow powder from the pollen of the tule rush, or, among the Navaho, of corn. It enters into every important ceremonial performance of the Apache and Navaho. The latter always sprinkle some upon the surface of the water before crossing a stream. The name of the medicine-man is written also Nakay-doklunni or Nockay Delklinne, and he was commonly called Bobbydoklinny by the whites. Dr Washington Matthews, the best authority on the closely related dialect of the Navaho, thinks the name might mean "spotted or freckled Mexican," *Nakai*, literally "white alien," being the name for Mexican in both dialects. The name would not necessarily indicate that the medicine-man was of Mexican origin, but might have been given, in accordance with the custom of some tribes, to commemorate the fact that he had killed a freckled Mexican.

eastern Kansas, by visiting Potawatomi, Winnebago, and Ojibwa from Wisconsin. As usual, the ritual part consists chiefly of a ceremonial dance. In doctrine it teaches the same code of morality enjoined by the ten commandments, and especially prohibits liquor drinking, gambling, and horse racing, for which reason the agents generally have not seen fit to interfere with it, and in some cases have rather encour-aged it as a civilizing influence among that portion of the tribes not yet enrolled in Christian denominations. The movement is entirely distinct from the Ghost dance, and may perhaps be a revival of the system preached by Känakûk more than fifty years before. In 1891 the majority of the two tribes, numbering in all 749, were reported as adherents of the doctrine. (*Comr., 5, 6, 7; also reports from the same agency for 1887 and 1889.*) A large number of the Sauk and Fox, Kick-apoo, and Potawatomi of Oklahoma are also believers in the religion.

In 1885 Agent Patrick says on this subject:

These Indians are chaste, cleanly, and industrious, and would be a valuable acquisition to the Prairie band if it were not for their intense devotion to a religious dance started among the northern Indians some years since. This dance was intro-duced to the Prairie band about two years ago by the Absentee Pottawatomies and Winnebagoes, and has spread throughout the tribes in the agency. They seem to have adopted the religion as a means of expressing their belief in the justice and mercy of the Great Spirit and of their devotion to him, and are so earnest in their convictions as to its affording them eternal happiness that I have thought it impoli-tic so far to interfere with it any further than to advise as few meetings as possible and to discountenance it in my intercourse with the individuals practicing the religion. It is not an unmixed evil, as under its teaching drunkenness and gambling have been reduced 75 per cent, and a departure from virtue on the part of its mem-bers meets with the severest condemnation. As some tenets of revealed religion are embraced in its doctrines, I do not consider it a backward step for the Indians who have not heretofore professed belief in any Christian religion, and believe its worst features are summed up in the loss of time it occasions and the fanatical train of thought involved in the constant contemplation of the subject. (*Comr., 6.*)

CHEEZ-TAH-PAEZH THE SWORD-BEARER

It is probable that something of the messiah idea entered into the promises held out to his followers by Sword-bearer, a Crow medicine-man, in Montana in 1887. The official records are silent on this point, although it is definitely stated that he asserted his own invulnerability, and that his claims in this respect were implicitly believed by his people. Cheez-tah-paezh, literally "Wraps his tail" (also written Chees-chapahdisch, Cheschopah, Chese-cha-pahdish, and Chese-Topah), was without any special prominence in his tribe until the summer of 1887, when, in company with several other young men of the Crows, he par-ticipated in the sun dance of the Cheyenne, and showed such fortitude in enduring the dreadful torture that he was presented by the Cheyenne with a medicine saber painted red, in virtue of which he took the title of Sword-bearer. This naturally brought him into notice at home, and he soon aspired to become a chief and medicine-man. Among other things, he asserted that no bullet or weapon had power to harm him.

What other claims he made are not known, but his words produced such an impression, it is said, that for a time every full-blood and half-blood among the Crows believed in him.

In a few months he had become one of the most influential leaders in the tribe, when, taking advantage of some dissatisfaction toward the agent, he headed a demonstration against the agency on September 30. Troops under General Ruger were called on to arrest him and the others concerned, and in attempting to do this, on November 5, 1887, a skirmish ensued in which Sword-bearer was killed. His death convinced his followers of the falsehood of his pretensions, and the tribe, which hitherto had always been loyal to the government, soon resumed its friendly attitude. (*Sec. War, 2; A. G. O., 3; additional details from a personal letter by Colonel Simon Snyder, Fifteenth infantry.*)

The action is graphically described by Roosevelt on the authority of one of the officers engaged. When the troops arrived, they found the Crow warriors awaiting them on a hill, mounted on their war ponies and in full paint and buckskin. In this author's words—

The Crows on the hilltop showed a sullen and threatening front, and the troops advanced slowly toward them, and then halted for a parley. Meanwhile a mass of black thunder clouds gathering on the horizon threatened one of those cloudbursts of extreme severity and suddenness so characteristic of the plains country. While still trying to make arrangements for a parley, a horseman started out of the Crow ranks and galloped headlong down toward the troops. It was the medicine chief Sword-bearer. He was painted and in his battle dress, wearing his war bonnet of floating, trailing eagle feathers, and with the plumes of the same bird braided in the mane and tail of his fiery little horse. On he came at a gallop almost up to the troops, and then began to circle around them, calling and singing, and throwing his red sword into the air, catching it by the hilt as it fell. Twice he rode completely around the troops, who stood in uncertainty, not knowing what to make of his performance, and expressly forbidden to shoot at him. Then, paying no further heed to them, he rode back toward the Crows. It appears that he had told the latter that he would ride twice around the hostile force, and by his incantations would call down rain from heaven, which would make the hearts of the white men like water, so that they would go back to their homes. Sure enough, while the arrangements for the parley were still going forward, down came the cloudburst, drenching the command, and making the ground on the hills in front nearly impassable; and before it dried a courier arrived with orders to the troops to go back to camp.

This fulfillment of Sword-bearer's prophecy of course raised his reputation to the zenith, and the young men of the tribe prepared for war, while the older chiefs, who more fully realized the power of the whites, still hung back. When the troops next appeared, they came upon the entire Crow force, the women and children with their tepees being off to one side beyond a little stream, while almost all the warriors of the tribe were gathered in front. Sword-bearer started to repeat his former ride, to the intense irritation of the soldiers. Luckily, however, this time some of his young men could not be restrained. They, too, began to ride near the troops, and one of them was unable to refrain from firing on Captain Edwards's troop, which was in the van. This gave the soldiers their chance. They instantly responded with a volley, and Edwards's troop charged. The fight lasted only a minute or two, for Sword-bearer was struck by a bullet and fell; and as he had boasted himself invulnerable and promised that his warriors should be invulnerable also if they would follow him, the hearts of the latter became as water, and they broke in every direction. (*Roosevelt, 1.*)

CHAPTER VI

THE SMOHALLA RELIGION OF THE COLUMBIA REGION

SMOHALLA

I have only one heart. Although you say, Go to another country, my heart is not that way. I do not want money for my land. I am here, and here is where I am going to be. I will not part with lands, and if you come again I will say the same thing. I will not part with my lands.—*Umatilla Chief.*

We have never made any trade. The earth is part of my body, and I never gave up the earth. So long as the earth keeps me I want to be let alone.—*Toohulhulsote.*

Their only troubles arise from the attempts of white men to encroach upon the reservations. I verily believe that were the snow-crowned summits of Mount Rainier set apart as an Indian reservation, white men would immediately commence jumping them.—*Superintendent Ross.*

About the time that the Paiute were preparing for the millennial dawn, we begin to hear of a "dreamer prophet" on the Columbia, called Smohalla, who was becoming a thorn in the flesh of the Indian agents in that quarter, and was reported to be organizing among the Indians a new religion which taught the destruction of the whites and resistance to the government, and made moral virtues of all the crimes in the catalog. One agent, in disregard of grammar if not of veracity, gravely reported that "the main object is to allow a plurality of wives, immunity from punishment for lawbreaking, and allowance of all the vices—especially drinking and gambling—are chief virtues in the believers of this religion." (*Comr., 8.*)

This was bad enough, but worse was behind it. It appeared that Smohalla and his followers, numbering perhaps about 2,000 Indians of various tribes along the Columbia in eastern Washington and Oregon, had never made treaties giving up any of their lands, and consequently claimed the right to take salmon in the streams and dig kamas in the prairies of their ancestral country undisturbed and unmolested, and stoutly objected to going on any of the neighboring reservations at Yakima, Umatilla, or Warmspring. There is no doubt that justice and common sense were on the side of the Indians, for by the reports of the agents themselves it is shown that the dwellers on the reservations were generally neglected, poor, and miserable, and subjected to constant encroachments by the whites in spite of treaties and treaty lines, while at the same time that agents and superintendents were invoking the aid of the military to compel Smohalla's followers to go on a reservation these same men were moving heaven and earth to force the Indians already on a reservation to give up their treaty rights and remove to another and less valuable location—to begin life anew under the fostering care of the government until such time as the white man should want them to move on again.

These matters are treated at length in the annual reports of the Commissioner of Indian Affairs, with the accompanying reports of superintendents and agents in charge of the reservations concerned, from 1870 to 1875. With regard to the Umatilla reservation, to which most strenuous efforts were made to remove the "renegades," as they were called, Agent Boyle reports in 1870 (*Comr., 9*) that the Indians are "dispirited . . . in consequence of the oft-repeated theme that their farms are to be taken from them and given to the white settlers." He continues, "It is hardly to be expected that the Indians can retain this reservation much longer unless the strong arm of the government protects them. Daily I am called upon to notify the white settlers that they are encroaching upon the Indian lands." He advises their removal to a permanent reservation, "knowing as I do that they must go sooner or later." Again, "The agency has been established for the space of ten years, and I regret exceedingly that I have been most completely disappointed with what I see about me." In discussing the removal of the Indians to a new reservation, Superintendent Meacham says of a considerable portion of them that it "would suit them better to be turned loose to look out for themselves." (*Comr., 10.*)

In 1873 Agent Cornoyer reported that the Indians numbered 837, by the census of 1870, which he believes was as correct as could then be taken, but "this number I think is now too high." He continues:

Of the appropriation of $4,000 per annum for beneficial objects, not one single dollar of that fund has been turned over to me since September, 1871; and of the appropriation for incidental expenses of $40,000 per annum for the Indian service in this state, only $200 of that appropriation has been turned over to me during the same period of two years. . . . I would also beg leave to call your attention to that portion of my last annual report wherein I called the attention of the Department to the unfulfilled stipulations of the treaty of June 9, 1855, with these Indians. (*Comr., 11.*)

Commissioner Brunot, in 1871, stated that the estimated number of Indians coming under the provisions of the treaty at the time it was made in 1855 was 3,500, and "by the census taken in 1870 the number was 1,622"—a decrease of nearly one-half in fifteen years. Of these only about half were on the reservation, the rest being on Columbia river, "never having partaken of the benefits of the treaty." On the next page he tells us what some of these benefits are: "Maladministration of agents, and the misapplication of funds, the failure of the government to perform the promises of the treaty, and the fact that the Indians have been constantly agitated by assertions that the government intended their removal, and that their removal was urged for several years in succession in the reports of a former agent, thus taking away from them all incentives to improve their lands." (*Comr., 12.*)

In 1871 a commission was sent to Umatilla and other reservations, which gave the Indians a chance to speak for themselves. The Cayuse chief, described as a Catholic Indian, in dress, personal appearance, and bearing superior to the average American farmer, said:

> This reservation is marked out for us. We see it with our eyes and our hearts. We all hold it with our bodies and our souls. Right out here are my father and mother, and brothers and sisters and children, all buried. I am guarding their graves. My friend, this reservation, this small piece of land, we look upon it as our mother, as if she were raising us. You come to ask me for my land. It is like as if we who are Indians were to be sent away and get lost. . . . What is the reason you white men who live near the reservation like my land and want to get it? You must not think so. My friends, you must not talk too strong about getting my land. I like my land and will not let it go.

The Wallawalla chief said:

> I have tied all the reservation in my heart and it can not be loosened. It is dear as our bodies to us.

The Umatilla chief said:

> Our red people were brought up here. . . . When my father and mother died, I was left here. They gave me rules and gave me their land to live upon. They left me to take care of them after they were buried. I was to watch over their graves. I do not wish to part with my land. I have felt tired working on my land, so tired that the sweat dropped off me on the ground. Where is all that Governor Stevens or General Palmer said [i. e., that it was to be a reservation for the Indians forever]? I am very fond of this land that is marked out for me. . . . Should I take only a small piece of ground and a white man sit down beside me, I fear there would be trouble all the time.

An old man said:

> I am getting old now, and I want to die where my father and mother and children have died. I do not wish to leave this land and go off to some other land. . . . I see where I have sweat and worked in trying to get food. I love my church, my mills, my farm, the graves of my parents and children. I do not wish to leave my land. That is all my heart, and I show it to you.

A young chief said:

> I have only one heart, one tongue. Although you say, Go to another country, my heart is not that way. I do not wish for any money for my land. I am here, and here is where I am going to be. . . . I will not part with lands, and if you come again I will say the same thing. I will not part with my lands.

The commissioner who was conducting the negotiations, after enumerating the promises made to the Indians in return for the lands which they had surrendered under the original treaty of 1855, tells how some of these promises have been fulfilled:

> . . . A miserably inadequate supply of worn-out agricultural implements. A group of eight or ten dilapidated shanties used for the agency buildings. The physician promised has never resided upon the reservation, but lives and practices his profession at Pendleton. The hospital promised (fifteen years ago) has not yet been erected.

Of their ever-living grievance Colonel Ross, superintendent of the Washington agencies, says:

> Their only troubles arise from the attempts of white men to encroach upon the reservations. A mania prevails among a certain class of citizens in this direction. I verily

believe that were the snow-crowned summits of Mount Rainier set apart as an Indian reservation, white men would immediately commence jumping them. (*Comr., 14.*)

JOSEPH AND THE NEZ PERCÉ WAR

We first hear officially of Smohalla and his people from A. B. Meacham, superintendent of Indian affairs in Oregon, who states, in September, 1870, that—

. . . One serious drawback [to the adoption of the white man's road] is the existence among the Indians of Oregon of a peculiar religion called Smokeller or Dreamers, the chief doctrine of which is that the red man is again to rule the country, and this sometimes leads to rebellion against lawful authority.

A few pages farther on we learn the nature of this rebellion:

The next largest band (not on a reservation) is Smokeller's, at Priest rapids, Washington territory. They also refused to obey my order to come in, made to them during the month of February last, of which full report was made. I would also recommend that they be removed to Umatilla by the military. (*Comr., 15.*)

Three months before this report Congress had passed a bill appointing commissioners to negotiate with the tribes of Umatilla reservation "to ascertain upon what terms they would be willing to sell their lands and remove elsewhere," and Meacham himself was the principal member of this commission. (*Comr., 15.*)

In 1872 Smohalla's followers along the Columbia were reported to number 2,000, and his apostles were represented as constantly traveling from one reservation to another to win over new converts to his teachings. Repeated efforts had been made to induce them to go on the reservations in eastern Oregon and Washington, but without success. We are told now that—

They have a new and peculiar religion, by the doctrines of which they are taught that a new god is coming to their rescue; that all the Indians who have died heretofore, and who shall die hereafter, are to be resurrected; that as they will then be very numerous and powerful, they will be able to conquer the whites, recover their lands, and live as free and unrestrained as their fathers lived in olden times. Their model of a man is an Indian. They aspire to be Indians and nothing else. . . . It is thought by those who know them best that they can not be made to go upon their reservations without at least being intimidated by the presence of a military force. (*Comr., 17.*)

We hear but little more of Smohalla and his doctrines for several years, until attention was again attracted to Indian affairs in the northwest by the growing dissatisfaction which culminated in the Nez Percé war of 1877. The Nez Percés, especially those who acknowledged the leadership of Chief Joseph, were largely under the influence of the Dreamer prophets, and there was reason to believe that an uprising inaugurated by so prominent a tribe would involve all the smaller tribes in sympathy with the general Indian belief. As soon therefore as it became evident that matters were approaching a crisis, a commission, of which General O. O. Howard was chief, was appointed to make some peaceable arrangement with the so-called "renegades" on the upper Columbia. The commissioners met Smohalla and his principal men at Wallula, Washington territory, on April 23, 1877, and as a result of the council then held these non-treaty tribes, although insisting as strongly as ever on their right to live undisturbed in their own country, yet refrained from taking part in the war which broke out a few weeks later.

It is foreign to our purpose to recount the history of the Nez Percé war of 1877. As is generally the case with Indian wars, it originated in the unauthorized intrusion of lawless whites on lands which the Indians claimed as theirs by virtue of occupancy from time immemorial. The Nez Percés, whom all authorities agree in representing as a superior tribe of Indians, originally inhabited the valleys of Clearwater and Salmon rivers in Idaho, with the country extending west of Snake river into Washington and Oregon as far as the Blue mountains. They are first officially noticed in the report of the Indian Commissioner for 1843, where they are described as "noble, industrious, sensible," and well disposed toward the whites, while "though brave as Cæsar, the whites have nothing to dread at their hands in case of their dealing out to them what they conceive to be right and equitable." (*Comr.*, *18.*) It being deemed advisable to bring them into more direct relations with the United States, the agent who made the report called the chiefs together in this year and "assured them of the kind intentions of our government, and of the sad consequences that would ensue to any white man, from this time, who should invade their rights." (*Comr.*, *19.*) On the strength of these fair promises a portion of the tribe, in 1855, entered into a treaty by which they ceded a large part of their territory, and were guaranteed possession of the rest. In 1860, however, gold was discovered in the country, and the usual result followed. "In defiance of law, and despite the protestations of the Indian agent, a townsite was laid off in October, 1861, on the reservation, and Lewiston, with a population of 1,200, sprung into existence." (*Comr.*, *20.*) A new treaty was then made in 1863, by which the intruders were secured in possession of what they had thus seized, and the Nez Percés were restricted within much narrower limits. By this treaty the Wallowa valley, in northeastern Oregon, the ancestral home of that part of the tribe under the leadership of Chief Joseph, was taken from the Indians. This portion of the tribe, however, had refused to have part in the negotiations, and "Chief Joseph and his band, utterly ignoring the treaty of 1863, continued to claim the Wallowa valley, where he was tacitly permitted to roam without restraint, until the encroachments of white settlers induced the government to take some definite action respecting this band of non-treaty Nez Percés." (*Comr.*, *21.*) At this time the tribe numbered about 2,800, of whom about 500 acknowledged Joseph as their chief.

Collisions between the whites and Indians in the valley became more frequent, and one of Joseph's band had been killed, when a commission was appointed in 1876 to induce the Indians to give up the Wallowa valley and remove to Lapwai reservation in Idaho. Joseph still refus-

CHIEF JOSEPH

ing to remove, the matter was turned over to General Howard. On May 3, 1877, he held the first council with Joseph and his followers at Fort Lapwai. Their ceremonial approach, which was probably in accord with the ritual teachings of the Dreamer religion, is thus described by the general:

A long rank of men, followed by women and children, with faces painted, the red paint extending back into the partings of the hair—the men's hair braided and tied up with showy strings—ornamented in dress, in hats, in blankets with variegated colors, in leggings of buckskin and moccasins beaded and plain; women with bright shawls or blankets, and skirts to the ankle and top moccasins. All were mounted on Indian ponies as various in color as the dress of the riders. These picturesque people, after keeping us waiting long enough for effect, came in sight from up the valley from the direction of their temporary camp just above the company gardens. They drew near to the hollow square of the post and in front of the small company to be interviewed. Then they struck up their song. They were not armed except with a few tomahawk pipes that could be smoked with the peaceful tobacco or penetrate the skull bone of an enemy, at the will of the holder. Yet somehow this wild sound produced a strange effect. It made one feel glad that there were but fifty of them, and not five hundred. It was shrill and searching; sad, like a wail, and yet defiant in its close. The Indians swept around outside the fence and made the entire circuit, still keeping up the song as they rode. The buildings broke the refrain into irregular bubblings of sound until the ceremony was completed. (*Howard, 1.*)

At this conference Toohulhulsote, the principal Dreamer priest of Joseph's band, acted as spokesman for the Indians, and insisted, according to the Smohalla doctrine, that the earth was his mother, that she should not be disturbed by hoe or plow, that men should subsist by the spontaneous productions of nature, and that the sovereignty of the earth could not be sold or given away. Continuing, he asserted, " We never have made any trade. Part of the Indians gave up their land. I never did. The earth is part of my body, and I never gave up the earth. So long as the earth keeps me I want to be left alone." General Howard finally ordered him under arrest, after which the Indians at last agreed to go on a reservation by June 14. (*Howard, 2.*) A few days later, councils were held with Smohalla and his people, and with Moses, another noted "renegade" chief with a considerable following farther up the Columbia. Both chiefs, representing at least 500 warriors, disclaimed any hostile intentions and agreed to go on reservations. Smohalla said, "Your law is my law. I say to you, yes. I will be on a reservation by September." (*Howard, 3.*) Parties under Joseph and other leading chiefs then went out to select suitable locations for reservations, Joseph and his band deciding in favor of Lapwai valley. Everything was moving smoothly toward a speedy and peaceful settlement of all difficulties, and the commission had already reported the successful accomplishment of the work, when a single act of lawless violence undid the labor of weeks and precipitated a bloody war. (*Comr., 22.*)

One of Joseph's band had been murdered by whites some time before, but the Indians had remained quiet. (*Comr., 23.*) Now, while the Nez Percés were gathering up their stock to remove to the reservation selected, a band of white robbers attacked them, ran off the cattle, and killed one of the party in charge. Joseph could no longer restrain his warriors, and on June 13, 1877—one day before the date that had been appointed for going on the reservation—the enraged Nez Percés attacked the neighboring settlement on White Bird creek, Idaho, and killed 21 persons.[1] The war was begun. The troops under Howard were ordered out. The first fight occurred on June 17 at Hangman's creek and resulted in the loss of 34 soldiers. Then came another on July 4 with a loss of 13 more. Then on July 12 another encounter by troops under General Howard himself, in which 11 soldiers were killed and 26 wounded. (*Comr., 24.*)

Then began one of the most remarkable exhibitions of generalship in the history of our Indian wars, a retreat worthy to be remembered with that of the storied ten thousand. With hardly a hundred warriors, and impeded by more than 350 helpless women and children—with General Howard behind, with Colonel (General) Miles in front, and with Colonel Sturgis and the Crow scouts coming down upon his flank—Chief Joseph led his little band up the Clearwater and across the mountains into Montana, turning at Big Hole pass long enough to beat back his pursuers with a loss of 60 men; then on by devious mountain trails southeast into Yellowstone park, where he again turned on Howard and drove him back with additional loss of men and horses; then out of Wyoming and north into Montana again, hoping to find safety on Canadian soil, until intercepted in the neighborhood of the Yellowstone by Colonel Sturgis in front with fresh troops and a detachment of Crow scouts, with whom they sustained two more encounters, this time with heavy loss of men and horses to themselves; then again eluding their pursuers, this handful of starving and worn-out warriors, now reduced to scarcely fifty able men, carrying their wounded and their helpless families, crossed the Missouri and entered the Bearpaw mountains. But new enemies were on their trail, and at last, when within 50 miles of the land of refuge, Miles, with a fresh army, cut off their retreat by a decisive blow, capturing more than half their horses, killing a number of the band, including Joseph's brother and the noted chief Looking Glass, and wounding 40 others. (*Comr., 25.*)

Forced either to surrender or to abandon the helpless wounded, the women, and children, Joseph chose to surrender to Colonel Miles, on October 5, 1877, after a masterly retreat of more than a thousand miles. He claimed that this was "a conditional surrender, with a distinct promise that he should go back to Idaho in the spring." (*Comr., 26.*) The statement of General Howard's aid-de-camp is explicit on this point:

It was promised Joseph that he would be taken to Tongue river and kept there till spring, and then be returned to Idaho. General Sheridan, ignoring the promises made

---

[1] The details of the attack on the cattle guards is given by Helen Hunt Jackson (Century of Dishonor, page 131). The Indian Commissioner, in his official report, says: "Open hostilities by these Indians began by the murder of 21 white men and women on White Bird creek, near Mount Idaho, in revenge for the murder of one of their tribe." (Comr. Rept., 1877, page 12.)

on the battlefield, ostensibly on account of the difficulty of getting supplies there from Fort Buford, ordered the hostiles to Leavenworth, . . . but different treatment was promised them when they held rifles in their hands. (*Sutherland, 1.*)

Seven ·years passed before the promise was kept, and in the meantime the band had been reduced by disease and death in Indian Territory from about 450 to about 280.

This strong testimony to the high character of Joseph and his people and the justice of their cause comes from the commissioner at the head of Indian affairs during and immediately after the outbreak:

I traveled with him in Kansas and the Indian Territory for nearly a week and found him to be one of the most gentlemanly and well-behaved Indians that I ever met. He is bright and intelligent, and is anxious for the welfare of his people. . . . The Nez Percés are very much superior to the Osages and Pawnees in the Indian Territory; they are even brighter than the Poncas, and care should be taken to place them where they will thrive. . . . It will be borne in mind that Joseph has never made a treaty with the United States, and that he has never surrendered to the government the lands he claimed to own in Idaho. . . . I had occasion in my last annual report to say that "Joseph and his followers have shown themselves to be brave men and skilled soldiers, who, with one exception, have observed the rules of civilized warfare, and have not mutilated their dead enemies." These Indians were encroached upon by white settlers on soil they believed to be their own, and when these encroachments became intolerable they were compelled, in their own estimation, to take up arms. (*Comr., 27a.*)

In all our sad Indian history there is nothing to exceed in pathetic eloquence the surrender speech of the Nez Percé chief:

I am tired of fighting. Our chiefs are killed. Looking Glass is dead. Toohulhulsote is dead. The old men are all dead. It is the young men who say yes or no. He who led the young men is dead. It is cold and we have no blankets. The little children are freezing to death. My people, some of them, have run away to the hills and have no blankets, no food. No one knows where they are—perhaps freezing to death. I want to have time to look for my children and see how many of them I can find. Maybe I shall find them among the dead. Hear me, my chiefs. I am tired. My heart is sick and sad. From where the sun now stands I will fight no more forever. (*Sec. War, 3.*)

CHAPTER VII

SMOHALLA AND HIS DOCTRINE

My young men shall never work. Men who work can not dream, and wisdom comes to us in dreams. . . . You ask me to plow the ground. Shall I take a knife and tear my mother's bosom? You ask me to dig for stone. Shall I dig under her skin for her bones? You ask me to cut grass and make hay and sell it and be rich like white men. But how dare I cut off my mother's hair?—*Smohalla.*

We hear little of Smohalla for several years after the Nez Percé war until the opening of the Northern Pacific railroad in 1883 once more brought to a focus the land grievances of the Indians in that section. Along Yakima valley the railroad "was located through Indian fields and orchards, with little respect for individual rights," while the host of prospective settlers who at once swarmed into the country showed the usual white man's consideration for the native proprietors. Some of the Indians, breaking away from their old traditions in order to obtain permanent homes before everything should be taken up by the whites, had gone out and selected homesteads under the law, and the agent was now using the Indian police to compel them to return to the reservation, "and the singular anomaly was presented of the United States Indian agent on the one hand applying for troops to drive the Indians from their homestead settlements to the reservation a hundred miles away, and on the other the Indians telegraphing to the military authorities to send troops to protect them from the Indian police." (*MacMurray MS.*) In addition to their land troubles the Yakima and their confederated tribes, among whom were many progressive and even prosperous Indians, were restive under constant interference with their religious (Smohalla) ceremonies, to which a large proportion adhered.

In order to learn the nature of the dissatisfaction of the Indians, and if possible to remove the cause, General Miles, then commanding the military department of the Columbia, sent Major J. W. MacMurray to the scene of the disturbance in June, 1884. He spent about a year in the work, visiting the various villages of the upper Columbia, especially P nä at Priest rapids, where he met Smohalla, the high priest of the Dreamer theology, and his report on the subject is invaluable.

Smohalla is the chief of the Wa'napûm, a small tribe in Washington, numbering probably less than 200 souls, commonly known rather indefinitely as "Columbia River Indians," and roaming along both banks of the Columbia from the neighborhood of Priest rapids down to the entrance of Snake river. They are of Shahaptian stock and closely akin to the Yakima and Nez Percés, and have never made a treaty with

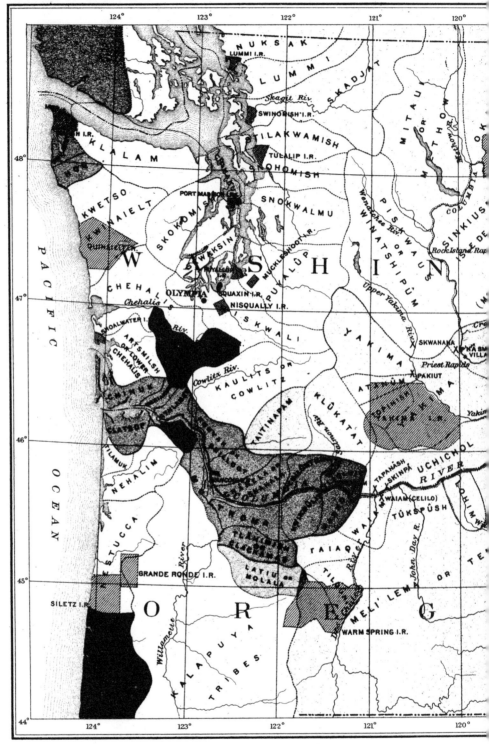

DISTRIBUTION OF TRIBES OF THE UPPER CO

INCLUDING ALL THOSE OF THE SN

JAMES

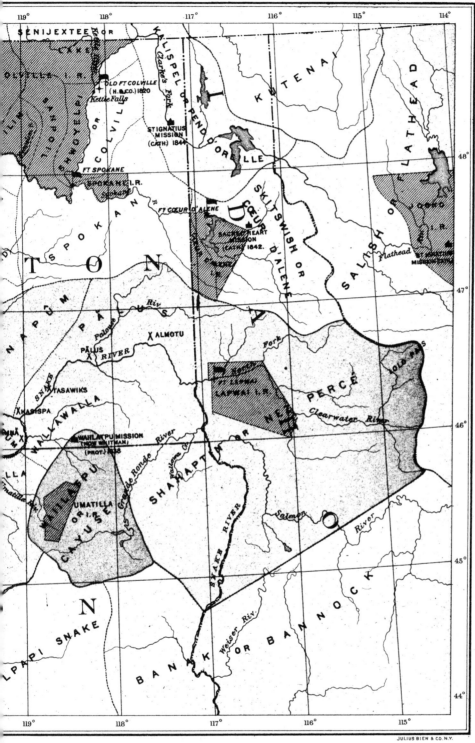

JULIUS BIEN & CO. N.Y.

A REGION IN WASHINGTON, OREGON AND IDAHO

A AND SHAKER RELIGIONS

NEY

the government.   Among his own people and his disciples in the neighboring tribes he is known as Shmóqûla, "The Preacher."[1]   He is also frequently called Yu'yunipī'tqana, "The Shouting Mountain," from a belief among his followers that a part of his revelation came to him from a mountain which became instinct with life and spoke into his soul while he lay dreaming upon it.   Still another name by which he is sometimes known is Waip-shwa, or "Rock Carrier," the reason for which does not appear.   The name which belonged to him in youth, before assuming his priestly function, is now forgotten.   For more than forty years he has resided at the Wanapûm village of P'nä on the west bank of the Columbia, at the foot of Priest rapids, in what is now Yakima county, Washington.   The name P'nä signifies "a fish weir," this point being a great rendezvous for the neighboring tribes during the salmon-fishing season.   These frequent gatherings afford abundant opportunity for the teaching and dissemination of his peculiar doctrines, as is sufficiently evident from the fact that, while his own tribe numbers hardly two score families, his disciples along the river are counted by thousands.

Smohalla was born about 1815 or 1820, and is consequently now an old man, although still well preserved, and with his few scattering locks unchanged in color.   At the time of the Nez Percé war he was in the full vigor of manhood.   His appearance in 1884 is thus described by Major MacMurray: "In person Smohalla is peculiar.   Short, thick-set, bald-headed and almost hunch-backed, he is not prepossessing at first sight, but he has an almost Websterian head, with a deep brow over bright, intelligent eyes.   He is a finished orator.   His manner is mostly of the bland, insinuating, persuasive style, but when aroused he is full of fire and seems to handle invectives effectively.   His audience seemed spellbound under his magic manner, and it never lost interest to me, though he spoke in a language comprehended by few white men and translated to me at second or third hand."   By another writer who met him a year later he is described as rather undersized and inclining toward obesity, with "a reserved and cunning but not ill-natured countenance, and a large, well-shaped head.   His manners were more suave and insinuating than is usual with Indians."   He had a comfortable appearance, his moccasins and leggins were new, and he rode a good pinto pony.   (*Huggins, 1.*)

In his youth he had frequented the Catholic mission of Atahnam among the Yakima, where he became familiar with the forms of that service and also acquired a slight knowledge of French.   Whether or not he was a regular member of the mission school is a disputed point, as it is asserted by some that he has never worn the white man's dress

---

[1] Bureau of Ethnology alphabet.   Like most Indian names, it appears in a variety of forms.   Other spellings are: Imoholla (misprint), Smawhola, Smohaller, Smohallow, Smohanlee, Smohollie, Smokeholer, Smokeller, Smuxale, Snohollie, Snooholler, Somahallie.   As the correct pronunciation is difficult to English speakers, I have chosen the popular form.   In one official report he is mentioned as "Smohal-ler, or Big-talk, or Four Mountains;" in another, probably by misprint, as "Big talk on four mountains."

or had his hair cut. The influence of the Catholic ceremonial is plainly visible in his own ritual performance. In his early manhood he distinguished himself as a warrior, and had already come to be regarded as a prominent man when he first began to preach his peculiar theology about the year 1850. There can be no question that the rapid spread of his doctrines among the tribes of the Columbia materially facilitated their confederation in the Yakima war of 1855–56. It is said that he aspired to be the leader in this war, and that, to attain this end, he invited all the neighboring bands to attend a council at his village of P nä, but failed to accomplish his object.

Shortly after the close of the war, probably about 1860, the incident occurred which wrought an entire change in his life, stamping him as an oracle and prophet beyond peradventure, and giving to his religious system the force of authority which it has ever since retained. He had already established a reputation as a medicine-man, and was believed to be "making medicine" against the life of Moses, the noted chief of a tribe farther up the river, who was greatly in dread of his occult powers, and forced a quarrel in order to rid himself forever of his rival. A fight resulted, and Smohalla was nearly killed. It is said that he was left on the ground as dead, but revived sufficiently to crawl away and get into a boat on the bank of the Columbia near by. Bleeding and disabled, he was carried down at the mercy of the current until he was finally rescued from his perilous position by some white men, far below. His recovery was slow. When it was completed, unwilling to return in disgrace to his own country and probably still dreading the anger of Moses, he determined to become a wanderer.

Then began one of the most remarkable series of journeyings ever undertaken by an uncivilized Indian. Going down the Columbia to Portland and the coast, he turned south, and, stopping on the way at various points in Oregon and California, continued beyond San Diego into Mexico. Then, turning again, he came back through Arizona, Utah, and Nevada to his former home on the Columbia, where he announced that he had been dead and in the spirit world and had now returned by divine command to guide his people. As he was thought to have been killed in the encounter with Moses, and as he had disappeared so completely until now, his awe-stricken hearers readily believed that they were actually in the presence of one who had been taken bodily into the spirit world, whence he was now sent back as a teacher.

On the occasion of MacMurray's visit, says that authority, "Smohalla asked me many geographic questions, and I spread out a railroad map, marking the situation of Priest rapids, Portland, and Vancouver barracks, and he traced with a straw down the coast line to below San Diego. He asked where San Bernardino was, and paused long over this. He recognized the ocean or ‘salt chuck,’ with many other geographic features and localities, but he would neither admit nor deny having been at Salt Lake City, although he admitted having been in Utah, knew the lake and adjacent mountain chains, and said that he had seen Mormon priests getting commands direct from heaven. He dwelt long over Arizona, and remarked, '*bad-a Inchun.*' "

Smohalla now declared to his people that the Sa'ghalee Tyee, the Great Chief Above, was angry at their apostasy, and commanded them through him to return to their primitive manners, as their present miserable condition in the presence of the intrusive race was due to their having abandoned their own religion and violated the laws of nature and the precepts of their ancestors. He then explained in detail the system to which they must adhere in future if they would conform to the expressed will of the higher power. It was a system based on the primitive aboriginal mythology and usage, with an elaborate ritual which combined with the genuine Indian features much of what he had seen and remembered of Catholic ceremonial and military parade, with perhaps also some additions from Mormon forms.

His words made a deep impression on his hearers. They had indeed abandoned their primitive simplicity to a great extent, and were now suffering the penalty in all the misery that had come to them with the advent of the white-skin race that threatened to blot them out from the earth. The voice of the prophet was accepted as a voice from the other world, for they knew that he had been dead and was now alive. What he said must be true and wise, for he had been everywhere and knew tribes and countries they had never heard of. Even the white men confirmed his words in this regard. He could even control the sun and the moon, for he had said when they would be dark, and they were dark.

If genius be a form of insanity, as has been claimed, intense religious enthusiasm would seem to have a close connection with physical as well as mental disease. Like Mohammed and Joan of Arc, and like the Shaker prophet of Puget sound, Smohalla is subject to cataleptic trances, and it is while in this unconscious condition that he is believed to receive his revelations. Says MacMurray:

He falls into trances and lies rigid for considerable periods. Unbelievers have experimented by sticking needles through his flesh, cutting him with knives, and otherwise testing his sensibility to pain, without provoking any responsive action. It was asserted that he was surely dead, because blood did not flow from the wounds. These trances always excite great interest and often alarm, as he threatens to abandon his earthly body altogether because of the disobedience of his people, and on each occasion they are in a state of suspense as to whether the Saghalee Tyee will send his soul back to earth to reoccupy his body, or will, on the contrary, abandon and leave them without his guidance. It is this going into long trances, out of which he comes as from heavy sleep and almost immediately relates his experiences in the spirit land, that gave rise to the title of "Dreamers," or believers in dreams, commonly given to his followers by the neighboring whites. His actions are similar to those of a trance medium, and if self-hypnotization be practicable that would seem to explain it. I questioned him as to his trances and hoped to have him explain them to me, but he avoided the subject and was angered when I pressed him. He manifestly believes all he says of what occurs to him in this trance state. As we

have hundreds of thousands of educated white people who believe in similar falla-
cies, this is not more unlikely in an Indian subjected to such influence.

In studying Smohalla we have to deal with the same curious mixture
of honest conviction and cunning deception that runs through the
history of priestcraft in all the ages. Like some other prophets before
him, he seeks to convey the idea that he is in control of the elements
and the heavenly bodies, and he has added greatly to his reputation
by predicting several eclipses. This he was enabled to do by the help
of an almanac and some little explanation from a party of surveyors.
In this matter, however, he was soon made to realize that a little
knowledge is a dangerous thing. He could not get another almanac,
and his astronomic prophecies came to an abrupt termination at the
end of the first year. Concerning this, Major MacMurray says:

> He showed me an almanac of a preceding year and asked me to readjust it for
> eclipses, as it did not work as it had formerly done. I explained that Washington
> (the Naval Observatory) made new ones every year, and that old ones could not be
> fixed up to date. He had probably obtained this one from the station agent at the
> railroad, now superseded by a new one, who had cut off Smohalla's supply of astro-
> nomical data. My inability to repair the 1882 almanac for use in prognosticating
> in 1884 cost me much of his respect as a wise man from the east. (*MacMurray MS.*)

Smohalla had also a blank book containing mysterious characters,
some of which resembled letters of the alphabet, and which he said
were records of events and prophecies. MacMurray was unable to
decide whether they were mnemonic or were simply unmeaning marks
intended to foster among his followers the impression of his superior
wisdom. It is probable that they were genuine mnemonic symbols
invented by himself for his own purposes, as such systems, devised
and used by single individuals or families, and unintelligible to others,
are by no means rare among those who may be called the literary men
of our aboriginal tribes.

As their principal troubles arose out of the disputed title to their
lands, Major MacMurray was asked by the Indians to explain the
Indian homestead law and how white men divided, land. This was
carefully done with the aid of a checkerboard, and they were shown
how the land was mapped out into equal squares arranged on straight
lines so that every man could find his own. They were then urged by
the officer to apply for homesteads and settle upon them so as to avoid
further trouble with the new settlers who were pouring into the country.
Smohalla replied that he knew all this, but he did not like the new law,
as it was against nature. He then went on to expound in detail the
Indian cosmogony. Said he:

> I will tell you about it. Once the world was all water and God lived alone. He
> was lonesome, he had no place to put his foot, so he scratched the sand up from the
> bottom and made the land, and he made the rocks, and he made trees, and he made
> a man; and the man had wings and could go anywhere. The man was lonesome, and
> God made a woman. They ate fish from the water, and God made the deer and other
> animals, and he sent the man to hunt and told the woman to cook the meat and to

SMOHALLA AND HIS PRIESTS

dress the skins. Many more men and women grew up, and they lived on the banks of the great river whose waters were full of salmon. The mountains contained much game and there were buffalo on the plains. There were so many people that the stronger ones sometimes oppressed the weak and drove them from the best fisheries, which they claimed as their own. They fought and nearly all were killed, and their bones are to be seen in the hills yet. God was very angry at this and he took away their wings and commanded that the lands and fisheries should be common to all who lived upon them; that they were never to be marked off or divided, but that the people should enjoy the fruits that God planted in the land, and the animals that lived upon it, and the fishes in the water. God said he was the father and the earth was the mother of mankind; that nature was the law; that the animals, and fish, and plants obeyed nature, and that man only was sinful. This is the old law.

I know all kinds of men. First there were my people (the Indians); God made them first. Then he made a Frenchman [referring to the Canadian voyagers of the Hudson Bay company], and then he made a priest [priests accompanied these expeditions of the Hudson Bay company]. A long time after that came Boston men [Americans are thus called in the Chinook jargon, because the first of our nation came into the Columbia river in 1796 in a ship from Boston], and then King George men [the English]. Later came black men, and last God made a Chinaman with a tail. He is of no account and has to work all the time like a woman. All these are new people. Only the Indians are of the old stock. After awhile, when God is ready, he will drive away all the people except those who have obeyed his laws.

Those who cut up the lands or sign papers for lands will be defrauded of their rights and will be punished by God's anger. Moses was bad. God did not love him. He sold his people's houses and the graves of their dead. It is a bad word that comes from Washington. It is not a good law that would take my people away from me to make them sin against the laws of God.

You ask me to plow the ground! Shall I take a knife and tear my mother's bosom? Then when I die she will not take me to her bosom to rest.

You ask me to dig for stone! Shall I dig under her skin for her bones? Then when I die I can not enter her body to be born again.

You ask me to cut grass and make hay and sell it, and be rich like white men! But how dare I cut off my mother's hair?

It is a bad law, and my people can not obey it. I want my people to stay with me here. All the dead men will come to life again. Their spirits will come to their bodies again. We must wait here in the homes of our fathers and be ready to meet them in the bosom of our mother. (*MacMurray MS.*)

The idea that the earth is the mother of all created things lies at the base, not only of the Smohalla religion, but of the theology of the Indian tribes generally and of primitive races all over the world. This explains Tecumtha's reply to Harrison: "The sun is my father and the earth is my mother. On her bosom I will rest." In the Indian mind the corn, fruits, and edible roots are the gifts which the earth-mother gives freely to her children. Lakes and ponds are her eyes, hills are her breasts, and streams are the milk flowing from her breasts. Earthquakes and underground noises are signs of her displeasure at the wrongdoing of her children. Especially are the malarial fevers, which often follow extensive disturbance of the surface by excavation or otherwise, held to be direct punishments for the crime of lacerating her bosom.

Smohalla's chief supporter and assistant at the ceremonies was Kotai'aqan, or Coteea'kun, as MacMurray spells it, of the Yakima tribe.

The name refers to a brood of young ducks scattering in alarm. He was the son of Kamai'äkan, the great war chief of the Yakima. He also gave MacMurray the story of the cosmos, which agrees with that obtained from Smohalla, but is more in detail:

The world was all water, and Saghalee Tyee was above it. He threw up out of the water at shallow places large quantities of mud, and that made the land. Some was piled so high that it froze hard, and the rains that fell were made into snow and ice. Some of the earth was made hard into rocks, and anyone could see that it had not changed — it was only harder. We have no records of the past; but we have it from our fathers from far back that Saghalee Tyee threw down many of the mountains he had made. It is all as our fathers told us, and we can see that it is true when we are hunting for game or berries in the mountains. I did not see it done. He made trees to grow, and he made a man out of a ball of mud and instructed him in what he should do. When the man grew lonesome, he made a woman as his companion, and taught her to dress skins, and to gather berries, and to make baskets of the bark of roots, which he taught her how to find.

She was asleep and dreaming of her ignorance of how to please man, and she prayed to Saghalee Tyee to help her. He breathed on her and gave her something that she could not see, or hear, or smell, or touch, and it was preserved in a little basket, and by it all the arts of design and skilled handiwork were imparted to her descendants.

Notwithstanding all the benefits they enjoyed, there was quarreling among the people, and the earth-mother was angry. The mountains that overhung the river at the Cascades were thrown down, and dammed the stream and destroyed the forests and whole tribes, and buried them under the rocks. (*MacMurray MS.*)

In connection with the wonderful little basket, MacMurray states that Kotai'aqan presented him with a very ancient drum-shape basket, about 2½ inches in diameter, to give to his wife, in order that she might likewise be inspired. Concerning the catastrophe indicated in the last paragraph, he goes on to say:

The Cascade range, where it crosses the Columbia river, exhibits enormous cross sections of lava, and at its base are petrified trunks of trees, which have been covered and hidden from view except where the wash of the mighty stream has exposed them. Indians have told me, of their knowledge, that, buried deep under these outpours of basalt, or volcanic tufa, are bones of animals of *siah*, or the long ago. Traditions of the great landslide at the Cascades are many, but vary little in form. According to one account, the mountain tops fell together and formed a kind of arch, under which the water flowed, until the overhanging rocks finally fell into the stream and made a dam or gorge. As the rock is columnar basalt, very friable and easily disintegrated, that was not impossible, and the landscape suggests some such giant avalanche. The submerged trees are plainly visible near this locality. Animal remains I have not seen, but these salmon-eating Indians have lived on the river's border through countless ages, and know every feature in their surroundings by constant association for generations, and naturally ally these facts with their religious theories. (*MacMurray MS.*)

In an article on "The submerged trees of the Columbia river," in *Science* of February 18, 1887, the geologist, Major Clarence E. Dutton, also notices the peculiar formation at the Cascades and mentions the Indian tradition of a natural bridge over the river at this point.

MacMurray continues:

Coteeakun went on to say that some day Saghalee Tyee would again overturn the mountains and so expose these bones, which, having been preserved through so long

SMOHALLA CHURCH ON YAKIMA RESERVATION

a time, would be reoccupied by the spirits which now dwell in the mountain tops, watching their descendants on earth and waiting for the resurrection to come. The voices of these spirits of the dead can be heard at all times in the mountains, and often they answer back when spoken to. Mourners who wail for their dead hear spirit voices replying, and know they will always remain near them. No man knows when it will come, and only those who have observed nature's laws and adhered to the faith of their ancestors will have their bones so preserved and be certain of an earthly tenement for their spirits. He wanted me to confirm this.

Coteeakun was pacific and gentle. He said all men were as brothers to him and he hoped all would dwell together. He had been told that white and black and all other kinds of men originally dwelt in tents, as the red men always have done, and that God in former times came to commune with white men. He thought there could be only one Saghalee Tyee, in which case white and red men would live on a common plane. We came from one source of life and in time would "grow from one stem again. It would be like a stick that the whites held by one end and the Indians by the other until it was broken, and it would be made again into one stick."

Some of the wilder Indians to the north have more truculent ideas as to the final cataclysm which is to reoverturn the mountains and bring back the halcyon days of the long past. As the whites and the others came only within the lifetime of the fathers of these Indians, they are not to be included in the benefits of the resurrection, but are to be turned over with all that the white man's civilization has put upon the present surface of the land.

Coteeakun was for progress—limited progress, it is true—to the extent of fixed homes and agriculture, but he did not want his people to go from their villages or to abandon their religious faith. They were nearly all disposed to work for wages among the farmers, and had orchards and some domestic animals upon whose produce they lived, besides the fish from the rivers. Smohalla opposed anything that pertained to civilization, and had neither cattle, sheep, goats, pigs, nor chickens, and not a tree or vegetable was grown anywhere in his vicinage. Kowse (*Peucedanum cous*), kamas (*Camassia esculenta*), berries, fish, and the game of the mountains alone furnished food to his people, whom he advised to resist every advance of civilization as improper for a true Indian and in violation of the faith of their ancestors. I found, however, that he was willing to advise his people to take up lands and adopt the white man's road, if the government would pension him as it had pensioned Chief Moses, so that while I thought he believed in his religion as much as other sectarians do in theirs, he was tainted by the mercenary desire to live upon his followers unless otherwise provided for by the government.

From Captain E. L. Huggins, Second cavalry, who visited Smohalla about the same time, we obtain further information concerning the prophet's personality and doctrines. When Smohalla was urged to follow the example of other Indians who had taken up the white man's road, he replied, "No one has any respect for these book Indians. Even the white men like me better and treat me better than they do the book Indians. My young men shall never work. Men who work can not dream, and wisdom comes to us in dreams."

When it was argued that the whites worked and yet knew more than the Indians, he replied that the white man's wisdom was poor and weak and of no value to Indians, who must learn the highest wisdom from dreams and from participating in the Dreamer ceremonies. Being pressed to explain the nature of this higher knowledge, he replied, "Each one must learn for himself the highest wisdom. It can not be taught. You have the wisdom of your race. Be content."

When the officer contended that even the Indians had to work hard during the fishing season to get food for winter, the prophet answered:

"This work lasts only for a few weeks. Besides it is natural work and does them no harm. But the work of the white man hardens soul and body. Nor is it right to tear up and mutilate the earth as white men do."

To the officer's assertion that the Indians also dug roots and were even then digging kamas in the mountains, he replied:

"We simply take the gifts that are freely offered. We no more harm the earth than would an infant's fingers harm its mother's breast. But the white man tears up large tracts of land, runs deep ditches, cuts down forests, and changes the whole face of the earth. You know very well this is not right. Every honest man," said he, looking at me searchingly, "knows in his heart that this is all wrong. But the white men are so greedy they do not consider these things."

He asserted that the Indians were now so helpless before the white men that they must cease to exist unless they had assistance from a higher power, but that if they heeded the sacred message they would receive strong and sudden help as surely as the spring comes after winter. When some doubt was expressed as to his own faith in these things, he asked pointedly:

"Do the white teachers believe what they teach?"

"It is said, Smohalla, that you hate all white men."

"It is not true. But the whites have caused us great suffering. Dr Whitman many years ago made a long journey to the east to get a bottle of poison for us. He was gone about a year, and after he came back strong and terrible diseases broke out among us. The Indians killed Dr Whitman, but it was too late. He had uncorked his bottle and all the air was poisoned. Before that there was little sickness among us, but since then many of us have died. I have had children and grandchildren, but they are all dead. My last grandchild, a young woman of 16, died last month. If only her infant could have lived"— his voice faltered slightly, but with scarcely a pause he continued in his former tone, "I labored hard to save them, but my medicine would not work as it used to."

He repelled the idea that the Indians had profited by the coming of the whites, and especially denied that they had obtained ponies from this source. His statement on this point may be of interest to those who hold that the horse is indigenous to America:

"What! The white man gave us ponies? Oh, no; we had ponies long before we ever saw white people. The Great Spirit gave them to us. Our horses were swifter and more enduring, too, in those days, before they were mixed with the white man's horses."

He went on to tell how the Indians had befriended the first explorers who came among them and how ungrateful had been their later recompense, and said: "We are now so few and weak that we can offer no resistance, and their preachers have persuaded them to let a few of us live, so as to claim credit with the Great Spirit for being generous and humane. But they begrudge us what little grass our ponies eat." At parting he repeated earnestly, "If they tell you Smohalla hates all white people, do not believe it." (*Huggins, 2.*)

Our knowledge of the Smohalla ritual is derived from the account given by Major MacMurray and from the statements of Yakima and Pälus informants. The officer's account is that of an intelligent observer, who noted ceremonies closely, but without fully comprehending their meaning. The Indian account is that of initiates and true believers, one of them being the regular interpreter of the Smohalla services on Yakima reservation.

The officer had already seen the ceremonial performances at the Indian villages at Celilo and Umatilla in Oregon, at Tumwater and Yakima gap in Washington, but found its greatest development at the fountain head, the home of Smohalla at Priest rapids. His account is so full of interest that we give it almost in its entirety.

While still several miles away, his party discovered the village, the houses extending along the bank of the river, with several flags attached to long poles fluttering in the wind. The trail from the mountains was winding and difficult, but at last—

We reached the plain and were met by a procession, headed by Smohalla in person, all attired in gorgeous array and mounted on their best chargers. We wended our way through sagebrush and sand dunes to the village street, not a soul being visible, but from the mat-roofed salmon houses there came forth the most indescribable chorus of bell ringing, drum beating, and screeching. I noticed that the street was neatly swept and well sprinkled—an unusual thing in any Indian village. This, Smohalla said, was in my honor and to show that his people had cleanly tastes. Our procession passed on beyond the village to a new canvas tent, which had a brush shade to keep off the sun and was lined and carpeted with new and very pretty matting. Smohalla said this had been prepared especially for me, and was to be my house as long as I should stay with him. To cap the climax, he had constructed a bench for me, having sent more than 90 miles for the nails. Fresh salmon, caught in a peculiar trap among the rocks and broiled on a plank, were regularly furnished my party, and with hard tack and coffee of our own supplying we got enough to eat and drink. Our own blankets furnished sleeping conveniences. The river was within two yards of our tent door and was an ample lavatory.

When I awoke the next morning, the sound of drums was again heard, and for days it continued. I do not remember that there was any intermission except for a few minutes at a time. Seven bass drums were used for the purpose. I was invited to be present, and took great interest in the ceremonies, which I shall endeavor to describe.

There was a small open space to the north of the larger house, which was Smohalla's residence and the village assembly room as well. This space was inclosed by a whitewashed fence made of boards which had drifted down the river. In the middle was a flagstaff with a rectangular flag, suggesting a target. In the center of the flag was a round red patch. The field was yellow, representing grass, which is there of a yellow hue in summer. A green border indicated the boundary of the world, the hills being moist and green near their tops. At the top of the flag was a small extension of blue color, with a white star in the center. Smohalla explained: "This is my flag, and it represents the world. God told me to look after my people—all are my people. There are four ways in the world—north and south and east and west. I have been all those ways. This is the center. I live here. The red spot is my heart—everybody can see it. The yellow grass grows everywhere around this place. The green mountains are far away all around the world. There is only water beyond, salt water. The blue [referring to the blue cloth strip] is the sky, and the star is the north star. That star never changes; it is always in the same place. I keep my heart on that star. I never change."

There are frequent services, a sort of processional around the outside of the fence, the prophet and a small boy with a bell entering the inclosure, where, after hoisting the flag, he delivers a sort of sermon. Captains or class leaders give instructions to the people, who are arranged according to stature, the men and women in different classes marching in single file to the sound of drums. There seems to be a regular system of signals, at command of the prophet, by the boy with the bell, upon which the people chant loud or low, quick or slow, or remain silent. These outdoor services occurred several times each day.

Smohalla invited me to participate in what he considered a grand ceremonial service within the larger house. This house was built with a framework of stout logs placed upright in the ground and roofed over with brush, or with canvas in rainy weather.

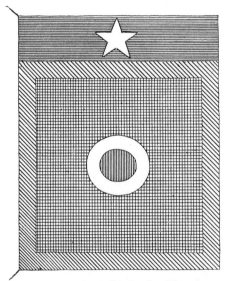

FIG. 64—Smohalla's flag (heraldic).

The sides consisted of bark and rush matting. It was about 75 feet long by 25 feet wide. Singing and drumming had been going on for some time when I arrived. The air resounded with the voices of hundreds of Indians, male and female, and the banging of drums. Within, the room was dimly lighted. Smoke curled from a fire on the floor at the farther end and pervaded the atmosphere. The ceiling was hung with hundreds of salmon, split and drying in the smoke.

The scene was a strange one. On either side of the room was a row of twelve women standing erect with arms crossed and hands extended, with finger tips at the shoulders. They kept time to the drums and their voices by balancing on the balls of their feet and tapping with their heels on the floor, while they chanted with varying pitch and time. The excitement and persistent repetition wore them out, and I heard that others than Smohalla had seen visions in their trances, but I saw none who would admit it or explain anything of it. I fancied they feared their own action, and that real death might come to them in this simulated death.

Those on the right hand were dressed in garments of a red color with an attempt at uniformity. Those on the left wore costumes of white buckskin, said to be very ancient ceremonial costumes, with red and blue trimmings. All wore large round silver plates or such other glittering ornaments as they possessed. A canvas covered the floor and on it knelt the men and boys in lines of seven. Each seven, as a rule, had shirts of the same color. The tallest were in front, the size diminishing regularly to the rear. Children and ancient hags filled in any spare space. In front on a mattress knelt Smohalla, his left hand covering his heart. On his right was the boy bell ringer in similar posture. Smohalla wore a white garment which he was pleased to call a priest's gown, but it was simply a white cloth shirt with a colored stripe down the back.

INTERIOR OF SMOHALLA CHURCH

I and my two assistants were seated on a mattress about 10 feet in front of the prophet, which fortunately placed us near the door and incidentally near fresh air. There were two other witnesses, Indians from distant villages, who sat at one side with Smohalla's son looking on.

Smohalla's son was said to be in training as his successor. He was a young man, apparently about 23 years old, tall, slender, and active in movement, and commonly kept himself apart from the body of the people. He was much darker than his father. His dress was brilliant in style and color. He ordinarily wore a short gown or surplice, sometimes yellow and at other times sky blue, with ornate decorations of stars or moons appliqué, cut from bright-colored cloths. The sleeves were extravagantly trimmed with beads and silver ornaments. He knelt at the right of the group as the place of honor. On his left was Coteeakun, the head man of the Indian village at Union gap, on the Yakima reservation. The third man was Coteeakun's brother, a most intelligent and progressive Indian. (*MacMurray MS.*)

From Charles Ike, an intelligent half-blood interpreter on Yakima reservation, who is also the regular interpreter of the Smohalla ritual services at the Yakima village of Pa'kiut, we obtain additional interesting details concerning the ceremony as there performed, with the underlying religious teachings.

As at present taught, the religion finds adherents among probably all the tribes along the Columbia from near the British border down to the Wushqûm tribe at The Dalles, with the exception, perhaps, of the Klikatat, who are nearly all Catholics. The two chief centers are at P'nä or Priest rapids, where Smohalla in person regularly preaches to about 120 hearers, and at Pa'kiut, at Union gap on Yakima reservation, where, until his death a short time ago, Tianä'ni as regularly conducted the services for about 300 of his tribe. At each place is a church or meeting-house built as already described.

The former high priest of the doctrine among the Yakima, and the right-hand man of Smohalla himself, was Kotai'aqan, already mentioned, the son of the great war chief Kamai'äkan. It is even asserted that he was the originator of the system. However this may be, it is certain that he had much to do with formulating both the dogmas and the ritual. In temper he was more gentle than Smohalla, and more disposed to meet civilization half-way. On his death, about 1890, he was succeeded by his stepson, Tianä'ni, or "Many Wounds," who filled the office until about October, 1892, when he was murdered near his home by two drunken Indians. He was succeeded in the chieftainship by a younger son of Kotai'aqan named Sha'awĕ (or Shaw-wawa Kootiacan), and in his priestly functions by a man known to the whites as Billy John.

The regular services take place on Sunday, in the morning, afternoon, and evening. Sunday has been held sacred among the Nez Percés and neighboring tribes for more than sixty years, as the result of the teachings of the Hudson Bay officers. The prairie tribes also, having learned that Sunday is the great "medicine day" of the whites, now select it by preference for their own religious ceremonies of the Ghost dance and the mescal. There are also services during the week, besides special periodic observances, such as the "lament" for the dead, particularly the dead chiefs, in early spring; the salmon dance, when the salmon begin to run in April, and the berry dance, when the wild berries ripen in autumn. The description of the ceremonial of the salmon

FIG. 65—Charles Ike, Smohalla interpreter.

dance will answer for the others, as it differs chiefly only by the addition of the feast.

As already stated, the house has the door at the eastern end, as is the common rule in all Indian structures. On the roof, at the eastern end of the building at Pa'kiut, are the flags, the center one blue, representing the sky; another one white, representing the earthly light, and the third yellow, representing the heavenly light of the spirit world. Blue, white, and yellow are the sacred colors of this system, as also of that of the Shakers, to be described later. On entering, the worshipers range themselves in two lines along the sides of the building, the men and boys standing along the northern wall, the women and girls along the southern wall, and all facing toward the center. The first man entering takes his place on the north nearest the door; the next one stands just beyond him, and so on; while the women and girls, when their turn comes, make the whole circuit along the northern side, and then, turning at the farther end, take their places in reverse order along the southern wall. In the open space between the rows is a floor-walker, whose business it is to see that everyone is in the right place. All are dressed as nearly as possible in the finest style of the old Indian costume, buckskin and shell ornaments, their faces painted yellow, white, or red with Indian paints, and carrying eagle feathers in their right hands (plates XC, XCI; figure 66).

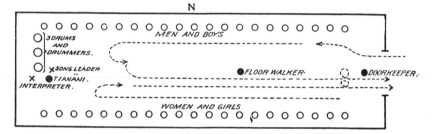

FIG. 66—Diagram showing arrangement of worshipers at Smohalla service.

At the farther end, facing the door, sits the high priest, while just behind him stands his "interpreter," and on his left are seated on the ground the three drummers with their large drums in front of them. The high priest carries a large bell in his left hand and a smaller one in his right.

Dishes of fresh-cooked salmon and jars of water, together with a plentiful supply of other food, are ranged in front of the devotees. After a preliminary ceremony in the nature of a litany, in which the principal articles of their theology are recited in the form of question and answer by the whole body of worshipers, the high priest gives the command, "Take water," when everyone raises a cup of water to his lips. Next comes the command, "Now drink," and each one takes a sip. At the words, "Now the salmon," each takes up a portion of fish, which he puts into his mouth at the next command, "Now eat." Last comes the command, "Now help yourselves," which is the signal for a general attack on the provisions.

When everyone has satisfied his hunger, the remains of the feast are cleared away and the "dance" begins. At a signal given by a single stroke of the bell in the left hand of the high priest all stand up in line on either side of the building. At another stroke of the bell all put their right hands on their breasts. Another tap of the bell and the right hand is brought out in front of the body. Another, and they begin to move their right hands backward and forward like fans in front of the breast, and thus continue throughout the dance, keeping time also to the singing by balancing alternately upon their toes and heels, as already described, without moving from their places. Ritual songs are sung throughout the remainder of the service, in time with the movements of the dancers and the sounds of the drums, and regulated by the strokes of the bell.

Between songs anyone who wishes to speak steps out into the open space. With a single tap of the bell the high priest then summons his "interpreter," standing behind him, who comes forward and stands beside the speaker, a few feet in front and at the right of the high priest. The speaker then in a low tone tells his story—usually a trance vision of the spirit world—to the interpreter, who repeats it in a loud voice to the company. At the end of the recital the high priest gives the signal with the bell, when all raise their right hands with a loud "Ai!" (Yes!). The high priest himself sometimes discourses also to the people through the interpreter; at other times directly.

Each song is repeated until the high priest gives the signal with the bell to stop. Most of the songs consist—in the native language—of seven lines. At the end of the first line the high priest taps once with the bell; at the end of the second line he taps twice, and so on to the end of the song, when he rings the bell hard and continuously, and all raise their hands with a loud "Ai!" Then the song leader, who stands with a feather fan between the high priest and the drummers, starts the next song.

The first song is given by all standing motionless, with the right hand on the breast and with eyes cast downward. It may be rendered:

> Verily, verily, Our Brother made the body.
> He gave it a spirit and the body moved.
> Then he counted out the words for us to speak.

Another begins:

> Verily, Our Brother put salmon in the water to be our food.

Another begins:

> O, brothers! O, sisters!
> When first the light struck this world, it lighted the world forever.

Our Brother (*Nämi Piäp*) is the term used in referring to the creating spirit, instead of "our father," as we might expect them to say.

On leaving, at the close of the ceremony, the man nearest the high priest passes around in front of him and down along in front of the line of women, and as he reaches the door he turns around and bows to the high priest. Each man in turn thus files around and passes out, after which the women—first the one nearest the high priest and then the others in regular order—pass out in the same manner. While the worshipers are thus going out, the high priest, standing up, rings continuously the small bell in his right hand, while with the larger bell in his left he gives a single stroke as each one passes through the door.

Tribes of the Columbia region

The following synopsis will give a good general idea of the location and numbers of the tribes of the Columbia region from the British line down to the Cascades, including all those under the influence of the Smohalla religion. Except when derived from such well-known authorities as Lewis and Clark, Stevens, Gibbs, etc, the information given is the result of personal investigation and work with Yakima and Pälus Indians. The general boundaries of the tribes west of the Cascade range, including the adherents of the Shaker religion, are also indicated on the accompanying map (plate LXXXVIII), but our information in regard to this region is too meager to be definite.

KUTENAI (Kitunahan stock).—*Synonyms:* Arcs Plats, Cotonné, Cottonoi, Coutanie, Flatbow, Kitunaha, Kootenai, Koutaine, Kutneha, Skalzi, Tushepaw (Lewis and Clark, 1805), White-tailed Deer People (Clark, Indian Sign Language). The Kutenai, properly Kituna'qa, form a distinct linguistic stock, and live chiefly on the Canadian side, around Kutenai river and lake, but extend across the line into northern Idaho and northwestern Montana. Their extension southward dates from their treaty of peace with the Flatheads about ninety years ago. In company with the Flatheads they were accustomed formerly to come down from the mountains in the fall to hunt the buffalo on the headwaters of the Missouri. They are mentioned by Lewis and Clark in 1805 under the name of Tushepaw, with bands distinguished as Ootlashoot, Micksucksealton (?), and Hohilpo living in the mountains and on Clark's fork within United States territory. According to Gatschet, Tu'shipa is a collective term applied by the Shoshoni to the tribes living north of them, including the Nez Percés and others, as well as the Kutenai. A part of the Kutenai joined with the Flatheads and Upper Pend d'Oreilles in a treaty with the government in 1855 and are now on Flathead (Jocko) reservation in Montana. They are probably all Catholics. Others, living in northern Idaho, have never entered into treaty relations, and may be followers of Smohalla. The best estimates for the last fifty years give those within the United States a population of from 400 to 450.

PEND D'OREILLE (Salishan stock).—*Synonyms:* Calispel, Coospellar (Lewis and Clark), Kahlispelm, Kalispelines, Kalispelusses, Kellespem, Kullas-Palus, Ku'shpĕlu (a Yakima or Pälus form), Papshpûn-'lĕma or "people of the great fir trees" (Yakima name), Pend d'Oreilles or "ear-rings" (French name), Ponderas. The Pend d'Oreilles held the country along the river and lake of the same name, in Idaho and Washington, immediately southwest of the Kutenai. They are commonly distinguished as Upper, on the lake, and Lower, on both banks of the river. They are the Coospellar mentioned by Lewis and Clark in 1805. They formerly crossed the mountains annually to hunt buffalo on the Missouri. Since 1844 they and most of the other Salishan tribes of this region have been under the influence of Catholic missionaries. The Upper Pend d'Oreilles joined with the Flatheads and Kutenai in a treaty with the government in 1855, and are now on Flathead reservation in Montana. Some of the Lower band joined them there in 1887. Others are on the Cœur d'Alêne reservation in Idaho, a few are with Moses on the Columbia in Washington, and the rest are still in their original country, never having entered into treaty stipulations. The whole tribe numbers about 1,000 souls.

COLVILLE (Salishan stock).—*Synonyms:* Chaudière (French name), Chualpay, Kettle Falls, Quiarlpi or "basket people" (Hale), Schrooyelpi, Schwogelpi, Schwoyelpi, Swielpee, Wheelpoo (Lewis and Clark). They originally occupied the country on Colville and Kettle rivers and on both sides of the Columbia from Kettle falls down to Spokane river, in Washington, and extending north into British territory to about the lower Arrow lake. They are mentioned by Lewis and Clark under the name of Wheelpoo. Kettle falls on the Columbia, within their territory, was the great salmon fishing resort for all the tribes of this region, and here, in 1846, was established the Catholic mission of Saint Paul. As a result of this missionary work, all of these Salishan tribes, excepting the Sanpoil, Nespelim, Mitaui, and a part of the Spokan are now Catholics. In 1854, according to Stevens, the original Shwoyelpi were nearly extinct and their places had been filled by Indians from neighboring tribes. Without ever having entered into any treaty with the government, they were assigned in 1872 to Colville reservation, Washington, which had been set apart for the tribes of that section. They were reported to number 616 in 1870, and only 301 in 1892.

LAKE or SENIJEXTEE (Salishan stock).—These owned the country on both sides of the Columbia, in Washington, from about Kettle falls northward into British Columbia to the vicinity of Arrow lake. They are now on Colville reservation in Washington and number about 350, with perhaps a few others across the boundary. They may be identical with the Lahannas of Lewis and Clark.

SPOKAN (Salishan stock).—*Synonyms:* Lartielo (Lewis and Clark), Sarlilso (Gibbs), Sinhumanish, Sinkoman (Kutenai name), Spokihnish, Spokomish, Zingomenes. They are commonly distinguished as Upper Spokan or Sineeguomenah, Middle or Sintootoo, and Lower or Chekisschee (*Winans, Comr., 1870*). Spokan is the name given them by the Cœur d'Alênes; Sinkoman is their Kutenai name, while the Lartielo or Sarlilso of Lewis and Clark is simply a bad misprint for Sintootoo, the name of the middle band. They are closely connected, linguistically and politically, with the Sanpoil and Nespelim. The lower Spokan are now Protestants, the rest are Catholics. They formerly owned the whole basin of Spokane river in Washington and extending into Idaho. They are now on Spokane reservation in Washington and the Cœur d'Alêne reservation in Idaho, and number in all about 900 or 1,000.

Cœur d'Alêne (Salishan stock).—*Synonyms:* Pointed Hearts, Q'ma'shpăl or "kamas people" (so called by the Yakima), Skeechaway, Skeetsomish (Lewis and Clark), Skitsămŭq (Pälus name), Skitswish, Stietshoi. They occupied the lake and river bearing their name in Idaho and the adjacent headwaters of the Spokane. A part of this territory they held jointly with the Spokan, whose language they speak. In 1892 they numbered 427, on Cœur d'Alêne reservation in Idaho.

Sanpoil (Salishan stock).—*Synonyms:* Hai-ai'nĭma (Yakima name), Hihighenimmo (Lewis and Clark), Ipoilq (another Yakima name), N'pochle•(Stevens), Sans Puelles, Sinapoils, Sinipouals, Sinpaivelish, Sinpohellechach, Sinpoilschne, Siur Poils. The name by which this tribe is commonly known is sometimes written as a French form Sans Poils, meaning "without bristles," or "hairless," but it is more probably an Indian word. They occupy the country on Sanpoil river in Washington, now included within Colville reservation, and are closely allied with the Nespelim. These two tribes are the most aboriginal in eastern Washington, and adhere strictly to their primitive customs and religion. The two tribes are thus described by Winans, the government farmer, in 1870:

They have never received any presents from the government, although they have been frequently asked to do so. They seem suspicious of the whites, are the least civilized and most independent of any of the tribes of the territory. They are rich in horses and cattle, possessing all the comforts they know how to enjoy, and it appears their only fear is that they will be interfered with by the government. They are perfectly contented with their condition, and would not accept anything from the government if offered, except a religious instructor and doctor.

Some years later they were brought under the reservation system and a change came o'er the spirit of their dream. In 1892 we are told officially that "the Sanpuell Indians are the worst people that I have anything to do with. . . . They are surly, ignorant, and filthy," notwithstanding which they still "have the same religious prejudice as the Nespelims about receiving aid from the government." Of the Nespelim the same intelligent witness tells us that "they are a peculiar class of Indians, having a religion of their own." The religion of the two tribes is aboriginal, and is similar to the Smohalla doctrine in principle, although not in ceremonial. In 1892 the Sanpoil were estimated at 300.

Nespelim (Salishan stock).—*Synonyms:* Inspellum, Sinspeelish. On the north bank of the Columbia, in Washington, along Nespelim river and down to the junction of the Okinagan, and on the opposite side of the Columbia down to about Grande Coulée. They speak the same language as the Sanpoils, and in aboriginal habit, religion, and organization are closely identified with them. They are within the limits of Colville reservation and were reported to number only 62 in 1892.

OKANAGAN (Salishan stock).—*Synonyms:* Oakinacken, Okinakane, Okiwahkine. They occupy the whole basin of Okanagan river in Washington, extending north into British Columbia, and including Similkameen river. The Okanagan were an important tribe or confederacy divided into a number of bands, some of which have also at times been considered as belonging to the Spokan, while others are commonly recognized as distinct tribes. Ross gives them "twelve tribes," as follows: Skamoynumach, Kewaughtchenunaugh, Pisscow (Piskwaus), Income-cane′took, Tsillane (Chelan), Intie′took (Entiatook), Battlelemuleemauch or Meatwho (Mitaui), Inspellum (Nespelim), Sinpohellechach (Sanpoil), Sinwhoyelppetook (Colville), Samilkanuigh (Similkameen), and Oakinacken (Okanagan). They are now included within the Colville agency, and are Catholics. They were estimated at 340 in 1870 and reported as numbering 405 in 1892.

MITAUI (Salishan stock).—*Synonyms:* Battlelemuleemauch, Meatwho, Meshons, Meteowwee (Lewis and Clark), Methows, Mithouies. They formerly lived on the west side of the Columbia, including the basins of the Methow, Lake Chelan, and Entiatook river. Lewis and Clark met some of them in 1805 below the mouth of the Wallawalla. They are closely connected with the Piskwaus and Isle de Pierres. They now reside in Nespelim valley on Colville reservation, confederated with the Isle de Pierres under Chief Moses. The two tribes were reported at 390 in 1892. A few others live in the neighborhood of Kittitas near the Yakima tribe. See *Piskwaus.*

ISLE DE PIERRE (Salishan stock).—*Synonyms:* Columbias, Linkinse, Sinkiuse. They originally occupied the country in Washington from the Columbia eastward to the Grande Coulée, extending from about the mouth of the Grande Coulée down nearly to Crab creek. Isle de Pierre is the French name of Rock island in the Columbia at the mouth of the Wenatchee. For a long time, under their noted chief Moses, they refused to recognize the authority of the government or to go on a reservation. Now, however, they are settled in Nespelim valley, on Colville reservation. They were reported to number 390 in 1892 and are described as "true, genuine Indians in every sense of the word." Their chief, Moses, the enemy and rival of Smohalla, was thus described in 1870: "Moses, the head chief, has been a great warrior. He was foremost in the fights of 1858 with Colonels Steptoe and Wright, and was severely wounded a number of times, but not dying, the Indians believe he has a charmed life. He is medium sized, about 45 years old, noble looking, straight as an arrow, and never breaks his word. He has more influence than any other chief east of the Cascade mountains in the territory. He comes nearer being such a chief as we read of than any I have ever met. He is kindly disposed toward the whites and invites them to come and settle in his country." (*Winans.*) Linguistically they are probably nearest related to the Piskwaus.

WA'NAPÛM (Shahaptian stock).—*Synonyms:* Columbia River Indians, Sokulks. This is the tribe of which Smohalla is the chief and high priest. They are a small band, numbering probably less than 200 souls, and closely connected linguistically and politically with the Yakima, Pälus, and Nez Percés. Wanapûm is the name by which they are known to these cognate tribes, and signifies "river people;" from *wana* or *wala*, "river" (particularly Columbia river), and *pûm* or *pam*, "people or tribal country." Together with the other non-treaty tribes of this region they are known to the whites under the indefinite name of "Columbia River Indians." They are identical with the Sokulk met by Lewis and Clark at the mouth of Snake river and described as living farther up on the Columbia. The name Sokulk seems to be entirely unknown among the Yakima and Pälus of today. The Wa'-napûm range along both banks of the Columbia, in Washington, from above Crab creek down to the mouth of Snake river. Their village, where Smohalla resides, is on the west bank of the Columbia, at the foot of Priest rapids, in the Yakima country. It is called P'nä, signifying "a fish weir," and is a great rendezvous for the neighboring tribes during the salmon fishing season. Having never made a treaty or gone on a reservation, they are not officially recognized by the government.

PÄ'LUS (Shahaptian stock).—*Synonyms* : Palouse, Pelloatpallah Chopunnish (Lewis and Clark), Peloose, Polonches, Sewatpalla. The Pälus owned the whole basin of Palouse river in Washington and Idaho, and extended also along the north bank of Snake river to its junction with the Columbia. They were, and are, closely connected with the Wanapûm and the Nez Percés. Pälus, the name by which the tribe is commonly known, is properly the name of Standing Rock, at the junction of Palouse and Snake rivers. They can not explain the meaning. They have four villages: Almotu, on the north bank of Snake river in Washington, about 30 miles above the mouth of Palouse river; Pälus, on the north bank of Snake river just below the junction of the Palouse; Ta'sawĭks, on the north bank of Snake river about 15 miles above its mouth; and Ḳasĭ'spä or Cosispa (meaning "at the point," from *kăsĭ's*, a point, and *pä*, the locative), at Ainsworth in the junction of the Snake and Columbia. This last village has a slight difference in dialect and is sometimes regarded as belonging to the Wanapûm. Although the Pä'lus are mentioned as parties to the Yakima treaty of 1855, they have never as a tribe recognized any treaty limitations or come upon a reservation. They are aboriginal in their ideas and among the most devoted adherents of the Smohalla doctrine. They were estimated at 500 in 1854, but, not being officially recognized, it is impossible to give their present number.

Pĭskwaus or Winä′tshipûm (Salishan stock).—*Synonyms:* Piscaous, Piscous, Pisquose.   The name by which this tribe is commonly known is properly the name of a fishing place on Wenatchee river, and is probably Salishan, but may be from the Yakima *pĭsko*, signifying "a bend in the river."   The Yakima call the river Winätshi, signifying a "river issuing from a cañon," and the tribe Winätshipûm.   The Pisk-waus proper, on Wenatchee river, with their connected bands or tribes living in the same neighborhood, west of the Columbia in Kittitas and Okanogan counties, Washington, are a southern extension of the Mitaui and speak the same language.   Under the name of Piskwaus, Stevens includes "the Indians on the Columbia between the Priests' and Ross rapids, on the Pisquose or Winatshapam river; the Enteatkeon, Chelaun lake, and the Mithaw on Barrier river.   The name of Pisquouse, however, properly refers to a single locality on the river known to the Yakamas as Winatshapam.   The Pisquouse themselves, as has before been remarked, are so much intermarried with the Yakamas that they have almost lost their nationality.   These bands were formerly all united under one principal chief, Stalkoosum, who is said to have been a man of great note among them.   He was killed a few years since in a fight with the Blackfeet, since which there has been no head of the tribe."   (*Stevens, Comr. Rept., 1854.*)   The Piskwaus and smaller connected tribes took part in the Yakima treaty of 1855, but do not live on the reservation.   Most of them live on the Wenatchee and the north branch of Yakima river in Kittitas county.   They are all Catholics. There is no official statement of their number.   Smaller tribes or bands connected with the Piskwaus proper and speaking the same language are:

1. K′′tätäs, K′tätäs-′lĕ′ma, Ketetas (Stevens), Pshwa′năpûm (Yakima name), Shanwappoms (Lewis and Clark).   K′′tätäs signifies "a shoal," ′lĕ′ma being a tribal suffix, and Pshwană-pûm in the Yakima language signifies "shoal people," the name referring to a shoal in Yakima river at Ellensburg.

2. Ska′utăl, or Skaddal (of Lewis and Clark).   About Boston creek and Kahchass lake, at the head of Yakima river.

3. W̱shä′nătu, or Shallattoos (of Lewis and Clark).   The word means "huckleberry" in Yakima, and is applied to a site on Yakima river just above Ellensburg.

4. Skwa′nănă, or Squannaroos (of Lewis and Clark).   A Yakima word meaning "whirlpool," and applied to a point on Yakima river about opposite the entrance of Selah creek, the village being on the west bank of the river.   This band may possibly speak the language of the Ätanûm, a Shahaptian tribe, whose territory adjoins them.

5. Qamĭl-′lĕma or Kahmiltpah.   The name is Yakima, and signifies "people of Qamĭ′lh."   Qamĭ′lh, or "Watching for Fish," was a chief who formerly lived with his band about Saddle mountain, on the east side of the Columbia, above Priest rapids.   They are called Kahmiltpah in

the Yakima treaty of 1855. They now live with the other tribes last named in Kittitas county.

6. SI′ĂPKAT or Seapcat. They reside now in Kittitas county, but probably lived originally at a place of the same name on the east bank of the Columbia, about Bishop rock and Milk creek, below Wenatchee river. They are called Seapcat in the Yakima treaty of 1855. The word is of the Piskwaus language.

YÄ′KĬMÂ (Shahaptian stock).—*Synonyms:* Cutsahnim (Lewis and Clark), Eyackimah, Pa′ʹkiut-lĕ′ma, Stobshaddat (by Puget sound tribes, *Tolmie*), Waptai′lmĭm, Yackamans, Yookoomans. The Yakima are the most important tribe of the Shahaptian stock, excluding the Nez Percés. They occupied the country of Natchess and middle Yakima rivers, in the present Yakima county, Washington, and are now on a reservation within the same county. Stevens says the name signifies "black bear" in the Wallawalla language, but Yakima informants state that it is a nickname signifying "coward" or "runaway," and say that the proper name of the tribe is Waptai′lmĭm, people of the "narrow river," or Pa′ʹkiut-ʹlĕma, "people of the gap," both names referring to the narrows in Yakima river at Union gap, near Yakima bridge. Their old village was on the west side of the river, just below the gap. They are the Cutsahnim of Lewis and Clark. This name may possibly come from the same root as Kû′tsano′t, "Lying Alongside," the name of an old Yakima chief who died about 1880. In 1854, according to Stevens, they were "divided into two principal bands, each made up of a number of villages and very closely connected, the one owning the country on the Natchess and lower Yakima, the other on the Wenass and its main branch above the forks." These latter, however, were chiefly of the Piskwaus connection. They had then several chiefs, of whom Kamaiakan was the most important. Like all the other Columbia tribes east of the Cascade range, they formerly crossed the Rocky mountains annually to hunt the buffalo on the waters of the Missouri. In 1855 the government made a treaty with the Yakima, Piskwaus, Pälus, and other tribes by which they were to cede a territory on both sides of the Columbia, extending generally from the Cascade range eastward to Palouse and Snake rivers, and southward from above Chelan lake to the Columbia, excepting a small portion between the Columbia and the lower Yakima. At the same time the Yakima reservation was established and an arrangement was made by which all the tribes and bands concerned were to be confederated under the title of the "Yakama Nation," with Kamaiakan as head chief. Shortly afterward the Yakima war broke out, and the treaty remained unratified until 1859. As already stated, the Pälus and several other tribes have never recognized it or come on the reservation, and their objection to such removal has become a religious principle of the Smoḥalla doctrine. In the original treaty of 1855 fourteen tribes are named as participating, as follows: Yakama (Yäkima), Palouse (Pä′lus), Pisquouse (Pi'skwaus), Wenatshapam (another name for Piskwaus), Klikatat (Klûkatät), Klinquit (not identified), Kowwassayee (K'kasawi), Liaywas (not identified), Skinpah (Skinpä), Wish-ham (Wushqûm), Shyiks (not identified), Ochechotes (Uchi'chol), Kahmiltpah (Qamil lĕma), and Seapcat (Si'apkat). Among these were represented at least six languages and three linguistic stocks. The majority of these Indians west of the Columbia, including the Yakima proper and others on the reservation, are Catholics, with also a number of adherents of the Shaker and Smohalla doctrines. Those on the reservation numbered 1,200 in 1892, with an estimated 1,500 outside the boundaries. Beside the principal band of Yakima, the Waptailmĭm already mentioned, there are also the Sĕ'tăs-'lĕma, or "people of the rye prairie," on Setass creek, a western tributary of the Yakima in the eastern part of the reservation, and the Pĭsko, or people of the "river bend," in a village also on the south side of the Yakima, between Topinish and Setass creeks. (See *Pishquitpah.*) Their dialects are said to differ slightly from that of the Waptailmĭm.

Ä'TĂNÛM-'LĔMA (Shahaptian stock) or "people (*lĕma*) of Ätanûm creek."—A small tribe on Atahnam creek, in Yakima county, Washington, on the northern boundary of the reservation. They are said to speak a language distinct from Yakima or Klûkatät, but cognate. They have no official recognition now or in the treaty of 1855. The name Ä'tănûm is Yakima, and refers to a stream "ascended" (by salmon).

KLÛ'KĂTÄT (Shahaptian stock).—*Synonyms:* Clickahut, Clickitat, Klikatat, Qwû'lh-hwai-pûm, Weyehhoo, Whulwhypum. The name by which this tribe is commonly known is from the Wasko language and signifies "beyond (the mountain)"—that is, east of the Cascade range—with reference to the Chinookan tribes on the lower Columbia. The same name was also at times extended to the Yakima. They call themselves Qwûlh-hwai-pûm, "prairie people;" from *qwûlh-hwai,* "prairie," and *pûm,* "people," referring particularly to their occupancy of Camass prairie. They formerly occupied the southern slopes of Mount Adams and Mount Helens, with the country of Klikatat and Lewis rivers, in the present Klickitat and Skamania counties, Washington. East of them were the Yakima and west were the Salishan and Chinookan tribes. At one time they lived farther east, but were driven west by the Cayuse. (*Stevens.*) About sixty years ago they crossed the Columbia and overran the Willamet country, and even penetrated as far south as the Umpqua, but afterward withdrew again to their proper country. Although but a small tribe, they were aggressive and enterprising and were the trade medium between the tribes west of the mountains and those east. They joined in the Yakima treaty of 1855 and are now chiefly on Yakima reservation, but a few are still on White Salmon river, in Klickitat county. Their number is unknown. The Taitinapam and Topinish speak the same language and may be considered as branches of this tribe.

Qaʹpnĭsh-ʹlĕma or Topinish (Shahaptian stock).—A small tribe on Topinish river in Yakima county, Washington, within the present limits of the reservation. They speak the Klûkatät language. The name signifies "people (*lĕma*) of the trail coming from the foot of the hill."

Taitinapam (Shahaptian stock).—*Synonym:* Tai-kie-a-pain (misprint). A small tribe speaking the Klûkatät language, formerly living on the western slopes of the Cascade mountains, between the heads of Lewis and Cowlitz rivers, in Skamania county, Washington, being the westernmost tribe of Shahaptian stock. If any are left, they are probably incorporated with the Klûkatät on Yakima reservation. They never had official recognition.

Chämnäʹpûm (Shahaptian stock).—*Synonyms:* Chimnahpum, Chimnapoos, Cuimnapum. A tribe which occupied the bend of the Columbia below Yakima river, together with the country on the lower Yakima, chiefly in the present Yakima county, Washington. They are the Chimnahpum of Lewis and Clark, and speak a dialect of the language of the Päʹlus and Wanapûm, with which tribes the few survivors are incorporated. A few are also still living on the west side of the Columbia, opposite Pasco. The name is of their own language and means "people (*pûm*) of Chämnäʹ," their old village about opposite Wallula.

Pishquitpah (Shahaptian stock).—This name occurs only in the narrative of Lewis and Clark as that of a tribe in 1805, "residing at the Muscleshell rapid and on the north side of the Columbia to the commencement of the high country, wintering on the borders of the Tapteal." The Tapteal (properly Waptail or Waptailmĭm) is Yakima river. This would locate them in eastern Klickitat and Yakima counties, Washington. They are probably identical with the Pĭsko band of the Yakima. In the name Pishquitpah the final *pah* is the Yakima or Päʹlus locative *pä*, "at."

Kʻkaʹsăwi or Kowwassayee (Shahaptian stock).—A small tribe speaking the Tenino language and formerly occupying a village of the same name, Kʻkaʹsăwi, on the north bank of the Columbia, in Klickitat county, Washington, about opposite the mouth of the Umatilla. The full name is Kʻkaʹsăwi-ʹlĕʹma, "people (ʹlĕma) of the arrow-making place," the local form being from kʻkaʹso, "arrow." They took part in the Yakima treaty of 1855 under the name of Kowwassayee, and are now on Yakima reservation.

Hăhauʹpûm or Wahowpum (Shahaptian stock).—A small tribe speaking the Tenino language and occupying a village, Hăhaʹu, on the north bank of the Columbia, about the mouth of Olive creek, in Klickitat county, Washington. The word means "willow people," from hăhaʹu, a species of willow, and pûm, "people." They are the Wahowpum of Lewis and Clark. They have never had official recognition.

UCHI'CHOL or OCHECHOTES (Shahaptian stock).—A small tribe speaking the Tenino language, living now, or formerly, on the north bank of the Columbia in Klickitat county, Washington. They are mentioned as Ochechotes in the Yakima treaty of 1855, and may now be incorporated with other tribes on Yakima reservation. The name, from the Tenino language, signifies the "hind dorsal fin" (of a salmon), and is the name of a rock on the north side of the Columbia, opposite the upper end of the island, at the mouth of the Des Chutes. See *Tapänäsh.*

SKĬ'NPÄ (Shahaptian stock).—*Synonyms:* Sawpaw (?), Skien, Skin, Skinpah. A small tribe speaking the Tenino language and formerly having a village on the north bank of the Columbia in Klickitat county, Washington, at the falls opposite Celilo. They took part in the Yakima treaty of 1855 under the name of Skinpah, and are now incorporated with the other tribes on Yakima reservation. The name is Tenino, and means "cradle place," or "at the cradle," from *skĭn,* "cradle," and *pä,* the locative, and refers to a prominent rock at the site of their former village having some resemblance to an Indian cradle. See *Tapänäsh.*

TAPÄNÄ'SH or ENEESHUR (Shahaptian stock).—A small tribe speaking the Tenino language, having a village on the north bank of the Columbia in Klickitat county, Washington, about opposite the mouth of Des Chutes river and a little above Celilo. The name is identical with the Eneeshur of Lewis and Clark, these explorers in 1805 having also included under this name the various bands speaking the Tenino language on both sides of the Columbia about the mouth of the Des Chutes. The Tapänäsh have no official recognition. See *Tenino.*

TLAQLUIT or WŬSHQÛM (Chinookan stock).—*Synonyms:* Echebool, Echeloot, Eloot, Helwit, Niculuita, Ouichram, Tchilouit, Tilhulhwit, Wisham, Wishham, Wishram, Wisswham. The Tlaqluit, with the Wasko, are the easternmost tribes of Chinookan stock on the Columbia, having immediately above them the Shahaptian tribes, speaking the Tenino language. The Tlaqluit territory lies along the north bank of the Columbia in Klickitat county, Washington, from Tenino, about 6 miles above The Dalles, down to the neighborhood of White Salmon river. They call themselves Tlaqluit (Echeloot of Lewis and Clark), and are called Wŭshqûmä-pûm, or "Wŭshqûm people," by the tribes speaking the Tenino language, Wŭshqûm being the name of their chief village near South Side at The Dalles, the great fishing and trading resort for the tribes of this section. The name appears also as Wishram. Both Tlaqluit and Wŭshqûm refer to a species of louse or flea abounding in that neighborhood. They took part in the Yakima treaty of 1855 under the name of Wishham, but most of them have probably never gone on the reservation. See *Wasko.*

There is a tradition in the tribe that long before the coming of the whites to the Columbia a band of Tlaqluit left their people on account of a petty quarrel as to whether a goose made a certain noise with its bill or with its wings, and went up the Columbia and the Spokane, and are supposed to be now about the headwaters of the latter stream and still retaining their language, although under a different tribal name.

Chilû′ktkwa or Chilluckittequaws (Chinookan stock).—A tribe formerly extending along the north bank of the Columbia in Klickitat and Skamania counties, Washington, from about White Salmon river down to some distance below the Cascades. They are called Chilluck-ittequaws in 1805 by Lewis and Clark, who speak also of a separate band of the same tribe under the name of Smackshop, a name which can not now be identified. The tribe now numbers less than 100. Until recently the remnant lived about the mouth of White Salmon river, but removed about thirteen years ago to the Cascades. Their language is nearly the same as that of the Wasko. They have never had official recognition.

Kwikwû′lĭt or Dog River (Chinookan stock).—*Synonyms:* Cascade Indians, Kigaltwalla, Upper Chinook, Wahclellah, Watlala. A small tribe formerly living at the Cascades and about Dog river, a small stream coming into the Columbia about half-way between the Cascades and The Dalles, in Wasco county, Oregon. They are identical, in part at least, with the Wahclellahs of Lewis and Clark (mentioned as a part of the "Shahala nation"), and are the "Ki-gal-twal-la band of the Wascoes" and the "Dog River band of the Wascoes" of the Wasco treaty of 1855. The "Dog River or Cascade Indians" were reported to number 80 souls in 1854. In the next year they, with other tribes, entered into the Wasco treaty, by which they agreed to remove to Warmspring reservation, where some of them now are, while the others are still about the Cascades. Their language is nearly the same as that of the Wasko.

Wasko (Chinookan stock).—*Synonyms:* Dalles Indians, Wascopum. A tribe formerly claiming the country about The Dalles, on the south bank of the Columbia, in Wasco county, Oregon. They, with the Tlaqluit on the opposite bank, are the easternmost extension of the Chinookan stock, and speak the same language. The name is said to be a Tenino word, meaning "grass," or "grass people." It has sometimes been made to include several cognate bands about The Dalles and Cascades, on both sides of the Columbia. Under the name of "The Dalles band of the Wascoes," they entered into the Wasco treaty of 1855, and are now on Warmspring reservation in Oregon. They numbered 260 in 1892.

Waiäm (Shahaptian stock).—*Synonyms:* (Lower) Des Chutes, Wai-äm-ʻlĕma, Wayyampa, Wyam. A tribe speaking the Tenino language and formerly living about the mouth of Des Chutes river, in the present Wasco and Sherman counties, Oregon. Their chief village was on the Columbia where Celilo now is, and was called Waiäm, whence their name of Waiäm-ʻlĕma or "people of Waiäm." They joined in the Wasco treaty of 1855 under the name of "Wyam or Lower De Chutes band of Walla-Wallas," and are now on Warmspring reservation in Oregon. Their number is not separately reported.

TAI'-ẊQ (Shahaptian stock).—*Synonyms:* Taigh, Ta-ih, Tairtla, Tyich. A tribe speaking the Tenino language and formerly occupying the country about Tygh and White rivers, in Wasco county, Oregon. The name Tai'-ăq refers to the stream and denotes "muddy, white water." They took part in the Wasco treaty of 1855 under the name of "Ta-ih or Upper De Chutes band of Walla-Wallas," and are now on Warmspring reservation, Oregon. Their number is not reported.

TǏ'LQÛNI (Shahaptian stock).—A tribe formerly claiming the country between Tygh valley and Warmspring river, west of Des Chutes river, in the present Wasco county, Oregon. They are now on Warmspring reservation, in the same neighborhood. They have never been officially mentioned under their Indian name, and may be considered the Warmspring proper, although this name is local rather than tribal. They speak the Tenino language. See *Tenino.*

TENINO or MĔLI'-LĔMA (Shahaptian stock).—The most important Shahaptian tribe of western Oregon. They formerly occupied middle Des Chutes river, and conquered the present Warmspring reservation from the Paiute or Snake tribes, but never occupied it until put there by the Wasco treaty of 1855. Since then they have been known indiscriminately as Tenino or Warmspring Indians, although this latter designation is commonly used to include other cognate tribes on the same reservation. For this reason it is impossible to give their number definitely. The Tenino language, in various dialects, is spoken, excepting by the Lohim, by all the tribes formerly living on both banks of the Columbia and on its tributaries from the country of the Wasko about The Dalles up to about the mouth of the Umatilla.

Most of this region, on the south or Oregon side of the Columbia, was formerly held by Shoshonean tribes of Paiute connection, which have been dispossessed by the Shahaptian tribes and driven farther back to the south. The only Shoshonean tribe which maintained its place on the Columbia was the Lohim, on Willow creek. The Tenino themselves conquered the present Warmspring reservation from the Snakes. The expulsion was in full progress when Lewis and Clark went down the Columbia in 1805, but had been practically completed when the first treaties were made with these tribes fifty years later. Lewis and Clark state that "on that (the south) side of the river none of the tribes have any permanent habitations, and on inquiry we were confirmed in our belief that it was from the fear of being attacked by the Snake Indians, with whom they are constantly at war. This nation they represent as being very numerous and residing in a great number of villages on the Towahnahiook (Wanwaui or Des Chutes), where they live principally on salmon, . . . the first villages of the Snake Indians being twelve days' journey on a course about southeast of this place." In the appendix, after mentioning various bands of Snakes on Snake and Willamette rivers, they speak of the main body as "residing in the fall and winter on the Multnomah (Willamet) river, southward of the Southwest mountains, and in spring and summer near the heads of the Towahnahiook (Des Chutes), Lepage (John Day), Yaumalolam (Umatilla), and Wollawollah rivers, and especially at the falls of the Towahnahiook, for the purpose of fishing." In the Wasco treaty of 1855 the Shahaptian tribes were recognized as owners of the whole country southward to the forty-fourth parallel, from the Cascade range east to the Blue mountains. See *Tapänäsh*.

TÛKSPÛ'SH or JOHN DAY INDIANS (Shahaptian stock).— *Synonyms:* Dock-spus, John Day Rivers, Tûkspûsh-'lĕma. A tribe speaking the Tenino language and formerly living along the lower part of John Day river, Oregon, having their principal village at the falls about 4 miles above the mouth. They are now on Warmspring reservation, and numbered 59 in 1892, with perhaps others off the reservation. Tûkspûsh is the name of John Day river in the Tenino language.

LOHĬM or WILLOW CREEK INDIANS (Shoshonean stock).—A tribe living on Willow creek, in Gilliam and Morrow counties, Oregon. They are of Shoshonean connection, being the only Indians of this stock who have been able to maintain their position on the Columbia against the inroads of the Shahaptian tribes. They have never made a treaty with the government, and are generally spoken of as renegades belonging to the Umatilla reservation. In 1870 they were reported to number 114, but are not mentioned in the recent official reports.

CAYUSE or WAILĔ''TPU (Waiilatpuan stock). — *Synonyms:* Cailloux, Kayuse, Shiwanish, Skyuse, Wailetma, Yeletpo Chopunnish (of Lewis and Clark). The Cayuse are a warlike tribe of distinct stock formerly occupying the mountain country on the heads of Wallawalla, Umatilla, and Grande Ronde rivers in Oregon and Washington, including the present Umatilla reservation. Further investigation may yet establish a linguistic connection with the Shahaptian tribes. The Molala, formerly on Molalla creek, west of the Cascades, are a separated band, of whose western migration the Cayuse and their neighbors still have a tradition. The Cayuse formerly bore a high reputation for intelligence and bravery, but on account of their fighting propensities, which led them to make constant war on the Snakes and other tribes to the west, they were never very numerous. In 1838 a Presbyterian mission, called Waiilatpu, had been established among the Cayuse, by Dr Whitman, where now is the town of Whitman, in Wallawalla county, Washington. In 1847 the smallpox, before unknown among them, carried off a large part of the tribe. The Cayuse, believing that the missionaries were the cause of it, attacked the mission on November 29, 1847, killed Dr Whitman and thirteen others, and destroyed the mission. As a matter of fact, there seems little question that the infection was brought into the country in supplies intended for the use of the mission or of emigrants temporarily stopping there.   In 1854, according to Stevens, "the tribe, though still dreaded by their neighbors on account of their courage and warlike spirit, is but a small one, numbering, according to the census of 1851, only 126.   Of these, individuals of the pure blood are few, the majority being intermixed with the Nez Percés and the Wallah-Wallahs, particularly with the former, to such a degree that their own language has fallen into disuse."   A few years ago only a few individuals, then living on Umatilla reservation, retained their old language.   In 1855 they joined in the treaty by which Umatilla reservation in Oregon was set apart, and most of those remaining are now there, while a few others are with the Nez Percés at Lapwai.   Joseph, the noted Nez Percé chief, is himself the son of a Cayuse father.   In 1892 the Cayuse on Umatilla reservation were reported to number 391, but it is evident that most of these are mixed-bloods of other tribes, particularly the Umatilla.   The name Cayuse is from the Nez Percé language. They call themselves Wailĕtpu.   They are known to the Yakima as Wi'alĕt-pûm or Wai'lĕtma, and to the Tenino as Shiwanish, or "strangers from up the river," a name extended also to the Nez Percés.

UMATILLA (Shahaptian stock). — *Synonym:* Utilla.   A tribe formerly occupying the lower portion of the river of the same name, with the adjacent bank of the Columbia, in Oregon.   They speak a distinct language of the Shahaptian stock.   By the treaty of 1855 they agreed to go on Umatilla reservation in Oregon, where in 1892 they were reported to number 216.   A large proportion of those now called Cayuse on the same reservation are Umatilla mixed-bloods.

WALLAWALLA (Shahaptian stock).—*Synonyms:* Oualla-Oualla, Walawaltz, Wollawollah, Wollaw-Wollah.   A tribe formerly occupying the country about the lower portion of the river of the same name and along the east bank of the Columbia from Snake river down nearly to the Umatilla, in Washington and Oregon.   They take their name from the river, the word being said to refer to "rushing water."   Their language is said to resemble closely that of the Nez Percés.   By the treaty of 1855 they agreed to go on Umatilla reservation, Oregon, where, in 1892, they were reported to number 474.

A small band of the same tribe, known to the Yakima as Walu'la-pûm, formerly lived on the west bank of the Columbia opposite the present Wallula.   Their dialect is said to have been more akin to the Pä'lus language.

SAHAPTIN or NEZ PERCÉS (Shahaptian stock).—*Synonyms:* Chohoptins, Chopunnish (Lewis and Clark), Copunnish, Laaptin (misprint), Â'dal-k'ato'igo, "people with hair cut across the forehead" (Kiowa name), Shi'wanĭsh (Tenino name, applied also to the Cayuse), Wa'pamĕtănt (Yakima name for the language).   The Nez Percés are said to call themselves Sahaptin, and were named Nez Percés, or "pierced noses," by the French from their former custom of wearing nose pendants.   They are the most important tribe of the Shahaptian stock, and formerly occupied a large territory in eastern Washington and Oregon and central Idaho, bounded on the east by the main divide of the Bitterroot mountains, and including lower Grande Ronde and Salmon rivers, with a large part of the Snake and all of the Clearwater. The Wallowa valley, the disputed title to which led to the Nez Percé war, lies on a branch of the Grande Ronde, in Oregon. They had the Salishan tribes to the northeast, the Shoshonean tribes to the south, and the Cayuse, Wallawalla, and Pälus, with all of whom they are much intermarried, on the west and northwest. Almost all authorities give them a high character for bravery, intelligence, and honorable conduct traits which were strikingly displayed in the Nez Percé war.

Lewis and Clark traversed their country in 1805, and speak of them and some connected tribes under the name of Chopunnish, distinguished as follows: Chopunnish nation (about the present Lapwai reservation), Pelloatpallah band (the Pälus), Kimooenim band (on Snake river, between the Salmon and the Clearwater), Yeletpo band (the Cayuse), Willewah band (in Wallowa valley, afterward Joseph's band), Soyennom band (on the north side of the upper Clearwater, in Idaho; these were really a part of the Pälus—the proper form is Tätqu'nma, whence Thatuna hills, referring to "a fawn" in the Pälus language, and was the name applied to their kamas ground about Camass creek), Chopunnish of Lewis river (on Snake river, below the Clearwater). In response to a request from the Nez Percés, who sent a delegation all the way to Saint Louis for that purpose in 1832, the first Protestant mission was established among them at Lapwai, Idaho, in 1837. Soon afterward they entered into relations with the government, and made their first treaty with the United States in 1855. By this treaty they ceded the greater portion of their territory, and were confirmed in the possession of a reservation including Wallowa valley. On the discovery of gold in the country, however, the miners rushed in, and in consequence a new treaty was made in 1863, by which they gave up all but the present Lapwai reservation in Idaho. Joseph, who occupied Wallowa valley with his band, refused to recognize this treaty or remove to Lapwai. This refusal finally led to the Nez Percé war in 1877, as already related. The main body of the tribe took no part in the war. After the surrender of Joseph his band was removed to Indian Territory, where the mortality among them was so great that in 1884 they were returned to the northwest. For several reasons, however, it was deemed unadvisable to settle them in the neighborhood of their old home, and a place was finally found for them in 1887 on Colville reservation in northern Washington. In 1892 there were 1,828 on Lapwai reservation and 138 on Colville reservation, a total population of 1,966.

CHAPTER VIII

THE SHAKERS OF PUGET SOUND

My breath was out and I died. All at once I saw a great shining light. Angels told me to look back. I did, and saw my own body lying dead. It had no soul. My soul left my body and went up to the judgment place of God. . . . My soul was told that I must come back and live on earth. When I came back, I told my friends, "There is a God. My good friends, be Christians. If you all try hard and help me, we shall be better men on earth." — *John Slocum.*

In 1881 there originated among the tribes of Puget sound in Washington a new religion, which, although apparently not founded on any doctrinal prophecy, yet deserves special attention for the prominent part which hypnotism holds in its ceremonial. Indeed, there is good reason to believe that the Paiute messiah himself, and through him

FIG. 67—John Slocum and Louis Yowaluch.

all the apostles of the Ghost dance, have obtained their knowledge of hypnotic secrets from the "Shakers" of Puget sound.

The founder of the religion is Squ-sacht-un, known to the whites as John Slocum. He is now (1896) about 58 years of age. His chief high priest is Louis Yowaluch, or Ai-yäl as he is called by the Yakima. Both are of the Squaxin tribe. In 1881 (Eells makes it 1882) he "died" or fell into a trance one morning about daylight and remained in that condition until the middle of the afternoon, when he awoke and announced that he had been to heaven, but had been met at the entrance by angels, who forbade him to enter on account of his wickedness, and gave him his choice either to go to hell or return to earth and teach his people what they must do to get to heaven. Accordingly, he came back to earth and began his divinely appointed mission, introducing into the new doctrine and ritual a great deal of what he had learned from the white missionaries. From the nervous twitchings which so peculiarly distinguished them, his followers soon became known as "Shakers." Although strongly opposed by the agent, who arrested and imprisoned the leaders and visited various minor penalties on their followers, the Shaker religion grew and flourished until it now has a regular organization with several houses of worship, and has received the official indorsement of the Presbyterian church.

The following account of the system, in response to a letter of inquiry, was obtained from the missionary, Reverend Myron Eells, brother of the agent:

A curious phase of religion sprang up in the fall of 1882 among some of the Indians on the southern part of Puget sound. It has prevailed mainly among the Squaxon, Nisqually, Skokomish, and Chehalis Indians, and has been called by its opponents the "Shake religion," and its followers have been called "Shakers" on account of a large amount of nervous shaking which is a part of the form of its observance. It is evidently based upon about the same principles of the mind as the jerks and shouting at camp meetings among the whites of the southern and western states fifty years ago, when they were more ignorant and less acquainted with real religion than they are now. When superstition, ignorance, dreams, imagination, and religion are all mingled together, either among whites, Indians, or people of any other race, they produce a strange compound. It has proven so in this case.

In the fall of 1882 an Indian named John Slocum, who was living on Skookum bay, in Mason county, apparently died. Some years previous he had lived on the Skokomish reservation, where he had attended a Protestant church, and had learned something of the white man's religion, God, Jesus Christ, and the morals inculcated. He had also learned something in his early life of the Catholic religion and its forms and ceremonies. Many Indians were present when he was sick and apparently died. They said his neck was broken, and that he remained dead for about six hours, when he returned to life, jumped up, and ran off a short distance, and soon began to converse with the people. Whether or not it was a case of suspended animation is a question. A white man, a near neighbor of his, who saw him before his apparent death, while he thus lay, and after his resuscitation, said he believed the Indian was "playing possum." But the Indians believed that he really died and rose again.

The Indian stated that he died and attempted to go to heaven, but could not enter it because he was so wicked. He was there told, however, the way of life, and that he must return to this earth and teach his people the way, and induce them to become Christians. He gained a small band of followers, a church was built for him, and he steadily preached to the people.

Affairs went on this way until the next August. Then, after consultation with other Indians who favored him, especially on the Skokomish reservation, it was decided to hold a big meeting. The Indians of the surrounding region were called to go. They were told that they would be lost if they did not; that four women would be turned into angels; that persons would die and be raised to life again, and that other wonderful things would be done.

Many went, about half of those on the Skokomish reservation being among the number, and they did hold a big meeting. Women did go around trying to fly like angels; four persons are said to have died, and, with the power which was said to have been given them from above, others were said to have brought them back to life again. This was a mixture of trying to perform miracles, as in Bible times, to prove the divinity of their religion, and some of the ceremonies of their old black *tomahnous*. This was a secret society of their savage days, in which persons went into a hypnotic condition, in which they became very rigid, and out of which they came in the course of time. The followers of this new religion dreamed dreams, saw visions, went through some disgusting ceremonies a la mode the black *tomahnous*, and were taken with a kind of shaking. With their arms at full length, their hands and arms would shake so fast that a common person not under the excitement could hardly shake half as fast. Gazing into the heavens, their heads would also shake very fast, sometimes for a few minutes and sometimes for hours, or half the night. They would also brush each other with their hands, as they said, to brush off their sins, for they said they were much worse than white people, the latter being bad only in their hearts, while the Indians were so bad that the badness came to the surface of their bodies and the ends of their finger nails, so that it could be picked off. They sometimes brushed each other lightly, and sometimes so roughly that the person brushed was made black for a week, or even sick.

In connection with this they held church services, prayed to God, believed in Christ as a savior, said much about his death, and used the cross, their services being a combination of Protestant and Catholic services, though at first they almost totally rejected the Bible, for they said they had direct revelations from Christ, and were more fortunate than the whites, who had an old, antiquated book.

After having kept up this meeting for about a week, they disbanded and went to their homes, but did not stop their shaking or services. They sometimes held meetings from 6 oclock in the evening until about midnight, lighting candles and putting them on their heads for a long time. They became very peculiar about making the sign of the cross many times a day, when they began to eat as they asked a blessing, and when they finished their meal and returned thanks; when they shook hands with anyone — and they shook hands very often — when they went to church and prayer meeting on Thursday evening, and at many other times, far more often than the Catholics do.

On the Skokomish reservation their indiscretions caused the death of a mother and her child, and an additional loss of time and property to the amount of $600 or $800 in a few weeks. It also became a serious question whether the constant shaking of their heads would not make some of them crazy, and from symptoms and indications it was the opinion of the agency physician, J. T. Martin, that it would do so. Accordingly, on the reservation the authority of the agent was brought to bear, and to a great extent the shaking was stopped, though they were encouraged to keep on in the practice of some good habits which they had begun, of ceasing gambling, intemperance, their old style incantations over the sick, and the like. Some at first said they could not stop shaking, but that at their prayer meetings and church services on the Sabbath their hands and heads would continue to shake in spite of themselves; but after a short time, when the excitement had died away, they found that they could stop.

But about Skookum bay, Mud bay, and Squaxon the shaking continued, and it spread to the Nisqually and Chehalis Indians. It seemed to be as catching, to use the expression of the Indians, as the measles. Many who at first ridiculed it and fought against it, and invoked the aid of the agent to stop it, were drawn into it after a little, and then they became its strong upholders. This was especially true of the medicine-men, or Indian doctors, and those who had the strongest faith in them. The Shakers declared that all the old Indian religion, and especially the cure of the sick by the medicine-men, was from the devil, and they would have nothing to do with it, those who at first originated and propagated it having been among the more intelligent and progressive of the uneducated Indians. Very few of those who had learned to read and had been in Sabbath school for a considerable length of time were drawn into it. It was the class between the most educated and the most superstitious who at first upheld it. They seemed to know too much to continue in the old-style religious ceremonies, but not to know enough and to be too superstitious to fully believe the Bible. Consequently, the medicine-men were at first bitterly opposed to it. About this time, however, an order came from the Indian department to stop all medicine-men from practicing their incantations over the sick. As a respectable number of the Indians had declared against the old style of curing the sick, it seemed to be a good time to enforce this order, as there was sufficient popular opinion in connection with the authority of the agent to enforce it. This was done, and then the medicine-men almost entirely joined the Shakers, as their style was more nearly in accordance with the old style than with the religion of the Bible.

As it spread, one Indian went so far as to declare himself to be Christ again come to earth, and rode through the streets of Olympia at the head of several scores of his followers with his hands outstretched as Christ was when he was crucified. But he was so ridiculed by other Indians and by the whites that he gave up this idea and simply declared himself to be a prophet who had received revelations from heaven.

For several years there has been very little of the shaking or this mode of worship among the Indians on the reservation, excepting secretly when persons were sick. Still, their native superstition and their intercourse with those off the reservation, who sometimes hold a special gathering and meeting when their followers grow cold and careless, has kept the belief in it as a religion firm in their hearts, so that lately, since they have become citizens, and are hence more free from the authority of the agent, the practice of it has become more common, especially when persons are sick.

In fact, while it is a religion for use at all times, yet it is practiced especially over the sick, and in this way takes the place of the medicine-men and their methods. Unlike the system of the medicine-men, it has no single performer. Though often they select for leader one who can pray the best, yet in his absence another may take the lead. Like the old system, it has much noise. Especially do they use bells, which are rung over the person where the sickness is supposed to be. The others present use their influence to help in curing the sick one, and so imitate the attendants on an Indian doctor, getting down upon their knees on the floor and holding up their hands, with a candle in each hand, sometimes for an hour. They believe that by so holding up their hands the man who is ringing the bell will get the sickness out more easily than he otherwise would. They use candles both when they attempt to cure the sick and in their general service, eschewing lamps for fear of being easily tempted, as they believe coal-oil lights to be from Satan.

In another point also this resembles very closely their old religion. For a long time before a person is taken sick they foretell that his spirit is gone to heaven and profess to be able to bring it back and restore it to him, so that he will not die as soon as he otherwise would. This was also a part of the old *tomahnous* belief.

They have also prophesied very much. Several times when a person has died they have told me that someone had foretold this event, but they have never told me this until after the event happened, except in one case. They have prophesied much in regard to the end of the world and the day of judgment. Generally, the time set has been on a Fourth of July, and many have been frightened as the time drew near, but, alas, in every instance the prophecy failed. Like Christians, they believe in a Supreme Being, in prayer, the sabbath, in heaven and hell, in man as a sinner, and Christ as a savior, and the system led its followers to stop drinking, gambling, betting, horse racing, the use of tobacco, and the old-style incantations over the sick. Of late years, however, some of them have fallen from grace.

It has been a somewhat strange freak of human nature, a combination of morals and immorals, of Protestantism, Catholicism, and old Indian practices, of dreams and visions—a study in mental philosophy, showing what the mind may do under certain circumstances. Yet it is all easily accounted for. These Indians have mingled with the whites for a long time, nearly ever since most of them were small. All classes of whites have made sport of their religion—the infidel, the profane man, the immoral one, the moral one, and the Christian—and they have been told that God and the Bible were against it, consequently they lost faith in it. But the Indian must have some religion. He can not do without one. They were not ready to accept the Bible in all its purity. They wanted more excitement. Like the Dakota Indians more recently, they saw that Christ was the great center of the most powerful religion of the most powerful, intelligent, successful, and wisest nations with whom they came in contact. Consequently they formulated a system for themselves that would fill all their required conditions, and when a few leaders had originated it, a large share of the rest were ripe to accept it, but having had more Christian teaching than the wild Dakotas, it took a somewhat different form, with no thought of war and with more of real Christianity.

James Wickersham, esquire, of Tacoma, Washington, the well-known historian of that region, is the regular attorney for these people as a religious organization, and is consequently in a position to speak with authority concerning them. In reply to a letter of inquiry, he states that the Shakers believe in an actual localized heaven and hell, and reverence the Bible, but regard John Slocum's revelations as of more authority. "They practice the strictest morality, sobriety, and honesty. Their 500 or 600 members are models, and it is beyond question that they do not drink whisky, gamble, or race, and are more free from vice than any other church. They practice a mixture of Catholic, Presbyterian, and old Indian ceremonies, and allow only Indians in the church. They have five churches, built by themselves, and the sect is growing quite rapidly." From all this it would appear that the Shaker religion is a distinct advance as compared with the old Indian system.

Under date of December 5, 1892, Mr Wickersham wrote again on this subject, as follows:

I read your letter to my Indian friends, and they beg me to write you and explain that they are not Ghost dancers, and have no sympathy with that ceremony or any other founded on the Dreamer religion. That they believe in heaven as do the orthodox Christians; also in Christ, and God, the Father of all; that they believe in future rewards and punishments, but not in the Bible particularly. They do believe in it as a history, but they do not value it as a book of revelation. They do not need it, for John Slocum personally came back from a conference with the angels at the gates of heaven, and has imparted to them the actual facts and the angelic words of the means of salvation.

This testimony is even better than the words of Christ contained in the Bible, for John Slocum comes 1800 years nearer; he is an Indian, and personally appears to them and in Indian language reports the facts. These people believe Slocum as firmly as the martyr at the stake believed in that for which he offered up his life; but it is the Christian religion which they believe, and not the Ghost dance or Dreamer religion.

In short, they have a mixture of Catholic, Protestant, and Indian ceremonies, with a thorough belief in John Slocum's personal visit to heaven, and his return with a mission to save the Indians and so guide them that they, too, shall reach the realms of bliss. Personally, I think they are honest, but mistaken; but the belief certainly has beneficial effect, and has reduced drinking and crime to a minimum among the members of the "Shaker" or "Tschaddam" church.

In conclusion, permit me to say that the general assembly of the Presbyterian church in this state has several times examined into the religion and character of the Shaker or Slocum church, and has highly indorsed its people and their character and actions. Yowaluch is their head now, and the strongest man mentally among them.

Some months later Mr Wickersham forwarded a circumstantial and carefully written statement of the history and present condition of the movement. In accordance with his request, we publish it as written, omitting only some paragraphs which do not bear directly on the general subject. It may be considered as an official statement of the Shaker case by their legally constituted representative. As might have been expected, he takes direct issue with those who have opposed the new religion. The reader will note the recurrence of the Indian sacred number, four, in Slocum's speech, as also the fact that his first trance was the culmination of a serious illness.

Tschaddam or Shaker religion

"On Christmas day, 1854, a treaty was signed at the mouth of Shenahnam or Medicine creek, on the south side of Puget sound, Washington, between Isaac I. Stevens, governor and ex officio superintendent of Indian affairs for the United States, and the chief and headmen of the Nisqually, Puyallup, and other small tribes of Indians residing around the south shores of Puget sound.

"One of these small tribes was the Squaxin, situated on the southwestern branch or arm of Puget sound, now known as Little Skookum bay, in Mason county, Washington, near Olympia. The remaining members of this tribe yet live on the old home places, having purchased small tracts of their old hunting grounds from the first settlers; and they now make a living by fishing and gathering oysters as in days of old. Of the fishy tribe of Squaxin was born John Slocum, as he is known to the 'Boston man,' but to his native friends he is known as Squ-sacht-un.

"John Slocum, Squ-sacht-un, is now (1893) about 51 years of age, about 5 feet 8 inches high, and weighs about 160 pounds; rather stoop shouldered, with a scattering beard, a shock of long black hair, a flat head (fashionably flat, and produced by pressure while a baby), bright eyes, but in all rather a common expression of countenance. He is modest and rather retiring, but has unquestioned confidence in himself and his mission. He is married, and up to the time of his translation was looked on as a common Indian, with a slight inclination to fire-water and pony racing, as well as a known fondness for Indian gambling.

"In the month of October, 1881, Slocum was unaccountably drawn to think of his evil courses. While in the woods he knelt and prayed to God, and began seriously to think of the error of his ways and of the evil days that had fallen on his few remaining native friends. Whisky, gambling, idleness, and general vice had almost exterminated his people. His eyes were opened to the folly of these facts, and he prayed. He, however, became sick; and as his sickness increased, these ideas became brighter in his mind and his duty more clear. He grew worse, and one day he died. He was pronounced dead by all present, and was laid out for burial. His brother went to Olympia for a coffin, and a grave was prepared. He died at 4 oclock in the morning, and late in the afternoon he again resumed life and recovered consciousness.

"His recovery was rapid, and immediately he told those present that during his term of death his soul had been to heaven, where it had been met by the angels, who, after a proper inquiry as to his name, etc., told him that he had been bad on earth, and reminded him very forcibly of his shortcomings while there, and finally wound up by informing him that he could not enter heaven, but that he could either go to hell or could go back to the earth and preach to the Indians and tell them the way to heaven. He accepted this latter proposition, and the result was that his soul again returned to earth, reentered its old body, and has from that day to this animated Slocum with the spirit of a crusader against gambling, whisky drinking, and other 'Boston' vices.

"About a year ago I was employed by these people as their attorney, and at their request attended the meetings in Mason county, and had a long conference with them. As a practical person would, Slocum undertook to demonstrate to me his honesty and the divine character of their religion, and at a large meeting composed only of Indians, members of his church, he made to me a long public statement of facts, and explained, through an intepreter, the character of their religion and of their belief. I wrote down at the time a synopsis of what was said to me, and now quote it at some length as being the exact words of Slocum, and as the best explanation of their religion.

"Standing before all his people, in the most solemn and impressive manner, in their church, he said in substance:

"The witnesses have spoken the truth. I was sick about two weeks, and had five Indian doctors. I grew very weak and poor. Dr Jim was there. He could not cure me. They wanted to save me, but my soul would die two or three hours at a time. At night my breath was out, and I died. All at once I saw a shining light — great light — trying my soul. I looked and saw my body had no soul — looked at my own body — it was dead.

"I came through the first time and told my friends, 'When I die, don't cry,' and then I died again. Before this I shook hands and told my friends I was going to die. Angels told me to look back and see my body. I did, and saw it lying down. When I saw it, it was pretty poor. My soul left body and went up to judgment place of God. I do not know about body after 4 oclock.

"I have seen a great light in my soul from that good land; I have understand all Christ wants us to do. Before I came alive I saw I was sinner. Angel in heaven said to me, 'You must go back and turn alive again on earth.' I learned that I must be good Christian man on earth, or will be punished. My soul was told that I must come back and live four days on earth. When I came back, I told my friends, 'There is a God — there is a Christian people. My good friends, be Christian.'

"When I came alive, I tell my friends, 'Good thing in heaven. God is kind to us. If you all try hard and help me we will be better men on earth.' And now we all feel that it is so.

"A good Christian man prayed with me four days. After four days, a voice said to me, 'You shall live on earth four weeks.' My soul was told that they must build a church for me in four weeks. I had lumber for a house, and my friends built church. Had it all done in four weeks but 6 feet of roof, and spread a mat over that. Soon as the church was finished the people came and filled the house and began to worship God. I felt strong—bigger than today—all these men know this. My friends worked hard, and I am here because they finished the house in four weeks. My soul was told to remain on earth four weeks more. All my friends came, and every Saturday we worshiped God. In four weeks more my soul was told that I should live on earth four years if I did right and preached for God. All felt thankful, and people joined the church—about fifty people. I was promised more time if we worshiped God.

"A bad man can't reach heaven. I believe in God. I saw how bad I used to be. God sends us light to see. They know in heaven what we think. When people are sick, we pray to God to cure us. We pray that he take the evil away and leave the good. If man don't be Christian, he will suffer and see what is bad. When we remember Jesus Christ's name, we always felt happy in our hearts. This is good road for us to travel if we hold on. If we do, God's angels are near to our souls. Power from this to help us. When we pray, it helps us lots in our hearts. We don't do good sometimes, because our hearts are not right. When our body and heart feel warm, we do good and sing good songs. As Christ said, he sends power to every believing soul on earth.

"While one man can try to start religion here on earth, it don't do much good; they won't believe him much. That's why we join to worship. Now we are preparing ourselves for judgment. For it is said, it don't make any difference if he prays good and does good. God gives him help and words to speak. Makes no difference if 'Boston' or Indian, if God helps we know it. These things are what we learned. We learn good while we pray—voice says, Do good.

"It is ten years, now, since we began, and we have good things. We all love these things and will follow them all time. We learn to help ourselves when sick. When our friend is sick, we kneel and ask for help to cure him. We learn something once in a while to cure him. Then we do as we know to help him and cure him. If we don't learn to help him, we generally lose him.

"This is a pretty accurate synopsis of the speech delivered to me by Slocum, and translated by another Indian, who spoke pretty good English. But that a more thorough knowledge may be given of their religious belief, I give also a brief synopsis of another speech made at the same meeting by Louis Yowaluch, a full-blood Indian, who is the legal head of this church. It is about as follows:

"Well, my friend, we was about the poorest tribe on earth. We was only tribe now full blood and nothing else. We would not believe anything. Minister came here, but we laugh at him. We loved bad habits—stealing—and John Slocum died. He was not a religious man—knew nothing of God—all of us same. We heard there was a God from Slocum—we could see it. Same time we heard God, we believe it. I was worst of lot. I was drunkard—was half starving—spent every cent for whisky. I gambled, raced horses, bet shirt, money, blankets—did not know any better.

"John Slocum brought good to us; his words civilized us. We could see. We all felt blind those times. We lost by drowning—our friends drink whisky and the canoes turn over—we died out in the bay. Today who stopped us from these things?

"John Slocum came alive, and I remember God and felt frightened. We never heard such a thing as a man dying and bring word that there was a God. I became sick for three weeks, four weeks. I hear a voice saying to soul, 'Tomorrow they will be coming to fix you up.' Had just heard about John Slocum, and knew it was punishment for my bad habits. My heart was black—it was a bad thing.

"Now I have quit swearing—my heart is upside down—it is changed. After I heard the voice I heard another say: 'There it is now—some one to fix you up. Have you prepared your heart? If you don't believe in Christ, you will go into a big fire and burn forever.' I saw a man's hand coming to my heart. That day I got up—was well—talked to my friends, advising them. I will remain a follower of Christ as long as I live.

"Long ago we knew nothing at all. When Slocum came back from God, we found out there was a God. From that time we have prayed for anything we want. We follow God's way. God teaches us if we do bad we will go to hell. That's why we pray and avoid bad habits. If we don't ask grace, bad things come when we eating. When we drink water, we think about God before drinking. If we don't think of him, may be we get sick from water. If traveling, may be we die if we don't think of God. We are afraid to do wrong against God. Long time ago we worked on Sundays, but no more now. Our brother Christ has given us six days to work. On Sunday pray to God. God put people here to grow—puts our soul in our body. That's why we pray so much. If we quit, like a man quit his job, he gets no pay. We would go to fire in hell. We have no power to put out hell fire.

"Louis Yowaluch is the strong man of the Shaker church. He is 6 feet tall, rawboned, muscular, and rather slow. While he may once have been, as he says, a drunkard, he is now a Christian man. His conservativeness makes him a fine leader for the organization, while all the Indians respect him for his humanity and charity, for his honesty and uprightness, for his fearlessness and love of right. He fully and freely places John Slocum at the head of the church, as the man who ascended to heaven and brought back a personal knowledge of the road, but at the same time he takes the lead in laying out work, building churches, and sending out preachers to new tribes.

"A new feature of this religion is found in Sam Yowaluch, the brother of Louis. He is younger than Louis, and has more of the native superstition in his character. He has by common consent been placed at the head of the faith-cure branch of the church. The following synopsis of his 'talk' will be an explanation of his position:

"Among the Shakers, John Slocum is first. Louis is next. I take power and cure people when they are sick. Long time ago I knew nothing—just like an animal. No doctoring, no medicine—no good. I was a drunkard, was a thief, and a robber. When I joined this religion, I was told to be good. When John Slocum was preaching, I heard that if I prayed I would have power and be a medicine-man, and could cure the sick. From time John Slocum preached I tried to be a good Christian man. I prayed and was sick—my soul was sick. I prayed to God and he pays me for that. There is lots of difference between this power and old Indian doctoring. This is not old power. I can cure people now. I have cured some white men and women, but they are ashamed to tell it. I cure without money. One big, rich man, Henry Walker, was sick—had great pains in his ear and leg. Doctor at Olympia failed to cure him, and he came to John Slocum and me. We worked for him, prayed, and he lay down and slept and was cured. He offered us twenty dollars—but no, we refused it. God will pay us when we die. This is our religion. When we die, we get our pay from God.

"No, we do not believe the Bible. We believe in God, and in Jesus Christ as the Son of God, and we believe in a hell. In these matters we believe the same as the Presbyterians. We think fully of God today. A good Christian man is a good medicine-man. A good Christian man in the dark sees a light toward God. God makes a fog—good Christian man goes straight through it to the end, like good medicine. I believe this religion. It helps poor people. Bad man can't see good — bad man can't get to heaven — can't find his way. We were sent to jail for this religion, but we will never give up. We all believe that John Slocum died and went to heaven, and was sent back to preach to the people. We all talk about that and believe it.

"The Shakers use candles, bells, crucifixes, Catholic pictures, etc, in their church and other ceremonies. As Mr Ellis says, they use para-phernalia of the Catholic, Presbyterian, and even some of the Indian religion. They cross themselves as the Catholics do; they say grace before and after meals; they stand and pray and chant in unison; they set candles around the dead as the Catholics do, and believe in the cure of the sick by faith and prayer. In times of excitement many of them twitch and shake, but in no instance do they conduct themselves in so nervous.a manner as I have seen orthodox Christians do at old Sandy Branch camp-meeting in Illinois. They believe that by praying with a man or woman and rubbing the person they could induce them to join their church, and could rub away their sins; but they have no rite, no ceremony, no belief, no policy, no form of religion that is not in use by some one or other of our orthodox people.

"Their religion, in brief, is a belief in God as the father and ruler of all, and in Jesus Christ as the Son of God and the Savior of mankind. They know there is a heaven, for John Slocum was there, and believe in a hell of fire for the punishment of sinners, because the angels in heaven told John Slocum about it. They do not care for the Bible. It is of no use to them, for they have a distinct revelation direct from heaven. This is the only practical difference between them and the orthodox believers, and this they do not care for."

Two of their songs, as recorded by Mr Wickersham, are as follows:

Stalib gwuch Kwē Shuck, or Song of Heaven

Alkwē klū sutlh akwē schelch huchum akwē shuck;

When we get warning from heaven;
Gwalch clah tlōwch kwē lehass;

Then the angels wi'l come;
Gwalch clah gwä tä äddō kwē kä-kä tēdtēd;

Then the wonderful bells will ring;
Gwalch clah ass kwä-buch kwē kä-kä tsille;

Then our souls will be ready;
Gwalch clah ōwhuh tu shuck;

Then they will go up to heaven;
Gwalch clah tālib tōbuch ah shō-shō-quille;

Then we will sing with Jesus;
Gwalch clah jōil tōbuch ah shō-shō-quille.

Then we will be happy with Jesus.

Quā-dä-tsits Stälib, or Preacher's Song

Chelch lä tä lä beuch;

Then we shall sing;
Chelch lä tä lä beuch;

Then we shall sing;
Chelch lä tä lä beuch;

Then we shall sing;
Al kwe shuck älläl.

Up in heaven's house.

Chelch lā jōilla;
>Then we'll be happy;
Chelch lā jōilla;
>Then we'll be happy;
Chelch lā jōilla,
>Then we'll be happy,
Al kwe shuck älläl.
>Up in heaven's house.

Chelch lā jōilla;
>Then we'll be happy;
Chelch lā jōilla;
>Then we'll be happy;
Chelch lā jōilla,
>Then we'll be happy,
Yuchquē shō-shō-quille.
>Up with Jesus.

Mr Wickersham then gives an account of the persecutions to which the rising sect was for a long time subjected, chiefly at the hands of agent Edwin Eells and his brother, Reverend Myron Eells, already quoted at length, who was at that time the missionary on the Skokomish reservation. As Mr Wickersham's statements in this regard are mainly in the form of extended quotations from Ten Years' Missionary Work at Skokomish, written by the Reverend Mr Eells himself, they may be regarded as conclusive. It is apparent that a part at least of this persecution, which took the shape of banishment, chains, and imprisonment, and even the forcible seizure of a dead body from the bereaved relatives, was due to the fact that the Shakers, who considered themselves a genuine branch of the Christian church, were disposed to lean toward Catholicity rather than toward the denominational form upheld by the agent and his brother.

However, religious persecution failed as utterly in its purpose in this case as it has and must in all others. Quoting from Mr Eells, "The chiefs did not care if they were deposed, were about to resign, and did not wish to have anything more to do with the 'Boston' religion or the agent. Billy Clams was ready, if need be, to suffer as Christ did. He was willing to be a martyr."

Mr Wickersham continues:

" While Billy Clams and some of his people publicly abandoned the forms of Shaker religion rather than be banished, yet John Slocum and his people refused to so surrender, and the agent sent out his police and arrested John Slocum, Louis Yowaluch, and two or three more of these people—good, true men—and, loading their limbs with chains, confined them for several weeks in the dirty little single room of a jail at the Puyallup agency, near Tacoma. Their only offense was worship of a different form from that adopted by the agent and his brother. They had broken no law, created no disorder, and yet they suffered ignominious incarceration in a vile dungeon, loaded with chains, at the pleasure of the agent. The Shakers believed in God, in Jesus Christ, in heaven and hell, in temperance, sobriety, and a virtuous life. They abandoned the old Indian religion and all its vices and forms, including the power of the doctors or medicine-men. These medicine-men had a great hold on the Indian mind, and they joined the minister and the agent in their fight on the Shakers, because the Shakers fought them; so that there was seen the unique spectacle of the savage shamanism of the American Indian and the supposed orthodox religion of civilization hand in hand fighting the followers of Jesus Christ.

"Imprisonment, banishment, threats, chains, and the general ill will of the agent and all his employees were visited on these Shakers who continued to practice their forms of worship, and yet they did continue it. In spite of the fact that they occupied a place only half-way between slaves and freemen, and were under the orders of the agent and subject to be harassed and annoyed all the time by him, yet they continued nobly and fearlessly to practice their religion and to worship God and Jesus Christ as they saw fit. To do it, however, they were forced to stay away from the reservations, where the greater number of employees were located, and their churches were built on Mud bay and Oyster bay, far away from the reservations.

"But a brighter day came for these people, a day when they could stand up and defy every form or force of persecution. In 1886 Congress passed the Indian land severalty bill, an act providing for dividing lands in severalty to Indians, and providing that those who took lands and adopted the habits of civilized life should be American citizens, with all the rights, privileges, and immunities of any other citizen. In 1892 I was appointed by Judge Hanford to defend a prisoner in the United States district court at Tacoma. The prisoner was accused of selling liquor to a Puyallup Indian, but it appeared on cross-examination that this Indian owned land in severalty, voted, paid taxes, and exercised other rights of citizenship. The question was then raised by me on motion to dismiss, that these land-holding, tax-paying Indians were citizens of the United States, free and independent. The United States prosecuting attorney appeared to contest the claim, but after an extended argument Judge Hanford held with me, and the prisoner was discharged.

"The effect of this decision was far-reaching. It meant that all land-holding Indians were no longer wards of the government, but free citizens and not under the control of the Indian agent. The Shaker people, hearing this, sent a deputation to see me, and I held a long consultation with them, assuring them that they were as free as the agent, and could establish their own church, own and build houses of worship, and do both in religious and worldly matters as other citizens of the United States could. This was glorious news to them. It meant freedom, it meant the cessation of persecution and annoyance by the agency employees, and they were jubilant.

"Accordingly they met on June 6, 1892, at Mud bay, at Louis Yowaluch's house, and organized their church on a regular business basis.

The following officers were elected: Headman, Louis Yowaluch; elders, John Slocum, Louis Yowaluch, John Smith, James Walker, Charles Walker, John W. Simmons, and William James. At this meeting the following persons were also appointed ministers of this church, and licenses were issued to them, to wit: Louis Yowaluch, John Slocum, James Tobin, John Powers, and Richard Jackson. Provision was made to establish a church at the Puyallup reservation, where the power of the agent had hitherto kept them out, and William James, a Puyallup landowner, gave land for a church. After much talk about sending out ministers, etc, the meeting adjourned, after a two days' session, and

FIG. 68—Shaker church at Mud bay.

tne Shaker church, after eleven years' fighting against persecutions, was an established fact, free and independent, with its own officers, ministers, and church property.

"The spectacle of an Indian church with Indian officers, preachers, and members, and of houses built by the Indians for church purposes, was too much for the average citizen of Puget sound, and the Shakers were continually disturbed, not only by the whites, but by the Indians who could not and did not appreciate the change to citizenship, so that I was constantly applied to for protection by the ministers and members of the Shaker church. A 'paper' has a great effect on the average Indian, and I issued on application several papers addressed in general terms to those who might be disposed to interfere with them, which had a quieting effect and caused evil-disposed persons to respect the Indians and their religion, or at least to let them alone. They now feel quite confident of their position, and are acting quite like the average citizen. Even the persons who persecuted them for eleven years now felt obliged to retire from the conflict, and a day of peace is reached at last.

"The Shaker church now reaches over nearly the whole of western Washington. The story of Slocum's death and visit to heaven, and his return to preach to the Indians, is accepted by them as a direct revelation of the will of God. They say that they do not need to read the Bible, for do they not have better and more recent testimony of the existence of heaven and of the way to that celestial home than is contained in the Bible? Here is John Slocum, alive, and has he not been to heaven? Then, why read the Bible to learn the road, when John can so easily tell them all about it? The Bible says there are many roads; the Catholics have one, the Presbyterians another, and the Congregationalists a third; but John Slocum gives them a short, straight road—and they choose that.

"The Shaker church now has a building for church purposes at Mud bay, at Oyster bay, at Cowlitz, Chehalis, and Puyallup. They have about a dozen ministers regularly licensed, and about 500 members. Most of the Indians at Skokomish belong, while the Squaxins, Chehalis, Nisqually, Cowlitz, and Columbia River Indians, and in fact the majority of the Indians of western Washington, either belong or are in sympathy with its teachings, so that it is now the strongest church among them. They are sending out runners to the Yakimas east of the Cascade mountains, and expect before long to make an effort to convert that tribe.

"The Indian is inclined to be weak, and to adopt the vices of the white man, but not his virtues. However, this is not true of the Shakers. They do not drink intoxicants of any kind, and make a special effort at all times to banish liquor. This is the strong element in their faith, and the one for which they fight hardest. They feel upon their honor in the matter, and contrast the members of their church at every place with those belonging to the other denominations— and it is too true that an Indian does not seem at all to be restrained from drink by belonging to the other churches as he does in the Shaker church. In the others he feels no personal interest. The honor of neither himself nor his people is involved, and if he disgraces himself it reflects, in his opinion, rather on the white man's church. Not so with the Shakers. No white man belongs to their church, and it is their boast that no white preacher can keep his Indian members from drink as they can—and it is true. After their opposition to liquor, next comes gambling. From these two vices flow nearly all troubles to the Indian, and the Shakers are certainly successful in extinguishing their spread among the Indians. They make special war on drunkenness, gambling, and horse racing, and preach honesty, sobriety, temperance, and right living.

"The Presbyterian church occupies a queer position with regard to these people. The Reverend M. G. Mann has been the missionary to the Indians of Puget sound for many years, and has succeeded in making a very favorable impression upon them. He has been specially attentive to the Shakers, and, to his credit be it said, has never tried to coerce them, and has only dealt with them kindly. So far has this gone that Louis Yowaluch was long ago taken into the Presbyterian church, and is now an accredited elder therein. Louis does not know, seemingly, how to escape from his dual position, or rather does not seem to think that he needs to escape. It all seems to be for the best interest of his people, so he continues to occupy the position of elder in the Presbyterian church and headman of the Shaker church.

"At a recent meeting of the Presbyterian ministers the position of these Shaker people was fully discussed, and the strongest language was used in saying only good about them, and every effort seems to be made by the Presbyterians to claim the Shakers in a body as members of the Presbyterian church. If this account were not already too long, the reports of the church on the subject would be quoted, but the fact speaks volumes for the character of the Shakers and their teaching.

"In conclusion: I have known the Shaker people now intimately, as their attorney, for more than a year, and out of the many drunken Indians I have seen in that time not one was a Shaker. Not one of their people has been arrested for crime in that time. They are good citizens, and are far more temperate and peaceable than those Indians belonging to the other churches. I feel that their church is a grand success in that it prevents idleness and vice, drunkenness and disorder, and tends to produce quiet, peaceable citizens, and good Christian people. I think the Presbyterians make a mistake in trying to bring the Shakers into their fold—they ought rather to protect them and give them every assistance in their autonomy. It adds the greatest incentive to their labors, and makes them feel as if they were of some account. It lets them labor for themselves, instead of feeling, as always heretofore, that some one else—they hardly knew who—was responsible. Their forms of Christianity are not very unorthodox—their Christianity is quite orthodox, not exactly because they take Slocum's revelation instead of the Bible, but the result is the same—a Christian.

"JAMES WICKERSHAM.

"TACOMA, WASHINGTON, *June 25, 1893.*"

From competent Indian informants of eastern Washington—Charles Ike, half-blood Yakima interpreter, and Chief Wolf Necklace of the Pä'lus, we gather additional particulars, from which it would appear that there are more things in the Shaker system than are dreamed of in the philosophy of the Presbyterian general assembly.

According to their statements, Yowaluch, or Ai-yäl, as he is known east of the Cascades, was noted as a gambler before he received his revelation. His followers are called *Shäpupu-'lĕma*, or "blowers," by the Yakima, from the fact that on meeting a stranger, instead of at once shaking hands with him in the usual manner, they first wave the hand gently in front of his face like a fan, and blow on him, in order to "blow away the badness" from him. They first appeared among the Yakima and other eastern tribes about six years ago, and are gradually gaining adherents, although as yet they have no regular time or place of assembly. They are much addicted to making the sign of the cross—the cross, it is hardly necessary to state, being as much an Indian as a Christian symbol—and are held in great repute as doctors, their treatment consisting chiefly of hypnotic performances over the patient, resulting in the spasmodic shaking already described. In doctoring a patient the "blowers" usually gather around him in a circle to the number of about twelve, dressed in a very attractive ceremonial costume, and each wearing on his head a sort of crown of woven cedar bark, in which are fixed two lighted candles, while in his right hand he carries a small cloth, and in the left another lighted candle. By fastening screens of colored cloth over the candles the light is made to appear yellow, white, or blue. The candle upon the forehead is yellow, symbolic of the celestial glory; that at the back of the head is white, typical of the terrestrial light, while the third is blue, the color of the sky.

Frequently also they carry in their hands or wear on their heads garlands of roses and other flowers of various colors, yellow, white, and blue being the favorite, which they say represent the colors of objects in the celestial world. While the leader is going through his hypnotic performance over the patient the others are waving the cloths and swinging in circles the candles held in their hands. In all this it is easy to see the influence of the Catholic ritual, with its censers, tapers, and flowers, with which these tribes have been more or less familiar for the last fifty years.

A single instance will suffice to show the methods of the blower doctors. The story is told from the Indian point of view, as related by the half-blood interpreter, who believed it all. About six years ago two of these doctors from the north, while visiting near Woodland on the Columbia, were called to the assistance of a woman who was seriously ill, and had received no benefit from the treatment of the native doctors. They came and almost immediately on seeing the patient announced to the relatives that the sickness had been put into her by the evil magic of a neighboring medicine-man, whom they then summoned into their presence. When the messenger arrived for him, the medicine-man refused to go, saying that the doctors were liars and that he had not made the woman ill. By their clairaudient power—or possibly by a shrewd anticipation of probabilities—the doctors in the other house knew of his refusal and sent another messenger to tell him that concealment or denial would not avail him, and that if he refused to come they would proceed to blow the sickness into his own body. Without further argument he accompanied the messengers to the sick woman's house. As he entered, the chief doctor stepped up to him and looking intently into his face, said, "I can see your heart within your body, and it is black with evil things. You are not fit to live. You are making this woman sick, but we shall take out the badness from her body." With the cloths and lighted candles the two doctors then approached the sick woman and commanded her to arise, which she did, although she had been supposed to be too weak to stand. Waving the cloths in front of her with a gentle fanning motion, and blowing upon her at the same time, they proceeded to drive the disease out of her body, beginning at the feet and working upward until, as they approached the head the principal doctor changed the movement to a rapid fanning and corresponding blowing, while the assistant stood ready with his cloth to seize the disease when it should be driven out. All this time the medicine-man standing a few feet away was shaking and quivering like one in a fit, and the trembling became more violent and spasmodic as the doctors increased the speed of their motions. Finally the leader brought his hands together over the woman's head, where, just as the disease attempted to escape, it was seized and imprisoned in the cloth held by his assistant. Then, going up to the medicine-man, with a few rapid passes they fanned the disease into his body and he fell down dead. The woman recovered, and with her sister has recently come up to the Yakima country as an apostle of the new religion, preaching the doctrines and performing the wonders which she has been taught by the Nisqually doctors.

This is the Indian story as told by the half-blood, who did not claim to have been an eye-witness, but spoke of it as a matter of common knowledge and beyond question. It is doubtless substantially correct. The hypnotic action described is the same which the author has repeatedly seen employed in the Ghost dance, resulting successively in involuntary trembling, violent spasmodic action, rigidity, and final deathlike unconsciousness. The Ghost dancers regard the process not only as a means of bringing them into trance communication with their departed friends, but also as a preventive and cure of disease, just as we have our faith healers and magnetic doctors. With the Indian's implicit faith in the supernatural ability of the doctor, it is easy to suppose that the mental effect on the woman, who was told and believed that she was to be cured, would aid recovery if recovery was possible. It is unlikely that death resulted to the medicine-man. It is more probable that under the hypnotic spell of the doctors he fell unconscious and apparently lifeless and remained so perhaps for a considerable time, as frequently happens with sensitive subjects in the Ghost dance. The fact that the same process should produce exactly opposite effects in the two subjects is easily explainable. The object of the hypnotic performance was simply to bring the mind of the subject under the control of the operator. This accomplished, the mental, and ultimately the physical, effect on either subject was whatever the operator wished it to be. After bringing both under mental control in the manner described, he suggested recovery to the woman and sickness or death to the medicine-man, and the result followed.

Until the advent of these women from beyond the mountains such hypnotic performances seem to have been unknown among the Yakima and other eastern tribes of the Columbia region, the trance condition in the Smohalla devotees being apparently due entirely to the effect of the rhythmic dances and songs acting on excited imaginations, without the aid of blowing or manual passes.

Hypnotism and so-called magnetism, however, appear to have been employed by the medicine-men of the Chinook tribes of the lower Columbia from ancient times. Especially wonderful in this connection are the stories told of one of these men residing at Wushqûm or Wisham, near The Dalles.

About the time the two blower doctors appeared at Woodland, other apostles of the same doctrine, or it may have been the same two men, went up Willamet river into central Oregon, teaching the same system and performing the same wonders among the tribes of that region. And here comes in a remarkable coincidence, if it be no more. It is said among the northern Indians that on this journey these apostles met, somewhere in the south, a young man to whom they taught their mysteries, in which he became such an apt pupil that he soon outstripped his teachers, and is now working even greater wonders among his own people. This young man can be no other than Wovoka, the messiah of the Ghost dance, living among the Paiute in western Nevada. The only question is whether the story told among the Columbia tribes is a myth based on vague rumors of the southern messiah and his hypnotic performances, so similar to that of the blower doctors, or whether Wovoka actually derived his knowledge of such things from these northern apostles. The latter supposition is entirely within the bounds of possibility. The time corresponds with the date of his original revelations, as stated by himself to the writer. He is a young man, and, although he has never been far from home, the tribe to which he belongs roams in scattered bands over the whole country to the Willamet and the watershed of the Columbia, so that communication with the north is by no means difficult. He himself stated that Indians from Warmspring reservation, in northern Oregon, have attended his dances near Walker lake.

CHAPTER IX

WOVOKA THE MESSIAH

When the sun died, I went up to heaven and saw God and all the people who had died a long time ago. God told me to come back and tell my people they must be good and love one another, and not fight, or steal, or lie. He gave me this dance to give to my people.—*Woroka*.

When Tävibo, the prophet of Mason valley, died, about 1870, he left a son named Wovoka, "The Cutter," about 14 years of age. The prophetic claims and teachings of the father, the reverence with which

FIG. 69—Wovoka.

he was regarded by the people, and the mysterious ceremonies which were doubtless of frequent performance in the little tulé wikiup at home must have made early and deep impression on the mind of the boy, who seems to have been by nature of a solitary and contemplative disposition, one of those born to see visions and hear still voices.

The physical environment was favorable to the development of such a character. His native valley, from which he has never wandered, is a narrow strip of level sage prairie some 30 miles in length, walled in by the giant sierras, their sides torn and gashed by volcanic convulsions and dark with gloomy forests of pine, their towering summits white with everlasting snows, and roofed over by a cloudless sky whose blue infinitude the mind instinctively seeks to penetrate to far-off worlds beyond. Away to the south the view is closed in by the sacred mountain of the Paiute, where their Father gave them the first fire and taught them their few simple arts before leaving for his home in the upper regions of the Sun-land. Like the valley of Rasselas, it seems set apart from the great world to be the home of a dreamer.

The greater portion of Nevada is an arid desert of rugged mountains and alkali plains, the little available land being confined to narrow mountain valleys and the borders of a few large lakes. These tracts are occupied by scattered ranchmen engaged in stock raising, and as the white population is sparse, Indian labor is largely utilized, the Paiute being very good workers. The causes which in other parts of the country have conspired to sweep the Indian from the path of the white man seem inoperative here, where the aboriginal proprietors are regarded rather as peons under the protection of the dominant race, and are allowed to set up their small camps of tulé lodges in convenient out-of-the-way places, where they spend the autumn and winter in hunting, fishing, and gathering seeds and piñon nuts, working at fair wages on ranches through spring and summer. In this way young Wovoka became attached to the family of a ranchman in Mason valley, named David Wilson, who took an interest in him and bestowed on him the name of Jack Wilson, by which he is commonly known among the whites. From his association with this family he gained some knowledge of English, together with a confused idea of the white man's theology. On growing up he married, and still continued to work for Mr Wilson, earning a reputation for industry and reliability, but attracting no special notice until nearly 30 years of age, when he announced the revelation that has made him famous among the tribes of the west.

Following are the various forms of his name which I have noticed: Wo'voka, or Wü'voka, which I have provisionally rendered "Cutter," derived from a verb signifying "to cut;" Wevokar, Wopokahte, Kwohitsauq, Cowejo, Koit-tsow, Kvit-Tsow, Quoitze Ow, Jack Wilson, Jackson Wilson, Jack Winson, John Johnson. He has also been confounded with Bannock Jim, a Mormon Bannock of Fort Hall reservation, Idaho, and with Johnson Sides, a Paiute living near Reno, Nevada, and bitterly opposed to Wovoka. His father's name, Tävibo, has been given also as Waughzeewaughber. It is not quite certain that the Paiute prophet of 1870 was the father of Wovoka. This is stated to have been the case by one of Captain Lee's informants (*A. G. O.*, *4*) and by Lieutenant Phister (*Phister*, *2*). Wovoka himself says that his father did not preach, but was a "dreamer" with supernatural powers. Certain it is that a similar doctrine was taught by an Indian living in the same valley in Wovoka's boyhood. Possibly the discrepancy might be explained by an unwillingness on the part of the messiah to share his spiritual honors.

In proportion as Wovoka and his doctrines have become subjects of widespread curiosity, so have they become subjects of ignorant misrepresentation and deliberate falsification. Different writers have made him a Paiute, a half-blood, and a Mormon white man. Numberless stories have been told of the origin and character of his mission and the day predicted for its final accomplishment. The most mischievous and persistent of these stories has been that which represents him as preaching a bloody campaign against the whites, whereas his doctrine is one of peace, and he himself is a mild-tempered member of a weak and unwarlike tribe. His own good name has been filched from him and he has been made to appear under a dozen different cognomens, including that of his bitterest enemy, Johnson Sides. He has been denounced as an impostor, ridiculed as a lunatic, and laughed at as a pretended Christ, while by the Indians he is revered as a direct messenger from the Other World, and among many of the remote tribes he is believed to be omniscient, to speak all languages, and to be invisible to a white man. We shall give his own story as told by himself, with such additional information as seems to come from authentic sources.

Notwithstanding all that had been said and written by newspaper correspondents about the messiah, not one of them had undertaken to find the man himself and to learn from his own lips what he really taught. It is almost equally certain that none of them had even seen a Ghost dance at close quarters—certainly none of them understood its meaning. The messiah was regarded almost as a myth, something intangible, to be talked about but not to be seen. The first reliable information as to his personality was communicated by the scout, Arthur Chapman, who, under instructions from the War Department, visited the Paiute country in December, 1890, and spent four days at Walker lake and Mason valley, and in the course of an interview with Wovoka obtained from him a detailed statement similar in all essentials to that which I obtained later on. (*Sec. War, 3.*)

After having spent seven months in the field, investigating the new religion among the prairie tribes, particularly the Arapaho, and after having examined all the documents bearing on the subject in the files of the Indian Office and War Department, the author left Washington in November, 1891, to find and talk with the messiah and to gather additional material concerning the Ghost dance. Before starting, I had written to the agent in charge of the reservation to which he was attached for information in regard to the messiah (Jack Wilson) and the dance, and learned in reply, with some surprise, that the agent had never seen him. The surprise grew into wonder when I was further informed that there were "neither Ghost songs, dances, nor ceremonials" among the Paiute.[1] This was discouraging, but not entirely convincing, and I set out once more for the west. After a few days with the Omaha and Winnebago in Nebraska, and a longer stay with the Sioux at Pine Ridge, where traces of the recent conflict were still fresh on every hand, I crossed over the mountains and finally arrived at Walker Lake reservation in Nevada.

On inquiry I learned that the messiah lived, not on the reservation, but in Mason valley, about 40 miles to the northwest. His uncle, Charley Sheep, lived near the agency, however, so I sought him out and made his acquaintance. He spoke tolerable—or rather intolerable—English, so that we were able to get along together without an interpreter, a fact which brought us into closer sympathy, as an interpreter is generally at best only a necessary evil. As usual, he was very suspicious at first, and inquired minutely as to my purpose. I explained to him that I was sent out by the government to the various tribes to study their customs and learn their stories and songs; that I had obtained a good deal from other tribes and now wanted to learn some songs and stories of the Paiute, in order to write them down so that the

---

[1] The letter is given as a sample of the information possessed by some agents in regard to the Indians in their charge:

"UNITED STATES INDIAN SERVICE,
"*Pyramid Lake, Nevada Agency, October 12, 1891.*

"JAMES MOONEY, Esq.,
"*Bureau of Ethnology.*

"MY DEAR SIR: Your letter of September 24 in regard to Jack Wilson, the 'Messiah,' at hand and duly noted. In reply will say that his Indian name is Ko-wee-jow ('Big belly'). I do not know as it will be possible to get a photo of him. I never saw him or a photo of him. He works among the whites about 40 miles from my Walker Lake reserve, and never comes near the agency when I visit it. My headquarters are at Pyramid lake, about 70 miles north of Walker. I am pursuing the course with him of nonattention or a silent ignoring. He seems to think, so I hear, that I will arrest him should he come within my reach. I would give him no such notoriety. He, like all other prophets, has but little honor in his own country. He has been visited by delegations from various and many Indian tribes, which I think should be discouraged all that is possible. Don't know what the 'Smoholler' religion, you speak of, is. He speaks English well, but is not educated. He got his doctrine in part from contact, living in and with a religious family. There are neither ghost songs, dances, nor ceremonials among them about my agencies. Would not be allowed. I think they died out with 'Sitting Bull.' This is the extent of the information I can give you.

"Very respectfully, yours,
C. C. WARNER, *United States Indian Agent.*"

Here is an agent who has under his special charge and within a few miles of his agency the man who has created the greatest religious ferment known to the Indians of this generation, a movement which had been engrossing the attention of the newspaper and magazine press for a year, yet he has never seen him; and while the Indian Office, from which he gets his commission, in a praiseworthy effort to get at an understanding of the matter, is sending circular letters broadcast to the western agencies, calling for all procurable information in regard to the messiah and his doctrines, he "pursues the course of nonattention." He has never heard of the Smohalla religion of the adjacent northern tribes, although the subject is repeatedly mentioned in the volumes of the Indian Commissioner's report from 1870 to 1879, which were, or should have been, on a shelf in the office in which the letter was written. He asserts that there are no ghost songs, dances, or ceremonies among his Indians, although these things were going on constantly and had been for at least three years, and only a short time before a large delegation from beyond the mountains had attended a Ghost dance near Walker lake which lasted four days and nights. Chapman in 1890, and the author in 1891, saw the cleared grounds with the willow frames where these dances were being held regularly at short intervals. I found the ghost songs familiar to all the Indians with whom I talked, and had no special trouble to find the messiah and obtain his picture. The peaceful character of the movement is sufficiently shown by the fact that while the eastern papers are teeming with rumors of uprising and massacre, and troops are being hurried to the front, the agent at the central point of the disturbance seems to be unaware that there is anything special going on around him and can "silently ignore" the whole matter.

white people could read them. In a casual way I then offered to show him the pictures of some of my Indian friends across the mountains, and brought out the photos of several Arapaho and Cheyenne who I knew had recently come as delegates to the messiah. This convinced him that I was all right, and he became communicative. The result was that we spent about a week together in the wikiups (lodges of tulé rushes), surrounded always by a crowd of interested Paiute, discussing the old stories and games, singing Paiute songs, and sampling the seed mush and roasted piñon nuts. On one of these occasions, at night, a medicine-man was performing his incantations over a sick child on one side of the fire while we were talking on the other. When the ice was well thawed, I cautiously approached the subject of the ghost songs and dance, and, as confidence was now established, I found no difficulty in obtaining a number of the songs, with a description of the ceremonial. I then told Charley that, as I had taken part in the dance, I was anxious to see the messiah and get from him some medicine-paint to bring back to his friends among the eastern tribes. He readily agreed to go with me and use his efforts with his nephew to obtain what was wanted.

It is 20 miles northward by railroad from Walker River agency to Wabuska, and 12 miles more in a southwesterly direction from there to the Mason valley settlement. There we met a young white man named Dyer, who was well acquainted with Jack Wilson, and who also spoke the Paiute language, and learned from him that the messiah was about 12 miles farther up the valley, near a place called Pine Grove. Enlisting his services, with a team and driver, making four in all, we started up toward the mountain. It was New Year's day of 1892, and there was deep snow on the ground, a very unusual thing in this part of the country, and due in this instance, as Charley assured us, to the direct agency of Jack Wilson. It is hard to imagine anything more monotonously unattractive than a sage prairie under ordinary circumstances unless it be the same prairie when covered by a heavy fall of snow, under which the smaller clumps of sagebrush look like prairie-dog mounds, while the larger ones can hardly be distinguished at a short distance from wikiups. However, the mountains were bright in front of us, the sky was blue overhead, and the road was good under foot.

Soon after leaving the settlement we passed the dance ground with the brush shelters still standing. We met but few Indians on the way. After several miles we noticed a man at some distance from the road with a gun across his shoulder. Dyer looked a moment and then exclaimed, "I believe that's Jack now!" The Indian thought so, too, and pulling up our horses he shouted some words in the Paiute language. The man replied, and sure enough it was the messiah, hunting jack rabbits. At his uncle's call he soon came over.

As he approached I saw that he was a young man, a dark full-blood, compactly built, and taller than the Paiute generally, being nearly 6

WINTER VIEW IN MASON VALLEY, SHOWING SNOW-COVERED SAGEBRUSH

feet in height. He was well dressed in white man's clothes, with the broad-brimmed white felt hat common in the west, secured on his head by means of a beaded ribbon under the chin. This, with a blanket or a robe of rabbit skins, is now the ordinary Paiute dress. He wore a good pair of boots. His hair was cut off square on a line below the base of the ears, after the manner of his tribe. His countenance was open and expressive of firmness and decision, but with no marked intellectuality. The features were broad and heavy, very different from the thin, clear-cut features of the prairie tribes.

As he came up he took my hand with a strong, hearty grasp, and inquired what was wanted. His uncle explained matters, adding that I was well acquainted with some of his Indian friends who had visited him a short time before, and was going back to the same people. After some deliberation he said that the whites had lied about him and he did not like to talk to them; some of the Indians had disobeyed his instructions and trouble had come of it, but as I was sent by Washington and was a friend of his friends, he would talk with me. He was hunting now, but if we would come to his camp that night he would tell us about his mission.

With another hand-shake he left us, and we drove on to the nearest ranch, arriving about dark. After supper we got ready and started across country through the sagebrush for the Paiute camp, some miles away, guided by our Indian. It was already night, with nothing to be seen but the clumps of snow-covered sagebrush stretching away in every direction, and after traveling an hour or more without reaching the camp, our guide had to confess that he had lost the trail. It was two years since he had been there, his sight was failing, and, with the snow and the darkness, he was utterly at a loss to know his whereabouts.

To be lost on a sage plain on a freezing night in January is not a pleasant experience. There was no road, and no house but the one we had left some miles behind, and it would be almost impossible to find our way back to that through the darkness. Excepting for a lantern there was no light but what came from the glare of the snow and a few stars in the frosty sky overhead. To add to our difficulty, the snow was cut in every direction by cattle trails, which seemed to be Indian trails, and kept us doubling and circling to no purpose, while in the uncertain gloom every large clump of sagebrush took on the appearance of a wikiup, only to disappoint us on a nearer approach. With it all, the night was bitterly cold and we were half frozen. After vainly following a dozen false trails and shouting repeatedly in hope of hearing an answering cry, we hit on the expedient of leaving the Indian with the wagon, he being the oldest man of the party, while the rest of us each took a different direction from the central point, following the cattle tracks in the snow and calling to each other at short intervals, in order that we might not become lost from one another. After going far enough to know that none of us had yet struck the right trail, the wagon was moved up a short distance and the same performance was repeated. At last a shout from our driver brought us all together. He declared that he had heard sounds in front, and after listening a few minutes in painful suspense we saw a shower of sparks go up into the darkness and knew that we had struck the camp. Going back to the wagon, we got in and drove straight across to the spot, where we found three or four little wikiups, in one of which we were told the messiah was awaiting our arrival.

On entering through the low doorway we found ourselves in a circular lodge made of bundles of tulé rushes laid over a framework of poles, after the fashion of the thatched roofs of Europe, and very similar to the grass lodges of the Wichita. The lodge was only about 10 feet in diameter and about 8 feet in height, with sloping sides, and was almost entirely open above, like a cone with the top cut off, as in this part of the country rain or snow is of rare occurrence. As already remarked, the deep snow at the time was something unusual. In the center, built directly on the ground, was a blazing fire of sagebrush, upon which fresh stalks were thrown from time to time, sending up a shower of sparks into the open air. It was by this means that we had been guided to the camp. Sitting or lying around the fire were half a dozen Paiute, including the messiah and his family, consisting of his young wife, a boy about 4 years of age, of whom he seemed very fond, and an infant. It was plain that he was a kind husband and father, which was in keeping with his reputation among the whites for industry and reliability. The only articles in the nature of furniture were a few grass woven bowls and baskets of various sizes and patterns. There were no Indian beds or seats of the kind found in every prairie tipi, no rawhide boxes, no toilet pouches, not even a hole dug in the ground for the fire. Although all wore white men's dress, there were no pots, pans, or other articles of civilized manufacture, now used by even the most primitive prairie tribes, for, strangely enough, although these Paiute are practically farm laborers and tenants of the whites all around them, and earn good wages, they seem to covet nothing of the white man's, but spend their money for dress, small trinkets, and ammunition for hunting, and continue to subsist on seeds, piñon nuts, and small game, lying down at night on the dusty ground in their cramped wikiups, destitute of even the most ordinary conveniences in use among other tribes. It is a curious instance of a people accepting the inevitable while yet resisting innovation.

Wovoka received us cordially and then inquired more particularly as to my purpose in seeking an interview. His uncle entered into a detailed explanation, which stretched out to a preposterous length, owing to a peculiar conversational method of the Paiute. Each statement by the older man was repeated at its close, word for word and sentence by sentence, by the other, with the same monotonous inflection. This done, the first speaker signified by a grunt of approval that it had been correctly repeated, and then proceeded with the next statement, which was duly repeated in like manner. The first time I had heard two old men conversing together in this fashion on the reservation I had supposed they were reciting some sort of Indian litany, and it required several such experiences and some degree of patience to become used to it.

At last he signified that he understood and was satisfied, and then in answer to my questions gave an account of himself and his doctrine, a great part of the interpretation being by Dyer, with whom he seemed to be on intimate terms. He said he was about 35 years of age, fixing the date from a noted battle[1] between the Paiute and the whites near Pyramid lake, in 1860, at which time he said he was about the size of his little boy, who appeared to be of about 4 years. His father, Tävibo, "White Man," was not a preacher, but was a *capita* (from the Spanish *capitan*) or petty chief, and was a dreamer and invulnerable. His own proper name from boyhood was Wovoka or Wüvoka, "The Cutter," but a few years ago he had assumed the name of his paternal grandfather, Kwohitsauq, or "Big Rumbling Belly." After the death of his father he had been taken into the family of a white farmer, David Wilson, who had given him the name of Jack Wilson, by which he is commonly known among the whites. He thus has three distinct names, Wovoka, Kwohitsauq, and Jack Wilson. He stated positively that he was a full-blood, a statement borne out by his appearance. The impression that he is a half-blood may have arisen from the fact that his father's name was "White Man" and that he has a white man's name. His followers, both in his own and in all other tribes, commonly refer to him as "our father." He has never been away from Mason valley and speaks only his own Paiute language, with some little knowledge of English. He is not acquainted with the sign language, which is hardly known west of the mountains.

When about 20 years of age, he married, and continued to work for Mr Wilson. He had given the dance to his people about four years before, but had received his great revelation about two years previously. On this occasion "the sun died" (was eclipsed) and he fell asleep in the daytime and was taken up to the other world. Here he saw God, with all the people who had died long ago engaged in their oldtime sports and occupations, all happy and forever young. It was a pleasant land and full of game. After showing him all, God told him he must go

---

[1] This battle, probably the most important conflict that ever occurred between the Paiute and the whites, was fought in April, 1860, near the present agency at Pyramid lake and about 8 miles from Wadsworth, Nevada. Some miners having seized and forcibly detained a couple of Indian women, their husbands raised a party and rescued them, without, however, inflicting any punishment on the guilty ones. This was considered an "Indian outrage" and a strong body of miners collected and marched toward Pyramid lake to wipe out the Indian camp. The Paiute, armed almost entirely with bows and arrows, surprised them in a narrow pass at the spot indicated, with the result that the whites were defeated and fled in disorder, leaving nearly fifty dead on the field. The whole affair in its causes and results was most discreditable to the whites.

back and tell his people they must be good and love one another, have no quarreling, and live in peace with the whites; that they must work, and not lie or steal; that they must put away all the old practices that savored of war; that if they faithfully obeyed his instructions they would at last be reunited with their friends in this other world, where there would be no more death or sickness or old age. He was then given the dance which he was commanded to bring back to his people. By performing this dance at intervals, for five consecutive days each time, they would secure this happiness to themselves and hasten the event. Finally God gave him control over the elements so that he could make it rain or snow or be dry at will, and appointed him his deputy to take charge of affairs in the west, while "Governor Harrison" would attend to matters in the east, and he, God, would look after the world above. He then returned to earth and began to preach as he was directed, convincing the people by exercising the wonderful powers that had been given him.

In 1890 Josephus, a Paiute informant, thus described to the scout Chapman the occasion of Wovoka's first inspiration: "About three years ago Jack Wilson took his family and went into the mountains to cut wood for Mr Dave Wilson. One day while at work he heard a great noise which appeared to be above him on the mountain. He laid down his ax and started to go in the direction of the noise, when he fell down dead, and God came and took him to heaven." Afterward on one or two other occasions "God came and took him to heaven again." Wovoka also told Chapman that he had then been preaching to the Indians about three years. In our conversation he said nothing about a mysterious noise, and stated that it was about two years since he had visited heaven and received his great revelation, but that it was about four years since he had first taught the dance to his people. The fact that he has different revelations from time to time would account for the discrepancy of statement.

He disclaimed all responsibility for the ghost shirt which formed so important a part of the dance costume among the Sioux; said that there were no trances in the dance as performed among his people — a statement confirmed by eye-witnesses among the neighboring ranchmen — and earnestly repudiated any idea of hostility toward the whites, asserting that his religion was one of universal peace. When questioned directly, he said he believed it was better for the Indians to follow the white man's road and to adopt the habits of civilization. If appearances are in evidence he is sincere in this, for he was dressed in a good suit of white man's clothing, and works regularly on a ranch, although living in a wikiup. While he repudiated almost everything for which he had been held responsible in the east, he asserted positively that he had been to the spirit world and had been given a revelation and message from God himself, with full control over the elements. From his uncle I learned that Wovoka has five songs for making it rain, the first of which brings on a mist or cloud, the second a snowfall, the third a shower, and the fourth a hard rain or storm, while when he sings the fifth song the weather again becomes clear.

I knew that he was holding something in reserve, as no Indian would unbosom himself on religious matters to a white man with whom he had not had a long and intimate acquaintance. Especially was this true in view of the warlike turn affairs had taken across the mountains. Consequently I accepted his statements with several grains of salt, but on the whole he seemed to be honest in his belief and his supernatural claims, although, like others of the priestly function, he occasionally resorts to cheap trickery to keep up the impression as to his miraculous powers. From some of the reports he is evidently an expert sleight-of-hand performer. He makes no claim to be Christ, the Son of God, as has been so often asserted in print. He does claim to be a prophet who has received a divine revelation. I could not help feeling that he was sincere in his repudiation of a number of the wonderful things attributed to him, for the reason that he insisted so strongly on other things fully as trying to the faith of a white man. He made no argument and advanced no proofs, but said simply that he had been with God, as though the statement no more admitted of controversy than the proposition that 2 and 2 are 4. From Mr J. O. Gregory, formerly employed at the agency, and well acquainted with the prophet, I learned that Wovoka had once requested him to draw up and forward to the President a statement of his supernatural claims, with a proposition that if he could receive a small regular stipend he would take up his residence on the reservation and agree to keep Nevada people informed of all the latest news from heaven and to furnish rain whenever wanted. The letter was never forwarded.

From a neighboring ranchman, who knew Wovoka well and sometimes employed him in the working season, I obtained a statement which seems to explain the whole matter. It appears that a short time before the prophet began to preach he was stricken down by a severe fever, during which illness the ranchman frequently visited and ministered to him. While he was still sick there occurred an eclipse of the sun, a phenomenon which always excites great alarm among primitive peoples. In their system the sun is a living being, of great power and beneficence, and the temporary darkness is caused by an attack on him by some supernatural monster which endeavors to devour him, and will succeed, and thus plunge the world into eternal night unless driven off by incantations and loud noises. On this occasion the Paiute were frantic with excitement and the air was filled with the noise of shouts and wailings and the firing of guns, for the purpose of frightening off the monster that threatened the life of their god. It was now, as Wovoka stated, "when the sun died," that he went to sleep in the daytime and was taken up to heaven. This means simply that the excitement and alarm produced by the eclipse, acting on a mind and body already enfeebled by sickness, resulted in delirium, in which he imagined himself to enter the portals of the spirit world. Constant dwelling on the subject in thought by day and in dreams by night would effect and perpetuate the exalted mental condition in which visions of the imagination would have all the seeming reality of actual occurrences. To those acquainted with the spiritual nature of Indians and their implicit faith in dreams all this is perfectly intelligible. His frequent trances would indicate also that, like so many other religious ecstatics, he is subject to cataleptic attacks.

I have not been able to settle satisfactorily the date of this eclipse. From inquiry at the Nautical Almanac office I learn that solar eclipses visible in Nevada and the adjacent territory from 1884 to 1890 occurred as follows: 1884, October 18, partial; 1885, March 16, partial; 1886, March 5, partial; 1887, none; 1888, none; 1889, January 1, total or partial; 1890, none. The total eclipse of January 1, 1889, agrees best with his statement to me on New Year's night, 1892, that it was about two years since he had gone up to heaven when the sun died. It must be noted that Indians generally count years by winters instead of by series of twelve calendar months, a difference which sometimes makes an apparent discrepancy of nearly a year.

In subsequent conversations he added a few minor details in regard to his vision and his doctrine. He asked many questions in regard to the eastern tribes whose delegates had visited him, and was pleased to learn that the delegates from several of these tribes were my friends. He spoke particularly of the large delegation—about twelve in number—from the Cheyenne and Arapaho, who had visited him the preceding summer and taken part in the dance with his people. Nearly all the members of this party were personally known to me, and the leader, Black Coyote, whose picture I had with me and showed to him, had been my principal instructor in the Ghost dance among the Arapaho. While this fact put me on a more confidential footing with Wovoka, it also proved of great assistance in my further investigation on my return to the prairie tribes, as, when they were satisfied from my statements and the specimens which I had brought back that I had indeed seen and talked with the messiah, they were convinced that I was earnestly desirous of understanding their religion aright, and from that time spoke freely and without reserve.

I had my camera and was anxious to get Wovoka's picture. When the subject was mentioned, he replied that his picture had never been made; that a white man had offered him five dollars for permission to take his photograph, but that he had refused. However, as I had been sent from Washington especially to learn and tell the whites all about him and his doctrine, and as he was satisfied from my acquaintance with his friends in the other tribes that I must be a good man, he would allow me to take his picture. As usual in dealing with Indians, he wanted to make the most of his bargain, and demanded two dollars and a half for the privilege of taking his picture and a like sum for each one of his family. I was prepared for this, however, and refused to pay any such charges, but agreed to give him my regular price per day for his services as informant and to send him a copy of the picture when finished. After some demur he consented and got ready for the operation by knotting a handkerchief about his neck, fastening an eagle feather at his right elbow, and taking a wide brim sombrero upon his knee. I afterward learned that the feather and sombrero were important parts of his spiritual stock in trade. After taking his picture I obtained from him, as souvenirs to bring back and show to my Indian friends in Indian Territory, a blanket of rabbit skins, some piñon nuts, some tail feathers of the magpie, highly prized by the Paiute for ornamentation, and some of the sacred red paint, endowed with most miraculous powers, which plays so important a part in the ritual of the Ghost-dance religion. Then, with mutual expressions of good will, we parted, his uncle going back to the reservation, while I took the train for Indian Territory.

As soon as the news of my arrival went abroad among the Cheyenne and Arapaho on my return, my friends of both tribes came in, eager to hear all the details of my visit to the messiah and to get my own impressions of the man. In comparing notes with some of the recent delegates I discovered something of Wovoka's hypnotic methods, and incidentally learned how much of miracle depends on the mental receptivity of the observer.

The Cheyenne and Arapaho, although for generations associated in the most intimate manner, are of very different characters. In religious matters it may be said briefly that the Arapaho are devotees and prophets, continually seeing signs and wonders, while the Cheyenne are more skeptical. In talking with Tall Bull, one of the Cheyenne delegates and then captain of the Indian police, he said that before leaving they had asked Wovoka to give them some proof of his supernatural powers. Accordingly he had ranged them in front of him, seated on the ground, he sitting facing them, with his sombrero between and his eagle feathers in his hand. Then with a quick movement he had put his hand into the empty hat and drawn out from it "something black." Tall Bull would not admit that anything more had happened, and did not seem to be very profoundly impressed by the occurrence, saying that he thought there were medicine-men of equal capacity among the Cheyenne. In talking soon afterward with Black Coyote, one of the Arapaho delegates and also a police officer, the same incident came up, but with a very different sequel. Black Coyote told how they had seated themselves on the ground in front of Wovoka, as described by Tall Bull, and went on to tell how the messiah had waved his feathers over his hat, and then, when he withdrew his hand, Black Coyote looked into the hat and there "saw the whole world." The explanation is simple. Tall Bull, who has since been stricken with paralysis, was a jovial, light-hearted fellow, fond of joking and playing tricks on his associates, but withal a man of good hard sense and disposed to be doubtful in regard to all medicine-men outside of his own tribe. Black Coyote, on the contrary, is a man of contemplative disposition, much given to speculation on the unseen world. His body and arms are covered with the scars of wounds which he has inflicted on himself in obedience to commands received in dreams. When the first news of the new religion came to the southern tribes, he had made a long journey, at his own expense, to his kindred in Wyoming, to learn the doctrine and the songs, and since his return had been drilling his people day and night in both. Now, on his visit to the fountain head of inspiration, he was prepared for great things, and when the messiah performed his hypnotic passes with the eagle feather, as I have so often witnessed in the Ghost dance, Black Coyote saw the whole spirit world where Tall Bull saw only an empty hat. From my knowledge of the men, I believe both were honest in their statements.

As a result of the confidence established between the Indians and myself in consequence of my visit to the messiah, one of the Cheyenne delegates named Black Sharp Nose, a prominent man in his tribe, soon after voluntarily brought down to me the written statement of the doctrine obtained from the messiah himself, and requested me to take it back and show it to Washington, to convince the white people that there was nothing bad or hostile in the new religion. The paper had been written by a young Arapaho of the same delegation who had learned some English at the Carlisle Indian school, and it had been taken down on the spot from the dictation of the messiah as his message to be carried to the prairie tribes. On the reverse page of the paper the daughter of Black Sharp Nose, a young woman who had also some school education, had written out the same thing in somewhat better English from her father's dictation on his return. No white man had any part, directly or indirectly, in its production, nor was it originally intended to be seen by white men. In fact, in one part the messiah himself expressly warns the delegates to tell no white man.

CHAPTER X

THE DOCTRINE OF THE GHOST DANCE

You must not fight. Do no harm to anyone. Do right always.—Woroka.

The great underlying principle of the Ghost dance doctrine is that the time will come when the whole Indian race, living and dead, will be reunited upon a regenerated earth, to live a life of aboriginal happiness, forever free from death, disease, and misery. On this foundation each tribe has built a structure from its own mythology, and each apostle and believer has filled in the details according to his own mental capacity or ideas of happiness, with such additions as come to him from the trance. Some changes, also, have undoubtedly resulted from the transmission of the doctrine through the imperfect medium of the sign language. The differences of interpretation are precisely such as we find in Christianity, with its hundreds of sects and innumerable shades of individual opinion. The white race, being alien and secondary and hardly real, has no part in this scheme of aboriginal regeneration, and will be left behind with the other things of earth that have served their temporary purpose, or else will cease entirely to exist.

All this is to be brought about by an overruling spiritual power that needs no assistance from human creatures; and though certain medicine-men were disposed to anticipate the Indian millennium by preaching resistance to the further encroachments of the whites, such teachings form no part of the true doctrine, and it was only where chronic dissatisfaction was aggravated by recent grievances, as among the Sioux, that the movement assumed a hostile expression. On the contrary, all believers were exhorted to make themselves worthy of the predicted happiness by discarding all things warlike and practicing honesty, peace, and good will, not only among themselves, but also toward the whites, so long as they were together. Some apostles have even thought that all race distinctions are to be obliterated, and that the whites are to participate with the Indians in the coming felicity; but it seems unquestionable that this is equally contrary to the doctrine as originally preached.

Different dates have been assigned at various times for the fulfillment of the prophecy. Whatever the year, it has generally been held, for very natural reasons, that the regeneration of the earth and the renewal of all life would occur in the early spring. In some cases July, and particularly the 4th of July, was the expected time. This, it may be noted, was about the season when the great annual ceremony of the sun dance formerly took place among the prairie tribes. The messiah himself has set several dates from time to time, as one prediction after another failed to materialize, and in his message to the Cheyenne and Arapaho, in August, 1891, he leaves the whole matter an open question. The date universally recognized among all the tribes immediately prior to the Sioux outbreak was the spring of 1891. As springtime came and passed, and summer grew and waned, and autumn faded again into winter without the realization of their hopes and longings, the doctrine gradually assumed its present form—that some time in the unknown future the Indian will be united with his friends who have gone before, to be forever supremely happy, and that this happiness may be anticipated in dreams, if not actually hastened in reality, by earnest and frequent attendance on the sacred dance.

On returning to the Cheyenne and Arapaho in Oklahoma, after my visit to Wovoka in January, 1892, I was at once sought by my friends of both tribes, anxious to hear the report of my journey and see the sacred things that I had brought back from the messiah. The Arapaho especially, who are of more spiritual nature than any of the other tribes, showed a deep interest and followed intently every detail of the narrative. As soon as the news of my return was spread abroad, men and women, in groups and singly, would come to me, and after grasping my hand would repeat a long and earnest prayer, sometimes aloud, sometimes with the lips silently moving, and frequently with tears rolling down the cheeks, and the whole body trembling violently from stress of emotion. Often before the prayer was ended the condition of the devotee bordered on the hysterical, very little less than in the Ghost dance itself. The substance of the prayer was usually an appeal to the messiah to hasten the coming of the promised happiness, with a petition that, as the speaker himself was unable to make the long journey, he might, by grasping the hand of one who had seen and talked with the messiah face to face, be enabled in his trance visions to catch a glimpse of the coming glory. During all this performance the bystanders awaiting their turn kept reverent silence. In a short time it became very embarrassing, but until the story had been told over and over again there was no way of escape without wounding their feelings. The same thing afterward happened among the northern Arapaho in Wyoming, one chief even holding out his hands toward me with short exclamations of *hŭ! hŭ! hŭ!* as is sometimes done by the devotees about a priest in the Ghost dance, in the hope, as he himself explained, that he might thus be enabled to go into a trance then and there. The hope, however, was not realized.

After this preliminary ordeal my visitors would ask to see the things which I had brought back from the messiah—the rabbit-skin robes, the piñon nuts, the gaming sticks, the sacred magpie feathers, and, above all, the sacred red paint. This is a bright-red ocher, about the color of brick dust, which the Paiute procure from the neighborhood of their sacred eminence, Mount Grant. It is ground, and by the help of water is made into elliptical cakes about 6 inches in length. It is the principal paint used by the Paiute in the Ghost dance, and small portions of it are given by the messiah to all the delegates and are carried back by them to their respective tribes, where it is mixed with larger quantities of their own red paint and used in decorating the faces of the participants in the dance, the painting being solemnly performed for each dancer by the medicine-man himself. It is believed to ward off sickness, to contribute to long life, and to assist the mental vision in the trance. On the battlefield of Wounded Knee I have seen this paint smeared on the posts of the inclosure about the trench in which are buried the Indians killed in the fight. I found it very hard to refuse the numerous requests for some of the paint, but as I had only one cake myself I could not afford to be too liberal. My friends were very anxious to touch it, however, but when I found that every man tried to rub off as much of it as possible on the palms of his hands, afterward smearing this dust on the faces of himself and his family, I was obliged in self-defense to put it entirely away.

The piñon nuts, although not esteemed so sacred, were also the subject of reverent curiosity. One evening, by invitation from Left Hand, the principal chief of the Arapaho, I went over to his tipi to talk with him about the messiah and his country, and brought with me a quantity of the nuts for distribution. On entering I found the chief and a number of the principal men ranged on one side of the fire, while his wife and several other women, with his young grandchildren, completed the circle on the other. Each of the adults in turn took my hand with a prayer, as before described, varying in length and earnestness according to the devotion of the speaker. This ceremony consumed a considerable time. I then produced the piñon nuts and gave them to Left Hand, telling him how they were used as food by the Paiute. He handed a portion to his wife, and before I knew what was coming the two arose in their places and stretching out their hands toward the northwest, the country of the messiah, made a long and earnest prayer aloud that *Hesûnanin*, "Our Father," would bless themselves and their children through the sacred food, and hasten the time of his coming. The others, men and women, listened with bowed heads, breaking in from time to time with similar appeals to "the Father." The scene was deeply affecting. It was another of those impressive exhibitions of natural religion which it has been my fortune to witness among the Indians, and which throw light on a side of their character of which the ordinary white observer never dreams. After the prayer the nuts were carefully divided among those present, down to the youngest infant, that all might taste of what to them was the veritable bread of life.

As I had always shown a sympathy for their ideas and feelings, and had now accomplished a long journey to the messiah himself at the cost of considerable difficulty and hardship, the Indians were at last fully satisfied that I was really desirous of learning the truth concerning their new religion. A few days after my visit to Left Hand, several of the delegates who had been sent out in the preceding August came down to see me, headed by Black Short Nose, a Cheyenne. After preliminary greetings, he stated that the Cheyenne and Arapaho were now convinced that I would tell the truth about their religion, and as they loved their religion and were anxious to have the whites know that it was all good and contained nothing bad or hostile they would now give me the message which the messiah himself had given to them, that I might take it back to show to Washington. He then took from a beaded pouch and gave to me a letter, which proved to be the message or statement of the doctrine delivered by Wovoka to the Cheyenne and Arapaho delegates, of whom Black Short Nose was one, on the occasion of their last visit to Nevada, in August, 1891, and written down on the spot, in broken English, by one of the Arapaho delegates, Casper Edson, a young man who had acquired some English education by several years' attendance at the government Indian school at Carlisle, Pennsylvania. On the reverse page of the paper was a duplicate in somewhat better English, written out by a daughter of Black Short Nose, a school girl, as dictated by her father on his return. These letters contained the message to be delivered to the two tribes, and as is expressly stated in the text were not intended to be seen by a white man. The daughter of Black Short Nose had attempted to erase this clause before her father brought the letter down to me, but the lines were still plainly visible. It is the genuine official statement of the Ghost-dance doctrine as given by the messiah himself to his disciples. It is reproduced here in duplicate and verbatim, just as received, with a translation for the benefit of those not accustomed to Carlisle English. In accordance with the request of the Indians, I brought the original to Washington, where it was read by the Indian Commissioner, Honorable T. J. Morgan, after which I had two copies made, giving one to the commissioner and retaining the other myself, returning the original to its owner, Black Short Nose.

The Messiah Letter (Arapaho version)

What you get home you make dance, and will give you the same. when you dance four days and in night one day, dance day time, five days and then fift, will wash five for every body. He likes you flok you give him good many things, he heart been satting feel good. After you get home, will give good cloud, and give you chance to make you feel good. and he give you good spirit. and he give you al a good paint.

You folks want you to come in three [months] here, any tribs from there. There will be good bit snow this year. Sometimes rain's, in fall, this year some rain, never give you any thing like that. grandfather said when he die never no cry. no hurt anybody. no fight, good behave always, it will give you satisfaction, this young man, he is a good Father and mother, dont tell no white man. Jueses was on ground, he just like cloud. Every body is alive again, I dont know when they will [be] here, may be this fall or in spring.

Every body never get sick, be young again,—(if young fellow no sick any more,) work for white men never trouble with him until you leave, when it shake the earth dont be afraid no harm any body.

You make dance for six ᵂᵉᵉᵏˢ night, and put you foot [food?] in dance to eat for every body and wash in the water. that is all to tell, I am in to you. and you will received a good words from him some time, Dont tell lie.

The Messiah Letter (*Cheyenne version*)

When you get home you have to make dance. You must dance four nights and one day time. You will take bath in the morning before you go to yours homes, for every body, and give you all the same as this. Jackson Wilson likes you all, he is glad to get good many things. His heart satting fully of gladness, after you get home, I will give you a good cloud and give you chance to make you feel good. I give you a good spirit, and give you all good paint, I want you people to come here again, want them in three months any tribs of you from there. There will be a good deal snow this year. Some time rains, in fall this year some rain, never give you any thing like that, grandfather, said, when they were die never cry, no hurt any body, do any harm for it, not to fight. Be a good behave always. It will give a satisfaction in your life. This young man is a good father and mother. Do not tell the white people about this, Juses is on the ground, he just like cloud. Every body is a live again. I don't know when he will be here, may be will be this fall or in spring. When it happen it may be this. There will be no sickness and return to young again. Do not refuse to work for white man or do not make any trouble with them until you leave them. When the earth shakes do not be afraid it will not hurt you. I want you to make dance for six weeks. Eat and wash good clean yourselves [The rest of the letter had been erased].

The Messiah Letter (*free Rendering*)

When you get home you must make a dance to continue five days. Dance four successive nights, and the last night keep up the dance until the morning of the fifth day, when all must bathe in the river and then disperse to their homes. You must all do in the same way.

I, Jack Wilson, love you all, and my heart is full of gladness for the gifts you have brought me. When you get home I shall give you a good cloud [rain?] which will make you feel good. I give you a good spirit and give you all good paint. I want you to come again in three months, some from each tribe there [the Indian Territory].

There will be a good deal of snow this year and some rain. In the fall there will be such a rain as I have never given you before.

Grandfather [a universal title of reverence among Indians and here meaning the messiah] says, when your friends die you must not cry. You must not hurt anybody or do harm to anyone. You must not fight. Do right always. It will give you satisfaction in life. This young man has a good father and mother. [Possibly this refers to Casper Edson, the young Arapaho who wrote down this message of Wovoka for the delegation].

Do not tell the white people about this. Jesus is now upon the earth. He appears like a cloud. The dead are all alive again. I do not know when they will be here; maybe this fall or in the spring. When the time comes there will be no more sickness and everyone will be young again.

Do not refuse to work for the whites and do not make any trouble with them until you leave them. When the earth shakes [at the coming of the new world] do not be afraid. It will not hurt you.

I want you to dance every six weeks. Make a feast at the dance and have food that everybody may eat. Then bathe in the water. That is all. You will receive good words again from me some time. Do not tell lies.

Every organized religion has a system of ethics, a system of mythology, and a system of ritual observance. In this message from the high priest of the Ghost dance we have a synopsis of all three. With regard to the ritual part, ceremonial purification and bathing have formed a part in some form or other of every great religion from the beginning of history, while the religious dance dates back far beyond the day when the daughter of Saul "looked through a window and saw King David leaping and dancing before the Lord." The feasting enjoined is a part of every Indian ceremonial gathering, religious, political, or social. The dance is to continue four successive nights, in accord with the regular Indian system, in which *four* is the sacred number, as *three* is in Christianity. In obedience to this message the southern prairie tribes, after the return of the delegation in August, 1891, ceased to hold frequent one-night dances at irregular intervals as formerly without the ceremonial bathing, and adopted instead a system of four-night dances at regular periods of six weeks, followed by ceremonial bathing on the morning of the fifth day.

The mythology of the doctrine is only briefly indicated, but the principal articles are given. The dead are all arisen and the spirit hosts are advancing and have already arrived at the boundaries of this earth, led forward by the regenerator in shape of cloud-like indistinctness. The spirit captain of the dead is always represented under this shadowy semblance. The great change will be ushered in by a trembling of the earth, at which the faithful are exhorted to feel no alarm. The hope held out is the same that has inspired the Christian for nineteen centuries—a happy immortality in perpetual youth. As to fixing a date, the messiah is as cautious as his predecessor in prophecy, who declares that "no man knoweth the time, not even the angels of God." His weather predictions also are about as definite as the inspired utterances of the Delphian oracle.

The moral code inculcated is as pure and comprehensive in its simplicity as anything found in religious systems from the days of Gautama Buddha to the time of Jesus Christ. "*Do no harm to any one. Do right always.*" Could anything be more simple, and yet more exact and exacting? It inculcates honesty—"*Do not tell lies.*" It preaches good will—"*Do no harm to any one.*" It forbids the extravagant mourning customs formerly common among the tribes—"*When your friends die, you must not cry,*" which is interpreted by the prairie tribes as forbidding the killing of horses, the burning of tipis and destruction of property, the cutting off of the hair and the gashing of the body with knives, all of which were formerly the sickening rule at every death until forbidden by the new doctrine. As an Arapaho said to me when his little boy died, "I shall not shoot any ponies, and my wife will not gash her arms. We used to do this when our friends died, because we thought we would never see them again, and it made us feel bad. But now we know we shall all be united again." If the Kiowa had held to the Ghost-dance doctrine instead of abandoning it as they had done, they would have been spared the loss of thousands of dollars in horses, tipis, wagons, and other property destroyed, with much of the mental suffering and all of the physical laceration that resulted in consequence of the recent fatal epidemic in the tribe, when for weeks and months the sound of wailing went up night and morning, and in every camp men and women could be seen daily, with dress disordered and hair cut close to the scalp, with blood hardened in clots upon the skin, or streaming from mutilated fingers and fresh gashes on face, and arms, and legs. It preaches peace with the whites and obedience to authority until the day of deliverance shall come. Above all, it forbids war— "*You must not fight.*" It is hardly possible for us to realize the tremendous and radical change which this doctrine works in the whole spirit of savage life. The career of every Indian has been the war-path. His proudest title has been that of warrior. His conversation by day and his dreams by night have been of bloody deeds upon the enemies of his tribe. His highest boast was in the number of his scalp trophies, and his chief delight at home was in the war dance and the scalp dance. The thirst for blood and massacre seemed inborn in every man, woman, and child of every tribe. Now comes a prophet as a messenger from God to forbid not only war, but all that savors of war—the war dance, the scalp dance, and even the bloody torture of the sun dance—and his teaching is accepted and his words obeyed by four-fifths of all the warlike predatory tribes of the mountains and the great plains. Only those who have known the deadly hatred that once animated Ute, Cheyenne, and Pawnee, one toward another, and are able to contrast it with their present spirit of mutual brotherly love, can know what the Ghost-dance religion has accomplished in bringing the savage into civilization. It is such a revolution as comes but once in the life of a race.

The beliefs held among the various tribes in regard to the final catastrophe are as fairly probable as some held on the same subject by more orthodox authorities. As to the dance itself, with its scenes of intense excitement, spasmodic action, and physical exhaustion even to unconsciousness, such manifestations have always accompanied religious upheavals among primitive peoples, and are not entirely unknown among ourselves. In a country which produces magnetic healers, shakers, trance mediums, and the like, all these things may very easily be paralleled without going far from home.

In conclusion, we may say of the prophet and his doctrine what has been said of one of his apostles by a careful and competent investigator: "He has given these people a better religion than they ever had before, taught them precepts which, if faithfully carried out, will bring them into better accord with their white neighbors, and has prepared the way for their final Christianization." (*G. D., 4,* and *A. G. O., 5.*)

We may now consider details of the doctrine as held by different tribes, beginning with the Paiute, among whom it originated. The best account of the Paiute belief is contained in a report to the War Department by Captain J. M. Lee, who was sent out in the autumn of 1890 to investigate the temper and fighting strength of the Paiute and other Indians in the vicinity of Fort Bidwell in northeastern California. We give the statement obtained by him from Captain Dick, a Paiute, as delivered one day in a conversational way and apparently without reserve, after nearly all the Indians had left the room:

Long time, twenty years ago, Indian medicine-man in Mason's valley at Walker lake talk same way, same as you hear now. In one year, maybe, after he begin talk he die. Three years ago another medicine-man begin same talk. Heap talk all time. Indians hear all about it everywhere. Indians come from long way off to hear him. They come from the east; they make signs. Two years ago me go to Winnemucca and Pyramid lake, me see Indian Sam, a head man, and Johnson Sides. Sam he tell me he just been to see Indian medicine-man to hear him talk. Sam say medicine-man talk this way:

"All Indians must dance, everywhere, keep on dancing. Pretty soon in next spring Big Man [Great Spirit] come. He bring back all game of every kind. The game be thick everywhere. All dead Indians come back and live again. They all be strong just like young men, be young again. Old blind Indian see again and get young and have fine time. When Old Man [God] comes this way, then all the Indians go to mountains, high up away from whites. Whites can't hurt Indians then. Then while Indians way up high, big flood comes like water and all white people die, get drowned. After that water go way and then nobody but Indians everywhere and game all kinds thick. Then medicine-man tell Indians to send word to all Indians to keep up dancing and the good time will come. Indians who don't dance, who don't believe in this word, will grow little, just about a foot high, and stay that way. Some of them will be turned into wood and be burned in fire." That's the way Sam tell me the medicine-man talk. (A. G. O., 6.)

Lieutenant N. P. Phister, who gathered a part of the material embodied in Captain Lee's report, confirms this general statement and gives a few additional particulars. The flood is to consist of mingled mud and water, and when the faithful go up into the mountains, the skeptics will be left behind and will be turned to stone. The prophet claims to receive these revelations directly from God and the spirits of the dead Indians during his trances. He asserts also that he is invulnerable, and that if soldiers should attempt to kill him they would fall down as if they had no bones and die, while he would still live, even though cut into little pieces. (Phister, 3.)

One of the first and most prominent of those who brought the doctrine to the prairie tribes was Porcupine, a Cheyenne, who crossed the mountains with several companions in the fall of 1889, visited Wovoka, and attended the dance near Walker lake, Nevada. In his report of his experiences, made some months later to a military officer, he states that Wovoka claimed to be Christ himself, who had come back again, many centuries after his first rejection, in pity to teach his children. He quotes the prophet as saying:

I found my children were bad, so I went back to heaven and left them. I told them that in so many hundred years I would come back to see my children. At the end of this time I was sent back to try to teach them. My father told me the earth was getting old and worn out and the people getting bad, and that I was to renew everything as it used to be and make it better.

He also told us that all our dead were to be resurrected; that they were all to come back to earth, and that, as the earth was too small for them and us, he would do away with heaven and make the earth itself large enough to contain us all; that we must tell all the people we met about these things. He spoke to us about fighting, and said that was bad and we must keep from it; that the earth was to be all good hereafter, and we must all be friends with one another. He said that in the fall of the year the youth of all good people would be renewed, so that nobody would be more than forty years old, and that if they behaved themselves well after this the youth of everyone would be renewed in the spring. He said if we were all good he would send people among us who could heal all our wounds and sickness by mere touch and that we would live forever. He told us not to quarrel or fight or strike each other, or shoot one another; that the whites and Indians were to be all one people. He said if any man disobeyed what he ordered his tribe would be wiped from the face of the earth; that we must believe everything he said, and we must not doubt him or say he lied; that if we did, he would know it; that he would know our thoughts and actions in no matter what part of the world we might be. (*G. D., 5.*)

Here we have the statement that both races are to live together as one. We have also the doctrine of healing by touch. Whether or not this is an essential part of the system is questionable, but it is certain that the faithful believe that great physical good comes to them, to their children, and to the sick from the imposition of hands by the priests of the dance, apart from the ability thus conferred to see the things of the spiritual world.

Another idea here presented, namely, that the earth becomes old and decrepit, and requires that its youth be renewed at the end of certain great cycles, is common to a number of tribes, and has an important place in the oldest religions of the world. As an Arapaho who spoke English expressed it, "This earth too old, grass too old, trees too old, our lives too old. Then all be new again." Captain H. L. Scott also found among the southern plains tribes the same belief that the rivers, the mountains, and the earth itself are worn out and must be renewed, together with an indefinite idea that both races alike must die at the same time, to be resurrected in new but separate worlds.

The Washo, Pit River, Bannock, and other tribes adjoining the Paiute on the north and west hold the doctrine substantially as taught by the messiah himself. We have but little light in regard to the belief as held by the Walapai, Cohonino, Mohave, and Navaho to the southward, beyond the general fact that the resurrection and return of the dead formed the principal tenet. As these tribes received their knowledge of the new religion directly from Paiute apostles, it is quite probable that they made but few changes in or additions to the original gospel.

A witness of the dance among the Walapai in 1891 obtained from the leaders of the ceremony about the same statement of doctrine already mentioned as held by the Paiute, from whom also the Walapai had adopted many of the songs and ceremonial words used in connection with the dance. They were then expecting the Indian redeemer to appear on earth some time within three or four years. They were particularly anxious to have it understood that their intentions were not hostile toward the whites and that they desired to live in peace with them until the redeemer came, but that then they would be unable to prevent their destruction even if they wished. (*J. F. L., 3.*)

The manner of the final change and the destruction of the whites has been variously interpreted as the doctrine was carried from its original center. East of the mountains it is commonly held that a deep sleep will come on the believers, during which the great catastrophe will be accomplished, and the faithful will awake to immortality on a new earth. The Shoshoni of Wyoming say this sleep will continue four days and nights, and that on the morning of the fifth day all will open their eyes in a new world where both races will dwell together forever. The Cheyenne, Arapaho, Kiowa, and others, of Oklahoma, say that the new earth, with all the resurrected dead from the beginning, and with the buffalo, the elk, and other game upon it, will come from the west and slide over the surface of the present earth, as the right hand might slide over the left. As it approaches, the Indians will be carried upward and alight on it by the aid of the sacred dance feathers which they wear in their hair and which will act as wings to bear them up. They will then become unconscious for four days, and on waking out of their trance will find themselves with their former friends in the midst of all the oldtime surroundings. By Sitting Bull, the Arapaho apostle, it is thought that this new earth as it advances will be preceded by a wall of fire which will drive the whites across the water to their original and proper country, while the Indians will be enabled by means of the sacred feathers to surmount the flames and reach the promised land. When the expulsion of the whites has been accomplished, the fire will be extinguished by a rain continuing twelve days. By a few it is believed that a hurricane with thunder and lightning will come to destroy the whites alone. This last idea is said to be held also by the Walapai of Arizona, who extend its provisions to include the unbelieving Indians as well. (*G. D., 6.*) The doctrine held by the Caddo, Wichita, and Delaware, of Oklahoma, is practically the same as is held by the Arapaho and Cheyenne from whom they obtained it. All these tribes believe that the destruction or removal of the whites is to be accomplished entirely by supernatural means, and they severely blame the Sioux for having provoked a physical conflict by their impatience instead of waiting for their God to deliver them in his own good time.

Among all the tribes which have accepted the new faith it is held that frequent devout attendance on the dance conduces to ward off disease and restore the sick to health, this applying not only to the actual participants, but also to their children and friends. The idea of obtaining temporal blessings as the reward of a faithful performance of religious duties is too natural and universal to require comment. The purification by the sweat-bath, which forms an important preliminary to the dance among the Sioux, while devotional in its purpose, is probably also sanitary in its effect.

Among the powerful and warlike Sioux of the Dakotas, already restless under both old and recent grievances, and more lately brought to the edge of starvation by a reduction of rations, the doctrine speedily assumed a hostile meaning and developed some peculiar features, for which reason it deserves particular notice as concerns this tribe. The earliest rumors of the new messiah came to the Sioux from the more western tribes in the winter of 1888–89, but the first definite account was brought by a delegation which crossed the mountains to visit the messiah in the fall of 1889, returning in the spring of 1890. On the report of these delegates the dance was at once inaugurated and spread so rapidly that in a few months the new religion had been accepted by the majority of the tribe.

Perhaps the best statement of the Sioux version is given by the veteran agent, James McLaughlin, of Standing Rock agency. In an official letter of October 17, 1890, he writes that the Sioux, under the influence of Sitting Bull, were greatly excited over the near approach of a predicted Indian millennium or "return of the ghosts," when the white man would be annihilated and the Indian again supreme, and which the medicine-men had promised was to occur as soon as the grass was green in the spring. They were told that the Great Spirit had sent upon them the dominant race to punish them for their sins, and that their sins were now expiated and the time of deliverance was at hand. Their decimated ranks were to be reinforced by all the Indians who had ever died, and these spirits were already on their way to reinhabit the earth, which had originally belonged to the Indians, and were driving before them, as they advanced, immense herds of buffalo and fine ponies. The Great Spirit, who had so long deserted his red children, was now once more with them and against the whites, and the white man's gunpowder would no longer have power to drive a bullet through the skin of an Indian. The whites themselves would soon be overwhelmed and smothered under a deep landslide, held down by sod and timber, and the few who might escape would become small fishes in the rivers. In order to bring about this happy result, the Indians must believe and organize the Ghost dance.

The agent continues:

It would seem impossible that any person, no matter how ignorant, could be brought to believe such absurd nonsense, but as a matter of fact a great many Indians of this agency actually believe it, and since this new doctrine has been ingrafted here from the more southern Sioux agencies the infection has been wonderful, and so pernicious that it now includes some of the Indians who were formerly numbered with the progressive and more intelligent, and many of our very best Indians appear dazed and undecided when talking of it, their inherent superstition having been thoroughly aroused. (*G. D.*, 7.)

The following extract is from a translation of a letter dated March 30, 1891, written in Sioux by an Indian at Pine Ridge to a friend at Rosebud agency:

And now I will tell another thing. Lately there is a man died and come to life again, and he say he has been to Indian nation of ghosts, and tells us dead Indian nation all coming home. The Indian ghost tell him come after his war bonnet. The Indian (not ghost Indian) gave him his war bonnet and he died again. (G. D., S.)

The Sioux, like other tribes, believed that at the moment of the catastrophe the earth would tremble. According to one version the landslide was to be accompanied by a flood of water, which would flow into the mouths of the whites and cause them to choke with mud. Storms and whirlwinds were also to assist in their destruction. The Indians were to surmount the avalanche, probably in the manner described in speaking of the southern tribes, and on reaching the surface of the new earth would behold boundless prairies covered with long grass and filled with great herds of buffalo and other game. When the time was near at hand, they must assemble at certain places of rendezvous and prepare for the final abandonment of all earthly things by stripping off their clothing. In accordance with the general idea of a return to aboriginal habits, the believers, as far as possible, discarded white man's dress and utensils. Those who could procure buckskin—which is now very scarce in the Sioux country—resumed buckskin dress, while the dancers put on "ghost shirts" made of cloth, but cut and ornamented in Indian fashion. No metal of any kind was allowed in the dance, no knives, and not even the earrings or belts of imitation silver which form such an important part of prairie Indian costume. This was at variance with the custom among the Cheyenne and other southern tribes, where the women always wear in the dance their finest belts studded with large disks of German silver. The beads used so freely on moccasins and leggings seem to have been regarded as a substitute for the oldtime wampum and porcupine quill work, and were therefore not included in the prohibition. No weapon of any kind was allowed to be carried in the Ghost dance by any tribe, north or south, a fact which effectually disposes of the assertion that this was another variety of war dance. At certain of the Sioux dances, however, sacred arrows and a sacred bow, with other things, were tied on the tree in the center of the circle.

Valuable light in regard to the Sioux version of the doctrine is obtained from the sermon delivered at Red Leaf camp, on Pine Ridge reservation, October 31, 1890, by Short Bull, one of those who had been selected to visit the messiah, and who afterward became one of the prime leaders in the dance:

My friends and relations: I will soon start this thing in running order. I have told you that this would come to pass in two seasons, but since the whites are interfering so much, I will advance the time from what my father above told me to do, so the time will be shorter. Therefore you must not be afraid of anything. Some of my relations have no ears, so I will have them blown away.

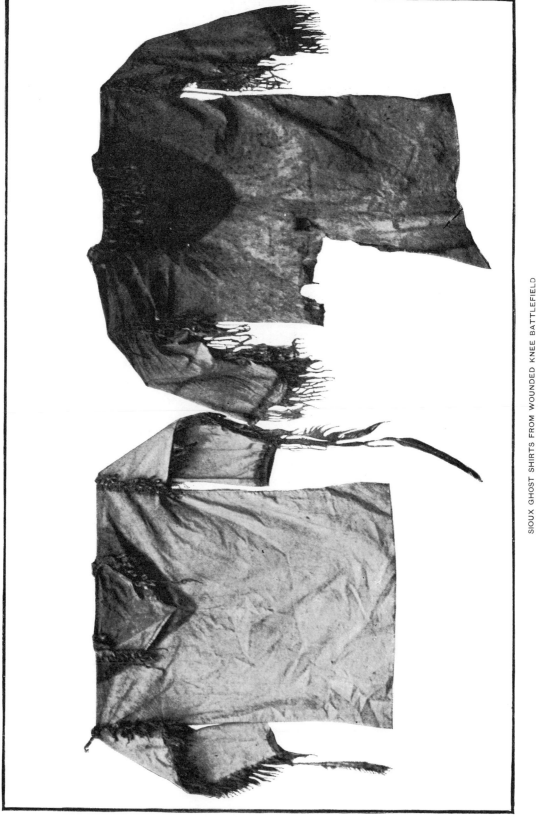

SIOUX GHOST SHIRTS FROM WOUNDED KNEE BATTLEFIELD

EXPLANATION OF PLATE XCIII

The originals of these ghost shirts, now in the National Museum, were taken, by scouts present during the fight, from the bodies of Indians killed at Wounded Knee, and were obtained by the author, at Pine Ridge, from Philip Wells and Louis Menard, mixed-blood interpreters, the former having also been present as interpreter for the Indian scouts during the fight. They are made of coarse white cloth, sewn with sinew. One of the shirts is partially burned, having probably been taken out of one of the tipis overturned and set on fire during the action. Two other ghost shirts, said to be from the same battlefield, are also in the National Museum.

Now, there will be a tree sprout up, and there all the members of our religion and the tribe must gather together. That will be the place where we will see our dead relations. But before this time we must dance the balance of this moon, at the end of which time the earth will shiver very hard. Whenever this thing occurs, I will start the wind to blow. We are the ones who will then see our fathers, mothers, and everybody. We, the tribe of Indians, are the ones who are living a sacred life. God, our father himself, has told and commanded and shown me to do these things.

Our father in heaven has placed a mark at each point of the four winds. First, a clay pipe, which lies at the setting of the sun and represents the Sioux tribe. Second, there is a holy arrow lying at the north, which represents the Cheyenne tribe. Third, at the rising of the sun there lies hail, representing the Arapaho tribe. Fourth, there lies a pipe and nice feather at the south, which represents the Crow tribe. My father has shown me these things, therefore we must continue this dance. If the soldiers surround you four deep, three of you, on whom I have put holy shirts, will sing a song, which I have taught you, around them, when some of them will drop dead. Then the rest will start to run, but their horses will sink into the earth. The riders will jump from their horses, but they will sink into the earth also. Then you can do as you desire with them. Now, you must know this, that all the soldiers and that race will be dead. There will be only five thousand of them left living on the earth. My friends and relations, this is straight and true.

Now, we must gather at Pass creek where the tree is sprouting. There we will go among our dead relations. You must not take any earthly things with you. Then the men must take off all their clothing and the women must do the same. No one shall be ashamed of exposing their persons. My father above has told us to do this, and we must do as he says. You must not be afraid of anything. The guns are the only things we are afraid of, but they belong to our father in heaven. He will see that they do no harm. Whatever white men may tell you, do not listen to them, my relations. This is all. I will now raise my hand up to my father and close what he has said to you through me. (*Short Bull; War, 4.*)

The pipe here referred to is the most sacred thing in Sioux mythology and will be more fully described in treating of the Sioux songs. The sacred object of the Cheyenne is the "medicine arrow," now in the keeping of the band living near Cantonment, Oklahoma. The Crow and Arapaho references are not so clear. The Arapaho are called by the Sioux the "Blue Cloud" people, a name which may possibly have some connection with hail. The sprouting tree at which all the believers must gather refers to the tree or pole which the Sioux planted in the center of the dance circle. The cardinal directions here assigned to the other tribes may refer to their former locations with regard to the Sioux. The Cheyenne and Arapaho, who now live far west and south of the Sioux, originally lived north and east of them, about Red river and the Saskatchewan.

The most noted thing connected with the Ghost dance among the Sioux is the "ghost shirt" which was worn by all adherents of the doctrine—men, women, and children alike. It is described by Captain Sword in his account of the Ghost dance, given in the appendix to this chapter, and will be noticed at length hereafter in treating of the ceremony of the dance. During the dance it was worn as an outside garment, but was said to be worn at other times under the ordinary dress. Although the shape, fringing, and feather adornment were practically the same in every case, considerable variation existed in regard to the painting, the designs on some being very simple, while the others were fairly covered with representations of sun, moon, stars, the sacred things of their mythology, and the visions of the trance. The feathers attached to the garment were always those of the eagle, and the thread used in the sewing was always the old-time sinew. In some cases the fringe or other portions were painted with the sacred red paint of the messiah. The shirt was firmly believed to be impenetrable to bullets or weapons of any sort. When one of the women shot in the Wounded Knee massacre was approached as she lay in the church and told that she must let them remove her ghost shirt in order the better to get at her wound, she replied: "Yes; take it off. They told me a bullet would not go through. Now I don't want it any more."

The protective idea in connection with the ghost shirt does not seem to be aboriginal. The Indian warrior habitually went into battle naked above the waist. His protecting "medicine" was a feather, a tiny bag of some sacred powder, the claw of an animal, the head of a bird, or some other small object which could be readily twisted into his hair or hidden between the covers of his shield without attracting attention. Its virtue depended entirely on the ceremony of the consecration and not on size or texture. The war paint had the same magic power of protection. To cover the body in battle was not in accordance with Indian usage, which demanded that the warrior should be as free and unincumbered in movement as possible. The so-called "war shirt" was worn chiefly in ceremonial dress parades and only rarely on the war-path.

Dreams are but incoherent combinations of waking ideas, and there is a hint of recollection even in the wildest visions of sleep. The ghost shirt may easily have been an inspiration from a trance, while the trance vision itself was the result of ideas derived from previous observation or report. The author is strongly inclined to the opinion that the idea of an invulnerable sacred garment is not original with the Indians, but, like several other important points pertaining to the Ghost-dance doctrine, is a practical adaptation by them of ideas derived from contact with some sectarian body among the whites. It may have been suggested by the "endowment robe" of the Mormons, a seamless garment of white muslin adorned with symbolic figures, which is worn by their initiates as the most sacred badge of their faith, and by many of the believers is supposed to render the wearer invulnerable. The Mormons have always manifested a particular interest in the Indians, whom they regard as the Lamanites of their sacred writings, and hence have made special efforts for their evangelization, with the result that a considerable number of the neighboring tribes of Ute, Paiute, Bannock, and Shoshoni have been received into the Mormon church and invested with the endowment robe. (See the appendix to this chapter: "The Mormons and the Indians;" also "Tell It All," by Mrs T. B. H. Stenhouse.) The Shoshoni and northern Arapaho occupy the same reservation in Wyoming, and anything which concerns one tribe is more or less talked of by the other. As the Sioux, Cheyenne, and other eastern tribes make frequent visits to the Arapaho, and as these Arapaho have been the great apostles of the Ghost dance, it is easy to see how an idea borrowed by the Shoshoni from the Mormons could find its way through the Arapaho first to the Sioux and Cheyenne and afterward to more remote tribes. Wovoka himself expressly disclaimed any responsibility for the ghost shirt, and whites and Indians alike agreed that it formed no part of the dance costume in Mason valley. When I first went among the Cheyenne and neighboring tribes of Oklahoma in January, 1891, the ghost shirt had not yet reached them. Soon afterward the first one was brought down from the Sioux country by a Cheyenne named White Buffalo, who had been a Carlisle student, but the Arapaho and Cheyenne, after debating the matter, refused to allow it to be worn in the dance, on the ground that the doctrine of the Ghost dance was one of peace, whereas the Sioux had made the ghost shirt an auxiliary of war. In consequence of this decision such shirts have never been worn by the dancers among the southern tribes. Instead they wear in the dance their finest shirts and dresses of buckskin, covered with painted and beaded figures from the Ghost-dance mythology and the visions of the trance.

The Ghost dance is variously named among the different tribes. In its original home among the Paiute it is called *Nänigükwa*, "dance in a circle" (*nüka*, dance), to distinguish it from the other dances of the tribe, which have only the ordinary up-and-down step without the circular movement. The Shoshoni call it *Tänä'räyün* or *Tämanä'rayära*, which may be rendered "everybody dragging," in allusion to the manner in which the dancers move around the circle holding hands, as children do in their ring games. They insist that it is a revival of a similar dance which existed among them fifty years ago. The Comanche call it *A'p-anĕka'ra*, "the Father's dance," or sometimes the dance "with joined hands." The Kiowa call it *Mânposo'ti guan*, "dance with clasped hands," and the frenzy, *guan â'dalka-i*, "dance craziness." The Caddo know it as *Ä'ă kakĭ'mbawi'ut*, "the prayer of all to the Father," or as the *Nänisana ka au'-shan*, "nänisana dance," from *nänisana*, "my children," which forms the burden of so many of the ghost songs in the language of the Arapaho, from whom they obtained the dance. By the Sioux, Arapaho, and most other prairie tribes it is called the "spirit" or "ghost" dance (Sioux, *Wana'ghi wa'chipi;* Arapaho, *Thigû'nawat*), from the fact that everything connected with it relates to the coming of the spirits of the dead from the spirit world, and by this name it has become known among the whites.

APPENDIX

THE MORMONS AND THE INDIANS

While the Indian excitement was at its height in 1892, a curious pamphlet was published anonymously at Salt Lake City in connection with a proposed series of lectures, from which we make some extracts for the light they give on the Mormon attitude toward the Indians. The pamphlet is headed, "The Mormons have stepped down and out of Celestial Government—the American Indians have stepped up and into Celestial Government." It begins by stating that the Messiah came to His people at the time appointed of the Father—March, 1890—notwithstanding the assertion in the Deseret Evening News, made January, 1892: '1890 has passed, and no Messiah has come.'" It goes on to say:

"1891 has passed, and no pruning of the vineyard." The vineyard of the Lord is the house of Israel.—Isa. 5: 7. In the part of the vineyard the American Indians, descendants of the righteous branch of Joseph, who were led to the Western Continent or hemisphere—Zion—we find the vine, the stone-power of the Latter Days. Ps. 80.

The celestial prophet, seer, and revelator, Joseph Smith, jr., prophesied on the 2d of April, 1843, that the Messiah would reveal himself to man in mortality in 1890. Doctrine and Covenants, 130, 15, 17, which reads: "I was once praying very earnestly to know the time of the coming of the Son of Man, when I heard a voice speak the following: 'Joseph, my son, if thou livest until thou art eighty-five years old, thou shalt see the face of the Son of Man.'"

   *   *   *   *   *   *   *

Five years later (than 1882) the sign that was to usher in the work of the Father was given to the American Indians, while March, 1890, witnesses the organization of a church under the restored order, where twelve disciples were chosen and ordained, whose first allegiance is given irrevocably to the Lord God, whereas that of the Celestial Church is given to the government fostering it.

   *   *   *   *   *   *   *

The following seven signs were to precede the fullness of the Gentiles upon the land of America; Zion, the time, place, and parties given with each. [The first, second, and third "signs" are omitted here.]

4. When the Bible and Book of Mormon become one in the hands of the Messiah. Ezk. 37: 19; III Nephi, 21: 1–7. In 1887, sixty years after the plates were delivered to Joseph Smith, jr., the Book of Mormon in Spanish was delivered to the American Indians, with the promise to those who are identified with the Gentiles that if they will not harden their hearts, but will repent and know the true points of my doctrine they shall be numbered with my covenant people, the Branch of Joseph. Doctrine and Covenant, 19:59–62; 20:8–17; III Nephi, 21:1–7.

5. The coming of the Messiah. Three years later, March, 1890, the people of God, who were notified by the three Nephites, met at Walkers lake, Esmeralda county, Nevada, where a dispensation of the Celestial kingdom of God—the gospel in the covenant of consecration, a perfect oneness in all things, temporal and spiritual—was given unto them. Twelve disciples were ordained, not by angels or men, but by the Messiah, in the presence of hundreds, representing scores of tribes or nations, who saw his face, heard and understood his voice as on the day of pentecost. Acts 2, also fulfilling sec. 90:9, 10, 11 of Doctrine and Covenant. Ezk. 20:33–37.

6. The Fulness of the Gentiles. In 1492, the Lord God let His vineyard to the nations of the Gentiles, to punish His people the Branch of Joseph for 400 years (Gen. 15: 13), bringing the fulness of the Gentiles the end of their rule over the American Indians. October, 1892, Rom. II: 25–26; Gen. 50: 25; New Trans. Matt. 21: 33–41.

7. The Pruning of the Vineyard. The husbandmen upon this land began the last pruning of the vineyard in 1891. Prominent among which stands our government in fulfilling Matt. 21: 33–41, saying, let us kill the heirs and hold the inheritance, as shown in the massacre of Wounded Knee; the butchery of Sitting Bull; the imprisonment of Short Bull and others; the breaking up of reservations, and the attempts to destroy the treaty stipulations above mentioned by forcing the mark of the Beast, citizenship and statehood, upon the American Indians, which will ultimately terminate in a war of extermination. Isa. 10: 24–27; Dan. 2: 34; Isa. 14: 21.

According to the astronomical, prophetic, and historical evidence found in the Bible, Book of Mormon, and Doctrine and Covenants for the redemption of Zion and the restoration of Israel, there are seven celestial keys of powers to be used which can not be handled by apostles, prophets, or angels. They can only be handled by the Messiah and his Father.

* * * * * * *

2. The key of power that restores the heirs, the American Indians, to their own lands consecrating to them the wealth of the Gentiles.

3. The key of power that turns away ungodliness from Jacob (the American Indians) enabling them to build the temple on the spot pointed out by the finger of God (Independence, Jackson County, Missouri), on which the true sign of Israel is to rest, the glory of the living God of the Hebrews, the cloud by day and the pillar of fire by night by the close of this generation, 1896.

* * * * * * *

On and after July 10, 1892, free lectures illustrated by figures, will be given weekly, on Sunday, Monday, and Tuesday, from 6.30 to 8.30 p. m. (weather permitting), at the book stand in the Nineteenth Ward, opposite Margett's Brewery, No. 312 North Second West.

First. On the coming of the Messiah to the Hebrews, at the sacrifice of Esau, near the close of the 400-year bondage of Jacob in the morning of the Abrahamic Covenant, B. C. 1491.

Second. On the coming of the Messiah to the Jews, at the Meridian sacrifice of Jacob at the close of the last 1921 years of the covenant, the year one A. D.

Third. On the coming of the Messiah to the American Indians, the remnants, at the evening sacrifice of Esau, near the expiration of the evening bondage of Jacob of 400 years, 1892, in the last 430 years of the covenant.

PORCUPINE'S ACCOUNT OF THE MESSIAH

The following statement was made to Major Carroll, in command of Camp Crook, at Tongue River agency, Montana, June 15, 1890, and transmitted through the War Department to the Indian Office:

In November last [1889] I left the reservation with two other Cheyennes. I went through [Fort] Washakie and took the Union Pacific railroad at Rawlins. We got on early in the morning about breakfast, rode all day on the railroad, and about dark reached a fort [Bridger?]. I stayed there two days, and then took a passenger train, and the next morning got to Fort Hall. I found some lodges of Snakes and Bannocks there. I saw the agent here, and he told me I could stay at the agency, but the chief of the Bannocks who was there took me to his camp near by. The Bannocks told me they were glad to see a Cheyenne and that we ought to make a treaty with the Bannocks.

The chief told me he had been to Washington and had seen the President, and that we ought all to be friends with the whites and live at peace with them and with each other. We talked these matters over for ten days. The agent then sent for me and some of the Bannocks and Shoshones, and asked me where I was going. I told him I was just traveling to meet other Indians and see other countries; that my people were at peace with the whites, and I thought I could travel anywhere I wished. He asked me why I did not have a pass. I said because my agent would not give me one. He said he was glad to see me anyhow, and that the whites and Indians were all friends. Then he asked me where I wanted a pass. I told him I wanted to go further and some Bannocks and Shoshones wanted to go along. He gave passes—five of them—to the chiefs of the three parties. We took the railroad to a little town near by, and then took a narrow-gauge road. We went on this, riding all night at a very fast rate of speed, and came to a town on a big lake [Ogden or Salt Lake City]. We stayed there one day, taking the cars at night, rode all night, and the next morning about 9 oclock saw a settlement of Indians. We traveled south, going on a narrow-gauge road. We got off at this Indian town. The Indians here were different from any Indians I ever saw. The women and men were dressed in white people's clothes, the women having their hair banged. These Indians had their faces painted white with black spots. We stayed with these people all day. We took the same road at night and kept on. We traveled all night, and about daylight we saw a lot of houses, and they told us there were a lot more Indians there; so we got off, and there is where we saw Indians living in huts of grass [tulé?]. We stopped here and got something to eat. There were whites living near by. We got on the cars again at night, and during the night we got off among some Indians, who were fish-eaters [Paiute]. We stayed among the Fish-eaters till morning, and then got into a wagon with the son of the chief of the Fish-eaters, and we arrived about noon at an agency on a big river. There was also a big lake near the agency.

The agent asked us where we were from and said we were a long ways from home, and that he would write to our agent and let him know we were all right. From this agency we went back to the station, and they told us there were some more Indians to the south. One of the chiefs of the Fish-eaters then furnished us with four wagons. We traveled all day, and then came to another railroad. We left our wagons here and took the railroad, the Fish-eaters telling us there were some more Indians along the railroad who wanted to see us. We took this railroad about 2 oclock and about sun down got to another agency, where there were more Fish-eaters. [From diagrams drawn and explanations given of them in addition to the foregoing, there seems to be no doubt that the lakes visited are Pyramid and Walker lakes, western Nevada, and the agencies those of the same name.]

They told us they had heard from the Shoshone agency that the people in this country were all bad people, but that they were good people there. All the Indians from the Bannock agency down to where I finally stopped danced this dance [referring to the late religious dances at the Cheyenne agency], the whites often dancing it themselves. [It will be recollected that he traveled constantly through the Mormon country.] I knew nothing about this dance before going. I happened to run across it, that is all. I will tell you about it. [Here all the Indian auditors removed their hats in token that the talk to follow was to be on a religious subject.] I want you all to listen to this, so that there will be no mistake. There is no harm in what I am to say to anyone. I heard this where I met my friends in Nevada. It is a wonder you people never heard this before. In the dance we had there [Nevada] the whites and Indians danced together. I met there a great many kinds of people, but they all seemed to know all about this religion. The people there seemed all to be good. I never saw any drinking or fighting or bad conduct among them. They treated me well on the cars, without pay. They gave me food without charge, and I found that this was a habit among them toward their neighbors. I thought it strange that the people there should have been so good, so different from those here.

What I am going to say is the truth. The two men sitting near me were with me, and will bear witness that I speak the truth. I and my people have been living in ignorance until I went and found out the truth. All the whites and Indians are brothers, I was told there. I never knew this before.

The Fish-eaters near Pyramid lake told me that Christ had appeared on earth again. They said Christ knew he was coming; that eleven of his children were also coming from a far land. It appeared that Christ had sent for me to go there, and that was why unconsciously I took my journey. It had been foreordained. Christ had summoned myself and others from all heathen tribes, from two to three or four from each of fifteen or sixteen different tribes. There were more different languages than I ever heard before and I did not understand any of them. They told me when I got there that my great father was there also, but did not know who he was. The people assembled called a council, and the chief's son went to see the Great Father [messiah], who sent word to us to remain fourteen days in that camp and that he would come to see us. He sent me a small package of something white to eat that I did not know the name of. There were a great many people in the council, and this white food was divided among them. The food was a big white nut. Then I went to the agency at Walker lake and they told us Christ would be there in two days. At the end of two days, on the third morning, hundreds of people gathered at this place. They cleared off a place near the agency in the form of a circus ring and we all gathered there. This space was perfectly cleared of grass, etc. We waited there till late in the evening anxious to see Christ. Just before sundown I saw a great many people, mostly Indians, coming dressed in white men's clothes. The Christ was with them. They all formed in this ring around it. They put up sheets all around the circle, as they had no tents. Just after dark some of the Indians told me that the Christ [Father] was arrived. I looked around to find him, and finally saw him sitting on one side of the ring. They all started toward him to see him. They made a big fire to throw light on him. I never looked around, but went forward, and when I saw him I bent my head. I had always thought the Great Father was a white man, but this man looked like an Indian. He sat there a long time and nobody went up to speak to him. He sat with his head bowed all the time. After awhile he rose and said he was very glad to see his children. "I have sent for you and am glad to see you. I am going to talk to you after awhile about your relatives who are dead and gone. My children, I want you to listen to all I have to say to you. I will teach you, too, how to dance a dance, and I want you to dance it. Get ready for your dance and then, when the dance is over, I will talk to you." He was dressed in a white coat with stripes. The rest of his dress was a white man's except that he had on a pair of moccasins. Then he commenced our dance, everybody joining in, the Christ singing while we danced. We danced till late in the night, when he told us we had danced enough.

The next morning, after breakfast was over, we went into the circle and spread canvas over it on the ground, the Christ standing in the midst of us. He told us he was going away that day, but would be back that next morning and talk to us.

In the night when I first saw him I thought he was an Indian, but the next day when I could see better he looked different. He was not so dark as an Indian, nor so light as a white man. He had no beard or whiskers, but very heavy eyebrows. He was a good-looking man. We were crowded up very close. We had been told that nobody was to talk, and even if we whispered the Christ would know it. I had heard that Christ had been crucified, and I looked to see, and I saw a scar on his wrist and one on his face, and he seemed to be the man. I could not see his feet. He would talk to us all day.

That evening we all assembled again to see him depart. When we were assembled, he began to sing, and he commenced to tremble all over, violently for a while, and then sat down. We danced all that night, the Christ lying down beside us apparently dead.

The next morning when we went to eat breakfast, the Christ was with us. After breakfast four heralds went around and called out that the Christ was back with us and wanted to talk with us. The circle was prepared again. The people assembled, and Christ came among us and sat down. He said he wanted to talk to us again and for us to listen. He said: "I am the man who made everything you see around you. I am not lying to you, my children. I made this earth and everything on it. I have been to heaven and seen your dead friends and have seen my own father and mother. In the beginning, after God made the earth, they sent me back to teach the people, and when I came back on earth the people were afraid of me and treated me badly. This is what they did to me [showing his scars]. I did not try to defend myself. I found my children were bad, so went back to heaven and left them. I told them that in so many hundred years I would come back to see my children. At the end of this time I was sent back to try to teach them. My father told me the earth was getting old and worn out, and the people getting bad, and that I was to renew everything as it used to be, and make it better."

He told us also that all our dead were to be resurrected; that they were all to come back to earth, and that as the earth was too small for them and us, he would do away with heaven, and make the earth itself large enough to contain us all; that we must tell all the people we meet about these things. He spoke to us about fighting, and said that was bad, and we must keep from it; that the earth was to be all good hereafter, and we must all be friends with one another. He said that in the fall of the year the youth of all the good people would be renewed, so that nobody would be more than 40 years old, and that if they behaved themselves well after this the youth of everyone would be renewed in the spring. He said if we were all good he would send people among us who could heal all our wounds and sickness by mere touch, and that we would live forever. He told us not to quarrel, or fight, nor strike each other, nor shoot one another; that the whites and Indians were to be all one people. He said if any man disobeyed what he ordered, his tribe would be wiped from the face of the earth; that we must believe everything he said, and that we must not doubt him, or say he lied; that if we did, he would know it; that he would know our thoughts and actions, in no matter what part of the world we might be.

When I heard this from the Christ, and came back home to tell it to my people, I thought they would listen. Where I went to there were lots of white people, but I never had one of them say an unkind word to me. I thought all of your people knew all of this I have told you of, but it seems you do not.

Ever since the Christ I speak of talked to me I have thought what he said was good. I see nothing bad in it. When I got back, I knew my people were bad, and had heard nothing of all this, so I got them together and told them of it and warned them to listen to it for their own good. I talked to them for four nights and five days. I told them just what I have told you here today. I told them what I said were the words of God Almighty, who was looking down on them. I wish some of you had been up in our camp here to have heard my words to the Cheyennes. The only bad thing that there has been in it at all was this: I had just told my people that the Christ would visit the sins of any Indian upon the whole tribe, when the recent trouble [killing of Ferguson] occurred. If any one of you think I am not telling the truth, you can go and see this man I speak of for yourselves. I will go with you, and I would like one or two of my people who doubt me to go with me.

The Christ talked to us all in our respective tongues. You can see this man in your sleep any time you want after you have seen him and shaken hands with him once. Through him you can go to heaven and meet your friends. Since my return I have seen him often in my sleep. About the time the soldiers went up the Rosebud I was lying in my lodge asleep, when this man appeared and told me that the Indians had gotten into trouble, and I was frightened. The next night he appeared to me and told me that everything would come out all right.

THE GHOST DANCE AMONG THE SIOUX

The following was written originally in the Teton Dakota dialect by George Sword, an Ogalala Sioux Indian, formerly captain of the Indian police at Pine Ridge agency and now judge of the Indian court. It was translated by an Indian for Miss Emma C. Sickels and is published by her courtesy. The copy of the original Sioux manuscript is in the archives of the Bureau of Ethnology:

In the story of ghost dancing, the Ogalala heard that the Son of God was truly on earth in the west from their country. This was in the year 1889. The first people knew about the messiah to be on earth were the Shoshoni and Arapaho. So in 1889 Good Thunder with four or five others visited the place where Son of God said to be. These people went there without permission. They said the messiah was there at the place, but he was there to help the Indians and not the whites; so this made the Indians happy to find out this. Good Thunder, Cloud Horse, Yellow Knife, and Short Bull visited the place again in 1890 and saw the messiah. Their story of visit to the messiah is as follows:

"From the country where the Arapaho and Shoshoni we start in the direction of northwest in train for five nights and arrived at the foot of the Rocky mountains. Here we saw him and also several tribes of Indians. The people said that the messiah will come at a place in the woods where the place was prepare for him. When we went to the place a smoke descended from heaven to the place where he was to come. When the smoke disappeared, there was a man of about forty, which was the Son of God. The man said:

"'My grandchildren! I am glad you have come far away to see your relatives. This are your people who have come back from your country.' When he said he want us to go with him, we looked and we saw a land created across the ocean on which all the nations of Indians were coming home, but, as the messiah looked at the land which was created and reached across the ocean, again disappeared, saying that it was not time for that to take place. The messiah then gave to Good Thunder some paints—Indian paint and a white paint—a green grass [sagebrush twigs?]; and said, 'My grandchildren, when you get home, go to farming and send all your children to school. And on way home if you kill any buffalo cut the head, the tail, and the four feet and leave them, and that buffalo will come to live again. When the soldiers of the white people chief want to arrest me, I shall stretch out my arms, which will knock them to nothingness, or, if not that, the earth will open and swallow them in. My father commanded me to visit the Indians on a purpose. I have came to the white people first, but they not good. They killed me, and you can see the marks of my wounds on my feet, my hands, and on my back. My father has given you life—your old life—and you have come to see your friends, but you will not take me home with you at this time. I want you to tell when you get home your people to follow my examples. Any one Indian does not obey me and tries to be on white's side will be covered over by a new land that is to come over this old one. You will, all the people, use the paints and grass I give you. In the spring when the green grass comes, your people who have gone before you will come back, and you shall see your friends then, for you have come to my call.'"

The people from every tipi send for us to visit them. They are people who died many years ago. Chasing Hawk, who died not long ago, was there, and we went to his tipi. He was living with his wife, who was killed in war long ago. They live in a buffalo skin tipi—a very large one—and he wanted all his friends to go there to live. A son of Good Thunder who died in war long ago was one who also took us to his tipi so his father saw him. When coming we come to a herd of buffaloes. We killed one and took everything except the four feet, head, and tail, and when we came a little ways from it there was the buffaloes come to life again and went off. This was one of the messiah's word came to truth. The messiah said, "I will short your journey when you feel tired of the long ways, if you call upon me." This we did when we were tired. The night came upon us, we stopped at a place, and we called upon the messiah to help us, because we were tired of long journey. We went to sleep and in the morning we found ourselves at a great distance from where we stopped.

The people came back here and they got the people loyal to the government, and those not favor of the whites held a council. The agent's soldiers were sent after them and brought Good Thunder and two others to the agency and they were confined to the prison. They were asked by the agent and Captain Sword whether they saw the Son of God and whether they hold councils over their return from visit, but Good Thunder refused to say "yes." They were confined in the prison for two days, and upon their promising not to hold councils about their visit they were released. They went back to the people and told them about their trouble with the agent. Then they disperse without a council.

In the following spring the people at Pine Ridge agency began to gather at the White Clay creek for councils. Just at this time Kicking Bear, from Cheyenne River agency, went on a visit to the Arapaho and said that the Arapaho there have ghost dancing. He said that people partaking in dance would get crazy and die, then the messiah is seen and all the ghosts. When they die they see strange things, they see their relatives who died long before. They saw these things when they died in ghost dance and came to life again. The person dancing becomes dizzy and finally drop dead, and the first thing they saw is an eagle comes to them and carried them to where the messiah is with his ghosts. The man said this:

The persons in the ghost dancing are all joined hands. A man stands and then a woman, so in that way forming a very large circle. They dance around in the circle in a continuous time until some of them become so tired and overtired that they became crazy and finally drop as though dead, with foams in mouth all wet by perspiration. All the men and women made holy shirts and dresses they wear in dance. The persons dropped in dance would all lie in great dust the dancing make. They paint the white muslins they made holy shirts and dresses out of with blue across the back, and alongside of this is a line of yellow paint. They also paint in the front part of the shirts and dresses. A picture of an eagle is made on the back of all the shirts and dresses. On the shoulders and on the sleeves they tied eagle feathers. They said that the bullets will not go through these shirts and dresses, so they all have these dresses for war. Their enemies weapon will not go through these dresses. The ghost dancers all have to wear eagle feather on head. With this feather any man would be made crazy if fan with this feather. In the ghost dance no person is allow to wear anything made of any metal, except the guns made of metal is carry by some of the dancers. When they come from ghosts or after recovery from craziness, they brought meat from the ghosts or from the supposed messiah. They also brought water, fire, and wind with which to kill all the whites or Indians who will help the chief of the whites. They made sweat house and made holes in the middle of the sweat house where they say the water will come out of these holes. Before they begin to dance they all raise their hands toward the northwest and cry in supplication to the messiah and then begin the dance with the song, "*Ate misunkala ceya omani-ye,*" etc.

SELWYN'S INTERVIEW WITH KUWAPI

On November 21, 1890, it was reported to Agent E. W. Foster, in charge of Yankton agency, South Dakota, that an Indian named Kuwapi, from Rosebud agency, was on the reservation teaching the doctrine and ceremony of the Ghost dance. He at once had the man arrested by a force in charge of William T. Selwyn, a full-blood Yankton Sioux, who had received a fair education under the patronage of a gentleman in Philadelphia, and who had for several years been employed in various capacities at different Sioux agencies. Selwyn had recently come from Pine Ridge, where he had learned and reported to Agent Gallagher something of the religious excitement among the

western Sioux, and had afterward repeated this information to the
agent at Yankton. While Kuwapi was in his custody Selwyn questioned him at length concerning the new doctrine, and forwarded the
following report (*G. D., Document 36861—1890*) of the interview to
Agent Foster:

YANKTON AGENCY, SOUTH DAKOTA,
November 22, 1890.

Colonel E. W. FOSTER,
United States Indian Agent, Yankton Agency, South Dakota.

DEAR SIR: It has been reported here a few days ago that there was an Indian
visitor up at White Swan from Rosebud agency who has been telling or teaching
the doctrines of the new messiah, and has made some agitation among the people
up there. According to the request of Captain Conrad, United States Army, of
Fort Randall, South Dakota, and by your order of the 21st instant, I went up to
White Swan and have arrested the wanted man (Kuwapi, or One they chased after).
On my way to the agency with the prisoner I have made little interview with him
on the subject of the new messiah. The following are the facts which he corroborated concerning the new messiah, his laws and doctrines to the Indians of this
continent:

Q. Do you believe in the new messiah?—A. I somewhat believe it.

Q. What made you believe it?—A. Because I ate some of the buffalo meat that he
(the new messiah) sent to the Rosebud Indians through Short Bull.

Q. Did Short Bull say that he saw the living herd of roaming buffaloes while he
was with the son of the Great Spirit?—A. Short Bull told the Indians at Rosebud
that the buffalo and other wild game will be restored to the Indians at the same
time when the general resurrection in favor of the Indians takes place.

Q. You said a "general resurrection in favor of the Indians takes place;" when or
how soon will this be?—A. The father sends word to us that he will have all these
caused to be so in the spring, when the grass is knee high.

Q. You said "father;" who is this father?—A. It is the new messiah. He has
ordered his children (Indians) to call him "father."

Q. You said the father is not going to send the buffalo until the resurrection takes
place. Would he be able to send a few buffaloes over this way for a sort of a sample,
so as to have his children (Indians) to have a taste of the meat?—A. The father
wishes to do things all at once, even in destroying the white race.

Q. You said something about the destroying of the white race. Do you mean to
say that all mankind except the Indians will be killed?—A. Yes.

Q. How, and who is going to kill the white people?—A. The father is going to
cause a big cyclone or whirlwind, by which he will have all the white people to perish.

Q. If it should be a cyclone or whirlwind, what are we going to do to protect ourselves?—A. The father will make some kind of provisions by which we will be saved.

Q. You said something about the coming destruction on the white people by your
father. Supposing your father is sick, tired out, forget, or some other accidental
cause by which he should not be able to accomplish his purpose, what would be
the case about the destroying of the white people?—A. There is no doubt about
these things, as the miracle performer or the father is going to do just as what he
said he would do.

Q. What other object could you come to by which you are led to believe that there
is such a new messiah on earth at present?—A. The ghost dancers are fainted
whenever the dance goes on.

Q. Do you believe that they are really fainted?—A. Yes.

Q. What makes you believe that the dancers have really fainted?—A. Because
when they wake or come back to their senses they sometimes bring back some news
from the unknown world, and some little trinkets, such as buffalo tail, buffalo
meat, etc.

Q. What did the fainted ones see when they get fainted?—A. They visited the happy hunting ground, the camps, multitudes of people, and a great many strange people.

Q. What did the ghost or the strange people tell the fainted one or ones?—A. When the fainted one goes to the camp, he is welcomed by the relatives of the visitor (the fainted one), and he is also invited to several feasts.

Q. Were the people at Rosebud agency anxiously waiting or expecting to see all of their dead relatives who have died several years ago?—A. Yes.

Q. We will have a great many older folks when all the dead people come back, would we not?—A. The visitors all say that there is not a single old man nor woman in the other world—all changed to young.

Q. Are we going to die when the dead ones come back?—A. No; we will be just the same as we are today.

Q. Did the visitor say that there is any white men in the other world?—A. No; no white people.

Q. If there is no white people in the other world, where did they get their provisions and clothing?—A. In the other world, the messenger tells us that they have depended altogether for their food on the flesh of buffalo and other wild game; also, they were all clad in skins of wild animals.

Q. Did the Rosebud agency Indians believe the new messiah, or the son of the Great Spirit?—A. Yes.

Q. How do they show that they have a believe in the new messiah?—A. They show themselves by praying to the father by looking up to heaven, and call him "father," just the same as you would in a church.

Q. Have you ever been in a church?—A. No.

Q. Do you faithfully believe in the new messiah?—A. I did not in the first place, but as I became more acquainted with the doctrines of the new messiah that I really believe in him.

Q. How many people at Rosebud, in your opinion, believe this new messiah?—A. Nearly every one.

Q. Did you not the Rosebud people prepare to attack the white people this summer? While I was at Pine Ridge agency this summer the Oglalla Sioux Indians say they will resist against the government if the latter should try to put a stop to the messiah question. Did your folks at Rosebud say the same thing?—A. Yes.

Q. Are they still preparing and thinking to attack the white people should the government send our soldiers with orders to put a stop to your new business of the messiah?—A. I do not know, but I think that the Wojaji band at Rosebud agency will do some harm at any time.

Q. You do not mean to say that the Rosebud Indians will try and cause an outbreak?—A. That seems to be the case.

Q. You said something about the "son of the Great Spirit," or "the father." What do you mean by the son of the Great Spirit?—A. This father, as he is called, said himself that he is the son of the Great Spirit.

Q. Have you talked to or with any Indian at White Swan about the new messiah, his laws and doctrines, or have you referred this to anyone while there?—A. I have told a few of them. I did not voluntarily express my wish for them to know and follow the doctrines of the new messiah.

Q. Yes, but you have explained the matter to the Indians, did you not?—A. Yes, I have.

Q. Do the Yankton Indians at White Swan believe in your teaching of the new messiah?—A. I did not intend to teach them, but as I have been questioned on the subject, that I have said something about it.

Q. Did any of them believe in you?—A. Some have already believed it, and some of them did not believe it.

Q. Those that have believed in you must be better men than the others, are they not?—A. I do not know.

Q. Do you intend to introduce the doctrines of the new messiah from Rosebud to this agency as a missionary of the gospel?—A. No, I did not.

Q. What brings you here, then?—A. I have some relatives here that I wanted to see, and this was the reason why I came here.

Q. Where does this new messiah question originate? I mean from the first start of it.—A. This has originated in White mountains.

Q. Where is this White mountain?—A. Close to the big Rocky mountains, near the country that belong to the Mexicans.

Q. Do you think that there will be a trouble in the west by next spring?—A. Yes.

Q. What makes you think so?—A. Because that is what I have heard people talk of.

This is all that I have questioned Kuwapi on the subject of the new messiah.

Respectfully, your obedient servant,

WILLIAM T. SELWYN.

CHAPTER XI

THE GHOST DANCE WEST OF THE ROCKIES

The first Ghost dance on Walker Lake reservation took place in January, 1889, about a mile above the railroad bridge near the agency. Wovoka's preaching had already been attracting general attention among his own people for some months. It is said that six Apache attended this first dance, but the statement is improbable, as this would imply that they had made a journey of 600 miles through a desert country to see a man as yet unknown outside of his own tribe. From this time, however, his fame went abroad, and another large dance in the same vicinity soon after was attended by a number of Ute from Utah. The Ute are neighbors of the Paiute on the east, as the Bannock are on the north, and these tribes were naturally the first to hear of the new prophet and to send delegates to attend the dance. The doctrine spread almost simultaneously to all the scattered bands of Paiute in Nevada, Oregon, and adjacent sections.

In its essential features the Ghost dance among the Paiute as conducted by the messiah himself was practically the same as among the majority of the prairie tribes, as will later be described. The Sioux, Kiowa, and perhaps some other tribes, however, danced around a tree or pole set up in the center of the ring, differing in this respect from the Paiute, as well as from the Cheyenne, Arapaho, Caddo, and others. No fire was allowed within the ring by any of the prairie tribes among whom the subject was investigated, but among the Paiute it seems that fires were built either within the circle or close to it. When I visited the messiah in January, 1892, deep snow was on the ground, which had caused the temporary suspension of dancing, so that I had no opportunity of seeing the performance there for myself. I saw, however, the place cleared for the dance ground—the same spot where the large delegation from Oklahoma had attended the dance the preceding summer—at the upper end of Mason valley. A large circular space had been cleared of sagebrush and leveled over, and around the circumference were the remains of the low round structures of willow branches which had sheltered those in attendance. At one side, within the circle, was a larger structure of branches, where the messiah gave audience to the delegates from distant tribes, and, according to their statements, showed them the glories of the spirit world through the medium of hypnotic trances. The Paiute always dance five nights, or perhaps more properly four nights and the morning of the fifth day, as enjoined by the messiah on the visiting delegates, ending the performance with a general shaking and waving of blankets, as among the prairie tribes, after which all go down and bathe in the nearest stream. The shaking of the blankets dispels all evil influences and drives sickness and disease away from the dancers. There is no previous consecration of the ground, as among the Arapaho, and no preliminary sweat bath, as among the Sioux. The sweat bath seems to be unknown to the Paiute, who are preeminently a dirty people, and I saw no trace of sweat-house frames at any of their camps. Nakash, the Arapaho who visited the messiah in 1889 and first brought the dance to the eastern tribes, confirmed the statements of the Paiute and ranchmen that there were no trances in the Paiute Ghost dance.

Besides the dance ground in Mason valley, where the messiah himself generally presided, there were several others on Walker River reservation, although, if we are to believe the agent, no Ghost dances were ever held on either reservation.

The following extract from Porcupine's account of his visit to the messiah in the fall of 1889 (see page 793) gives some idea of the Paiute Ghost dance and throws light on the cataleptic peculiarities of the messiah:

I went to the agency at Walker lake, and they told us Christ would be there in two days. At the end of two days, on the third morning, hundreds of people gathered at this place. They cleared off a place near the agency in the form of a circus ring and we all gathered there. This space was perfectly cleared of grass, etc. We waited there till late in the evening, anxious to see Christ. Just before sundown I saw a great many people, mostly Indians, coming dressed in white men's clothes. The Christ was with them. They all formed in this ring in a circle around him. They put up sheets all around the circle, as they had no tents. Just after dark some of the Indians told me that the Christ (father) was arrived. I looked around to find him, and finally saw him sitting on one side of the ring. They all started toward him to see him. They made a big fire to throw light on him. I never looked around, but went forward, and when I saw him I bent my head. . . . He sat there a long time and nobody went up to speak to him. He sat with his head bowed all the time. After awhile he rose and said he was very glad to see his children. "I have sent for you and am glad to see you. I am going to talk to you after awhile about your relatives who are dead and gone. My children, I want you to listen to all I have to say to you. I will teach you, too, how to dance a dance, and I want you to dance it. Get ready for your dance, and then when the dance is over I will talk to you." He was dressed in a white coat with stripes. The rest of his dress was a white man's, except that he had on a pair of moccasins. Then he commenced our dance, everybody joining in, the Christ singing while we danced. We danced till late in the night; then he told us we had danced enough.

The next morning after breakfast was over, we went into the circle and spread canvas over it on the ground, the Christ standing in the midst of us. He told us he was going away that day, but would be back the next morning and talk to us. . . . He had no beard or whiskers, but very heavy eyebrows. He was a good-looking man. We were crowded up very close. We had been told that nobody was to talk, and that even if we whispered the Christ would know it. . . . He would talk to us all day.

That evening we all assembled again to see him depart. When we were assembled he began to sing, and he commenced to tremble all over violently for a while and then sat down. We danced all that night, the Christ lying down beside us apparently dead.

The next morning when we went to eat breakfast, the Christ was with us. After breakfast four heralds went around and called out that the Christ was back with us and wanted to talk with us. The circle was prepared again. The people assembled, and Christ came among us and sat down. (*G. D., 9.*)

We come now to the other tribes bordering on the Paiute. First in order are the Washo, a small band dwelling on the slopes of the sierras in the neighborhood of Carson, Nevada, and speaking a peculiar language of unknown affinity. They are completely under the domination of the Paiute. They had no separate dance, but joined in with the nearest camps of Paiute and sang the same songs. Occupying practically the same territory as the Paiute, they were among the first to receive the new doctrine.

Farther to the south, in California, about Bridgeport and Mono lake and extending across to the westward slope of the sierras, are several small Shoshonean bands closely akin to the Paiute and known locally as the "Diggers." The Paiute state that bands of these Indians frequently came up and participated in the dance on the reservation. They undoubtedly had their own dances at home also.

According to the statement of the agent in charge of the Mission Indians in southern California in 1891, the doctrine reached them also, and the medicine-men of Potrero began to prophesy the destruction of the whites and the return of Indian supremacy. Few believed their predictions, however, until rumors brought the news of the overflow of Colorado river and the birth of "Salton sea" in the summer of 1891. Never doubting that the great change was near at hand, the frightened Indians fled to the mountains to await developments, but after having gone hungry for several days the millennial dawn seemed still as far away as ever, and they returned to their homes with disappointment in their hearts. Although the agent mentions specifically only the Indians of Potrero, there can be no doubt that the inhabitants of the other Mission rancherias in the vicinity were also affected, and we are thus enabled to fix the boundary of the messiah excitement in this direction at the Pacific ocean. (*Comr., 27.*)

In northern California the new doctrine was taken up late in 1890 by the Pit River Indians, a group of tribes constituting a distinct linguistic stock and scattered throughout the whole basin of Pit river, from Goose lake to the Sacramento, which may have formed the boundary of the Ghost-dance movement in this direction. (*A. G. O., 7.*) As a number of these Indians are living also on Round Valley reservation in California, it is possible that the doctrine may have reached there also. Having obtained the dance ritual directly from the Paiute, their neighbors on the east, the ceremony and belief were probably the same with both tribes.

So far as can be learned from the reports of agents, and from the statement of Wovoka himself, the dance was never taken up by the Indians of Hoopa Valley reservation in California; of Klamath, Siletz,

Grande Ronde, or Umatilla reservations in Oregon; by any of the tribes in Washington; by those of Lapwai or Cœur d'Alêne reservations in Idaho; or on Jocko reservation in Montana. Wovoka stated that he had been visited by delegates from Warmspring agency, in Oregon, who also had taken part in the dance, but these may have been some of the Paiute living on that reservation. The small band of Paiute living with the Klamath probably also attended the dance at some time.[1]

A single Nez Percé visited the messiah, but the visit had no effect on his tribe at home. In a general way it may be stated that the doctrine of the Ghost dance was never taken up by any tribes of the Salishan or Shahaptian stocks, occupying practically the whole of the great Columbia basin. This is probably due to the fact that the more important of these tribes have been for a long time under the influence of Catholic or other Christian missionaries, while most of the others are adherents of the Smohalla or the Shaker doctrine.

Of the tribes southward from the Paiute, according to the best information obtainable, the Ghost dance never reached the Yuma, Pima, Papago, Maricopa, or any of the Apache bands in Arizona or New Mexico, neither did it affect any of the Pueblo tribes except the Taos, who performed the dance merely as a pastime. As before stated, it is said that six Apache attended the first large dance at Walker lake in 1889. This seems improbable, but if true it produced no effect on any part of the tribe at large. Later on the Jicarilla Apache, in northern New Mexico, may have heard of it through the southern Ute, but, so far as is known officially, neither of these tribes ever engaged in the dance. The agent of the Jicarilla states that the tribe knew nothing of the doctrine until informed of it by himself. (*G. D., 10.*) It seems never to have been taken up by the Mescalero Apache in southern New Mexico, although they are in the habit of making frequent visits to the Kiowa, Comanche, Apache, and other Ghost-dancing tribes of Oklahoma. The agent of the Mohave states officially that these Indians knew nothing about it, but this must be a mistake, as there is constant communication between the Mohave and the southern Paiute, and, according to Wovoka's statement, Mohave delegates attended the dance in 1890, while the 700 Walapai and Chemehuevi associated with the Mohave are known to have been devoted adherents of the doctrine.

The dance was taken up nearly simultaneously by the Bannock, Shoshoni, Gosiute, and Ute in the early part of 1889. All these tribes are neighbors (on the east) of the Paiute and closely cognate to them, the Bannock particularly having only a slight dialectal difference of language, so that communication between them is an easy matter. The

---

[1]Hoopa Valley, Siletz, and Grande Ronde reservations are occupied by the remnants of a number of small tribes. Klamath reservation is occupied by the Klamath, Modoc, and Paiute. On Umatilla reservation are the Cayuse, Umatilla, and Wallawalla. The Nez Percé are at Lapwai to the number of over 1,800. On the Cœur d'Alêne reservation are the Cœur d' Alênes, Kutenai, Pend d'Oreilles, and part of the Spokan. On Jocko reservation in Montana are the Flatheads, Kutenai, and a part of the Pend d'Oreilles. Warmspring reservation in Oregon is occupied by the Warmspring, Wasco, Tenine Paiute, and John Day Indians.

Bannock are chiefly on Fort Hall and Lemhi reservations in Idaho. The Shoshoni are on the Western Shoshone (Duck Valley) reservation in Nevada, on Fort Hall and Lemhi reservations in Idaho, and on Wind River reservation in Wyoming. The Ute are on Uintah and Uncompahgre reservations in Utah, and on the Southern Ute reservation in Colorado. There are also a considerable number of Bannock and Shoshoni not on reservations. The Ute of Utah sent delegates to the messiah soon after the first Ghost dance in January, 1889, but it is doubtful if the southern Ute in Colorado were engaged in the dance. Although aware of the doctrine, they ridiculed the idea of the dead returning to earth. (*G. D., 11.*)

In regard to the dance among the Shoshoni and Paiute on the Western Shoshoni reservation, in Nevada and Idaho, their agent writes, under date of November 8, 1890:

The Indians of this reservation and vicinity have just concluded their second medicine dance, the previous one having taken place in August last. They are looking for the coming of the Indian Christ, the resurrection of the dead Indians, and the consequent supremacy of the Indian race. Fully one thousand people took part in the dance. While the best of order prevailed, the excitement was very great as morning approached. When the dancers were worn out mentally and physically, the medicine-men would shout that they could see the faces of departed friends and relatives moving about the circle. No pen can paint the picture of wild excitement that ensued. All shouted in a chorus, Christ has come, and then danced and sung until they fell in a confused and exhausted mass on the ground. . . . I apprehend no trouble beyond the loss of time and the general demoralizing effect of these large gatherings of people. Several of the leading men have gone to Walker lake to confer with a man who calls himself Christ. Others have gone to Fort Hall to meet Indians from Montana and Dakota, to get the news from that section. In fact, the astonishing part of the business is the fact that all the Indians in the country seem to possess practically the same ideas and expect about the same result. (*G. D., 12.*)

On December 6 he writes that another Ghost dance had then been in progress for six days, and that the Indians had announced their intention to dance one week in each month until the grass grew, at which time the medicine-men had told them the messiah would come, bringing with him all their dead friends. (*G. D., 13.*) This dance, however, was attended by a much smaller number of Indians, and skeptics had already arisen among them to scoff at the new believers. The leaven was working, and only a little shrewd diplomacy was needed to turn the religious scale, as is shown by an extract from a third letter, dated January 10, 1891, from which it would seem that Agent Plumb is a man of practical common sense, as likewise that Esau was not the only one who would sell his birthright for a mess of pottage:

Christmas day was the day set for commencing another dance. On learning this, I told the Indians that it was my intention to give them all a big feast and have a general holiday on Christmas, but that I would not give them anything if they intended to dance. I told them they could play all of their usual games, in fact, have a good time, but that dancing was forbidden. I showed them how continued dancing at various Sioux agencies had ended in soldiers being sent to stop them. I stated the case as clearly as I could; the Indians debated it two days, and then reported that while they hoped their dead friends would come back, and believed that dancing would help to bring them, yet they were friends of the government, and friends of the whites, and my friends, and would not hold any more resurrection dances without my consent. Up to this date they have kept their word. I have no hope of breaking up their dances altogether, but I have strong hopes of controlling them. (*G. D., 14.*)

The Bannock and Shoshoni of Fort Hall reservation in Idaho have served as the chief medium of the doctrine between the tribes west of the mountains and those of the plains. Situated almost on the summit of the great divide, they are within easy reach of the Paiute to the west, among whom the dance originated, and whose language the Bannock speak, while at no great distance to the east, on Wind River reservation in Wyoming, the remaining Shoshoni are confederated with the Arapaho, who have been from the first the great apostles of the doctrine among the prairie tribes. There is constant visiting back and forth between the tribes of these two reservations, while the four railroads coming in at Fort Hall, together with the fact of its close proximity to the main line of the Union Pacific, tend still more to make it a focus and halting point for Indian travel. Almost every delegation from the tribes east of the mountains stopped at this agency to obtain the latest news from the messiah and to procure interpreters from among the Bannock to accompany them to Nevada. In a letter of November 26, 1890, to the Indian Commissioner, the agent in charge states that during the preceding spring and summer his Indians had been visited by representatives from about a dozen different reservations. In regard to the dance and the doctrine at Fort Hall, he also says that the extermination and resurrection business was not a new thing with his tribes by any means, but had been quite a craze with them every few years for the last twenty years or more, only varying a little according to the whim of particular medicine-men. (*G. D., 15.*) This may have referred to the doctrine already mentioned as having been taught by Tävibo.

Early in 1889 a Bannock from Fort Hall visited the Shoshoni and Arapaho of Wind River reservation in Wyoming and brought them the first knowledge of the new religion. He had just returned from a visit to the Paiute country, where he said he had met messengers who had told him that the dead people were coming back, and who had commanded him to go and tell all the tribes. "And so," said the Shoshoni, "he came here and told us all about it." Accordingly, in the summer of that year a delegation of five Shoshoni, headed by Täbinshi, with Nakash ("Sage"), an Arapaho, visited the messiah of Mason valley, traveling most of the way by railroad and occupying several days in the journey. They attended a Ghost dance, which, according to their accounts, was a very large one, and after dancing all night were told by the messiah that they would meet all their dead in two years from that time at the turning of the leaves, i. e., in the autumn of 1891. They were urged to dance frequently, "because the dance moves the dead." One of the Shoshoni delegates understood the Bannock and Paiute language and interpreted for the rest. The information was probably conveyed by the Shoshoni to the Arapaho through the medium of the sign language.

In accord with the report of the delegates, on their return home the Shoshoni and Arapaho at once began to dance. A year later, in the fall of 1890, a dense smoke from forest fires in the mountains drifted down and obscured the air in the lower country to such an extent that horses were lost in the haze. This was regarded by the Indians as an indication of the approach of the great change, and the dance was continued with increased fervor, but at last the atmosphere began to clear and the phenomenon ended as it had begun—in smoke. The dance was kept up, however, without abatement for another year, until the predicted time had come and gone, when the Shoshoni—who seem to share the skeptical nature of their southern kinsmen, the Comanche— concluded that they had been deceived, and abandoned the dance. The Arapaho, who have greater faith in the unseen things of the spirit world, kept it up, and were still dancing when I visited them in the summer of 1892. A part of the Arapaho, headed by their chief, Black Coal, and encouraged by the Catholic missionaries, had steadily opposed the dance from the first. After considerable discussion of the matter it was decided, on Black Coal's proposition, to send another delegation to the messiah, under the guidance of Yellow Eagle, a graduate of a government Indian school, to learn as to the truth or falsity of the new doctrine. They returned early in 1891 and reported against the movement. Their report confirmed the doubters in their skepticism, but produced little effect on the rest of the tribe.

When I visited Wind River reservation in Wyoming in June, 1892, the agent in charge informed me that there was no Ghost dancing on his reservation; that he had explained how foolish it was and had strictly forbidden it, and that in consequence the Indians had abandoned it. However, he expressed interest in my investigation, and as the Arapaho, with whom I had most to do, were then camped in a body a few miles up in the mountains cutting wood, he very kindly furnished a conveyance and camping outfit, with two of the agency employees— a clerk and an interpreter—to take me out. It appeared afterward that the escort had received instructions of their own before starting. Having reached the camp and set up our tent, the Arapaho soon came around to get acquainted, over a pipe and a cup of coffee; but, in answer to questions put by one of my companions, a white man, who assumed the burden of the conversation, it seemed that the Indians had lost all interest in the dance. In fact, some of them were so ignorant on the subject that they wanted to know what it meant.

After trying in vain to convince me that it was useless to waste time further with the Indians, the clerk started back again after supper, satisfied that that part of the country was safe so far as the Ghost dance was concerned. By this time it was dark, and the Indians invited the interpreter and myself to come over to a tipi about half a mile away, where we could meet all the old men. We started, and had gone but a short distance when we heard from a neighboring hill the familiar measured cadence of the ghost songs. On turning with a questioning look to my interpreter—who was himself a half-blood—he quietly said: "Yes; they are dancing the Ghost dance. That's something I have never reported, and I never will. It is their religion and they have a right to it." Not wishing to be an accomplice in crime, I did not go over to the dance; but it is needless to state that the old men in the tipi that night, and for several successive nights thereafter, knew all about the songs and ceremonies of the new religion. As already stated, the Shoshoni had really lost faith and abandoned the dance.

Among the Shoshoni the dance was performed around a small cedar tree, planted in the ground for that purpose. Unlike the Sioux, they hung nothing on this tree. The men did not clasp each other's hands, but held on to their blankets instead; but a woman standing between two men took hold of their hands. There was no preliminary medicine ceremony. The dance took place usually in the morning, and at its close the performers shook their blankets in the air, as among the Paiute and other tribes, before dispersing. However novel may have been the doctrine, the Shoshoni claim that the Ghost dance itself as performed by them was a revival of an old dance which they had had fully fifty years before.

The selection of the cedar in this connection is in agreement with the general Indian idea, which has always ascribed a mystic sacredness to that tree, from its never-dying green, which renders it so conspicuous a feature of the desert landscape; from the aromatic fragrance of its twigs, which are burned as incense in sacred ceremonies; from the durability and fine texture of its wood, which makes it peculiarly appropriate for tipi poles and lance shafts; and from the dark-red color of its heart, which seems as though dyed in blood. In Cherokee myth the cedar was originally a pole, to the top of which they fastened the fresh scalps of their enemies, and the wood was thus stained by the blood that trickled slowly down along it to the ground. The Kiowa also selected a cedar for the center of their Ghost-dance circle.

We go back now to the southern tribes west of the mountains. Some time in the winter of 1889–90 Paiute runners brought to the powerful tribe of the Navaho, living in northern New Mexico and Arizona, the news of the near advent of the messiah and the resurrection of the dead. They preached and prophesied for a considerable time, but the Navaho were skeptical, laughed at the prophets, and paid but little attention to the prophesies. (*Matthews, 1.*) According to the official report for 1892, these Indians, numbering somewhat over 16,000 souls, have, in round numbers, 9,000 cattle, 119,000 horses, and 1.600.000

sheep and goats; and, as suggested by Dr Matthews, the authority on
that tribe, it may be that, being rich in herds and wealth of silver, they
felt no special need of a redeemer.   While with the Navaho in the winter of 1892–93 I made inquiry in various parts of their wide-extended
territory, but could not learn that the Ghost dance had ever been

FIG. 70—Navaho Indians.

performed among them, and it was evident that in their case the doctrinal seed had fallen on barren ground.

Before visiting the tribe, I had written for information to Mr A. M.
Stephen, of Keams Cañon, Arizona, since deceased, who had studied
the Navaho and Hopi for years and spoke the Navaho language
fluently. I quote from him on the subject. It may be noted that

Keams Cañon is about 125 miles northwest of Fort Wingate, the point from which Dr Matthews writes, and nearer by that much to the Paiute, Cohonino, and Walapai, all of whom have accepted the new religion. Mr Stephen states that some time in February or March, 1890, he first heard rumors among the Navaho that "the old men long dead" had returned to some foreign tribes in the north or east, the vague far away. The intelligence was brought to the Navaho either by the Ute or Paiute, or both. The rumor grew and the idea became commonly current among the Navaho that the mythic heroes were to return and that under their direction they were to expel American and Mexican and restrict the Zuñi and Hopi close to their villages, and, in fact, to reestablish their old domain from San Francisco mountains to Santa Fé. (*Stephen, 1.*) On November 22, 1891, he further writes:

While out this last time I camped over night with some Navajo friends, and over a pipe brought up the messiah topic. This family belongs to the Bitter-Water gens, and this is the gist of what I got from them: A Pah-ute came to a family of their gens living near Navajo mountain and told them that *Na'-Keh-tkla-ĭ* was to return from the under world and bring back all the Tinneh (Navajo) he had killed. *Na'-keh-tkla-ĭ* (i. e., "foreigner with white foot sole") in the long ago had a puma and a bear. These were his pets. He would call puma from the east and bear from the west, and just before dawn they met in the center. Thus they met four times. On the fourth meeting puma reached back with his forepaw and plucked his mane, tossing the hair aloft, and for every hair a Tinneh died. This fatal sorcery continued for a long time, and great numbers were killed. Now, the Pah-ute said, this sorcerer was to return, and would call his pets, and they would come east and west, and following their trail would be all the people whose death they had caused. These Navajo said they had heard of other Pah-ute prophecies a year or more ago, all to the effect that long dead people were to return alive from the under world. These resurrected ones were also to bring back the departed game, and the Tinneh would again dominate the region. But, said my informant, *datsaigi yelti*, " it is worthless talk." (*Stephen, 2.*)

In connection with hypnotism as seen in the Ghost dance, Dr Matthews states that in one curious Navaho ceremony he has several times seen the patient hypnotized or pretend to be hypnotized by a character dressed in evergreens. The occurrence of the hypnotic trance is regarded as a sign that the ceremony has been effective. If the trance does not occur, some other ceremony must be tried. (*Matthews, 2.*)

West of the Navaho in northeastern Arizona live the Hopi, or Moki, a Pueblo tribe occupying several villages on the tops of nearly inaccessible mesas. In July, 1891, four of these Indians, while on a visit to the Cohonino, living farther to the west, first heard of the new doctrine and witnessed a Ghost dance, as will be described hereafter. They brought back the news to their people, but it made no impression on them and the matter was soon forgotten. (*Stephen, 3.*) In this connection Mr Stephen states, in response to a letter of inquiry, that although he does not recollect any Hopi myth concerning rejuvenation of the world and reunion with the resurrected dead on this earth, yet the doctrine of a reunion with the revivified dead in the under world is a commonly accepted belief of the Hopi. They have also a curious myth

of a fair-hair god and a fair-skin people who came up from the under
world with the Hopi, and who then left them with a promise to return.
This suggests the idea of a messiah, but Mr Stephen has not yet been
able to get the myth in its entirety.   He does not think it derived from

Fig. 71—Vista in the Hopi pueblo of Walpi.

any corrupt source, however, through Spanish or other missionaries, as
the allusions are all of archaic tendency.   (*Stephen, 4.*)

The Cohonino or Havasupai are a small tribe occupying the canyon
of Cataract creek, an affluent of the Colorado, in northern Arizona,

about 120 miles west of the Hopi, with whom they have a considerable trade in buckskins and mesquite bread. They probably obtained the doctrine and the dance directly from the Paiute to the northward. Our only knowledge of the Cohonino dance is derived through Hopi informants, and as the two tribes speak languages radically different the ideas conveyed were neither complete nor definite, but it is evident that the general doctrine was the same, although the dance differed in some respects from that of the other tribes.

We quote again from Stephen's letter of November 22, 1891:

During a quiet interval, in one of the kivas I found the Hopi who brought the tidings of the resurrection to his people. His name is Pütci and his story is very meager and confused. He went on a customary trading visit to the Cojonino in their home at Cataract creek, and I could not determine just when. The chief of the Cojonino is named Navajo, and when Pütci got there, Navajo had but lately returned from a visit to the westward. He had been with the Walapai, the Mohave, and perhaps still farther west, and had been gone nearly three months. He told his people a vague mystic story that he had heard during his travels, to the effect that the long-time dead people of the Antelope, Deer, and Rabbit [Antelope, Deer, etc, are probably Cohonino gentes—J. M.] were to come back and live in their former haunts; that they had reached to a place where were the people of the Puma, the Wolf, and the Bear; that this meeting delayed the coming, but eventually all these people would appear, and in the sequence here related. Pütci was accompanied by three other Hopi, and they said they did not very well understand this strange story. While they were stopping in Cataract cañon a one-night dance was held by the Cojonino, at which these Hopi were present. During the night a long pole, having the tail of an eagle fastened to the end, was brought out and securely planted in the ground, and the dancers were told by their shamans that anyone who could climb this pole and put his mouth on the tail would see his dead mother (maternal ancestor). One man succeeded in climbing it and laid his mouth on the feathers, and then fell to the bottom in a state of collapse. They deemed him dead, but before dawn he recovered and then said that he had seen his dead mother and several other dead ancestors, who told him they were all on their way back. The Hopi on their return home related these marvels, but apparently it made little impression, and it was only with difficulty I could gather the above meager details.

Through the kindness of Mr Thomas V. Keam, trader for the Hopi and Navaho, we get a revision of Pütci's story. Pütci states that in July, 1891, he with three other Hopi went on a visit to the Cohonino to trade for buckskins. When they arrived in the vicinity of the Cohonino camp, they were met by one of the tribe, who informed the visitors that all the Indians were engaged in a very important ceremony, and that before they could enter the camp they must wash their bodies and paint them with white clay. Accordingly, when this had been done, they were escorted to the camp and introduced to the principal chief and headmen, all of whom they found engaged in washing their heads, decorating themselves, and preparing for the ceremony, which took place on a clear space near the camp late in the afternoon. Here a very tall straight pole had been securely fastened upright in the ground. At the top were tied two eagle-tail feathers. A circle was formed around this pole by the Indians, and, after dancing around it until almost dark, one of the men climbed the pole to the top, and remained there until exhausted, when he would slide to the ground, clinging insensible to the pole. After remaining in this state for some time, the medicine-men resuscitated him. On recovery he stood up and told them he had been into another world, where he saw all the old men who had died long ago, and among them his own people. They told him they would all come back in time and bring the deer, the antelope, and all other good things they had when they dwelt on this earth. This cere-mony lasted four days, including the cleansing and decorating of the dancers and the climbing of the pole, with an account of what had been seen by the Indian during the time he was in an apparently life-less state. Each day the ceremony was attended by the whole tribe. (*Keam*, *1*.) Resuscitation by the medicine-men, as here mentioned, is something unknown among the prairie tribes, where the unconscious subject is allowed to lie undisturbed on the ground until the senses return in the natural way.

Beyond the Cohonino, and extending for about 200 miles along Colo-rado river on the Arizona side, are the associated tribes of Mohave, Walapai, and Chemehuevi, numbering in all about 2,800 souls, of whom only about one-third are on a reservation. The Chemehuevi, being a branch of the Paiute and in constant communication with them, undoubtedly had the dance and the doctrine. The Mohave also have much to do with the Paiute, the two tribes interchanging visits and mutually borrowing songs and games. They sent delegates to the messiah and in all probability took up the Ghost dance, in spite of the agent's statement to the contrary. As only 660 of more than 2,000 Mohave are reported as being on the reservation, the agent may have a good reason for not keeping fully informed in regard to them.

Concerning the Walapai we have positive information. In Septem-ber, 1890, the commanding officer at Fort Whipple was informed that a Paiute from southern Utah was among the Walapai, inciting them to dance for the purpose of causing hurricanes and storms to destroy the whites and such Indians as would not participate in the dances. It was stated also that these dances had then been going on for several months and were participated in by a large portion of the tribe, and that each dance lasted four or five nights in succession. On investi-gation it appeared that this Paiute was one of a party who had come down and inaugurated the Ghost dance among the Walapai the preced-ing year. (*G. D.*, *17*.)

We find an account of the Walapai Ghost dance in a local paper a year later. The article states that all the songs were in the language of the Paiute, from whom the doctrine had originally come. The Wala-pai version of the doctrine has been already noted. The dance itself, and the step, as here described, are essentially the same as among other tribes. Each dance lasted five nights, and on the last night was kept up until daylight. Just before daylight on the morning of the last night the medicine men ascended a small butte, where they met and talked with the expected god, and on coming down again delivered his message to the people. The dance was held at irregular intervals, according to the instructions received on the butte by the medicine-men.

The dance place was a circular piece of ground a hundred feet in diameter, inclosed by a fence of poles and bushes, and surrounded by high mountain walls of granite, which reflected the light from half a dozen fires blazing within the circle. The dancers, to the number of 200, clad in white robes with fancy trimmings, their faces and hair painted white in various decorative designs, moved slowly around in a circle, keeping time with a wild chant, while 200 more stood or crouched around the fires, awaiting their turn to participate. The dancers faced toward the center, each holding the hands of the ones next to him and joining in the chant in unison. The dust issued in clouds from beneath their feet, and with the dust and exertion together the performers were soon exhausted and dropped out, when others took their places. After each circuit they rested a few minutes and then started round again. At each circuit a different chant was sung, and thus the dance continued until midnight, when, with a loud clapping of hands, it ended, and the people separated and went to their homes. Throughout the performance two or three chiefs or medicine-men were constantly going about on the outside of the circle to preserve order and reprimand any merriment, one of them explaining to the visitors that, as this was a religious ceremony, due solemnity must be observed. (*F. L. J., 2.*)

CHAPTER XII

THE GHOST DANCE EAST OF THE ROCKIES—AMONG THE SIOUX

In 1889 the Ogalala heard that the son of God had come upon earth in the west. They said the Messiah was there, but he had come to help the Indians and not the whites, and it made the Indians happy to hear this.—*George Sword.*

They signed away a valuable portion of their reservation, and it is now occupied by white people, for which they have received nothing. They understood that ample provision would be made for their support; instead, their supplies have been reduced and much of the time they have been living on half and two-thirds rations. Their crops, as well as the crops of white people, for two years have been almost a total failure. The disaffection is widespread, especially among the Sioux, while the Cheyennes have been on the verge of starvation and were forced to commit depredations to sustain life. These facts are beyond question, and the evidence is positive and sustained by thousands of witnesses.—*General Miles.*

Among the tribes east of the mountains and north of Oklahoma, it appears from official documents in the Indian Office and from other obtainable information that the Ghost dance and the doctrine, if known at all, were never accepted by the Blackfeet of Montana; the Ojibwa of Turtle mountain and Devils lake in North Dakota, or by the rest of the tribe farther to the east in Minnesota, Wisconsin, and Michigan; the Omaha, Winnebago, and Ponka in Nebraska; the small band of Sauk and Fox in Iowa; the still smaller band of Sauk and Fox, the Potawatomi, Kickapoo, Iowa, and Ojibwa in northeastern Kansas; or by the Sioux of Devils lake in North Dakota, Lake Traverse (Sisseton agency) and Flandreau in South Dakota, and Santee agency in Nebraska. All or most of these Sioux belong to the Santee or eastern division of the tribe, and have long been under civilizing influences. According to official statements the dance was not taken up by any of the Sioux of Crow Creek or Yankton agencies in South Dakota, but they were certainly more or less affected by it, as they knew all about it and are in constant communication with the wilder bands of Sioux which were concerned in the outbreak. I was informed by the Omaha and Winnebago in 1891 that they had been told of the new messiah by visiting Sioux from Pine Ridge agency in April, 1890, and later on by other Sioux from Yankton agency, but had put no faith in the story, and had never organized a Ghost dance. According to the agent in charge, the Crow of Montana were not affected. This, if true, is remarkable, in view of the fact that the Crow are a large tribe and comparatively primitive, and have living near them the wildest of the Ghost-dancing tribes, the northern Cheyenne especially occupying practically the same reservation. It is possible that their experience in the Sword-bearer affair in 1887, already mentioned, had a tendency to weaken their faith in later prophets. Dr George Bird Grinnell, a competent authority, states, in reply to a personal letter, that nothing was known about the dance by the Blackfeet of Montana or by the Blackfeet, Sarsi, or Plains Cree on the Canadian side of the boundary line.

Within the same general region, east of the Rocky mountains and north of Oklahoma, the doctrine and the dance were accepted by the Asiniboin (Fort Belknap and Fort Peck agencies), Grosventres (Arapaho subtribe, Fort Belknap agency), northern Cheyenne of Montana; the Arikara, Grosventres (Minitari), and Mandan of Fort Berthold agency, North Dakota; the Shoshoni and northern Arapaho on Wind River reservation in Wyoming, as already mentioned; and by the great body of the Sioux, at Fort Peck agency (Yanktonais), Montana, and at Standing Rock, Cheyenne River, Lower Brulé, Pine Ridge, and Rosebud agencies in North Dakota and South Dakota. The whole number of Sioux concerned was about 20,000, of whom 16,000 belonged to the Teton division, among the wildest and most warlike of all the western tribes. A few Cheyenne are also associated with the Sioux at Pine Ridge.

The northern Arapaho and the Shoshoni of Wyoming were the medium by which the doctrine of the new messiah was originally communicated to all these tribes. In the spring of 1889, Nakash, "Sage," the Arapaho chief already mentioned, crossed the mountains to investigate the reports of the new religion, and brought back a full confirmation of all that had been told them from the west. A visiting Grosventre, then among the Arapaho, heard the story and brought back the wonderful news to the Grosventres and Asiniboin of Fort Belknap, but although his account was received by some with unquestioning faith, the excitement had in it nothing of a dangerous character. (*G. D.*, *18*.)

In a short time the news spread to the Cheyenne in Montana and the Sioux of the Dakotas, and in the fall of 1889 delegates from these two tribes arrived at Fort Washakie to learn more about the messiah in the west. The principal Cheyenne delegate was Porcupine, while Short Bull and Kicking Bear were the leaders of the Sioux party. After hearing the statements of the Arapaho and Shoshoni, it was decided that some of the Cheyenne should return and report to their tribe, while Porcupine and one or two others, with the Sioux delegates, several Shoshoni, and the Arapaho, Sitting Bull, and Friday, should go to Nevada, interview the messiah himself, and learn the whole truth of the matter. Accordingly, about November, 1889, Porcupine and his companions left Fort Washakie in Wyoming for Fort Hall reservation in Idaho, where they met the Shoshoni and Bannock and were well received and entertained by them. The tribes at this place were firm believers in the new doctrine, and Porcupine states that from there on to the end of the journey all the Indians they met were dancing the Ghost dance.   After stopping a few days at Fort Hall, they went on again, accompanied by several Bannock and Shoshoni, and going rapidly by railroad soon found themselves in the country of the Paiute, and after stopping at one or two camps arrived at the agency at Pyramid lake.   Here the Paiute furnished them conveyances and guides to the other agency farther south at Walker river.   Porcupine is our principal authority for the events of the trip, and although he claims that he undertook this journey of a thousand miles without any definite purpose or destination in view, it is evident enough from his own narrative that he left Wyoming with the fixed intention of verifying. the rumors of a messiah.   He has much to say of the kindness of the whites they met west of the mountains, who, it will be remembered, were largely Mormons, who have always manifested a special interest in the Indians.   He also states that many of the whites took part with the Indians in the dance.

They were now in the messiah's country.   "The Fisheaters, near Pyramid lake, told me that Christ had appeared on earth again.   They said Christ knew he was coming; that eleven of his children were also coming from a far land.   It appeared that Christ had sent for me to go there, and that was why, unconsciously, I took my journey.   It had been foreordained.   Christ had summoned myself and others from all heathen tribes.   There were more different languages than I had ever heard before, and I did not understand any of them."   The delegation of which Porcupine was a member was probably the one mentioned by the agent in charge at Pyramid lake as having arrived in the spring of 1890, and consisting of thirty-four Indians of different tribes.   (*G. D., 19.*)

In a few days preparations were made for a great dance near Walker lake, with all the delegates from the various tribes and hundreds of Indians in attendance.   They danced two nights or longer, the messiah himself—Wovoka—coming down from his home in Mason valley to lead the ceremony.   After the dance Wovoka went into a trance, and on awaking announced to those assembled that he had been to the other world and had seen the spirits of their dead friends and of his own father and mother, and had been sent back to teach the people. According to Porcupine he claimed to be the returned Christ and bore on his body the scars of the crucifixion.   He told them that the dead were to be resurrected, and that as the earth was old and worn out it would be renewed as it used to be and made better; that when this happened the youth of everyone would be renewed with each return of spring, and that they would live forever; that there would be universal peace, and that any tribe that refused his message would be destroyed from the face of the earth.

It was early in the spring of 1890 when Porcupine and his Cheyenne companions returned to their tribe at Tongue River agency in Montana with the news of the appearance of the messiah.   A council was called and Porcupine made a full report of the journey and delivered the divine message, talking five days in succession. The report aroused the wildest excitement among the Cheyenne, and after several long debates on the subject the Ghost dance was inaugurated at the various camps in accordance with the instructions from beyond the mountains. In June the matter came to the attention of the military officer on the reservation, who summoned Porcupine before him and obtained from him a full account of the journey and the doctrine. (See page 793.) Porcupine insisted strongly on the sacred character of the messiah and his message, and challenged any doubters to return with him to Nevada and investigate for themselves. He claimed also that the messiah could speak all languages. As a matter of fact, Wovoka speaks only his native Paiute and a little English, but due allowance must be made for the mental exaltation of the narrator.

Grinnell states that the failure of certain things to happen according to the predictions of the messiah, in September, 1890, caused a temporary loss of faith on the part of the Cheyenne, but that shortly afterward some visiting Shoshoni and Arapaho from Wyoming reported that in their journey as they came over they had met a party of Indians who had been dead thirty or forty years, but had been resurrected by the messiah, and were now going about as if they had never died. It is useless to speculate on the mental condition of men who could seriously report or believe such things; but, however that may be, the result was that the Cheyenne returned to the dance with redoubled fervor. (*J. F. L., 5.*)

The Sioux first heard of the messiah in 1889. According to the statement of Captain George Sword, of that tribe, the information came to the Ogalala (Sioux of Pine Ridge) in that year, through the Shoshoni and Arapaho. Later in the same year a delegation consisting of Good Thunder and several others started out to the west to find the messiah and to investigate the truth of the rumor. On their return they announced that the messiah had indeed come to help the Indians, but not the whites. Their report aroused a fervor of joyful excitement among the Indians and a second delegation was sent out in 1890, consisting of Good Thunder, Cloud Horse, Yellow Knife, and Short Bull. They confirmed the report of the first delegation, and on this assurance the Ghost dance was inaugurated among the Sioux at Pine Ridge in the spring of 1890.

The matter is stated differently and more correctly by William Selwyn, an educated Sioux, at that time employed as postmaster at Pine Ridge. He says there was some talk on the subject by Indians from western tribes who visited the agency in the fall of 1888 (?), but that it did not excite much attention until 1889, when numerous letters concerning the new messiah were received by the Indians at Pine Ridge from tribes in Utah, Wyoming, Montana, Dakota, and Oklahoma. As Selwyn was postmaster, the Indians who could not read usually brought their letters to him to read for them, so that he was thus in position to get accurate knowledge of the extent and nature of the excitement. It may be remarked here that, under present conditions, when the various tribes are isolated upon widely separated reservations, the Ghost dance could never have become so widespread, and would probably have died out within a year of its inception, had it not been for the efficient aid it received from the returned pupils of various eastern government schools, who conducted the sacred correspondence for their friends at the different agencies, acted as interpreters for the delegates to the messiah, and in various ways assumed the leadership and conduct of the dance.

In the fall of 1889, at a council held at Pine Ridge by Red Cloud, Young Man Afraid, Little Wound, American Horse, and other Sioux chiefs, a delegation was appointed to visit the western agencies to learn more about the new messiah. The delegates chosen were Good Thunder, Flat Iron, Yellow Breast, and Broken Arm, from Pine Ridge; Short Bull and another from Rosebud, and Kicking Bear from Cheyenne River agency. They started on their journey to the west, and soon began to write from Wyoming, Utah, and beyond the mountains, confirming all that had been said of the advent of a redeemer. They were gone all winter, and their return in the spring of 1890 aroused an intense excitement among the Sioux, who had been anxiously awaiting their report. All the delegates agreed that there was a man near the base of the Sierras who said that he was the son of God, who had once been killed by the whites, and who bore on his body the scars of the crucifixion. He had now returned to punish the whites for their wickedness, especially for their injustice toward the Indians. With the coming of the next spring (1891) he would wipe the whites from the face of the earth, and would then resurrect all the dead Indians, bring back the buffalo and other game, and restore the supremacy of the aboriginal race. He had before come to the whites, but they had rejected him. He was now the God of the Indians, and they must pray to him and call him "father," and prepare for his awful coming. Selwyn's account of this delegation, which was accompanied by representatives of several other tribes, including Porcupine the Cheyenne, and Sitting Bull the Arapaho, agrees with the statements of the Arapaho as given in chapter XIV. Three of the Sioux delegates found their way to Umatilla reservation in Oregon and remained there several days discussing the new doctrine. (Comr., 30—Dorchester, 529.)

The delegates made their report at Pine Ridge in April, 1890. A council was at once called to discuss the matter, but Selwyn informed the agent, Colonel Gallagher, who had Good Thunder and two others arrested and imprisoned. They were held in confinement two days, but refused to talk when questioned. The intended council was not held, but soon afterward Kicking Bear returned from a visit to the northern Arapaho in Wyoming with the news that those Indians were already dancing, and could see and talk with their dead relatives in the trance. The excitement which the agent had thought to smother by the arrest of the leaders broke out again with added strength. Red Cloud himself, the great chief of the Ogalala, declared his adhesion to the new doctrine and said his people must do as the messiah had commanded. Another council was called on White Clay creek, a few miles from Pine Ridge agency, and the Ghost dance was formally inaugurated among the Sioux, the recent delegates acting as priests and leaders of the ceremony.

As the result of all he could learn, Selwyn, in November, 1890, warned the agent in charge of Yankton agency that the Indians intended a general outbreak in the spring. Six months earlier, and before Porcupine's statement had been made to the officer at Camp Crook, a letter dated May 29, 1890, had been addressed to the Interior Department from a citizen of Pierre, South Dakota, stating that the Sioux, or a portion of them, were secretly planning for an outbreak in the near future. This was the first intimation of trouble ahead. (*G. D., 20.*)

Wonderful things were said of the messiah by the returned delegates. It was claimed that he could make animals talk and distant objects appear close at hand, and that he came down from heaven in a cloud. He conjured up before their eyes a vision of the spirit world, so that when they looked they beheld an ocean, and beyond it a land upon which they saw "all the nations of Indians coming home," but as they looked the vision faded away, the messiah saying that the time had not yet come. Curiously enough, although he came to restore the old life, he advised his hearers to go to work and to send their children to school. Should the soldiers attempt to harm him, he said he need only stretch out his arms and his enemies would become powerless, or the ground would open and swallow them. On their way home if they should kill a buffalo—the messiah had evidently not read Allen's monograph— they must cut off its head and tail and feet and leave them on the ground and the buffalo would come to life again. They must tell their people to follow his instructions. Unbelievers and renegade Indians would be buried under the new earth which was to come upon the old. They must use the sacred red and white paint and the sacred grass (possibly sagebrush) which he gave them, and in the spring, when the green grass came, their people who were gone before would return, and they would see their friends again.

Now comes the most remarkable part, quoting from the statement given to Captain Sword:

The people from every tipi send for us to visit them; they are people who died many years ago. Chasing Hawk, who died not long ago, was there and we went to his tipi. He was living with his wife, who was killed in war long ago. They live in a buffalo skin tipi—a very large one—and he wanted all his friends to go there to live. A son of Good Thunder, who died in war long ago, was one who also took us to his tipi, so his father saw him. When coming we come to a herd of buffaloes. We killed one and took everything except the four feet, head, and tail, and when we came a little ways from it there was the buffaloes come to life again and went off. This was one of the messiah's word came to truth. The messiah said, "I will short your journey when you feel tired of the long ways, if you call upon me." This we did when we were tired. The night came upon us, we stopped at a place and we called upon the messiah to help us because we were tired of long journey. We went to sleep and in the morning we found ourselves at a great distance from where we stopped.

It is useless to assert that these men, who had been selected by the chiefs of their tribe to investigate and report upon the truth or falsity of the messiah rumors, were all liars, and that all the Cheyenne, Arapaho, and other delegates who reported equally wonderful things were liars likewise. They were simply laboring under some strange psychologic influence as yet unexplained. The story of the revivified buffalo became so widely current as to form the subject of a Kiowa ghost song.

Having mentioned some characteristics of the Ghost dance west of the Rockies, we shall notice here some of the peculiar features of the dance as it existed among the Sioux. The ceremony will be described in detail later on.

Before going into the dance the men, or at least the leaders, fasted for twenty-four hours, and then at sunrise entered the sweat-house for the religious rite of purification preliminary to painting themselves for the dance. The sweat-house is a small circular framework of willow branches driven into the ground and bent over and brought together at the top in such a way that when covered with blankets or buffalo robes the structure forms a diminutive round-top tipi just high enough to enable several persons to sit or to stand in a stooping posture inside. The doorway faces the east, as is the rule in Indian structures, and at the distance of a few feet in front of the doorway is a small mound of earth, on which is placed a buffalo skull, with the head turned as if looking into the lodge. The earth of which the mound is formed is taken from a hole dug in the center of the lodge. Near the sweat-house, on the outside, there is frequently a tall sacrifice pole, from the top of which are hung strips of bright-colored cloth, packages of tobacco, or other offerings to the deity invoked by the devotee on any particular occasion.

The sweat bath is in frequent use, both as a religious rite of purification and as a hygienic treatment. Like everything else in Indian life, even the sanitary application is attended with much detail of religious ceremony. Fresh bundles of the fragrant wild sage are strewn upon the ground inside of the sweat-house, and a fire is kindled outside a short distance away. In this fire stones are heated by the medicine-men, and when all is ready the patient or devotee, stripped to the breech-cloth, enters the sweat-house. The stones are then handed in to him by the priests by means of two forked sticks, cut especially for the purpose, and with two other forked sticks he puts the stones into the hole already mentioned as having been dug in the center of the lodge. Water is then passed in to him, which he pours over the hot stones until the whole interior is filled with steam; the blankets are pulled

SIOUX SWEAT-HOUSE AND SACRIFICE POLE

tight to close every opening, and he sits in this aboriginal Turkish bath until his naked body is dripping with perspiration. During this time the doctors outside are doing their part in the way of praying to the gods and keeping up the supply of hot stones and water until in their estimation he has been sufficiently purified, physically or morally, when he emerges and resumes his clothing, sometimes first checking the perspiration and inducing a reaction by a plunge into the neighboring stream. The sweat bath in one form or another was common to almost every tribe in the United States, but as an accompaniment to the Ghost dance it seems to have been used only by the Sioux. It may have been used in this connection among the Shoshoni or northern Cheyenne, but was not among any of the tribes of the southern plains. The Ghost-dance sweat-house of the Sioux was frequently made sufficiently large to accommodate a considerable number of persons standing inside at the same time.

After the sweating ceremony the dancer was painted by the medicine-men who acted as leaders, of whom Sitting Bull was accounted the greatest among the Sioux. The design and color varied with the individual, being frequently determined by a previous trance vision of the subject, but circles, crescents, and crosses, representing respectively the sun, the moon, and the morning star, were always favorite figures upon forehead, face, and cheeks. As this was not a naked dance, the rest of the body was not usually painted. After the painting the dancer was robed in the sacred ghost shirt already described. This also was painted with symbolic figures, among which were usually represented sun, moon, or stars, the eagle, magpie, crow, or sage-hen, all sacred to the Ghost dance among the Sioux. In connection with the painting the face and body were rubbed with the sweet-smelling vernal grass (*Hierochloe*), used for this purpose by many of the prairie tribes, and sometimes also burned as incense in their sacred ceremonies or carried as a perfume in small pouches attached to the clothing.

The painting occupied most of the morning, so that it was about noon before the participants formed the circle for the dance. Among the Sioux, unlike the southern and western tribes generally, a small tree was planted in the center of the circle, with an American flag or colored streamers floating from the top. Around the base of this tree sat the priests. At a great dance at No Water's camp on White river near Pine Ridge, shortly before the arrival of the troops, a young woman standing within the circle gave the signal for the performance by shooting into the air toward the cardinal points four sacred arrows, made after the old primitive fashion with bone heads, and dipped in the blood of a steer before being brought to the dance. These were then gathered up and tied to the branches of the tree, together with the bow, a gaming wheel and sticks, and a peculiar staff or wand with horns. (See plates XC, XCI.) Another young woman, or the same one, remained standing near the tree throughout the dance, holding a sacred redstone pipe stretched out toward the west, the direction from which the messiah was to appear.

At the beginning the performers, men and women, sat on the ground in a large circle around the tree. A plaintive chant was then sung, after which a vessel of some sacred food was passed around the circle until everyone had partaken, when, at a signal by the priests, the dancers rose to their feet, joined hands, and began to chant the opening song and move slowly around the circle from right to left. The rest of the performance, with its frenzies, trances, and recitals of visions, was the same as with the southern tribes, as will be described in detail hereafter. Like these tribes also, the Sioux usually selected Sunday, the great medicine day of the white man, for the ceremony.

We come now to the Sioux outbreak of 1890, but before going into the history of this short but costly war it is appropriate to state briefly the causes of the outbreak. In the documentary appendix to this chapter these causes are fully set forth by competent authorities—civilian, military, missionary, and Indian. They may be summarized as (1) unrest of the conservative element under the decay of the old life, (2) repeated neglect of promises made by the government, and (3) hunger.

The Sioux are the largest and strongest tribe within the United States. In spite of wars, removals, and diminished food supply since the advent of the white man, they still number nearly 26,000. In addition to these there are about 600 more residing in Canada. They formerly held the headwaters of the Mississippi, extending eastward almost to Lake Superior, but were driven into the prairie about two centuries ago by their enemies, the Ojibwa, after the latter had obtained firearms from the French. On coming out on the buffalo plains they became possessed of the horse, by means of which reinforcement to their own overpowering numbers the Sioux were soon enabled to assume the offensive, and in a short time had made themselves the undisputed masters of an immense territory extending, in a general way, from Minnesota to the Rocky mountains and from the Yellowstone to the Platte. A few small tribes were able to maintain their position within these limits, but only by keeping close to their strongly built permanent villages on the Missouri. Millions of buffalo to furnish unlimited food supply, thousands of horses, and hundreds of miles of free range made the Sioux, up to the year 1868, the richest and most prosperous, the proudest, and withal, perhaps, the wildest of all the tribes of the plains.

In that year, in pursuance of a policy inaugurated for bringing all the plains tribes under the direct control of the government, a treaty was negotiated with the Sioux living west of the Missouri by which they renounced their claims to a great part of their territory and had "set apart for their absolute and undisturbed use and occupation"— so the treaty states—a reservation which embraced all of the present state of South Dakota west of Missouri river. At the same time agents were appointed and agencies established for them; annuities and rations, cows, physicians, farmers, teachers, and other good things were promised them, and they agreed to allow railroad routes to be surveyed and built and military posts to be established in their territory and neighborhood. At one stroke they were reduced from a free nation to dependent wards of the government. It was stipulated also that they should be allowed to hunt within their old range, outside the limits of the reservation, so long as the buffalo abounded—a proviso which, to the Indians, must have meant forever.

The reservation thus established was an immense one, and would have been ample for all the Sioux while being gradually educated toward civilization, could the buffalo have remained and the white man kept away. But the times were changing. The building of the railroads brought into the plains swarms of hunters and emigrants, who began to exterminate the buffalo at such a rate that in a few years the Sioux, with all the other hunting tribes of the plains, realized that their food supply was rapidly going. Then gold was discovered in the Black hills, within the reservation, and at once thousands of miners and other thousands of lawless desperadoes rushed into the country in defiance of the protests of the Indians and the pledges of the government, and the Sioux saw their last remaining hunting ground taken from them. The result was the Custer war and massacre, and a new agreement in 1876 by which the Sioux were shorn of one-third of their guaranteed reservation, including the Black hills, and this led to deep and widespread dissatisfaction throughout the tribe. The conservatives brooded over the past and planned opposition to further changes which they felt themselves unable to meet. The progressives felt that the white man's promises meant nothing.

On this point Commissioner Morgan says, in his statement of the causes of the outbreak:

Prior to the agreement of 1876 buffalo and deer were the main support of the Sioux. Food, tents, bedding were the direct outcome of hunting, and with furs and pelts as articles of barter or exchange it was easy for the Sioux to procure whatever constituted for them the necessaries, the comforts, or even the luxuries of life. Within eight years from the agreement of 1876 the buffalo had gone and the Sioux had left to them alkali land and government rations. It is hard to overestimate the magnitude of the calamity, as they viewed it, which happened to these people by the sudden disappearance of the buffalo and the large diminution in the numbers of deer and other wild animals. Suddenly, almost without warning, they were expected at once and without previous training to settle down to the pursuits of agriculture in a land largely unfitted for such use. The freedom of the chase was to be exchanged for the idleness of the camp. The boundless range was to be abandoned for the circumscribed reservation, and abundance of plenty to be supplanted by limited and decreasing government subsistence and supplies. Under these circumstances it is not in human nature not to be discontented and restless, even turbulent and violent. (*Comr., 28.*)

It took our own Aryan ancestors untold centuries to develop from savagery into civilization. Was it reasonable to expect that the Sioux could do the same in fourteen years?

The white population in the Black hills had rapidly increased, and it had become desirable to open communication between eastern and western Dakota. To accomplish this, it was proposed to cut out the heart of the Sioux reservation, and in 1882, only six years after the Black hills had been seized, the Sioux were called on to surrender more territory. A commission was sent out to treat with them, but the price offered—only about 8 cents per acre—was so absurdly small, and the methods used so palpably unjust, that friends of the Indians interposed and succeeded in defeating the measure in Congress. Another agreement was prepared, but experience had made the Indians suspicious, and it was not until a third commission went out, under the chairmanship of General Crook, known to the Indians as a brave soldier and an honorable man, that the Sioux consented to treat. (*Welsh, 1.*) The result, after much effort on the part of the commission and determined opposition by the conservatives, was another agreement, in 1889, by which the Sioux surrendered one-half (about 11,000,000 acres) of their remaining territory, and the great reservation was cut up into five smaller ones, the northern and southern reservations being separated by a strip 60 miles wide.

Then came a swift accumulation of miseries. Dakota is an arid country with thin soil and short seasons. Although well adapted to grazing it is not suited to agriculture, as is sufficiently proven by the fact that the white settlers in that and the adjoining state of Nebraska have several times been obliged to call for state or federal assistance on account of failure of crops. To wild Indians hardly in from the warpath the problem was much more serious. As General Miles points out in his official report, thousands of white settlers after years of successive failures had given up the struggle and left the country, but the Indians, confined to reservations, were unable to emigrate, and were also as a rule unable to find employment, as the whites might, by which they could earn a subsistence. The buffalo was gone. They must depend on their cattle, their crops, and the government rations issued in return for the lands they had surrendered. If these failed, they must starve. The highest official authorities concur in the statement that all of these did fail, and that the Indians were driven to outbreak by starvation. (See appendix to this chapter.)

In 1888 their cattle had been diminished by disease. In 1889 their crops were a failure, owing largely to the fact that the Indians had been called into the agency in the middle of the farming season and kept there to treat with the commission, going back afterward to find their fields trampled and torn up by stock during their absence. Then followed epidemics of measles, grippe, and whooping cough, in rapid succession and with terribly fatal results. Anyone who understands the Indian character needs not the testimony of witnesses to know the mental effect thus produced. Sullenness and gloom, amounting almost to despair, settled down on the Sioux, especially among the wilder portion. "The people said their children were all dying from the face of the earth, and they might as well be killed at once." Then came another entire failure of crops in 1890, and an unexpected reduction of rations, and the Indians were brought face to face with starvation. They had been expressly and repeatedly told by the commission that their rations would not be affected by their signing the treaty, but immediately on the consummation of the agreement Congress cut down their beef rations by 2,000,000 pounds at Rosebud, 1,000,000 at Pine Ridge, and in less proportion at other agencies. Earnest protest against this reduction was made by the commission which had negotiated the treaty, by Commissioner Morgan, and by General Miles, but still Congress failed to remedy the matter until the Sioux had actually been driven to rebellion. As Commissioner Morgan states, "It was not until January, 1891, *after the troubles*, that an appropriation of $100,000 was made by Congress for additional beef for the Sioux." The protest of the commission, a full year before the outbreak, as quoted by Commissioner Morgan (see page 829), is strong and positive on this point.

Commissioner Morgan, while claiming that the Sioux had before been receiving more rations than they were justly entitled to according to their census number, and denying that the reduction was such as to cause even extreme suffering, yet states that the reduction was especially unwise at this juncture, as it was in direct violation of the promises made to the Indians, and would be used as an argument by those opposed to the treaty to show that the government cared nothing for the Indians after it had obtained their lands. It is quite possible that the former number of rations was greater than the actual number of persons, as it is always a difficult matter to count roving Indians, and the difficulties were greater when the old census was made. The census is taken at long intervals and the tendency is nearly always toward a decrease. Furthermore, it has usually been the policy with agents to hold their Indians quiet by keeping them as well fed as possible. On the other hand, it must be remembered that the issue is based on the weight of the cattle as delivered at the agency in the fall, and that months of exposure to a Dakota winter will reduce this weight by several hundred pounds to the animal. The official investigation by Captain Hurst at Cheyenne River agency shows conclusively that the essential food items of meat, flour, and coffee were far below the amount stipulated by the treaty. (See page 837.)

In regard to the effect of this food deficiency Bishop Hare says: "The people were often hungry and, the physicians in many cases said, died, when taken sick, not so much from disease as for want of food." General Miles says: "The fact that they had not received sufficient food is admitted by the agents and the officers of the government who have had opportunities of knowing," and in another place he states that in spite of crop failures and other difficulties, after the sale of the reservation "instead of an increase, or even a reasonable supply for their support, they have been compelled to live on half and two-thirds rations and received nothing for the surrender of their lands." The testimony from every agency is all to the same effect.

There were other causes of dissatisfaction, some local and others general and chronic, which need not be detailed here. Some of these are treated in the documents appended to this chapter. Prominent among them were the failure of Congress to make payment of the money due the Sioux for the lands recently ceded, or to have the new lines surveyed promptly so that the Indians might know what was still theirs and select their allotments accordingly; failure to reimburse the friendly Indians for horses confiscated fourteen years before; the tardy arrival of annuities, consisting largely of winter clothing, which according to the treaty were due by the 1st of August, but which seldom arrived until the middle of winter; the sweeping and frequent changes of agency employees from the agent down, preventing anything like a systematic working out of any consistent policy, and almost always operating against the good of the service, especially at Pine Ridge, where so brave and efficient a man as McGillycuddy was followed by such a one as Royer—and, finally, the Ghost dance.

The Ghost dance itself, in the form which it assumed among the Sioux, was only a symptom and expression of the real causes of dissatisfaction, and with such a man as McGillycuddy or McLaughlin in charge at Pine Ridge there would have been no outbreak, in spite of broken promises and starvation, and the Indians could have been controlled until Congress had afforded relief. That it was not the cause of the outbreak is sufficiently proved by the fact that there was no serious trouble, excepting on the occasion of the attempt to arrest Sitting Bull, on any other of the Sioux reservations, and none at all among any of the other Ghost-dancing tribes from the Missouri to the Sierras, although the doctrine and the dance were held by nearly every tribe within that area and are still held by the more important. Among the Paiute, where the doctrine originated and the messiah has his home, there was never the slightest trouble. It is significant that Commissioner Morgan in his official statement of the causes of the outbreak places the "messiah craze" eleventh in a list of twelve, the twelfth being the alarm created by the appearance of troops. The Sioux outbreak of 1890 was due entirely to local grievances, recent or long standing. The remedy and preventive for similar trouble in the future is sufficiently indicated in the appended statements of competent authorities.

APPENDIX—CAUSES OF THE OUTBREAK

COMMISSIONER MORGAN'S STATEMENT

[From the Report of the Commissioner of Indian Affairs for 1891, Vol. I, 132-135.]

In stating the events which led to this outbreak among the Sioux, the endeavor too often has been merely to find some opportunity for locating blame. The causes are complex, and many are obscure and remote. Among them may be named the following:

First. A feeling of unrest and apprehension in the mind of the Indians has naturally grown out of the rapid advance in civilization and the great changes which this advance has necessitated in their habits and mode of life.

Second. Prior to the agreement of 1876 buffalo and deer were the main support of the Sioux. Food, tents, bedding were the direct outcome of hunting, and, with furs and pelts as articles of barter or exchange, it was easy for the Sioux to procure whatever constituted for them the necessaries, the comforts, or even the luxuries of life. Within eight years from the agreement of 1876 the buffalo had gone, and the Sioux had left to them alkali land and government rations. It is hard to overestimate the magnitude of the calamity, as they viewed it, which happened to these people by the sudden disappearance of the buffalo and the large diminution in the numbers of deer and other wild animals. Suddenly, almost without warning, they were expected at once and without previous training to settle down to the pursuits of agriculture in a land largely unfitted for such use. The freedom of the chase was to be exchanged for the idleness of the camp. The boundless range was to be abandoned for the circumscribed reservation, and abundance of plenty to be supplanted by limited and decreasing government subsistence and supplies. Under these circumstances it is not in human nature not to be discontented and restless, even turbulent and violent.

Third. During a long series of years, treaties, agreements, cessions of land and privileges, and removals of bands and agencies have kept many of the Sioux, particularly those at Pine Ridge and Rosebud, in an unsettled condition, especially as some of the promises made them were fulfilled tardily or not at all. (A brief history of negotiations with the Sioux was given in my letter of December 24, 1890, to the Department, which will be found in the appendix, page 182.)

Fourth. The very large reduction of the great Sioux reservation, brought about by the Sioux commission through the consent of the large majority of the adult males, was bitterly opposed by a large, influential minority. For various reasons, they regarded the cession as unwise, and did all in their power to prevent its consummation, and afterwards were constant in their expressions of dissatisfaction and in their endeavors to awaken a like feeling in the minds of those who signed the agreement.

Fifth. There was diminution and partial failure of the crops for 1889, by reason of their neglect by the Indians, who were congregated in large numbers at the council with the Sioux commission, and a further diminution of ordinary crops by the drought of 1890. Also, in 1888, the disease of black leg appeared among the cattle of the Indians.

Sixth. At this time, by delayed and reduced appropriations, the Sioux rations were temporarily cut down. Rations were not diminished to such an extent as to bring the Indians to starvation or even extreme suffering, as has been often reported; but short rations came just after the Sioux commission had negotiated the agreement for the cession of lands, and, as a condition of securing the signatures of the majority, had assured the Indians that their rations would be continued unchanged. To this matter the Sioux commission called special attention in their report dated December 24, 1889, as follows:

"During our conference at the different agencies we were repeatedly asked whether the acceptance or rejection of the act of Congress would influence the action of the government with reference to their rations, and in every instance the Indians were assured that subsistence was furnished in accordance with former treaties, and that signing would not affect their rations, and that they would continue to receive them as provided in former treaties. Without our assurances to this effect it would have been impossible to have secured their consent to the cession of their lands. Since our visit to the agencies it appears that large reductions have been made in the amounts of beef furnished for issues, amounting at Rosebud to 2,000,000 pounds and at Pine Ridge to 1,000,000 pounds, and lesser amounts at the other agencies. This action of the Department, following immediately after the successful issue of our negotiations, can not fail to have an injurious effect. It will be impossible to convince the Indians that the reduction is not due to the fact that the government, having obtained their land, has less concern in looking after their material interests than before. It will be looked upon as a breach of faith and especially as a violation of the express statements of the commissioners. Already this action is being used by the Indians opposed to the bill, notably at Pine Ridge, as an argument in support of the wisdom of their opposition."

In forwarding this report to Congress the Department called special attention to the above-quoted statements of the commission and said: "The commission further remarks that as to the quality of the rations furnished there seems to be no just cause for complaint, but that it was particularly to be avoided that there should be any diminution of the rations promised under the former treaties at this time, as the Indians would attribute it to their assent to the bill. Such diminution certainly should not be allowed, as the government is bound in good faith to carry into effect the former treaties where not directly and positively affected by the act, and if under the provisions of the treaty itself the ration is at any time reduced, the commissioners recommend that the Indians should be notified before spring opens, so that crops may be cultivated. It is desirable that the recent reduction made should be restored, as it is now impossible to convince the Indians that it was not due to the fact that the government, having obtained their lands, had less concern in looking after their material interests."

Notwithstanding this plea of the commission and of the Department, the appropriation made for the subsistence and civilization of the Sioux for 1890 was only $950,000, or $50,000 less than the amount estimated and appropriated for 1888 and 1889, and the appropriation not having been made until August 19, rations had to be temporarily purchased and issued in limited quantities pending arrival of new supplies to be secured from that appropriation. It was not until January, 1891, after the troubles, that an appropriation of $100,000 was made by Congress for additional beef for the Sioux.

Seventh. Other promises made by the Sioux commission and the agreement were not promptly fulfilled; among them were increase of appropriations for education, for which this office had asked an appropriation of $150,000; the payment of $200,000 in compensation for ponies taken from the Sioux in 1876 and 1877; and the reimbursement of the Crow Creek Indians for a reduction made in their per capita allowance of land, as compared with the amount allowed other Sioux, which called for an appropriation of $187,039. The fulfillment of all these promises except the last named was contained in the act of January 19, 1891.

Eighth. In 1889 and 1890 epidemics of la grippe, measles, and whooping cough, followed by many deaths, added to the gloom and misfortune which seemed to surround the Indians.

Ninth. The wording of the agreement changed the boundary line between the Rosebud and Pine Ridge diminished reservations and necessitated a removal of a portion of the Rosebud Indians from the lands which, by the agreement, were included in the Pine Ridge reservation to lands offered them in lieu thereof upon the diminished Rosebud reserve. This, although involving no great hardship to any considerable number, added to the discontent.

Tenth. Some of the Indians were greatly opposed to the census which Congress ordered should be taken. The census at Rosebud, as reported by Special Agent Lea and confirmed by a special census taken by Agent Wright, revealed the somewhat startling fact that rations had been issued to Indians very largely in excess of the number actually present, and this diminution of numbers as shown by the census necessitated a diminution of the rations, which was based, of course, upon the census.

Eleventh. The Messiah craze, which fostered the belief that "ghost shirts" would be invulnerable to bullets, and that the supremacy of the Indian race was assured, added to discontent the fervor of fanaticism and brought those who accepted the new faith into the attitude of sullen defiance, but defensive rather than aggressive.

Twelfth. The sudden appearance of military upon their reservation gave rise to the wildest rumors among the Indians of danger and disaster, which were eagerly circulated by disaffected Indians and corroborated by exaggerated accounts in the newspapers, and these and other influences connected with and inseparable from military movements frightened many Indians away from their agencies into the bad lands and largely intensified whatever spirit of opposition to the government existed

EX-AGENT McGILLYCUDDY'S STATEMENT

[*Letter of Dr V. T. McGillycuddy, formerly agent at Pine Ridge, written in reply to inquiry from General L. W. Colby, commanding Nebraska state troops during the outbreak, and dated January 15, 1891. From article on "The Sioux Indian War of 1890-91," by General L. W. Colby, in Transactions and Reports of the Nebraska State Historical Society, III, 1892, pages 176-180.*]

SIR: In answer to your inquiry of a recent date, I would state that in my opinion to no one cause can be attributed the recent so-called outbreak on the part of the Sioux, but rather to a combination of causes gradually cumulative in their effect and dating back through many years—in fact to the inauguration of our practically demonstrated faulty Indian policy.

There can be no question but that many of the treaties, agreements, or solemn promises made by our government with these Indians have been broken. Many of them have been kept by us technically, but as far as the Indian is concerned have been misunderstood by him through a lack of proper explanation at time of signing, and hence considered by him as broken.

It must also be remembered that in all of the treaties made by the government with the Indians, a large portion of them have not agreed to or signed the same. Noticeably was this so in the agreement secured by us with them the summer before last, by which we secured one-half of the remainder of the Sioux reserve, amounting to about 16,000 square miles. This agreement barely carried with the Sioux nation as a whole, but did not carry at Pine Ridge or Rosebud, where the strong majority were against it; and it must be noted that wherever there was the strongest opposition manifested to the recent treaty, there, during the present trouble, have been found the elements opposed to the government.

The Sioux nation, which at one time, with the confederated bands of Cheyennes and Arapahos, controlled a region of country bounded on the north by the Yellowstone, on the south by the Arkansas, and reaching from the Missouri river to the Rocky mountains, has seen this large domain, under the various treaties, dwindle down to their now limited reserve of less than 16,000 square miles, and with the land has disappeared the buffalo and other game. The memory of this, chargeable by them to the white man, necessarily irritates them.

There is back of all this the natural race antagonism which our dealings with the aborigine in connection with the inevitable onward march of civilization has in no degree lessened. It has been our experience, and the experience of other nations, that defeat in war is soon, not sooner or later, forgotten by the coming generation, and as a result we have a tendency to a constant recurrence of outbreak on the part of the weaker race. It is now sixteen years since our last war with the Sioux in 1876—a time when our present Sioux warriors were mostly children, and therefore have no memory of having felt the power of the government. It is but natural that these young warriors, lacking in experience, should require but little incentive to induce them to test the bravery of the white man on the war path, where the traditions of his people teach him is the only path to glory and a chosen seat in the "happy hunting grounds." For these reasons every precaution should be adopted by the government to guard against trouble with its disastrous results. Have such precautions been adopted? Investigation of the present trouble does not so indicate.

Sitting Bull and other irreconcilable relics of the campaign of 1876 were allowed to remain among their people and foment discord. The staple article of food at Pine Ridge and some of the other agencies had been cut down below the subsisting point, noticeably the beef at Pine Ridge, which from an annual treaty allowance of 6,250,000 pounds gross was cut down to 4,000,000 pounds. The contract on that beef was violated, insomuch as that contract called for northern ranch beef, for which was substituted through beef from Texas, with an unparalleled resulting shrinkage in winter, so that the Indians did not actually receive half ration of this food in winter—the very time the largest allowance of food is required. By the fortunes of political war, weak agents were placed in charge of some of the agencies at the very time that trouble was known to be brewing. Noticeably was this so at Pine Ridge, where a notoriously weak and unfit man was placed in charge. His flight, abandonment of his agency, and his call for troops have, with the horrible results of the same, become facts in history.

Now, as for facts in connection with Pine Ridge, which agency has unfortunately become the theater of the present "war," was there necessity for troops? My past experience with those Indians does not so indicate. For seven long years, from 1879 to 1886, I, as agent, managed this agency without the presence of a soldier on the reservation, and none nearer than 60 miles, and in those times the Indians were naturally much wilder than they are to-day. To be sure, during the seven years we occasionally had exciting times, when the only thing lacking to cause an outbreak was the calling for troops by the agent and the presence of the same. As a matter of fact, however, no matter how much disturbed affairs were, no matter how imminent an outbreak, the progressive chiefs, with their following, came to the front enough in the majority, with the fifty Indian policemen, to at once crush out all attempts at rebellion against the authority of the agent and the government.

Why was this? Because in those times we believed in placing confidence in the Indians; in establishing, as far as possible, a home-rule government on the reservation. We established local courts, presided over by the Indians, with Indian juries; in fact, we believed in having the Indians assist in working out their own salvation. We courted and secured the friendship and support of the progressive and orderly element, as against the mob element. Whether the system thus inaugurated was practicable, was successful, comparison with recent events will decide.

When my Democratic successor took charge in 1886, he deemed it necessary to make general changes in the system at Pine Ridge, i. e., a Republican system. All white men, half-breeds, or Indians who had sustained the agent under the former administration were classed as Republicans and had to go. The progressive chiefs, such as Young Man Afraid, Little Wound, and White Bird, were ignored, and the backing of the element of order and progress was alienated from the agent and the government, and in the place of this strong backing that had maintained order for seven years was substituted Red Cloud and other nonprogressive chiefs, sustainers of the ancient tribal system.

If my successor had been other than an amateur, or had had any knowledge or experience in the inside Indian politics of an Indian tribe, he would have known that if the element he was endeavoring to relegate to the rear had not been the balance of power, I could not for seven years have held out against the mob element which he now sought to put in power. In other words, he unwittingly threw the balance of power at Pine Ridge against the government, as he later on discovered to his cost. When still later he endeavored to maintain order and suppress the ghost dance, the attempt resulted in a most dismal failure.

The Democratic agent was succeeded in October last by the recently removed Republican agent, a gentleman totally ignorant of Indians and their peculiarities; a gentleman with not a qualification in his make-up calculated to fit him for the position of agent at one of the largest and most difficult agencies in the service to manage; a man selected solely as a reward for political services. He might possibly have been an average success as an Indian agent at a small, well-regulated agency. He endeavored to strengthen up matters, but the chiefs and leaders who could have assisted him in so doing had been alienated by the former agent. They virtually said among themselves, "We, after incurring the enmity of the bad element among our people by sustaining the government, have been ignored and ill-treated by that government, hence this is not our affair." Being ignorant of the situation, he had no one to depend on. In his first clash with the mob element he discovered that the Pine Ridge police, formerly the finest in the service, were lacking in discipline and courage, and, not being well supplied with those necessary qualities himself, he took the bluff of a mob for a declaration of war, abandoned his agency, returned with troops—and you see the result.

As for the ghost dance, too much attention has been paid to it. It was only the symptom or surface indication of deep-rooted, long-existing difficulty; as well treat the eruption of smallpox as the disease and ignore the constitutional disease.

As regards disarming the Sioux, however desirable it may appear, I consider it neither advisable nor practicable. I fear that it will result as the theoretical enforcement of prohibition in Kansas, Iowa, and Dakota; you will succeed in disarming the friendly Indians, because you can, and you will not so succeed with the mob element, because you can not. If I were again to be an Indian agent and had my choice, I would take charge of 10,000 armed Sioux in preference to a like number of disarmed ones; and, furthermore, agree to handle that number, or the whole Sioux nation, without a white soldier.

Respectfully, etc,   V. T. McGILLYCUDDY.

P. S.—I neglected to state that up to date there has been neither a Sioux outbreak nor war. No citizen in Nebraska or Dakota has been killed, molested, or can show the scratch of a pin, and no property has been destroyed off the reservation.

STATEMENT OF GENERAL MILES

[*From the Report of the Secretary of War for 1891, Vol. I, pp, 133, 134, and 149. He enumerates specific causes of complaint at each of the principal Sioux agencies, all of whicl. causes may be summarized as hunger and unfulfilled promises.*]

Cause of Indian dissatisfaction.—The causes that led to the serious disturbance of the peace in the northwest last autumn and winter were so remarkable that an explanation of them is necessary in order to comprehend the seriousness of the situation. The Indians assuming the most threatening attitude of hostility were the Cheyennes and Sioux. Their condition may be stated as follows: For several years following their subjugation in 1877, 1878, and 1879 the most dangerous element of the Cheyennes and the Sioux were under military control. Many of them were disarmed and dismounted; their war ponies were sold and the proceeds returned to them in domestic stock, farming utensils, wagons, etc. Many of the Cheyennes, under the charge of military officers, were located on land in accordance with the laws of Congress, but after they were turned over to civil agents and the vast herds of buffalo and large game had been destroyed their supplies were insufficient, and they were forced to kill cattle belonging to white people to sustain life.

The fact that they had not received sufficient food is admitted by the agents and the officers of the government who have had opportunities of knowing. The majority of the Sioux were under the charge of civil agents, frequently changed and often inexperienced. Many of the tribes became rearmed and remounted. They claimed that the government had not fulfilled its treaties and had failed to make large enough appropriations for their support; that they had suffered for want of food, and the evidence of this is beyond question and sufficient to satisfy any unprejudiced intelligent mind. The statements of officers, inspectors, both of the military and the Interior departments, of agents, of missionaries, and civilians familiar with their condition, leave no room for reasonable doubt that this was one of the principal causes. While statements may be made as to the amount of money that has been expended by the government to feed the different tribes, the manner of distributing those appropriations will furnish one reason for the deficit.

The unfortunate failure of the crops in the plains country during the years of 1889 and 1890 added to the distress and suffering of the Indians, and it was possible for them to raise but very little from the ground for self-support; in fact, white settlers have been most unfortunate, and their losses have been serious and universal throughout a large section of that country. They have struggled on from year to year; occasionally they would raise good crops, which they were compelled to sell at low prices, while in the season of drought their labor was almost entirely lost. So serious have been their misfortunes that thousands have left that country within the last few years, passing over the mountains to the Pacific slope or returning to the east of the Missouri or the Mississippi.

The Indians, however, could not migrate from one part of the United States to another; neither could they obtain employment as readily as white people, either upon or beyond the Indian reservations. They must remain in comparative idleness and accept the results of the drought—an insufficient supply of food. This created a feeling of discontent even among the loyal and well disposed and added to the feeling of hostility of the element opposed to every process of civilization.

Reports forwarded by Brigadier-General Ruger, commanding Department of Dakota, contained the following:

The commanding officer at Fort Yates, North Dakota, under date of December 7, 1890, at the time the Messiah delusion was approaching a climax, says, in reference to the disaffection of the Sioux Indians at Standing Rock agency, that it is due to the following causes:

(1) Failure of the government to establish an equitable southern boundary of the Standing Rock agency reservation.

(2) Failure of the government to expend a just proportion of the money received from the Chicago, Milwaukee and St. Paul railroad company, for right of way privileges, for the benefit of the Indians of said agency. Official notice was received October 18, 1881, by the Indian agent at the Standing Rock agency, that the said railroad company had paid the government under its agreement with the Sioux Indians, for right of way privileges, the sum of $13,911. What additional payments, if any, have been made by the said railroad company, and what payments have been made by the Dakota Central railroad company, the records of the agency do not show. In 1883, and again in 1885, the agent, upon complaints made by the Indians, wrote to the Commissioner of Indian Affairs, making certain recommendations as regards the expenditure of the money received from the said railroad company, but was in each instance informed that until Congress took action with respect to the funds referred to nothing could be done. No portion of the money had been expended up to that time (December, 1890) for the benefit of the Indians of the agency, and frequent complaints had been made to the agent by the Indians because they had received no benefits from their concessions to the said railroad companies.

(3) Failure of the government to issue the certificates of title to allotments, as required by article 6 of the treaty of 1868.

(4) Failure of the government to provide the full allowance of seeds and agricultural implements to Indians engaged in farming, as required in article 8, treaty of 1868.

(5) Failure of the government to issue to such Indians the full number of cows and oxen provided in article 10, treaty of 1876.

(7) Failure of the government to issue to the Indians the full ration stipulated in article 5, treaty of 1876. (For the fiscal year beginning July 1, 1890, the following shortages in the rations were found to exist: 485,275 pounds of beef [gross], 761,212 pounds of corn, 11,937 pounds of coffee, 281,712 pounds of flour, 26,234 pounds of sugar, and 39,852 pounds of beans. Although the obligations of the government extend no further than furnishing so much of the ration prescribed in article 5 as may be necessary for the support of the Indians, it would seem that, owing to the almost total failure of crops upon the Standing Rock reservation for the past four years, and the absence of game, the necessity for the issue of the full ration to the Indians here was never greater than at the present time—December, 1890.)

(8) Failure of the government to issue to the Indians the full amount of annuity supplies to which they were entitled under the provisions of article 10, treaty of 1868.

(9) Failure of the government to have the clothing and other annuity supplies ready for issue on the first day of August of each year. Such supplies have not been ready for issue to the Indians, as a rule, until the winter season is well advanced. (After careful examination at this agency, the commanding officer is convinced that not more than two-thirds of the supplies provided in article 10 have been issued there, and the government has never complied with that provision of article 10 which requires the supplies enumerated in paragraphs 2, 3, and 4 of said article to be delivered on or before the first day of August of each year. Such supplies for the present fiscal year, beginning July 1, 1890, had not yet reached (December, 1890) the nearest railway station, about 60 miles distant, from which point they must, at this season of the year, be freighted to this agency in wagons. It is now certain that the winter will be well advanced before the Indians at this agency receive their annual allowance of clothing and other annuity supplies.)

(10) Failure of the government to appropriate money for the payment of the Indians for the ponies taken from them, by the authority of the government, in 1876.

In conclusion, the commanding officer says: "It, however, appears from the foregoing, that the government has failed to fulfill its obligations, and in order to render the Indians law-abiding, peaceful, contented, and prosperous it is strongly recommended that the treaties be promptly and fully carried out, and that the promises made by the commission in 1889 be faithfully kept."

[*The reports from Pine Ridge, Rosebud, Cheyenne River, and Yankton agencies are of similar tenor. Following are two telegrams sent from the field by General Miles at the beginning of the trouble.*]

RAPID CITY, SOUTH DAKOTA, *December 19, 1890.*

Senator DAWES,
   Washington, District of Columbia:

You may be assured of the following facts that can not be gainsaid:

First. The forcing process of attempting to make large bodies of Indians self-sustaining when the government was cutting down their rations and their crops almost a failure, is one cause of the difficulty.

Second. While the Indians were urged and almost forced to sign a treaty presented to them by the commission authorized by Congress, in which they gave up a valuable portion of their reservation which is now occupied by white people, the government has failed to fulfill its part of the compact, and instead of an increase or even a reasonable supply for their support, they have been compelled to live on half and two-thirds rations, and received nothing for the surrender of their lands, neither has the government given any positive assurance that they intend to do any differently with them in the future.

Congress has been in session several weeks and could, if it were disposed, in a few hours confirm the treaties that its commissioners have made with these Indians and appropriate the necessary funds for its fulfillment, and thereby give an earnest of their good faith or intention to fulfill their part of the compact. Such action, in my judgment, is essential to restore confidence with the Indians and give peace and protection to the settlements. If this be done, and the President authorized to place the turbulent and dangerous tribes of Indians under the control of the military, Congress need not enter into details, but can safely trust the military authorities to subjugate and govern, and in the near future make self-sustaining, any or all of the Indian tribes of this country.

RAPID CITY, SOUTH DAKOTA, *December 19, 1890.*

General JOHN M. SCHOFIELD,

Commanding the Army, Washington, District of Columbia:

Replying to your long telegram, one point is of vital importance—the difficult Indian problem can not be solved permanently at this end of the line. It requires the fulfillment by Congress of the treaty obligations which the Indians were entreated and coerced into signing. They signed away a valuable portion of their reservation, and it is now occupied by white people, for which they have received nothing. They understood that ample provision would be made for their support; instead, their supplies have been reduced, and much of the time they have been living on half and two-thirds rations. Their crops, as well as the crops of the white people, for two years have been almost a total failure. The disaffection is widespread, especially among the Sioux, while the Cheyennes have been on the verge of starvation and were forced to commit depredations to sustain life. These facts are beyond question, and the evidence is positive and sustained by thousands of witnesses. Serious difficulty has been gathering for years. Congress has been in session several weeks and could in a single hour confirm the treaties and appropriate the necessary funds for their fulfillment, which their commissioners and the highest officials of the government have guaranteed to these people, and unless the officers of the army can give some positive assurance that the government intends to act in good faith with these people, the loyal element will be diminished and the hostile element increased. If the government will give some positive assurance that it will fulfill its part of the understanding with these 20,000 Sioux Indians, they can safely trust the military authorities to subjugate, control, and govern these turbulent people, and I hope that you will ask the Secretary of War and the Chief Executive to bring this matter directly to the attention of Congress.

REPORT OF CAPTAIN HURST

(*A. G. O. Doc. 6266–1891.*)

FORT BENNETT, SOUTH DAKOTA, *January 9, 1891.*

ASSISTANT ADJUTANT-GENERAL,

Department of Dakota, Saint Paul, Minnesota.

SIR: In compliance with instructions of the department commander—copy attached marked A—I have the honor to submit the following report as the result of my investigations into the matters referred to therein.

I have been at this post continuously since August 6, 1887, and inspector of Indian supplies at the Cheyenne River Indian agency, located here, during that period, and am at the present time.

The Indians of this agency have a standing list of grievances which they present at every opportunity, and talk about in council when they assemble at every monthly ration issue. The Indians most persistent in recounting and proclaiming their grievances are those least willing to help in bettering their condition, and who are opposed to any change or improvement of their old habits and customs, and oppose all progress. Of this class I cite Big Foot's band of irreconcilables—who have now ceased to complain—and those in accord with them. Except in the matter of short rations, the story of their wrongs needs no attention. It commences with a recital of the wrong done them by the white race sharing the earth with them.

The other class, comprising a large majority of Indians of the reservation, have accepted the situation forced upon them, and have been for years bravely struggling in the effort to reconcile themselves to the ways of civilization and moral progress, with a gratifying degree of success. It is this class whose complaints and grievances demand considerate attention. They complain in true Indian style that they only have kept faith in all treaties made with them, and that somehow the treaties when they appeared in print were not in many respects the treaties which they signed.

They complain principally —

(1) That the boundaries of the reservation in the treaty of 1877 are not what they agreed to and thought they were signing on the paper, and they especially emphasize the point that the line of the western boundary should be a *straight line* at the Black Hills, instead of as it appears on the maps.

(2) That they have never received full recompense for the ponies taken from them in 1876.

(3) That the game has been destroyed and driven out of the country by the white people.

(4) That their children are taken from them to eastern schools and kept for years, instead of being educated among them.

(5) That when these eastern graduates return to them with civilized habits, education, and trades, there is no provision made on the reservation for their employment and improvement to the benefit of themselves and their people.

(6) That the agents and employees sent out to them have not all been "good men" and considerate of their (the Indians') interests and welfare.

(7) That the issue of their annuity goods is delayed so late in the winter as to cause them much suffering.

(8) That they are expected to plow the land and raise grain when the climate will not permit them to reap a crop. They think cattle should be issued to them for breeding purposes instead of farming implements for useless labor.

(9) That the rations issued to them are insufficient in quantity and frequently (beef and flour) very poor in quality.

Complaints 2, 3, 4, 5, 7, 8, and 9 are all well founded and justified by the facts in each case, No. 9 especially so, and this through no fault or negligence of the agent. The agent makes his annual estimate for sustenance in kind for the number of people borne on his rolls, based on the stipulated ration in treaty of 1877. This estimate is modified or cut down in the Indian Commissioner's office to meet the requirements of a limited or reduced Congressional appropriation, and when it returns to the agent's hands approved, he finds that he has just so many pounds of beef and flour, etc, placed to his credit for the year, without regard to whether they constitute the full number of treaty rations or not. There is no allowance given him for loss by shrinkage, wastage, or other unavoidable loss, and with the very best efforts and care in the distribution throughout the year of this usually reduced allowance there can not be issued to each Indian his treaty ration nor enough to properly sustain life. As a general thing the Indians of this reservation have been compelled to purchase food according to their means, between ration issues. Those having no means of purchase have suffered.

The half pound of flour called for by the treaty ration could not be issued in full, and the half pound of corn required has never been issued nor anything in lieu of it. In the item of beef but 1 pound was issued instead of the pound and a half called for in the treaty, and during the early spring months, when the cattle on the range are thin and poor, the pound of beef issued to the Indian is but a fraction of the pound issued to him on the agent's returns, and, under the system of purchase in practice until the present fiscal year, must necessarily be so. The agent's purchase of the beef supply on the hoof for the year, under contract, is closed in the month of November, from which time he has to herd them the balance of the year as best he can. He is responsible for the weight they show on the scales when *fat and in prime condition*, so that a steer weighing 1,200 pounds in the fall must represent 1,200 pounds in April, while in fact it may be but skin, horns, and bones, and weigh scarcely 600 pounds, while he has done his best to care for them during the severity of a Dakota winter. The Indians do not understand why they should be made to suffer all this shrinkage and loss, and it is a useless and humiliating attempt to explain. The agent is not to blame. The department of Indian affairs can do only the best it can with a limited and tardy appropriation. The remedy in the matter of food supply seems to be: A sufficient and earlier appropriation of funds. All contracts for the beef supply should call for delivery when required by the agent. The agent should be allowed a percentage of wastage to cover unavoidable loss in issue by shrinkage and wastage. The government should bear this loss and not the Indians.

Complaint 1: No remarks.

Complaint 2: Is before Congress.

Complaint 4: Should be remedied by adequate home schools.

Complaint 5: Suggests its proper remedy.

Complaint 6: No remarks.

Complaint 7: Can be remedied only by earlier appropriations.

Complaint 8: This reservation is not agricultural land. The climate makes it a grazing country. The Indians now can raise cattle successfully and care for them in winter. All attempts at general farming must result in failure on account of climatic conditions.

In connection with complaint 9, I respectfully invite attention to tabular statement accompanying this report, marked B, showing rations as issued up to December 6 in present fiscal year and amount required to make the issues according to article 5, treaty of February 27, 1877, and special attention to columns 6 and 7 therein.

Appended to this report, marked C, is an extract copy of treaties of 1877 and 1868.

In submitting this report, I desire to commend the administration of the affairs of this agency, as it has appeared under my daily observation since August, 1887. So far as this reservation is concerned, the present unrest among the Indians is not attributable to any just cause of complaint against the former or present agent or employees; nor is it due entirely or largely to failure on the part of the government to fulfill treaty obligations.

Very respectfully, your obedient servant,

J. H. HURST,
Captain, Twelfth Infantry, Commanding Post.

APPENDIX C.—EXTRACT COPY—TREATIES OF 1877 AND 1868

TREATY OF 1877

ARTICLE 3. The said Indians also agree that they will hereafter receive all annuities provided by the said treaty of 1868, and all subsistence and supplies which may be provided for them under the present or any future act of Congress, at such points and places on the said reservation and in the vicinity of the Missouri river as the President of the United States shall designate.

ARTICLE 5. In consideration of the foregoing cession of territory and rights, and upon full compliance with each and every obligation assumed by the said Indians, the United States agree to provide all necessary aid to assist the said Indians in the work of civilization; to furnish to them schools and instruction in mechanical and agricultural arts, as provided for by the treaty of 1868. Also to provide the said Indians with subsistence consisting of a ration for each individual of a pound and a half of beef (or in lieu thereof, one-half pound of bacon), one-half pound of flour, and one-half pound of corn; and for every one hundred rations, four pounds of coffee, eight pounds of sugar, and three pounds of beans, or in lieu of said articles the equivalent thereof, in the discretion of the Commissioner of Indian Affairs. Such rations, or so much thereof as may be necessary, shall be continued until the Indians are able to support themselves. Rations shall in all cases be issued to the head of each separate family; and whenever schools shall have been provided by the government for said Indians, no rations shall be issued for children between the ages of six and fourteen years (the sick and infirm excepted), unless such children shall regularly attend school. Whenever the said Indians shall be located upon lands which are suitable for cultivation, rations shall be issued only to the persons and families of those persons who labor (the aged, sick, and infirm excepted); and as an incentive to industrious habits the Commissioner of Indian Affairs may provide that persons be furnished in payment for their labor such other necessary articles as are requisite for civilized life. . . .

ARTICLE 8. The provisions of the said treaty of 1868, except as herein modified, shall continue in full force. . . .

TREATY OF 1868

ARTICLE 8. When the head of a family or lodge shall have selected lands in good faith and received a certificate therefor and commenced farming in good faith, he is to receive not to exceed one hundred dollars for the first year in seeds and agricultural implements, and for a period of three years more not to exceed twenty-five dollars in seeds and implements.

ARTICLE 10. In lieu of all sums of money or other annuities provided to be paid to the Indians herein named under any treaty or treaties heretofore made, the United States agrees to deliver at the agency house on the reservation herein named on (or before) the first day of August of each year for thirty years, the following articles, to wit:

For each male person over fourteen years of age, a suit of good, substantial woolen clothing, consisting of coat, pantaloons, flannel shirt, hat, and a pair of home-made socks.

For each female over twelve years of age, a flannel skirt or the goods necessary to make it, a pair of woolen hose, twelve yards of calico, and twelve yards of cotton domestics.

For the boys and girls under the ages named, such flannel and cotton goods as may be needed to make each a suit aforesaid, with a pair of hose for each. And in addition to the clothing herein named, the sum of ten dollars for each person entitled to the beneficial effects of this treaty, shall be annually appropriated for a period of thirty years, while such persons roam and hunt, and twenty dollars for each person who engages in farming, to be used by the Secretary of the Interior in the purchase of such articles as from time to time the condition and necessities of the Indians may indicate to be proper. And if within thirty years at any time it shall appear that the amount of money needed for clothing, under this article, can be appropriated to better uses for the Indians named herein, Congress may, by law, change the appropriation to other purposes, but in no event shall the amount of the appropriation be withdrawn or discontinued for the period named.

Article 10 further stipulates that each lodge or family which shall commence farming shall receive within sixty days thereafter one good American cow and one good well-broken pair of American oxen.

Extract from tabular statement, showing articles of subsistence received or to be received, rations as issued up to date, and amount required to make the issues according to Article 5 of treaty of February 27, 1877, in fiscal year 1891—At Cheyenne River agency, Fort Bennett, South Dakota.

3	5	7
Name of articles.	Quantity allowed to 100 rations up to date.	Quantity per 100 rations as allowed per treaty 1877.
	Pounds.	*Pounds.*
Bacon	3	16⅔
Beans........................	3	3
Baking powder	1½	....
Beef, gross....................	*a* 100	*b* 100
Coffee........................	2½–3	4
Flour	45	50
Sugar........................	4¾	8
Salt..........................	1	....
Soap.........................	2	....
Mess pork	3	....
Hard bread (in lieu of bacon)	25	....
Corn (in lieu of flour)	None.	50

a Net. *b* Net, or 150 without bacon.

Rations as fixed by treaty of 1877: 1½ pounds beef or ½ pound bacon; ½ pound flour and ½ pound corn; 4 pounds coffee, 8 pounds sugar, and 3 pounds beans to every 100 rations; "or, in lieu of said articles, the equivalent thereof, in the discretion of the Commissioner of Indian Affairs."

STATEMENT OF AMERICAN HORSE

[*Delivered in council at Pine Ridge agency to Agent Royer, and forwarded to the Indian Office, November 27, 1890. G. D. Doc. 37002—1890.*]

American Horse, Fast Thunder, Spotted Horse, Pretty Back, and Good Lance present, with American Horse as spokesman:

"I think the late Sioux commissioners (General Crook, Major Warner, and Governor Foster) had something to do with starting this trouble. I was speaker for the whole tribe. In a general council I signed the bill (the late Sioux bill) and 580 signed with me. The other members of my band drew out and it divided us, and ever since these two parties have been divided. The nonprogressive started the ghost dance to draw from us. We were made many promises, but have never heard from them since. The Great Father says if we do what he directs it will be to our benefit; but instead of this they are every year cutting down our rations, and we do not get enough to keep us from suffering. General Crook talked nice to us; and after we signed the bill they took our land and cut down our allowance of food. The commission made us believe that we would get full sacks if we signed the bill, but instead of that our sacks are empty. We lost considerable property by being here with the commissioners last year, and have never got anything for it. Our chickens were all stolen, our cattle some of them were killed, our crops were entirely lost by us being absent here with the Sioux commission, and we have never been benefited one bit by the bill; and, in fact, we are worse off than we were before we signed the bill. We are told if we do as white men we will be better off, but we are getting worse off every year.

"The commissioners promised the Indians living on Black Pipe and Pass creeks that if they signed the bill they could remain where they were and draw their rations at this agency, showing them on the map the line, and our people want them here, but they have been ordered to move back to Rosebud agency. This is one of the broken promises. The commission promised to survey the boundary line, and appropriate $1,000 for the purpose, but it has not been done. When we were at Washington, the President, the Secretary of the Interior, and the Commissioner all promised us that we would get the million pounds of beef that were taken from us, and I heard the bill appropriating the money passed Congress, but we never got the beef. The Commissioner refused to give it to us. American Horse, Fast Thunder, and Spotted Horse were all promised a spring wagon each, but they have never heard anything of it. This is another broken promise."

In forwarding the report of the council, the agent says: "After American Horse was through talking, I asked the other men present if his statement voiced their sentiments and they all answered, Yes."

STATEMENT OF BISHOP HARE

[*Bishop W. H. Hare is the veteran Episcopal missionary bishop among the Sioux. The following extracts are from a communication by him to Secretary Noble, dated January 7, 1891. G. D. Doc. 2440—1891.*]

The evidence compels the conclusion that, among the Pine Ridge Indians at least, *hunger has been an important element* in the causes of *discontent* and *insubordination*. In the farming season of 1889 [July] the Indians were all called into the agency and kept there for a month by the Sioux commission. During their absence their cattle broke into their fields and trod down, or ate up, their crops. The Indians reaped practically nothing. In the year 1890, drought, the worst known for many years, afflicted the western part of South Dakota, and the Indian crops were a total failure. There is ample evidence that, during this period, the rations issued lasted, even when carefully used, for only two-thirds the time for which they were intended. To add to their distress, this period, 1889 and 1890, was marked by extraordinary misfortune. The measles prevailed with great virulence in 1889, the grippe in 1890. Whooping cough also attacked the children. The sick died from want. In this statement Inspector Gardiner, Dr McGillycuddy, late agent, Miss Elaine Goodale, who has been in the camps a good deal, the missionary force, and many others whose testimony is of the highest value because of their character and their knowledge of the situation, all agree. . . .

The time seemed now to have come to take a further step and divide the Great Sioux reservation up into separate reserves for each important tribe, and to open the surplus land to settlement. The needs of the white population, with their business and railroads, and the welfare of the Indians, seemed alike to demand this. Commissioners were therefore sent out to treat with the people for the accomplishment of this end, and an agreement which, after much debate, had won general approval was committed to them for presentation to the Indians. The objections of the Indians to the bill, however, were many and they were ardently pressed. Some preferred their old life, the more earnestly because schools and churches were sapping and undermining it. Some wished delay. All complained that many of the engagements solemnly made with them in former years when they had surrendered valued rights had been broken, and here they were right. They suspected that present promises of pay for their lands would prove only old ones in a new shape (when milch cows were promised, cows having been promised in previous agreements, the Indians exclaimed, "There's that same old cow"), and demanded that no further surrender should be expected until former promises had been fulfilled. They were assured that a new era had dawned, and that all past promises would be kept. So we all thought. The benefits of the proposed agreement were set before them, and verbal promises, over and above the stipulations of the bill, were made, that special requests of the Indians would be met. The Indians have no competent representative body. The commissioners had to treat at each agency with a crowd, a crowd composed of full-bloods, half-breeds, and squaw men, a crowd among whom all sorts of sinister influences and brute force were at work. Commissioners with such a business in hand have the devil to fight, and can fight him, so it often seems, only with fire, and many friends of the Indians think that in this case the commission, convinced that the acceptance of the bill was essential, carried persuasion to the verge of intimidation. I do not blame them if they sometimes did. The wit and patience of an angel would fail often in such a task.

But the requisite number, three-fourths of the Indians, signed the bill, and expectation of rich and prompt rewards ran high. The Indians understand little of the complex forms and delays of our government. Six months passed, and nothing came. Three months more, and nothing came. A bill was drawn up in the Senate under General Crook's eye and passed, providing for the fulfillment of the promises of the commission, but it was pigeon-holed in the House. But in the midst of the winter's pinching cold the Indians learned that the transaction had been declared complete and half of their land proclaimed as thrown open to the whites. Surveys were not promptly made; perhaps they could not be, and no one knew what land was theirs and what was not. The very earth seemed sliding from beneath their feet. Other misfortunes seemed to be crowding on them. On some reserves their rations were being reduced, and lasted, even when carefully husbanded, but one-half the period for which they were issued. (The amount of beef *bought* for the Indians is not a fair criterion of the amount he *receives*. A steer will lose 200 pounds or more of its flesh during the course of the winter.) In the summer of 1889 all the people on the Pine Ridge reserve, men, women, and children, were called in from their farms to the agency to treat with the commissioners and were kept there a whole month, and, on returning to their homes, found that their cattle had broken into their fields and trampled down or eaten up all their crops. This was true in a degree elsewhere. In 1890 the crops, which promised splendidly early in July, failed entirely later, because of a severe drought. The people were often hungry, and, the physicians in many cases said, died when taken sick, not so much from disease as for want of food. (This is doubtless true of all the poor—the poor in our cities and the poor settlers in the west.)

No doubt the people could have saved themselves from suffering if industry, economy, and thrift had abounded; but these are just the virtues which a people merging from barbarism lack. The measles prevailed in 1889 and were exceedingly fatal. Next year the grippe swept over the people with appalling results. Whooping cough followed among the children. Sullenness and gloom began to gather, especially among the heathen and wilder Indians. A witness of high character told me that a marked discontent amounting almost to despair prevailed in many quarters. The people said their children were all dying from diseases brought by the whites, their race was perishing from the face of the earth, and they might as well be killed at once. Old chiefs and medicine men were losing their power. Withal new ways were prevailing more and more which did not suit the older people. The old ways which they loved were passing away. In a word, all things were against them, and to add to the calamity, many Indians, especially the wilder element, had nothing to do but to brood over their misfortunes. While in this unhappy state, the story of a messiah coming, with its ghost dance and strange hallucinations, spread among the heathen part of the people. . . .

But these things we do want. A profound conviction in the mind not only of a few, but of the *people*, that the Indian problem is worth attending to. Next, that the officials placed in charge of the difficult Indian problem should be protected from the importunity of hungry politicians, and that the employees in the Indian country, agents, teachers, farmers, carpenters, should not be changed with every shuffling of the political cards. The abuse here has been shameful. Next, that Congress, especially the House of Representatives, shall consider itself bound in honor to make provision for the fulfillment of promises made to the Indians by commissioners duly appointed and sent to the Indians by another branch of the government. The evils which have arisen from a violation of this comity have been most serious. Next, that testimony regarding Indian affairs should not be swallowed until careful inquiry has been made as to the disinterestedness of the witness. An honest man out here burns with indignation when he reads in the papers that so and so, represented as being fully informed on the whole question, affirms that Indians have no grievances and ought to receive no quarter, when he knows that the lots which the witness owns in a town near the Indian country would no longer be a drug in the market if Indians could be gotten out of the way. Next, let it be remembered that the crisis has lifted evils in the Indian country up to the light, and left the good things in the shade. But the good things are real and have shown their vigor under trial. There is no reason for losing faith or courage. Let all kind and honest men unite with the higher officials of the government, all of whom, I believe, mean well, in a spirit of forbearance toward each other, of willingness to learn, and of mutual helpfulness, to accomplish the results which they all desire.

Chapter XIII

THE SIOUX OUTBREAK—SITTING BULL AND WOUNDED KNEE

We were made many promises, but have never heard from them since. — *American Horse.*

Congress has been in session several weeks and could, if it were disposed, in a few hours confirm the treaty that its commissioners have made with these Indians, and appropriate the necessary funds for their fulfillment, and thereby give an earnest of good faith or intention to fulfill their part of the compact. Such action in my judgment is essential to restore confidence with the Indians and give peace and protection to the settlements. — *General Miles.*

Approximate cost of outbreak in one month: Forty-nine whites and others on the government side, and three hundred Indians, killed; $1,200,000 expense to government and individuals.

Short Bull and the other Sioux delegates who had gone to see the messiah in the fall of 1889 returned in March, 1890. Short Bull, on Rosebud reservation, at once began to preach to his people the doctrine and advent of the messiah, but desisted on being warned to stop by Agent Wright. (*Comr., 29.*) The strange hope had taken hold of the Indians however, and the infection rapidly, although quietly, spread among all the wilder portion of the tribe. The first warning of trouble ahead came in the shape of a letter addressed to Secretary Noble by Charles L. Hyde, a citizen of Pierre, South Dakota, under date of May 29, 1890, in which he stated that he had trustworthy information that the Sioux, or a part of them, were secretly planning an outbreak in the near future. His informant appears to have been a young half-blood from Pine Ridge, who was at that time attending school in Pierre, and was in correspondence with his Indian relatives at home. (*G. D., 20.*) The letter was referred to the Commissioner of Indian Affairs, who forwarded a copy of it to the agents of the several western Sioux reservations, with a request for further information. They promptly and unanimously replied that there was no ground for apprehension, that the Indians were peaceably disposed, and that there was no undue excitement beyond that occasioned by the rumors of a messiah in the west. This excitement they thought would continue to increase as the predicted time drew near, and would die a natural death when the prophecy failed of its fulfillment.

All the agents are positive in the opinion that at this time, about the middle of June, 1890, the Indians had no hostile intentions. McLaughlin, the veteran agent of Standing Rock, who probably knew the Sioux better than any other white man having official relations with them, states that among his people there was nothing in word or action to justify such a suspicion, and that he did not believe such an imprudent step was seriously contemplated by any of the tribe, and concludes by saying that he has every confidence in the good intentions of the Sioux as a people, that they would not be the aggressors in any hostile act, and that if justice were only done them no uneasiness need be entertained. He complains, however, of the evil influence exercised by Sitting Bull and a few other malcontents attached to his agency and advises their removal from among the Indians. Wright, at Rosebud, also advised the removal of Crow Dog and some other mischief-makers. These men had led the opposition to the late treaty and to every advance

FIG. 72—A Sioux warrior—Weasel Bear.

of civilization, by which they felt their former influence undermined, and between them and the progressive party there was uncompromising hostility. (*G. D.*, *21*.) Although the trouble did come six months later, it is sufficiently evident that at this time there was no outbreak intended. Certain it is that the Sioux as a tribe—25,000 strong—did not engage in the outbreak, and in view of all the circumstances it will hardly be claimed that they were deliberate aggressors.

The first mutterings of dissatisfaction came from Pine Ridge. This is the largest of the Sioux agencies, having 6,000 of the wildest and most warlike of the tribe, largely under the influence of the celebrated chief Red Cloud, the twin spirit of Sitting Bull in wily disposition and hatred of the white man. It is the most remote from the white settlements along Missouri river, and joins Rosebud reservation, with 4,000 more Sioux of about the same condition and temper, thus making a compact body of 10,000 of the most warlike Indians of the plains. Above all other reservations in the United States this was the very one where there was most urgent and obvious necessity for efficient and vigorous administration and for prompt and honest fulfillment of pledges.

From 1879 to 1886 this agency was in charge of Dr V. T. McGillycuddy, a man of unflinching courage, determined will, and splendid executive ability. Taking charge of these Indians when they had come in fresh from the warpath, he managed them, as he himself says, for seven years without the presence of a soldier on the reservation, and with none nearer than 60 miles. Relying on the Indians themselves, he introduced the principle of home rule by organizing a force of 50 Indian police, drilled in regular cavalry and infantry tactics. With these he was able to thwart all the mischievous schemes of Red Cloud, maintain authority, and start the Indians well on the road to civilization.

Then came a political change of administration, with a resulting train of changes all through the service. Out of 58 Indian agents more than 50 were removed and new men appointed. Some of these appointments were for the better, but the general result was bad, owing mainly to the inexperience of the new officials. In the meantime commissioners were negotiating with the Sioux for a further cession of lands, which was finally effected in spite of the opposition of a large part of the tribe, especially of those under the influence of Red Cloud and Sitting Bull at Pine Ridge and Standing Rock. Then rations were reduced and the Indians began to suffer and, consequently, to be restless, their unrest being intensified but not caused by the rumors of a messiah soon to appear to restore the former conditions. According to the official statement of General Brooke, the beef issue at Pine Ridge was reduced from 8,125,000 pounds in 1886 to 4,000,000 pounds in 1889, a reduction of more than one-half in three years. (*War, 5.*) In April, 1890, Gallagher, the agent then in charge, informed the Department that the monthly beef issue was only 205,000 pounds, whereas the treaty called for 470,400. He was informed that it was better to issue half rations all the time than to issue three-fourths or full rations for two months and none for the rest of the year. From other sources also the warning now came to the Department that the Sioux of Pine Ridge were becoming restless from hunger. (*G. D., 22.*) Repeated representations failed to bring more beef, and at last in the summer of 1890 the Indians at Pine Ridge made the first actual demonstration by refusing to accept the deficient issue and making threats against the agent. They were finally persuaded to take the beef, but Agent Gallagher, finding that the dissatisfaction was growing and apparently without remedy, resigned, and his successor took charge in the beginning of October, 1890.

By this time the Ghost dance was in full progress among the western Sioux and was rapidly spreading throughout the tribe. The principal

FIG. 73—Red Cloud.

dance ground on Pine Ridge reservation was at No Water's camp on White Clay creek, about 20 miles from the agency. At a great Ghost dance held here about the middle of June the ghost shirts were worn probably for the first time. (*Comr., 30.*) In August about 2,000 Indians had assembled for a dance at the same rendezvous, when Agent Gallagher sent out several police with orders to the dancers to quit and go home. They refused to do so, and the agent himself went out with more police to enforce the order. On repeating his demand a number of the warriors leveled their guns toward him and the police, and told him that they were ready to defend their religion with their lives. Under the circumstances the agent, although known to be a brave man, deemed it best to withdraw and the dance went on. (*Comr.*, *31; G. D.*, *23.*)

On Rosebud reservation, which adjoins Pine Ridge on the east and is occupied by the turbulent and warlike Brulés, the warning given to Short Bull had such an effect that there was no open manifestation until September, when the Ghost dance was inaugurated at the various camps under the leadership of Short Bull the medicine-man, Crow Dog, and Two Strike. Agent Wright, then in charge, went out to the Indians and told them the dance must be stopped, which was accordingly done. He expressly states that no violence was contemplated by the Indians, and that no arms were carried in the dance, but that he forbade it on account of its physical and mental effect on the participants and its tendency to draw them from their homes. In some way a rumor got among the Indians at this time that troops had arrived on the reservation to attack them, and in an incredibly short time every Indian had left the neighborhood of the agency and was making preparations to meet the enemy. It was with some difficulty that Agent Wright was able to convince them that the report was false and persuade them to return to their homes. Soon afterward circumstances obliged him to be temporarily absent, leaving affairs in the meantime in charge of a special agent. The Indians took advantage of his absence to renew the Ghost dance and soon defied control. The agent states, however, that no Indians left the agency until the arrival of the troops, when the leaders immediately departed for Pine Ridge, together with 1,800 of their followers. (*G. D.*, *24; Comr.*, *32.*)

On October 9 Kicking Bear of Cheyenne River agency, the chief high priest of the Ghost dance among the Sioux, went to Standing Rock by invitation of Sitting Bull and inaugurated the dance on that reservation at Sitting Bull's camp on Grand river. The dance had begun on Cheyenne river about the middle of September, chiefly at the camps of Hump and Big Foot. On learning of Kicking Bear's arrival, Agent McLaughlin sent a force of police, including two officers, to arrest him and put him off the reservation, but they returned without executing the order, both officers being in a dazed condition and fearing the power of Kicking Bear's " medicine." Sitting Bull, however, had promised that his visitors would go back to their own reservation, which they did a day or two later, but he declared his intention to continue the dance, as they had received a direct message from the spirit world through Kicking Bear that they must do so to live. He promised that he would suspend the dance until he could come and talk the matter over with the agent, but this promise he failed to keep. Considering Sitting Bull the leader and instigator of the excitement on the reservation, McLaughlin again advised his removal, and that of several other mischief makers, and their confinement in some military prison at a distance. (*G. D., 25.*)

The two centers of excitement were now at Standing Rock reservation, where Sitting Bull was the open and declared leader, and at Pine Ridge, where Red Cloud was a firm believer in the new doctrine, although perhaps not an instigator of direct opposition to authority. At Rosebud the movement had been smothered for the time by the prompt action of Agent Wright, as already described. At the first-named reservation McLaughlin met the emergency with bravery and ability reinforced by twenty years of experience in dealing with Indians, and, while recommending the removal of Sitting Bull, expressed confidence in his own ability to allay the excitement and suppress the dance. At Pine Ridge, however, where the crisis demanded a man of most positive character—somebody of the McGillycuddy stamp—Gallagher had resigned and had been succeeded in October by D. F. Royer, a person described as "destitute of any of those qualities by which he could justly lay claim to the position—experience, force of character, courage, and sound judgment." (*Welsh, 2.*) This appears in every letter and telegram sent out by him during his short incumbency, and is sufficiently evidenced in the name by which the Sioux soon came to know him, Lakota Kokipa-Koshkala, "Young-man-afraid-of-Indians." Before he had been in charge a week, he had so far lost control of his Indians as to allow a half dozen of them to release and carry off a prisoner named Little, whom the police had arrested and brought to the agency. On October 12 he reported that more than half of his 6,000 Indians were dancing, and that they were entirely beyond the control of the police, and suggested that it would be necessary to call out the military. (*G. D., 26.*)

About the same time Agent Palmer at Cheyenne River reported to the Department that Big Foot's band (afterward engaged at Wounded Knee) was very much excited over the coming of the messiah, and could not be kept by the police from dancing. In reply, both agents were instructed to use every prudent measure to stop the dance and were told that military assistance would be furnished if immediate need should arise. (*L. B., 1.*) Instructions were also sent to agents in Nevada to warn the leaders of the dance in that quarter to desist. A few days later the agent at Cheyenne River had a talk with the dancers, and so far convinced them of the falsity of their hopes that he was able to report that the excitement was dying out, but recommended the removal of Hump, as a leader of the disaffection. (*G. D., 27.*)

By the advice of the Department, Royer had consulted General Miles, at that time passing on his way to the west, as to the necessity for troops, and, after hearing a full statement, the general expressed the opinion that the excitement would die out of itself. The next day the general had a talk with the Indians, who informed him that they intended to continue the dance. He gave them some good advice and told them that they must stop. Had the matter rested here until the words of the commanding officer could have been deliberated in their minds—for the mental process of an Indian can not well be hurried—all might have been well. Unfortunately, however, the agent, now thoroughly frightened, wrote a long letter to the Department on October 30, stating that the only remedy for the matter was the use of military, and that about 600 or 700 troops would be necessary. On November 11 he telegraphed for permission to come to Washington to "explain," and was refused. Then came other telegraphic requests, at the rate of one every day, for the same permission, all of which were refused, with pointed intimation that the interests of the service required that the agent should remain at his post of duty. Finally the matter was reported by the Indian Office to the War Department, and on November 15 Royer was instructed to report the condition of affairs to the commander of the nearest military post, Fort Robinson, Nebraska. On the same day he had telegraphed that the Indians were wild and crazy and that at least a thousand soldiers were needed. The agent at Rosebud also now reported that his Indians were beyond control by the police. Special agents were sent to both agencies and confirmed the reports as to the alarming condition of affairs. The agent at Crow Creek and Lower Brulé agency reported at the same time that his Indians were under good control and that the police were sufficient for all purposes. (*G. D., 28; L. B., 2.*)

On the last day of October, Short Bull, one of those who had been to see the messiah, made an address to a large gathering of Indians near Pine Ridge, in which he said that as the whites were interfering so much in the religious affairs of the Indians he would advance the time for the great change and make it nearer, even within the next month. He urged them all to gather in one place and prepare for the coming messiah, and told them they must dance even though troops should surround them, as the guns of the soldiers would be rendered harmless and the white race itself would soon be annihilated. (See his speech, page 788.)

Soon afterward, McLaughlin personally visited Sitting Bull at his camp on Grand river and attempted to reason with the Indians on the absurdity of their belief. In reply, Sitting Bull proposed that they should both go with competent attendants to the country of the messiah and see and question him for themselves, and rest the truth or falsity of the new doctrine on the result. The proposition was not accepted. (*G. D., 29.*) There can be no question that the leaders of the Ghost dance among the Sioux were fully as much deceived as their followers.

As the local agents had declared the situation beyond their control, the War Department was at last called on and responded. On November 13 the President had directed the Secretary of War to assume a military responsibility to prevent an outbreak (*G. D., 30*), and on November 17 troops, under command of General John R. Brooke, were ordered to the front. The general plan of the campaign was under the direction of General Nelson A. Miles, in command of the military department of the Missouri. On November 19 the first troops arrived at Pine Ridge from Fort Robinson, Nebraska, and were speedily reinforced by others. Within a few days there were at Pine Ridge agency, under immediate command of General Brooke, eight troops of the Seventh cavalry, under Colonel Forsyth; a battalion of the Ninth cavalry (colored), under Major Henry; a battalion of the Fifth artillery, under Captain Capron, and a company of the Eighth infantry and eight companies of the Second infantry, under Colonel Wheaton. At Rosebud were two troops of the Ninth cavalry, with portions of the Eighth and Twenty-first infantry, under Lieutenant-Colonel Poland. Between Rosebud and Pine Ridge were stationed seven companies of the First infantry, under Colonel Shafter. West and north of Pine Ridge were stationed portions of the First, Second, and Ninth cavalry, under command of Colonel Tilford and Lieutenant-Colonel Sanford. Farther west, at Buffalo Gap, on the railroad, were stationed three troops from the Fifth and Eighth cavalry, under Captain Wells. Farther north on the railroad, at Rapid City, was Colonel Carr with six troops of the Sixth cavalry. Along the south fork of Cheyenne river Lieutenant-Colonel Offley took position with seven companies of the Seventeenth infantry, and east of him was stationed Lieutenant-Colonel Sumner with three troops of the Eighth cavalry, two companies of the Third infantry, and Lieutenant Robinson's company of Crow Indian scouts. Small garrisons were also stationed at Forts Meade, Bennett, and Sully. Most of the force was placed in position between the Indians now gathering in the Bad Lands, under Short Bull and Kicking Bear, and the scattered settlements nearest them. Seven companies of the Seventh infantry, under Colonel Merriam, were also placed along Cheyenne river to restrain the Indians of Cheyenne River and Standing Rock reservations. In a short time there were nearly 3,000 troops in the field in the Sioux country. General Miles established his headquarters at Rapid City, South Dakota, close to the center of disturbance. (*War, 6.*) On December 1 the Secretary of the Interior directed that the agents be instructed to obey and cooperate with the military officers in all matters looking to the suppression of an outbreak. (*G. D., 31.*)

Upon the first appearance of the troops a large number of Indians of Rosebud and Pine Ridge, led by Short Bull, Kicking Bear, and others, left their homes and fled to the rough broken country known as the Bad Lands, northwest of White river in South Dakota, on the edge

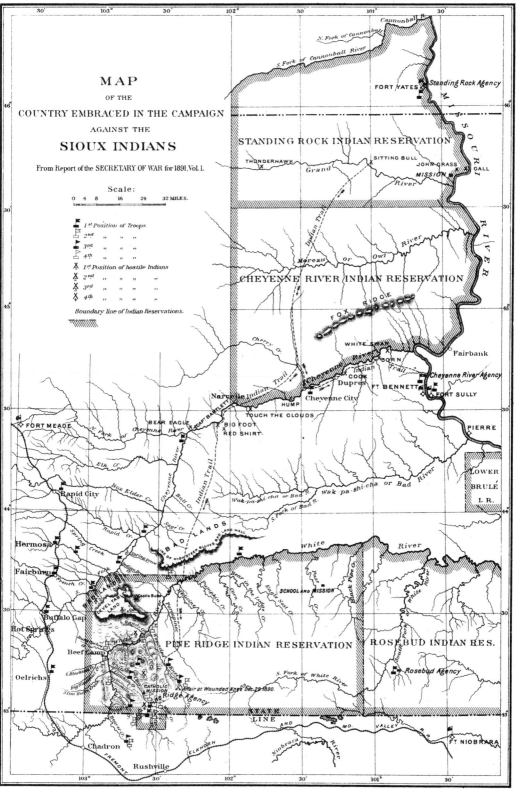

MAP

OF THE

COUNTRY EMBRACED IN THE CAMPAIGN

AGAINST THE

SIOUX INDIANS

From Report of the SECRETARY OF WAR for 1891, Vol. 1.

Scale:

0   4   8   16   24   32 MILES.

1st Position of Troops
2nd   "   "   "
3rd   "   "   "
4th   "   "   "
1st Position of hostile Indians
2nd   "   "   "   "
3rd   "   "   "   "
4th   "   "   "   "

Boundary line of Indian Reservations.

of Pine Ridge reservation and about 50 miles northwest of the agency. In their flight they destroyed the houses and other property of the friendly Indians in their path and compelled many to go with them. They succeeded also in capturing a large portion of the agency beef herd. Others rapidly joined them until soon a formidable body of

FIG. 74—Short Bull.

3,000 Indians had gathered in the Bad Lands, where, protected by the natural fastnesses and difficulties of the country, their future intentions became a matter of anxious concern to the settlers and the authorities.

From the concurrent testimony of all the witnesses, including Indian Commissioner Morgan and the Indians themselves, this flight to the

Bad Lands was not properly a hostile movement, but was a stampede caused by panic at the appearance of the troops. In his official report Commissioner Morgan says:

> When the troops reached Rosebud, about 1,800 Indians—men, women, and children— stampeded toward Pine Ridge and the Bad Lands, destroying their own property before leaving and that of others en route.

After the death of Sitting Bull he says:

> Groups of Indians from the different reservations had commenced concentrating in the Bad Lands, upon or in the vicinity of the Pine Ridge reservation. Killing of cattle and destruction of other property by these Indians, almost entirely within the limits of Pine Ridge and Rosebud reservations, occurred, but no signal fires were built, no warlike demonstrations were made, no violence was done to any white settlers, nor was there any cohesion or organization among the Indians themselves. Many of them were friendly Indians who had never participated in the ghost dance. but had fled thither from fear of soldiers, in consequence of the Sitting Bull affair or through the overpersuasion of friends. The military gradually began to close in around them and they offered no resistance, and a speedy and quiet capitulation of all was confidently expected. (*Comr., 33.*)

The Sioux nation numbers over 25,000, with between 6,000 and 7,000 warriors. Hardly more than 700 warriors were concerned altogether, including those of Big Foot's band and those who fled to the Bad Lands. None of the Christian Indians took any part in the disturbance.

While it is certain that the movement toward the Bad Lands with the subsequent events were the result of panic at the appearance of the troops, it is equally true that the troops were sent only on the request of the civilian authorities. On this point General Miles says: "Not until the civil agents had lost control of the Indians and declared themselves powerless to preserve peace, and the Indians were in armed hostility and defiance of the civil authorities, was a single soldier moved from his garrison to suppress the general revolt." (*War, 7.*) Throughout the whole trouble McGillycuddy at Standing Rock consistently declared his ability to control his Indians without the presence of troops.

In accord with instructions from the Indian Office, the several agents in charge among the Sioux had forwarded lists of disturbers whom it would be advisable to arrest and remove from among the Indians, using the military for the purpose if necessary. The agents at the other reservations sent in all together the names of about fifteen subjects for removal, while Royer, at Pine Ridge, forwarded as a "conservative estimate" the names of sixty-four. Short Bull and Kicking Bear being in the Bad Lands, and Red Cloud being now an old man and too politic to make much open demonstration, the head and front of the offenders was Sitting Bull, the irreconcilable; but McLaughlin, within whose jurisdiction he was, in a letter of November 22, advised that the arrest be not attempted until later in the season, as at the date of writing the weather was warm and pleasant—in other words, favorable to the Indians in case they should make opposition. (*G. D., 32.*) The worst

element had withdrawn to the Bad Lands, where they were making no
hostile demonstrations, but were apparently badly frightened and
awaiting developments to know whether to come in and surrender or
to continue to retreat. The dance had generally been discontinued on
the reservations, excepting at Sitting Bull's camp on Grand river and

Fig. 75— Kicking Bear.

Big Foot's camp on Cheyenne river. The presence of troops had
stopped the dances near the agencies, and the Secretary of the Interior,
in order to allay the dissatisfaction, had ordered that the full rations
due under the treaty should be issued at all the Sioux agencies, which
at the same time were placed under the control of the military. (*G.*

D., 33; L. B., 3.) Such were the conditions on the opening of December, 1890. Everything seemed to be quieting down, and it was now deemed a favorable time to forestall future disturbance by removing the ringleaders.

Agent McLaughlin at Standing Rock had notified the Department some weeks before that it would be necessary to remove Sitting Bull and several others at no distant day to put an end to their harmful influence among the Sioux, but stated also that the matter should not be precipitated, and that when the proper time came he could accomplish the undertaking with his Indian police without the aid of troops. As soon as the War Department assumed control of the Sioux agencies, it was determined to make an attempt to secure Sitting Bull by military power. Accordingly, orders were given to the noted scout, William F. Cody, better known as Buffalo Bill, who was well acquainted with Sitting Bull and was believed to have influence with him, to proceed to Standing Rock agency to induce him to come in, with authority to make such terms as might seem necessary, and, if unsuccessful, to arrest him and remove him from his camp to the nearest post, Fort Yates. Cody arrived at Fort Yates on November 28, and was about to undertake the arrest, when his orders were countermanded at the urgent remonstrance of Agent McLaughlin, who represented that such a step at that particular time was unwise, as military interference was liable to provoke a conflict, in which the Indians would have the advantage, as the warm weather was in their favor. He insisted that there was no immediate danger from the dancing, and that at the proper time—when the weather grew colder—he could take care of Sitting Bull and the other disturbers whose removal he advised with the aid of the Indian police, whom, in all his years of service, he had always found equal to the emergency. The attempt was accordingly postponed. In the meantime Sitting Bull had promised to come into the agency to talk over the situation with the agent, but failed to keep his engagement. A close watch was kept over his movements and the agent was instructed to make no arrests except by authority from the military or the Secretary of the Interior. (*G. D., 34.*)

There is no question that Sitting Bull was plotting mischief. His previous record was one of irreconcilable hostility to the government, and in every disturbance on the reservation his camp had been the center of ferment. It was at his camp and on his invitation that Kicking Bear had organized the first Ghost dance on the reservation, and the dance had been kept up by Sitting Bull ever since in spite of the repeated remonstrance of the agent. At the same time the turbulent followers of the medicine-man took every opportunity to insult and annoy the peaceable and progressive Indians who refused to join them until these latter were forced to make complaint to the agent. In October, while the dance was being organized at his camp, Sitting Bull had deliberately broken the "pipe of peace" which he had kept

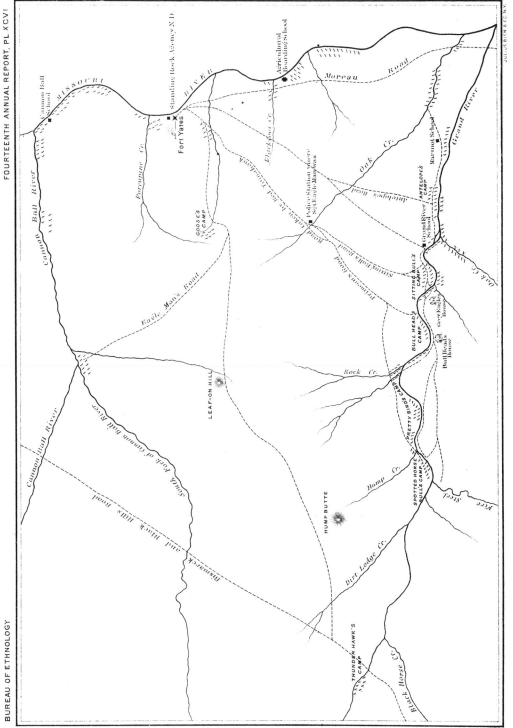

STANDING ROCK AGENCY AND VICINITY

in his house since his surrender in 1881, and when askeᴅ why he had broken it, replied that he wanted to die and wanted to fight. From that time he discontinued his regular visits to the agency. It became known that he contemplated leaving the reservation to visit the other leaders of dissatisfaction at the southern Sioux agencies, and to frustrate such an attempt the agent had gradually increased the number of police in the neighborhood of his camp, and had arranged for speedy information and prompt action in case of any sudden move on his part. (*G. D., 35.*)

Foreseeing from the active movements of the military that the arrest of Sitting Bull was liable to be ordered at any moment, and fearing that such action might come at an inopportune time, and thus result in trouble, McLaughlin made arrangements to have him and several other disturbers arrested by the Indian police on the night of December 6, the weather and other things being then, in his opinion, most favorable for the attempt. On telegraphing to the Indian department, however, for authority, he was directed to make no arrests excepting upon order from the military authorities or the Secretary of the Interior. In reply to a telegram from General Ruger, McLaughlin stated that there was no immediate need of haste, and that postponement was preferable, as the winter weather was cooling the ardor of the dancers.

On December 12 the military order came for the arrest of Sitting Bull. Colonel Drum, in command at Fort Yates, was directed to make it his personal duty to secure him and to call on the agent for assistance and cooperation in the matter. On consultation between the commandant and the agent, who were in full accord, it was decided to make the arrest on the 20th, when most of the Indians would be down at the agency for rations, and there would consequently be less danger of a conflict at the camp. On the 14th, however, late Sunday afternoon, a courier came from Grand river with a message from Mr Carignan, the teacher of the Indian school, stating, on information given by the police, that an invitation had just come from Pine Ridge to Sitting Bull asking him to go there, as God was about to appear. Sitting Bull was determined to go, and sent a request to the agent for permission, but in the meantime had completed his preparations to go anyhow in case permission was refused. With this intention it was further stated that he had his horses already selected for a long and hard ride, and the police urgently asked to be allowed to arrest him at once, as it would be a difficult matter to overtake him after he had once started.

It was necessary to act immediately, and arrangements were made between Colonel Drum and Agent McLaughlin to attempt the arrest at daylight the next morning, December 15. The arrest was to be made by the Indian police, assisted, if necessary, by a detachment of troops, who were to follow within supporting distance. There were already twenty-eight police under command of Lieutenant Bull Head in the immediate vicinity of Sitting Bull's camp on Grand river, about 40 miles southwest of the agency and Fort Yates, and couriers were at once dispatched to these and to others in that direction to concentrate at Sitting Bull's house, ready to make the arrest in the morning. It was then sundown, but with loyal promptness the police mounted their ponies and by riding all night from one station to another assembled a force of 43 trained and determined Indian police, including four volunteers, at the rendezvous on Grand river before daylight. In performing this courier service Sergeant Red Tomahawk covered the distance of 40 miles between the agency and the camp, over an unfamiliar road,

Fig. 76—Red Tomahawk.

in four hours and a quarter; and another, Hawk Man, made 100 miles, by a roundabout way, in twenty-two hours. In the meantime two troops of the Eighth cavalry, numbering 100 men, under command of Captain E. G. Fechét, and having with them a Hotchkiss gun, left Fort Yates at midnight, guided by Louis Primeau, and by a rapid night march arrived within supporting distance near Sitting Bull's camp just before daybreak. It was afterward learned that Sitting Bull, in anticipation of such action, had had a strong guard about his house for his protection for several nights previous, but on this particular night the

Indians had been dancing until nearly morning, and the house was consequently left unguarded.

At daybreak on Monday morning, December 15, 1890, the police and volunteers, 43 in number, under command of Lieutenant Bull Head, a cool and reliable man, surrounded Sitting Bull's house. He had two log cabins, a few rods apart, and to make sure of their man, eight of the police entered one house and ten went into the other, while the rest remained on guard outside. They found him asleep on the floor in the larger house. He was aroused and told that he was a prisoner and must go to the agency. He made no objection, but said "All right; I will dress and go with you." He then sent one of his wives to the other house for some clothes he desired to wear, and asked to have his favorite horse saddled for him to ride, which was done by one of the police. On looking about the room two rifles and several knives were found and taken by the police. While dressing, he apparently changed his mind and began abusing the police for disturbing him, to which they made no reply. While this was going on inside, his followers, to the number of perhaps 150, were congregating about the house outside and by the time he was dressed an excited crowd of Indians had the police entirely surrounded and were pressing them to the wall. On being brought out, Sitting Bull became greatly excited and refused to go, and called on his followers to rescue him. Lieutenant Bull Head and Sergeant Shave Head were standing on each side of him, with Second Sergeant Red Tomahawk guarding behind, while the rest of the police were trying to clear the way in front, when one of Sitting Bull's followers, Catch-the-Bear, fired and shot Lieutenant Bull Head in the side. Bull Head at once turned and sent a bullet into the body of Sitting Bull, who was also shot through the head at the same moment by Red Tomahawk. Sergeant Shave Head was shot by another of the crowd, and fell to the ground with Bull Head and Sitting Bull. Catch-the-Bear, who fired the first shot, was immediately shot and killed by Alone Man, one of the police, and it became a desperate hand-to-hand fight of less than 43 men against more than a hundred. The trained police soon drove their assailants into the timber near by, and then returned and carried their dead and wounded into the house and held it for about two hours, until the arrival of the troops under Captain Fechét, about half past seven. The troops had been notified of the perilous situation of the police by Hawk Man, who had volunteered to carry the information from Sitting Bull's camp. He succeeded in getting away, assisted by Red Tomahawk, although so closely pursued that several bullets passed through his clothing. In spite of the efforts of the hostiles, the police also held possession of the corral, which Sitting Bull had filled with horses in anticipation of his flight. When the cavalry came in sight over a hill, about 1,500 yards distant from the camp, the police at the corral raised a white flag to show where they were, but the troops, mistaking them for hostiles, fired two shells at them from the Hotchkiss, when Sergeant Red Tomahawk, who had taken command after the wounding of his superior officers, paraded his men in line and then rode out alone with a white flag to meet the troops. On the approach of the soldiers Sitting Bull's warriors fled up Grand river a short distance and then turned south across the prairie toward Cherry creek and Cheyenne river. Not wishing to create such a panic among them as to drive them into the hostile camp in the Bad Lands, Captain Fechét pursued them only a short distance and then left them to be handled by the other detachments in that direction. Their wives and families, their property and their dead, were left behind in the flight.

Fig. 77—Sitting Bull the Sioux medicine-man.

As soon as possible Captain Fechét also sent word to them by some Indian women to return to their homes and they would not be molested. To further reassure them, the troops at once began their march back to the post. As a result of this sensible policy, very few of the Sitting Bull band joined the hostiles. They had made no resistance to the troops, but fled immediately on their appearance.

The fight lasted only a few minutes, but with terribly fatal result. Six policemen were killed or mortally wounded, including the officers Bull Head and Shave Head, and one other less seriously wounded. The hostiles lost eight killed, including Sitting Bull and his son Crow

Foot, 17 years of age, with several wounded. During the fight the women attacked the police with knives and clubs, but notwithstanding the excitement the police simply disarmed them and put them in one of the houses under guard.

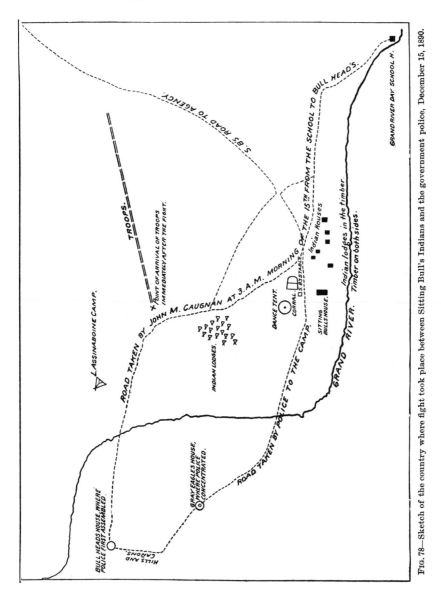

Fig. 78—Sketch of the country where fight took place between Sitting Bull's Indians and the government police, December 15, 1890.

The warmest praise is given the Indian police for their conduct on this occasion by those who are most competent to judge. Some who thus faced death in obedience to orders had near relatives among those opposed to them. Agent McLaughlin in one official letter says that he can not too strongly commend their splendid courage and ability in the action, and in another letter says: "The details of the battle show that the Indian police behaved nobly and exhibited the best of judgment and bravery, and a recognition by the government for their services on this occasion is richly deserved. . . . I respectfully urge that the Interior Department cooperate with the War Department in obtaining Congressional action which will secure to these brave survivors and to the families of the dead a full and generous reward." Colonel Drum, under whose orders the arrest was made, after stating that Sitting Bull was not hurt until he began struggling to escape and until one of the police had been shot, adds: "It is also remarkable that no squaws or children were hurt. The police appear to have constantly warned the other Indians to keep away, until they were forced to fight in self-defense. It is hardly possible to praise their conduct too highly." Notwithstanding the recommendation of the Commissioner of Indian Affairs, Congress has taken no action in recognition of their services on this occasion.

Before the action orders had been sent to the police to have with them a wagon, in order to convey Sitting Bull quickly away from the camp, so as to avoid trouble, but in the excitement of preparation this was overlooked. The police returned to the agency late in the afternoon, bringing with them their dead and wounded, together with two prisoners and the body of Sitting Bull, which was turned over to the military authorities at Fort Yates. The four dead policemen were buried at the agency next day with military honors. Bull Head and Shave Head died in the hospital soon afterward, with the consolation of having their friends around them in their last moments. The agent states that the large majority of the Indians were loyal to the government, and expressed satisfaction at what they considered the termination of the disturbance. Couriers were again sent after the fleeing Indians by McLaughlin, warning them to return to the agency, where they would be safe, or suffer the consequences if found outside the reservation. Within a few days nearly 250 had come in and surrendered, leaving only about one-third still out. Most of these soon afterward surrendered with Hump on Cherry creek, while the remainder, about 50, joined Big Foot or went on to Pine Ridge. (*G. D., 36; War, 8.*)

Thus died Tata′nka I′yota′nke, Sitting Bull, the great medicine-man of the Sioux, on the morning of December 15, 1890, aged about 56 years. He belonged to the Uncpapa division of the Teton Sioux. Although a priest rather than a chief, he had gained a reputation in his early years by organizing and leading war parties, and became prominent by his participation in the battle of Little Bighorn, in Montana, on June 25, 1876, by which Custer's command was wiped out of existence. Being pursued by General Terry, Sitting Bull and his band made their escape northward into Canada, where they remained until 1881, when he surrendered, through the mediation of the Canadian authorities, on a promise of pardon. To obtain subsistence while in Canada, his people had been obliged to sell almost all they possessed, including their fire-arms, so that they returned to their old homes in an impoverished condition. After confinement as a prisoner of war until 1883, Sitting Bull took up his residence on Grand river, where he remained until he met his death. Here he continued to be the leader of the opposition to civilization and the white man, and his camp became the rallying point for the dissatisfied conservative element that clung to the old order of things, and felt that innovation meant destruction to their race. For seven years he had steadily opposed the treaty by which the great Sioux reservation was at last broken up in 1889. After the treaty had been signed by the requisite number to make it a law, he was asked by a white man what the Indians thought about it. With a burst of pas-sionate indignation he replied, "Indians! There are no Indians left now but me." However misguided he may have been in thus continu-ing a losing fight against the inevitable, it is possible that from the Indian point of view he may have been their patriot as he was their high priest. He has been mercilessly denounced as a bad man and a liar; but there can be no doubt that he was honest in his hatred of the whites, and his breaking of the peace pipe, saying that he "wanted to fight and wanted to die," showed that he was no coward. But he rep-resented the past. His influence was incompatible with progress, and his death marks an era in the civilization of the Sioux. In the language of General Miles, "His tragic fate was but the ending of a tragic life. Since the days of Pontiac, Tecumseh, and Red Jacket no Indian has had the power of drawing to him so large a following of his race and molding and wielding it against the authority of the United States, or of inspiring it with greater animosity against the white race and civilization." (*War, 9.*)

On December 18 the Indians who had already fled to the Bad Lands attacked a small party of men on Spring creek of Cheyenne river. Major Tupper with 100 men of Carr's division was sent to their rescue, and a skirmish ensued with the Indians, who were concealed in the bushes along the creek. The government wagons, while crossing the creek, were also attacked by the hostiles, who were finally driven off by reinforcements of cavalry under Captain Wells. On the same date over a thousand Indians returned to Pine Ridge. News was received that there were still about 1,500 fugitives camped on Cheyenne river in the neighborhood of Spring creek. (*Colby, 1.*)

The most dangerous leader of dissatisfaction in the north after the death of Sitting Bull was considered to be Hump, on Cheyenne River reservation. The agent in charge had long before recommended his removal, but it was thought that it would now be next to impossible to arrest him. Hump with his band of about 400 persons, and Big Foot with nearly as many, had their camps about the junction of Cherry creek and Cheyenne river. For several weeks they had been dancing almost constantly, and were very sullen and apparently very hostile. After serious consideration of the matter, the task of securing Hump was assigned to Captain E. P. Ewers of the Fifth infantry, who had had charge of this chief and his band for seven years and had their full confidence and respect. He was then on duty in Texas, but was ordered forward and reported soon after at Fort Bennett on the border of the reservation. So dangerous was Hump considered to be that the civil agents did not think it possible even for the officer to communicate with him. However, Captain Ewers, without troops and attended only by Lieutenant Hale, at once left the fort and rode out 60 miles to Hump's camp. "Hump at the time was 20 miles away and a runner was sent for him. Immediately upon hearing that Captain Ewers was in the vicinity he came to him and was told that the division commander desired him to take his people away from the hostiles and bring them to the nearest military post. He replied that if General Miles sent for him, he would do whatever he desired. He immediately brought his people into Fort Bennett and complied with all the orders and instructions given him, and subsequently rendered valuable service for peace. Thus an element regarded as among the most dangerous was removed." After coming into the fort, Hump enlisted as a scout under Captain Ewers, and soon afterward, in connection with the same Lieutenant Hale, proved his loyalty by bringing about the surrender of the Sitting Bull fugitives. Subsequently Captain Ewers further distinguished himself by conducting the northern Cheyenne—who were considered as particularly dangerous, but who regarded Captain Ewers with absolute affection—from Pine Ridge to Tongue river, Montana, a distance of 300 miles, and in the most rigorous of the winter season, without an escort of troops and without the loss of a single life or the commission by an Indian of a single unlawful act. (*War, 10.*)

The Sitting Bull fugitives who had not come in at once had fled southward toward their friends and near relatives of Cheyenne River reservation, and were camped on Cherry creek a few miles above its junction with Cheyenne river at Cheyenne City. As their presence there could serve only to increase the unrest among the other Indians in that vicinity, and as there was great danger that they might attempt to join those already in the Bad Lands, Captain Hurst, of the Twelfth infantry, commanding at Fort Bennett, directed Lieutenant H. E. Hale on December 18 to go out and bring them in. On arriving at Cheyenne City the officer found it deserted, all the citizens excepting one man having fled in alarm a short time before on the report of a half-blood that the Sitting Bull Indians were coming and had sworn to kill the first white man they met. Having succeeded in frightening the whole population, the half-blood himself, Narcisse Narcelle, left at once for the fort.

After some difficulty in finding anyone to assist him, Hale sent a policeman to bring back Narcelle and sent out another Indian to learn the situation and condition of the Indian camp. His only interpreter for the purpose was Mr Angell, the single white man who had remained, and who had learned some of the Sioux language during his residence among them. While thus waiting, a report came that the Indians had raided a ranch about 10 miles up the creek. Not hearing from his scouts, the lieutenant determined to go alone and find the camp, and was just about to start, when Hump, the late dangerous hostile, but now an enlisted scout, rode in with the news that the Sitting Bull Indians were approaching only a short distance away, and armed. Although from the reports there was every reason to believe that they had just destroyed a ranch and were now coming to attack the town, the officer, with rare bravery, kept his determination to go out and meet them, even without an interpreter, in the hope of preventing their hostile purpose. Hump volunteered to go with him. The two rode out together and soon came up with the Indians, who received them in a friendly manner. There were 46 warriors in the party, besides women and children, wagons and ponies. Says the officer: "I appreciated the importance of the situation, but was absolutely powerless to communicate with the Indians. I immediately formed the opinion that they could be easily persuaded to come into the agency if I could but talk with them. While I was trying by signs to make them understand what I wanted, Henry Angell rode into the circle and took his place at my side. This generous man had not liked the idea of my going among these Indians, and from a true spirit of chivalry had ridden over to 'see it out.'" Verily, while such men as Ewers, Hale, and Angell live, the day of chivalry is not gone by.

With Angell's assistance as interpreter, the officer told the Indians that if they would stay where they were for one day, he would go back to the agency and return within that time with the chief (Captain J. H. Hurst) and an interpreter and no soldiers. They replied that they would not move, and, having directed Angell to kill a beef for them, as they were worn-out and well-nigh starving, and leaving Hump with them to reassure them, the lieutenant rode back to Fort Bennett, 40 miles away, notified Captain Hurst, and returned with him, Sergeant Gallagher, and two Indian scouts as interpreters, the next day. Knowing the importance of haste, they started out on this winter ride of 40 miles without blankets or rations.

On arriving Captain Hurst told them briefly what he had come for, and then, being exhausted from the rapid ride, and knowing that an Indian must not be hurried, he ordered some beef and a plentiful supply of tobacco for them, and said that after he and they had eaten and rested they could talk the matter over. In the evening the principal men met him and told him over a pipe that they had left Standing Rock agency forever; that their great chief and friend Sitting Bull had been killed there without cause; that they had come down to talk with their friends on Cherry creek about it, but had found them gone, and were consequently undecided as to what they should do. The captain replied that he had come as a friend; that if they would surrender their arms and go back with him to Fort Bennett, they would be provided for and would not be harmed; that he could make no promises as to their future disposition; that if they chose to join Big Foot's camp, only a few miles up the river, the result would be their certain destruction. After deliberating among themselves until midnight, they came in a body, delivered a number of guns, and said they would go back to the fort. Accordingly they broke camp next morning and arrived at Fort Bennett on December 24. The entire body numbered 221, including 55 belonging on Cherry creek. These last were allowed to join their own people camped near the post. The Sitting Bull Indians, with some others from Standing Rock, numbering 227 in all, were held at Fort Sully, a few miles below Fort Bennett, until the close of the trouble. Thirty-eight others of the Sitting Bull band had joined Big Foot and afterward fled with him. (*War, 11.*)

After the death of Sitting Bull and the enlistment of Hump in the government service, the only prominent leader outside of the Bad Lands who was considered as possibly dangerous was Sitanka or Big Foot, whose village was at the mouth of Deep creek, a few miles below the forks of Cheyenne river. The duty of watching him was assigned to Lieutenant-Colonel E. V. Sumner of the Eighth cavalry, who had his camp just above the forks. Here he was visited by Big Foot and his head men, who assured the officer that they were peaceable and intended to remain quietly at home. Friendly relations continued until the middle of December, when Big Foot came to bid good bye, telling Sumner that his people were all going to the agency to get their annuities. A day or two later the order came to arrest Big Foot and send him as a prisoner to Fort Meade. Believing that the chief was acting in good faith to control his warriors, who might easily go beyond control were he taken from them, Colonel Sumner informed General Miles that the Indians were already on their way to the agency; that if Big Foot should return he (Sumner) would try to get him, and that otherwise he could be arrested at the agency, if necessary. Soon after, however, the report came that Big Foot had stopped at Hump's camp on the way to the agency, to meet the fugitives coming south from Sitting Bull's camp.

On receipt of this information, Sumner at once marched down the river with the intention of stopping Big Foot. When about half way to Hump's camp, Big Foot himself came up to meet him, saying that he was friendly, and that he and his men would obey any orders that the officer might give. He stated that he had with him 100 of his own Indians and 38 from Standing Rock (Sitting Bull's band). When asked why he had received these last, knowing that they were refugees from their reservation, he replied that they were his brothers and relations; that they had come to his people hungry, footsore, and almost naked; and that he had taken them in and fed them, and that no one with a heart could do any less.

Sumner then directed one of his officers, Captain Hennisee, to go to the Indian camp with Big Foot and bring in all the Indians. That officer started and returned the next day, December 21, with 333 Indians. This large number was a matter of surprise in view of Big Foot's statement shortly before, but it is possible that in speaking of his party he intended to refer only to the warriors. They went into camp as directed, turned out their ponies to graze, and were fed, and on the next morning all started quietly back with the troops. As they had all along appeared perfectly friendly and compliant with every order, no attempt was made to disarm them. On arriving near their own village, however, it became apparent that Big Foot could not control their desire to go to their homes. The chief came frankly to Sumner and said that he himself would go wherever wanted, but that there would be trouble to force the women and children, who were cold and hungry, away from their village. He protested also that they were now at home, where they had been ordered by the government to stay, and that none of them had done anything to justify their removal. As it was evident that they would not go peaceably, Colonel Sumner determined to bring his whole force on the next day to compel them. In the meantime he sent a white man named Dunn, who had a friendly acquaintance with Big Foot, to tell him that the Indians must obey the order to remove. Dunn delivered the message and returned, being followed later by the interpreter, with the statement that the Indians had consented to go to the agency, and would start the next morning, December 23. That evening, however, scouts came in with the word that the Indians had left their village and were going southward. It was at first thought that they intended turning off on another trail to the agency, but instead of doing so they kept on in the direction of Pine Ridge and the refugees in the Bad Lands, taking with them only their ponies and tipi poles.

The cause of this precipitate flight after the promise given by Big Foot is somewhat uncertain. The statement of the interpreter, Felix Benoit, would make it appear that the Indians were frightened by Dunn, who told them that the soldiers were coming in the morning to carry them off and to shoot them if they refused to go. While this doubtless had the effect of alarming them, the real cause of their flight was probably the fact that just at this critical juncture Colonel Merriam was ordered to move with his command up Cheyenne river to join forces with Sumner in compelling their surrender. Such is the opinion of General Ruger, who states officially that "Big Foot and adherents who had joined him, probably becoming alarmed on the movement of Colonel Merriam's command from Fort Bennett and a rumor that Colonel Sumner would capture them, eluded Colonel Sumner's command and started for the Pine Ridge reservation." This agrees with the statement of several of the survivors that they had been frightened from their homes by the news of Merriam's approach. Sumner, in his report, calls attention to the fact that they committed no depredations in their flight, although they passed several ranches and at one time even went through a pasture filled with horses and cattle without attempting to appropriate them. He also expresses the opinion that Big Foot was compelled unwillingly to go with his people. The whole number of fugitives was at least 340, including a few from the bands of Sitting Bull and Hump. Immediately on learning of their flight Colonel Sumner notified General Carr, commanding in the direction of the Bad Lands. (*War, 12.*)

The situation at this crisis is thus summed up by Indian Commissioner Morgan:

> Groups of Indians from the different reservations had commenced concentrating in the Bad Lands upon or in the vicinity of the Pine Ridge reservation. Killing of cattle and destruction of other property by these Indians, almost entirely within the limits of Pine Ridge and Rosebud reservations, occurred, but no signal fires were built, no warlike demonstrations were made, no violence was done to any white settler, nor was there cohesion or organization among the Indians themselves. Many of them were friendly Indians, who had never participated in the ghost dance, but had fled thither from fear of soldiers, in consequence of the Sitting Bull affair or through the overpersuasion of friends. The military gradually began to close in around them and they offered no resistance, and a speedy and quiet capitulation of all was confidently expected. (*Comr., 34.*)

Nearly 3,000 troops were now in the field in the Sioux country. This force was fully sufficient to have engaged the Indians with success, but as such action must inevitably have resulted in wholesale killing on both sides, with the prospect of precipitating a raiding warfare unless the hostiles were completely annihilated, it was thought best to bring about a surrender by peaceful means.

The refugees in the Bad Lands who had fled from Pine Ridge and Rosebud had been surrounded on the west and north by a strong cordon of troops, operating under General Brooke, which had the effect of gradually forcing them back toward the agency. At the same time that officer made every effort to expedite the process by creating dissensions in the Indian camp, and trying in various ways to induce them to come in by small parties at a time. To this end the Indians were promised that if they complied with the orders of the military their rights and interests would be protected, so far as it was within the power of the military department to accomplish that result. Although they had about lost confidence in the government, these assurances had a good effect, which was emphasized by the news of the death of Sitting Bull, the arrest of Big Foot, and return of Hump to his agency, and the steady pressure of the troops from behind; and on December 27, 1890, the entire force broke camp and left their stronghold in the Bad Lands and began moving in toward the agency at Pine Ridge. The several detachments of troops followed behind, within supporting distance of one another, and so closely that the fires were still burning in the Indian camps when the soldiers moved in to occupy the same ground. (*War, 13.*)

As early as December 6 a conference had been brought about at Pine Ridge, through the efforts of Father Jutz, the priest of the Catholic mission, between General Brooke and the leading chiefs of both friendlies and "hostiles." Although no definite conclusion was reached, the meeting was a friendly one, ending with a feast and an Indian dance. The immediate effect was a division in the hostile camp, culminating in a quarrel between the two factions, with the result that Two Strike and his party left the rest and moved in toward the agency, while Short Bull and Kicking Bear retreated farther into the Bad Lands. On learning of this condition of affairs, General Brooke sent out American Horse and Big Road with a large party of warriors to meet Two Strike and go back with him to persuade the others, if possible, to come in. At the same time the troops were moved up to intercept the flight of the hostiles. (*Colby, 2; G. D., 37.*)

On Christmas day the Cheyenne scouts, camped on Battle creek north of the Bad Lands, were attacked by a party of hostiles led by Kicking Bear in person. The fight was kept up until after dark, several being killed or wounded on both sides, but the hostiles were finally driven off. (*Colby, 3.*)

But the tragedy was near at hand. Orders had been given to intercept Big Foot's party in its flight from Cheyenne river toward the Bad Lands. This was accomplished on December 28, 1890, by Major Whitside of the Seventh cavalry, who came up with him a short distance west of the Bad Lands. Not having succeeded in communicating with the refugees who had fled there and who were already on their way to the agency, Big Foot had made no stop, but continued on also toward Pine Ridge. On sighting the troops he raised a white flag, advanced into the open country, and asked for a parley. This was refused by Major Whitside, who demanded an unconditional surrender, which was at once given, and the Indians moved on with the troops to Wounded Knee creek, about 20 miles northeast of Pine Ridge agency, where they camped as directed by Major Whitside. In order to make assurance complete, General Brooke sent Colonel Forsyth to join Major Whitside with four additional troops of the Seventh cavalry, which, with the scouts under Lieutenant Taylor, made up a force of eight troops of cavalry, one company of scouts, and four pieces of light artillery (Hotchkiss guns), with a total force of 470 men, as against a total of 106 warriors then present in Big Foot's band. A scouting party of Big Foot's band was out looking for the camp under Kicking Bear and Short Bull, but as these chiefs, with their followers, were already on their way to the agency, the scouting party was returning to rejoin Big Foot when the fight occurred the next morning. It was the intention of General Miles to send Big Foot and his followers back to their own reservation, or to remove them altogether from the country until the excitement had subsided. (*War, 14.*)

At this time there were no Indians in the Bad Lands. Two Strike and Crow Dog had come in about a week before and were now camped close to the agency. Kicking Bear and Short Bull, with their follow-ers, had yielded to the friendly persuasions of American Horse, Little Wound, Standing Bear, and others who had gone out to them in the interests of peace, and both parties were now coming in together and had arrived at the Catholic mission, 5 miles from the agency, when the battle occurred.

On the morning of December 29, 1890, preparations were made to disarm the Indians preparatory to taking them to the agency and thence to the railroad. In obedience to instructions the Indians had pitched their tipis on the open plain a short distance west of the creek and surrounded on all sides by the soldiers. In the center of the camp the Indians had hoisted a white flag as a sign of peace and a guarantee of safety. Behind them was a dry ravine running into the creek, and on a slight rise in the front was posted the battery of four Hotchkiss machine guns, trained directly on the Indian camp. In front, behind, and on both flanks of the camp were posted the various troops of cav-alry, a portion of two troops, together with the Indian scouts, being dismounted and drawn up in front of the Indians at the distance of only a few yards from them. Big Foot himself was ill of pneumonia in his tipi, and Colonel Forsyth, who had taken command as senior officer, had provided a tent warmed with a camp stove for his reception.

Shortly after 8 oclock in the morning the warriors were ordered to come out from the tipis and deliver their arms. They came forward and seated themselves on the ground in front of the troops. They were then ordered to go by themselves into their tipis and bring out and surrender their guns. The first twenty went and returned in a short time with only two guns. It seemed evident that they were unwilling to give them up, and after consultation of the officers part of the soldiers were ordered up to within ten yards of the group of war-riors, while another detachment of troops was ordered to search the tipis. After a thorough hunt these last returned with about forty rifles, most of which, however, were old and of little value. The search had consumed considerable time and created a good deal of excitement among the women and children, as the soldiers found it necessary in the process to overturn the beds and other furniture of the tipis and in some instances drove out the inmates. All this had its effect on their husbands and brothers, already wrought up to a high nervous tension and not knowing what might come next. While the soldiers had been looking for the guns Yellow Bird, a medicine-man, had been walking about among the warriors, blowing on an eagle-bone whistle, and urging them to resistance, telling them that the soldiers would become weak and powerless, and that the bullets would be

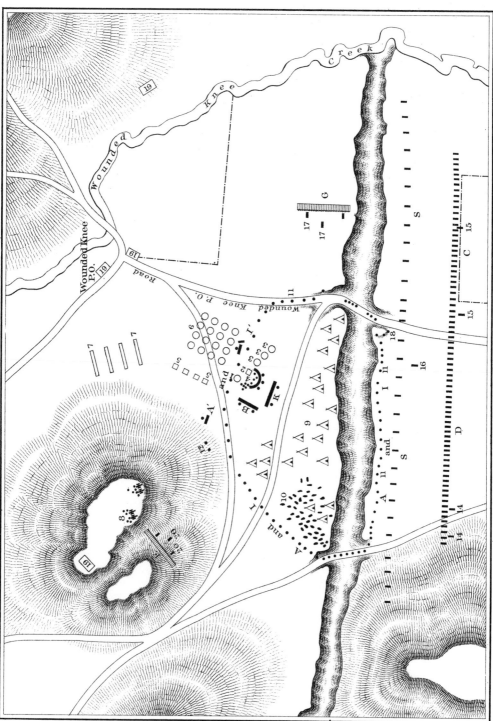

WOUNDED KNEE BATTLEFIELD

JULIUS BIEN & CO. N.Y.

EXPLANATION OF PLATE XCVII

Compiled from map by Lieutenant T. Q. Donaldson, Seventh United States cavalry, kindly loaned by Dr J. D. Glennan, United States Army.

A and I. Seventy-six men from A and I troops forming dismounted line of sentinels.

B. Troop B dismounted and in line.

C. Troop C mounted and in line (sorrel troop).

D. Troop D mounted and in line (black troop).

E. Troop E mounted and in line (bay troop).

G. Troop G mounted and in line (gray troop).

K. Troop K dismounted and in line.

S. Indian scouts.

1. Tent from which a hostile warrior shot two soldiers.

2. Tent occupied by Big Foot and his wife and in front of which the former was killed.

3. Tents put up for the use of Big Foot's band.

4. Council ring in or near which were General Forsyth, Major Whitside, Captain Varnum, Captain Hoff, Captain Wallace, Doctor Glennan, Lieutenant Robinson, Lieutenant Nicholson, Lieutenant McCormick, and the reporters.

5. Officers' tents, first battalion.

6. Enlisted mens' tents, first battalion.

7. Bivouac of second battalion on night of December 28, 1890.

8. Four Hotchkiss guns and detachment of First artillery, under Captain Capron, First artillery, and Lieutenant Hawthorne, Second artillery.

9. Indian village.

10. Indian ponies.

11. Dismounted line of sentinels.

12. Captains Ilsley and Moylan.

13. Lieutenants Garlington and Waterman.

14. Captain Godfrey and Lieutenant Tompkins.

15. Captain Jackson and Lieutenant Donaldson.

16. Lieutenant Taylor, Ninth cavalry, commanding Indian scouts (S).

17. Captain Edgerly and Lieutenant Brewer.

18. Captain Nowlan and Lieutenant Gresham.

19. Indian houses.

20. Lieutenants Sickel and Rice.

Just beyond the limit of the map, toward the west, the ravine forms a bend, in which a number of hostiles took refuge, and from which Lieutenant Hawthorne was shot. Captain Wallace was found near the center of the council ring. Big Foot was killed two or three yards in front of his tent. Father Craft was near the center of the ring when stabbed. The Indians broke to the west through B and K troops. While in the council ring all the warriors had on blankets, with their arms, principally Winchester rifles, concealed under them. Most of the warriors, including the medicine-man, were painted and wore ghost shirts.

unavailing against the sacred " ghost shirts," which nearly every one of the Indians wore. As he spoke in the Sioux language, the officers did not at once realize the dangerous drift of his talk, and the climax came too quickly for them to interfere. It is said one of the searchers now attempted to raise the blanket of a warrior. Suddenly Yellow Bird stooped down and threw a handful of dust into the air, when, as if this were the signal, a young Indian, said to have been Black Fox from Cheyenne river, drew a rifle from under his blanket and fired at the soldiers, who instantly replied with a volley directly into the crowd of warriors and so near that their guns were almost touching. From the number of sticks set up by the Indians to mark where the dead fell, as seen by the author a year later, this one volley must have killed nearly half the warriors (plate XCIX). The survivors sprang to their feet, throwing their blankets from their shoulders as they rose, and for a few minutes there was a terrible hand to hand struggle, where every man's thought was to kill. Although many of the warriors had no guns, nearly all had revolvers and knives in their belts under their blankets, together with some of the murderous warclubs still carried by the Sioux. The very lack of guns made the fight more bloody, as it brought the combatants to closer quarters.

At the first volley the Hotchkiss guns trained on the camp opened fire and sent a storm of shells and bullets among the women and children, who had gathered in front of the tipis to watch the unusual spectacle of military display. The guns poured in 2-pound explosive shells at the rate of nearly fifty per minute, mowing down everything alive. The terrible effect may be judged from the fact that one woman survivor, Blue Whirlwind, with whom the author conversed, received fourteen wounds, while each of her two little boys was also wounded by her side. In a few minutes 200 Indian men, women, and children, with 60 soldiers, were lying dead and wounded on the ground, the tipis had been torn down by the shells and some of them were burning above the helpless wounded, and the surviving handful of Indians were flying in wild panic to the shelter of the ravine, pursued by hundreds of maddened soldiers and followed up by a raking fire from the Hotchkiss guns, which had been moved into position to sweep the ravine.

There can be no question that the pursuit was simply a massacre, where fleeing women, with infants in their arms, were shot down after resistance had ceased and when almost every warrior was stretched dead or dying on the ground. On this point such a careful writer as Herbert Welsh says: "From the fact that so many women and children were killed, and that their bodies were found far from the scene of action, and as though they were shot down while flying, it would look as though blind rage had been at work, in striking contrast to the moderation of the Indian police at the Sitting Bull fight when they were assailed by women." (*Welsh, 3.*) The testimony of American Horse and other friendlies is strong in the same direction. (See page

839.) Commissioner Morgan in his official report says that "Most of the men, including Big Foot, were killed around his tent, where he lay sick. The bodies of the women and children were scattered along a distance of two miles from the scene of the encounter." (*Comr., 35.*)

This is no reflection on the humanity of the officer in charge. On the contrary, Colonel Forsyth had taken measures to guard against such an occurrence by separating the women and children, as already stated, and had also endeavored to make the sick chief, Big Foot, as comfortable as possible, even to the extent of sending his own surgeon, Dr Glennan, to wait on him on the night of the surrender. Strict orders had also been issued to the troops that women and children were not to be hurt. The butchery was the work of infuriated soldiers whose comrades had just been shot down without cause or warning. In justice to a brave regiment it must be said that a number of the men were new recruits fresh from eastern recruiting stations, who had never before been under fire, were not yet imbued with military discipline, and were probably unable in the confusion to distinguish between men and women by their dress.

After examining all the official papers bearing on the subject in the files of the War Department and the Indian Office, together with the official reports of the Commissioner of Indian Affairs and of the Secretary of War and the several officers engaged; after gathering all that might be obtained from unofficial printed sources and from conversation with survivors and participants in the engagement on both sides, and after going over the battle-ground in company with the interpreter of the scouts engaged, the author arrives at the conclusion that when the sun rose on Wounded Knee on the fatal morning of December 29, 1890, no trouble was anticipated or premeditated by either Indians or troops; that the Indians in good faith desired to surrender and be at peace, and that the officers in the same good faith had made preparations to receive their surrender and escort them quietly to the reservation; that in spite of the pacific intent of Big Foot and his band, the medicine-man, Yellow Bird, at the critical moment urged the warriors to resistance and gave the signal for the attack; that the first shot was fired by an Indian, and that the Indians were responsible for the engagement; that the answering volley and attack by the troops was right and justifiable, but that the wholesale slaughter of women and children was unnecessary and inexcusable.

Authorities differ as to the number of Indians present and killed at Wounded Knee. General Ruger states that the band numbered about 340, including about 100 warriors, but Major Whitside, to whom they surrendered, reported them officially as numbering 120 men and 250 women and children, a total of 370. (*War, 15; G. D., 38.*) This agrees almost exactly with the statement made to the author by Mr Asay, a trader who was present at the surrender. General Miles says that there were present 106 warriors, a few others being absent at the time in search of the party under Kicking Bear and Short Bull. (*War, 16.*) Among those who surrendered were about 70 refugees from the bands of Sitting Bull and Hump. (*G. D., 39.*) No exact account of the dead could be made immediately after the fight, on account of a second attack by another party of Indians coming up from the agency. Some of the dead and wounded left on the field were undoubtedly carried off by their friends before the burial party came out three days later, and of those brought in alive a number afterward died of wounds and exposure, but received no notice in the official reports. The Adjutant-General, in response to a letter of inquiry, states that 128 Indians were killed and 33 wounded. Commissioner Morgan, in his official report, makes the number killed 146. (*Comr., 36.*) Both these estimates are evidently too low. General Miles, in his final report, states that about 200 men, women, and children were killed. (*War, 17.*) General Colby, who commanded the Nebraska state troops, says that about 100 men and over 120 women and children were found dead on the field, a total of about 220. (*Colby, 4.*) Agent Royer telegraphed immediately after the fight that about 300 Indians had been killed, and General Miles, telegraphing on the same day, says, "I think very few Indians have escaped." (*G. D., 40.*) Fifty-one Indians were brought in the same day by the troops, and a few others were found still alive by the burial party three days later. A number of these afterward died. No considerable number got away, being unable to reach their ponies after the fight began. General Miles states that 98 warriors were killed on the field. (*War, 18.*) The whole number killed on the field, or who later died from wounds and exposure, was probably very nearly 300.

According to an official statement from the Adjutant-General, 31 soldiers were killed in the battle. About as many more were wounded, one or two of whom afterward died. All of the killed, excepting Hospital Steward Pollock and an Indian scout named High Backbone, belonged to the Seventh cavalry, as did probably also nearly all of the wounded. The only commissioned officer killed was Captain Wallace. He received four bullet wounds in his body and finally sank under a hatchet stroke upon the head. Lieutenant E. A. Garlington, of the Seventh cavalry, and Lieutenant H. L. Hawthorne, of the Second artillery, were wounded. (*War, 19.*) The last-named officer owed his life to his watch, which deflected the bullet that otherwise would have passed through his body.

Below is given a complete list of officers and enlisted men who were killed, or died of wounds or exposure, in connection with the Sioux campaign. The statement is contained in an official letter of reply from the Adjutant-General's office dated May 26, 1894. Unless otherwise noted all were of the Seventh cavalry and were killed on December 29, the date of the battle of Wounded Knee. In addition to these, two others, Henry Miller, a herder, and George Wilhauer, of the Nebraska militia, were killed in the same connection. With the 6

Indian police killed in arresting Sitting Bull, this makes a total of 49 deaths on the government side, including 7 Indians and a negro:

Adams, William.

Bone, Albert S. (corporal, died of wounds).

Casey, Edward W. (first lieutenant Twenty-second infantry, January 7).

Coffey, Dora S. (first sergeant).

Cook, Ralph L.

Corwine, Richard W. (sergeant major).

Costello, John.

Cummings, Pierce.

De Vreede, Jan.

Dyer, Arthur C. (sergeant).

Elliott, George (died of wounds, January 13).

Francischetti, Dominic (December 30).

Forrest, Harry R. (corporal).

Frey, Henry.

Grauberg, Herman (died of wounds, December 30).

Haywood, Charles (Ninth cavalry, colored, December 30).

High Backbone (Indian scout).

Hodges, William T. (sergeant).

Howard, Henry (sergeant, died of wounds, January 23).

Johnson, George P.

Kelley, James E.

Kellner, August.

Korn, Gustav (blacksmith).

Logan, James.

McClintock, William F.

McCue, John M.

Mann, James D. (first lieutenant, died of wounds, January 15).

Meil, John W. (killed in railroad accident, January 26).

Mezo, William S.

Murphy, Joseph.

Nettles, Robert H. (sergeant).

Newell, Charles H. (corporal, died of wounds).

Pollock, Oscar (hospital steward).

Regan, Michael.

Reinecky, Frank T.

Schartel, Thomas (First artillery, killed in railroad accident, January 26).

Schwenkey, Philip.

Stone, Harry B. (died of wounds, January 12).

Twohig, Daniel.

Wallace, George B. (captain).

Zehnder, Bernhard (died of wounds).

The heroic missionary priest, Father Craft, who had given a large part of his life to work among the Sioux, by whom he was loved and respected, had endeavored at the beginning of the trouble to persuade the stampeded Indians to come into the agency, but without success, the Indians claiming that no single treaty ever made with them had been fulfilled in all its stipulations. Many of the soldiers being of his own faith, he accompanied the detachment which received the surrender of Big Foot, to render such good offices as might be possible to either party. In the desperate encounter he was stabbed through the lungs, but yet, with bullets flying about him and hatchets and warclubs circling through the air, he went about his work, administering the last religious consolation to the dying until he fell unconscious from loss of blood. He was brought back to the agency along with the other wounded, and although his life was despaired of for some time, he finally recovered. In talking about Wounded Knee with one of the friendly warriors who had gone into the Bad Lands to urge the hostiles to come in, he spoke with warm admiration of Father Craft, and I asked why it was, then, that the Indians had tried to kill him. He replied, "They did not know him. Father Jutz [the priest at the Drexel Catholic mission, previously mentioned] always wears his black robe, but Father Craft on that day wore a soldier's cap and overcoat. If he had worn his black robe, no Indian would have hurt him." On

MARY IRVIN WRIGHT

AFTER THE BATTLE

inquiring afterward I learned that this was not correct, as Father Craft did have on his priestly robes. From the Indian statement, however, and the well-known affection in which he was held by the Sioux, it is probable that the Indian who stabbed him was too much excited at the moment to recognize him.

The news of the battle was brought to the agency by Lieutenant Guy Preston, of the Ninth cavalry, who, in company with a soldier and an Indian scout, made the ride of 16 or 18 miles in a little over an hour, one horse falling dead of exhaustion on the way. There were then at the agency, under command of General Brooke, about 300 men of the Second infantry and 50 Indian police.

The firing at Wounded Knee was plainly heard by the thousands of Indians camped about the agency at Pine Ridge, who had come in from the Bad Lands to surrender. They were at once thrown into great excitement, undoubtedly believing that there was a deliberate purpose on foot to disarm and massacre them all, and when the fugitives—women and children, most of them—began to come in, telling the story of the terrible slaughter of their friends and showing their bleeding wounds in evidence, the camp was divided between panic and desperation. A number of warriors mounted in haste and made all speed to the battle-ground, only about two hours distant, where they met the troops, who were now scattered about, hunting down the fugitives who might have escaped the first killing, and picking up the dead and wounded. The soldiers were driven in toward the center, where they threw up entrenchments, by means of which they were finally able to repel the attacking party. With the assistance of a body of Indian scouts and police, they then gathered up the dead and wounded soldiers, with some of the wounded Indians and a few other prisoners to the number of 51, and came into the agency. In the meantime the hostiles under Two Strike had opened fire on the agency from the neighboring hills and endeavored to approach, by way of a deep ravine, near enough to set fire to the buildings. General Brooke, desiring to avoid a general engagement, ordered out the Indian police—a splendidly drilled body of 50 brave men—who gallantly took their stand in the center of the agency inclosure, in full view of the hostiles, some of whom were their own relatives, and kept them off, returning the fire of besiegers with such good effect as to kill two and wound several others. The attacking party, as well as those who rode out to help their kinsmen at Wounded Knee, were not the Pine Ridge Indians (Ogalala) but the Brulé from Rosebud under the lead of Two Strike, Kicking Bear, and Short Bull. On the approach of the detachment returning from Wounded Knee almost the entire body that had come in to surrender broke away and fell back to a position on White Clay creek, where the next day found a camp of 4,000 Indians, and including more than a thousand warriors now thoroughly hostile. On the evening of the battle General Miles telegraphed to military headquarters,

"Last night everything looked favorable for getting all the Indians under control; since report from Forsyth it looks more serious than at any other time." (*G. D., 41.*) It seemed that all the careful work of the last month had been undone.

At the first indication of coming trouble in November all the outlying schools and mission stations on Pine Ridge reservation had been abandoned, and teachers, farmers, and missionaries had fled to the agency to seek the protection of the troops, all but the members of the Drexel Catholic mission, 5 miles northwest from the agency. Here the two or three priests and five Franciscan sisters remained quietly at their post, with a hundred little children around them, safe in the assurance of the "hostiles" that they would not be molested. While the fighting was going on at Wounded Knee and hundreds of furious warriors were firing into the agency, where the handful of whites were shivering in spite of the presence of troops and police, these gentle women and the kindly old German priest were looking after the children, feeding the frightened fugitive women, and tenderly caring for the wounded Indians who were being brought in from Wounded Knee and the agency. Throughout all these weeks of terror they went calmly about the duties to which they had consecrated their lives, and kept their little flock together and their school in operation, without the presence of a single soldier, completely cut off from the troops and the agency and surrounded by thousands of wild Indians.

Some time afterward, in talking with the Indians about the events of the campaign, the warrior who had spoken with such admiration of Father Craft referred with the same affectionate enthusiasm to Father Jutz, and said that when the infuriated Indians attacked the agency on hearing of the slaughter at Wounded Knee they had sent word to the mission that no one there need be afraid. "We told him to stay where he was and no Indian would disturb him," said the warrior. He told how the priest and the sisters had fed the starving refugees and bound up the wounds of the survivors who escaped the slaughter, and then after a pause he said: "He is a brave man; braver than any Indian." Curious to know why this man had not joined the hostiles, among whom were several of his near relatives, I asked him the question. His reply was simple: "I had a little boy at the Drexel mission. He died and Father Jutz put a white stone over him. That is why I did not join the hostiles."

While visiting Pine Ridge in 1891 I went out to see the Drexel school and found Father John Jutz, a simple, kindly old German from the Tyrol, with one or two other German lay brothers and five Franciscan sisters, Americans. Although but a recent establishment, the school was in flourishing condition, bearing in everything the evidences of orderly industry. Like a true German of the Alps, Father Jutz had already devised a way to make jelly from the wild plums and excellent wine from the chokecherry. While talking, the recess hour arrived and

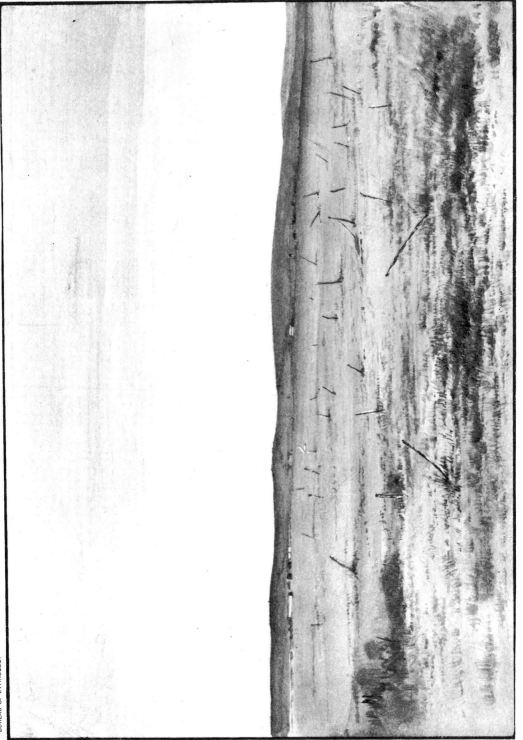

BATTLEFIELD OF WOUNDED KNEE

a bevy of small children came trooping in, pushing over one another in the effort to get hold of a finger of the good father, or at least to hold on to his robe while he led them into another room where one of the sisters gave to each a ginger cake, hot from the oven. The room was filled with the shouts and laughter of the children and the father explained, "Children get hungry, and we always have some cakes for the little ones at recess. I let the boys be noisy in the playroom as long as they don't fight. It is good for them." Looking at the happy, noisy crowd around the black-gowned missionary and sister, it was easy to see how they had felt safe in the affection of the Indians through all the days and nights when others were trembling behind breastworks and files of soldiers. Referring to what the Indians had told me, I asked Father Jutz if it was true that the hostiles had sent word to them not to be afraid. He replied, "Yes; they had sent word that no one in the mission need be alarmed," and then, with a gentle smile, he added, "But it was never our intention to leave." It was plain enough that beneath the quiet exterior there burned the old missionary fire of Jogues and Marquette.

The conflict at Wounded Knee bore speedy fruit. On the same day, as has been said, a part of the Indians under Two Strike attacked the agency and the whole body of nearly 4,000 who had come in to surrender started back again to intrench themselves in preparation for renewed hostilities. On the morning of December 30, the next day after the fight, the wagon train of the Ninth cavalry (colored) was attacked within 2 miles of the agency while coming in with supplies. One soldier was killed, but the Indians were repulsed with the loss of several of their number.

On the same day news came to the agency that the hostiles had attacked the Catholic mission 5 miles out, and Colonel Forsyth with eight troops of the Seventh cavalry and one piece of artillery was ordered by General Brooke to go out and drive them off. It proved that the hostiles had set fire to several houses between the mission and the agency, but the mission had not been disturbed. As the troops approached the hostiles fell back, but Forsyth failed to occupy the commanding hills and was consequently surrounded by the Indians, who endeavored to draw him into a canyon and pressed him so closely that he was obliged to send back three times for reinforcements. Major Henry had just arrived at the agency with a detachment of the Ninth cavalry, and on hearing the noise of the firing started at once to the relief of Forsyth with four troops of cavalry and a Hotchkiss gun. On arriving on the ground he occupied the hills and thus succeeded in driving off the hostiles without further casualty, and rescued the Seventh from its dangerous position. In this skirmish, known as the "mission fight," the Seventh lost one officer, Lieutenant Mann, and a private, Dominic Francischetti, killed, and seven wounded. (*War, 20; G. D., 42.*)

The conduct of the colored troops of the Ninth calvary on this occasion deserves the highest commendation. At the time of the battle at Wounded Knee, the day before, they were in the Bad Lands, about 80 or 90 miles out from Pine Ridge, when the order was sent for them to come in to aid in repelling the attack on the agency. By riding all night they arrived at the agency at daylight, together with two Hotchkiss guns, in charge of Lieutenant John Hayden of the First artillery. Hardly had they dismounted when word arrived that their wagon train, coming on behind, was attacked, and they were obliged to go out again to its relief, as already described. On coming in again they lay down to rest after their long night ride, when they were once more called out to go to the aid of the Seventh at the mission. Jumping into the saddle they rode at full speed to the mission, 5 miles out, repelled the hostiles and saved the command, and returned to the agency, after having ridden over 100 miles and fought two engagements within thirty hours. Lieutenant Hayden, with his Hotchkiss, who had come in with them from the Bad Lands, took part also with them in the mission fight.

On the same evening Standing Soldier, an Indian scout, arrived at the agency with a party of 65 Indians, including 18 men. These were a part of Big Foot's or Short Bull's following, who had lost their way during the flight from Cheyenne river and were hunting for the rest of the band when captured by the scouts. They were not aware of the death of Big Foot and the extermination of his band, but after having been disarmed and put under guard they were informed of it, but only in a mild way, in order not to provoke undue excitement. (*G. D., 43.*)

Immediately after the battle of Wounded Knee, in consequence of the panic among the frontier settlers of Nebraska, the Nebraska state troops were called out under command of General L. W. Colby. They were stationed at the most exposed points between the settlements and the reservation and remained in the field until the surrender of the hostiles two weeks later. The only casualty among them was the death of private George Wilhauer, who was accidentally shot by a picket. (*Colby, 5.*)

On New Year's day of 1891, three days after the battle, a detachment of troops was sent out to Wounded Knee to gather up and bury the Indian dead and to bring in the wounded who might be still alive on the field. In the meantime there had been a heavy snowstorm, culminating in a blizzard. The bodies of the slaughtered men, women, and children were found lying about under the snow, frozen stiff and covered with blood (plate XCVIII). Almost all the dead warriors were found lying near where the fight began, about Big Foot's tipi, but the bodies of the women and children were found scattered along for 2 miles from the scene of the encounter, showing that they had been killed while trying to escape. (*Comr., 37; Colby, 6.*) A number of women and children were found still alive, but all badly wounded or frozen, or both, and most of them died after being brought in. Four babies were found

BURYING THE DEAD

alive under the snow, wrapped in shawls and lying beside their dead mothers, whose last thought had been of them. They were all badly frozen and only one lived. The tenacity of life so characteristic of wild

Fig. 79—Survivors of Wounded Knee—Blue Whirlwind and children (1891).

people as well as of wild beasts was strikingly illustrated in the case of these wounded and helpless Indian women and children who thus lived three days through a Dakota blizzard, without food, shelter, or attention to their wounds. It is a commentary on our boasted Christian civilization that although there were two or three salaried missionaries at the agency not one went out to say a prayer over the poor mangled bodies of these victims of war.   The Catholic priests had reasons for not being present, as one of them, Father Craft, was lying in the hospital with a dangerous wound received on the battlefield while bravely administering to the dying wants of the soldiers in the heat of the encounter, and the other, Father Jutz, an old man of 70 years, was at the mission school 5 miles away, still attending to his little flock of 100 children

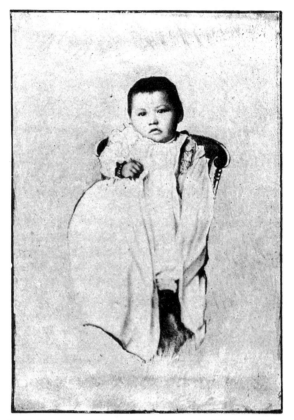

Fig. 80—Survivors of Wounded Knee—Marguerite Zitkala-noni (1891).

as before the trouble began, and unaware of what was transpiring at the agency.

A long trench was dug and into it were thrown all the bodies, piled one upon another like so much cordwood, until the pit was full, when the earth was heaped over them and the funeral was complete (plate c). Many of the bodies were stripped by the whites, who went out in order to get the " ghost shirts," and the frozen bodies were thrown into the trench stiff and naked.   They were only dead Indians.   As one of the burial party said, " It was a thing to melt the heart of a man, if it was

GRAVE OF THE DEAD AT WOUNDED KNEE

of stone, to see those little children, with their bodies shot to pieces, thrown naked into the pit." The dead soldiers had already been brought in and buried decently at the agency. When the writer visited the spot the following winter, the Indians had put up a wire fence around the trench and smeared the posts with sacred red medicine paint (plate CI).

A baby girl of only three or four months was found under the snow, carefully wrapped up in a shawl, beside her dead mother, whose body was pierced by two bullets. On her head was a little cap of buckskin,

FIG. 81—Survivors of Wounded Knee—Jennie Sword (1891).

upon which the American flag was embroidered in bright beadwork. She had lived through all the exposure, being only slightly frozen, and soon recovered after being brought in to the agency. Her mother being killed, and, in all probability, her father also, she was adopted by General Colby, commanding the Nebraska state troops. The Indian women in camp gave her the poetic name of Zitkala-noni, "Lost Bird," and by the family of her adoption she was baptized under the name of Marguerite (figure 80). She is now (1896) living in the general's family at Washington, a chubby little girl 6 years of age, as happy with her dolls and playthings as a little girl of that age ought to be.

Another little girl about 5 years of age was picked up on the battle-field and brought in by the Indian police on the afternoon of the fight. She was adopted by George Sword, captain of the Indian police, and is now living with him under the name of Jennie Sword, a remarkably pretty little girl, gentle and engaging in her manners (figure 81).

A little boy of four years, the son of Yellow Bird, the medicine-man, was playing on his pony in front of a tipi when the firing began. As

FIG. 82—Survivors of Wounded Knee—Herbert Zitkalazi (1892).

he described it some time ago in lisping English: "My father ran and fell down and the blood came out of his mouth [he was shot through the head], and then a soldier put his gun up to my white pony's nose and shot him, and then I ran and a policeman got me." As his father was thus killed and his mother was already dead, he was adopted by Mrs Lucy Arnold, who had been a teacher among the Sioux and knew his

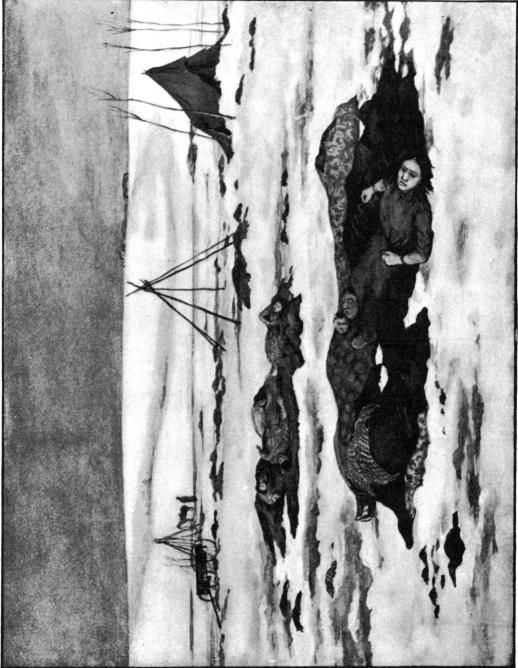

BATTLEFIELD AFTER THE BLIZZARD

family before the trouble began. She had already given him his name, Herbert Zitkalazi, the last word being the Sioux form of his father's name, "Yellow Bird." She brought him back with her to Washington, where he soon learned English and became a general favorite of all who knew him for his affectionate disposition and unusual intelligence, with genuine boyish enthusiasm in all he undertook. His picture here given (figure 82) is from a photograph made in Lafayette park, Washington, in 1892. His adopted mother having resumed her school work among his tribe, he is now back with her, attending school under her supervision at Standing Rock, where, as in Washington, he seems to be a natural leader among those of his own age. When we think of these children and consider that only by the merest accident they escaped the death that overtook a hundred other children at Wounded Knee, who may all have had in themselves the same possibilities of affection, education, and happy usefulness, we can understand the sickening meaning of such affairs as the Chivington massacre in Colorado and the Custer fight on the Washita, where the newspaper reports merely that "the enemy was surprised and the Indian camp destroyed."

The Indian scouts at Wounded Knee, like the Indian police at Grand river and Pine Ridge, were brave and loyal, as has been the almost universal rule with Indians when enlisted in the government service, even when called on, as were these, to serve against their own tribe and relatives. The prairie Indian is a born soldier, with all the soldier's pride of loyalty to duty, and may be trusted implicitly after he has once consented to enter the service. The scouts at Wounded Knee were Sioux, with Philip Wells as interpreter. Other Sioux scouts were ranging the country between the agency and the hostile camp in the Bad Lands, and acted as mediators in the peace negotiations which led to the final surrender. Fifty Cheyenne and about as many Crow scouts were also employed in the same section of country. Throughout the entire campaign the Indian scouts and police were faithful and received the warmest commendation of their officers.

On New Year's day, 1891, Henry Miller, a herder, was killed by Indians a few miles from the agency. This was the only noncombatant killed by the Indians during the entire campaign, and during the same period there was no depredation committed by them outside of the reservation. On the next day the agent reported that the school buildings and Episcopal church on White Clay creek had been burned by hostiles, who were then camped to the number of about 3,000 on Grass creek, 15 miles northeast of the agency. They had captured the government beef herd and were depending on it for food. Red Cloud, Little Wound, and their people were with them and were reported as anxious to return, but prevented by the hostile leaders, Two Strike, Short Bull, and Kicking Bear, who threatened to kill the first one who made a move to come in. (*G. D., 44.*) A few days later a number of

Red Cloud's men came in and surrendered and reported that the old chief was practically a prisoner and wanted the soldiers to come and rescue him from the hostiles, who were trying to force him into the war. They reported further that there was much suffering from cold and hunger in the Indian camp, and that all the Ogalala (Red Cloud's people of Pine Ridge) were intending to come in at once in a body.

On the 3d of January General Miles took up his headquarters at Pine Ridge and directed General Brooke to assume immediate command of the troops surrounding the hostile camp. Brooke's men swung out to form the western and northern part of a circle about the hostiles, cutting them off from the Bad Lands, while the troops under General Carr closed in on the east and northeast in such a way that the Indians were hemmed in and unable to make a move in any direction excepting toward the agency.

On January 3 a party of hostiles attacked a detachment of the Sixth cavalry under Captain Kerr on Grass creek, a few miles north of the agency, but were quickly repulsed with the loss of four of their number, the troops having been reinforced by other detachments in the vicinity. In this engagement the Indian scouts again distinguished themselves. (*War*, *21*.) The effect of this repulse was to check the westward movement of the hostiles and hold them in their position along White Clay creek until their passion had somewhat abated.

On January 5 there was another encounter on Wounded Knee creek. A small detachment which had been sent out to meet a supply train coming into the agency found the wagons drawn up in a square to resist an attack made by a band of about 50 Indians. The soldiers joined forces with the teamsters, and by firing from behind the protection of the wagons succeeded in driving off the Indians and killing a number of their horses. The hostiles were reinforced, however, and a hard skirmish was kept up for several hours until more troops arrived from the agency about dark, having been sent in answer to a courier who managed to elude the attacking party. The troops charged on a gallop and the Indians retreated, having lost several killed and wounded, besides a number of their horses. (*Colby*, *7*.)

Amid all these warlike alarms the gentle muse Calliope hovered over the field and inspired W. H. Prather, a colored private of troop I of the Ninth cavalry, to the production of the ballad given below, one of the few good specimens of American ballad poetry, and worthy of equal place with "Captain Lovewell's Fight," "Old Quebec," or anything that originated in the late rebellion. It became a favorite among the troops in camp and with the scattered frontiersmen of Dakota and Nebraska, being sung to a simple air with vigor and expression and a particularly rousing chorus, and is probably by this time a classic of the barracks. It is here reproduced verbatim from the printed slip published for distribution among the soldiers during the campaign.

The Indian Ghost Dance and War

The Red Skins left their Agency, the Soldiers left their Post,
All on the strength of an Indian tale about Messiah's ghost
Got up by savage chieftains to lead their tribes astray;
But Uncle Sam wouldn't have it so, for he ain't built that way.
They swore that this Messiah came to them in visions sleep,
And promised to restore their game and Buffalos a heap,
So they must start a big ghost dance, then all would join their band,
And may be so we lead the way into the great Bad Land.

Chorus :

They claimed the shirt Messiah gave, no bullet could go through,
But when the Soldiers fired at them they saw this was not true.
The Medicine man supplied them with their great Messiah's grace,
And he, too, pulled his freight and swore the 7th hard to face.

About their tents the Soldiers stood, awaiting one and all,
That they might hear the trumpet clear when sounding General call
Or Boots and Saddles in a rush, that each and every man
Might mount in haste, ride soon and fast to stop this devilish band
But Generals great like Miles and Brooke don't do things up that way,
For they know an Indian like a book, and let him have his sway
Until they think him far enough and then to John they'll say,
"You had better stop your fooling or we'll bring our guns to play."

Chorus.—They claimed the shirt, etc.

The 9th marched out with splendid cheer the Bad Lands to explo'e—
With Col. Henry at their head they never fear the foe;
So on they rode from Xmas eve 'till dawn of Xmas day;
The Red Skins heard the 9th was near and fled in great dismay;
The 7th is of courage bold both officers and men,
But bad luck seems to follow them and twice has took them in;
They came in contact with Big Foot's warriors in their fierce might
This chief made sure he had a chance of vantage in the fight.

Chorus.—They claimed the shirt, etc.

A fight took place, 'twas hand to hand, unwarned by trumpet call,
While the Sioux were dropping man by man—the 7th killed them all,
And to that regiment be said "Ye noble braves, well done,
Although you lost some gallant men a glorious fight you've won."
The 8th was there, the sixth rode miles to swell that great command
And waited orders night and day to round up Short Bull's band.
The Infantry marched up in mass the Cavalry's support,
And while the latter rounded up, the former held the fort.

Chorus.—They claimed the shirt, etc.

E battery of the 1st stood by and did their duty well,
For every time the Hotchkiss barked they say a hostile fell.
Some Indian soldiers chipped in too and helped to quell the fray,
And now the campaign's ended and the soldiers marched away.
So all have done their share, you see, whether it was thick or thin,
And all helped break the ghost dance up and drive the hostiles in.
The settlers in that region now can breathe with better grace;
They only ask and pray to God to make John hold his base.

Chorus.—They claimed the shirt, etc.

(W. H. Prather, I, 9th Cavalry).

APPENDIX—THE INDIAN STORY OF WOUNDED KNEE

[*From the Report of the Commissioner of Indian Affairs for 1891, volume 1, pages 179-181. Extracts from verbatim stenographic report of council held by delegations of Sioux with Commissioner of Indian Affairs, at Washington, February 11, 1891.*]

TURNING HAWK, Pine Ridge (Mr Cook, interpreter). Mr Commissioner, my purpose to-day is to tell you what I know of the condition of affairs at the agency where I live. A certain falsehood came to our agency from the west which had the effect of a fire upon the Indians, and when this certain fire came upon our people those who had farsightedness and could see into the matter made up their minds to stand up against it and fight it. The reason we took this hostile attitude to this fire was because we believed that you yourself would not be in favor of this particular mischief-making thing; but just as we expected, the people in authority did not like this thing and we were quietly told that we must give up or have nothing to do with this certain movement. Though this is the advice from our good friends in the east, there were, of course, many silly young men who were longing to become identified with the movement, although they knew that there was nothing absolutely bad, nor did they know there was anything absolutely good, in connection with the movement.

In the course of time we heard that the soldiers were moving toward the scene of trouble. After awhile some of the soldiers finally reached our place and we heard that a number of them also reached our friends at Rosebud. Of course, when a large body of soldiers is moving toward a certain direction they inspire a more or less amount of awe, and it is natural that the women and children who see this large moving mass are made afraid of it and be put in a condition to make them run away. At first we thought that Pine Ridge and Rosebud were the only two agencies where soldiers were sent, but finally we heard that the other agencies fared likewise. We heard and saw that about half our friends at Rosebud agency, from fear at seeing the soldiers, began the move of running away from their agency toward ours (Pine Ridge), and when they had gotten inside of our reservation they there learned that right ahead of them at our agency was another large crowd of soldiers, and while the soldiers were there, there was constantly a great deal of false rumor flying back and forth. The special rumor I have in mind is the threat that the soldiers had come there to disarm the Indians entirely and to take away all their horses from them. That was the oft-repeated story.

So constantly repeated was this story that our friends from Rosebud, instead of going to Pine Ridge, the place of their destination, veered off and went to some other direction toward the "Bad Lands." We did not know definitely how many, but understood there were 300 lodges of them, about 1,700 people. Eagle Pipe, Turning Bear, High Hawk, Short Bull, Lance, No Flesh, Pine Bird, Crow Dog, Two Strike, and White Horse were the leaders.

Well, the people after veering off in this way, many of them who believe in peace and order at our agency, were very anxious that some influence should be brought upon these people. In addition to our love of peace we remembered that many of these people were related to us by blood. So we sent out peace commissioners to the people who were thus running away from their agency.

I understood at the time that they were simply going away from fear because of so many soldiers. So constant was the word of these good men from Pine Ridge agency that finally they succeeded in getting away half of the party from Rosebud, from the place where they took refuge, and finally were brought to the agency at Pine Ridge. Young-Man-Afraid-of-his-Horses, Little Wound, Fast Thunder, Louis Shangreau, John Grass, Jack Red Cloud, and myself were some of these peacemakers.

The remnant of the party from Rosebud not taken to the agency finally reached the wilds of the Bad Lands. Seeing that we had succeeded so well, once more we sent to the same party in the Bad Lands and succeeded in bringing these very Indians out of the depths of the Bad Lands and were being brought toward the agency. When we were about a day's journey from our agency we heard that a certain party of Indians (Big Foot's band) from the Cheyenne River agency was coming toward Pine Ridge in flight.

CAPTAIN SWORD. Those who actually went off of the Cheyenne River agency probably number 303, and there were a few from the Standing Rock reserve with them, but as to their number I do not know. There were a number of Ogalallas, old men and several school boys, coming back with that very same party, and one of the very seriously wounded boys was a member of the Ogalalla boarding school at Pine Ridge agency. He was not on the warpath, but was simply returning home to his agency and to his school after a summer visit to relatives on the Cheyenne river.

TURNING HAWK. When we heard that these people were coming toward our agency we also heard this. These people were coming toward Pine Ridge agency, and when they were almost on the agency they were met by the soldiers and surrounded and finally taken to the Wounded Knee creek, and there at a given time their guns were demanded. When they had delivered them up, the men were separated from their families, from their tipis, and taken to a certain spot. When the guns were thus taken and the men thus separated, there was a crazy man, a young man of very bad influence and in fact a nobody, among that bunch of Indians fired his gun, and of course the firing of a gun must have been the breaking of a military rule of some sort, because immediately the soldiers returned fire and indiscriminate killing followed.

SPOTTED HORSE. This man shot an officer in the army; the first shot killed this officer. I was a voluntary scout at that encounter and I saw exactly what was done, and that was what I noticed; that the first shot killed an officer. As soon as this shot was fired the Indians immediately began drawing their knives, and they were exhorted from all sides to desist, but this was not obeyed. Consequently the firing began immediately on the part of the soldiers.

TURNING HAWK. All the men who were in a bunch were killed right there, and those who escaped that first fire got into the ravine, and as they went along up the ravine for a long distance they were pursued on both sides by the soldiers and shot down, as the dead bodies showed afterwards. The women were standing off at a different place from where the men were stationed, and when the firing began, those of the men who escaped the first onslaught went in one direction up the ravine, and then the women, who were bunched together at another place, went entirely in a different direction through an open field, and the women fared the same fate as the men who went up the deep ravine.

AMERICAN HORSE. The men were separated, as has already been said, from the women, and they were surrounded by the soldiers. Then came next the village of the Indians and that was entirely surrounded by the soldiers also. When the firing began, of course the people who were standing immediately around the young man who fired the first shot were killed right together, and then they turned their guns, Hotchkiss guns, etc., upon the women who were in the lodges standing there under a flag of truce, and of course as soon as they were fired upon they fled, the men fleeing in one direction and the women running in two different directions. So that there were three general directions in which they took flight.

There was a women with an infant in her arms who was killed as she almost touched the flag of truce, and the women and children of course were strewn all along the circular village until they were dispatched. Right near the flag of truce a mother was shot down with her infant; the child not knowing that its mother was dead was still nursing, and that especially was a very sad sight. The women as they were fleeing with their babes were killed together, shot right through, and the women who were very heavy with child were also killed. All the Indians fled in these three directions, and after most all of them had been killed a cry was made that all those who were not killed or wounded should come forth and they would be safe. Little boys who were not wounded came out of their places of refuge, and as soon as they came in sight a number of soldiers surrounded them and butchered them there.

Of course we all feel very sad about this affair. I stood very loyal to the government all through those troublesome days, and believing so much in the government and being so loyal to it, my disappointment was very strong, and I have come to Washington with a very great blame on my heart. Of course it would have been all right if only the men were killed; we would feel almost grateful for it. But the fact of the killing of the women, and more especially the killing of the young boys and girls who are to go to make up the future strength of the Indian people, is the saddest part of the whole affair and we feel it very sorely.

I was not there at the time before the burial of the bodies, but I did go there with some of the police and the Indian doctor and a great many of the people, men from the agency, and we went through the battlefield and saw where the bodies were from the track of the blood.

TURNING HAWK. I had just reached the point where I said that the women were killed. We heard, besides the killing of the men, of the onslaught also made upon the women and children, and they were treated as roughly and indiscriminately as the men and boys were.

Of course this affair brought a great deal of distress upon all the people, but especially upon the minds of those who stood loyal to the government and who did all that they were able to do in the matter of bringing about peace. They especially have suffered much distress and are very much hurt at heart. These peacemakers continued on in their good work, but there were a great many fickle young men who were ready to be moved by the change in the events there, and consequently, in spite of the great fire that was brought upon all, they were ready to assume any hostile attitude. These young men got themselves in readiness and went in the direction of the scene of battle so they might be of service there. They got there and finally exchanged shots with the soldiers. This party of young men was made up from Rosebud, Ogalalla (Pine Ridge), and members of any other agencies that happened to be there at the time. While this was going on in the neighborhood of Wounded Knee — the Indians and soldiers exchanging shots — the agency, our home, was also fired into by the Indians. Matters went on in this strain until the evening came on, and then the Indians went off down by White Clay creek. When the agency was fired upon by the Indians from the hillside, of course the shots were returned by the Indian police who were guarding the agency buildings.

Although fighting seemed to have been in the air, yet those who believed in peace were still constant at their work. Young-Man-Afraid-of-his-Horses, who had been on a visit to some other agency in the north or northwest, returned, and immediately went out to the people living about White Clay creek, on the border of the Bad Lands, and brought his people out. He succeeded in obtaining the consent of the people to come out of their place of refuge and return to the agency. Thus the remaining portion of the Indians who started from Rosebud were brought back into the agency. Mr Commissioner, during the days of the great whirlwind out there, those good men tried to hold up a counteracting power, and that was "Peace." We have now come to realize that peace has prevailed and won the day. While we were engaged in bringing about peace our property was left behind, of course, and most of us have lost everything, even down to the matter of guns with which to kill ducks, rabbits, etc, shotguns, and guns of that order. When Young-Man-Afraid brought the people in and their guns were asked for, both men who were called hostile and men who stood loyal to the government delivered up their guns.

CHAPTER XIV

CLOSE OF THE OUTBREAK—THE GHOST DANCE IN THE SOUTH

In the meantime overtures of peace had been made by General Miles to the hostiles, most of whose leaders he knew personally, having received their surrender on the Yellowstone ten years before, at the close of the Custer war. On the urgent representations of himself and others Congress had also appropriated the necessary funds for carrying out the terms of the late treaty, by the disregard of which most of the trouble had been caused, so that the commander was now able to assure the Indians that their rights and necessities would receive attention. They were urged to come in and surrender, with a guaranty that the general himself would represent their case with the government. At the same time they were informed that retreat was cut off and that further resistance would be unavailing. As an additional step toward regaining their confidence, the civilian agents were removed from the several disturbed agencies, which were then put in charge of military officers well known and respected by the Indians. Cheyenne River agency was assigned to Captain J. H. Hurst, and Rosebud agency to Captain J. M. Lee, while Royer, at Pine Ridge, was superseded on January 8 by Captain F. E. Pierce. The last-named officer was afterward relieved by Captain Charles G. Penney, who is now in charge. (*War, 22; Comr., 38; G. D., 45.*)

The friendly overtures made by General Miles, with evidences that the government desired to remedy their grievances, and that longer resistance was hopeless, had their effect on the hostiles. Little Wound, Young-man-afraid-of-his-horses (more properly, "Young-man-of-whose-horses-they-are-afraid), Big Road, and other friendly chiefs, also used their persuasions with such good effect that by January 12 the whole body of nearly 4,000 Indians had moved in to within sight of the agency and expressed their desire for peace. The troops closed in around them, and on the 16th of January, 1891, the hostiles surrendered, and the outbreak was at an end. They complied with every order and direction given by the commander, and gave up nearly 200 rifles, which, with other arms already surrendered, made a total of between 600 and 700 guns, more than had ever before been surrendered by the Sioux at one time. As a further guaranty of good faith, the commander demanded the surrender of Kicking Bear and Short Bull, the principal leaders, with about twenty other prominent warriors, as hostages. The demand was readily complied with, and the men designated came forward voluntarily and gave themselves up as sureties for the good conduct of their people. They were sent to Fort Sheridan, Illinois, near Chicago, where they were kept until there was no further apprehension, and were then returned to their homes. (*War, 23; Colby, 8.*) After the surrender the late hostiles pitched their camp, numbering in all 742 tipis, in the bottom along White Clay creek, just west of the agency, where General Miles had supplies of beef, coffee, and sugar issued to them from the commissary department, and that night they enjoyed the first full meal they had known in several weeks.

Thus ended the so called Sioux outbreak of 1890–91. It might be better designated, however, as a Sioux panic and stampede, for, to quote the expressive letter of McGillycuddy, writing under date of January 15, 1891, "Up to date there has been neither a Sioux outbreak or war. No citizen in Nebraska or Dakota has been killed, molested, or can show the scratch of a pin, and no property has been destroyed off the reservation." (*Colby, 9.*) Only a single noncombatant was killed by the Indians, and that was close to the agency. The entire time occupied by the campaign, from the killing of Sitting Bull to the surrender at Pine Ridge, was only thirty-two days. The late hostiles were returned to their homes as speedily as possible. The Brulé of Rosebud, regarded as the most turbulent of the hostiles, were taken back to the agency by Captain Lee, for whom they had respect, founded on an acquaintance of several years' standing, without escort and during the most intense cold of winter, but without any trouble or dissatisfaction whatever. The military were returned to their usual stations, and within a few weeks after the surrender affairs at the various agencies were moving again in the usual channel.

An unfortunate event occurred just before the surrender in the killing of Lieutenant E. W. Casey of the Twenty-second infantry by Plenty Horses, a young Brulé, on January 7. Lieutenant Casey was in command of a troop of Cheyenne scouts, and was stationed at the mouth of White Clay creek, charged with the special duty of watching the hostile camp, which was located 8 miles farther up the creek at No Water's place. On the day before his death several of the hostiles had visited him and held a friendly conference. The next morning, in company with two scouts, he went out avowedly for the purpose of observing the hostile camp more closely. He rode up to within a short distance of the camp, meeting and talking with several of the Indians on the way, and had stopped to talk with a half-blood relative of Red Cloud, when Plenty Horses, a short distance away, deliberately shot him through the head, and he fell from his horse dead. His body was not disturbed by the Indians, but was brought in by some of the Cheyenne scouts soon after. Plenty Horses was arraigned before a United States court, but was acquitted on the ground that as the Sioux were then at war and the officer was practically a spy upon the Indian camp, the act was not murder in the legal sense of the word. Lieutenant Casey had been for a year in charge of the Cheyenne scouts and had taken great interest in their welfare and proficiency, and his death was greatly deplored by the Indians as the insane act of a boy overcome by the excitement of the times. (*War, 24; Comr., 39; Colby, 10; G. D., 46.*)

On January 11 an unprovoked murder was committed on a small party of peaceable Indians on Belle Fourche, or North fork of Cheyenne river, by which the Indians who had come in to surrender were once more thrown into such alarm that for a time it seemed as if serious trouble might result. A party of Ogalala from Pine Ridge, consisting of Few Tails, a kindly, peaceable old man, with his wife, an old woman, and One Feather, with his wife and two children—one a girl about 13 years of age and the other an infant—had been hunting in the Black Hills under a pass from the agency. They had had a successful hunt, and were returning with their two wagons well loaded with meat, when they camped for the night at the mouth of Alkali creek. During the evening they were visited by some soldiers stopping at a ranch a few miles distant, who examined their pass and pronounced it all right. In the morning, after breakfast, the Indians started on again toward the agency, but had gone only a few hundred yards when they were fired upon by a party of white men concealed near the road. The leaders of the whites were three brothers named Culbertson, one of whom had but recently returned from the penitentiary. One of the murderers had visited the Indians in their camp the night before, and even that very morning. At the first fire Few Tails was killed, together with both ponies attached to the wagon. His wife jumped out and received two bullets, which brought her to the ground. The murderers rode past her, however, to get at the other Indian, who was coming up behind in the other wagon with his wife and two children. As soon as he saw his companion killed, One Feather turned his wagon in the other direction, and, telling his wife, who had also been shot, to drive on as fast as she could to save the children, he jumped upon one of the spare ponies and held off the murderers until his family had had time to make some distance. He then turned and joined his family and drove on for some 8 or 10 miles until the pursuers came up again, when he again turned and fought them off, while his wife went ahead with the wagon and the children. The wounded woman bravely drove on, while the two little children lay down in the wagon with their heads covered up in the blankets. As they drove they passed near a house, from which several other shots were fired at the flying mother, when her husband again rode up and kept off the whole party until the wagon could get ahead. Finally, as the ponies were tired out, this heroic man abandoned the wagon and put the two children on one of the spare ponies and his wounded wife and himself upon another and continued to retreat until the whites gave up the pursuit. He finally reached the agency with the wife and children.

The wife of Few Tails, after falling wounded by two bullets beside the wagon in which was her dead husband, lay helpless and probably unconscious upon the ground through all the long winter night until morning, when she revived, and finding one of the horses still alive, mounted it and managed by night to reach a settler's house about 15 miles away. Instead of meeting help and sympathy, however, she was driven off by the two men there with loaded rifles, and leaving her horse in her fright, she hurried away as well as she could with a bullet in her leg and another in her breast, passing by the trail of One Feather's wagon with the tracks of his pursuers fresh behind it, until she came near a trader's store about 20 miles farther south. Afraid to go near it on account of her last experience, the poor woman circled around it, and continued, wounded, cold, and starving as she was, to travel by night and hide by day until she reached the Bad Lands. The rest may be told in her own words:

After that I traveled every night, resting daytime, until I got here at the beef corral. Then I was very tired, and was near the military camp, and early in the morning a soldier came out and he shouted something back, and in a few minutes fifty men were there, and they got a blanket and took me to a tent. I had no blanket and my feet were swelled, and I was about ready to die. After I got to the tent a doctor came in—a soldier doctor, because he had straps on his shoulders—and washed me and treated me well.

A few of the soldiers camped near the scene of the attack had joined in the pursuit at the beginning, on the representations of some of the murderers, but abandoned it as soon as they found their mistake. According to all the testimony, the killing was a wanton, unprovoked, and deliberate murder, yet the criminals were acquitted in the local courts. The apathy displayed by the authorities of Meade county, South Dakota, in which the murder was committed, called forth some vigorous protests. Colonel Shafter, in his statement of the case, concludes, referring to the recent killing of Lieutenant Casey: "So long as Indians are being arrested and held for killing armed men under conditions of war, it seems to me that the white murderers of a part of a band of peaceful Indians should not be permitted to escape punishment." The Indians took the same view of the case, and when General Miles demanded of Young-man-afraid-of-his-horses the surrender of the slayers of Casey and the herder Miller, the old chief indignantly replied: "No; I will not surrender them, but if you will bring the white men who killed Few Tails, I will bring the Indians who killed the white soldier and the herder; and right out here in front of your tipi I will have my young men shoot the Indians and you have your soldiers shoot the white men, and then we will be done with the whole business."

In regard to the heroic conduct of One Feather, the officer then in charge of the agency says: "The determination and genuine courage, as well as the generalship he manifested in keeping at a distance the six men who were pursuing him, and the devotion he showed toward his family, risking his life against great odds, designate him as entitled to a place on the list of heroes." (*War, 25; Comr., 40; G. D., 47.*)

On the recommendation of General Miles, a large delegation of the principal leaders of both friendly and hostile parties among the Sioux was allowed to visit Washington in February, 1891, to present their grievances and suggest remedies for dissatisfaction in the future. Among the principal speakers were: From Pine Ridge, American Horse, Captain George Sword, Big Road, and He Dog; from Rosebud, White Bird and Turning Hawk; from Cheyenne River, Little No Heart and Straight Head; from Standing Rock, John Grass and Mad Bear. The interpreters were Reverend C. S. Cook, David Zephier, Louis Primeau, Louis Richard, Clarence Three Stars, and Louis Shangreau. Their visit was eminently satisfactory and resulted in the inauguration of a more efficient administration of Sioux affairs for the future. Steps were taken to reimburse those whose ponies had been confiscated at the time of the Custer war in 1876, and additional appropriations were made for rations, so that before the end of the year the Indians were receiving half as much more as before the outbreak. (*War, 26.*) On returning to their homes the Indians of the various Sioux agencies went to work in good faith putting in their crops and caring for their stock, and in a short time all further apprehension was at an end.

The discussion of Indian affairs in connection with the outbreak led to the passage by Congress of a bill which enacted that all future vacancies in the office of Indian agent should be filled by military officers selected by the Indian office and detailed for the purpose from the army. At the same time a plan was originated to enlist Indians as a component part of the regular army. Small parties from various tribes had long been attached to various posts and commands in an irregular capacity as scouts. These bodies of scouts were now reduced in number or disbanded altogether, and in their stead were organized Indian troops or companies to be regularly attached to the different cavalry or infantry regiments. In the spring of 1891 officers were sent out to various western reservations, and succeeded in thus recruiting a number of regular troops from among the most warlike of the tribes, a considerable part of these coming from the late hostile Sioux.

Although the campaign lasted only about a month the destruction of life was great, for an Indian war, and the money loss to the government and to individuals was something enormous. Three officers and 28 privates were killed or mortally wounded during the campaign, and 4 officers and 38 privates were less seriously wounded, several of these dying later on. (*War, 27.*) The Indian loss can not be stated exactly. In the arrest of Sitting Bull there were killed or mortally wounded 8 of Sitting Bull's party and 6 police, a total of 14. Those killed in the Wounded Knee fight, or who afterward died of wounds or exposure, numbered, according to the best estimates, at least 250. Those afterward killed in the various small skirmishes, including the Few Tails affair, may have numbered 20 or 30. In all, the campaign cost the lives of 49 whites and others on the government side and about 300 or more Indians.

The direct or incidental expenses of the campaign were as follows: Expenses of the Department of Justice for defending Plenty Horses and prosecuting the murderers of Few Tails, unknown; appropriation by Congress to reimburse Nebraska national guard for expense of service during the campaign, $43,000; paid out under act of Congress to reimburse friendly Indians and other legal residents on the reservations for property destroyed by hostiles, $97,646.85 (*Comr., 41*); extra expense of Commissary department of the army, $37,764.69; extra expense of the Medical department of the army, $1,164, besides extra supplies purchased by individuals; extra expenses of Ordnance department of the army, for ammunition, not accounted for; total extra expense of Quartermaster's department of the army, $915,078.81, including $120,634.17 for transportation of troops over bonded railroads. (*A. G. O., 8.*) The total expense, public or private, was probably but little short of $1,200,000, or nearly $40,000 per day, a significant commentary on the bad policy of breaking faith with Indians.

According to the report of the agency farmer sent out after the trouble to learn the extent of property of the friendly Indians destroyed by the hostiles on Pine Ridge agency, there were burned 53 Indian dwellings, 1 church, 2 schoolhouses, and a bridge, all on White Clay creek, while nearly every remaining house along the creek had the windows broken out. A great deal of farming machinery and nearly all of the hay were burned, while stoves were broken to pieces and stock killed. A few of the friendly Indians had been so overcome by the excitement that they had burned their own houses and run their machinery down high hills into the river, where it was found frozen in the ice several months later. (*G. D., 48.*)

In view of the fact that only one noncombatant was killed and no depredations were committed off the reservation, the panic among the frontier settlers of both Dakotas, Nebraska, and Iowa was something ludicrous. The inhabitants worked themselves into such a high panic that ranches and even whole villages were temporarily abandoned and the people flocked into the railroad cities with vivid stories of murder, scalping, and desolation that had no foundation whatever in fact. A reliable authority who was on the ground shortly after the scare had subsided gives this characteristic instance among others:

In another city, a place of 3,000 inhabitants, 75 miles from any Indians and 150 miles from any hostiles, word came about 2 o'clock Sunday morning for the militia to be in readiness. The company promptly assembled, were instructed and drilled. In an evening church service one of the pastors broke out in prayer: "O Lord, prepare us for what awaits us. We have just been listening to the sweet sounds of praise, but ere the morning sun we may hear the war whoop of the red man." The effect on children and nervous persons may be imagined. The legislature was in session and the impression upon that body was such as to lead it to make an appropriation for the benefit of the state militia at the expense of one to the state agricultural fair. (*Comr., 42.*)

The crisis produced the usual crop of patriots, all ready to serve their country—usually for a consideration. Among these was a lady of Utica,

New York, claiming to be of the renowned Iroquois blood, and styling herself the "Doctor Princess Viroqua," who, with her sister "Wynima," wrote to the Indian Office for a commission to go out to try the effect of moral suasion on the belligerent Sioux, representing that by virtue of her descent from a long line of aboriginal princes she would be welcomed with enthusiasm and accomplish her mission of peace. (*G. D., 49.*) As a matter of fact, neither of the names Viroqua or Wynima could be pronounced by a genuine Iroquois knowing only his own tongue, and the second one, Wynima, is borrowed from Meacham's sensational history of the Modoc war in California.

The proprietor of a "wild west" show in New York, signing himself Texas Ben, wrote also volunteering his services and submitting as credentials his museum letter-head, stating that he had served with Quantrell, and had the written indorsement of Cole Younger. An old veteran of the Iowa soldiers' home wrote to Secretary Noble, with a redundance of capitals and much bad spelling, offering his help against the hostiles, saying that he had been "RAZeD" among them and could "ToLK The TUN" and was ready to "Do eneThin FoR mY CuntRY." (*G. D., 50.*)

A band of patriots in Minnesota, whose early education appears to have been somewhat neglected, wrote to the Secretary of the Interior offering to organize a company of 50 men to put down the outbreak, provided the government would look after a few items which they enumerated: "The government to Furnish us with Two good Horses Each a good Winchester Rifle, Two good Cotes Revolvers and give us $300.00 Bounty and say a Salary of Fifty Per Month, Each and our own judgment and we will settel this Indian question For Ever, and Rations and Ammunition. We Should Have in addition to this say Five dollars a Head." (*G. D., 51.*)

A man named Albert Hopkins appeared at Pine Ridge in December, 1890, wearing a blanket and claiming to be the Indian messiah, and announced his intention of going alone into the Bad Lands to the Indians, who were expecting his arrival, with the "Pansy Banner of Peace." His claims were ridiculed by Red Cloud and others, and he was promptly arrested and put off the reservation. However, he was not dead, but only sleeping, and on March, 1893, having come to Washington, he addressed an urgent letter to Secretary Noble requesting official authority to visit the Sioux reservations and to preach to the Indians, stating that "with the help of the Pansy and its motto and manifest teaching, 'Union, Culture, and Peace,' and the star-pansy banner, of which I inclose an illustration, I hope to establish the permanent peace of the border." He signs himself "Albert C. Hopkins, Pres. Pro. tem. The Pansy Society of America."

The letter was referred to the Indian Office, which refused permission. This brought a reply from Hopkins, who this time signs himself "The Indian Messiah," in which he states that as the Indians were expecting the messiah in the spring, "in accordance with the prophecy of Sitting

Bull," it was necessary that he should go to them at once, so that they might "accept the teaching of the pansy and its motto, which now they only partially or very doubtfully accept."

Receiving no answer, he wrote again about the end of March, both to the Secretary and to the Indian Commissioner, stating that messiahs, being human, were subject to human limitations, of which fact the Indians were well aware, but warning these officials that if these limitations were set by the government it would be held responsible for his nonappearance to the Indians, as he had promised, "before the native pansies blossom on the prairies." He ends by stating that he would leave on Easter Sunday for the Sioux country, but as nothing was heard of him later, it is presumed that he succumbed to the limitations. (*G. D.*, *52.*)

The first direct knowledge of the messiah and the Ghost dance came to the northern Arapaho in Wyoming, through Nakash, "Sage," who, with several Shoshoni, visited the messiah in the early spring of 1889, and on his return brought back to his people the first songs of the dance, these being probably some of the original Paiute songs of the messiah himself. The Ghost dance was at once inaugurated among the Shoshoni and northern Arapaho. In the summer of the same year the first rumors of the new redeemer reached the southern Arapaho and Cheyenne in Oklahoma, through the medium of letters written by returned pupils of eastern government schools.

Fresh reports of wonderful things beyond the mountains were constantly coming to the northern prairie tribes, and the excitement grew until the close of the year 1889, when a large delegation, including Sioux, northern Cheyenne, and northern Arapaho, crossed the mountains to the Paiute country to see and talk with the messiah. Among the Sioux delegates were Short Bull, Fire Thunder, and Kicking Bear, as already stated. Among the Cheyenne were Porcupine and several others, including one woman. The Arapaho representatives were Sitting Bull (Hänä′chä-thi′ăk) and Friday. The delegates from the different tribes met at Wind River reservation, in Wyoming, which they left about Christmas, and after stopping a short time among the Bannock and Shoshoni at Fort Hall, went on to Walker lake, in Nevada. They were gone some time and returned to Wyoming in March of 1890, the Sioux and Cheyenne continuing on to their homes farther east. According to the statement of Nakash they had a five days' conference with the messiah, who at one time went into a trance, but his visitors did not.

Before their return the southern Arapaho, in Oklahoma, had sent up Wa′tän-ga′a, "Black Coyote," an officer of the Indian police, and Washee, a scout at Fort Reno, to their relatives in Wyoming to learn definitely as to the truth or falsity of the rumors. Washee went on to Fort Hall, where his faith failed him, and he came back with the report that the messiah was only a half-blood. This was not correct, but Washee himself afterward acknowledged that he had based his report

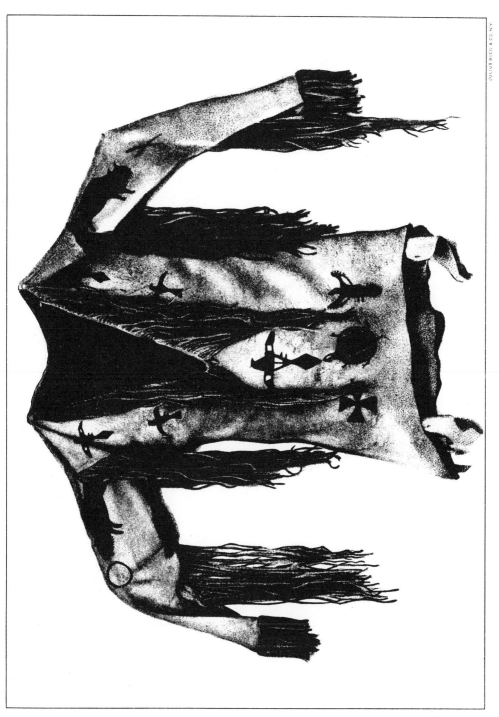

JULIUS BIEN & CO. N.Y.

ARAPAHO GHOST SHIRT, SHOWING COLORING

on hearsay. Black Coyote remained until the other delegates returned from the Paiute country with the announcement that all that had been said of the messiah and the advent of a new earth was true. He listened eagerly to all they had to tell, took part with the rest in the dance, learned the songs, and returned in April, 1890, and inaugurated the first Ghost dance in the south among the Arapaho.

The Cheyenne, being skeptical by nature, were unwilling to trust entirely to the report of Black Coyote and so sent up two delegates of their own, Little Chief and Bark, to investigate the story in the north. Somewhat later White Shield, another Cheyenne, went up alone on the same errand. Their report being favorable, the Cheyenne also took up the Ghost dance in the summer of 1890. They never went into it with the same fervor, however, and although they had their separate dance with songs in their own language, they more commonly danced together with the Arapaho and sang with them the Arapaho songs. For several years the old Indian dances had been nearly obsolete with these tribes, but as the new religion meant a revival of the Indian idea they soon became common again, with the exception of the war dance and others of that kind which were strictly prohibited by the messiah.

From this time the Ghost dance grew in fervor and frequency among the Arapaho and Cheyenne. In almost every camp the dance would be held two or three times a week, beginning about sunset and often continuing until daylight. The excitement reached fever heat in September, 1890, when Sitting Bull came down from the northern Arapaho to instruct the southern tribes in the doctrine and ceremony.

At a great Ghost dance held on South Canadian river, about 2 miles below the agency at Darlington, Oklahoma, it was estimated that 3,000 Indians were present, including nearly all of the Arapaho and Cheyenne, with a number of Caddo, Wichita, Kiowa, and others. The first trances of the Ghost dance among the southern tribes occurred at this time through the medium of Sitting Bull. One informant states that a leader named Howling Bull had produced trances at a dance on the Washita some time before, but the statement lacks confirmation.

As Sitting Bull was the great apostle of the Ghost dance among the southern tribes, being regarded almost in the same light as the messiah himself, he merits special notice. He is now about 42 years of age and at the beginning of his apostleship in 1890 was but 36. He is a full-blood Arapaho, although rather light in complexion and color of eyes, and speaks only his native language, but converses with ease in the universal sign language of the plains. It was chiefly by means of this sign language that he instructed his disciples among the Caddo, Wichita, and Kiowa. He is about 5 feet 8 inches tall, dignified but plain in his bearing, and with a particularly winning smile. His power over those with whom he comes in contact is evident from the report of Lieutenant (now Captain) Scott, who had been ordered by the War Department to investigate the Ghost dance, and who for weeks had been denouncing him as a humbug, but who, on finally meeting him for the first time, declares that the opinion formed before seeing him began to change in his favor almost immediately. (*G. D.*, *53*.) In conversation with the author Sitting Bull stated that he was originally a southern Arapaho, but went up to live with the northern branch of the tribe, in Wyoming, about 1876. When a boy in the south he was known as Bítäye, "Captor," but on reaching manhood his name was changed, in conformity with a common Indian custom, to Hänä′chä-thi′ăk, "Sitting Bull." On returning to the south, after having visited the messiah, he found his brother known under the same name, and to avoid confusion the brother then adopted the name of Scabby Bull, by which he is now known. It should be mentioned that an Indian

Fig. 83—Sitting Bull the Arapaho apostle.

"brother" may be only a cousin, as no distinction is made in the Indian system. On removing to the south he fixed his abode near Cantonment, Oklahoma, where he now resides.

With regard to the reverence in which he was held by his disciples at this time, and of his own sincerity, Captain Scott says:

It was very difficult to get an opportunity to talk with him quietly on account of the persistent manner in which he was followed about. All sorts of people wanted to touch him, men and women would come in, rub their hands on him, and cry, which demonstration he received with a patient fortitude that was rather ludicrous at times. While he by no means told us everything he knew, it was easy to believe that he was not the rank impostor that I had before considered him. He makes no demands for presents while at these camps. This trip entailed a ride of 200 miles in

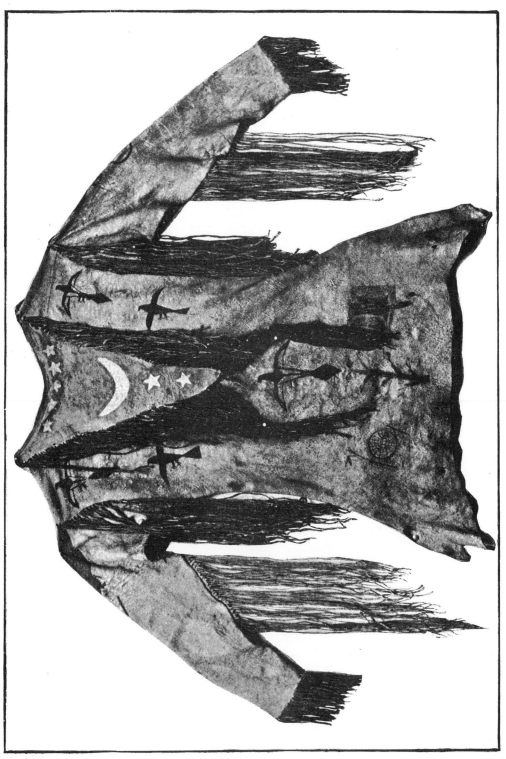

the winter season, at the request of the Wichitas, for which I understand they paid him $50 before starting, but everything that was given him while at this camp was a voluntary gift, prompted entirely by the good wishes of the giver. He took but little property away when he left, and I saw but one horse that I thought he had not brought down with him.

Upon being asked concerning his religion, he said that all I had heard must not be attributed to him, as some of it was false; that he does not believe that he saw the veritable "Jesus" alive in the north, but he did see a man there whom "Jesus" had helped or inspired. This person told him that if he persevered in the dance it would cause sickness and death to disappear. He avoided some of the questions about the coming of the buffalo, etc, and under the circumstances it was not possible to draw him out further, and the subject of religion was then dropped, with the intention of taking it up at a more favorable time, but this time never came. A great many of the doings seen at these dances are the afterthoughts of all kinds of people. I have seen some of them arise and have watched their growth. These are not the teachings of Sitting Bull, although he refrains from interfering with them through policy. He took no part in the humbuggery going on, but danced and sang like the humblest individual there. These things, taken in connection with Äpiatañ's letter, would make it seem that Sitting Bull has been a dupe himself partly, and there is a possibility that he is largely sincere in his teachings. There is this to be said in his favor, that he has given these people a better religion than they ever had before, taught them precepts which if faithfully carried out will bring them into better accord with their white neighbors, and has prepared the way for their final Christianization. For this he is entitled to no little credit. (*G. D., 54.*)

He made no claim to be a regular medicine-man, and so far as known never went into a trance himself. Since the failure of his predictions, especially with regard to the recovery of the ceded reservation, he has fallen from his high estate. Truth compels us also to state that, in spite of his apostolic character, he is about as uncertain in his movements as the average Indian.

After Sitting Bull, the principal leader of the Ghost dance among the southern Arapaho is Wa'tän-ga'a or Black Coyote, from whom the town of Watonga, in Canadian county, derives its name. Black Coyote is a man of considerable importance both in his tribe and in his own estimation, and aspires to be a leader in anything that concerns his people. With a natural predisposition to religious things, it is the dream of his life to be a great priest and medicine-man. At the same time he keeps a sharp lookout for his temporal affairs, and has managed to accumulate considerable property in wagons and livestock, including three wives. Although still a young man, being but little more than 40 years of age, he has had his share of the world's honors, being not only a leader in the Ghost dance and other Indian ceremonies, tribal delegate to Washington, and captain of the Indian police, but also, in his new character of an American citizen, deputy sheriff of Canadian county. He is a good-natured fellow, and vain of his possessions and titles, but at the same time thoroughly loyal and reliable in the discharge of his duties, and always ready to execute his orders at whatever personal risk. His priestly ambition led him to make the journey to the north, in which he brought back the first songs of the Ghost dance, and thus became a leader, and a year later he headed a delegation from Oklahoma to the messiah of Walker lake.   He has repeatedly asked me to get for him a permanent license from the government to enable him to visit the various reservations at will as a general evangel of Indian medicine and ceremony.   Black Coyote in full uniform, with official badge, a Harrison medal, and an immense police overcoat, which he procured in Washington, and riding with his three wives in his own double-seated coach, is a spectacle magnificent and impressive.   Black Coyote in breechcloth, paint, and feathers, leading the Ghost dance, or sitting flat on the ground and beating the earth with his hand in excess of religious fervor, is equally impressive.   It was this combination of vanity of leadership and sense of duty as a government officer that made him my first and most willing informant on the Ghost dance, and enabled me through him to do so much with the Arapaho.

In his portrait (plate CV) a number of scars will be noticed on his chest and arms.   The full number of these scars is seventy, arranged in various patterns of lines, circles, crosses, etc, with a long figure of the sacred pipe on one arm.   According to his own statement they were made in obedience to a dream as a sacrifice to save the lives of his children.   Several of his children had died in rapid succession, and in accordance with Indian custom he undertook a fast of four days as an expiation to the overruling spirit.   During this time, while lying on his bed, he heard a voice, somewhat resembling the cry of an owl or the subdued bark of a dog.   The voice told him that if he wished to save his other children he must cut out seventy pieces of skin and offer them to the sun.   He at once cut out seven pieces, held them out to the sun and prayed, and then buried them.   But the sun was not satisfied, and soon after he was warned in a vision that the full number of seventy must be sacrificed if he would save his children.   He then did as directed, cutting out the pieces of skin in the various patterns indicated, offering each in turn to the sun with a prayer for the health of his family, and then burying them.   Since then there has been no death in his family.   In cutting out the larger pieces, some of which were several inches long and nearly half an inch wide, the skin was first lifted up with an awl and then sliced away with a knife.   This had to be done by an assistant, and Black Coyote was particular to show me by signs, sitting very erect and bracing himself firmly, that he had not flinched during the process.

As has been stated, the first trances in the southern Ghost dance occurred at the great dance held near the Cheyenne and Arapaho agency under the auspices of Sitting Bull in September, 1890.   On this occasion Cheyenne and Arapaho, Caddo, Wichita, Kiowa, and Apache to the number of perhaps 3,000 assembled, and remained together for about two weeks, dancing every night until daylight.   This was the largest Ghost dance ever held in the south.   After dances had been held for two or three nights Sitting Bull announced that at the next one he would perform a great wonder in the sight of all the people, after

BLACK COYOTE

which they would be able to make songs for themselves. He said no more, but dismissed them to their tipis, wondering what this miracle could be. On the next night he appeared wearing a wide-brim hat with a single eagle feather, the same hat in which he is generally seen. Nearly all of the two tribes of Cheyenne and Arapaho were present, and probably 600 or 800 were in the dance circle at one time. Nothing unusual occurred for several hours until the dancers had gradually worked themselves up to a high state of excitement, when Sitting Bull stepped into the circle, and going up close in front of a young Arapaho woman, he began to make hypnotic passes before her face with the eagle feather. In a few seconds she became rigid and then fell to the ground unconscious. Sitting Bull then turned his attention to another and another, and the same thing happened to each in turn until nearly a hundred were stretched out on the ground at once. As usual in the trances some lay thus for a long time, and others recovered sooner, but none were disturbed, as Sitting Bull told the dancers that these were now beholding happy visions of the spirit world. When next they came together those who had been in the trance related their experiences in the other world, how they had met and talked with their departed friends and joined in their oldtime amusements. Many of them embodied their visions in songs, which were sung that night and afterward in the dance, and from that time the Ghost dance was naturalized in the south and developed rapidly along new lines. Each succeeding dance resulted in other visions and new songs, and from time to time other hypnotists arose, until almost every camp had its own.

About this time a commission arrived to treat with the Cheyenne and Arapaho for the sale of their reservation. The Indians were much divided in opinion, the great majority opposing any sale whatsoever, even of their claim in the Cherokee strip, which they believed was all that the agreement was intended to cover. While the debate was in progress Left Hand, chief of the Arapaho, went to Sitting Bull and asked his opinion on the matter. Sitting Bull advised him to sell for what they could get, as they had need of the money, and in a short time the messiah would come and restore the land to them. On this advice Left Hand signed the agreement, in the face of threats from those opposed to it, and his example was followed by nearly all of his tribe. This incident shows how thoroughly Sitting Bull and the other Arapaho believed in the new doctrine. In view of the misery that has come on these tribes from the sale of their reservation, it is sad to think that they could have so deceived themselves by false hopes of divine interposition. A large party of the Cheyenne refused to have anything to do with the sale or to countenance the transaction by accepting their share of the purchase money, even after the whites had taken possession of the lands.

The troubles in the Sioux country now began to attract public attention, and there was suggestion of military interference. The newspaper liar has reached an abnormal development in Oklahoma, and dispatches from Guthrie, El Reno, and Oklahoma City were filled with vivid accounts of war dances, scalping parties, and imminent outbreaks, mingled with frantic appeals for troops. A specimen dispatch stated that a thousand Kickapoo were dancing, whereas in fact the whole tribe numbers only 325, very few of whom were in any way concerned with the Ghost dance. Indian Commissioner Morgan was at this time (November, 1890) on a tour of inspection among the western tribes of Oklahoma, and satisfied himself that all such sensational reports were false, and that there was no danger to be apprehended from the dance. (*G. D., 55*.) At the same time the War Department commissioned Lieutenant (now Captain) H. L. Scott, of the Seventh cavalry, then and now stationed at Fort Sill, Oklahoma, to investigate the meaning of the excitement and the possibility of an outbreak. Captain Scott was eminently fitted for the work by his intimate acquaintance with the Indians and his perfect knowledge of the sign language. In the course of December, 1890, and January and February, 1891, he visited the various camps of the western tribes of the territory, attended a number of dances, and talked with the leaders. His reports on the Ghost dance are most valuable, and confirmed the War Department in its previous opinion that no danger was to be apprehended, and that the true policy was one of noninterference.

The dance constantly gathered strength among the Arapaho and Cheyenne, in spite of the failure of the first prediction, and spread rapidly to the neighboring tribes, Sitting Bull himself being the high priest and chief propagandist. The adverse report brought back by Ä'piatañ, the Kiowa, in the spring of 1891 had no effect outside of his own tribe. In the early part of that year the Arapaho and Cheyenne sent a delegation, including one woman, to visit the messiah in Nevada and bring back the latest news from heaven. They were gone a considerable time and returned with some of the sacred medicine paint given them by Wovoka, after having taken part with the Paiute in a Ghost dance under his leadership at the regular dance ground near Mason valley. Tall Bull, captain of the Cheyenne police, was one of this party, and Arnold Woolworth, a Carlisle student, acted as interpreter.

In August, 1891, another delegation went out, consisting of Black Coyote, Little Raven, Red Wolf, Grant Left Hand, and Casper Edson (Arapaho), and Black Sharp Nose and Standing Bull (Cheyenne). Grant Left Hand and Casper Edson, Carlisle students, acted as interpreters, wrote down the words of the messiah, and delivered his message to their people on their return. This message, as written down at the time by Casper Edson, is given in the preceding chapter on the doctrine of the Ghost dance. In accord with the messiah's instructions the two tribes now changed their manner of dancing from frequent small dances at each camp at irregular intervals to larger dances participated in by several camps together at regular intervals of six weeks, each dance continuing for five consecutive days. The Caddo and Wichita also adopted the new rule in agreement with instructions brought back by a delegation sent out about the same time. The change was opposed by Sitting Bull and some others, but the delegates, having the authority of the messiah for the innovation, succeeded in carrying their point, and thereafter assumed a leadership on equal terms with Sitting Bull, who from that time lost much of his interest in the dance. They were gone about two weeks, and brought back with them a quantity of the sacred paint and a large number of magpie feathers, the kind commonly worn by the Paiute in the Ghost dance. This started a demand for magpie feathers, and the shrewd traders soon turned the fact to their own advantage by importing selected crow feathers, which they sold to the unsuspecting Indians for the genuine article at the rate of two feathers for a quarter. While in the land of the Paiute the delegates took part in the Ghost dance at Mason valley, and were thrown into a trance by Wovoka, as related in chapter IX.

The Ghost dance practically superseded all other dances among the Cheyenne and Arapaho, and constantly developed new features, notably the auxiliary "crow dance," which was organized by Grant Left Hand. This was claimed as a dance seen in a trance vision of the spirit world, but is really only a modification of the "Omaha dance," common to the northern prairie tribes. The opening of the reservation and the influx of the whites served to intensify the religious fervor of the Indians, who were now more than ever made to feel their dependent and helpless condition. It was impossible, however, that the intense mental strain could endure forever, and after the failure of the predictions on the appointed dates the wild excitement gradually cooled and crystallized into a fixed but tranquil expectation of ultimate happiness under the old conditions in another world.

In October, 1892, another delegation, consisting of Sitting Bull and his wife, with Washee and two other Arapaho, and Edward Guerrier, a half-blood Cheyenne, visited the messiah. They brought back a very discouraging report, which was in substance that the messiah was tired of so many visitors and wanted them to go home and tell their tribes to stop dancing. Although the Indians generally refused to accept the message as genuine, the effect was naturally depressing. A year later, in October, 1893, Black Coyote and several others dictated through me a letter to Wovoka, asking him to send them some of the sacred paint or anything else that would make them think of him, with "some good words to help us and our children," and requesting to know whether he had been truthfully reported by the delegates of the preceding year. To one who knows these people their simple religious faith is too touching to be a subject of amusement.

The messiah doctrine never gained many converts among the Comanche, excepting those of the Penätĕ'ka division and a few others living on the Little Washita and other streams on the northern boundary of the reservation, adjoining the tribes most interested in the Ghost dance. These Comanche held a few Ghost dances and made a few songs, but the body of the tribe would have nothing to do with it.   This lack of interest was due partly to the general skeptical temperament of the Comanche, evinced in their carelessness in regard to ceremonial forms, and partly to their tribal pride, which forbade their following after the strange gods of another people, as they considered their own mescal rite sufficient to all their needs.   Quanah Parker, their head chief, a shrewd half-blood, opposed the new doctrine and prevented its spread among his tribe.

The Ghost dance was brought to the Pawnee, Ponca, Oto, Missouri, Kansa, Iowa, Osage, and other tribes in central Oklahoma by delegates from the Arapaho and Cheyenne in the west.   The doctrine made slow progress for some time, but by February, 1892, the majority of the Pawnee were dancing in confident expectation of the speedy coming of the messiah and the buffalo.   Of all these tribes the Pawnee took most interest in the new doctrine, becoming as much devoted to the Ghost dance as the Arapaho themselves.   The leader among the Pawnee was Frank White, and among the Oto was Buffalo Black.   The agent in charge took stringent measures against the dance, and had the Oto prophet arrested and confined in the Wichita jail, threatening at the same time to cut off supplies from the tribe.   As the confederated Oto and Missouri number only 362 in all, they were easily brought into subjection, and the dance was abandoned.   The same method was pursued with the Pawnee prophet and his people, but as they are stronger in number than the Oto, they were proportionately harder to deal with, but the final result was the same.   (Comr., 43.)   The Osage gave but little heed to the story, perhaps from the fact that, as they are the wealthiest tribe in the country, they feel no such urgent need of a redeemer as their less fortunate brethren.   The Sauk, Fox, Kickapoo, and Potawatomi engaged in the dance only to a limited extent, for the reason that a number of the natives of these tribes, particularly the Potawatomi, are under Catholic influences, while most of the others adhere to the doctrine of Känakûk, the Potawatomi prophet mentioned in chapter v.

The Ghost dance doctrine was communicated directly to the Caddo, Wichita, Kichai, Delaware, and Kiowa by the Arapaho and Cheyenne, their neighbors on the north.   We shall speak now of the tribes first mentioned, leaving the Kiowa until the last.   The Caddo, Wichita, Kichai, and several remnants of cognate tribes, with a small band of the Delaware, numbering in all about a thousand Indians, occupy a reservation between the Washita and the South Canadian in western Oklahoma, having the Arapaho and Cheyenne on the north and west, the Kiowa on the south, and the whites of Oklahoma and the Chickasaw nation on the east.   The Caddo are the leading tribe, numbering more than half of the whole body. They were the first of these to take up the dance, and have manifested the greatest interest in it from the time it was introduced among them.

A number of Caddo first attended the great Ghost dance held by the Cheyenne and Arapaho on the South Canadian in the fall of 1890 on the occasion when Sitting Bull came down from the north and inaugurated the trances. On returning to their homes they started the Ghost dance, which they kept up, singing the Arapaho songs as they had heard them on the Canadian, until Sitting Bull came down about December, 1890, to give them further instruction in the doctrine and to "give the feather" to the seven persons selected to lead the ceremony. From this time the Caddo had songs and trances of their own, the chief priest and hypnotist of the dance being Nĭshkû′ntŭ, "Moon Head," or John Wilson. The Caddo and the Delaware usually danced together on Boggy creek. The Wichita and the Kichai, who took the doctrine from the Caddo, usually danced together on Sugar creek about 15 miles from the agency at Anadarko, but manifested less interest in the matter until Sitting Bull came down about the beginning of February, 1891, and "gave the feather" to the leaders. From this time all these tribes went into the dance heart and soul, on some occasions dancing for days and nights together from the middle of the afternoon until the sun was well up in the morning. The usual custom was to continue until about midnight. Cold weather had no deterrent effect, and they kept up the dance in the snow, the trance subjects sometimes lying unconscious in the snow for half an hour at a time. At this time it was confidently expected that the great change would occur in the spring, and as the time drew near the excitement became most intense. The return of the Kiowa delegate, Ä′piatañ, in the middle of February, 1891, with a report adverse to the messiah, produced no effect on the Caddo and their confederates, who refused to put any faith in his statements, claiming that he had not seen the real messiah or else had been bribed by the whites to make a false report.

About the time that Black Coyote and the others went out to see the messiah in the fall of 1891 the Caddo and their confederates sent out a delegation for the same purpose. The delegates were Billy Wilson and Squirrel (Caddo), Nashtowi and Lawrie Tatum (Wichita), and Jack Harry (Delaware). Tatum was a schoolboy and acted as interpreter for the party. Like the Arapaho they came back impressed with reverence for the messiah, and at once changed the time and method of the dancing, in accordance with his instructions, to periodical dances at intervals of six weeks, continuing for five consecutive days, the dance on the last night being kept up until daylight, when all the participants went down to bathe in the stream and then dispersed to their homes. They were dancing in this fashion when last visited in the fall of 1893.

The principal leader of the Ghost dance among the Caddo is Nĭshkû′ntŭ, "Moon Head," known to the whites as John Wilson. Although considered a Caddo, and speaking only that language, he is very much of a mixture, being half Delaware, one-fourth Caddo, and one-fourth French. One of his grandfathers was a Frenchman. As the Caddo lived originally in Louisiana, there is a considerable mixture of French blood among them, which manifests itself in his case in a fairly heavy beard. He is about 50 years of age, rather tall and well built, and wears his hair at full length flowing loosely over his shoulders. With a good head and strong, intelligent features, he presents the appearance of a natural leader. He is also prominent in the mescal rite, which has recently come to his tribe from the Kiowa and Comanche. He was one of the first Caddo to go into a trance, the occasion being the great Ghost dance held by the Arapaho and Cheyenne near Darlington agency, at which Sitting Bull presided, in the fall of 1890. On his return to consciousness he had wonderful things to tell of his experiences in the spirit world, composed a new song, and from that time became the high priest of the Caddo dance. Since then his trances have been frequent, both in and out of the Ghost dance, and in addition to his leadership in this connection he assumes the occult powers and authority of a great medicine-man, all the powers claimed by him being freely conceded by his people.

When Captain Scott was investigating the Ghost dance among the Caddo and other tribes of that section, at the period of greatest excitement, in the winter of 1890–91, he met Wilson, of whom he has this to say:

John Wilson, a Caddo man of much prominence, was especially affected, performing a series of gyrations that were most remarkable. At all hours of the day and night his cry could be heard all over camp, and when found he would be dancing in the ring, possibly upon one foot, with his eyes closed and the forefinger of his right hand pointed upward, or in some other ridiculous posture. Upon being asked his reasons for assuming these attitudes he replied that he could not help it; that it came over him just like cramps.

Somewhat later Captain Scott says:

John Wilson had progressed finely, and was now a full-fledged doctor, a healer of diseases, and a finder of stolen property through supernatural means. One day, while we were in his tent, a Wichita woman entered, led by the spirit. It was explained to us that she did not even know who lived there, but some force she could not account for brought her. Having stated her case to John, he went off into a fit of the jerks, in which his spirit went up and saw "his father" [i. e., God], who directed him how to cure this woman. When he came to, he explained the cure to her, and sent her away rejoicing. Soon afterwards a Keechei man came in, who was blind of one eye, and who desired to have the vision restored. John again consulted his father, who informed him that nothing could be done for that eye because that man held aloof from the dance.

While the author was visiting the Caddo on Sugar creek in the fall of 1893, John Wilson came down from his own camp to explain his part in the Ghost dance. He wore a wide-brim hat, with his hair flowing down to his shoulders, and on his breast, suspended from a cord about his neck, was a curious amulet consisting of the polished end of a buffalo horn, surrounded by a circlet of downy red feathers, within another circle of badger and owl claws. He explained that this was the source of his prophetic and clairvoyant inspiration. The buffalo horn was "God's heart," the red feathers contained his own heart, and the circle of claws represented the world. When he prayed for help, his heart communed with "God's heart," and he learned what he wished to know. He had much to say also of the moon. Sometimes in his trances he went to the moon and the moon taught him secrets. It must be remembered that sun, moon, stars, and almost every other thing in nature are considered by the Indians as endowed with life and spirit. He claimed an intimate acquaintance with the other world and asserted positively that he could tell me "just what heaven is like." Another man who accompanied him had a yellow sun with green rays painted on his forehead, with an elaborate rayed crescent in green, red, and yellow on his chin, and wore a necklace from which depended a crucifix and a brass clock-wheel, the latter, as he stated, representing the sun.

On entering the room where I sat awaiting him, Nĭshkû′ntŭ approached and performed mystic passes in front of my face with his hands, after the manner of the hypnotist priests in the Ghost dance, blowing upon me the while, as he afterward explained to blow evil things away from me before beginning to talk on religious subjects. He was good enough to state also that he had prayed for light before coming, and had found that my heart was good. Laying one hand on my head, and grasping my own hand with the other, he prayed silently for some time with bowed head, and then lifting his hand from my head, he passed it over my face, down my shoulder and arm to the hand, which he grasped and pressed slightly, and then released the fingers with a graceful upward sweep, as in the minuet. The first part of this—the laying of the hands upon the head, afterward drawing them down along the face and chest or arms—is the regular Indian form of blessing, reverential gratitude, or prayerful entreaty, and is of frequent occurrence in connection with the Ghost dance, when the believers ask help of the priests or beg the prayers of the older people. The next day about twenty or more Caddo came by on their way to the agency, all dressed and painted for a dance that was to be held that night. They stopped awhile to see us, and on entering the room where we were the whole company, men, women, and children, went through the same ceremony, with each one of the inmates in turn, beginning with Wilson and myself, and ending with the members of the family. The ceremony occupied a considerable time, and was at once beautiful and impressive. Not a word was said by either party during the while, excepting as someone in excess of devotion would utter prayerful exclamations aloud like the undertone of a litany. Every face wore a look of reverent solemnity, from the old men and women down to little children of 6 and 8 years. Several of them, the women especially, trembled while praying, as under the excitement of the Ghost dance. The religious greeting being over, the women of the family, with those of the party, went out to prepare the dinner, while the rest remained to listen to the doctrinal discussion.

The Kiowa were predisposed to accept the doctrine of the Ghost dance. No tribe had made more desperate resistance to the encroachments of the whites upon their hunting grounds, and even after the failure of the last effort of the confederated tribes in 1874–75, the Kiowa were slow to accept the verdict of defeat. The result of this unsuccessful struggle was to put an end to the boundless freedom of the prairie, where they had roamed unquestioned from Dakota almost to central Mexico, and henceforth the tribes were confined within the narrow limits of reservations. Within five years the great southern buffalo herd was extinct and the Indians found themselves at once prisoners and paupers. The change was so swift and terrible in its effects that they could not believe it real and final. It seemed to them like a dream of sorrow, a supernatural cloud of darkness to punish their derelictions, but which could be lifted from them by prayer and sacrifice. Their old men told of years when the buffalo was scarce or had gone a long way off, but never since the beginning of the world of a time when there was no buffalo. The buffalo still lived beyond their horizon or in caves under the earth, and with its return would come back prosperity and freedom. Before we wonder at their faith we must remember that the disappearance of these millions of buffalo in the space of a few years has no parallel in the annals of natural history.

In 1881 a young Kiowa named Da'tekañ, "Keeps-his-name-always," began to "make medicine" to bring back the buffalo. He set up a sacred tipi, in front of which he erected a pole with a buffalo skin at the top, and made for himself a priestly robe of red color, trimmed with rows of eagle feathers. Then standing in front of his tipi he called the people around him and told them that he had been commanded and empowered in a dream to bring back the buffalo, and if they observed strictly the prayers and ceremonies which he enjoined the great herds would once more cover the prairie. His hearers believed his words, promised strict obedience, and gave freely of their blankets and other property to reward his efforts in their behalf. Da'tekañ retired to his sacred tipi, where, in his feathered robe of office, he continued to prophesy and make buffalo medicine for a year, when he died without seeing the realization of his hopes. The excitement caused by his predictions came to the notice of the agent then in charge, who mentions it in his annual report, without understanding the cause. On a Kiowa calendar obtained by the author the event is recorded in a pictograph which represents the medicine-man in his tipi, with his scarlet robe over his shoulders and a buffalo beneath his feet (figure 84).

About six years later, in 1887, another prophet, named Pa'-iñgya, "In the Middle," revived the prophecy, claiming to be heir to all the supernatural powers of his late predecessor. He amplified the doctrine by asserting, logically enough, that as the whites were responsible for the disappearance of the buffalo, the whites themselves would be destroyed by the gods when the time was at hand for the return of the buffalo. He preached also his own invulnerability and claimed the power to kill with a look those who might offend him, as far as his glance could reach. He fixed his headquarters on Elk creek, near the western limit of the reservation, where he inaugurated a regular series of ritual observances, under the management of ten chosen assistants. Finally he announced that the time was at hand when the whites would be removed and the buffalo would return. He ordered all the tribe to assemble on Elk creek, where after four days he would bring down fire from heaven which would destroy the agency, the schools, and the white race, with the Indian unbelievers all together. The faithful need not fear pursuit by the troops, for the soldiers who might follow would wither before his glance and their bullets would have no effect on the Indians. On the same Kiowa calendar this prediction is recorded in another pictograph intended to represent flying bullets. The whole Kiowa tribe caught the infection of his words. Every camp was abandoned, parents took their children from the schools, and all fled to the rendezvous on Elk creek. Here they waited patiently for their deliverance till the predicted day came and passed without event, when they returned

FIG. 84—Two Kiowa prophecies (from a Kiowa calendar).

with sadness to their camps and their government rations of white man's beef. Pa'-iñgya still lives, but the halo of prophecy no longer surrounds him. To account for the disappointment he claimed that his people had violated some of the ordinances and thereby postponed the destined happiness. In this way their minds were kept dwelling on the subject, and when at last the rumor of a messiah came from the north he hailed it as the fulfillment of the prediction.

Early in the summer of 1890 the news of the advent of the messiah reached the Kiowa, and in June of that year they sent a delegation of about twenty men under the leadership of Pa'tadal, "Poor Buffalo," to Cheyenne and Arapaho agency at Darlington to learn more about the matter. They brought back a favorable report and also a quantity of the sacred red paint procured originally from the country of the messiah. Soon after there was a great gathering of the Kiowa and Apache at the agency at Anadarko to receive a payment of "grass money" due from the cattlemen for the lease of pasturage on the reservation. On this occasion the Ghost dance was formally inaugurated among the Kiowa, Poor Buffalo assuming direction of the ceremony, and painting the principal participants with the sacred red paint with his own hands. The dance was carried back to their various camps and became a part of the tribal life.

FIG. 85—Poor Buffalo.

About this time a Sioux chief, High Wolf, came down from the north to visit the Cheyenne, Arapaho, Kiowa, and other tribes in that section. He remained some time among them, and on his return to the north invited a young Kiowa named Ä'piatañ, "Wooden Lance," whose grandmother had been a Sioux captive, to come up and visit his relatives at Pine Ridge. The invitation was accepted by Ä'piatañ, partly for the pleasure of seeing a new tribe and meeting his mother's kindred, but chiefly for the purpose of investigating for himself and for the Kiowa the truth of the messiah story. Äpiatañ, who speaks but little English, and who was then about 30 years of age, had recently lost a child to whom he had been very much attached. He brooded over his loss until the new doctrine came with its promise of a reunion with departed friends and its possibility of seeing and talking with them in visions of the trance. Moved by parental affection, which is the ruling passion with an Indian, he determined on this long journey in search of the messiah, who was vaguely reported to be somewhere in the north, to learn from his own lips the wonderful story, and to see if it were possible to talk again with his child. He discussed the matter with the chiefs, who decided to send him as a delegate to find the messiah and

BI'ÄÑK'I, THE KIOWA DREAMER

learn the truth or falsity of the reports, in order that the Kiowa might be guided by the result on his return. A sufficient sum of money was raised for his expenses, and he left for the north in September, 1890. Almost the whole tribe had assembled at the agency to witness his departure, and each in turn of the principal men performed over him a ceremony of blessing, such as has already been described. His going and return are both recorded on the calendar previously mentioned.

In October, 1890, shortly after Ä'piatañ's departure, Sitting Bull, the Arapaho prophet of the Ghost dance, came down from his tribe and gave new impetus to the excitement among the Kiowa. This event also is recorded on the same Kiowa calendar in a well-drawn picture representing a buffalo standing beside the figure of a man (figure 86). It is also indicated less definitely on another calendar obtained from the tribe. Sitting Bull confirmed, as by personal knowledge, all that had been told of the messiah, and predicted that the new earth would arrive in the following spring, 1891. The Kiowa assembled on the Washita, at the mouth of Rainy Mountain creek, and here, at the largest Ghost dance ever held by the tribe, Sitting Bull consecrated seven men

Fig. 86—Sitting Bull comes down (from a Kiowa calendar).

and women as leaders of the dance and teachers of the doctrine by giving to each one a sacred feather to be worn in the dance as the badge of priesthood. Until the Ghost dance came to the prairie tribes their women had never before been raised to such dignity as to be allowed to wear feathers in their hair. After "giving the feather" to the leaders thus chosen, they were taught the songs and ritual of the dance. At first the songs were all in the Arapaho language, but after the trances, which now began to be frequent, the Kiowa composed songs of their own.

Among the dreamers and prophets who now came to the front was one who merits more than a passing notice. His original name was Bi'äñk'i, "Eater," but on account of his frequent visits to the spirit world he is now known as Äsa'tito'la, which may be freely rendered "The Messenger." For a long time he had been in the habit of going alone upon the mountain, there to fast and pray until visions came to him, when he would return and give to his people the message of inspiration. Frequently these vigils were undertaken at the request of friends of sick people to obtain spiritual knowledge of the proper remedies to be applied, or at the request of surviving relatives who wished to hear from their departed friends in the other world.   He is now about 55 years of age, quiet and dignified in manner, with a thoughtful cast of countenance which accords well with his character as a priest and seer.   His intellectual bent is further shown by the fact that he has invented a system of ideographic writing which is nearly as distinct from the ordinary Indian pictograph system as it is from our own alphabet.   It is based on the sign language of the plains tribes, the primary effort being to convey the idea by a pictured representation of the gesture sign; but, as in the evolution of the alphabet, a part is frequently put for the whole, and numerous arbitrary or auxiliary characters are added, until the result is a well-developed germ of an alphabetic system.   He has taught the system to his sons, and by this means was able to keep up a correspondence with them while they were attending Carlisle school. It is unintelligible to the rest of the tribe.   I have specimens of this curious graphic method, obtained from the father and his sons, which may be treated at length at some future time.   In the picture of Äsa'ti-to'la (plate CVI), he holds in one hand a paper on which is depicted one of his visions, while in the other is the pointer with which he explains its meaning.

Plate CVII herewith represents this vision.   On this occasion, after reaching the spirit world he found himself on a vast prairie covered with herds of buffalo and ponies, represented respectively in the picture by short black and green lines at the top.   He went on through the buffalo, the way being indicated by the dotted green lines, until he came to a large Kiowa camp, in which, according to their old custom, nearly every tipi had its distinctive style of painting or ornamentation to show to what family it belonged, all these families being still represented in the tribe.   He went on to the point indicated by the first heavy blue mark, where he met four young women, whom he knew as having died years before, returning on horseback with their saddle-pouches filled with wild plums.   After some conversation he asked them about two brothers, his relatives, who had died some time ago. He went in the direction pointed out by the young women and soon met the two young men coming into camp with a load of fresh buffalo meat hung at their saddles.   Their names were Emanki'na, "Can't-hold-it," a policeman, and E''pea, "Afraid-of-him," who had died while held as a prisoner of war in Florida about fifteen years before. It will be noted that they are represented in the picture as armed only with bows and arrows, in agreement with the Ghost-dance doctrine of a return to aboriginal things.   After proceeding some distance he retraced his steps and met two curious beings, represented in the picture by green figures with crosses instead of heads.   These told him

BIĂÑ

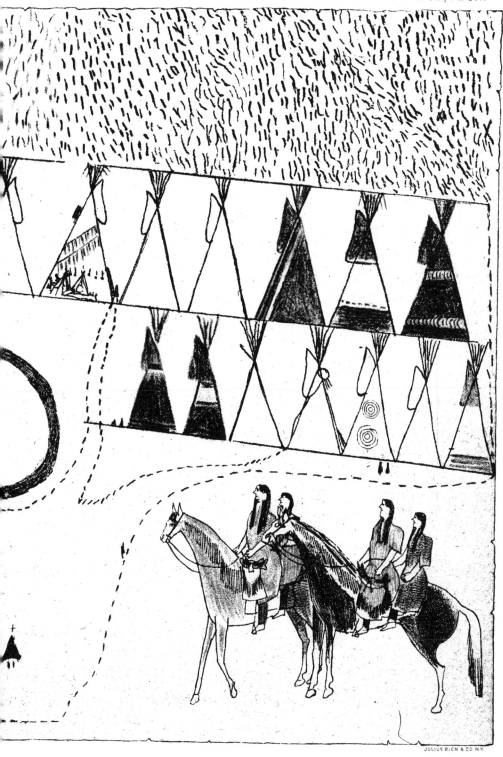

ION.

to go on, and on doing so he came to an immense circle of Kiowa dancing the Ghost dance around a cedar tree, indicated by the black circle
with a green figure resembling a tree in the center. He stood for a
while near the tree, shown by another blue mark, when he saw a woman,
whom he knew, leave the dance. He hurried after her until she reached
her own tipi and went into it—shown by the blue mark beside the red
tipi with red flags on the ends of the tipi poles—when he turned around
and came back. She belonged to the family of the great chief Set-
t'aiñti, "White Bear," as indicated by the red tipi with red flags, no
other warrior in the tribe having such a tipi. On inquiring for his
own relatives he was directed to the other side of the camp, where he
met a man—represented by the heavy black mark—who told him his
own people were inside of the next tipi. On entering he found the
whole family, consisting of his father, two brothers, two sisters, and
several children, feasting on fresh buffalo beef from a kettle hung
over the fire. They welcomed him and offered him some of the meat,
which for some reason he was afraid to taste. To convince him that it
was good they held it up for him to smell, when he awoke and found
himself lying alone upon the mountain.

Ä'piatañ went on first to Pine Ridge, where he was well received by
the Sioux, who had much to say of the new messiah in the west. He
was urged to stop and join them in the Ghost dance, but refused and
hurried on to Fort Washakie, where he met the northern Arapaho and
the Shoshoni, whom he called the "northern Comanches." Here the new
prophecy was the one topic of conversation, and after stopping only
long enough to learn the proper route to the Paiute country, he went
on over the Union Pacific railroad to Nevada. On arriving at the
agency at Pyramid lake the Paiute furnished him a wagon and an
Indian guide across the country to the home of Wovoka in the upper
end of Mason valley. The next day he was admitted to his presence.
The result was a complete disappointment. A single interview convinced him of the utter falsity of the pretensions of the messiah and the
deceptive character of the hopes held out to the believers.

Saddened and disgusted, Ä'piatañ made no stay, but started at once
on his return home. On his way back he stopped at Bannock agency
at Fort Hall, Idaho, and from there sent a letter to his people, stating
briefly that he had seen the messiah and that the messiah was a fraud.
This was the first intimation the Kiowa had received from an Indian
source that their hopes were not well grounded. The author was present when the letter was received at Anadarko and read to the assembled Indians by Ä'piatañ's sister, an educated woman named Laura
Dunmoi, formerly of Carlisle school. The result was a division of
opinion. Some of the Indians, feeling that the ground had been taken
from under them, at once gave up all hope and accepted the inevitable
of despair. Others were disposed to doubt the genuineness of the letter, as it had come through the medium of a white man, and decided

to withhold their decision until they could hear directly from the delegate himself. Ä'piatañ returned in the middle of February, 1891. The
agent sent notice to the various camps on the reservation for the Indians

Fig. 87—Ä'piatañ.

to assemble at the agency to hear his report, and also sent a request to
Cheyenne and Arapaho agency to have Sitting Bull come down at the
same time so that the Indians might hear both sides of the story.

KIOWA SUMMER SHELTER

The council was held at the agency at Anadarko, Oklahoma, on February 19, 1891, the author being among those present on the occasion. It was a great gathering, representing every tribe on the reservation, there being also in attendance a number of Arapaho who had accompanied Sitting Bull from the other agency. Everything said was interpreted in turn into English, Kiowa, Comanche, Caddo, Wichita, and Arapaho. This was a slow process, and necessitated frequent repetition, so that the talk occupied all day. Ä'piatañ first made his report, which was interpreted into the various languages. Questions were asked by the agent, Mr Adams, and by leading Indians, and after the full details had been obtained in this manner Sitting Bull, the Arapaho, was called on to make his statement. The scene was dramatic in the highest degree. Although in a certain sense Sitting Bull himself was on trial, it meant more than that to the assembled tribe. Their power, prosperity, and happiness had gone down, their very race was withering away before the white man. The messiah doctrine promised a restoration of the old conditions through supernatural assistance. If this hope was without foundation, the Indian had no future and his day was forever past.

After some preliminaries Ä'piatañ arose and told his story. He had gone on as related until he arrived at the home of Wovoka in Mason valley. Here he was told that the messiah could not be seen until the next day. On being finally admitted to his presence he found him lying down, his face covered with a blanket, and singing to himself. When he had finished the song the messiah uncovered his face and asked Ä'piatañ, through an interpreter, what he wanted. As Ä'piatañ had approached with great reverence under the full belief that the messiah was omniscient, able to read his secret thoughts and to speak all languages, this question was a great surprise to him, and his faith at once began to waver. However, he told who he was and why he had come, and then asked that he be permitted to see some of his dead relatives, particularly his little child. Wovoka replied that this was impossible, and that there were no spirits there to be seen. With their mixture of Christian and aboriginal ideas many of the Indians had claimed that this messiah was the veritable Christ and bore upon his hands and feet the scars of the crucifixion. Not seeing these scars, Ä'piatañ expressed some doubt as to whether Wovoka was really the messiah he had come so far to see, to which Wovoka replied that he need go no farther for there was no other messiah, and went on to say that he had preached to Sitting Bull and the others and had given them a new dance, but that some of them, especially the Sioux, had twisted things and made trouble, and now Ä'piatañ had better go home and tell his people to quit the whole business. Discouraged and sick at heart Ä'piatañ went out from his presence, convinced that there was no longer a god in Israel.

After the story had been told and interpreted to each of the tribes, Sitting Bull was called on for his statement. He told how he had visited the messiah a year before and what the messiah had said to

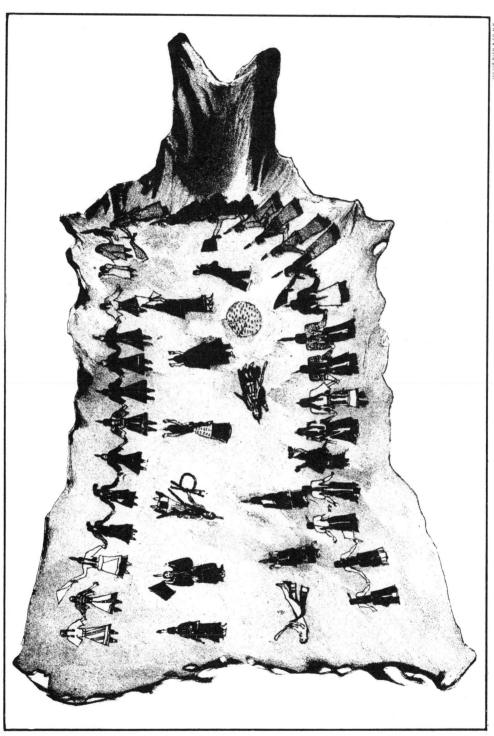

JULIUS BIEN & CO. N.Y.

GHOST DANCE PAINTING ON BUCKSKIN

EXPLANATION OF PLATE CIX

The original of this picture was drawn in colored inks on buckskin by Yellow Nose, a Ute captive among the Cheyenne, in 1891. It was obtained from him by the author and is now deposited in the National Museum at Washington. Besides being a particularly fine specimen of Indian pictography, it gives an excellent idea of the ghost dance as it was at that time among the Cheyenne and Arapaho. The dancers are in full costume, with paint and feathers. The women of the two tribes are plainly distinguished by the arrangement of their hair, the Cheyenne women having the hair braided at the side, while the Arapaho women wear it hanging loosely. Two of the women carry children on their backs. One of the men carries the *bä'qati* wheel, another a shinny stick, and a woman holds out the sacred crow, while several wave handkerchiefs which aid in producing the hypnotic effect. In the center are several persons with arms outstretched and rigid, while at one side is seen the medicine-man hypnotizing a subject who stretches out toward him a blue handkerchief. The spotted object on the ground behind the medicine-man is a shawl which has fallen from the shoulders of the woman standing near.

CHAPTER XV

THE CEREMONY OF THE GHOST DANCE

In chapter XI we have spoken of the Ghost dance as it existed among the Paiute, Shoshoni, Walapai, and Cohonino, west of the mountains. We shall now give a more detailed account of the ceremony and connected ritual among the prairie tribes.

AMONG THE NORTHERN CHEYENNE

According to Dr Grinnell the Ghost dance among the northern Cheyenne had several features not found in the south. Four fires were built outside of the dance circle and about 20 yards back from it, toward each of the cardinal points. These fires were built of long poles set up on end, so as to form a rude cone, much as the poles of a tipi are erected. The fires were lighted at the bottom, and thus made high bonfires, which were kept up as long as the dance continued. (*J. F. L., 5.*)

AMONG THE SIOUX

Perhaps the most important feature in connection with the dance among the Sioux was the "ghost shirt," already noticed and to be described more fully hereafter. On account of the scarcity of buckskin, these shirts were almost always made of white cloth cut and figured in the Indian fashion. The Sioux wore no metal of any kind in the dance, differing in this respect from the southern tribes, who wore on such occasions all their finery of German silver ornaments. The Sioux also began the dance sometimes in the morning, as well as in the afternoon or evening. Another important feature not found among the southern tribes, excepting the Kiowa, was the tree planted in the center of the circle and decorated with feathers, stuffed animals, and strips of cloth.

At a Ghost dance at No Water's camp, near Pine Ridge, as described by J. F. Asay, formerly a trader at the agency, the dancers first stood in line facing the sun, while the leader, standing facing them, made a prayer and waved over their heads the "ghost stick," a staff about 6 feet long, trimmed with red cloth and feathers of the same color. After thus waving the stick over them, he faced the sun and made another prayer, after which the line closed up to form a circle around the tree and the dance began. During the prayer a woman standing near the tree held out a pipe toward the sun, while another beside her held out several (four?) arrows from which the points had been removed. On another occasion, at a Ghost dance at the same camp, four arrows, headed with bone in the olden fashion, were shot up into the air from the center of the circle and afterward gathered up and hung upon the tree, together with the bow, a gaming wheel and sticks, and a staff of peculiar shape (ghost stick?). See plate CXI. The ceremonies of fasting, painting, and the sweat-bath in connection with the Ghost dance among the Sioux have been already described.

The best account of the dance itself and of the ghost shirt is given by Mrs Z. A. Parker, at that time a teacher on the Pine Ridge reservation, writing of a Ghost dance observed by her on White Clay creek, on June 20, 1890. We quote at length from her description:

We drove to this spot about 10.30 oclock on a delightful October day. We came upon tents scattered here and there in low, sheltered places long before reaching the dance ground. Presently we saw over three hundred tents placed in a circle, with a large pine tree in the center, which was covered with strips of cloth of various colors, eagle feathers, stuffed birds, claws, and horns—all offerings to the Great Spirit. The ceremonies had just begun. In the center, around the tree, were gathered their medicine-men; also those who had been so fortunate as to have had visions and in them had seen and talked with friends who had died. A company of fifteen had started a chant and were marching abreast, others coming in behind as they marched. After marching around the circle of tents they turned to the center, where many had gathered and were seated on the ground.

I think they wore the ghost shirt or ghost dress for the first time that day. I noticed that these were all new and were worn by about seventy men and forty women. The wife of a man called Return-from-scout had seen in a vision that her friends all wore a similar robe, and on reviving from her trance she called the women together and they made a great number of the sacred garments. They were of white cotton cloth. The women's dress was cut like their ordinary dress, a loose robe with wide, flowing sleeves, painted blue in the neck, in the shape of a three-cornered handkerchief, with moon, stars, birds, etc, interspersed with real feathers, painted on the waist and sleeves. While dancing they wound their shawls about their waists, letting them fall to within 3 inches of the ground, the fringe at the bottom. In the hair, near the crown, a feather was tied. I noticed an absence of any manner of bead ornaments, and, as I knew their vanity and fondness for them, wondered why it was. Upon making inquiries I found they discarded everything they could which was made by white men.

The ghost shirt for the men was made of the same material—shirts and leggings painted in red. Some of the leggings were painted in stripes running up and down, others running around. The shirt was painted blue around the neck, and the whole garment was fantastically sprinkled with figures of birds, bows and arrows, sun, moon, and stars, and everything they saw in nature. Down the outside of the sleeve were rows of feathers tied by the quill ends and left to fly in the breeze, and also a row around the neck and up and down the outside of the leggings. I noticed that a number had stuffed birds, squirrel heads, etc, tied in their long hair. The faces of all were painted red with a black half-moon on the forehead or on one cheek.

As the crowd gathered about the tree the high priest, or master of ceremonies, began his address, giving them directions as to the chant and other matters. After he had spoken for about fifteen minutes they arose and formed in a circle. As nearly as I could count, there were between three and four hundred persons. One stood directly behind another, each with his hands on his neighbor's shoulders. After walking about a few times, chanting, "Father, I come," they stopped marching, but

SACRED OBJECTS FROM THE SIOUX GHOST DANCE

remained in the circle, and set up the most fearful, heart-piercing wails I ever heard—crying, moaning, groaning, and shrieking out their grief, and naming over their departed friends and relatives, at the same time taking up handfuls of dust at their feet, washing their hands in it, and throwing it over their heads. Finally, they raised their eyes to heaven, their hands clasped high above their heads, and stood straight and perfectly still, invoking the power of the Great Spirit to allow them to see and talk with their people who had died. This ceremony lasted about fifteen minutes, when they all sat down where they were and listened to another address, which I did not understand, but which I afterwards learned were words of encouragement and assurance of the coming messiah.

When they arose again, they enlarged the circle by facing toward the center, taking hold of hands, and moving around in the manner of school children in their play of "needle's eye." And now the most intense excitement began. They would go as fast as they could, their hands moving from side to side, their bodies swaying, their arms, with hands gripped tightly in their neighbors', swinging back and forth with all their might. If one, more weak and frail, came near falling, he would be jerked up and into position until tired nature gave way. The ground had been worked and worn by many feet, until the fine, flour-like dust lay light and loose to the depth of two or three inches. The wind, which had increased, would sometimes take it up, enveloping the dancers and hiding them from view. In the ring were men, women, and children; the strong and the robust, the weak consumptive, and those near to death's door. They believed those who were sick would be cured by joining in the dance and losing consciousness. From the beginning they chanted, to a monotonous tune. the words—

> Father, I come;
> Mother, I come;
> Brother, I come;
> Father, give us back our arrows.

All of which they would repeat over and over again until first one and then another would break from the ring and stagger away and fall down. One woman fell a few feet from me. She came toward us, her hair flying over her face, which was purple, looking as if the blood would burst through; her hands and arms moving wildly; every breath a pant and a groan; and she fell on her back, and went down like a log. I stepped up to her as she lay there motionless, but with every muscle twitching and quivering. She seemed to be perfectly unconscious. Some of the men and a few of the women would run, stepping high and pawing the air in a frightful manner. Some told me afterwards that they had a sensation as if the ground were rising toward them and would strike them in the face. Others would drop where they stood. One woman fell directly into the ring, and her husband stepped out and stood over her to prevent them from trampling upon her. No one ever disturbed those who fell or took any notice of them except to keep the crowd away.

They kept up dancing until fully 100 persons were lying unconscious. Then they stopped and seated themselves in a circle, and as each one recovered from his trance he was brought to the center of the ring to relate his experience. Each told his story to the medicine-man and he shouted it to the crowd. Not one in ten claimed that he saw anything. I asked one Indian—a tall, strong fellow, straight as an arrow—what his experience was. He said he saw an eagle coming toward him. It flew round and round, drawing nearer and nearer until he put out his hand to take it, when it was gone. I asked him what he thought of it. "Big lie," he replied. I found by talking to them that not one in twenty believed it. After resting for a time they would go through the same performance, perhaps three times a day. They practiced fasting, and every morning those who joined in the dance were obliged to immerse themselves in the creek. (*Comr., 44.*)

SONG REHEARSALS

As with church choirs, the leaders, both men and women, frequently assembled privately in a tipi to rehearse the new or old songs for the next dance. During the first winter spent among the Arapaho I had frequent opportunity of being present at these rehearsals, as for a long time the snow was too deep to permit dancing outside. After having obtained their confidence the Arapaho police invited me to come up to their camp at night to hear them practice the songs in anticipation of better weather for dancing. Thenceforth rehearsals were held in Black Coyote's tipi almost every night until the snow melted, each session usually lasting about three hours.

On these occasions from eight to twelve persons were present, sitting in a circle on the low beds around the fire in the center. Black Coyote acted as master of ceremonies and opened proceedings by filling and lighting the redstone pipe, offering the first whiff to the sun, then reversing the stem in offering to the earth, next presenting the pipe to the fire, and then to each of the four cardinal points. He then took a few puffs himself, after which he passed the pipe to his next neighbor, who went through the same preliminaries before smoking, and thus the pipe went round the circle, each one taking only a few puffs before passing it on. The pipe was then put back into its pouch, and Black Coyote, standing with his face toward the northwest, the messiah's country, with eyes closed and arms outstretched, made a fervent prayer for help and prosperity to his tribe, closing with an earnest petition to the messiah to hasten his coming. The others listened in silence with bowed heads. The prayer ended, they consulted as to the song to be sung first, which Black Coyote then started in a clear musical bass, the others joining. From time to time explanations were made where the meaning of the song was not clear. They invited me to call for whatever songs I wished to hear, and these songs were repeated over and over again to give me an opportunity to write them down, but they waived extended discussion until another time. Usually the men alone were the singers, but sometimes Black Coyote's wives or other women who were present joined in the songs. It was noticeable that even in these rehearsals the women easily fell under the excitement of the dance. Finally, about 10 oclock, all rose together and sang the closing song, *Ni'ninitubi'na Huhu*, "The Crow has given the signal," and the rehearsal was at an end. On one occasion, before I had obtained this song, I called for it in order that I might write it down, but they explained that we must wait awhile, as it was the closing song, and if they sung it then they must quit for the night.

PREPARATIONS FOR THE DANCE

On several occasions the dance ground was consecrated before the performance, one of the leaders going all about the place, sprinkling some kind of sacred powder over the ground and praying the while.

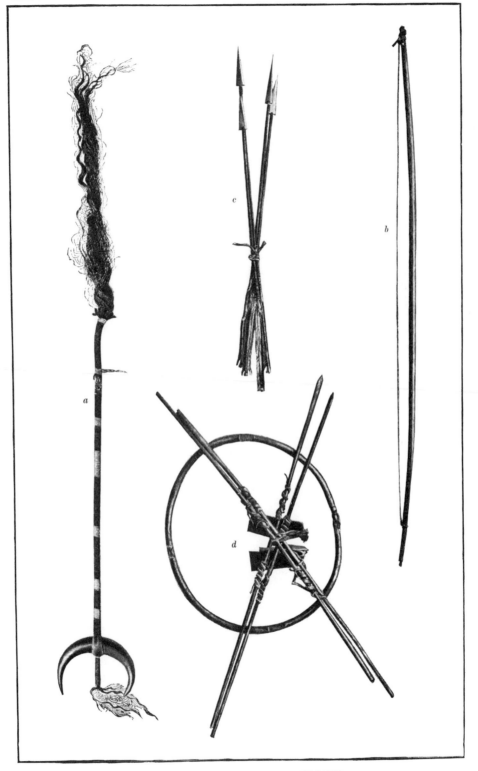

SACRED OBJECTS FROM THE SIOUX GHOST DANCE

a, Staff; *b*, *c*, Bow and bone-head arrows; *d*, Gaming wheel and sticks

Frequently in the dance one or more of the leaders while sitting within the circle would beat upon the earth with his extended palm, then lay his hand upon his head, afterward blow into his hand, and then repeat the operation, praying all the time. Sometimes the hypnotist would beat the ground in the same way and then lay his hand on the head of the subject (plate CXV). No satisfactory explanation of this ceremony was obtained beyond the general idea that the earth, like the sun, the fire, and the water, is sacred.

GIVING THE FEATHER

The ceremony of "giving the feather" has been already noticed. This was an official ordination of the priests in the dance, conferred on them by the apostle who first brought the ceremony to the tribe. Among the Arapaho, Caddo, Kiowa, and adjoining tribes in the south the feather was conferred by Sitting Bull himself. The feather was thus given to seven leaders, or sometimes to fourteen, that is, seven men and seven women, the number seven being sacred with most tribes and more particularly in the Ghost dance. The feather, which was worn upon the head of the dancers, was either that of the crow, the sacred bird of the Ghost dance, or of the eagle, sacred in all Indian religions. If from the crow, two feathers were used, being attached at a slight angle to a small stick which was thrust into the hair. (See Arapaho song 8.) The feathers were previously consecrated by the priest with prayer and ceremony. The chosen ones usually reciprocated with presents of ponies, blankets, or other property. After having thus received the feather the tribe began to make songs of its own, having previously used those taught them by the apostle from his own language.

Besides the seven leaders who wear the sacred crow feathers as emblems of their leadership, nearly all the dancers wear feathers variously painted and ornamented, and the preparation of these is a matter of much concern. The dancer who desires instruction on this point usually takes with him six friends, so as to make up the sacred number of seven, and goes with them to one who has been in a trance and has thus learned the exact method in vogue in the spirit world. At their request this man prepares for each one a feather, according to what he has seen in some trance vision, for which they return thanks, usually with a small present. The feathers are painted in several colors, each larger feather usually being tipped with a small down feather painted in a different color. On certain occasions a special day is set apart for publicly painting and preparing the feathers for all the dancers, the work being done by the appointed leaders of the ceremony.

THE PAINTING OF THE DANCERS

The painting of the dancers is done with the same ceremonial exactness of detail, each design being an inspiration from a trance vision. Usually the dancer adopts the particular style of painting which, while in the trance, he has seen worn by some departed relative. If he has not yet been in a trance, the design is suggested by a vision of one who does the painting. In making the request the dancer lays his hands upon the head of the leader and says, "My father, I have come to be painted, so that I may see my friends; have pity on me and paint me," the sacred paint being held to sharpen the spiritual vision as well as to be conducive to physical health. The painting consists of elaborate designs in red, yellow, green, and blue upon the face, with a red or yellow line along the parting of the hair. Suns, crescents, stars, crosses, and birds (crows) are the designs in most common use.

THE CEREMONY

The dance commonly begins about the middle of the afternoon or later, after sundown. When it begins in the afternoon, there is always an intermission of an hour or two for supper. The announcement is made by the criers, old men who assume this office apparently by tacit understanding, who go about the camp shouting in a loud voice to the people to prepare for the dance. The preliminary painting and dressing is usually a work of about two hours. When all is ready, the leaders walk out to the dance place, and facing inward, join hands so as to form a small circle. Then, without moving from their places they sing the opening song, according to previous agreement, in a soft undertone. Having sung it through once they raise their voices to their full strength and repeat it, this time slowly circling around in the dance. The step is different from that of most other Indian dances, but very simple, the dancers moving from right to left, following the course of the sun, advancing the left foot and following it with the right, hardly lifting the feet from the ground. For this reason it is called by the Shoshoni the "dragging dance." All the songs are adapted to the simple measure of the dance step. As the song rises and swells the people come singly and in groups from the several tipis, and one after another joins the circle until any number from fifty to five hundred men, women, and children are in the dance. When the circle is small, each song is repeated through a number of circuits. If large, it is repeated only through one circuit, measured by the return of the leaders to the starting point. Each song is started in the same manner, first in an undertone while the singers stand still in their places, and then with full voice as they begin to circle around. At intervals between the songs, more especially after the trances have begun, the dancers unclasp hands and sit down to smoke or talk for a few minutes. At such times the leaders sometimes deliver short addresses or sermons, or relate the recent trance experience of the dancer. In holding each other's hands the dancers usually intertwine the fingers instead of grasping the hand as with us. Only an Indian could keep the blanket in place as they do under such circumstances. Old people hobbling along with sticks, and little children hardly past the toddling period sometimes form a part of the circle, the more vigorous dancers

THE GHOST DANCE—SMALL CIRCLE

accommodating the movement to their weakness. Frequently a woman will be seen to join the circle with an infant upon her back and dance with the others, but should she show the least sign of approaching excitement watchful friends lead her away that no harm may come to the child. Dogs are driven off from the neighborhood of the circle lest they should run against any of those who have fallen into a trance and thus awaken them. The dancers themselves are careful not to disturb the trance subjects while their souls are in the spirit world. Full Indian dress is worn, with buckskin, paint, and feathers, but among the Sioux the women discarded the belts ornamented with disks of German silver, because the metal had come from the white man. Among the southern tribes, on the contrary, hats were sometimes worn in the dance, although this was not considered in strict accordance with the doctrine.

No drum, rattle, or other musical instrument is used in the dance, excepting sometimes by an individual dancer in imitation of a trance vision. In this respect particularly the Ghost dance differs from every other Indian dance. Neither are any fires built within the circle, so far as known, with any tribe excepting the Walapai. The northern Cheyenne, however, built four fires in a peculiar fashion outside of the circle, as already described. With most tribes the dance was performed around a tree or pole planted in the center and variously decorated. In the southern plains, however, only the Kiowa seem ever to have followed this method, they sometimes dancing around a cedar tree. On breaking the circle at the end of the dance the performers shook their blankets or shawls in the air, with the idea of driving away all evil influences. On later instructions from the messiah all then went down to bathe in the stream, the men in one place and the women in another, before going to their tipis. The idea of washing away evil things, spiritual as well as earthly, by bathing in running water is too natural and universal to need comment.

The peculiar ceremonies of prayer and invocation, with the laying on of hands and the stroking of the face and body, have several times been described and need only be mentioned here. As trance visions became frequent the subjects strove to imitate what they had seen in the spirit world, especially where they had taken part with their departed friends in some of the old-time games. In this way gaming wheels, shinny sticks, hummers, and other toys or implements would be made and carried in future dances, accompanied with appropriate songs, until the dance sometimes took on the appearance of an exhibition of Indian curios on a small scale.

THE CROW DANCE

Within the last few years the southern Arapaho and Cheyenne have developed an auxiliary dance called the "crow dance," which is performed in the afternoon as a preliminary to the regular Ghost dance at night. As it is no part of the original Ghost dance and is confined to these two tribes, it deserves no extended notice in this connection. Although claimed by its inventors as a direct inspiration from the other world, where they saw it performed by "crows," or spirits of departed friends, it is really only a modification of the picturesque Omaha dance of the prairie tribes, with the addition of religious features borrowed from the new doctrine. The men participating are stripped to the breechcloth, with their whole bodies painted as in the Omaha dance, and wear elaborate pendants of varicolored feathers hanging down behind from the waist. An immense drum is an important feature. Men and women take part, and the songs refer to the general subject of the crow and the messiah, but are set to a variety of dance steps and evolutions performed by the dancers. As the leaders, who are chiefly young men, are constantly studying new features, the crow dance has become one of the most attractive ceremonies among the prairie tribes. Hypnotism and trances form an essential feature of this as of the Ghost dance proper. (See plate CXIX.)

THE HYPNOTIC PROCESS

The most important feature of the Ghost dance, and the secret of the trances, is hypnotism. It has been hastily assumed that hypnotic knowledge and ability belong only to an overripe civilization, such as that of India and ancient Egypt, or to the most modern period of scientific investigation. The fact is, however, that practical knowledge, if not understanding, of such things belongs to people who live near to nature, and many of the stories told by reliable travelers of the strange performances of savage shamans can be explained only on this theory. Numerous references in the works of the early Jesuit missionaries, of the Puritan writers of New England and of English explorers farther to the south, would indicate that hypnotic ability no less than sleight-of-hand dexterity formed part of the medicine-man's equipment from the Saint Lawrence to the Gulf. Enough has been said in the chapters on Smohalla and the Shakers to show that hypnotism exists among the tribes of the Columbia, and the author has had frequent opportunity to observe and study it in the Ghost dance on the plains. It can not be said that the Indian priests understand the phenomenon, for they ascribe it to a supernatural cause, but they know how to produce the effect, as I have witnessed hundreds of times. In treating of the subject in connection with the Ghost dance the author must be understood as speaking from the point of view of an observer and not as a psychologic expert.

Immediately on coming among the Arapaho and Cheyenne in 1890, I heard numerous stories of wonderful things that occurred in the Ghost dance—how people died, went to heaven and came back again, and how they talked with dead friends and brought back messages from the other world. Quite a number who had thus "died" were mentioned and their adventures in the spirit land were related with great particularity of

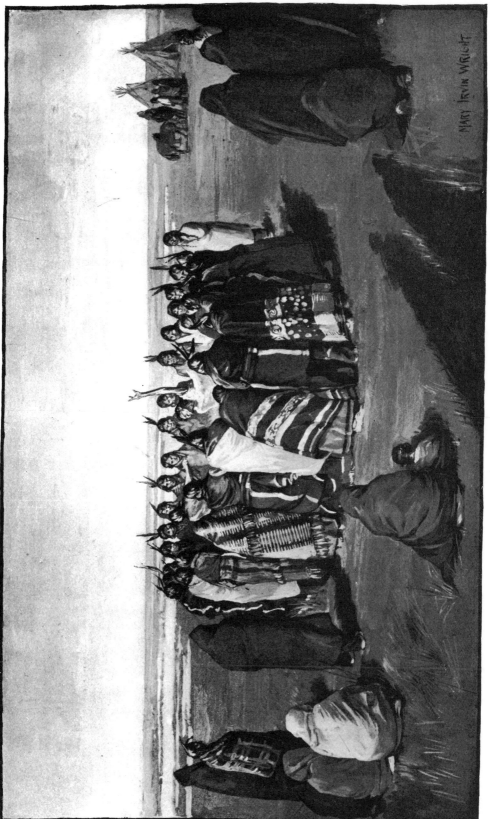

MARY IRVIN WRIGHT

THE GHOST DANCE—LARGER CIRCLE

detail, but as most of the testimony came from white men, none of whom had seen the dance for themselves, I preserved the scientific attitude of skepticism. So far as could be ascertained, none of the intelligent people of the agency had thought the subject sufficiently worthy of serious consideration to learn whether the reports were true or false. On talking with the Indians I found them unanimous in their statements as to the visions, until I began to think there might be something in it.

The first clew to the explanation came from the statement of his own experience in the trance, given by Paul Boynton, a particularly bright Carlisle student, who acted as my interpreter. His brother had died some time before, and as Paul was anxious to see and talk with him, which the new doctrine taught was possible, he attended the next Ghost dance, and putting his hands upon the head of Sitting Bull, according to the regular formula, asked him to help him see his dead brother. Paul is of an inquiring disposition, and, besides his natural longing to meet his brother again, was actuated, as he himself said, by a desire to try "every Indian trick." He then told how Sitting Bull had hypnotized him with the eagle feather and the motion of his hands, until he fell unconscious and did really see his brother, but awoke just as he was about to speak to him, probably because one of the dancers had accidentally brushed against him as he lay on the ground. He embodied his experience in a song which was afterward sung in the dance. From his account it seemed almost certain that the secret was hypnotism. The explanation might have occurred to me sooner but for the fact that my previous Indian informants, after the manner of some other witnesses, had told only about their trance visions, forgetting to state how the visions were brought about.

This was in winter and the ground was covered deeply with snow, which stopped the dancing for several weeks. In the meantime I improved the opportunity by visiting the tipis every night to learn the songs and talk about the new religion. When the snow melted, the dances were renewed, and as by this time I had gained the confidence of the Indians I was invited to be present and thereafter on numerous occasions was able to watch the whole process by which the trances were produced. From the outside hardly anything can be seen of what goes on within the circle, but being a part of the circle myself I was able to see all that occurred inside, and by fixing attention on one subject at a time I was able to note all the stages of the phenomenon from the time the subject first attracted the notice of the medicine-man, through the staggering, the rigidity, the unconsciousness, and back again to wakefulness. On two occasions my partner in the dance, each time a woman, came under the influence and I was thus enabled to note the very first nervous tremor of her hand and mark it as it increased in violence until she broke away and staggered toward the medicine-man within the circle.

Young women are usually the first to be affected, then older women, and lastly men. Sometimes, however, a man proves as sensitive as the average woman. In particular I have seen one young Arapaho become rigid in the trance night after night. He was a Carlisle student, speaking good English and employed as clerk in a store. He afterward took part in the sun dance, dancing three days and nights without food, drink, or sleep. He is of a quiet, religious disposition, and if of white parentage would perhaps have become a minister, but being an Indian, the same tendency leads him into the Ghost dance and the sun dance. The fact that he could endure the terrible ordeal of the sun dance would go to show that his physical organization is not frail, as is frequently the case with hypnotic or trance subjects. So far as personal observation goes, the hypnotic subjects are usually as strong and healthy as the average of their tribe. It seems to be a question more of temperament than of bodily condition or physique. After having observed the Ghost dance among the southern tribes at intervals during a period of about four years, it is apparent that the hypnotic tendency is growing, although the original religious excitement is dying out. The trances are now more numerous among the same number of dancers. Some begin to tremble and stagger almost at the beginning of the dance, without any effort on the part of the medicine-man, while formerly it was usually late in the night before the trances began, although the medicine-men were constantly at work to produce such result. In many if not in most cases the medicine-men themselves have been in trances produced in the same fashion, and must thus be considered sensitives as well as those hypnotized by them.

Not every leader in the Ghost dance is able to bring about the hypnotic sleep, but anyone may try who feels so inspired. Excepting the seven chosen ones who start the songs there is no priesthood in the dance, the authority of such men as Sitting Bull and Black Coyote being due to the voluntary recognition of their superior ability or interest in the matter. Any man or woman who has been in a trance, and has thus derived inspiration from the other world, is at liberty to go within the circle and endeavor to bring others to the trance. Even when the result is unsatisfactory there is no interference with the performer, it being held that he is but the passive instrument of a higher power and therefore in no way responsible. A marked instance of this is the case of Cedar Tree, an Arapaho policeman, who took much interest in the dance, attending nearly every performance in his neighborhood, consecrating the ground and working within the circle to hypnotize the dancers. He was in an advanced stage of consumption, nervous and excitable to an extreme degree, and perhaps it was for this reason that those who came under his influence in the trance constantly complained that he led them on the "devil's road" instead of the "straight road;" that he made them see monstrous and horrible shapes, but never the friends whom they wished to see. On this account they all dreaded to see him at work within the circle, but no one commanded him to desist as it was held that he was controlled by a stronger power and was to be pitied rather than blamed for his ill success. A similar idea

THE GHOST DANCE—LARGE CIRCLE

exists in Europe in connection with persons reputed to possess the evil eye. Cedar Tree himself deplored the result of his efforts and expressed the hope that by earnest prayer he might finally be able to overcome the evil influence.

We shall now describe the hypnotic process as used by the operators, with the various stages of the trance. The hypnotist, usually a man, stands within the ring, holding in his hand an eagle feather or a scarf or handkerchief, white, black, or of any other color. Sometimes he holds the feather in one hand and the scarf in the other. As the dancers circle around singing the songs in time with the dance step the excitement increases until the more sensitive ones are visibly affected. In order to hasten the result certain songs are sung to quicker time, notably the Arapaho song beginning *Nŭ'nanŭ'naatani'na Hu'hu*. We shall assume that the subject is a woman. The first indication that she is becoming affected is a slight muscular tremor, distinctly felt by her two partners who hold her hands on either side. The medicine-man is on the watch, and as soon as he notices the woman's condition he comes over and stands immediately in front of her, looking intently into her face and whirling the feather or the handkerchief, or both, rapidly in front of her eyes, moving slowly around with the dancers at the same time, but constantly facing the woman. All this time he keeps up a series of sharp exclamations, Hu! Hu! Hu! like the rapid breathing of an exhausted runner. From time to time he changes the motion of the feather or handkerchief from a whirling to a rapid up-and-down movement in front of her eyes. For a while the woman continues to move around with the circle of dancers, singing the song with the others, but usually before the circuit is completed she loses control of herself entirely, and, breaking away from the partners who have hold of her hands on either side, she staggers into the ring, while the circle at once closes up again behind her. She is now standing before the medicine-man, who gives his whole attention to her, whirling the feather swiftly in front of her eyes, waving his hands before her face as though fanning her, and drawing his hand slowly from the level of her eyes away to one side or upward into the air, while her gaze follows it with a fixed stare. All the time he keeps up the Hu! Hu! Hu! while the song and the dance go on around them without a pause. For a few minutes she continues to repeat the words of the song and keep time with the step, but in a staggering, drunken fashion. Then the words become unintelligible sounds, and her movements violently spasmodic, until at last she becomes rigid, with her eyes shut or fixed and staring, and stands thus uttering low pitiful moans (plate CXVII). If this is in the daytime, the operator tries to stand with his back to the sun, so that the full sunlight shines in the woman's face (plate CXVI). The subject may retain this fixed, immovable posture for an indefinite time, but at last falls heavily to the ground, unconscious and motionless (plate CXVIII). The dance and the song never

stop, but as soon as the woman falls the medicine-man gives his attention to another subject among the dancers. The first one may lie
unconscious for ten or twenty minutes or sometimes for hours, but no
one goes near to disturb her, as her soul is now communing with the
spirit world. At last consciousness gradually returns. A violent tremor
seizes her body as in the beginning of the fit. A low moan comes from
her lips, and she sits up and looks about her like one awaking from
sleep. Her whole form trembles violently, but at last she rises to her
feet and staggers away from the dancers, who open the circle to let
her pass. All the phenomena of recovery, except rigidity, occur in
direct reverse of those which precede unconsciousness.

Sometimes before falling the hypnotized subject runs wildly around
the circle or out over the prairie, or goes through various crazy evolutions like those of a lunatic. On one occasion—but only once—I have
seen the medicine-man point his finger almost in the face of the hypnotized subject, and then withdrawing his finger describe with it a large
circle about the tipis. The subject followed the direction indicated,
sometimes being hidden from view by the crowd, and finally returned,
with his eyes still fixed and staring, to the place where the medicine-
man was standing. There is frequently a good deal of humbug mixed
with these performances, some evidently pretending to be hypnotized
in order to attract notice or to bring about such a condition from force
of imitation, but the greater portion is unquestionably genuine and
beyond the control of the subjects. In many instances the hypnotized
person spins around for minutes at a time like a dervish, or whirls the
arms with apparently impossible speed, or assumes and retains until
the final fall most uncomfortable positions which it would be impossible
to keep for any length of time under normal conditions. Frequently a
number of persons are within the ring at once, in all the various stages
of hypnotism. The proportion of women thus affected is about three
times that of men.

THE AREA COVERED BY THE DANCE

It is impossible to give more than an approximate statement as to
the area of the Ghost dance and the messiah doctrine and the number
of Indians involved. According to the latest official report, there are
about 146,000 Indians west of Missouri river, exclusive of the five
civilized nations in Indian Territory. Probably all these tribes heard of
the new doctrine, but only a part took any active interest in it. Generally speaking, it was never taken up by the great tribe of the Navaho,
by any of the Pueblos except the Taos, or by any of the numerous tribes
of the Columbia region. The thirty or thirty-five tribes more or less
concerned with the dance have an aggregate population of about 60,000
souls. A number of these were practically unanimous in their acceptance of the new doctrine, notably the Paiute, Shoshoni, Arapaho, Cheyenne, Caddo, and Pawnee, while of others, as the Comanche, only a

THE GHOST DANCE—PRAYING

small minority ever engaged in it. Only about one-half of the 26,000 Sioux took an active part in it. It may safely be said, however, that the doctrine and ceremony of the Ghost dance found more adherents among our tribes than any similar Indian religious movement within the historic period, with the single possible exception of the crusade inaugurated by Tenskwatawa, the Shawano prophet, in 1805. (See plate LXXXV.)

PRESENT CONDITION OF THE DANCE

Among most of these tribes the movement is already extinct, having died a natural death, excepting in the case of the Sioux. The Shoshoni and some others lost faith in it after the failure of the first predictions. The Sioux probably discontinued the dance before the final surrender, as the battle of Wounded Knee and the subsequent events convinced even the most fanatic believers that their expectations of invulnerability and supernatural assistance were deceptive. The Paiute were yet dancing a year ago, and as their dream has received no such rude awakening as among the Sioux, they are probably still patiently awaiting the great deliverance, in spite of repeated postponements, although the frenzied earnestness of the early period has long ago abated. The Kiowa, who discarded the doctrine on the adverse report of Ä'piatañ, have recently taken up the dance again and are now dancing as religiously as ever under the leadership of the old men, although the progressive element in the tribe is strongly opposed to it. Among the other tribes in Oklahoma—especially the Arapaho, Cheyenne, Caddo, Wichita, Pawnee, and Oto—the Ghost dance has become a part of the tribal life and is still performed at frequent intervals, although the feverish expectation of a few years ago has now settled down into something closely approaching the Christian hope of a reunion with departed friends in a happier world at some time in the unknown future.

As for the great messiah himself, when last heard from Wovoka was on exhibition as an attraction at the Midwinter fair in San Francisco. By this time he has doubtless retired into his original obscurity.

CHAPTER XVI

PARALLELS IN OTHER SYSTEMS

I will pour out my spirit upon all flesh; and your sons and your daughters shall prophesy, your old men shall dream dreams, your young men shall see visions.—*Joel.*

How is it then, brethren? When ye come together every one of you hath a doctrine, hath a revelation.—*I Corinthians.*

THE BIBLICAL PERIOD

The remote in time or distance is always strange. The familiar present is always natural and a matter of course. Beyond the narrow range of our horizon imagination creates a new world, but as we advance in any direction, or as we go back over forgotten paths, we find ever a continuity and a succession. The human race is one in thought and action. The systems of our highest modern civilizations have their counterparts among all the nations, and their chain of parallels stretches backward link by link until we find their origin and interpretation in the customs and rites of our own barbarian ancestors, or of our still existing aboriginal tribes. There is nothing new under the sun.

The Indian messiah religion is the inspiration of a dream. Its ritual is the dance, the ecstasy, and the trance. Its priests are hypnotics and cataleptics. All these have formed a part of every great religious development of which we have knowledge from the beginning of history.

In the ancestors of the Hebrews, as described in the Old Testament, we have a pastoral people, living in tents, acquainted with metal working, but without letters, agriculture, or permanent habitations. They had reached about the plane of our own Navaho, but were below that of the Pueblo. Their mythologic and religious system was closely parallel. Their chiefs were priests who assumed to govern by inspiration from God, communicated through frequent dreams and waking visions. Each of the patriarchs is the familiar confidant of God and his angels, going up to heaven in dreams and receiving direct instructions in waking visits, and regulating his family and his tribe, and ordering their religious ritual, in accord with these instructions. Jacob, alone in the desert, sleeps and dreams, and sees a ladder reaching to heaven, with angels going up and down upon it, and God himself, who tells him of the future greatness of the Jewish nation. So Wovoka, asleep on the mountain, goes up to the Indian heaven and is told by the Indian god of the coming restoration of his race. Abraham is "tempted" by God and commanded to sacrifice his son, and proceeds to carry out the supernatural injunction. So Black Coyote dreams and is commanded to sacrifice himself for the sake of his children.

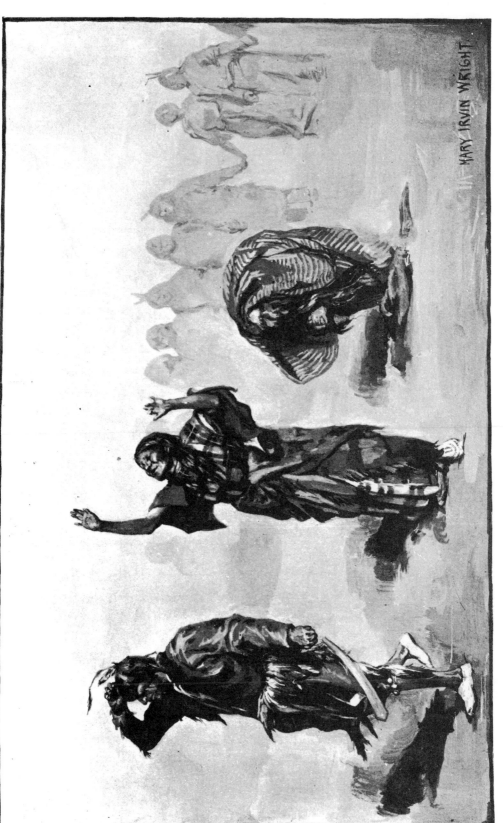

MARY IRVIN WRIGHT

THE GHOST DANCE—INSPIRATION

Coming down to a later period we find the Chaldean Job declaring that God speaketh "in a dream, in a vision of the night, when deep sleep falleth upon men; then he openeth the ears of men and sealeth their instruction." The whole of the prophecies are given as direct communications from the other world, with the greatest particularity of detail, as, for instance, in the beginning of the book of Ezekiel, where he says that "it came to pass in the thirtieth year, in the fourth month, in the fifth day of the month, as I was among the captives by the river of Chebar, that the heavens were opened and I saw visions of God."

In the New Testament, representing the results of six centuries of development beyond the time of the prophets and in intimate contact with more advanced civilizations, we still have the dream as the controlling influence in religion. In the very beginning of the new dispensation we are told that, while Joseph slept, the angel of the Lord appeared to him in a dream, and as a result "Joseph being raised from sleep did as the angel of the Lord had bidden him." The most important events in the history of the infant redeemer are regulated, not in accordance with the ordinary manner of probabilities, but by dreams.

The four gospels are full of inspirational dreams and trances, such as the vision of Cornelius, and that of Peter, when he went up alone upon the housetop to pray and "fell into a trance and saw heaven opened," and again when "a vision appeared to Paul in the night," of a man who begged him to come over into Macedonia, so that "immediately we endeavored to go into Macedonia, assuredly gathering that the Lord had called us." In another place Paul—the same Paul who had that wonderful vision on the road to Damascus—declares that he knew a man who was caught up into paradise and heard unspeakable words. In Paul, we have the typical religious evangel, a young enthusiast, a man of sensibility and refinement above his fellows, so carried away by devotion to his ideal that he attaches himself to the most uncompromising sect among his own people, and when it seems to be assailed by an alien force, not content simply to hold his own belief, he seeks and obtains official authority to root out the heresy. As he goes on this errand, "breathing out threatenings and slaughter," the mental strain overcomes him. He falls down in the road, hears voices, and sees a strange light. His companions raise him up and lead him by the hand into the city, where for several days he remains sightless without food or drink. From this time he is a changed man. Without any previous knowledge or investigation of the new faith he believes himself called by heaven to embrace it, and the same irrepressible enthusiasm which had made him its bitterest persecutor leads him now to defend it against all the world and even to cross the sea into a far country in obedience to a dream to spread the doctrine. In many respects he reminds us forcibly of such later evangelists as Fox and Wesley.

The cloudy indistinctness which Wovoka and his followers ascribe to the Father as he appears to them in their trance visions has numerous parallels in both Testaments. At Sinai the Lord declares to Moses, "I come unto thee in a thick cloud," and thereafter whenever Moses went up the mountain or entered into the tabernacle to receive revelations "the Lord descended upon it in a cloudy pillar." Job also tells us that "thick clouds are a covering to him," and Isaiah says that he "rideth upon a swift cloud," which reminds us of the Ghost song of the Arapaho representing the Indian redeemer as coming upon the whirlwind. Moses goes up into a mountain to receive inspiration like Wovoka of the Paiute and Bi'äñk'i of the Kiowa. As Wovoka claims to bring rain or snow at will, so Elijah declares that "there shall not be dew nor rain these years, but according to my word," while of the Jewish Messiah himself his wondering disciples say that even the winds and the sea obey him.

Fasting and solitary contemplation in lonely places were as powerful auxiliaries to the trance condition in Bible days as now among the tribes of the plains. When Daniel had his great vision by the river Hiddekel, he tells us that he had been mourning for three full weeks, during which time he "ate no pleasant bread, neither came flesh nor wine in my mouth, neither did I anoint myself at all." When the vision comes, all the strength and breath leave his body and he falls down, and "then was I in a deep sleep on my face, and my face toward the ground." Six hundred years later, Christ is "led by the spirit into the wilderness, being forty days tempted by the devil, and in those days he did eat nothing." Another instance occurs at his baptism, when, as he was coming out of the water, he saw the heavens opened and the spirit like a dove, and heard a voice, and immediately was driven by the spirit into the wilderness. In the transfiguration on the mountain, when "his face did shine as the sun," and in the agony of Gethsemane, with its mental anguish and bloody sweat, we see the same phenomena that appear in the lives of religious enthusiasts from Mohammed and Joan of Arc down to George Fox and the prophets of the Ghost dance.

Dancing, which forms so important a part of primitive rituals, had a place among the forms of the ancient Hebrew and of their neighbors, although there are but few direct references to it in the Bible. The best example occurs in the account of the transfer of the ark to Zion, where there were processions and sacrifices, and King David himself "danced before the Lord with all his might."

MOHAMMEDANISM

Six hundred years after the birth of Christianity another great religion, which numbers its adherents by the hundred million, had its origin in the same region and among a kindred Semitic race. Its prophet and high priest was the cataleptic Mohammed, who was born about the year 570 and died in 642. In infancy and all through life he was afflicted with epileptic attacks and fainting fits, during which he would lose all appearance of life without always losing inner consciousness. It was while in this condition that he received the visions and revelations on which he built his religious system. Frequently at such times it was necessary to wrap him up to preserve life in his body, and

THE GHOST DANCE—RIGID

at other times he was restored by being drenched with cold water. At one time for a period of two years he was in such a mental condition—subject to hallucinations—that he doubted his own sanity, believing himself to be possessed by evil spirits, and contemplated suicide. "It is disputed whether Mohammed was epileptic, cataleptic, hysteric, or what not. Sprenger seems to think that the answer to this medical question is the key to the whole problem of Islam." (*"Mohammedanism,"* in *Encyclopedia Britannica.*) To how many other systems might such an answer be the key?

We are told that ordinarily his body had but little natural warmth, but that whenever the angel appeared to him, as the Mohammedan biographers express it, the perspiration burst out on his forehead, his eyes became red, he trembled violently, and would bellow like a young camel—all the accompaniments of the most violent epileptic fit. Usually the fit ended in a swoon. There is no question that he was sincere in his claim of divine inspiration. His last hours were serene and peaceful, and there is no evidence of the slightest misgiving on his part as to the reality of his mission as a prophet sent from God. Some of his inspiration came in dreams, and he was accustomed to say that a prophet's dream is a revelation. At times the revelation came to him without any painful or strange accompaniment.

The fit during which he received the revelation of his religious mission is thus described, as it came to him after a long period of despondency and mental hallucinations: "In this morbid state of feeling he is said to have heard a voice, and on raising his head, beheld Gabriel, who assured him he was the prophet of God. Frightened, he returned home, and called for covering. He had a fit, and they poured cold water on him, and when he came to himself he heard these words: 'Oh, thou covered one, arise, and preach, and magnify thy Lord;' and henceforth, we are told, he received revelations without intermission. Before this supposed revelation he had been medically treated on account of the evil eye, and when the Koran first descended to him he fell into fainting fits, when, after violent shudderings, his eyes closed, and his mouth foamed." (*Gardner, Faiths of the World.*)

Solitude also had much to do with his visions, as a great part of his early life was spent in the lonely occupation of a shepherd among the Arabian mountains. Like other prophets he asserted that the various angels had offered him control over the stars, the sun, the mountains, and the sea. Further, it is claimed most positively by all his followers that his great ascent into the seven heavens was made bodily and in full wakefulness, and not merely in spirit while asleep, and this assertion they supported by "the declarations of God and his prophet, the imâms of the truth, the verses of the Koran, and thousands of traditions," as earnestly as religious enthusiasts the world over have ever backed up the impossible.

The kinship of the late Semitic idea to the old is well exemplified in Mohammed's account of this vision, in which he is conducted to Mount

Sinai, where he is directed to alight and pray, because there God had spoken to Moses, after which he is conducted to Bethlehem, where again he is directed to alight and pray, because there Jesus was born, after which again he is brought into the presence of Abraham, Moses, Enoch, John the Baptist, and Jesus, by all of whom he was hailed as a worthy brother and prophet. The direct descent becomes plainer still when we learn how Mohammed, on his return from talking with God in the seventh heaven, again meets Moses, who persuades him that the religious exercises prescribed by God for the faithful are too onerous, and goes back with him to plead with the Lord for a reduction of the daily prayers from fifty to five as Abraham pleaded for Sodom.

The spirit world of our Indians is a place where death and old age are unknown, and where every one is happy in the simple happiness which he knew on earth—hunting, feasting, and playing the old-time games with former friends, but without war, for there all is peace. The ideal happiness is material, perhaps, but it is such happiness as the world might long for, with nothing in it gross or beyond reasonable probability. The Semitic ideal, from which our own is derived, is very different. We get one conception in the book of Revelation and another six hundred years later in the vision of Mohammed, which is puerile to the last degree. Among its wonders are an houri, who comes out of a quince, and whose body is composed of camphor, amber, and musk. Then there is a cock which stands with his feet on the lowest earth, while his head reaches the empyrean and his wings outstretched the limits of space, whose business is every morning to praise the Lord and set all the cocks on earth to crowing after him. There is an angel who bathes daily in a river, after which he flaps his wings, and from every drop that falls from them there is created an angel with 20,000 faces and 40,000 tongues, each of which speaks a distinct language, unintelligible to the rest. But the masterpiece is the tree *tooba*, whose fruit is the food of the inhabitants of paradise. Every branch produces a hundred thousand different-colored fruits, while from its roots run rivers of water, milk, wine, and honey. As if this were not enough, the tree produces also ready-made clothing. "On the tree were baskets filled with garments of the brocade and satin of paradise. A million of baskets are allotted to each believer, each basket containing a hundred thousand garments, all of different class and fashion"—and so on ad nauseam. (*Merrick's Mohammed.*) When we reflect that this is accepted by more than 150,000,000 civilized Orientals, from whom we have derived much of our own culture, we may, perhaps, be more tolerantly disposed toward the American Indian belief.

JOAN OF ARC

The most remarkable, the most heroic and pathetic instance of religious hallucination in Europe is that of Joan of Arc, known as the Maid of Orleans, born in 1412 and burned at the stake in 1431, and recently

THE GHOST DANCE—UNCONSCIOUS

beatified as the patron saint of France.   Naturally of a contemplative disposition, she was accustomed from earliest childhood to long fasts and solitary communings, in which she brooded over the miserable condition of her country, then overrun by English armies.   When 13 years of age, she had a vision in which a voice spoke to her from out of a great light, telling her that God had chosen her to restore France. She immediately fell on her knees and made a vow of virginity and entire devotion to the cause, and from that day to the time of her cruel death she believed herself inspired and guided by supernatural voices to lead her countrymen against the invader.   A simple peasant girl, she sought out the royal court and boldly announced to the king her divine mission.   Her manner made such an impression that she was assigned a command, and putting on a soldier's dress and carrying a sword which she claimed had come to her through miraculous means, she led the armies of France, performing superhuman feats of courage and endurance and winning victory after victory for three years until she was finally captured.   After a long and harassing mockery of a trial, in which the whole machinery of the law and the church was brought into action for the destruction of one poor girl barely 19 years of age, she was finally condemned and burned at Rouen, ostensibly as a witch and a heretic, but really as the most dangerous enemy of English tyranny in France.

She was forever hearing these spirit voices, which she called "her voices" or "her counsel."   They spoke to her with articulate words in the ripple of the village fountain, in the vesper bells, in the rustling of the leaves, and in the sighing of the wind.   Sometimes it was the war-like archangel Michael, but oftener it was the gentle Saint Katherine, who appeared to her as a beautiful woman wearing a crown.   Her visions must be ascribed to the effect of the troubled times in which she lived, acting on an enthusiastic, unquestioning religious temper-ament.   She is described as physically robust and intellectually keen, aside from her hallucination, as was proven in her trial, and there is no evidence that she was subject to epilepsy or other abnormal condi-tions such as belonged to Mohammed and most others of the same class.   Her long and frequent fasts unquestionably aided the result. She claimed no supernatural powers outside of her peculiar mission, and in every public undertaking relied entirely on the guidance of her voices.

Toward the end these voices were accompanied by other hallucina-tions, together with presentiments of her coming death.   On one occasion, while assaulting a garrison, her men fled, leaving her stand-ing on the moat with only four or five soldiers.   Seeing her danger, a French officer galloped up to rescue her and impatiently asked her why she stood there alone.   Lifting her helmet from her face she looked at him with astonishment and replied that she was not alone—that she had 50,000 men with her—and then, despite his entreaties, she turned to her phantom army and shouted out her commands to bring logs to bridge the moat.   It was in April, while standing alone on the ramparts of Mélun, that the voices first told her that she would be taken before midsummer. From that time the warning was constantly repeated, and although she told no one and still exposed herself fearlessly, she no longer assumed the responsibility of command. Two months later she was in the hands of her enemies.

Throughout the trial every effort was made by her enemies to shake her statement as to the voices, or, failing in that, to prove them from the devil, but to the last she steadfastly maintained that the voices were with her and came from heaven. According to her own statement these voices were three—one remained always with her, another visited her at short intervals, while both deliberated with the third. On one occasion, when hard pressed by her enemies, she answered solemnly, "I believe firmly, as firmly as I believe the Christian faith and that God has redeemed us from the pains of hell, that the voice comes from God and by his command." And again she asserted, "I have seen Saint Michael and the two saints so well that I know they are saints of paradise. I have seen them with my bodily eyes, and I believe they are saints as firmly as I believe that God exists."

When questioned as to her original inspiration, she stated that the voice had first come to her when she was about 13 years of age. "The first time I heard it I was very much afraid. It was in my father's garden at noon in the summer. I had fasted the day before. The voice came from the right hand by the church, and there was a great light with it. When I came into France, I heard it frequently. I believe it was sent me from God. After I heard it three times, I knew it was the voice of an angel. I understand perfectly what it says. It bade me be good and go to church often, and it told me I must go into France. Two or three times a week it said I must go into France, until I could no longer rest where I was. It told me I should raise the siege of Orleans, and that Robert de Baudricourt would give me people to conduct me. Twice he repulsed me, but the third time he received me and sped me on my way."

The examiners were very curious to know by what sign she had recognized the king when she had first seen him in the midst of his courtiers. To this question she said she must first consult with Saint Katherine before replying, and afterward continued: "The sign was a crown. The first time I saw the king he had the sign, and it signified that he should hold the kingdom of France. I neither touched it nor kissed it. The angel came by the command of God and entered by the door of the room. I came with the angel up the steps to the king's room and the angel came before the king and bowed and inclined himself before the king, and said: 'My lord, here is your sign; take it.' He departed by the way he had come. There were a number of other angels with him, and Saint Katherine and Saint Margaret. In the little chapel he left me. I was neither glad nor afraid, but I was very sorrowful, and I wish he had taken away my soul with him."

THE CROW DANCE

To another question she replied emphatically: "If I were at judgment, if I saw the fire kindled and the fagots ablaze and the executioner ready to stir the fire, and if I were in the fire, I would say no more, and to the death I would maintain what I have said in the trial."

The end came at last in the market place of Rouen, when this young girl, whose name for years had been a terror to the whole English army, was dragged in her white shroud and bound to the stake, and saw the wood heaped up around her and the cruel fire lighted under her feet. "Brother Martin, standing almost in the draft of the flames, heard her sob with a last sublime effort of faith, bearing her witness to God whom she trusted: 'My voices have not deceived me!' And then came death." (*Parr, Jeanne d'Arc.*)

DANCE OF SAINT JOHN

In 1374 an epidemic of maniacal religious dancing broke out on the lower Rhine and spread rapidly over Germany, the Netherlands, and into France. The victims of the mania claimed to dance in honor of Saint John. Men and women went about dancing hand in hand, in pairs, or in a circle, on the streets, in the churches, at their homes, or wherever they might be, hour after hour without rest until they fell into convulsions. While dancing they sang doggerel verses in honor of Saint John and uttered unintelligible cries. Of course they saw visions. At last whole companies of these crazy fanatics, men, women, and children, went dancing through the country, along the public roads, and into the cities, until the clergy felt compelled to interfere, and cured the dancers by exorcising the evil spirits that moved them. In the fifteenth century the epidemic broke out again. The dancers were now formed into divisions by the clergy and sent to the church of Saint Vitus at Rotestein, where prayers were said for them, and they were led in procession around the altar and dismissed cured. Hence the name of Saint Vitus' dance given to one variety of abnormal muscular tremor. (*Schaff, Religious Encyclopedia.*)

THE FLAGELLANTS

About the same time another strange religious extravagance spread over western Europe. Under the name of Flagellants, thousands of enthusiasts banded together with crosses, banners, hymns, and all the paraphernalia of religion, and went about in procession, publicly scourging one another as an atonement for their sins and the sins of mankind in general. They received their first impetus from the preaching of Saint Anthony of Padua in the thirteenth century. About the year 1260 the movement broke out nearly simultaneously in Italy, France, Germany, Austria, and Poland, and afterward spread into Denmark and England. It was at its height in the fourteenth century. In Germany in 1261 the devotees, preceded by banner and crosses, marched with faces veiled and bodies bared above the waist, and scourged themselves twice a day for thirty-three successive days in memory of the thirty-three years of Christ's life. The strokes of the whip were timed to the music of hymns. Men and women together took part in the scourging. The mania finally wore itself out, but reappeared in 1349 with more systematic organization. According to Schaff, "When they came to towns, the bands marched in regular military order and singing hymns. At the time of flagellation they selected a square or churchyard or field. Taking off their shoes and stockings and forming a circle, they girded themselves with aprons and laid down flat on the ground. . . . The leader then stepped over each one, touched them with the whip, and bade them rise. As each was touched they followed after the leader and imitated him. Once all on their feet the flagellation began. The brethren went two by two around the whole circle, striking their backs till the blood trickled down from the wounds. The whip consisted of three thongs, each with four iron teeth. During the flagellation a hymn was sung. After all had gone around the circle the whole body again fell on the ground, beating upon their breasts. On arising they flagellated themselves a second time. While the brethren were putting on their clothes a collection was taken up among the audience. The scene was concluded by the reading of a letter from Christ, which an angel had brought to earth and which commended the pilgrimages of the Flagellants. The fraternities never tarried longer than a single day in a town. They gained great popularity, and it was considered an honor to entertain them." (*Schaff, Religious Encyclopedia.*) The society still exists among the Latin races, although under the ban of the church. As late as 1820 a procession of Flagellants passed through the streets of Lisbon. Under the name of Penitentes they have several organizations in the Mexican towns of our southwest, where they periodically appear in processions, inflicting horrible self-torture on themselves, even to the extent of binding one of their number upon a cross, which is then set up in the ground, while the blood streams down the body of the victim from the wounds made by a crown of cactus thorns and from innumerable gashes caused by the thorny whips. Such things among people called civilized enables us to understand the feeling which leads the Indian to offer himself a willing sacrifice in the sun dance and other propitiatory rites.

RANTERS, QUAKERS, AND FIFTH-MONARCHY MEN

The middle of the seventeenth century was a time of great religious and political upheaval in England. Hatreds were intense and persecutions cruel and bitter, until men's minds gave way under the strain. "The air was thick with reports of prophecies and miracles, and there were men of all parties who lived on the border land between sanity and insanity." This was due chiefly to the long-continued mental tension which bore on the whole population during this troublous period, and in particular cases to wholesale confiscations, by which families were ruined, and to confinement in wretched prisons, suffering from insufficient food and brutal treatment. Individuals even in the established church began to assert supernatural power, while numerous new sects sprang up, with prophecy, miracle working, hypnotism, and convulsive ecstasy as parts of their doctrine or ritual. Chief among these were the Ranters, the Quakers, and the Fifth-Monarchy Men. The first and last have disappeared with the conditions which produced them; but the Quakers, being based on a principle, have outlasted persecution, and, discarding the extravagances which belonged to the early period, are now on a permanent foundation under the name of the "Society of Friends." One of the Ranter prophets, in 1650, claimed to be the reincarnation of Melchizedek, and even declared his divinity. He asserted that certain persons then living were Cain, Judas, Jeremiah, etc, whom he had raised from the dead, and the strangest part of it was that the persons concerned stoutly affirmed the truth of his assertion. Others of them claimed to work miracles and to produce lights and apparitions in the dark. In Barclay's opinion all the evidence "supports the view that these persons were mad, and had a singular power of producing a kind of sympathetic madness or temporary aberration of intellect in others."

We are better acquainted with the Quakers (Friends), although it is not generally known that they were originally addicted to similar practices. Such, however, is the fact, as is shown by the name itself. Their founder, George Fox, claimed and believed that he had the gift of prophecy and clairvoyance, and of healing by a mere word, and his biographer, Janney, of the same denomination, apparently sees no reason to doubt that such was the case. As might have been expected, he was also a believer in dreams.

We are told that on one occasion, on coming into the town of Lichfield, "a very remarkable exercise attended his mind, and going through the streets without his shoes he cried, 'Woe to the bloody city of Lichfield.' His feelings were deeply affected, for there seemed to be a channel of blood running down the streets, and the market place appeared like a pool of blood." On inquiry he learned that a large number of Christians had been put to death there during the reign of the Emperor Diocletian thirteen centuries before. "He therefore attributed the exercise which came upon him to the sense that was given him of the blood of the martyrs."

We are also told that he "received an evidence" of the great fire of London in 1666, before the event, and Janney narrates at length a "still more remarkable vision" of the same fire by another Friend, "whose prophecy is well attested." According to the account, this man rode into the city, as though having come in haste, and went up and down the streets for two days, prophesying that the city would be destroyed by fire. To others of his own denomination he declared that he had had a vision of the event some time before, but had delayed to declare it as commanded, until he felt the fire in his own bosom.

When the fire did occur as he had predicted, he stood before the flames with arms outstretched, as if to stay their advance, until forcibly brought away by his friends.

In mental and physical temperament Fox seems to have closely resembled Mohammed and the Indian prophets of the Ghost dance. We are told that he had much mental suffering and was often under great temptation. "He fasted much, and walked abroad in solitary places. Taking his Bible, he sat in hollow trees or secluded spots, and often at night he walked alone in silent meditation." At one time "he fell into such a condition that he looked like a corpse, and many who came to see him supposed him to be really dead. In this trance he continued fourteen days, after which his sorrow began to abate, and with brokenness of heart and tears of joy he acknowledged the infinite love of God." (*Janney, George Fox.*)

The sect obtained the name of Quakers from the violent tremblings which overcame the worshipers in the early days, and which they regarded as manifestations of divine power on them. So violent were these convulsions that, as their own historian tells us, on one occasion the house itself seemed to be shaken. According to another authority, men and women sometimes fell down and lay upon the ground struggling as if for life. Their ministers, however, seem not to have encouraged such exhibitions, but strove to relieve the fit by putting the patient to bed and administering soothing medicines. ("*Quakers,*" *Encyclopedia Britannica.*)

The Fifth-Monarchy Men were a small band of religionists who arose about the same time, proclaiming that the "Fifth Monarchy" prophesied by Daniel was at hand, when Christ would come down from heaven and reign visibly upon earth for a thousand years. In 1657 they formed a plot to kill Cromwell, and in 1661 they broke out in insurrection at night, parading the streets with a banner on which was depicted a lion, proclaiming that Christ had come and declaring that they were invulnerable and invincible, as "King Jesus" was their invisible leader. Troops were called out against them, but the Fifth-Monarchy Men, expecting supernatural assistance, refused to submit, and fought until they were nearly all shot down. The leaders were afterward tried and executed. (*Janney's George Fox* and *Schaff's Religious Encyclopedia.*)

FRENCH PROPHETS

Forty years later, about the end of the seventeenth century, another sect of convulsionists, being driven out of France, "found an asylum in Protestant countries [and] carried with them the disease, both of mind and body, which their long sufferings had produced." They spread into Germany and Holland, and in 1706 reached England, where they became known as "French prophets." Their meetings were characterized by such extravagance of convulsion and trance performance that they became the wonder of the ignorant and the scandal of the more intelligent classes, notwithstanding which the infection spread far and wide. We are told that they " were wrought upon in a very extraordinary manner, not only in their minds, but also in their physical systems. They had visions and trances and were subject to violent agitations of body. Men and women, and even little children, were so exercised that spectators were struck with great wonder and astonishment. Their powerful admonitions and prophetic warnings were heard and received with reverence and awe."

At one time Charles Wesley had occasion to stop for the night with a gentleman who belonged to the sect. Wesley was unaware of the fact until, as they were about to go to bed, his new friend suddenly fell into a violent fit and began to gobble like a turkey. Wesley was frightened and began exorcising him, so that he soon recovered from the fit, when they went to bed, although the evangelist confesses that he himself did not sleep very soundly with Satan so near him.

Some time afterward Wesley with several companions visited a prophetess of the sect, as he says, to try whether the spirits came from God. She was a young woman of agreeable speech and manner. "Presently she leaned back in her chair and had strong workings in her breast and uttered deep sighs. Her head and her hands and by turns every part of her body were affected with convulsive motions. This continued about ten minutes. Then she began to speak with a clear, strong voice, but so interrupted with the workings, sighings, and contortions of her body that she seldom brought forth half a sentence together. What she said was chiefly in spiritual words, and all as in the person of God, as if it were the language of immediate inspiration." (*Southey's Wesley, I,* and *Evans' Shakers.*)

JUMPERS

About 1740 a similar extravagant sect, known as the Jumpers, arose in Wales. According to the description given by Wesley, their exercises were a very exact parallel of the Ghost dance. "After the preaching was over anyone who pleased gave out a verse of a hymn, and this they sung over and over again, with all their might and main, thirty or forty times, till some of them worked themselves into a sort of drunkenness or madness; they were then violently agitated, and leaped up and down in all manner of postures frequently for hours together." A contemporary writer states that he had seen perhaps ten thousand at a single meeting of the Jumpers shouting out in the midst of the sermon and ready to leap for joy. (*Southey's Wesley,* II.)

METHODISTS

About the same time the Methodists originated in England under Wesley and Whitefield, and their assemblies were characterized by all the hysteric and convulsive extravagance which they brought with them to this country, and which is not even yet extinct in the south.

The most remarkable of these exhibitions took place under the preaching of Wesley, following him, as we are told, wherever he went. Whitefield, although more forcible and sensational in his preaching, did not at first produce the same effect on his hearers, and considered such manifestations as but doubtful signs of the presence of the Lord and by no means to be encouraged. On preaching, however, to a congregation in which Wesley had already produced such convulsions, and where, consequently, there was a predisposition in this direction, several persons were thus seized and sank down upon the floor, and we are told by the biographer "this was a great triumph to Wesley."

Wesley himself describes several instances. At one time, he states, a physician suspecting fraud attended a meeting during which a woman was thrown into a fit, crying aloud and weeping violently, until great drops of sweat ran down her face and her whole body shook. The doctor stood close by, noting every symptom, and not knowing what to think, being convinced that it was not fraud or any natural disorder. "But when both her soul and body were healed in a moment he acknowledged the finger of God." On another occasion, Wesley tells us, "While I was earnestly inviting all men to enter into the Holiest by this new and living way, many of those that heard began to call upon God with strong cries and tears. Some sank down, and there remained no strength in them. Others exceedingly trembled and quaked. Some were torn with a kind of convulsive motion in every part of their bodies, and that so violently that often four or five persons could not hold one of them. I have seen many hysterical and epileptic fits, but none of them were like these in many respects. I immediately prayed that God would not suffer those who were weak to be offended; but one woman was greatly, being sure that they might help it if they would, no one should persuade her to the contrary; and she was got three or four yards, when she also dropped down in as violent an agony as the rest."

At another time, "while he was speaking one of his hearers dropped down, and in the course of half an hour seven others, in violent agonies. The pains as of hell, he says, came about them; but notwithstanding his own reasoning neither he nor his auditors called in question the divine origin of these emotions, and they went away rejoicing and praising God. . . . Sometimes he scarcely began to speak before some of his believers, overwrought with expectation, fell into the crisis, for so it may be called in this case, as properly as in animal magnetism. Sometimes his voice could scarcely be heard amid the groans and cries of these suffering and raving enthusiasts. It was not long before men, women, and children began to act the demoniac as well as the convert. Wesley had seen many hysterical fits and many fits of epilepsy, but none that were like these, and he confirmed the patients in their belief that they were torn of Satan. One or two indeed perplexed him a little, for they were tormented in such an unaccountable manner that they seemed to be lunatic, he says, as well as sore vexed. But suspicions of this kind made little impression upon his intoxicated understanding; the fanaticism which he had excited in others was now reacting upon himself. How should it have been otherwise? A Quaker, who was present at one meeting and inveighed against what he called the dissimulation of these creatures, caught the contagious emotion himself, and even while he was biting his lips and knitting his brows, dropped down as if he had been struck by lightning." (*Southey's Wesley.*)

SHAKERS

About the year 1750 there originated in England another peculiar body of sectarians calling themselves the "United Society of Believers in Christ's Second Appearing," but commonly known, for obvious reasons, as Shakers. Their chief prophetess and founder was "Mother" Ann Lee, whom they claim as the actual reincarnation of Christ. They claim also the inspiration of prophecy, the gift of healing, and sometimes even the gift of tongues, and believe in the reality of constant intercourse with the spirit world through visions. In consequence of persecution in England, on account of their public dancing, shouting, and shaking, they removed to this country about 1780 and settled at New Lebanon, New York, where the society still keeps up its organization.

The best idea of the Shakers is given in a small volume by Evans, who was himself a member of the sect. Speaking of the convulsive manifestations among them, he says: "Sometimes, after sitting awhile in silent meditation, they were seized with a mighty trembling, under which they would often express the indignation of God against all sin. At other times they were exercised with singing, shouting, and leaping for joy at the near prospect of salvation. They were often exercised with great agitation of body and limbs, shaking, running, and walking the floor, with a variety of other operations and signs, swiftly passing and repassing each other like clouds agitated with a mighty wind. These exercises, so strange in the eyes of the beholders, brought upon them the appellation of Shakers, which has been their most common name of distinction ever since." With regard to their dancing, he says: "It is pretty generally known that the Shakers serve God by singing and dancing; but why they practice this mode of worship is not so generally understood. . . . When sin is fully removed, by confessing and forsaking it, the cause of heaviness, gloom, and sorrow is gone, and joy and rejoicing, and thanksgiving and praise are then the spontaneous effects of a true spirit of devotion. And whatever manner the spirit may dictate, or whatever the form into which the spirit may lead, it is acceptable to Him from whom the spirit proceeds." On one particular occasion, "previous to our coming we called a meeting and there was [sic] so many gifts (such as prophecies, revelations, visions, and dreams) in confirmation of a former revelation for us to come that some could hardly wait for others to tell their gifts. We had a joyful meeting and danced till morning."

Of Ann Lee, their founder, he asserts that she saw Jesus Christ in open vision and received direct revelations from this source. On a certain occasion she herself declared to her followers: " The room over your head is full of angels of God. I see them, and you could see them if you were redeemed. I look in at the windows of heaven and see what there is in the invisible world. I see the angels of God, and hear them sing. I see the glories of God. I see Ezekiel Goodrich flying from one heaven to another!" And, turning to the company present, she said, "Go in and join his resurrection." She then began to sing, and they praised the Lord in the dance. On another occasion she said: " The apostles, in their day, saw as through a glass darkly, but we see face to face, and see things as they are, and converse with spirits and see their states. The gospel is preached to souls who have left the body. I see thousands of the dead rising and coming to judgment, now at this present time." At another time she declared that she had seen a certain young woman in the spirit world, "praising God in the dance;" and of a man deceased, " He has appeared to me again, and has arisen from the dead and come into the first heaven and is traveling on to the second and third heaven."

Their dance is performed regularly at their religious gatherings at the New Lebanon settlement. The two sexes are arranged in ranks opposite and facing each other, in which position they listen to a sermon by one of the elders, after which a hymn is sung. They then form a circle around a party of singers, to whose singing they keep time in the dance. At times the excitement and fervor of spirit become intense, and their bodily evolutions as rapid as those of the dervishes, although still preserving the order of the dance. (*Evans' Shakers* and encyclopedia articles on *Shakers.*)

KENTUCKY REVIVAL

About the year 1800 an epidemic of religious frenzy, known as the Kentucky Revival, broke out in Kentucky and Tennessee, chiefly among the Methodists and Baptists, with accompaniments that far surpassed the wildest excesses of the Ghost dance. Fanatic preachers taught their deluded followers that the spiritual advent of the kingdom was near at hand, when Christ would reign on earth and there would be an end of all sin. The date generally fixed for the consummation was the summer of 1805, and the excitement continued and grew in violence for several years until the time came and passed without extraordinary event, when the frenzy gradually subsided, leaving the ignorant believers in a state of utter collapse. The performances at the meetings of these enthusiasts were of the most exaggerated camp-meeting order, such as may still be witnessed in many parts of the south, especially among the colored people. Evans, the Shaker historian, who is strong in the gift of faith, tells us that "the subjects of this work were greatly exercised in dreams, visions, revelations, and the spirit of prophecy. In these gifts of the spirit they saw and testified that the great day of

God was at hand, that Christ was about to set up his kingdom on earth, and that this very work would terminate in the full manifestation of the latter day of glory."

From another authority, endowed perhaps with less of fervor but with more of common sense, we get a description of these "exercises" which has a familiar ring that seems to bring it very near home. "The people remained on the ground day and night, listening to the most exciting sermons, and engaging in a mode of worship which consisted in alternate crying, laughing, singing, and shouting, accompanied with gesticulations of a most extraordinary character. Often there would be an unusual outcry; some bursting forth into loud ejaculations of thanksgiving; others exhorting their careless friends to 'turn to the Lord;' some struck with terror, and hastening to escape; others trembling, weeping, and swooning away, till every appearance of life was gone, and the extremities of the body assumed the coldness of a corpse. At one meeting not less than a thousand persons fell to the ground, apparently without sense or motion. It was common to see them shed tears plentifully about an hour before they fell. They were then seized with a general tremor, and sometimes they uttered one or two piercing shrieks in the moment of falling. This latter phenomenon was common to both sexes, to all ages, and to all sorts of characters." (*Caswall, The Prophet of the Nineteenth Century*, quoted by *Remy*.)

After a time these crazy performances in the sacred name of religion became so much a matter of course that they were regularly classified in categories as the rolls, the jerks, the barks, etc. "The rolling exercise was affected by doubling themselves up, then rolling from one side to the other like a hoop, or in extending the body horizontally and rolling over and over in the filth like so many swine. The jerk consisted in violent spasms and twistings of every part of the body. Sometimes the head was twisted round so that the head was turned to the back, and the countenance so much distorted that not one of its features was to be recognized. When attacked by the jerks, they sometimes hopped like frogs, and the face and limbs underwent the most hideous contortions. The bark consisted in throwing themselves on all fours, growling, showing their teeth, and barking like dogs. Sometimes a number of people crouching down in front of the minister continue to bark as long as he preached. These last were supposed to be more especially endowed with the gifts of prophecy, dreams, rhapsodies, and visions of angels." (*Remy, Journey to Great Salt Lake City, I.*)

Twenty years later the jerking epidemic again broke out in Tennessee, and is described in a letter by the famous visionary and revivalist, Lorenzo Dow, who was then preaching in the same region. His description agrees with that given the author by old men who lived at this time in eastern Tennessee. We quote from Dow's letter: "There commenced a trembling among the wicked. One and a second fell from their seats. I think for eleven hours there was no cessation of the loud cries. Of the people, some who were standing and sitting fell like men shot on the field of battle, and I felt it like a tremor to run through my soul and veins so that it took away my limb power, so that I fell to the floor, and by faith saw a greater blessing than I had hitherto experienced." At another place he says: "After taking a cup of tea, I began to speak to a vast audience, and I observed about thirty to have the jerks, though they strove to keep as still as they could. These emotions were involuntary and irresistible, as any unprejudiced mind might see." At Marysville "many appeared to feel the word, but about fifty felt the jerks. On Sunday, at Knoxville, the governor being present, about one hundred and fifty had the jerking exercise, among them a circuit preacher, Johnson, who had opposed them a little while before. Camp meeting commenced at Liberty. Here I saw the jerks, and some danced. The people are taken with jerking irresistibly, and if they strive to resist it it worries them more than hard work. Their eyes, when dancing, seem to be fixed upward as if upon an invisible object, and they are lost to all below. I passed by a meeting house where I observed the undergrowth had been cut down for a camp meeting, and from fifty to a hundred saplings left breast high, which appeared to me so slovenish that I could not but ask my guide the cause, who observed they were topped so high and left for the people to jerk by. This so excited my attention that I went over the ground to view it, and found where the people had laid hold of them and jerked so powerfully that they kicked up the earth as a horse stamping flies. Persecutors are more subject to the jerks than others, and they have cursed and swore and damned it while jerking." Then he says: "I have seen Presbyterians, Methodists, Quakers, Baptists, Church of England, and Independents exercised with the jerks—gentlemen and ladies, black and white, rich and poor—without exception. Those naturalists who wish to get it to philosophize upon it and the most godly are excepted from the jerks. The wicked are more afraid of it than of the smallpox or yellow fever."

It is worthy of note that, according to his account, investigators who wished to study the phenomenon were unable to come under the influence, even though they so desired.

ADVENTISTS

About 1831 William Miller, a licensed minister, began to preach the advent of Christ and the destruction of the world, fixing the date for the year 1843. Like most others of his kind who have achieved notoriety, he based his prediction on the prophecies of the Bible, which he figured out with mathematical exactness. He began preaching in New York and New England, but afterward traveled southward, delivering, it is said, over three thousand lectures in support of his theory. His predictions led to the formation of a new sect commonly known as

Adventists, who are said at one time to have numbered over fifty thousand. Carried away by blind enthusiasm they made their preparations for the end of all things, which they confidently expected in the summer of 1843. As the time drew near the believers made all preparations for their final departure from the world, many of them selling their property, and arraying themselves in white "ascension robes," which were actually put on sale by the storekeepers for the occasion. But the day and the year went by without the fulfillment of the prophecy. Miller claimed to have discovered an error in his calculations and fixed one or two other dates later on, but as these also proved false, his followers lost faith and the delusion died out. The Adventists still number fifteen or twenty thousand, the largest body being in southern Michigan, but although they hold the doctrine of the near advent of the final end, and endeavor to be at all times ready, they no longer undertake to fix the date.

It may be noted here that the idea of a millennium, when the Messiah shall come in person upon the earth and reign with the just for a thousand years, was so firmly held by many of the early Christians that it may almost be said to have formed a part of the doctrinal tradition of the church. The belief was an inheritance from the Jews, many of whose sacred writers taught that time was to endure through seven great "years" of a thousand years each, the seventh and last being the Sabbatical year or millennium, when their Messiah would appear and make their kingdom the mistress of the world. For this materialistic view of the millennium the Christian fathers substituted a belief in the spiritual triumph of religion, when the armies of antichrist would be annihilated, but the expectation of the return of Christ to rule in person over his church before the last days was an essential part of the doctrine, founded on numerous prophecies of both the Old and the New Testament.

OTHER PARALLELS

BEEKMANITES

It would require a volume to treat of the various religious abnormalisms, based on hypnotism, trances, and the messiah idea, which have sprung up and flourished in different parts of our own country even within the last twenty years. Naturally these delusions thrived best among the ignorant classes, but there were some notable exceptions, particularly in the case of the Beekmanites or "Church of the Redeemed." About 1875 Mrs Dora Beekman, the wife of a Congregational minister in Rockford, Illinois, began preaching that she was the immortal reincarnation of Jesus Christ. Absurd as this claim may appear, she found those who believed her, and as her converts increased in numbers they established their headquarters, which they called "heaven," near Rockford, built a church, and went zealously to work to gather proselytes. Beekman refused to believe the new doctrine, but being unable to convince his wife of her folly he was finally driven to insanity. In the meantime the female Christ found an able disciple in the Reverend George Schweinfurth, a young Methodist minister of considerable cultivation and ability, who was installed as bishop and apostle of the new sect. Mrs Beekman dying soon after, in spite of her claim to immortality, Schweinfurth at once stepped into her place, declaring that the Christly essence had passed from her into himself. His claim was accepted, and when last heard from, about three years ago, he was worshiped by hundreds of followers drawn from the most prominent denominations of the vicinity as the risen Christ, the lord of heaven and the immortal maker and ruler of the earth. (*J. F. L.*, *6*, and current newspapers.)

PATTERSON AND BROWN'S MISSION

In 1888 a man named Patterson, in Soddy, a small town in eastern Tennessee, began preaching that a wonderful thing was about to happen, and after the matter had been talked about sufficiently for his purpose, he announced that Christ had come in the person of A. J. Brown, who had served as Patterson's assistant. Later on Brown disappeared, and it was announced that he had gone up into the mountain to fast for forty days and nights in order to be fittingly prepared for his mission. At the end of this period, on a Sunday morning in June, his followers went out toward the hills, where he suddenly appeared before them, clothed in white, with his hands uplifted. A great shout went up, and the people rushed toward him, falling upon their knees and kissing his feet. Many who were ill declared themselves healed by his touch. So great was the fanaticism of these people that one girl declared she was ready to die to prove her faith, and the nonbelievers became so fearful that human life would be sacrificed that they sent for the sheriff at Chattanooga, and it required all his power to compel Patterson and Brown to leave the neighborhood that quiet might be restored. (*J. F. L.*, *6*.)

WILDERNESS WORSHIPERS

In 1889 and 1890 a remarkable messianic excitement developed among the negroes along Savannah river in Georgia and South Carolina, where one man after another proclaimed himself as Christ, promised miracles, drew crowds of excited men and women from their work, and created a general alarm among the white population of the whole section. The most prominent of these Christs was a mulatto named Bell, who went about preaching his divinity and exhorting all who would be saved to give up everything and follow him. Hundreds of negroes abandoned the cotton fields, the sawmills, and the turpentine woods to follow him, obeying his every word and ready to fall down and worship him. They assumed the name of "Wilderness Worshipers," and set up in the woods a "temple" consisting of a series of circular seats around an oak. The excitement became so demoralizing and dangerous that Bell was finally arrested. His frenzied disciples would have resisted the officers, but he commanded them to be patient, declaring that he could not be harmed and that an angel would come and open his prison doors by night. As no specific charge could be formulated against him, he was released after a short time, and continued his preaching to greater crowds than before. At last he announced that the world would come to an end on August 16, 1890; that all the negroes would then turn white and all white men black, and that all who wished to ascend on the last day must purchase wings from him. (*J. F. L., 6.*) He was finally adjudged insane and sent to the asylum. Successors arose in his place, however, and kept up the excitement for a year afterward in spite of the efforts of the authorities to put a stop to it. One of these claimed to be King Solomon, while another asserted that he was Nebuchadnezzar, and emphasized his claim by eating grass on all fours. In addition to the " temple" in the woods they set up an "ark," and were told by the leaders that any persecutors who should sacrilegiously attempt to touch it would fall down dead. Notwithstanding this warning, the officers destroyed both ark and temple in their efforts to end the delusion. At last a woman was killed by the enthusiasts, and a series of wholesale arrests followed. King Solomon, Nebuchadnezzar, and others who were clearly insane were sent to join Bell in the asylum, and the others were released from custody after the excitement had waned.

HEAVENLY RECRUITS

Within the last five years various local revivalists have attracted attention in different sections of Indiana, Illinois, and Missouri, by their extravagances, among which prophecies, visions, trances, and frenzied bodily exercises were all prominent. Particularly at the meetings of the " Heavenly Recruits" in central Indiana, and at other gatherings under the direction of Mrs Woodworth, cataleptic trances were of nightly occurrence. The physical and mental demoralization at last became so great that the meetings were suppressed by the authorities.

From the beginning of history the dance and kindred physical exercises have formed a part of the religious ritual of various oriental sects, while hypnotic powers and practices have been claimed for their priests. This is especially true of the Mohammedan sect or order of the Dervishes, of which some account is given in the appendix to this chapter.

APPENDIX—HYPNOTISM AND THE DANCE AMONG THE DERVISHES

[From Brown's Dervishes]

HYPNOTISM.—It is through the performance of the Zikr, by khalvet (pious retirement for purposes of deep devotion), by the Tevejjuh (or turning the face or mind devoutly toward God in prayer), by the Murakebeh (or fearful contemplation of God), the Tesarruf (or self-abandonment to pious reflection and inspiration), and the Tesavvuf (or mystical spiritualism), that the fervent Dervish reaches peculiar spiritual powers called *Kuvveh i roohee batinee* (a mystical, internal, spiritual power). The life or biography of every eminent sheikh or peer details innumerable evidences of this power exercised in a strange and peculiar manner. This exercise is called the Kuvveh Iradat, or the "Power of the Will," and, as a theory, may be traced historically to the Divine Power—the soul of man being connected with the Divine Spirit—from which it emanates, and with which, through the means before mentioned, it commences. Some sheikhs are more celebrated than others for their peculiar and strange powers, and it is to their superiority that their reputation and reverence in the Mussulman world in general, and among Dervishes in particular, is to be attributed. With the supposition that the details given of them by their biographers, disciples, or successors are not invented, or even exaggerated, their powers are certainly very remarkable. Whilst among them an implicit belief in them is firmly sustained, sultans and princes have evidently doubted them, and, being alarmed with the influence the possessors acquired and sustained among the public generally, they have often shown a direful exercise of their own arbitrary will and power, which resulted in the untimely end of the unfortunate sheikh. Many, on the other hand, have survived the frequent exercise of their "spiritual powers," and either because they acquired a power and influence over the minds of their temporal rulers, or whether they used them for their own private purposes, so as to conciliate the more religious or fanatic, they succeeded in reaching advanced ages and a peaceful end of their remarkable careers. When the ruler of the country has not cared to order the execution of the sheikh who declared himself possessed of these spiritual powers, he has simply exiled him from his capital or his territory, and permitted him freely to exercise his powers and renown in some less objectionable locality. These powers can only be acquired through the long instruction of a superior spiritual director, or Murshid, or As-hâb i Yekeen, for whom the disciples ever retain a most grateful remembrance and attachment.

Among the practices of these powers is the faculty of foreseeing coming events; of predicting their occurrence; of preserving individuals from the harm and evil which would otherwise certainly result for them; of assuring to one person success over the machinations of another, so that he may freely attack him and prevail over him; of restoring harmony of sentiment between those who would otherwise be relentless enemies; of knowing when others devised harm against themselves, and through certain spells of preserving themselves and causing harm to befall the evil minded, and even of causing the death of anyone against whom they wish to proceed. All this is done as well from a distance as when near.

In other parts of the world, and among other people, these attainments would have been attributed to sorcery and witchcraft; in modern times they would be ascribed to spiritism, or magnetic influences, either of the spirit or of the body; but to the instructed Dervish they all derive their origin in the spirit of the holy sheikh—the special gift of the great Spirit of God, which commences with the spirit of man, from which it directly emanated. The condition or disposition necessary for these effects is called the Hâl (state or frame), and is much the same as that required by the magnetized, and the object of his operation. The powers of the body are enfeebled by fasting and mental fatigue in prayer, and the imagination kept in a fervid state, fully impressed with the conviction that such powers are really possessed by the sheikh, and that he can readily exercise them over the willing mind and body of the disciple. How the sheikh can produce such strange results on a distant and unconscious person is left to the admiration and imagination of the faithful disciple, as an incentive to exertions in the same true path as that of his sheikh.

To exercise the power of the will, it is necessary to contract the thoughts suddenly upon the object designed to be affected so perfectly as to leave no room for the mind to dwell, possibly, upon any other. The mind must not doubt for an instant of the success of this effort, nor the possibility of failure; it must, in fact, be completely absorbed by the one sole idea of performing the determination strongly taken and firmly relied upon. The persons must, from time to time, practice this; and as they proceed, they will be able to see how much propinquity exists between themselves and the Hazret i Asmâ (God?) and how much they are capable of exercising this power.

As an example, the author of the Reshihât narrates the following:

In my youth, I was ever with our Lord Molâná Sa'eed ed Deen Kâshgharee at Hereed. It happened that we, one day, walked out together and fell in with an assembly of the inhabitants of the place who were engaged in wrestling. To try our powers we agreed to aid with our "powers of the will" one of the wrestlers, so that the other should be overcome by him, and after doing so, to change our design in favor of the discomfited individual. So we stopped and, turning toward the parties, gave the full influence of our united wills to one, and immediately he was able to subdue his opponent. As the person we chose, each in turn, conquered the other, whichever we willed to prevail became the most powerful of the two, the power of our own wills was thus clearly manifested.

On another occasion two other persons possessed of these same powers fell in with an assembly of people at a place occupied by prize fighters. "To prevent any of the crowd from passing between and separating us we joined our hands together. Two persons were engaged fighting; one was a powerful man, while the other was a spare and weak person. The former readily overcame the latter; and seeing this I proposed to my companion to aid the weak one by the power of our wills. So he bade me aid him in the project, while he concentrated his powers upon the weaker person. Immediately a wonderful occurrence took place; the thin, spare man seized his giant-like opponent and threw him on the ground with surprising force. The crowd cried out with astonishment as he turned him over on his back and held him down with apparent ease. No one present except ourselves knew the cause. Seeing that my companion was much affected by the effort which he had made, I bade him remark how perfectly successful we had been, and adding that there was no longer any necessity for our remaining there, we walked away." (Pages 129–132.)

* * * * * * * *

Many individuals who have seriously wronged and oppressed his friends received punishments through the powers of the sheikh. Several instances are related wherein some such even fell sick and died, or were only restored to health by open declarations of repentance and imploring his prayerful intercession with God. His spirit seems to have accompanied those in whose welfare he took an active interest, and enabled them to commune with him, though far distant from him. His power of hearing them was well known to his friends, and several instances are cited to prove the fact. His power of affecting the health of those who injured him or his friends was greatly increased while he was excited by anger, and on such occasions his whole frame would be convulsed and his beard move about as if moved by electricity. On learning details of cruelty done to innocent individuals, the sheikh would be strangely affected, so much so that no one dared to address him until the paroxysm was passed; and on such occasions he never failed to commune spiritually with the sovereign or prince in such a mysterious manner as to inspire him to deal justly with the guilty person and secure his merited punishment.

Through his "mystical powers" many persons were impressed with the unrighteousness of their course, and, having repented of the same, became good and pious and firm believers in his spiritual influences. These powers were always connected with his prayers, and it was during these that he was enabled to assure the parties interested of their salutary results and the acceptation of their desires. It scarcely needs to be added, that these prayers were in conformance with Islamism, and were offered up to Allah, whom he adored, and to whose supreme will he attributes his powers. He constantly performed the Zikr Jehree, or "audibly called God's name," and the frequent repetition of this practice fitted him for such holy purposes. Sometimes he would affect the mind of the individual upon whom he exercised his powers in such a manner as to throw him into a species of trance, after which he could remember nothing that he had previously known, and continued in this state until the sheikh chose to restore him to the enjoyment of his ordinary faculties. Notwithstanding all of these eminent powers, this great sheikh is reputed to have spent the latter days of his life at Herat in extreme indigence, much slighted and neglected by those who had so admired him while in the vigor of his career. All fear of his mystical influences seems to have disappeared, and it is narrated that these greatly declined with his ordinary strength of mind and body. (Pages 137–139.)

*　　　*　　　*　　　*　　　*　　　*　　　*

DERVISH DANCE.—The exercises which are followed in these halls are of various kinds, according to the rules of each institution; but in nearly all they commence by the recital, by the sheikh, of the seven mysterious words of which we have spoken. He next chants various passages of the Koran, and at each pause, the Dervishes, placed in a circle round the hall, respond in chorus by the word "Allah!" or "Hoo!" In some of the societies they sit on their heels, the elbows close to those of each other, and all making simultaneously light movements of the head and the body. In others, the movement consists in balancing themselves slowly, from the right to the left, and from the left to the right, or inclining the body methodically forward and aft. There are other societies in which these motions commence seated, in measured cadences, with a staid countenance, the eyes closed or fixed upon the ground, and are continued on foot. These singular exercises are concentrated under the name of Murâkebeh (exaltation of the Divine glory), and also under that of the Tevheed (celebration of the Divine unity), from which comes the name Tevheed Khâneh, given to the whole of the halls devoted to these religious exercises.

In some of these institutions—such as the Kâdirees, the Rufâ'ees, the Khalwettees, the Bairâmees, the Gulshenees, and the Ushâkees—the exercises are made each holding the other by the hand, putting forward always the right foot and increasing at every step the strength of the movement of the body. This is called the Devr, which may be translated the "dance" or "rotation." The duration of these dances is arbitrary—each one is free to leave when he pleases. Everyone, however, makes it a point to remain as long as possible. The strongest and most robust of the number, and the most enthusiastic, strive to persevere longer than the others; they uncover their heads, take off their turbans, form a second circle within the other, entwine their arms within those of their brethren, lean their shoulders against each other, gradually raise the voice, and without ceasing repeat "Yâ Allah!" or "Yâ Hoo!" increasing each time the movement of the body, and not stopping until their entire strength is exhausted.

Those of the order of the Rufâ'ees excel in these exercises. They are, moreover, the only ones who use fire in their devotions. Their practices embrace nearly all those of the other orders; they are ordinarily divided into five different scenes, which last more than three hours, and which are preceded, accompanied, and followed by certain ceremonies peculiar to this order. The first commences with praises which all the Dervishes offer to their sheikhs, seated before the altar. Four of the more ancient come forward the first, and approach their superior, embrace each other as if to give the kiss of peace, and next place themselves two to his right and two to his left. The remainder of the Dervishes, in a body, press forward in a procession, all having their arms crossed and their heads inclined. Each one, at first, salutes by a profound bow the tablet on which the name of his founder is inscribed. Afterwards, putting his two hands over his face and his beard, he kneels before the sheikh, kisses his hand respectfully, and then they all go on with a grave step to take their places on the sheepskins, which are spread in a half circle around the interior of the hall. So soon as a circle is formed, the Dervishes together chant the Tekbeer and the Fâtiha. Immediately afterwards the sheikh pronounces the words "Lâ ilâha ill' Allah!" and repeats them incessantly; to which the Dervishes repeat "Allah!" balancing themselves from side to side, and putting their hands over their faces, on their breasts and their abdomens, and on their knees.

The second scene is opened by the Hamdee Mohammedee, a hymn in honour of the prophet, chanted by one of the elders placed on the right of the sheikh. During this chant the Dervishes continue to repeat the word "Allah!" moving, however, their bodies forward and aft. A quarter of an hour later they all rise up, approach each other, and press their elbows against each other, balancing from right to left and afterwards in a reverse motion, the right foot always firm, and the left in a periodical movement, the reverse of that of the body, all observing great precision of measure and cadence. In the midst of this exercise they cry out the words "Yâ Allah!" followed by that of "Yâ Hoo!" Some of the performers sigh, others sob, some shed tears, others perspire great drops, and all have their eyes closed, their faces pale, and the eyes languishing.

A pause of some minutes is followed by a third scene. It is performed in the middle of an Ilahee, chanted by the two elders on the right of the sheikh. The Ilahees, as has already been said, are spiritual cantiques, composed almost exclusively in Persian by sheikhs deceased in the odor of sanctity. The Dervishes then hasten their movements, and, to prevent any relaxation, one of the first among them puts himself in their center, and excites them by his example. If in the assembly there be any strange Dervishes, which often happens, they give them, through politeness, this place of honor; and all fill it successively, the one after the other, shaking themselves as aforesaid. The only exception made is in favor of the Mevevees; these never perform any other dance than that peculiar to their own order, which consists in turning round on each heel in succession.

After a new pause commences the fourth scene. Now all the Dervishes take off their turbans, form a circle, bear their arms and shoulders against each other, and thus make the circuit of the hall at a measured pace, striking their feet at intervals against the floor, and all springing up at once. This dance continues during the Ilahees chanted alternately by the two elders to the left of the sheikh. In the midst of this chant the cries of "Yâ Allah!" are increased doubly, as also those of "Yâ Hoo!" with frightful howlings, shrieked by the Dervishes together in the dance. At the moment that they would seem to stop from sheer exhaustion the sheikh makes a point of exerting them to new efforts by walking through their midst, making also himself most violent movements. He is next replaced by the two elders, who double the quickness of the step and the agitation of the body; they even straighten themselves up from time to time, and excite the envy or emulation of the others in their astonishing efforts to continue the dance until their strength is entirely exhausted.

The fourth scene leads to the last, which is the most frightful of all, the wholly prostrated condition of the actors becoming converted into a species of ecstasy which they call Halet. It is in the midst of this abandonment of self, or rather of religious delirium, that they make use of red-hot irons. Several cutlasses and other instruments of sharp-pointed iron are suspended in the niches of the hall, and upon a part of the wall to the right of the sheikh. Near the close of the fourth scene two Dervishes take down eight or nine of these instruments, heat them red hot, and present them to the sheikh. He, after reciting some prayers over them, and invoking the founder of the order, Ahmed er Rufâ'ee, breathes over them, and raising them slightly to the mouth, gives them to the Dervishes, who ask for them with the greatest eagerness. Then it is that these fanatics, transported by frenzy, seize upon these irons, gloat upon them tenderly, lick them, bite them, hold them between their teeth, and end by cooling them in their mouths. Those who are unable to procure any seize upon the cutlasses hanging on the wall with fury, and stick them into their sides, arms, and legs.

Thanks to the fury of their frenzy, and to the amazing boldness which they deem a merit in the eyes of the Divinity, all stoically bear up against the pain which they

experience with apparent gaiety. If, however, some of them fall under their sufferings, they throw themselves into the arms of their confrères, but without a complaint
or the least sign of pain. Some minutes after this, the sheikh walks round the hall,
visits each one of the performers in turn, breathes upon their wounds, rubs them
with saliva, recites prayers over them, and promises them speedy cures. It is said
that twenty-four hours afterward nothing is to be seen of their wounds. (Pages
218–222.)

*   *   *   *   *   *   *

There was no regularity in their dancing, but each seemed to be performing the
antics of a madman; now moving his body up and down; the next moment turning
round, then using odd gesticulations with his arms, next jumping, and sometimes
screaming; in short, if a stranger observing them was not told that this was the
involuntary effect of enthusiastic excitement, he would certainly think that these
Durweeshes were merely striving to excel one another in playing the buffoon.
(Page 260.)

*   *   *   *   *   *   *

THE FIT.—After this preface, the performers began the Zikr. Sitting in the manner above described, they chanted, in slow measure, Lá iláha illa 'lláh (there is no
deity but God), to the following air: Lá i-lá hailla-lláh. Lá i-lá-ha-illa-l-lá-h. Lá
i-lá ha illa-l-láh. Bowing the head twice on each repetition of "Lá iláha illa 'lláh."
Thus they continued about a quarter of an hour, and then, for about the same space
of time, they repeated the same words to the same air, but in a quicker measure,
and with correspondingly quicker motion. . . .

They next rose, and, standing in the same order in which they had been sitting,
repeated the same words to another air. During this stage of their performance
they were joined by a tall, well-dressed, black slave, whose appearance induced me
to inquire who he was. I was informed that he was a eunuch, belonging to the
basha. The Zikkeers, still standing, next repeated the same words in a very deep
and hoarse tone, laying the principal emphasis upon the word "Lá," and the first
syllable of the last word, Allah, and uttering, apparently with a considerable effort.
The sound much resembled that which is produced by beating the rim of a tambour-
ine. Each Zikkeer turned his head alternately to the right and left at each repetition of "Lá iláha illa 'llah." The eunuch above mentioned, during this part of the
Zikr, became what is termed melboos, or "possessed." Throwing his arms about, and
looking up with a very wild expression of countenance, he exclaimed, in a very high
tone and with great vehemence and rapidity, Allah! Allah! Allah! Allah! Allah! la!
la! la! la! la! la! la! la! la! la! la! la! láh! Yá ʿammee! Yá ʿammee! Yá ʿammee! Ashmáwee! Yá Ashmáwee! Yá Ashmáwee! (Yá ʿammee signifies O, my uncle!) His voice
gradually became faint, and when he had uttered those words, though he was held
by a Durweesh who was next him, he fell on the ground, foaming at the mouth, his
eyes closed, his limbs convulsed, and his fingers clenched over his thumbs. It was
an epileptic fit. No one could see it and believe it to be the effect of feigned
emotions; it was undoubtedly the result of a high state of religious excitement.
Nobody seemed surprised at it, for occurrences of this kind at Zikrs are not uncommon. All the performers now appeared much excited, repeating their ejaculations
with greater rapidity, violently turning their heads, and sinking the whole body at
the same time, some of them jumping. The eunuch became melboos again several
times, and I generally remarked that his fits happened after one of the Moonshids
had sung a line or two, and exerted himself more than usually to excite his hearers.
The singing was, indeed, to my taste, very pleasing. Toward the close of the Zikr
a private soldier, who had joined through the whole performance, also seemed
several times to be melboos, growling in a horrible manner and violently shaking
his head from side to side. The contrast presented by the vehement and distressing
exertions of the performers at the close of the Zikr, and their calm gravity and
solemnity of manner at the commencement, was particularly striking. Money was
collected during the performance for the Moonshid. The Zikkeers receive no pay.
(Pages 252–255.)

THE SONGS

INTRODUCTORY

The Ghost-dance songs are of the utmost importance in connection with the study of the messiah religion, as we find embodied in them much of the doctrine itself, with more of the special tribal mythologies, together with such innumerable references to old-time customs, ceremonies, and modes of life long since obsolete as make up a regular symposium of aboriginal thought and practice. There is no limit to the number of these songs, as every trance at every dance produces a new one, the trance subject after regaining consciousness embodying his experience in the spirit world in the form of a song, which is sung at the next dance and succeeding performances until superseded by other songs originating in the same way. Thus, a single dance may easily result in twenty or thirty new songs. While songs are thus born and die, certain ones which appeal especially to the Indian heart, on account of their mythology, pathos, or peculiar sweetness, live and are perpetuated. There are also with each tribe certain songs which are a regular part of the ceremonial, as the opening song and the closing song, which are repeated at every dance. Of these the closing song is the most important and permanent. In some cases certain songs constitute a regular series, detailing the experiences of the same person in successive trance visions. First in importance, for number, richness of reference, beauty of sentiment, and rhythm of language, are the songs of the Arapaho.

THE ARAPAHO

TRIBAL SYNONYMY

Ähyä'to—Kiowa name; meaning unknown; the Kiowa call the wild plum by the same name.

Ano's-anyotskano—Kichai name.

Ärä'păho—popular name; derivation uncertain; but, perhaps, as Dunbar suggests, from the Pawnee word *tirapihu* or *larapĭhu*, "he buys or trades," in allusion to the Arapaho having formerly been the trading medium between the Pawnee, Osage, and others on the north, and the Kiowa, Comanche, and others to the southwest (*Grinnell letter*).

Äräpăkata—Crow name, from word Arapaho.

Bĕtidĕĕ—Kiowa Apache name.

Detseka'yaa—Caddo name, "dog eaters."

Hitäniwo'ĭv—Cheyenne name, "cloud men."

Inûna-ina—proper tribal name, "our people," or "people of our kind."

Kaninahoic or *Kaninä'vish*—Ojibwa name; meaning unknown.

Komse'ka-K'iñahyup—former Kiowa name; "men of the worn-out leggings;" from *komse'*, "smoky, soiled, worn out;" *kati*, "leggings;" *k'iñahyup*, "men."

Maqpi'ăto—Sioux name, "blue cloud," i. e., clear sky; reason unknown.

Niă'rhari's-kŭrikiwă's-hŭski—Wichita name.

Sani'ti'ka—Pawnee name, from the Comanche name.

Särètika—Comanche and Shoshoni name, "dog eaters," in allusion to their special liking for dog flesh.

Sarĕtika—Wichita name, from the Comanche name.

TRIBAL SIGNS

Southern Arapaho, "*rub noses;*" northern Arapaho, "*mother people;*" Gros Ventres of the Prairie, "*belly people.*"

SKETCH OF THE TRIBE

The Arapaho, with their subtribe, the Gros Ventres, are one of the westernmost tribes of the wide-extending Algonquian stock. According to their oldest traditions they formerly lived in northeastern Minnesota and moved westward in company with the Cheyenne, who at that time lived on the Cheyenne fork of Red river. From the earliest period the two tribes have always been closely confederated, so that they have no recollection of a time when they were not allies. In the westward migration the Cheyenne took a more southerly direction toward the country of the Black hills, while the Arapaho continued more nearly westward up the Missouri. The Arapaho proper probably ascended on the southern side of the river, while the Gros Ventres went up the northern bank and finally drifted off toward the Blackfeet, with whom they have ever since been closely associated, although they have on several occasions made long visits, extending sometimes over several years, to their southern relatives, by whom they are still regarded as a part of the "Inûna-ina." The others continued on to the great divide between the waters of the Missouri and those of the Columbia, then turning southward along the mountains, separated finally into two main divisions, the northern Arapaho continuing to occupy the head streams of the Missouri and the Yellowstone, in Montana and Wyoming, while the southern Arapaho made their camps on the head of the Platte, the Arkansas, and the Canadian, in Colorado and the adjacent states, frequently joining the Comanche and Kiowa in their raids far down into Mexico. From their earliest recollection, until put on reservations, they have been at war with the Shoshoni, Ute, Pawnee, and Navaho, but have generally been friendly with their other neighbors. The southern Arapaho and Cheyenne have usually acted in concert with the Comanche, Kiowa, and Kiowa Apache.

They recognize among themselves five original divisions, each having a different dialect. They are here given in the order of their importance:

1. *Na'kasinĕ'na, Ba'achinĕna* or *Northern Arapaho.* Nakasinĕna, "sagebrush men," is the original name of this portion of the tribe and the divisional name used by themselves. The name Baachinĕna, by which they are commonly known to the rest of the tribe, is more

modern and may mean "red willow (i. e., kinikinik) men," or possibly "blood-pudding men," the latter meaning said to have been an allusion to a kind of sausage formerly made by this band. They are commonly known as northern Arapaho, to distinguish them from the other large division living now in Oklahoma. The Kiowa distinguished them as Tägyä'ko, "sagebrush people," a translation of their proper name, Baachinĕna. Although not the largest division, the Baachinĕna claim to be the "mother people" of the Arapaho, and have in their keeping the grand medicine of the tribe, the sĕicha or sacred pipe.

2. *Na'wunĕna*, "southern men," or *Southern Arapaho*, called *Nawathi'nĕha*, "southerners," by the northern Arapaho. This latter is said to be the archaic form. The southern Arapaho, living now in Oklahoma, constitute by far the larger division, although subordinate in the tribal sociology to the northern Arapaho. In addition to their everyday dialect, they are said to have an archaic dialect, some words of which approximate closely to Cheyenne.

3. *Aä'ninĕna, Hitu'nĕna*, or *Gros Ventres of the Prairie*. The first name, said to mean "white clay people" (from *aäti*, "white clay"), is that by which they call themselves. Hitunĕna or Hitunĕnina, "begging men," "beggars," or, more exactly, "spongers," is the name by which they are called by the other Arapaho, on account, as these latter claim, of their propensity for filling their stomachs at the expense of someone else. The same idea is intended to be conveyed by the tribal sign, which signifies "belly people," not "big bellies" (Gros Ventres), as rendered by the French Canadian trappers. The Kiowa call them Bot-k'iñ'ago, "belly men." By the Shoshoni, also, they are known as Sä'pani, "bellies," while the Blackfeet call them Atsina, "gut people." The Ojibwa call them Bahwetegow-ēninnewug, "fall people," according to Tanner, whence they have sometimes been called Fall Indians or Rapid Indians, from their former residence about the rapids of the Saskatchewan. To the Sioux they are known as Sku'tani. Lewis and Clark improperly call them "Minnetarees of Fort de Prairie." The Hidatsa or Minitari are sometimes known as Gros Ventres of the Missouri.

4. *Bä'sawunĕ'na*, "wood lodge men," or, according to another authority, "big lodge people." These were formerly a distinct tribe and at war with the other Arapaho. They are represented as having been a very foolish people in the old times, and many absurd stories are told of them, in agreement with the general Indian practice of belittling conquered or subordinate tribes. They have been incorporated with the northern Arapaho for at least a hundred and fifty years, according to the statements of the oldest men of that band. Their dialect is said to have differed very considerably from the other Arapaho dialects. There are still about one hundred of this lineage among the northern Arapaho, and perhaps a few others with the two other main divisions. Weasel Bear, the present keeper of the sacred pipe, is of the Bäsawunĕna.

5. *Ha'nahawunĕna* or *Aanŭ'hawă* (meaning unknown). These, like the Bäsawunĕna, lived with the northern Arapaho, but are now practically extinct.

There seems to be no possible trace of a clan or gentile system among the Arapaho, and the same remark holds good of the Cheyenne, Kiowa, and Comanche. It was once assumed that all Indian tribes had the clan system, but later research shows that it is lacking over wide areas in the western territory. It is very doubtful if it exists at all among the prairie tribes generally. Mr Ben Clark, who has known and studied the Cheyenne for half a lifetime, states positively that they have no clans, as the term is usually understood. This agrees with the result of personal investigations and the testimony of George Bent, a Cheyenne half-blood, and the best living authority on all that relates to his tribe. With the eastern tribes, however, and those who have removed from the east or the timbered country, as the Caddo, the gentile system is so much a part of their daily life that it is one of the first things to attract the attention of the observer.

In regard to the tribal camping circle, common to most of the prairie tribes, the Arapaho state that on account of their living in three main divisions they have had no common camping circle within their recollection, but that each of these three divisions constituted a single circle when encamped in one place.

Among the northern Arapaho, on the occasion of every grand gathering, the sacred pipe occupied a special large tipi in the center of the circle, and the taking down of this tipi by the medicine keeper was the signal to the rest of the camp to prepare to move. On the occasion of a visit of several hundred Cheyenne and Arapaho to the Kiowa and Comanche at Anadarko, in the summer of 1892, each of the visiting tribes camped in a separate circle adjacent to the other. The opening of the circle, like the door of each tipi, always faces the east.

Under the name of Kanenăvish the Arapaho proper are mentioned by Lewis and Clark in 1805, as living southwest of the Black hills. As a tribe they have not been at war with the whites since 1868, and took no part in the outbreak of the Cheyenne, Kiowa, and Comanche in 1874. At present they are in three main divisions. First come the Gros Ventres, numbering 718 in 1892, associated with the Asiniboin on Fort Belknap reservation in Montana. There are probably others of this band with the Blackfeet on the British side of the line. Next come the northern Arapaho, numbering 829, associated with the Shoshoni on Wind River reservation in Wyoming. They were placed on this reservation in 1876, after having made peace with the Shoshoni, their hereditary enemy, in 1869. They are divided into three bands, the "Forks of the River Men" under Black Coal, the head chief of the whole division; the "Bad Pipes" under Short Nose, and the "Greasy Faces" under Spotted Horse. The third division, the southern Arapaho, associated with the Cheyenne in Oklahoma, constitute the main body of the tribe and numbered 1,091 in 1892. They have five bands: 1, Wa'quithi, "bad faces," the principal band and the one to which the head chief, Left Hand, belongs; 2, Aqa'thině'na, "pleasant men;" 3, Gawuně'na or Ga'wuněhäna (Kawinahan, "black people"—*Hayden*), "Blackfeet," so called because said to be of part Blackfoot blood, the same name being applied to the Blackfoot tribe; 4, Ha'qihana, "wolves," because they had a wolf (not coyote) for medicine; 5, Säsa'bä-ithi, "looking up," or according to another authority, "looking around, i. e., watchers or lookouts." Under the treaty of Medicine Lodge in 1867, they and the southern Cheyenne were placed on the reservation which they sold in 1890 to take allotments and become citizens. Their present

FIG. 88—Arapaho tipi and windbreak.

chief is Left Hand (Nawat), who succeeded the celebrated Little Raven (Hosa) a few years ago. The whole number of the Arapaho and Gros Ventres, including a few in eastern schools, is about 2,700.

Until very recently the Arapaho have been a typical prairie tribe, living in skin tipis and following the buffalo in its migrations, yet they retain a tradition of a time when they were agricultural. They are of a friendly, accommodating disposition, religious and contemplative, without the truculent, pugnacious character that belongs to their confederates, the Cheyenne, although they have always proven themselves brave warriors. They are also less mercenary and more tractable than the prairie Indians generally, and having now recognized the inevitable of civilization have gone to work in good faith to make the best of it.

Their religious nature has led them to take a more active interest in the Ghost dance, which, together with the rhythmic character of their language, has made the Arapaho songs the favorite among all the tribes of Oklahoma. The chief study of the Ghost dance was made among the Arapaho, whom the author visited six times for this purpose. One visit was made to those in Wyoming, the rest of the time being spent with the southern branch of the tribe.

SONGS OF THE ARAPAHO

1. Opening Song—Eyehe′! Nä′nisa′na

E-ye-he′! A - nä′-ni-sa′ - na,   E-ye-he′! A - nä′-ni-sa′ - na,   Hi′ - nä chä′-säq

ä-ti-cha′ nĭ-na He′- e - ye′! Hi′-nä chä′-säq ä-ti-cha′ nĭ′-na He′-e - ye′! Na′-hă-ni nä′-ni-

thä′-tu-hŭ′-na   He′-e-ye′!   Na′-hă-ni nä′-ni-thä′-tu-hŭ′-na   He′-e-ye′!   Bĭ′-ta-a′-wu′

da′ - na - a′ - bä -na′-wa He′-e - ye′! Bĭ′-ta - a′-wu′ da′ - na - a′ - bä - na′-wa He′-e - ye′!

Eyehe′! nä′nisa′na,
Eyehe′! nä′nisa′na,
Hi′nä chä′sä′ ätīcha′nĭ′na He′eye′!
Hi′nä chä′sä′ ätīcha′nĭ′na He′eye′!
Na′häni nä′nithä′tuhŭ′na He′eye′!
Na′häni nä′nithä′tuhŭ′na He′eye′!
Bi′taa′wu′ da′naa′bäna′wa He′eye′!
Bi′taa′wu′ da′naa′bäna′wa He′eye′!

Translation

O, my children! O, my children!
Here is another of your pipes—*He′eye′!*
Here is another of your pipes—*He′eye′!*
Look! thus I shouted—*He′eye′!*
Look! thus I shouted—*He′eye′!*
When I moved the earth—*He′eye′!*
When I moved the earth—*He′eye′!*

This opening song of the Arapaho Ghost dance originated among the northern Arapaho in Wyoming and was brought down to the southern branch of the tribe by the first apostles of the new religion. By "another pipe" is probably meant the newer revelation of the messiah, the pipe being an important feature of all sacred ceremonies, and all their previous religious tradition having centered about the sĕicha or flat pipe, to be described hereafter. The pipe, however, was not commonly carried in the dance, as was the case among the Sioux. In this song, as in many others of the Ghost dance, the father or messiah, *Hesúna'nin*, is supposed to be addressing "my children," *nänisa'na*. The tune is particularly soft and pleasing, and the song remains a standard favorite. The second reference is to the new earth which is supposed to be already moving rapidly forward to slide over and take the place of this old and worn-out creation.

2. SĔ'ICHA HEI'TA'WUNI'NA

Sĕ'icha' hei'ta'wuni'na — E'yahe'eye,
Sĕ'icha hei'ta'wuni'na — E'yahe'eye.
He'sûna'nini — Yahe'eye',
He'sûna'nini — Yahe'eye'.
Ûtnitha'wuchä'wahänänina — E'yahe'eye',
Ûtnitha'wuchä'wahänänina — E'yahe'eye'.
He'sana'nini — E'yahe'eye,
He'sana'nini — E'yahe'eye.

Translation

The sacred pipe tells me — *E'yahe'eye!*
The sacred pipe tells me — *E'yahe'eye!*
Our father — *Yahe'eye'!*
Our father — *Yahe'eye'!*
We shall surely be put again (with our friends) — *E'yahe'eye!*
We shall surely be put again (with our friends) — *E'yahe'eye!*
Our father — *E'yahe'eye!*
Our father — *E'yahe'eye!*

The sĕicha or flat pipe is the sacred tribal medicine of the Arapaho. According to the myth it was given to their ancestors at the beginning of the world after the Turtle had brought the earth up from under the water. It was delivered to them by the Duck, which was discovered swimming about on the top of the water after the emergence of the land. At the same time they were given an ear of corn, from which comes all the corn of the world. The Arapaho lost the art of agriculture when they came out upon the buffalo plains, but the sacred pipe the Turtle long since changed to stone, and the first ear of corn, also transformed to stone, they have cherished to this day as their great medicine. The pipe, turtle, and ear of corn are preserved among the northern Arapaho in Wyoming, who claim to be the "mother people" of the tribe. They are handed down in the keeping of a particular family from generation to generation, the present priestly guardian being Se'hiwûq, "Weasel Bear" (from *sea*, weasel, and *wûq*, bear; the name has also been rendered "Gray Bear," from *se*, gray, and *wûq*, bear), of the Bäsawunĕ'na division.

The three sacred things are preserved carefully wrapped in deerskins, and are exposed only on rare occasions, always within the sacred tipi and in the presence of but a small number of witnesses, who take this opportunity to smoke the sacred pipe and pray for the things which they most desire. The pipe itself is of stone, and is described as apparently made in double, one part being laid over the other like the bark of a tree, the outer part of both bowl and stem being of the regular red pipestone, while the inner part of both is of white stone. The stem is only about 10 inches long, while the bowl is large and heavy, with the characteristic projection for resting the end upon the ground. Both bowl and stem are rounded, but with a flange of perhaps an inch in width along each side of the stem and up along the bowl. From this comes its name of sĕicha, or "flat pipe." When exposed on such occasions, the devotees sit around the fire in a circle, when the bundle is opened upon the ground so that all may see the sacred objects. The medicine keeper then lights the pipe and after taking one or two whiffs passes it to the one next him, who takes a single whiff and passes it on to the next. It thus goes sunwise (?) around the circle. In taking the sĕicha the devotees do not grasp the stem, as when smoking on other occasions, but receive it upon the outstretched palm of the right hand, smoke, and pass it on around the circle. The flanges along the side of the pipe allow it to rest flat upon the hand. After all have smoked, the priest recites the genesis myth of the origin of the land, and the manner in which the pipe and the corn were given to their ancestors. The corresponding myth of the Cheyenne occupies "four smokes" (i. e., four consecutive nights) in the delivery, but I am unable to state whether or not this is the case with the Arapaho. So sacred is this tradition held that no one but the priest of the pipe dares to recite it, for fear of divine punishment should the slightest error be made in the narration. At the close of the recital the devotees send up their prayers for the blessings of which they stand most in need, after which the priest again carefully wraps up the sacred objects in the skins. Before leaving the lodge the worshipers cover the bundle with their offerings of blankets or other valuables, which are taken by the medicine keeper as his fee.

When encamped in the tribal circle, the sacred pipe and its keeper occupied a large tipi, reserved especially for this purpose, which was set up within the circle and near its western line, directly opposite the doorway on the east. In the center of the circle, between the doorway and the sacred tipi, was erected the sweat-house of the Chi'nachichinĕ'na or old men of the highest degree of the warrior order. The taking down of the sacred tipi by the attendants of the pipe keeper was the signal for moving camp, and no other tipi was allowed to be taken down before it. When on the march, the pipe keeper proceeded on foot—never on horse—carrying the sacred bundle upon his back and attended by a retinue of guards. As a matter of course, the sacred pipe was not carried by war parties or on other expeditions requiring celerity of movement. Of late years the rules have so far relaxed that its present guardian sometimes rides on horseback while carrying the pipe, but even then he carries the bundle upon his own back instead of upon the saddle. He never rides in a wagon with it. Since the tribe is permanently divided under the modern reservation system, individuals or small parties of the southern Arapaho frequently make the long journey by railroad and stage to the reservation in Wyoming in order to see and pray over the sĕicha, as it is impossible, on account of the ceremonial regulations, for the keeper to bring it down to them in the south.

So far as known, only one white man, Mr J. Roberts, formerly superintendent of the Arapaho school in Wyoming, has ever seen the sacred pipe, which was shown to him on one occasion by Weasel Bear as a special mark of gratitude in return for some kindness. After having spent several months among the southern Arapaho, from whom I learned the songs of the pipe with much as to its sacred history, I visited the messiah in Nevada and then went to the northern Arapaho in Wyoming, with great hope of seeing the sĕicha and hearing the tradition in full. On the strength of my intimate acquaintance with their relatives in the south and with their great messiah in the west, the chiefs and head-men were favorable to my purpose and encouraged me to hope, but on going out to the camp in the mountains, where nearly the whole tribe was then assembled cutting wood, my hopes were dashed to the ground the first night by hearing the old priest, Weasel Bear, making the public announcement in a loud voice throughout the camp that a white man was among them to learn about their sacred things, but that these belonged to the religion of the Indian and a white man had no business to ask about them. The chief and those who had been delegates to the messiah came in soon after to the tipi where I was stopping, to express their deep regret, but they were unable to change the resolution of Weasel Bear, and none of themselves would venture to repeat the tradition.

3. Ate'bĕ tiăwu'nănu'

Ate'bĕ tiăwu'nănu', nä'nisa'nă,
Ate'bĕ tiăwu'nănu', nä'nisa'nă,
Nĭ'athu'ă', Nĭ'athu'ă',
Nĭ'binu' ga'awa'ti'na,
Nĭ'binu' ga'awa'ti'na.

Translation

My children, when at first I liked the whites,
My children, when at first I liked the whites,
I gave them fruits,
I gave them fruits.

This song referring to the whites was composed by Nawat or Left Hand, chief of the southern Arapaho, and can hardly be considered dangerous or treasonable in character. According to his statement, in his trance vision of the other world the father showed him extensive orchards, telling him that in the beginning all these things had been given to the whites, but that hereafter they would be given to his children, the Indians. *Nia′tha*, plural *Nia′thuă*, the Arapaho name for the whites, signifies literally, expert, skillful, or wise.

4. A′BĂ′NI′HI′

A′bä′ni′hi′,
A′bä′ni′hi′,
Ätichä′bi′näsänä,
Ätichä′bi′näsänä,
Chi′chita′nĕ,
Chi′chita′nĕ.

Translation

My partner, my partner,
Let us go out gambling,
Let us go out gambling,
At *chi′chita′nĕ*, at *chi′chita′nĕ*.

Chi′chita′nĕ is a favorite game of contest with the boys, in which the player, while holding in his hands a bow and an arrow ready to shoot, keeps in the hand which grasps the string a small wisp of grass bound with sinew. He lets this drop and tries to shoot it with the arrow before it touches the ground. The wisp is about the size of a man's finger.

The song came from the north, and was suggested by a trance vision in which the dreamer saw his former boy friends playing this game in the spirit world.

5. A′-NISÛNA′A′HU ĂCHĬSHINĬ′QAHI′NA

A′-nisûna′a′hu′,
A′-nisûna′a′hu′,
Ä′chĭshinĭ′qahi′na,
Ä′chĭshinĭ′qahi′na,
E′hihä′sina′käwu′hu′nĭt,
E′hihä′sina′käwu′hu′nĭt.

Translation

My father, my father,
While he was taking me around,
While he was taking me around,
He turned into a moose,
He turned into a moose.

This song relates the trance experience of Waqui′si or "Ugly Face Woman." In his vision of the spirit world he went into a large Arapaho camp, where he met his dead father, who took him around to the various tipis to meet others of his departed friends. While they were thus going about, a change came o'er the spirit of his dream, as so often

ARAPAHO BED

happens in this fevered mental condition, and instead of his father
he found a moose standing by his side. Such transformations are
frequently noted in the Ghost-dance songs.

6. E′YEHE′! Wû′NAYU′UHU′

E′yehe′! Wû′nayu′uhu′ —
E′yehe′! Wû′nayu′uhu′ —
A′ga′nä′,
A′ga′nä′.

Translation

E′yehe′! they are new —
E′yehe′! they are new —
The bed coverings,
The bed coverings.

The composer of this song is a woman who, in her trance, was taken
to a large camp where all the tipis were of clean new buffalo skins,
and the beds and interior furniture were all in the same condition.

FIG. 89—Bed of the prairie tribes.

The bed of the prairie tribes is composed of slender willow rods,
peeled, straightened with the teeth, laid side by side and fastened
together into a sort of mat by means of buckskin or rawhide strings
passed through holes at the ends of the rods. The bed is stretched upon
a platform raised about a foot above the ground, and one end of the
mat is raised up in hammock fashion by means of a tripod and buckskin hanger. The rods laid across the platform, forming the bed proper,
are usually about 3½ or 4 feet long (the width of the bed), while those
forming the upright part suspended from the tripod are shorter as they

approach the top, where they are only about half that length. The bed is bordered with buckskin binding fringed and beaded, and the exposed rods are painted in bright colors. The hanging portion is distinct from the part resting upon the platform, and in some cases there is a hanger at each end of the bed. Over the platform portion are spread the buckskins and blankets, which form a couch by day and a bed by night. A pillow of buckskin, stuffed with buffalo hair and elaborately ornamented with beads or porcupine quills, is sometimes added. The bed is placed close up under the tipi. In the largest tipis there are usually three beds, one being opposite the doorway and the others on each side, the fire being built in a hole scooped out in the ground in the center of the lodge. They are used as seats during waking hours, while the ground, with a rawhide spread upon it, constitutes the only table at meal time (plate CXXI; figure 89). In going to bed there is no undressing, each person as he becomes sleepy simply stretching out and drawing a blanket over himself, head and all, while the other occupants of the tipi continue their talking, singing, or other business until they too lie down to pleasant dreams.

7. HI'SÄHI'HI

Hi'sähi'hi, Hi'sähi'hi,
Ha'nä ta'wŭnä ga'awä'ha,
Ha'nä ta'wŭnä ga'awä'ha.
A'tanä'tähinä'na,
A'tanä'tähinä'na.

Translation

My partner! My partner!
Strike the ball hard—
Strike the ball hard.
I want to win,
I want to win.

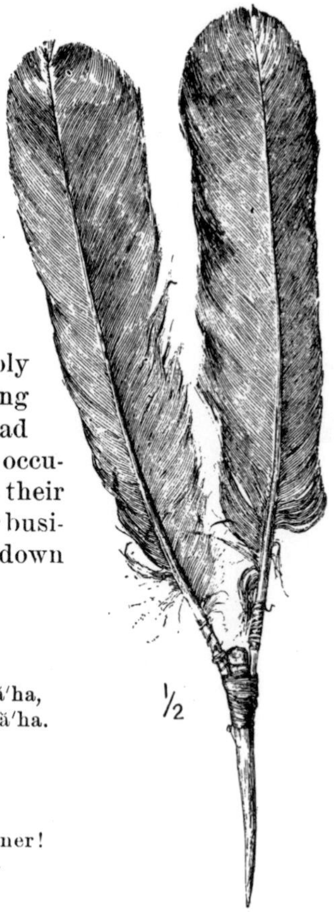

FIG. 90—Shinny stick and ball.

½

FIG. 91—Wakuna or head-feathers.

This song refers to the woman's game of *gŭ'gä'hawa't* or "shinny," played with curved sticks and a ball like a baseball, called *gaawä'ha*, made of (buffalo) hair and covered with buckskin (figure 90). Two stakes are set up as goals at either end of the ground, and the object of each party is to drive the ball through the goals of the other. Each inning is a game. The song was composed by a woman, who met her former girl comrade in the spirit world and played this game with her against an opposing party.

8. Ä′-NANI′NI′BI′NÄ′SI WAKU′NA

Nä′nisa′na, Nä′nisa′na,
Ä′-nani′ni′bi′nä′si waku′na,
Ä′-nani′ni′bi′nä′si waku′na.
Nä′nisa′na, Nä′nisa′na.

Translation

My children, my children.
The wind makes the head-feathers sing—
The wind makes the head-feathers sing.
My children, my children.

By the *wakuna* or head-feathers (figure 91) is meant the two crow feathers mounted on a short stick and worn on the head by the leaders of the dance, as already described.

9. HE′! NÄNE′TH BI′SHIQA′WÄ

He′! näne′th bi′shiqa′wä,
He′! näne′th bi′shiqa′wä,
Nä′nisa′na, nä′nisa′na,
Nä′ina′ha′tdä′bä′naq,
Nä′ina′ha′tdä′bä′naq.

Translation

He! When I met him approaching—
He! When I met him approaching—
My children, my children—
I then saw the multitude plainly,
I then saw the multitude plainly.

This song was brought from the north to the southern Arapaho by Sitting Bull. It refers to the trance vision of a dancer, who saw the

messiah advancing at the head of all the spirit army.   It is an old
favorite, and is sung with vigor and animation.

10. HÄNA′NA′WUNĂNU NI′TAWU′NA′NA′

Nä′nisa′na, nä′nisa′na,
Häna′na′wunănu ni′tawu′na′na′,
Häna′na′wunănu ni′tawu′na′na′,
Di′chin niănita′wa′thi,
Di′chin niănita′wa′thi.
Nithi′na hesûna′nĭn,
Nithi′na hesûna′nĭn.

Translation

My children, my children,
I take pity on those who have been taught,
I take pity on those who have been taught,
Because they push on hard,
Because they push on hard.
Says our father,
Says our father.

This is a message from the messiah to persevere in the dance.   In
the expressive idiom of the prairie tribes, as also in the sign language,
the term for persevering signifies to "push hard."

11. A-NI′QU WA′WANÄ′NIBÄ′TIA′

A-ni′qu wa′wanä′nibä′tia′ — Hi′ni′ni′!
A-ni′qu wa′wanä′nibä′tia′ — Hi′ni′ni′!
Hi′niqa′agayetu′sa,
Hi′niqa′agayetu′sa,
Hi′ni ni′nitu′sa nibä′tia — Hi′ni′ni′!
Hi′ni ni′nitu′sa nibä′tia — Hi′ni′ni′!

Translation

Father, now I am singing it — *Hi′ni′ni!*
Father, now I am singing it — *Hi′ni′ni!*
That loudest song of all,
That loudest song of all —
That resounding song — *Hi′ni′ni!*
That resounding song — *Hi′ni′ni!*

This is another of the old favorites.   The rolling effect of the vocalic
Arapaho syllables renders it particularly sonorous when sung by a full
chorus.   *Ni′qa* or *a-ni′qu*, "father," is a term of reverential affection,
about equivalent to "our father" in the Lord's prayer.   The ordinary
word is *hesûna′nin*, from *nisû′na*, "my father."

12. HA′YANA′-USI′YA′

Ha′yana′-usi′ya′!
Ha′yana′-usi′ya′!
Bi′ga ta′cha′wagu′na,
Bi′ga ta′cha′wagu′na.

Translation

How bright is the moonlight!
How bright is the moonlight!
Tonight as I ride with my load of buffalo beef,
Tonight as I ride with my load of buffalo beef.

The author of this song, on meeting his friends in the spirit world, found them preparing to go on a great buffalo hunt, the prairies of the new earth being covered with the countless thousands of buffalo that have been swept from the plains since the advent of the white man. They returned to camp at night, under the full moonlight, with their ponies loaded down with fresh beef. There is something peculiarly touching in this dream of the old life—this Indian heaven where—

> "In meadows wet with moistening dews,
> In garments for the chase arrayed,
> The hunter still the deer pursues—
> The hunter and the deer a shade."

13. Ha′ti ni′bät—E′he′eye′

Ha′ti ni′bät—E′he′eye′!
Ha′ti ni′bät—E′he′eye′!
Nä′nibä′tawa′,
Nä′nibä′tawa′,
He′yäya′ahe′ye!
He′yäya′ahe′ye!

Translation

The cottonwood song— *E′he′eye′!*
The cottonwood song— *E′he′eye′!*
I am singing it,
I am singing it,
He′yäya′ahe′ye!
He′yäya′ahe′ye!

The cottonwood (*Populus monilifera*) is the most characteristic tree of the plains and of the arid region between the Rockies and the Sierras. It is a species of poplar and takes its name from the white downy blossom fronds, resembling cotton, which come out upon it in the spring. The cottonwood and a species of stunted oak, with the mesquite in the south, are almost the only trees to be found upon the great plains extending from the Saskatchewan southward into Texas. As it never grows out upon the open, but always close along the borders of the few streams, it is an unfailing indication of water either on or near the surface, in a region well-nigh waterless. Between the bark and the wood there is a sweet milky juice of which the Indians are very fond—as one who had been educated in the east said, "It is their ice cream"—and they frequently strip off the bark and scrape the trunk in order to procure it. Horses also are fond of this sweet juice, and in seasons when the grass has been burned off or is otherwise scarce, the

Indian ponies sometimes resort to the small twigs and bark of the cottonwood to sustain life. In extreme cases their owners have sometimes been driven to the same shift. In winter the camps of the prairie tribes are removed from the open prairie to the shelter of the cottonwood timber along the streams. The tree is held almost sacred, and the sun-dance lodge is usually or always constructed of cottonwood saplings.

14. Eyehe′! A′nie′sa′na

Eyehe′! A′nie′sa′na′,
Eyehe′! A′nie′sa′na′,
He′ee′ä′ehe′yuhe′yu!
He′ee′ä′ehe′yuhe′yu!
A′-baha′ ni′esa′na′,
A′-baha′ ni′esa′na′.

Translation

Eyehe′! The young birds,
Eyehe′! The young birds,
He′ee′ä′ehe′yuhe′yu!
He′ee′ä′ehe′yuhe′yu!
The young Thunderbirds,
The young Thunderbirds.

Among the Algonquian tribes of the east, the Sioux, Cheyenne, Arapaho, Kiowa, Comanche, and prairie tribes generally, as well as among those of the northwest coast and some parts of Mexico, thunder and lightning are produced by a great bird, whose shadow is the thunder cloud, whose flapping wings make the sound of thunder, and whose flashing eyes rapidly opening or closing send forth the lightning. Among some tribes of the northwest this being is not a bird, but a giant who puts on a dress of bird skin with head, wings, and all complete, by means of which he flies through the air when in search of his prey. The myth is not found among the Iroquois or the Cherokee, or, perhaps, among the Muskhogean tribes.

The Thunderbird usually has his dwelling on some high mountain or rocky elevation of difficult access. Within the territory of the myth several places are thus designated as the Thunder's Nest. Thunder bay of Lake Huron, in lower Michigan, derives its name in this way. Such a place, known to the Sioux as *Waqkiñ′a-oye′*, "The Thunder's Nest," is within the old territory of the Sisseton Sioux in eastern South Dakota in the neighborhood of Big Stone lake. At another place, near the summit of the Coteau des Prairies, in eastern South Dakota, a number of large round bowlders are pointed out as the eggs of the Thunderbird. According to the Comanche there is a place on upper Red river where the Thunderbird once alighted on the ground, the spot being still identified by the fact that the grass remains burned off over a space having the outline of a large bird with outstretched wings. The same people tell how a hunter once shot and wounded a large bird which fell to the ground. Being afraid to attack it alone on account of its size, he returned to camp for help, but on again approaching the spot the hunters heard the thunder rolling and saw flashes of lightning shooting out from the ravine where the bird lay wounded. On coming nearer, the lightning blinded them so that they could not see the bird, and one flash struck and killed a hunter. His frightened companions then fled back to camp, for they knew it was the Thunderbird.

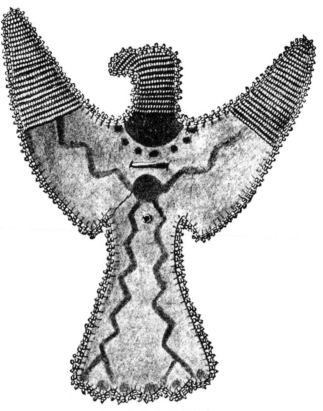

FIG. 92—The Thunderbird.

With both Cheyenne and Arapaho the thunder (*ba'a'*) is a large bird, with a brood of smaller ones, and carries in its talons a number of arrows with which it strikes the victim of lightning. For this reason they call the eagle on our coins *baa*. When it thunders, they say *ba'a' nänitŭ'-hut*, "the thunder calls." In Indian pictography the Thunderbird is figured with zigzag lines running out from its heart to represent the lightning. A small figure of it (represented in figure 92), cut from rawhide and ornamented with beads, is frequently worn on the heads of the dancers.

15. A′HE′SÛNA′NINI NĂYA′QÛTI′HI

A′he′sûna′nini năya′qûti′hi,
A′he′sûna′nini năya′qûti′hi,
Hä′ni′nihiga′hŭna′,
Hä′ni′nihiga′hŭna′,
He′sûna′nin hä′ni na′ha′waŭ′.
He′sûna′nin hä′ni na′ha′waŭ′.

Translation

Our father, the Whirlwind,
Our father, the Whirlwind —
By its aid I am running swiftly,
By its aid I am running swiftly,
By which means I saw our father,
By which means I saw our father.

The idea expressed in this song is that the dreamer "rides the whirlwind" in order sooner to meet the messiah and the spirit hosts. Father or grandfather are terms of reverence and affection, applied to anything held sacred or awful.

16. A′HE′SÛNA′NINI NĂYA′QÛTI′

A′he′sûna′nini năya′qûti′,
A′he′sûna′nini năya′qûti′,
Wa′wă chä′nĭ′nagu′nĭti hu′na,
Wa′wă chä′nĭ′nagu′nĭti hu′na.

Translation

Our father, the Whirlwind,
Our father, the Whirlwind,
Now wears the headdress of crow feathers,
Now wears the headdress of crow feathers.

In this song the Whirlwind, personified, wears on his head the two crow feathers, by which the dancers are to be borne upward to the new spirit world.

17. NINAÄ′NIAHU′NA

Ninaä′niahu′na,
Ninaä′niahu′na
Bi′taa′wu hä′näi′säĭ,
Bi′taa′wu hä′näi′säĭ,
Hi′nää′thi nä′niwu′hŭnă,
Hi′nää′thi nä′niwu′hŭnă.

Translation

I circle around —
I circle around
The boundaries of the earth,
The boundaries of the earth —
Wearing the long wing feathers as I fly,
Wearing the long wing feathers as I fly.

This song probably refers to the Thunderbird.   There is an energetic swing to the tune that makes it a favorite.   In Indian belief the earth is a circular disk, usually surrounded on all sides by water, and the sky is a solid concave hemisphere coming down at the horizon to the level of the earth.   In Cherokee and other Indian myth the sky is continually lifting up and coming down again to the earth, like the upper blade of the scissors.   The sun, which lives upon the outside of this hemisphere, comes through from the east in the morning while there is a momentary opening between the earth and the edge of the sky, climbs along upon the underside of the sky from east to west, and goes out at the western horizon in the evening, to return during the night to its starting point in the east.

18. Ha′nahawu′nĕn bĕni′ni′na

Ha′nahawu′nĕn bĕni′ni′na,
Ha′nahawu′nĕn bĕni′ni′na,
Hina′wûn ga′na′ni′na,
Hina′wûn ga′na′ni′na.

Translation

The *Hanahawunĕn* gave to me,
The *Hanahawunĕn* gave to me,
His paint—He made me clean,
His paint—He made me clean.

The author of this song met in the spirit world a man of the now extinct Arapaho band of the *Hanahawunĕna*, who washed the face of the visitor and then painted him afresh with some of the old-time mineral paint of the Indians.   In accord with the Indian belief, all the extinct and forgotten tribes have now their home in the world of shades.

19. Ate′be′tana′-ise′ti he′sûna′nini′

Ate′be′tana′-ise′ti he′sûna′nini′ — Ahe′eye′!
Ate′be′tana′-ise′ti he′sûna′nini′ — Ahe′eye′!
Na′waa′tănû′, Na′waa′tănû,
Danatinĕnawaŭ,
Nita-isa, nita-isa,
He′yahe′eȳe′!

Translation

When first our father came — *Ahe′eye′!*
When first our father came — *Ahe′eye′!*
I prayed to him, I prayed to him —
My relative, my relative —
He′yahe′eȳe′!

This song was composed by Paul Boynton (Bääku′ni, "Red Feather"), a Carlisle student, after having been in a trance.   His brother had died some time before, and being told by the Indians that he might be able to see and talk with him by joining the dance, Paul went to Sitting Bull, the leader of the dance, at the next gathering, and asked him to help him to see his dead brother. The result was that he was hypnotized by Sitting Bull, fell to the ground in a trance, and saw his brother. While talking with him, however, he suddenly awoke, much to his regret, probably from some one of the dancers having touched against him as he lay upon the ground. According to his statement, the words were spoken by him in his sleep after coming from the dance and were overheard by some companions who questioned him about it in the morning, when he told his experience and put the words into a song. The "father" here referred to is Sitting Bull, the great apostle of the Arapaho Ghost dance. It was from Paul's statement, intelligently told in good English before I had yet seen the dance, that I was first led to suspect that hypnotism was the secret of the trances.

20. A-NI′ÄNĔ′THĂHI′NANI′NA NISA′NA

A-ni′änĕ′thăhi′nani′na nisa′na,
A-ni′änĕ′thăhi′nani′na nisa′na.
He′chä′ na′hăbi′na,
He′chä′ na′hăbi′na,
Hewa-u′sa häthi′na,
Hewa-u′sa häthi′na.

Translation

My father did not recognize me (at first),
My father did not recognize me (at first).
When again he saw me,
When again he saw me,
He said, "You are the offspring of a crow,"
He said, "You are the offspring of a crow."

This song was composed by Sitting Bull, the Arapaho apostle of the dance, and relates his own experience in the trance, in which he met his father, who had died years before. The expression, "You are the child of a crow," may refer to his own sacred character as an apostle, the crow being regarded as the messenger from the spirit world.

21. NI′-ATHU′-A-U′ A′HAKÄ′NITH′IĬ

I′yehe′! anä′nisa′nă′ — Uhi′yeye′heye′!
I′yehe′! anä′nisa′nă′ — Uhi′yeye′heye′!
I′yehe′! ha′dawu′hana′ — Eye′äe′yuhe′yu!
I′yehe′! ha′dawu′hana′ — Eye′äe′yuhe′yu!
Ni′athu′-a-u′ a′hakä′nith′iĭ — Ahe′yuhe′yu!

Translation

I′yehe′! my children — *Uhi′yeye′heye′!*
I′yehe′! my children — *Uhi′yeye′heye′!*
I′yehe′! we have rendered them desolate — *Eye′äe′yuhe′yu!*
I′yehe′! we have rendered them desolate — *Eye′äe′yuhe′yu!*
The whites are crazy — *Ahe′yuhe′yu!*

In this song the father tells his children of the desolation, in consequence of their folly and injustice, that would come upon the whites when they will be left alone upon the old world, while the Indians will be taken up to the new earth to live in happiness forever.

22. Na′ha′ta bitaa′wu

Nä′nisa′nă, nä′nisa′nă,
Na′ha′ta bi′taa′wu hätnaa′waa′-u′hu′,
Na′ha′ta bi′taa′wu hätnaa′waa′-u′hu′.
Häthi′na hi′nisû′na-hu′,
Häthi′na hi′nisû′na-hu′.

Translation

My children, my children,
Look! the earth is about to move,
Look! the earth is about to move.
My father tells me so,
My father tells me so.

In this song the dreamer tells his friends, on the authority of the messiah, that the predicted spiritual new earth is about to start to come over and cover up this old world. It was also taught, as appears from the messiah's letter, that at the moment of contact this world would tremble as in an earthquake.

23. Ahe′sûna′nini Ächiqa′hă′wa-ŭ′

Ahe′sûna′nini, ahe′sûna′nini,
Ächiqa′hă′wa-ŭ′, Ächiqa′hă′wa-ŭ′,
E′hihä′sĭni′ĕhi′nĭt,
E′hihä′sĭni′ĕhi′nĭt.

Translation

My father, my father—
I am looking at him,
I am looking at him.
He is beginning to turn into a bird,
He is beginning to turn into a bird.

In this, as in the fifth Arapaho song, we have a transformation. According to the story of the author, his father is transformed into a bird even while he looks at him. The song is sung in quick time to hasten the trance.

24. Ha′änake′i

Ha′änake′i, ha′änake′i,
Dä′nasa′ku′tăwa′,
Dä′nasa′ku′tăwa′,
He′sûna′nin hä′ni na′ha′waŭ′,
He′sûna′nin hä′ni na′ha′waŭ′.

Translation

The rock, the rock,
I am standing upon it,
I am standing upon it.
By its means I saw our father,
By its means I saw our father.

This is one of the old songs now obsolete, and its meaning is not clear. It may mean simply that the author of it climbed a rock in order to be able to see farther, but it is more likely that it contains some mythic reference.

25. WA′WA′NA′DANÄ′DIÄ′

Nä′nisa′naăñ′, nä′nisa′naăñ′,
Wa′wa′na′danä′diä′,
Wa′wa′na′danä′diä′,
Nänisa′na, nänisa′na.

Translation

My children, my children,
I am about to hum.
I am about to hum.
My children, my children.

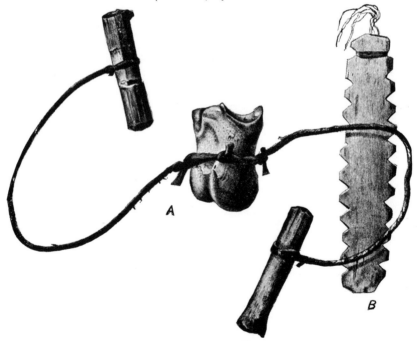

Fig. 93—Hummer and bull-roarer.

The author of this song saw her children in the other world playing with the *hätiku′tha*, or hummer. On going home after awaking from her trance, she made the toy and carried it with her to the next dance and twirled it in the air while singing the song. The *hätiku'tha*, or hummer, is used by the boys of the prairie tribes as our boys use the "cut-water," a circular tin disk, suspended on two strings passed through holes in the middle, and set in rapid revolution, so as to produce a humming sound, by alternately twisting the strings upon each other and allowing them to untwist again. One of these which I examined consists of a bone from a buffalo hoof, painted in different colors, with four buckskin strings tied around the middle and running out on each side and fastened at each end to a small peg, so as to be more firmly grasped by the fingers. It was carried in the dance in 1890 by an old Arapaho named Tall Bear, who had had it in his possession for twenty years. Another specimen, shown in figure 93,*a*, now in possession of the National Museum, is similar in construction, but with only one string on each side.

A kindred toy—it can hardly be considered a musical instrument— is that known among the whites as the "bull-roarer." It is found among most of the western tribes, as well as among our own children and primitive peoples all over the world. It is usually a simple flat piece of wood, about 6 inches long, sometimes notched on the edges and fancifully painted, attached to a sinew or buckskin string of convenient length. It is held in one hand, and when twirled rapidly in the air produces a sound not unlike the roaring of a bull or of distant thunder. With most tribes it is simply a child's toy, but among the Hopi, according to Fewkes, and the Apache, according to Bourke, it has a sacred use to assist the prayers of the medicine-man in bringing on the storm clouds and the rain.

26. A-te'bĕ' dii'nĕtita'nĭĕg

A-te'bĕ' dii'nĕtita'nĭĕg — I'yehe'eye'!
A-te'bĕ' dii'nĕtita'nĭĕg — I'yehe'eye'!
Nii'te'gu be'na nĕ'chäi'hit — I'yehe'eye'!
Bi'taa'wuu — I'yahe'eye'!
Nii'te'gu be'na nĕ'chäi'hit — I'yehe'eye'!
Bi'taa'wuu — I'yahe'eye'!
De'tawu'ni'na ni'sa'na — Ahe'eye'-he'eye'!
De'tawu'ni'na ni'sa'na' — Ahe'eye'-he'eye'!

Translation

At the beginning of human existence — *I'yehe'eye'!*
At the beginning of human existence — *I'yehe'eye'!*
It was the turtle who gave this grateful gift to me —
The earth — *I'yahe'eye'!*
It was the turtle who gave this grateful gift to me —
The earth — *I'yahe'eye'!*
(Thus) my father told me — *Ahe'eye'-he'eye'!*
(Thus) my father told me — *Ahe'eye'-he'eye'!*

In the mythology of many primitive nations, from the ancient Hindu to our own Indian tribes, the turtle or tortoise is the supporter of the earth, the Atlas on whose back rests the burden of the whole living universe. A reason for this is found in the amphibious character of the turtle, which renders it equally at home on land and in the water, and in its peculiar shape, which was held to be typical of the world, the world itself being conceived as a huge turtle swimming in a limitless ocean, the dome of the sky being its upper shell, and the flat surface of the earth being the bony breastplate of the animal, while inclosed between them was the living body, the human, animal, and vegetal creation. In Hindu mythology, when the gods are ready to destroy mankind, the turtle will grow weary and sink under his load and then the waters will rise and a deluge will overwhelm the earth. (*Fiske.*)

The belief in the turtle as the upholder of the earth was common to all the Algonquian tribes, to which belong the Arapaho and Cheyenne, and to the northern Iroquoian tribes. Earthquakes were caused by his shifting his position from time to time. In their pictographs the turtle was frequently the symbol of the earth, and in their prayers it was sometimes addressed as mother. The most honored clan was the Turtle clan; the most sacred spot in the Algonquian territory was Mackinaw, the "Island of the Great Turtle;" the favorite medicine bowl of their doctors is the shell of a turtle; the turtle is pictured on the ghost shirts of the Arapaho, and farther south in Oklahoma it is the recognized stock brand by which it is known that a horse or cow belongs to one of the historic Delaware tribe.

27. Tahu′na′änä′nia′huna

Nä′nisa′na, nä′nisa′na,
Nä′näni′na ta′hu′na′änä′nia′hunä′,
    Tahu′na′änä′nia′huna,
Nä′nisa′na, nä′nisa′na,
Nä′näni′na ta′hĕti′nia′hunä′,
    Ta′hĕti′nia′hunä′.

Translation

My children, my children,
It is I who make the thunder as I circle about—
    The thunder as I circle about.
My children, my children,
It is I who make the loud thunder as I circle about—
    The loud thunder as I circle about.

This song evidently refers to the Thunderbird. It is one of the old favorites from the north, and is sung to a sprightly tune in quick time. It differs from the others in having only a part instead of all of the line repeated.

28. Ani'qu ne'chawu'nani'

Moderato.

A - ni' - qu ne' - cha - wu' - na - ni',   a - ni' - qu ne' - cha - wu' - na - ni';

a - wa' - wa bi' - qă - na' - ka - ye' - na,   a - wa' - wa bi' - qă - na' - ka - ye' - na;

i - ya - hu'h ni' - bi - thi' - ti,   i - ya - hu'h ni' - bi - thi' - ti.

Ani'qu ne'chawu'nani',
Ani'qu ne'chawu'nani';
Awa'wa biqăna'kaye'na,
Awa'wa biqăna'kaye'na;
Iyahu'h ni'bithi'ti,
Iyahu'h ni'bithi'ti.

Translation

Father, have pity on me,
Father, have pity on me;
I am crying for thirst,
I am crying for thirst;
All is gone—I have nothing to eat,
All is gone—I have nothing to eat.

This is the most pathetic of the Ghost-dance songs. It is sung to a plaintive tune, sometimes with tears rolling down the cheeks of the dancers as the words would bring up thoughts of their present miserable and dependent condition. It may be considered the Indian paraphrase of the Lord's prayer.

29. A-ni'niha'niahu'na

A-ni'niha'niahu'na,
A-ni'niha'niahu'na,
Yeni's-iti'na ku'niahu'na,
Yeni's-iti'na ku'niahu'na,
Hi'chäbä'i—He'e'e'!
Hi'chäbä'i—He'e'e'!

Translation

I fly around yellow,
I fly around yellow,
I fly with the wild rose on my head,
I fly with the wild rose on my head,
On high—*He'e'e'*!
On high—*He'e'e'*!

The meaning of this song is not clear. It may refer to the Thunder-bird or to the Crow, the sacred bird of the Ghost dance. The *ye'nis* or wild rose is much esteemed among the prairie tribes for its red seed berries, which are pounded into a paste and dried for food. It is frequently mentioned in the ghost songs, and is sometimes pictured on the ghost shirts. Although rather insipid, the berries possess nutritive qualities. They are gathered in winter, and are sometimes eaten raw, but more generally are first boiled and strained to get rid of the seeds. This dough-like substance is sometimes mixed with marrow from broken bones and pasted around sticks and thus roasted before the fire. It is never packed away for future use. The Cherokee call the same plant by a name which means "rabbit food," on account of this animal's fondness for the berries.

30. NIHA'NATA'YECHE'TI

He'yoho'ho'! He'yoho'ho'!
Niha'nata'yeche'ti, na'naga'qanĕ'tihi,
Wa'waga'thänŭhu,
Wa'waga'thänŭhu,
Wa'wa ne'hawa'wŭna'nahu',
Wa'wa ne'hawa'wŭna'nahu'.
He'yoho'ho'! He'yoho'ho'!

Translation

He'yoho'ho'! He'yoho'ho'!
The yellow-hide, the white-skin (man).
I have now put him aside—
I have now put him aside—
I have no more sympathy with him,
I have no more sympathy with him.
He'yoho'ho'! He'yoho'ho'!

This is another song about the whites, who are spoken of as "yellow hides" or "white skins." The proper Arapaho name for a white man is *Nia'tha*, "skillful." A great many names are applied to the whites by the different Indian tribes. By the Comanche, Shoshoni, and Paiute they are called *Tai'vo*, "easterners;" by the Hopi, of the same stock as the three tribes mentioned, they are known as *Paha'na*, "eastern water people;" by the Kiowa they are called *Be'dălpago*, "hairy mouths," or *Ta'ka'-i*, "standing ears." It is very doubtful if the "pale face" of romance ever existed in the Indian mind.

31. A-BÄÄ'THINA'HU

A-bää'thina'hu, a-bää'thina'hu,
Ha'tnithi'aku'ta'na,
Ha'tnithi'aku'ta'na,
Ha'-bätä'nani'hi,
Ha'-bätä'nani'hi.
Ha'tnithi'aku'ta'na,
Ha'tnithi'aku'ta'na.

The cedar tree, the cedar tree,
We have it in the center,
We have it in the center
When we dance,
When we dance.
We have it in the center,
We have it in the center.

The Kiowa, the Sioux, and perhaps some other tribes performed the Ghost dance around a tree set up in the center of the circle. With the Kiowa this tree was a cedar, and such was probably the case with the other tribes, whenever a cedar could be obtained, as it is always a sacred tree in Indian belief and ceremonial. The southern Arapaho and Cheyenne never had a tree in connection with the Ghost dance, so that this song could not have originated among them. The cedar is held sacred for its evergreen foliage, its fragrant smell, its red heart wood, and the durable character of its timber. On account of its fine grain and enduring qualities the prairie tribes make their tipi poles of its wood, which will not warp through heat or moisture. Their flageolets or flutes are also made of cedar, and in the mescal and other ceremonies its dried and crumbled foliage is thrown upon the fire as incense. In Cherokee and Yuchi myth the red color of the wood comes from the blood of a wizard who was killed and decapitated by a hero, and whose head was hung in the top of several trees in succession, but continued to live until, by the advice of a medicine-man, the people hung it in the topmost branches of a cedar tree, where it finally died. The blood of the severed head trickled down the trunk of the tree and thus the wood was stained.

32. WA′WA NŮ′NANŮ′NAKU′TI

Nä′nisa′na, nä′nisa′na,
Wa′wa nŭ′nanŭ′naku′ti waku′hu,
Wa′wa nŭ′nanŭ′naku′ti waku′hu.
Hi′yu nä′nii′bä′-i,
Hi′yu nä′nii′bä′-i.
Hä′tä-i′naku′ni häthi′na nisŭ′nahu,
Hä′tä-i′naku′ni häthi′na nisŭ′nahu.

Translation

My children, my children,
Now I am waving an eagle feather,
Now I am waving an eagle feather.
Here is a spotted feather for you,
Here is a spotted feather for you.
You may have it, said my father,
You may have it, said my father.

While singing this song the author of it waved in his right hand an eagle feather prepared for wearing in the hair, while he carried a spotted hawk feather in the other hand. In his trance vision he had received such a spotted feather from the messiah.

33. A-NI′QANA′GA

A-ni′qana′ga,
A-ni′qana′ga,
Ha′tăni′i′na′danĕ′na,
Ha′tăni′i′na′danĕ′na.

Translation

There is a solitary bull,
There is a solitary bull—
I am going to use him to "make medicine,"
I am going to use him to "make medicine."

From the buffalo they had food, fuel, dress, shelter, and domestic furniture, shields for defense, points for their arrows, and strings for their bows. As the old Spanish chronicles of Coronado put it: "To be short, they make so many things of them as they have need of, or as many as suffice them in the use of this life."

Among Indians the professions of medicine and religion are inseparable. The doctor is always a priest, and the priest is always a doctor. Hence, to the whites in the Indian country the Indian priest-doctor has come to be known as the "medicine-man," and anything sacred, mysterious, or of wonderful power or efficacy in Indian life or belief is designated as "medicine," this term being the nearest equivalent of the aboriginal expression in the various languages. To "make medicine" is to perform some sacred ceremony, from the curing of a sick child to the consecration of the sun-dance lodge. Among the prairie tribes the great annual tribal ceremony was commonly known as the "medicine dance," and the special guardian deity of every warrior was spoken of as his "medicine."

The buffalo was to the nomad hunters of the plains what corn was to the more sedentary tribes of the east and south—the living, visible symbol of their support and existence; the greatest gift of a higher being to his children. Something of the buffalo entered into every important ceremony. In the medicine dance—or sun dance, as it is frequently called—the head and skin of a buffalo hung from the center pole of the lodge, and in the fearful torture that accompanied this dance among some tribes, the dancers dragged around the circle buffalo skulls tied to ropes which were fastened to skewers driven through holes cut in their bodies and limbs. A buffalo skull is placed in front of the sacred sweat-lodge, and on the battlefield of Wounded Knee I have seen buffalo skulls and plates of dried meat placed at the head of the graves. The buffalo was the sign of the Creator on earth as the sun was his glorious manifestation in the heavens. The hair of the buffalo was an important element in the preparation of "medicine," whether for war, hunting, love, or medicine proper, and for such

THE SWEAT-LODGE—KIOWA CAMP ON THE WASHITA

purpose the Indian generally selected a tuft taken from the breast close under the shoulder of the animal. When the Kiowa, Comanche, and Apache delegates visited Washington in the spring of 1894, they made an earnest and successful request for some buffalo hair from the animals in the Zoological Park, together with some branches from the cedars in the grounds of the Agricultural Department, to take home with them for use in their sacred ceremonies.

34. A-NĔÄ′THIBIWÄ′HANÄ

A′-nĕä′thibiwă′hană,
A′-nĕä′thibiwă′hană—
Thi′äya′nĕ,
Thi′äya′nĕ.

Translation

The place where crying begins,
The place where crying begins —
The *thi′äya*,
The *thi′äya*.

This song refers to the sweat-lodge already described in treating of the Ghost dance among the Sioux. In preparing the sweat-lodge a small hole, perhaps a foot deep, is dug out in the center of the floor space, to serve as a receptacle for the heated stones over which the water is poured to produce the steam. The earth thus dug out is piled in a small hillock a few feet in front of the entrance to the sweat-lodge, which always faces the east. This small mound is called *thi′äya* in the Arapaho language, the same name being also applied to a memorial stone heap or to a stone monument. It is always surmounted by a buffalo skull, or in these days by the skull of a steer, placed so as to face the doorway of the lodge. The *thi′äya* is mentioned in several of the Ghost-dance songs, and usually, as here, in connection with crying or lamentation, as though the sight of these things in the trance vision brings up sad recollections.

35. THI′ÄYA HE′NÄÄ′AWÄ′

Thi′äya′ he′nää′awă′ —
Thi′äya′ he′nää′awă′,
Nä′hibiwa′huna′,
Nä′hibiwa′huna′.

Translation

When I see the *thi′äya*—
When I see the *thi′äya*,
Then I begin to lament,
Then I begin to lament.

This song refers to a trance vision in which the dreamer saw a sweat-lodge, with the *thi′äya*, or mound, as described in the preceding song.

36. A-HU′HU HA′GENI′STI′TI BA′HU

A-hu′hu ha′geni′sti′ti ba′hu,
Ha′geni′sti′ti ba′hu.
Hä′nisti′ti,
Hä′nisti′ti.
Hi′nisa′nă,
Hi′nisa′nă —
Ne′a-i′qaha′ti,
Ne′a-i′qaha′ti.

Translation

The crow is making a road,
He is making a road;
He has finished it,
He has finished it.
His children,
His children—
Then he collected them,
Then he collected them (i. e., on the farther side).

The crow (*ho*) is the sacred bird of the Ghost dance, being revered as the messenger from the spirit world because its color is symbolic of death and the shadow land. The raven, which is practically a larger crow, and which lives in the mountains, but occasionally comes down into the plains, is also held sacred and regarded as a bringer of omens by the prairie tribes, as well as by the Tlinkit and others of the northwest coast and by the Cherokee in the east. The crow is depicted on the shirts, leggings, and moccasins of the Ghost dancers, and its feathers are worn on their heads, and whenever it is possible to kill one, the skin is stuffed as in life and carried in the dance, as shown in the picture of Black Coyote (plate CV). At one time the dancers in Left Hand's camp had a crow which it was claimed had the power of speech and prophetic utterance, and its hoarse inarticulate cries were interpreted as inspired messages from the spirit world. Unfortunately the bird did not thrive in confinement, and soon took its departure for the land of spirits, leaving the Arapaho once more dependent on the guidance of the trance revelations. The eagle, the magpie, and the sagehen are also sacred in the Ghost dance, the first being held in veneration by Indians, as well as by other peoples throughout the world, while the magpie and the sage-hen are revered for their connection with the country of the messiah and the mythology of his tribe.

The crow was probably held sacred by all the tribes of the Algonquian race. Roger Williams, speaking of the New England tribes, says that although the crows sometimes did damage to the corn, yet hardly one Indian in a hundred would kill one, because it was their tradition that this bird had brought them their first grain and vegetables, carrying a grain of corn in one ear and a bean in the other, from the field of their great god Cautantouwit in Sowwani′u, the southwest, the happy spirit world where dwelt the gods and the souls of the great and good. The souls of the wicked were not permitted to enter this elysium after death, but were doomed to wander without rest or home. (*Williams, Key into the Language of America, 1643.*)

In Arapaho belief, the spirit world is in the west, not on the same level with this earth of ours, but higher up, and separated also from it by a body of water. In their statement of the Ghost-dance mythology referred to in this song, the crow, as the messenger and leader of the spirits who had gone before, collected their armies on the other side and advanced at their head to the hither limit of the shadow land. Then, looking over, they saw far below them a sea, and far out beyond it toward the east was the boundary of the earth, where lived the friends they were marching to rejoin. Taking up a pebble in his beak, the crow then dropped it into the water and it became a mountain towering up to the land of the dead. Down its rocky slope he brought his army until they halted at the edge of the water. Then, taking some dust in his bill, the crow flew out and dropped it into the water as he flew, and it became a solid arm of land stretching from the spirit world to the earth. He returned and flew out again, this time with some blades of grass, which he dropped upon the land thus made, and at once it was covered with a green sod. Again he returned, and again flew out, this time with some twigs in his bill, and dropping these also upon the new land, at once it was covered with a forest of trees. Again he flew back to the base of the mountain, and is now, for the fourth time, coming on at the head of all the countless spirit host which has already passed over the sea and is marshaling on the western boundary of the earth.

37. Bi′taa′wu hu′hu′

Bi′taa′wu hu′hu′,
Bi′taa′wu hu′hu′—
Nû′nagûna′-ua′ti hu′hu′,
Nû′nagûna′-ua′ti hu′hu′—
A′hene′heni′ă′ă′! A′he′yene′hene′!

Translation

The earth—the crow,
The earth—the crow—
The crow brought it with him,
The crow brought it with him—
A′hene′heni′ă′ă′! A′he′yene′hene′!

The reference in this song is explained under the song immediately preceding.

38. Ni′nini′tubi′na hu′hu′—I

Ni′nini′tubi′na hu′hu′,
Ni′nini′tubi′na hu′hu′.
Nana′thina′ni hu′hu,
Nana′thina′ni hu′hu.
Ni′nita′naû,
Ni′nita′naû.

Translation

The crow has called me,
The crow has called me.
When the crow came for me,
When the crow came for me,
I heard him,
I heard him.

The reference in this song is explained under number 36. The song is somewhat like the former closing song, number 52.

39. Nŭ′nanŭ′naa′tăni′na hu′hu′—I

Nŭ′nanŭ′naa′tăni′na hu′hu′,
Nŭ′nanŭ′naa′tăni′na hu′hu′.
Da‘chi′nathi′na hu′hu′,
Da‘chi′nathi′na hu′hu′.

Translation

The crow is circling above me,
The crow is circling above me,
The crow having come for me,
The crow having come for me.

The author of this song, in his trance vision, saw circling above his head a crow, the messenger from the spirit world, to conduct him to his friends who had gone before. The song is a favorite one, and is sung with a quick forcible tune when the excitement begins to grow more intense, in order to hasten the trances, the idea conveyed to the dancers being that their spirit friends are close at hand.

40. I′yu hä′thäbĕ′nawa′

Ä′näni′sa′na—E′e′ye′!
Ä′näni′sa′na—E′e′ye′!
I′yu hä′thäbĕ′nawa′.
Bi′taa′wu—E′e′ye′!
Bi′taa′wu—E′e′ye′!

Translation

My children—*E′e′ye′!*
My children—*E′e′ye′!*
Here it is, I hand it to you.
The earth—*E′e′ye′!*
The earth—*E′e′ye′!*

In this song the father speaks to his children and gives them the new earth.

41. Ha′naĕ′hi ya′ga′ahi′na

Ha′naĕ′hi ya′ga′ahi′na—
Ha′naĕ′hi ya′ga′ahi′na—
Să′niya′gu′nawa′—Ahe′e′ye′!
Să′niya′gu′nawa′—Ahe′e′ye′!
Nä′yu hä′nina′ta i′tha′q,
Nä′yu hä′nina′ta i′tha′q.

Translation

Little boy, the coyote gun —
Little boy, the coyote gun —
I have uncovered it — *Ahe'e'ye'*!
I have uncovered it — *Ahe'e'ye'*!
There is the sheath lying there,
There is the sheath lying there.

This song was composed by Nakash, or "Sage," one of the northern Arapaho delegates to the messiah. It evidently refers to one of his trance experiences in the other world, and has to do with an interesting feature in the sociology of the Arapaho and other prairie tribes. The *ga'ahinĕ'na* or *gaahi'na*, "coyote men," were an order of men of middle age who acted as pickets or lookouts for the camp. When the band encamped in some convenient situation for hunting or other business, it was the duty of these men, usually four or six in a band, to take their stations on the nearest hills to keep watch and give timely warning in case of the approach of an enemy. It was an office of danger and responsibility, but was held in corresponding respect. When on duty, the *gaahi'nĕn* wore a white buffalo robe and had his face painted with white clay and carried in his hand the *ya'haga'ahi'na* or "coyote gun," a club decorated with feathers and other ornaments and usually covered with a sheath of bear gut (*i'tha'q*). He must be unmarried and remain so while in office, finally choosing his own successor and delivering to him the "coyote gun" as a staff of authority. They were never all off duty at the same time, but at least half were always on guard, one or more coming down at a time to the village to eat or sleep. They built no shelter on the hills, but slept there in their buffalo robes, or sometimes came down in turn and slept in their own tipis. They usually, however, preferred to sleep alone upon the hills in order to receive inspiration in dreams. If attacked or surprised by the enemy, they were expected to fight. The watcher was sometimes called *higa'ahi'na-ĭt*, "the man with the coyote gun." The corresponding officer among the Cheyenne carried a bow and arrows instead of a club.

42. HE'SÛNA' NA'NAHATHA'HI

He'sûna' na'nahatha'hi,
He'sûna' na'nahatha'hi.
Ni'itu'qawigû'niĕ',
Ni'itu'qawigû'niĕ'.

Translation

The father showed me,
The father showed me,
Where they were coming down,
Where they were coming down.

In his trance vision the author of this song saw the spirit hosts descending from the upper shadow land to the earth, along the mountain raised up by the crow, as already described in song number 36. The song comes from the northern Arapaho.

43. Nänisa'tăqu'thi Chĭnachi'chibä'iha'

Nänisa'tăqu'thi Chĭnachi'chibä'iha',
Nänisa'tăqu'thi Chĭnachi'chibä'iha' —
Ni'nahawa'na,
Ni'nahawa'na.
Nibäi'naku'nithi —
Nibäi'naku'nithi —
Ä-bäna'änahu'u',
Ä-bäna'änahu'u'.
Nä'hibi'wahuna'na,
Nä'hibi'wahuna'na.

Translation

The seven venerable *Chĭ'nachichi'bät* priests,
The seven venerable *Chĭ'nachichi'bät* priests —
We see them,
We see them.
They all wear it on their heads —
They all wear it on their heads —
The Thunderbird,
The Thunderbird.
Then I wept,
Then I wept.

In his trance vision the author of this song saw a large camp of Arapaho, and in the midst of the camp circle, as in the old days, were sitting the seven priests of the *Chĭ'nachichi'bät*, each wearing on his head the Thunderbird headdress, already described and figured under song number 14. This vision of the old life of the tribe brought up sorrowful memories and caused him to weep. In the similar song next given the singer laments for the *Chĭ'nachichi'bät* and the *bä'qati* gaming wheel. The priests here referred to were seven in number, and constituted the highest order of the military and social organization which existed among the Blackfeet, Sioux, Cheyenne, Kiowa, and probably all the prairie tribes excepting the Comanche in the south, among whom it seems to have been unknown. The society, so far as it has come under the notice of white men, has commonly been designated by them as the "Dog Soldier" society—a misapprehension of a name belonging probably to only one of the six or eight orders of the organization. The corresponding Blackfoot organization, the *Ikunuhkatsi* or "All Comrades," is described by Grinnell in his "Blackfoot Lodge Tales." The Kiowa organization will be noted later.

Among the Arapaho the organization was called *Běni'něna*, "Warriors," and consisted of eight degrees or orders, including nearly all the men of the tribe above the age of about seventeen. Those who were not enrolled in some one of the eight orders were held in but little respect, and were not allowed to take part in public ceremonies or to accompany war expeditions. Each of the first six orders had its own peculiar dance, and the members of the principal warrior orders had also their peculiar staff or badge of rank.

First and lowest in rank were the *Nuhinĕ'na* or Fox men, consisting of young men up to the age of about 25 years. They had no special duties or privileges, but had a dance called the *Nuha'wŭ* or fox dance.

Next came the *Hă'thahu'ha* or Star men, consisting of young warriors about 30 years of age. Their dance was called the *Ha'thahŭ*.

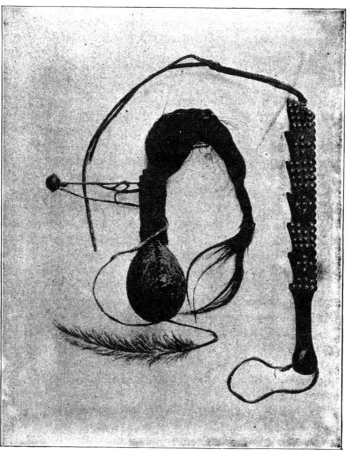

FIG. 94—Dog-soldier insignia—rattle and quirt.

The third order was that of the *Hichăă'quthi* or Club men. Their dance was called *Hichăă'qawŭ*. They were an important part of the warrior organization, and were all men in the prime of life. The four leaders carried wooden clubs, bearing a general resemblance in shape to a gun, notched along the edges and variously ornamented. In an attack on the enemy it was the duty of these leaders to dash on ahead and strike the enemy with these clubs, then to ride back again and take their places in the front of the charge. It hardly need be said that the position of leader of the *Hichăä'quthi* was a dangerous honor, but the honor was in proportion to the very danger, and there were always candidates for a vacancy. It was one of those offices where the holder sometimes died but never resigned. The other members of the order carried sticks carved at one end in the rude semblance of a horse head and pointed at the other. In desperate encounters they were expected to plant these sticks in the ground in line in front of the body of warriors and to fight beside them to the death unless a retreat should be ordered by the chief in command.

The fourth order was called *Bitahi'nĕna* or Spear men, and their dance was called *Bitaha'wŭ*. This order came originally from the Cheyenne. Their duties and peculiar insignia of office were about the same among all the tribes. They performed police duty in camp, when traveling, and on the hunt, and were expected to see that the orders of the chief were obeyed by the tribe. For instance, if any person violated the tribal code or failed to attend a general dance or council, a party of *Bitahi'nĕna* was sent to kill his dogs, destroy his tipi, or in extreme cases to shoot his ponies. On hunting expeditions it was their business to keep the party together and see that no one killed a buffalo until the proper ceremonies had been performed and the order was given by the chief. They were regarded as the representatives of the law and were never resisted in performing their duty or inflicting punishments. In war they were desperate warriors, equaling or surpassing even the *Hichăä'quthi*. Of the leaders of the order, two carried a sort of shepherd's crook called *nu'sa-icha'tha*, having a lance point at its lower end; two others carried lances wrapped around with otter skin; four carried lances painted black; one carried a club shaped like a baseball bat, and one carried a rattle made of the scrotum of a buffalo and ornamented with its hair. In battle, if the enemy took shelter behind defenses, it was this man's duty to lead the charge, throw his rattle among the enemy, and then follow it himself.

The fifth order was called *Aha'känĕ'na* or Crazy men. They were men more than 50 years of age, and were not expected to go to war, but must have graduated from all the lower orders. Their duties were religious and ceremonial, and their insignia consisted of a bow and a bundle of blunt arrows. Their dance was the *Ahaka'wŭ* or crazy dance, which well deserved the name. It will be described in another place.

The sixth was the order of the *Hĕthĕ'hinĕ'na* or Dog men. Their dance was called *Hĕthĕwa'wŭ'*. They had four principal leaders and two lesser leaders. The four principal leaders were the generals and directors of the battle. Each carried a rattle and wore about his neck a buckskin strap (two being yellow, the other two black) which hung down to his feet. On approaching the enemy, they were obliged to go forward, shaking their rattles and chanting the war song, until some other warriors of the party took the rattles out of their hands. When forming for the attack, they dismounted, and, driving their lances into

DOG-SOLDIER INSIGNIA—LANCE AND SASH

the ground, tied themselves to them by means of the straps, thus anchoring themselves in front of the battle. Here they remained until, if the battle seemed lost, they themselves gave the order to retreat. Even then they waited until some of their own society released them by pulling the lances out of the ground and whipping them away from the place with a peculiar quirt carried only by the private members of this division. No one was allowed to retreat without their permission, on penalty of disgrace, nor were they themselves allowed to retire until thus released. Should their followers forget to release them in the confusion of retreat, they were expected to die at their posts. They could not be released excepting by one of their own division, and anyone else attempting to pull up the lances from the ground was resisted as an enemy. When pursued on the retreat, they must give up their horses to the women, if necessary, and either find other horses or turn and face the enemy alone on foot. They seldom accompanied any but large war parties, and, although they did but little actual fighting, their very presence inspired the warriors with desperate courage, and the driving of their lances into the ground was always understood as the signal for an encounter to the death.

The seventh order was that of the *Nûnaha'wŭ*, a word of which the meaning is now unknown. This was a secret order. They had no dance and their ceremonies were witnessed only by themselves. They did not fight, but accompanied the war parties, and every night in secret performed ceremonies and prayers for their success.

The eighth and highest order was that of the *Chĭ'nachinĕ'na* or Water-pouring men, the "seven venerable priests" to whom the song refers. They were the high priests and instructors of all the other orders, and were seven in number, from among the oldest warriors of the tribe. Their name refers to their pouring the water over the heated stones in the sweat-house to produce steam. They had no dance, and were not expected to go to war, although one of the seven was allowed to accompany the war party, should he so elect. Their ceremonies were performed in a large sweat-lodge, called *chĭnachichi'bät*, which, when the whole tribe was camped together, occupied the center of the circle, between the entrance and the lodge in which was kept the sacred medicine pipe. Unlike the ordinary sweat-lodge, this one had no mound and buffalo skull in front of the entrance.

The warrior organization of the Kiowa is called *Yä'ʻpähe*, "Soldiers," and consisted of six orders, each with its own dance, songs, and ceremonial dress. 1. *Polänyup* or *Tsän'yui*, "Rabbits." These were boys and young men from 8 to 15 years of age. Their dance, in which they were drilled by certain old men, has a peculiar step, in imitation of the jumping movement of a rabbit; 2. *Ädalto'yui*, or *Te'ñbiyu'i*, "Young Mountain Sheep," literally "Herders or Corralers;" 3. *Tsentä'nmo*, "Horse Head-dress (?) people;" 4. "*Toñkoñ'ko* (?) "Black-leg people;" 5. *Tʻäñpe'ko*, "Skunkberry (?) people;" 6. *Kâ'itseñ'ko*, "Principal Dogs or Real Dogs." These last were the highest warrior order, and also the camp police, combining the functions of the *Bita-hi'něna* and the *Hěthě'bině'na* of the Arapaho organization. Their two leaders carried an arrow-shape lance, with which they anchored themselves in the front of the battle by means of buckskin straps brought over the shoulders. The *Toñkoñ'ko* captains carried in a similar way a crook-shape lance, called *pabo'n*, similar to that of the *Bitahi'něna* of the Arapaho.

44. Nănisa'tăqi Chĭ'năchi'chibă̈'iha'

Nä'ni-sa'-tă-qi   Chĭ'-nă-chĭ' - chi - bă̈' - ĭ - ha',   nä'-ni-sa'-tă̈-qi

Chĭ'-nă-chĭ' - chi - bă̈' - ĭ - ha',   bă̈' - hi-bĭ' - wă̈'-hĭ-nă,   bă̈-hi-bĭ' - wă̈-hĭ-nă'.

Bă̈'-qă̈-tĭ'   hä'-ni-bĭ' - wă̈'-hĭ-nă',   bă̈'-qă̈-tĭ'   hä'-ni-bi - wă̈'hĭ - nă'.

Nä'nisa'tăqi Chĭ'năchi'chibä'iha' —
Nä'nisa'tăqi Chĭ'năchi'chibä'iha' —
Bä'hibi'wă̈'hĭnă',
Bä'hibi'wă̈'hĭnă'.
Bä'qăti hä'nibi'wă̈'hĭnă',
Bä'qăti hä'nibi'wă̈'hĭnă'.

Translation

The seven venerable *Chĭnachichi'bät* priests—
The seven venerable *Chĭnachichi'bät* priests—
For them I am weeping,
For them I am weeping.
For the gaming wheel I am weeping,
For the gaming wheel I am weeping.

The first reference in this song is explained under number 43. The *bä'qati* or gaming wheel will be described later.

45. Nû'nanû'naatani'na hu'hu'—II

Nû'-na-nû'-naa'-ta - nĭ' - na   hu'-hu',   nû'-na-nû'-naa'-ta - nĭ' - na   hu'-hu'.

Da'-chĭ' - bi - nĭ'-na hä - thĭ'-na,   da'-chĭ' - bi - nĭ'-na hä - thĭ'-na.

Nû'nanû'naatani'na hu'hu',
Nû'nanû'naatani'na hu'hu'.
Da'chi'bini'na häthi'na,
Da'chi'bini'na häthi'na.

Translation

The crow is circling above me,
The crow is circling above me.
He says he will give me a hawk feather,
He says he will give me a hawk feather.

This song is very similar to number 39, and requires no further explanation. It is sung to the same quick time.

46. NA'TĂNU'YA CHĔ'BI'NH

Na'tănu'ya chĕ'bi'nh—
Na'tănu'ya chĕ'bi'nh,
Na'chicha'ba'n,
Na'chicha'ba'n.

Translation

The pemmican that I am using—
The pemmican that I am using,
They are still making it,
They are still making it.

This song refers to the pemmican or preparation of dried and pounded meat, which formerly formed a favorite food of the prairie tribes, and which the author of the song evidently tasted as it was being prepared by the women in the spirit world. (See Sioux song 7.) One must be an Indian to know the thrill of joy that would come to the heart of the dancers when told that some dreamer had seen their former friends in the spirit world still making and feasting on pemmican. During the first year or two of the excitement, it several times occurred at Ghost dances in the north and south, among Sioux as well as among Arapaho and others, that meat was exhibited and tasted as genuine buffalo beef or pemmican brought back from the spirit world by one of the dancers. It is not necessary to explain how this deception was accomplished or made successful. It is sufficient to know that it was done, and that the dancers were then in a condition to believe anything.

47. HÄĬ'NAWA' HÄ'NI'TA'QUNA'NI

Häĭ'nawa' hä'ni'ta'quna'ni—
Häĭ'nawa' hä'ni'ta'quna'ni—
Ninĕ'n nänä' hänita'quna'ni,
Ninĕ'n nänä' hänita'quna'ni.

Translation

I know, in the pitfall—
I know, in the pitfall—
It is tallow they use in the pitfall,
It is tallow they use in the pitfall.

This song refers to the vision of a northern Arapaho, who found one of his friends in the spirit world preparing a pitfall trap to catch eagles.

Wherever found, the eagle was regarded as sacred among the Indian tribes both east and west, and its feathers were highly prized for orna- mental and "medicine" purposes, and an elaborately detailed ritual of prayer and ceremony was the necessary accompaniment to its capture. Among all the tribes the chief purpose of this ritual was to obtain the help of the gods in inducing the eagle to approach the hunter, and to turn aside the anger of the eagle spirits at the necessary sacrilege. The feathers most valued were those of the tail and wings. These were used to ornament lances and shields, to wear upon the head, and to decorate the magnificent war bonnets, the finest of which have a pendant or trail of eagle-tail feathers reaching from the warrior's head to the ground when he stands erect. The whistle used in the sun dance and other great ceremonies is made of a bone from the leg or wing of the eagle, and the fans carried by the warriors on parade and used also to sprinkle the holy water in the mescal ceremony of the southern prairie tribes is commonly made of the entire tail or wing of that bird. Hawk feathers are sometimes used for these various purposes, but are always considered far inferior to those of the eagle. The smaller feath- ers are used upon arrows. Eagle feathers and ponies were formerly the standard of value and the medium of exchange among the prairie tribes, as wampum was with those of the Atlantic coast. The standard varied according to place and season, but in a general way from two to four eagles were rated as equal to a horse. In these days the eagle-feather war bonnets and eagle-tail fans are the most valuable parts of an Indian's outfit and the most difficult to purchase from him. Among the pueblo tribes eagles are sometimes taken from the nest when young and kept in cages and regularly stripped of their best feathers. Among the Caddo, Cherokee, and other tribes of the timbered country in the east they were shot with bow and arrow or with the gun, but always according to certain ritual ceremonies. Among the prairie tribes along the whole extent of the plains they were never shot, but must be cap- tured alive in pitfalls and then strangled or crushed to death, if possi- ble without the shedding of blood. A description of the Arapaho method will answer with slight modifications for all the prairie tribes.

The hunter withdrew with his family away from the main camp to some rough hilly country where the eagles were abundant. After some preliminary prayers he went alone to the top of the highest hill and there dug a pit large enough to sit or lie down in, being careful to carry the earth taken out of the hole so far away from the place that it would not attract the notice of the eagle. The pit was roofed over with a covering of light willow twigs, above which were placed earth and grass to give it a natural appearance. The bait was a piece of fresh meat, or, as appears from this song, a piece of tallow stripped from the ribs of the buffalo. This was tied to a rawhide string and laid upon the top of the pit, while the rope was passed down through the roof into the cavity below. A coyote skin, stuffed and set up erect as in life, was sometimes placed near the bait to add to the realistic effect. Having sat up all night, singing the eagle songs and purifying himself for the ceremony, the hunter started before daylight, without eating any breakfast or drinking water, and went up the hill to the pit, which he entered, and, having again closed the opening, he seated himself inside holding the end of the string in his hands, to prevent a coyote or other animal from taking the bait, and waiting for the eagles to come.

Should other birds come, he drove them away or paid no attention to them. When at last the eagle came the other birds at once flew away. The eagle swooped down, alighting always at one side and then walking over upon the roof of the trap to get at the bait, when the hunter, putting up his hand through the framework, seized the eagle by the legs, pulled it down and quickly strangled it or broke its neck. He then rearranged the bait and the roof and sat down to wait for another eagle. He might be so lucky as to capture several during the day, or so unfortunate as to take none at all. At night, but not before, he repaired to his own tipi to eat, drink, and sleep, and was at the pit again before daylight. While in the pit he did not eat, drink, or sleep. The eagle hunt, if it may be so called, lasted four days, and must end then, whatever might have been the good or bad fortune of the hunter.

At the expiration of four days he returned to his home with the dead bodies of the eagles thus caught. A small lodge was set up outside his tipi and in this the eagles were hung up by the neck upon a pole laid across two forked sticks driven into the ground. After some further prayers and purifications the feathers were stripped from the bodies as they hung.

The Blackfoot method, as described by Grinnell, in his Blackfoot Lodge Tales, was the same in all essentials as that of the Arapaho. He adds several details, which were probably common to both tribes and to others, but which my Arapaho informants failed to mention. While the hunter was away in the pit his wife or daughters at home must not use an awl for sewing or for other purposes, as, should they do so, the eagle might scratch the hunter. He took a human skull with him into the pit, in order that he might be as invisible to the eagle as the spirit of the former owner of the skull. He must not eat the berries of the wild rose during this period, or the eagle would not attack the bait, and he must put a morsel of pemmican into the mouth of the dead eagle in order to gain the good will of its fellows and induce them to come in and be caught.

The eagle-catching ceremony of the Caddo, Cherokee, and other eastern tribes will be noticed in treating of the Caddo songs.

48. Bä′hinä̈′ninä′tä̈ ni′tabä̈′na

Bä′hinä̈′nina′tä̈ ni′tabä̈′na,
Bä′hinä̈′nina′tä̈ ni′tabä̈′na.
Nänä̈′nina hu′hu,
Nänä̈′nina hu′hu.

Translation

I hear everything,
I hear everything.
I am the crow,
I am the crow.

This is another song expressive of the omniscience of the crow, which, as their messenger from the spirit world, hears and knows everything, both on this earth and in the shadow land. The tune is one of the prettiest of all the ghost songs.

49. A-BÄ'QATI' HÄ'NICHÄ'BI'HINÄ'NA

A-bä′qati′ hä′nichä′bi′hinä′na,
A-bä′qati′ hä′nichä′bi′hinä′na.
A-wa′täna′ni ani′ä′tähi′näna,
A-wa′täna′ni ani′ä′tähi′näna.

Translation

With the *bä′qati* wheel I am gambling,
With the *bä′qati* wheel I am gambling.
With the black mark I win the game,
With the black mark I win the game.

This song is from the northern Arapaho. The author of it, in his visit to the spirit world, found his former friends playing the old game of the *bä′qati* wheel, which was practically obsolete among the prairie tribes, but which is being revived since the advent of the Ghost dance. As it was a favorite game with the men in the olden times, a great many of the songs founded on these trance visions refer to it, and the wheel and sticks are made by the dreamer and carried in the dance as they sing.

The game is played with a wheel (*bä′qati*, "large wheel") and two pairs of throwing sticks (*qa′qa-u′nûtha*). The Cheyenne call the wheel *ä′ko′yo* or *äkwi′u*, and the sticks *hoo′isi′yonots*. It is a man's game, and there are three players, one rolling the wheel, while the other two, each armed with a pair of throwing sticks, run after it and throw the sticks so as to cross the wheel in a certain position. The two throwers are the contestants, the one who rolls the wheel being merely an assistant. Like most Indian games, it is a means of gambling, and high stakes are sometimes wagered on the result. It is common to the Arapaho, Cheyenne, Sioux, and probably to all the northern prairie tribes, but is not found among the Kiowa or Comanche in the south.

The wheel is about 18 inches in diameter, and consists of a flexible young tree branch, stripped of its bark and painted, with the two ends fastened together with sinew or buckskin string. At equal distances around the circumference of the wheel are cut four figures, the two opposite each other constituting a pair, but being distinguished by different colors, usually blue or black and red, and by lines or notches on the face. These figures are designated simply by their colors. Figures of birds, crescents, etc, are sometimes also cut or painted upon the wheel, but have nothing to do with the game. (See plate CXI.)

The sticks are light rods, about 30 inches long, tied in pairs by a peculiar arrangement of buckskin strings, and distinguished from one another by pieces of cloth of different colors fastened to the strings. There is also a pile of tally sticks, usually a hundred in number, about the size of lead pencils and painted green, for keeping count of the game. The sticks are held near the center in a peculiar manner between the fingers of the closed hand. When the wheel is rolled, each player runs from the same side, and endeavors to throw the sticks so as to strike the wheel in such a way that when it falls both sticks of his pair shall be either over or under a certain figure. It requires dexterity to do this, as the string has a tendency to strike the wheel in such a way as to make one stick fall under and the other over, in which case the throw counts for nothing. The players assign their own value to each figure, the usual value being five points for one and ten for the other figure, with double that number for a throw which crosses the two corresponding figures, and one hundred tallies to the game.

The wheel-and-stick game, in some form or another, was almost universal among our Indian tribes. Another game among the prairie tribes is played with a netted wheel and a single stick or arrow, the effort being to send the arrow through the netting as nearly as possible to the center or bull's-eye. This game is called *ana'wati'n-hati,* "playing wheel," by the Arapaho.

50. Ani'äsa'kua'na dä'chäbi'hati'tani

Ani'äsa'kua'na dä'chäbi'hati'tani bä'qati'bä,
Ani'äsa'kua'na dä'chäbi'hati'tani bä'qati'bä.
Ni'ati'biku'thahu' bä'qatihi,
Ni'ati'biku'thahu' bä'qatihi.
Di'chäbi'häti'ta'ni',
Di'chäbi'häti'ta'ni'.

Translation

I am watching where they are gambling with the *bä'qati* wheel,
I am watching where they are gambling with the *bä'qati* wheel.
They are rolling the *bä'qati,*
They are rolling the *bä'qati.*
While they gamble with it,
While they gamble with it.

In this song the dancer tells how he watched a group of his friends in the spirit world playing the game of the *bä'qati,* as has been explained in the song last treated.

51. Ni'chi'a i'theti'hi

Ni'chi'ä i'theti'hi,
Ni'chi'ä i'theti'hi,
Chana'ha'ti i'nĭt—
Chana'ha'ti i'nĭt—
Gu'n baa'-ni'binä thi'aku'-u,
Gu'n baa'-ni'binä thi'aku'-u.

Translation

(There) is a good river,
(There) is a good river,
Where there is no timber—
Where there is no timber—
But thunder-berries are there,
But thunder-berries are there.

This song refers to a trance vision in which the dreamer found his people camped by a good, i. e., perennial, river, fringed with abundant bushes or small trees of the *baa-ni'bin* or "thunder-berry," which appears to be the black haw, being described as a sort of wild cherry, in size between the chokecherry and the wild plum. It was eaten raw, or dried and boiled, the seeds having first been taken out. It is very scarce, if found at all, in the southern plains.

52. NI'NINI'TUBI'NA HU'HU' (former closing song)

Ni'nini'tubi'na hu'hu',
Ni'nini'tubi'na hu'hu'.
Bäta'hina'ni hu'hu',
Bäta'hina'ni hu'hu',
Nä'hinä'ni häthi'na,
Nä'hinä'ni hä"thi'na.

Translation

The crow has given me the signal,
The crow has given me the signal.
When the crow makes me dance,
When the crow makes me dance,
He tells me (when) to stop,
He tells me (when) to stop.

This was formerly the closing song of the dance, but is now super. seded as such by number 73, beginning *Ahu'yu häthi'na.* It was also the last song sung when a small party gathered in the tipi at night for a private rehearsal, and was therefore always held in reserve until the singers were about ready to separate. The tune is one of the best.

The special office of the crow as the messenger from the spirit world and representative of the messiah has been already explained. He is supposed to direct the dance and to give the signal for its close.

53. ANIHÄ′YA ATANI′TÄ′NU′NAWA′

Anihä′ya atani′tä′nu′nawa′,
Anihä′ya atani′tä′nu′nawa′,
Häthi′na hesûna′nĭn,
Häthi′na hesûna′nĭn,
Da‵chä′-ihi′na he′sûna′nĭn,
Da‵chä′-ihi′na he′sûna′nĭn—Ih! Ih!

Translation

I use the yellow (paint),
I use the yellow (paint),
Says the father,
Says the father,
In order to please me, the father,
In order to please me, the father—*Ih! Ih!*

The meaning of this song is somewhat obscure. It seems to be a message from the messiah to the effect that he paints himself with yellow paint, because it pleases him, the inference being that it would please him to have his children do the same. Those who take part in the sun dance are usually painted yellow, that being the color of the sun. This song is peculiar in having at the end two sharp yelps, in the style of the ordinary songs of the warrior dances.

54. NI′NAÄ′NIAHU′TAWA BI′TAA′WU

A′-näni′sa′na, a′-näni′sa′na,
Ni′naä′niahu′tawa bi′taa′wu,
Ni′naä′niahu′tawa bi′taa′wu,
A′-tini′ehi′ni′na nä′nisa′na,
A′-tini′ehi′ni′na nä′nisa′na,
Häthi′na hesûna′nĭn,
Häthi′na hesûna′nĭn.

Translation

My children, my children,
I am flying about the earth,
I am flying about the earth.
I am a bird, my children,
I am a bird, my children,
Says the father,
Says the father.

In this song the messiah, addressing his children, is represented as a bird (crow?) flying about the whole earth, symbolic of his omniscience. The song has one or two variants.

55. I′nita′ta′—usä′na

I′nita′ta′-usä′na,
I′nita′ta′-usä′na.
Hä′tini′tubibä′ hu′hu,
Hä′tini′tubibä′ hu′hu.
Hä′tina′ha′wa′bä hu′hu,
Hä′tina′ha′wa′bä hu′hu.

Translation

Stand ready,
Stand ready.
(So that when) the crow calls you,
(So that when) the crow calls you.
You will see him,
You will see him.

This song was composed by Little Raven, one of the delegation of seven from the southern Arapaho and Cheyenne which visited the messiah in Nevada in August, 1891. It is a message to the believers to be ready for the near coming of the new earth. The first line is sometimes sung *I′nita′ta-u′sä-hu′na.*

56. WA′WÄTHÄ′BI

Nä′nisa′na-ŭ′, nä′nisa′na-ŭ′,
Wa′wäthä′bichä′chinĭ′nabä′nagu′wa-u′i′naga′thi—He′e′ye′!
Häthi′na ne′nahu′,
Häthi′na ne′nahu′.

Translation

My children, my children,
I have given you magpie feathers again to wear on your heads—*He′e′ye′!*
Thus says our mother,
Thus says our mother.

This song affords a good specimen of the possibilities of Indian word building. The second word might serve as a companion piece to Mark Twain's picture of a complete word in German. It consists of seventeen syllables, all so interwoven to complete the sense of the word sentence that no part can be separated from the rest without destroying the whole. The verbal part proper indicates that "I have given you (plural) a headdress again." The final syllables, *wa-u′i-naga′thi*, show that the headdress consists of the tail feathers (*wagathi*) of the magpie (*wa-u-i*). The syllable *cha* implies repetition or return of action, this being probably not the first time that the messiah had given magpie feathers to his visitors.

The magpie (*Pica hudsonica* or *mittalii*) of the Rocky mountains and Sierra Nevada and the intermediate region of Nevada and Utah is perhaps the most conspicuous bird in the Paiute country. It bears a general resemblance to a crow or blackbird, being about the size of the latter, and jet black, with the exception of the breast, which is white, and a white spot on each wing. In its tail are two long feathers with beautiful changeable metallic luster. It is a home bird, frequenting the neighborhood of the Paiute camps in small flocks. It is held sacred among the Paiute, by whom the long tail feathers are as highly prized for decorative purposes as eagle feathers are among the tribes of the plains. The standard price for such feathers in 1891 was 25 cents a pair. The delegates who crossed the mountains to visit the messiah brought back with them quantities of these feathers, which thenceforth filled an important place in the ceremonial of the Ghost dance. In fact they were so eagerly sought after that the traders undertook to meet the demand, at first by importing genuine magpie feathers from the mountains, but later by fraudulently substituting selected crow feathers from the east at the same price.

The song is also peculiar in referring to the messiah as "my mother" (*nena*) instead of "our father" (*hesúnanin*), as usual.

57. Ani'qa hĕ'tabi'nuhu'ni'na

Ani'qa hĕ'tabi'nuhu'ni'na,
Ani'qa hĕ'tabi'nuhu'ni'na.
Hatăna'wunăni'na hesûna'nĭn,
Hatăna'wunăni'na hesûna'nĭn.
Ha'tăni'ni'ahu'hi'na he'sûna'nĭn,
Ha'tăni'ni·ahu'hi'na he'sûna'nĭn.

Translation

My father, I am poor,
My father, I am poor.
Our father is about to take pity on me,
Our father is about to take pity on me.
Our father is about to make me fly around.
Our father is about to make me fly around.

This song refers to the present impoverished condition of the Indians, and to their hope that he is now about to take pity on them and remove them from this dying world to the new earth above; the feathers worn on their heads in the dance being expected to act as wings, as already explained, to enable them to fly to the upper regions.

58. Nä'nisa'taqu'thi hu'na

Nä'nisa'taqu'thi hu'na—Hi'ă hi'ni'ni'!
Nä'nisa'taqu'thi hu'na—Hi'ă hi'ni'ni'!
Hi'bithi'ni'na gasi'tu—Hi'ă hi'ni'ni'!
Hi'bithi'ni'na gasi'tu—Hi'ă hi'ni'ni'!

Translation

The seven crows—*Hi'ă hi'ni'ni'!*
The seven crows—*Hi'ă hi'ni'ni'!*
They are flying about the carrion—*Hi'ă hi'ni'ni'!*
They are flying about the carrion—*Hi'ă hi'ni'ni'!*

In this song the dreamer tells of his trance visit to the spirit world, where he found his friends busily engaged cutting up the meat after a successful buffalo hunt, while the crows were hovering about the carrion. Four and seven are the constant sacred numbers of the Ghost dance, as of Indian ritual and story generally.

59. AHU′NÄ HE′SÛNA′NĬN

Ahu′nä he′sûna′nĭn—
Ahu′nä he′sûna′nĭn—
Ni′tabä′tani′ bäta′hina′ni,
Ni′tabä′tani′ bäta′hina′ni,
Ha kä hä′sabini′na he′sûna′nĭn,
Ha′kä hä′sabini′na he′sûna′nĭn.

Translation

There is our father—
There is our father—
We are dancing as he wishes (makes) us to dance,
We are dancing as he wishes (makes) us to dance,
Because our father has so commanded us,
Because our father has so commanded us.

The literal meaning of the last line is "because our father has given it to us," the prairie idiom for directing or commanding being to "give a road" or to "make a road" for the one thus commanded. To disobey is to "break the road" and to depart from the former custom is to "make a new road." The idea is expressed in the same way both in the various spoken languages and in the sign language.

60. GA′AWA′HU

Ga′awa′hu, ga′awa′hu,
Ni′hji′nä gu′shi′nä,
Ni′hii′nä gu′shi′nä.
A′tanä′tähinä′na,
A′tanä′tähinä′na.

Translation

The ball, the ball—
You must throw it swiftly,
You must throw it swiftly.
I want to win,
I want to win.

The author of this song was a woman who in her trance vision saw her girl friends in the other world playing the ball game, as described in song number 7. In this case, however, her partner is urged to *throw* the ball, instead of to strike it.

61. AHU′ NI′HIGA′HU

Ahu′ ni′higa′hu,
Ahu′ ni′higa′hu.
Ha′tani′ni′tani′na,
Ha′tani′ni′tani′na.

Translation

The Crow is running,
The Crow is running.
He will hear me.
He will hear me.

This song implies that the Crow (messiah) is quick to hear the prayer of the dancer and comes swiftly to listen to his petition.

62. YA′THÄ-YÛ′NA TA′NA-U′QAHE′NA

Ne′sûna′—He′e′ye′!
Ne′sûna′—He′e′ye′!
Ya′thä-yûna ta′na-u′qahe′na—He′e′ye′!
Ya′thä-yûna ta′na-u′qahe′na—He′e′ye′!
Ta′bini′na hi′ticha′ni—He′e′ye′!
Ta′bini′na hi′ticha′ni—He′e′ye′!
Bi′taa′wu ta′thi′aku′tawa′—He′e′ye′!
Bi′taa′wu ta′thi′aku′tawa′—He′e′ye′!

Translation

My father—*He′e′ye′!*
My father—*He′e′ye′!*
He put me in five places—*He′e′ye′!*
He put me in five places—*He′e′ye′!*
I stood upon the earth—*He′e′ye′!*
I stood upon the earth—*He′e′ye′!*

The author of this song tells how in his trance he went up to the other world, where he stood upon the new earth and saw the messiah, who took him around to five different places and gave him a pipe. The number five may here have some deeper mythic meaning besides that indicated in the bare narrative.

63. NI′NAÄQA′WA CHIBÄ′TI

Ni′naäqa′wa chibä′ti,
Ni′naäqa′wa chibä′ti.
Ha′-ina′tä be′yi thi′äya′na,
Ha′-ina′tä be′yi thi′äya′na.

Translation

I am going around the sweat-house,
I am going around the sweat-house.
The shell lies upon the mound,
The shell lies upon the mound.

The maker of this song saw in his vision a sweat-house with a white shell lying upon the mound in front, where a buffalo skull is usually placed. The song evidently refers to some interesting religious cere-mony, but was heard only once, and from a young man who could give no fuller explanation. I have never seen a shell used in this connec-tion. It may be, as suggested by Reverend H. R. Voth, that the word shell is really a figurative expression for skull. In the old days the whole buffalo head was used, instead of the mere skull

64. Hise′hi, hise′hi

Hise′hi, hise′hi,
Hä′tine′bäku′tha′na,
Hä′tine′bäku′tha′na,
Häti′ta-u′seta′na,
Häti′ta-u′seta′na.

Translation

My comrade, my comrade,
Let us play the awl game,
Let us play the awl game,
Let us play the dice game,
Let us play the dice game.

The woman who composed this song tells how, on waking up in the spirit world, she met there a party of her former girl companions and sat down with them to play the two games universally popular with the women of all the prairie tribes.

The first is called *ně′bäku′thana* by the Arapaho and *tsoñä* or "awl game" (from *tsoñ*, an awl) by the Kiowa, on account of an awl, the Indian woman's substitute for a needle, being used to keep record of the score.

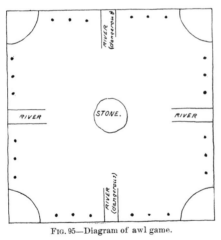

FIG. 95—Diagram of awl game.

The game is becoming obsolete in the north, but is the everyday summer amusement of the women among the Kiowa, Comanche, and Apache in the southern plains. It is very amusing on account of the unforeseen "rivers" and "whips" that are constantly turning up to disappoint the expectant winner, and a party of women will frequently sit around the blanket for half a day at a time, with a constant ripple of laughter and good-humored jokes as they follow the chances of the play. It would make a very pretty picnic game, or could readily be adapted to the parlor of civilization.

The players sit upon the ground around a blanket marked in charcoal with lines and dots, and quadrants in the corners, as shown in figure 95. In the center is a stone upon which the sticks are thrown. Each dot, excepting those between the parallels, counts a point, making twenty-four points for dots. Each of the parallel lines, and each end of the curved lines in the corners, also counts a point, making sixteen points for the lines or forty points in all. The players start from the bottom, opposing players moving in opposite directions, and with each throw of the sticks the thrower moves her awl forward and sticks it into the blanket at the dot or line to which her throw carries her. The parallels on each of the four sides are called "rivers," and the dots within these parallels do not count in the game. The rivers at the top and bottom are "dangerous" and can not be crossed, and when the player is so unlucky as to score a throw which brings her upon the edge of the river (i. e., upon the first line of either of these pairs of parallels), she "falls into the river" and must lose all she has hitherto gained, and begin again at the start. In the same way, when a player moving around in one direction makes a throw which brings her awl to the place occupied by the awl of her opponent coming around from the other side, the said opponent is "whipped back" to the starting point and must begin all over again. Thus there is a constant succession of unforeseen accidents which furnish endless amusement to the players.

The game is played with four sticks, each from 6 to 10 inches long,

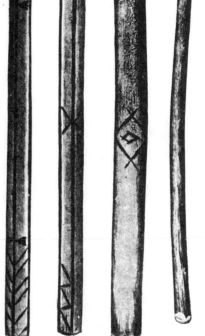

FIG. 96—Sticks used in awl game.

flat on one side and round on the other (figure 96). One of these is the trump stick and is marked in a distinctive manner in the center on both sides, and is also distinguished by having a green line along the flat side (figure 97), while the others have each a red line. The Kiowa call this trump stick *sahe*, "green," on account of the green stripe, while the others are called *guadal*, "red." There are also a number of small green sticks, about the size of lead

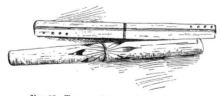

FIG. 97—Trump sticks used in awl game.

pencils, for keeping tally. Each player in turn takes up the four sticks together in her hand and throws them down on end upon the stone in the center. The number of points depends on the number of flat or round sides which turn up. A lucky throw with the green or trump stick generally gives the thrower another trial in addition. The formula is:

One flat side up counts 1
One flat side (if *sahe*) counts .... 1 and another throw.
Two flat sides up, with or without *sahe*, count............... 2
Three flat sides up count 3
Three flat sides up, including *sahe*, count.................... 3 and another throw.
All four flat sides up count................................... 6 and another throw.
All four round sides up count.................................. 10 and another throw.

Only the flat sides count except when all the sticks turn round side up. This is the best throw of all, as it counts ten points and another throw. On completing one round of forty points the player takes one of the small green tally sticks from the pile and she who first gets the number of tally sticks previously agreed on wins the game. Two, four, or any even number of persons may play the game, half on each side. When two or more play on a side, all the partners move up the same number of points at each throw, but only the lucky thrower gets a second trial in case of a trump throw.

The other woman's game mentioned, the dice game, is called *ta-u'sĭta'tina* (literally, "striking," or "throwing against" something) by the Arapaho, and *mo'nshimûnh* by the Cheyenne, the same name being now given to the modern card games. It was practically universal among all the tribes east and west, and under the name of "hubbub" is described by a New England writer as far back as 1634, almost precisely as it exists today among the

Fig. 98—Baskets used in dice game.

prairie tribes. The only difference seems to have been that in the east it was played also by the men, and to the accompaniment of a song such as is used in the hand games of the western tribes.

The requisites are a small wicker bowl or basket (*hatĕchi'na*), five dice made of bone or of plum stones, and a pile of tally sticks such as are used in the awl game. The bowl is 6 or 8 inches in diameter and about 2 inches deep, and is woven in basket fashion of the tough fibers of the yucca (figure 98). The dice may be round, elliptical, or diamond-shape and are variously marked on one side with lines and figures, the turtle being a favorite design among the Arapaho (figure 99). Two of the five must be alike in shape and marking. The other three are marked with another design and may also be of another shape. Any number of women or girls may play, each throwing in turn, and sometimes one set of partners playing against another. The players toss up the dice from the basket, letting them drop again into it, and score points according to the way the dice turn up in the basket. The first throw by each player is made from the hand instead of from the basket. One hundred points usually count a game, and stakes are wagered on the result as in almost every other Indian contest of skill or chance. For the purpose of explanation, we shall designate two of the five as "rounds" and the other three as "diamonds," it being understood that only the marked side counts in the game, excepting when the throw happens to turn up the three diamonds blank while the other two show the marked side, or, as sometimes happens, when all five dice turn up blank. In

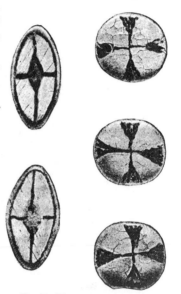

FIG. 99—Dice used in dice game.

every case all of one kind at least must turn up to score a point. A successful throw entitles the player to another throw, while a failure obliges her to pass the basket to some one else. The formula is:

1 only of either kind	0
2 rounds	3
3 diamonds (both rounds with blank side up)	3
3 diamonds blank (both rounds with marked side up)	3
4 marked sides up	1
5 (all) blank sides up	1
5 (all) marked sides up	8

A game similar in principle, but played with six dice instead of five, is also played by the Arapaho women, as well as by those of the Comanche and probably also of other tribes.

65. NA'TU'WANI'SA

Nänisa'na, nänisa'na,
Na'tu'wani'sa, na'tu'wani'sa—
Hä'nätä'hĭ'näti',
Hä'nätä'hĭ'näti'.

Translation

My children, my children,
My top, my top—
It will win the game,
It will win the game.

The man who made this song when he entered the spirit world in his vision met there one of his boy friends who had died long years before, and once more spun tops with him as in childhood.

Tops are used by all Indian boys, and are made of wood or bone. They are not thrown or spun with a string, but are kept in motion by whipping with a small quirt or whip of buckskin. In winter they are spun upon the ice. The younger children make tops to twirl with the fingers by running a stick through a small seed berry.

66. HE'NA'GA'NAWA'NEN

He'na'ga'nawa'nen näa'wu'nani'nä bi'gushi'shi He'sûna'nini'—Ahe'e'ye'!
He'na'ga'nawa'nen näa'wu'nani'nä bi'gushi'shi He'sûna'nini'—Ahe'e'ye'!
Nithi'na hesûna'nini'—Ahe'e'ye'!
Nithi'na hesûna'nini'—Ahe'e'ye'!

Translation

When we dance until daylight our father, the Moon, takes pity on us—*Ahe'e'ye'!*
When we dance until daylight our father, the Moon, takes pity on us—*Ahe'e'ye'!*
The father says so—*Ahe'e'ye'!*
The father says so—*Ahe'e'ye'!*

With the Arapaho, as with many other tribes, the moon is masculine, and the sun is feminine. In mythology the two are brother and sister. There are various myths to account for the spots on the moon's surface, some discerning in them a large frog, while to others they bear a likeness to a kettle hung over the fire. The Arapaho name for the moon, *bi'gushish*, means literally "night sun," the sun itself being called *hishinishish*, "day sun." A similar nomenclature exists among most other tribes.

67. NI'NÄ'NINA'TI'NAKU'NI'NA NA'GA'QU'

A'nä-ni'-sa'-na, a'nä-ni'-sa'-na,   ni'-nä'-ni-na'-ti'-na-ku'   ni'-na na'-ga'-qu',

ni'-nä'-ni-na'-ti'-na-ku'   ni'-na na'-ga'-qu';   ti'-na-ha'-thi-hu' nä'-ni-sa'-na,

ti'-na-ha'-thi-hu' nä'-ni-sa'-na,   hä-thi'-na He'-sû-na'-nĭn, hä-thi'-na He'-sû-na'-nĭn.

A'näni'sa'na, a'näni'sa'na,
Ni'nä'nina'ti'naku'ni'na na'ga'qu',
Ni'nä'nina'ti'naku'ni'na na'ga'qu';
Ti'naha'thihu' nä'nisa'na,
Ti'naha'thihu' nä'nisa'na,
Häthi'na He'sûna'nĭn,
Häthi'na He'sûna'nĭn.

Translation

My children, my children,
It is I who wear the morning star on my head,
It is I who wear the morning star on my head;
I show it to my children,
I show it to my children,
Says the father,
Says the father.

This beautiful song originated among the northern Arapaho, and is a favorite north and south. In it the messiah is supposed to be addressing his children. There is a rhythmic swing to the vocalic syllables that makes the tune particularly pleasing, and the imagery of thought expressed is poetry itself. The same idea occurs in European ballad and legend, and has a parallel in the angel of the evangelist, "clothed with a cloud, and a rainbow upon his head."

68. A'-NENA' TABI'NI'NA

A'-nena' tabi'ni'na nĕ'tĭqta'wa'hu',
A'-nena' tabi'ni'na nĕ'tĭqta'wa'hu'.
Ä'nii'nahu'gahu'nahu,
Ä'nii'nahu'gahu'nahu.
Tahu'naha'thihi'na nä'nisa'na,
Tahu'naha'thihĭ'na nä'nisa'na.

Translation

My mother gave me my *ti'qtawa* stick,
My mother gave me my *ti'qtawa* stick.
I fly around with it,
I fly around with it,
To make me see my children,
To make me see my children.

This song was composed by a woman of the southern Arapaho. The reference is not entirely clear, but it is probable that in her trance vision she saw her children in the other world playing the game mentioned, and that afterward she made the game sticks and carried them in the dance, hoping by this means to obtain another vision of the spirit world, where she could again talk with her children who had gone before her to the shadow land. In one Ghost dance seven different women carried these game sticks.

The *băti'qtŭba* (abbreviated *ti'qtŭp*) game of the Arapaho and other prairie tribes somewhat resembles the Iroquois game of the "snow snake," and is played by children or grown persons of both sexes. It is a very simple game, the contestants merely throwing or sliding the sticks along the ground to see who can send them farthest. Two persons or two parties play against each other, boys sometimes playing against girls or men against women. It is, however, more especially a girl's game. The game sticks (*băti̭qta'wa*) are slender willow rods about 4 feet long, peeled and painted and tipped with a point of buffalo horn to enable them to slide more easily along the ground. In throwing, the player holds the stick at the upper end with the thumb and fingers, and, swinging it like a pendulum, throws it out with a sweeping motion. Young men throw arrows about in the same way, and small boys sometimes throw ordinary reeds or weed stalks. Among the Omaha, according to Dorsey, bows, unstrung, are made to slide along the ground or ice in the same manner.

69. YĬ′HÄ′Ä′Ä′HI′HĬ′

Yĭ′hä′ä′ä′hi′hĭ′, Yĭ′hä′ä′ä′hi′hĭ,
Hä′nänä′hi′gutha′-u ga′qaä-hu′hu′,
Hä′nänä′hi′gutha′-u ga′qaä-hu′hu′.

Translation

Yĭ′hä′ä′ä′hi′hĭ′, Yĭ′hä′ä′ä′hi′hĭ′,
I throw the "button,"
I throw the "button."

In his trance vision the author of this song entered a tipi and found it filled with a circle of his old friends playing the *ga'qutit*, or "hunt the button" game. This is a favorite winter game with the prairie tribes, and was probably more or less general throughout the country. It is played both by men and women, but never by the two sexes together. It is the regular game in the long winter nights after the scattered families have abandoned their exposed summer positions on the open prairie, and moved down near one another in the shelter of the timber along the streams. When hundreds of Indians are thus camped together, the sound of the drum, the rattle, and the gaming song resound nightly through the air. To the stranger there is a fascination about such a camp at night, with the conical tipis scattered about under the trees, the firelight from within shining through the white canvas and distinctly outlining upon the cloth the figures of the occupants making merry inside with jest and story, while from half a dozen different directions comes the measured tap of the Indian drum or the weird chorus of the gaming songs. Frequently there will be a party of twenty to thirty men gaming in one tipi, and singing so that their voices can be heard far out from the camp, while from another tipi a few rods away comes a shrill chorus from a group of women engaged in another game of the same kind.

The players sit in a circle around the tipi fire, those on one side of the fire playing against those on the other. The only requisites are the "button" or *ga'qaä*, usually a small bit of wood, around which is tied a piece of string or otter skin, with a pile of tally sticks, as has been already described. Each party has a "button," that of one side being painted black, the other being red. The leader of one party takes the button and endeavors to move it from one hand to the other, or to pass it on to a partner, while those of the opposing side keep a sharp lookout, and try to guess in which hand it is. Those having the button try to deceive their opponents as to its whereabouts by putting one hand over the other, by folding their arms, and by putting their hands behind them, so as to pass the *ga'qaä* on to a partner, all the while keeping time to the rhythm of a gaming chorus sung by the whole party at the top of their voices. The song is very peculiar, and well-nigh indescribable. It is usually, but not always or entirely, unmeaning, and jumps, halts, and staggers in a most surprising fashion, but always in perfect time with the movements of the hands and arms of the singers. The greatest of good-natured excitement prevails, and every few minutes some more excitable player claps his hands over his mouth or beats the ground with his flat palms, and gives out a regular war-whoop. All this time the opposing players are watching the hands of the other, or looking straight into their faces to observe every tell-tale movement of their features, and when one thinks he has discovered in which hand the button is, he throws out his thumb toward that hand with a loud *"that!"* Should he guess aright, his side scores a certain number of tallies, and in turn takes the button and begins another song. Should the guess be wrong, the losing side must give up an equivalent number of tally sticks. So the play goes on until the small hours of the night. It is always a gambling game, and the stakes are sometimes very large.

The first line of the song here given is an imitation of one of these gambling songs. Among the prairie tribes each song has one or perhaps two words with meaning bearing on the game, the rest of the song being a succession of unmeaning syllables. Among some other tribes, particularly among the Navaho, as described by Dr Washington Matthews, the songs have meaning, being prayers to different animal or elemental gods to assist the player.

As specimens of another variety of gambling songs, we give here two heard among the Paiute of Nevada when visiting the messiah in the winter of 1891–92. They have pretty tunes, very distinct from those of the prairie tribes, and were borrowed by the Paiute from the Mohave, in whose language they may have a meaning, although unintelligible to the Paiute.

Paiute gambling song

Yo'-ho' ma-ho'-yo o-wa'-na, ha'-yă-mă ha'-yă-mă kă-ni'-yo-wi'. Yo'-ho' ma-ho'-yo o-wa'-na, ha'yă-mă ha'-yă-mă kă-ni-yo-wi'. Ho'-tsă-ni'-ă-ni tsai'-o-wi'-a-ni,

i - ha' - ha' tsi - ma'-ni-mi-na,   ha - tsi-ma'-ni-mi-na'.   Ho' - tsă - ni'-ă - ni

tsai' -o - wi'-a - ni',   i - ha' - ha tsi-ma'-ni-mi-na'.   ha - tsi-ma'-ni-mi - na'.

1. Yo'ho' maho'yo owa'na,
   Ha'yămă ha'yămă kăni'yowĭ'.   (*Repeat.*)
2. Ho'tsăni'ăni tsai'-owi'ani',
   Iha'ha' tsima'nimina' ha' tsima'nimina'.   (*Repeat.*)

70. NI'QA-HU'HU'

Ni'qa-hu'hu', ni'qa-hu'hu',
Hu'wĭ'säna', hu'wĭ'säna' —
Ga'qa'ä-hu'hu', ga'qa'ä-hu'hu'.

Translation

My father, my father,
I go straight to it, I go straight to it—
The *ga'qaä*, the *ga'qaä*.

This song also refers to the game of *ga'qutit*, just described. The *ga'qaä* is the "button."

71. A'HU'NAWU'HU'

A'hu'nawu'hu'-u'-u', a'hu'nawu'hu'-u'-u',
Hă'tani'i'bii'na—He'e'ye'!
Hă'tani'i'bii'na—He'e'ye'!
Ga'qu'tina'ni,
Ga'qu'tina'ni,
Hi'nä'ähä'k ga'qa'ä—He'e'ye'!
Hi'nä'ähä'k ga'qa'ä—He'e'ye'!

Translation

With red paint, with red paint,
I want to paint myself— *He'e'ye'!*
I want to paint myself— *He'e'ye'!*
When I play *ga'qutit*,
When I play *ga'qutit*.
It is the "button"— *He'e'ye*
It is the "button"— *He'e'ye'!*

This song refers to the same game described under songs 69 and 70, and like them is based on the trance experience of the composer.

72. ANI'QA NAGA'QU

Ani'qa naga'qu !
Ani'qa naga'qu !
Ina'habi'ä nina'gănawa'ni,
Ina'habi'ä nina'gănawa'ni.
Awu'năni'ä — Hi'i'i' !
Awu'năni'ä — Hi'i'i' !

Father, the Morning Star !
Father, the Morning Star !
Look on us, we have danced until daylight,
Look on us, we have danced until daylight.
Take pity on us — *Hi′i′i′!*
Take pity on us — *Hi′i′i′!*

This song is sung about daylight, just before the closing song, after the dancers have danced all night and are now ready to quit and go home. When the new doctrine came among the prairie tribes, the Ghost dance was held at irregular and frequent intervals, almost every other night, in fact—lasting sometimes until about midnight, sometimes until daylight, without any rule. As the ceremonial became crystallized, however, the messiah gave instructions that the dance should be held only at intervals of six weeks, and should then continue four consecutive nights, lasting the first three nights until about midnight, but on the fourth night to continue all night until daylight of the next morning. The original letter containing these directions is given in chapter x. For a long time these directions were implicitly followed, but the tendency now is to the original fashion of one-night dances, at short intervals. This song to the morning star was sung just before daylight on the final morning of the dance.

With all the prairie tribes the morning star is held in great reverence and is the subject of much mythological belief and ceremony. It is universally represented in their pictographs as a cross, usually of the Maltese pattern. In this form it is frequently pictured on the ghost shirts. The Arapaho name, *nagaq′*, means literally "a cross." The Kiowa know it as *t′aiñso*, "the cross," or sometimes, as *dä-e′dal*, "the great star."

73. Ahu′yu häthi′na (closing song)

A - hu′ - yu hä - thi′ - na he - sû - na′ - ni - ni hu′ - hu, a - hu′ - yu hä-

thi′ - na he - sû - na′ - ni - ni hu′ - hu, ya - thû′n ä - ta′ - u - sä′ - bä, ya - thû′n ä-

ta′ - u - sä′ - bä, ni - thi′ - na he - sû - na′ - nîn, ni - thi′ - na he - sû - na′ - nîn.

Ahu′yu häthi′na hesûna′nini hu′hu,
Ahu′yu häthi′na hesûna′nini hu′hu,
Yathû′n äita′-usä′bä—

Yathû'n äta'-usä'bä—
Nithi'na hesûna'nĭn,
Nithi'na hesûna'nĭn.

Translation

Thus says our father, the Crow,
Thus says our father, the Crow.
Go around five times more—
Go around five times more—
Says the father,
Says the father.

This is the closing song of the dance since the return of the great delegation of southern Arapaho and Cheyenne who visited the messiah in August, 1891. Before that time the closing song had been number 52, beginning *Ni'nini'tubi'na hu'hu'*. The literal rendering of the second part is "stop five times," the meaning and practice being that they must make five circuits singing this song and then stop. As already stated, in accordance with the instructions of the messiah, the Ghost dance is now held (theoretically) at intervals of six weeks and continues for four consecutive nights, closing about midnight, excepting on the last night, when the believers dance until daylight. As daylight begins to appear in the east, they sing the song to the morning star, as just given (number 72), and then, after a short rest, the leaders start this, the closing song, which is sung while the dancers make five circuits, resting a few moments between circuits. Then they unclasp hands, wave their blankets in the air to fan away all evil influences, and go down to the river to bathe, the men in one place and the women in another. After bathing, they resume their clothing and disperse to their various camps, and the Ghost dance is over.

ARAPAHO GLOSSARY

In this and the other glossaries here given it is intended only to give a concise definition of the meaning of each word without going into details of grammar or etymology. The Ghost dance was studied for its mythology, psychology, ritual, and history, and language in this connection was only the means to an end, as it was impossible in a few months of time to devote close attention to the numerous languages spoken by the tribes represented in the dance.

The Arapaho language, as will be seen from the specimens given, is eminently vocalic, almost every syllable ending in a vowel, and there being almost no double consonant sounds. Like the Cheyenne language, it lacks *l* and *r*. The most prominent vowel sounds are *a, ä,* and *i,* and in some instances there are combinations of several vowel sounds without any intervening consonant. The soft *th* sound is also prominent. The *g* and *d* frequently approximate to *k* and *t*, respectively, and *b* in the standard dialect becomes *v* among the northern Arapaho. The only sound of the language (excepting the medial *k* and *t*) not found in English is the guttural *q*, and the language is entirely devoid of the hissing effect of Cheyenne or the choking sounds of Kiowa.

In the songs it is common to prefix *a*, and to add *i*, *hi*, *hu*, *huhu*, etc, to the ends of words in order to fill out the meter. In a few cases changes are made in the body of the word for the same purpose. In the glossary these unmeaning syllables are not given where they occur at the end of words. Words beginning with a vowel sound may sometimes be written as beginning with the breathing *h*, and *s* is sometimes pronounced· *sh*.

Aä'ninĕ'na— the name by which the Arapaho Grosventres of the Prairie, one of the five principal divisions of the Arapaho, call themselves. It is said to signify "white clay men," from *aäti*, "white clay," and *hinĕ'na*, "men." They are called *Hitu'nĕna*, or "beggars," by the rest of the tribe, and are commonly known to the whites under the French name of Grosventres, "big bellies."

Aanû'hawa— another name for the Ha'nahawunĕ'na division of the Arapaho. The meaning of the word is unknown.

Abää'thina'hu— for *Bääthi'na*.

A'baha'— for *Ba'haa'*.

Ä'bäna'änahu'u'— for *Bänaä'na*.

Abä'nihi— for *Bä'ni*.

Abä'qati— for *Bä'qăti*.

Ächiqa'hăwa— I am looking at him. Also *Nina'hawa*, I look at him. *Nă'hănĭ*, Here! Look! *nahata*, look at it (imperative singular); *ina'habi'ä*, look on us. Compare *Hätina'hawa'bä*.

Ächĭshinĭ'qahi'na— he was taking me around.

A'gană'— bed-covers of buffalo skin; singular, *a'gă'*.

Aha'kănĕ'na— "crazy men," one of the degrees of the Arapaho military organization. The word is derived from *aha'ka*, crazy, and *hinĕna*, men. The "fire moth," which flies around and into the fire, is called *aha'kăă'*, or "crazy," and the *Aha'kănĕna* are supposed to imitate the action of this moth in the fire dance. See Arapaho song 43 and Cheyenne song 10.

Aha'känithi'ĭ— they are crazy. In the Indian idea "foolĭsh" and "crazy" are generally synonymous. Compare *Aha'känen'a* and *Ahaka'wŭ*.

Ahaka'wŭ— the crazy dance. It is called *Psam* by the Cheyenne, from *psa*, crazy. See Arapaho song 43 and Cheyenne song 10.

Ahe'eye'!— an unmeaning exclamation used in the songs.

A'hene'heni'ăă!— an unmeaning exclamation used in the songs.

A'hesûna'nini— for *Hesûna'nĭn*.

A'heye'ne'hene'!— an unmeaning exclamation used in the songs.

Ahe'yuhe'yu!— an unmeaning exclamation used in the songs.

Ahu'— for *Ho*.

Ahu'hu— for *Ho*.

Ahu'nä— there it is; there he is.

Ahu'nawu'hu— for *Hĭnăw'*, paint. Compare *Hĭna'wûn*.

Ahu'yu— thus; in this way.

Änani'nibinä'si— for *Nani'nibinä'sĭ*.

Anä'nisa'na— for *Näni'sanäû*.

Ana'wati'n-hati— "playing wheel" (*hati*, wheel); a netted gaming wheel. See Arapaho song 50.

Anĕä'thibiwä'hana— for *Nĕä'thibiwa'na*.

Ane'na— for *Ne'na*.

Ani'anethahi'nani'na— for *Ni'anĕ'hahi'nani'na*.

Aniäsa'kua'na— for *Ni'äsa'kua'na*.

Ani'ätähĭ'näna— for *Hänä'tähĭnä'na*.

A'niesa'na— for *Niesa'na*.

Anihä'ya— the yellow (paint).

Ä'nii'nahu'gahu'nahu— for *Häni'inĭahu'na*.

Ani'niha'niahu'na— for *Niniha'niahu'na*.

Ani'qa— for *Ni'qa*.

Ani'qu— for *Ni'qa*.

Ani'qana'ga— for *Ni'qana'ga*.

A'nisûna'ahu— for *Nisû'na*.

Aqa'thinĕ'na— "pleasant men," from *aqa'thi*, "pleasant," and *hinĕ'na*, "men." One of the five bands of the southern Arapaho.

Ärä'pʜo— the popular name for the Arapaho tribe. The derivation is uncertain, but it may be, as Dunbar suggests, from the Pawnee verb *tirapihu* or *larapihu*, "he buys or trades," in allusion to the Arapaho having formerly been the trading medium between the Pawnee, Osage, and others in the north, and the Kiowa, Comanche, and others to the southwest (*Grinnell*). It is worthy of note that old frontiersmen pronounce the name Arä́pihu. It is not the name by which they are called by the Cheyenne, Sioux, Shoshoni, Kiowa, Comanche, Apache, Caddo, or Wichita.

ÄRÄPA'KATA—the Crow name for the Arapaho, evidently another form of the word Arapaho.

Atănätähinä'na—I wish to win or beat.

Atani'tanu'newa—I use it. *Ati'tänu'wä*, use it! (imperative singular).

Äta'-usä'bä—stop *so many* times (plural imperative). The verb applies only to walking, etc; the generic imperative for stopping or quitting is *nä'hinä'ni*, q. v.; *Hithĕta'-usä*, stop! (singular imperative).

Ate'be—for *Tĕ'bĕ*.

Atĕ'betana'-ise'ti—for *Tĕ'bĕ'tana'-isĕt*.

Äti'ʻchäbi'näsä'nă—let us go out gambling.

Äti'chani'na—your pipes. *Hicha*, a pipe; *hiti'cha*, this pipe; *sĕ'icha*, the sacred "flat pipe." See Arapaho song 2.

Atini'ehini'na—for *Thĕni'ehi'nina*.

ATSI'NA — the Blackfoot name for the *Aä'ninĕna* or Arapaho Grosventres. The word signifies "gut people."

Awawa—for *Wa'wa*.

Awatänani—for *Watäna'ni*.

Awu'năni'ä—another form of *ne'chawu'nani*—take pity on us.

Ba(-hu)—a road or trail.

Ba'achinĕ'na—Another name for the *Nakasinĕ'na* (q. v.) or northern Arapaho. The word may mean "red willow (i. e., kinikinik) men," or "blood-pudding men," the latter etymology being derived from *bä*, blood, and *chini'niki*, to put liquid into a bladder.

Bääku'ni—"Red Feather," the Arapaho name of Paul Boynton, a Carlisle student, and formerly interpreter at Cheyenne and Arapaho agency.

Baa'-ni'bina — "thunder-berries," from *băa'*, thunder, and *ni'bin*, berry; a wild fruit, perhaps the black haw. See Arapaho song 51.

Bääthi'na—cedar tree. See Arapaho song 31.

BAD PIPES—one of the three bands of the northern Arapaho. Their present chief is Sharp Nose.

Băĕ'na—turtle. See Arapaho song 25.

Ba'haa', or *Băa'*—the Thunder. See Arapaho song 14.

Bähibiwă'hina—on their account I am made to cry (immediate present). *Băniwa'nă* or *nibiwa'na*, I am crying; *hä'nibiwähina*, on its account I am made to cry, for its sake I am crying; *năhibiwa'huna'na*, then I wept; *năhibiwa'huna*, then I began to cry or lament; *nĕä thibiwa'na*, the place where crying begins.

Bä'hinänina'tä—everything.

BAHWETEGOW-ENINNEWAY—the Ojibwa name for the *Aä'ninĕna* or Arapaho Grosventres (*Tanner*). It signifies "men, or people of the falls," from *bawitig*, "falls," and *ininiwăg*, "men, or people." They are so called on account of their former residence at the rapids of the Saskatchewan.

Bänaä'na—the thunderbirds; singular *Ba'haa'*, or *Ba'awa*.

Bä'ni—my (male) comrade. Vocative. Used by a boy or young man speaking to his comrade or partner of the same sex. The corresponding female term is *hisä*.

Bä'qati—"great wheel," from —— great, and *hati'*, a gaming wheel, a wagon. An ordinary wheel is called *ni'nae'găti*, "turner." See Arapaho song 49.

Bä'qătibä—with the *bä'qăti*, q. v.

Bäsawunĕ'na—one of the five divisions of the Arapaho, and formerly a distinct tribe. The name is variously rendered "wood lodge men" or "big lodge men," or people, the terminal part being derived from *hinĕ'na* "men."

Băta'hina'ni—he makes me dance. (In the songs *when*, *where*, etc., are sometimes understood with verbs). *Băta't*, a dance; *nibä'tană*, I dance; *nitabä'tani*, we are dancing; *bätäna'ni*, when we dance; *Thi'gănăwa't*, the Ghost dance. Compare also *Hena'gana'wanĕn*.

Bätäna'ni—when we dance. Compare *Băta'hina'ni*.

Bătĭ'qtawa—the throwing-stick used in the *bătĭ'qtăba* game. See Arapaho song 68.

Bătĭ'qtŭba—the game of the "throwing-stick" or "snow-snake" among the prairie tribes. See Arapaho song 68.

Bena—for *Băĕ'na*.

Běni'něna—"warriors," the military organization of the Arapaho. See Arapaho song 43.

Běni'nina—he gave it to me. *Běni'na*, I gave it to him; *bě'nině'thǐn*, I gave it to you; *niibi'nu*, I gave it to them; *häsabini'na*, he has given it to us; *tabini'na*, he (she) gave it to me; *da'chi'bini'na*, he will give me a hawk-feather.

Bětiděě—the Kiowa Apache name for the Arapaho.

Beyi—a (white) shell.

Bi'ga—night.

Bi'gushish—the moon, literally "night sun," from *bi'ga*, night, and *hishi'sh*, sun, or celestial luminary. The sun is distinquished as *hishi-nishi'sh*, or "day sun," from *hishǐ*, day, and *hishi'sh*. In many Indian languages the sun and moon have but one name, with an adjective prefix or suffix to distinguish between day and night. See Arapaho song 66. The morning star is called *naga'q*, "the cross;" the milky way is *hi'thina'na-ba*, "the buffalo road," or *thi'gûni-ba*, "the spirit or ghost road;" the pleiades are *bä'naküth*, "the group (sitting)."

Biqăna'kaye'na—I am crying on account of thirst. *Naka'yena*, I am thirsty.

Bishiqa'wa—coming into sight, approaching from a distance. (Third person, singular.)

Bitaa'wu—the earth.

Bitaha'wŭ—the dance of the *Bita'hiněna*. See Arapaho song 43.

Bita'hiněna—"spear men;" one of the degrees of the Arapaho military organization. The name comes from the Cheyenne word for spear, *bitahä'na;* the Arapaho word for spear is *qawă'*. See Arapaho song 43.

Bi'täye—captor, seizer; the name by which the Arapaho *Hänä'chäthi'äk*, "Sitting Bull," was called when a boy.

Chăna'ha't—where there is none. *Iyahu'h*, it is all gone.

Chänii'nagu'nǐt—he wears them, he is wearing them.

Cha'qtha (singular, *Chaq*)—"enemies," the Arapaho name for the Comanche.

Chä'säq—another, another of them; from *chä'saiy'*, one. See *Yathûn*.

Chěbi'nh—greasy, something greasy; figuratively used for pemmican. See Arapaho song 46.

Chi'bät—a sweat-house.

Chǐ'chita'nǔ—literally, a target, a mark to shoot at. A boy's game. See Arapaho song 4.

Chǐnachǐ'chibä'iha—venerable, (memorable or ancient) priests of the *Chǐ'nachichi'bät*, or sacred sweat-lodge, from *chǐnachichi'bät*, the sacred sweat-lodge, and *bäiä*, old man. See Arapaho song 43.

Chǐ'nachichi'bät—the sacred large sweat-house; from *chi'bät*, sweat-house. See Arapaho song 43.

Chǐnăchǐ'chibä'tina—immortal, venerable, or never-to-be-forgotten priests of the sweat-house; from *chi'bät*, sweat-house. See Arapaho song 43.

Chǐ'nachiněě'na—water-pouring men; the highest degree of the Arapaho military organization. See Arapaho song 43.

Dă'chäbi'hati'tanǐǐ—where there is gambling; where they are gambling. In the Arapaho language there is no generic term for playing for amusement only. *Chäbi'hǐnä'na*, I am gambling; *häni'chäbihǐnäna*, I am gambling with it; *di'chäbihäti'tani'ǐ*, while or when they are gambling with it.

Da'chä'-ihi'na—in order to please me.

Da'chi'binina—he will give me a (chicken-) hawk feather. Compare *Běni'nina*.

Da'chinathi'na—he having come for me (participle). *Nichǐnǔ'ti'ha*, I come for him.

Da'naa'bäna'wa—I moved it ("when" is sometimes understood).

Dä'nasaku'tawa—I am standing upon it.

Dăna'tiněnawa'ŭ—because I longed, or wished, to see him; *da* in composition gives the idea of "because."

De'tawuni'na—he told me. Compare *Häthi'na*.

Di'chäbihäti'tani'ǐ—while or when, they are gambling with it. Compare *Dă'chäbi'hati'tanǐǐ*.

Di'chin—because. *Haka* is also sometimes used.

Diině'tita'niěg—living people; human existence.

DOG SOLDIER—a popular but incorrect name given by the whites to the military organizations of the prairie tribes. See Arapaho song 43.

E'eye'!—an unmeaning exclamation used in the songs.

Ehe'eye'!—ibid.

E'hihänakuwu'hunĭt—he turned into a moose. *Naku'wu*, moose; *iwä'qu*, elk.

Ehihä'sina'kawu'hunĭt—for *E'hihänakuwu'hunĭt*.

Ehihä'sinĭĕhi'nĭt—he is beginning to be a bird, he is turning into a bird; *ni'ĕhi*, a bird.

E'yahe'eye'!—an unmeaning exclamation used in the songs.

Eye'ae'yuhe'yu!—ibid.

E'yehe'!—ibid.

FORKS-OF-THE-RIVER MEN—the principal of the three bands of the northern Arapaho. Their present chief is Black Coal.

Gaahi'na—another form of *Ga'ahinĕ'na*.

Ga'ahinĕ'na—"coyote men," from *ga'a*, coyote, and *hinĕ'na*, men; singular, *ga'ahinĕ'n*. The camp guards or pickets of the Arapaho. See Arapaho song 41.

Ga'awä', or *ga'awäha*—a ball, used in the woman's game of *gä̆'ga'hawa't* or shinny. See Arapaho song 7.

Gaäwa'tina—canned goods, c a n n e d fruits.

Ga'näni'na—he wiped me off, he cleaned me. *Ganĕ'naa*, I wipe him off.

Ga'qaä—the "button" or small object hidden by the players in the *ga'qutit* game. See Arapaho song 69.

Ga'qutina'ni—when I play *ga'qutit*. See Arapaho song 69.

Ga'qutit—the "hunt the button" game of the western tribes. See Arapaho song 69.

Gasi'tu—carrion.

Ga'wunĕ'häna—another form of *Gawunĕ'na*.

Gawunĕ'na—one of the five bands of the southern Arapaho. The name is the same applied by the Arapaho to the Blackfeet, from whom this band is said to be derived. It is also the Arapaho name for the Blackfoot band of Sioux. The name is of foreign origin and can not be explained by the Arapaho. The Blackfeet are sometimes also called by them *Watä'nitä'si*, "black feet."

GREASY FACES—one of the three bands of the northern Arapaho. Their present chief is Spotted Horse.

GROSVENTRES (OF THE PRAIRIE)—the name by which the *Aä'ninĕ'na* (Arapaho division) are commonly known to the whites.

The correct French form is Gros Ventres des Prairies, "Big Bellies of the Prairie," to distinguish them from the Minitari', or Hidatsa, who were called Gros Ventres du Missouri. The term *Gros Ventres*, as applied to this division of the Arapaho, is derived from a misconception of the Indian gesture sign for the tribe, which really denotes "belly people," i. e. "spongers" or "beggars."

Gä̆'gä'hawa't—the woman's game of shinny. See Arapaho song 7.

Gun—but.

Gushi'nä—throw it! (imperative singular). *Asegŭ'*, I throw it; *chegŭ'*, throw it here!

Ha'änake'ĭ—rock, the rock.

Ha'anúnä—forcibly, violently.

Habätä'nani'hi—for *Bätäna'ni*.

Ha'dä'wuha'na—we have made them desolate; we have deprived them of all happiness.

Hageni'stit—he is making it across the water. Compare *Hani'stit*.

Ha'hat—the cottonwood tree (*Populus monilifera*).

Ha-ina'tä—it lies there, it lies upon it.

Häï'nawa—I know. *Ni'hawa*, I do not know.

Ha'ka—because. *Dichin* has the same meaning.

Ha'nä—for *Ha'änúnä*.

Hänä'chä-thi'ä'k—Sitting Bull, the Arapaho apostle of the ghost dance; from *hänä'chä*, a buffalo bull, and *thi'äk*, he is sitting. In early youth, before going to Wyoming, he was called *Bi'täye*, "Captor."

Ha'naĕ'hĭ—little boy (vocative).

Ha'nahawu'nĕn (singular).

Ha'nahawunĕ'na—one of the five divisions of the Arapaho, but now practically extinct. The meaning of the name is unknown, but the final syllables are from *hinĕ'na*, signifying "men," or "people."

Hänäi'säi—at the boundaries.

Hä'nänä'higu'tha-u—for *Nä'higu'tha*.

Häna'nawu'nänu—those who have been taught (?).

Hänä'tähĭnä'na—I win the game (by means of something).

Hä'nätä'hĭ'nät—It will win the game. *Ä'nätähĭ'nänä*, I win.

Hänĭ—for *Häni'ĭnĭ*.

Hä'nibiwă'hĭnă—on its account I am made to cry; for its sake I am crying. Compare *Bähibiwă'hĭna*.

Hänĭ'chäbihĭ'näna—I am gambling with it. Compare *Dă'chäbi'hati'tanĭ*.

Hänĭ'ĭnĭ—by this means, by its means; abbreviated to *hänĭ* or *häni*.

Häni'inĭahu'na—I fly around with it.

Hänina'ta—it is lying there (inanimate). *Säshĭ'năna*, I lie down.

Häni'nihiga'huna' — for *Häni'ĭnĭ nĭhiga'-huna*,—by its means I am running swiftly.

Hani'stit—he has finished it, now he has finished it. Compare *Hageni'stit*.

Hänĭta'quna'nĭ—in the pitfall; from *ta'quna*, a pitfall. See Arapaho song 47.

Ha'qihana—"wolves," one of the five bands of the southern Arapaho.

Hä'sabini'na—he has given it to us. Compare *Bĕni'nina*.

Hä'täi'naku'ni—you may have it. *Näni'-thana'na*, I have it.

Hatăna'wunăni'na—he is about to take pity on me. *Nä'awu'năna*, I pity him; *awu'nanĭ* or *ne'chawu'nani*, have pity on me; *nitawu'nana*, I take pity on them. Compare *Tĭ'awawu'nănu*.

Hă'tanbii'na—I wish to paint myself with it. *Bii'nanihä'ya*, I paint myself.

Hă'tani'i'bii'na—for *Ha'tanbii'na*.

Hatäni'ina'danĕ'na—I am about to use him to "make medicine," i. e., to perform a sacred ceremony (remote future). The immediate future is *hatăni'nada-nĕ'na; inĭ* is the root of *to use; nada-nĕ'na*, is to "make medicine," from the root *nĕ'na*, to sing. The gesture sign for "song" and "medicine" are also nearly the same. See Arapaho song 33.

Hatăni'niahu'hi'na—he is going to make me fly around. *Hăni'niahu'na*, I am flying; *gaya'ahuha*, I make him fly.

Ha'tani'nitani'na—for *Hatni'tăni'na*.

Hatĕchi'na—the basket bowl used in the dice game. See Arapaho song 64.

Hä'thäbĕ'na (-*wa*)—I hand it to you.

Ha'thahŭ—star dance; the dance of the *Hă'thahu'ha*. See Arapaho song 43.

Hă'thahu'ha—star people, from *hă'tha*, star; one of the degrees of the Arapaho military organization. See Arapaho song 43.

Häthi'na—he tells me, he says to me. Present, *häthi'na;* future, *nĭhiithi'na;*

perfect, *hatnithi'na; he'ităwuni'na*, it tells me; *de'tawuni'na*, another form for "he told me."

Ha'ti—for *Ha'hat*.

Hätiku'tha—the humming toy used by boys of the prairie tribes. See Arapaho song 25.

Hätina'hawa'bä—you (plural) will see him; *nana'hawă*, I see him; *ni'naha-wa'na*, we see them; *nahăbi'na*, he saw me; *na'hawû*, I saw him; *he'nă̆'awă̆*, when I see it; *tahu'naha'thihi'na*, to make me see them. *Nina'hawa*, I look at him.

Hätinĕ'bäku'thana—let us play *nĕ'bäku'-thana*, the awl game. See Arapaho song 64.

Hätini'tubi'bä—he is calling you (plural); *nini'tuwa*, I call him.

Häti'ta-usĕta'na—let us play *ta'-usĕta'na*. See Arapaho song 64.

Hä'tnaa'waa'—it is about to move (immediate future).

Hätnaawaa-uhu—for *Hä'tnaa'waa'*.

Hatni'tani'na—he will hear me. *Näni'-ta'nă̆*, I hear him; *nitabä'na*, I hear it; *nini'dănă̆'û*, I heard him. In the form in Arapaho song 61, *Hatani'nitani'na*, the syllable *ni* is repeated in the body of the word to fill in the meter.

Hatni'thi'aka'tana—we have it in the center. *Nahi'thaä'ntană̆*, I am the center; *nähi'thiăni'na'ta*, it is in the center.

Hayana'-u'si'ya—for *Yaʳna-u'si'ya*.

He!—an unmeaning exclamation used in the songs.

Hechä'—when again.

He'e'e'!—an unmeaning exclamation used in the songs.

He'ee'ä'ehe'yuhe'yu!—ibid.

He'eye'!—ibid.

He'ităwuni'na—it tells me. Compare *Häthi'na*.

He'nă̆'awă̆—when I see it. Compare *Hätina'hawa'bä*.

He'nagana'ʳwanĕn—when we dance until daylight. The root is *naga'nh*, daylight, or dawn. *Nibä'tanä*, I dance; *ni'nagăn-awa'ni*, we have danced until daylight. Compare *Bäta'hina'ni*.

Hesû'na—the father. *Hesûna'nĭn*, our father; *nisû'na*, my father, whence *hi-nisû'na-hu* of the songs.

Hesûna'nĭn—our father. Compare *He-sû'na*.

Hĕtabi'nuhu'ni'na—I am poor; I am needy.

Hĕthĕʼhinĕʼna—Dog men, from *hĕth*, dog, and *hinĕʼna*, men; one of the degrees of the Arapaho military organization. See Arapaho song 43.

Hĕthĕwaʼwŭ—The dance of the *Hĕthĕhinĕʼna.* See Arapaho song 43.

Heʼwa-uʼsa—you are a young crow, you are the offspring of the crow; *ho* or *hu*, crow; *hosa*, a young crow, a little crow. This was the Indian name of Little Raven, the noted Arapaho chief, who died a few years ago.

Heʼyaheʼeye!—an unmeaning exclamation used in the songs.

Heʼyäyaʼaheʼye!—ibid.

Heʼyohoʼho!—ibid.

Hiʼa!—ibid.

Hiʼbithiniʼna—they are flying about it. *Ninaäʼniahuʼtawa*, I am flying about it. Compare *Näniiʼahuʼna.*

Hichääʼqawŭ—the dance of the *Hichääʼquthi.* See Arapaho song 43.

Hichääʼquthi—Club men, from *chääʼtha*, a club; one of the degrees of the Arapaho military organization. See Arapaho song 43.

Hiʼchäbäʼ-i—high up, on high, i. e., in heaven, in the sky, or in a tree top.

Higaʼahinaʼ-ĭt—"The man with the coyote gun;" from *gaahiʼna*, the "coyote men;" a camp guard or picket among the Arapaho. See Arapaho song 41.

Hiii!—an unmeaning exclamation used in the songs.

Hiʼnä—here; here it is.

Hinäʼähäʼk—it is! (strongly affirmative). Compare *Hiʼnä.*

Hinäʼäthi—the long wing-feather (referring to the longest wing pinion, worn on the head).

Hĭnaʼwûn—his paint; *hĭnäʼwʼ*, (red) paint, the Indian clay paint; *ninaʼwʼ*, my paint; *henaʼwʼ*, your paint.

Hĭʼni or *ĭʼnĭ*—that, that one.

Hiʼnini'!—an unmeaning song terminal.

Hiʼniqaʼagaʼyetuʼsa—for *Hĭʼnĭ niqagaʼyätusă.*

Hinisaʼna—his children. Compare *Nänisaʼnäŭ.*

Hinisûʼnahu—for *Nisûʼna.*

Hĭsäʼ—my female comrade, or companion (vocative).

Hiʼsähihi—for *Hĭsäʼ.*

Hiseʼhi—ibid.

Hĭtäsiʼna—(singular, *Hĭʼtäsi*)—"scarred people," the Arapaho name for the Cheyenne. From *hĭtäshiʼni*, scarred or cut.

Hitiʼcha—this pipe. Compare *Ätiʼchaniʼna.*

Hiticha'ni—for *Hitiʼcha.*

Hituʼnena—the name by which the *Aäʼninĕʼna* or Arapaho Grosventres of the Prairie are known to the rest of the tribe. Another form is *Hituʼnĕniʼna.* It signifies "begging men," or more exactly "spongers," the terminal part being from *hinĕʼna*, "men." The Arapaho call the Sioux *Natni*, and the Asiniboin *Tu-natni*, or "begging Sioux."

Hiʼyu—here it is. *Näyu*, there it is; *häyu*, where is it? what is it?

Ho—crow; usually duplicated as *Huhu* or *Ahuhu* in the songs. The crow is the sacred bird of the Ghost dance, and is also held sacred by the Algonquian tribes generally. See Arapaho song 36.

Hoʼsa—"Little Crow," better known as "Little Raven," the celebrated chief of the southern Arapaho. He died a few years ago and was succeeded by the present head chief *Naʼwat* or Left Hand. The name is derived from *ho*, "crow," and *sa*, the diminutive.

Hu!—an unmeaning exclamation sometimes used by devotees and priests in the Ghost dance when under strong excitement, as *Hu! Hu! Hu!*

HUBBUB—the name given by old New England writers to the Indian dice game. See Arapaho song 68.

Huhu—for *Ho.*

Huʼnă—crows; plural of *ho* or *hu*; figuratively used in the songs for crow feathers worn on the head.

Huʼnakuʼnithi—wearers of the crow feathers; the name given to the seven leaders of the Ghost dance who wear crow feathers on their heads. *Ho*, crow; plural, *hona* or *huna.*

Huʼwisäʼna—I go straight to it. *Huwĭʼsä*, you go, etc; *qănuʼwĭsät*, he goes, etc.

Huyu—another form of *Hiʼyu.*

Ih!—an unmeaning exclamation used in the songs.

IKUNUHKATSI — "All Comrades," the military society of the Blackfeet. See Arapaho song 43.

Inaʼhabiʼä—Look on us! *Ninaʼhawa*, I look at him. Compare *Achiqaʼhăwa.*

I'nĭt—timber.

Inita'ta-usä'na—stand ready! (imperative plural) *Näni'tata'-usä'na*, I am ready.

Inŭ'na-i'na—the name used by the Arapaho to designate themselves. It signifies "our people," or "people of our kind."

I'thaq—a gut; a sheath or case made of bear gut. See Arapaho song 41.

I'thetihi—good.

Iyahu'h—gone, it is all gone.

Iyehe'!—an unmeaning exclamation used in the songs.

I'yehe'eye—ibid.

Iyu—another form of *Hi'yu*.

KANINAHOIC—the Ojibwa name for the Arapaho.

KANINA'VISH—ibid.

Kawinahan—the form used by Hayden for *Gawunĕ'na* or *Gawunĕ'häna*, q. v.

Ku'niahu'na—I fly with it on my head.

MAQPĬ'ATO—the Sioux name for the Arapaho. It signifies "blue cloud, i.e., a clear sky;" reason unknown.

MINNETAREES OF FORT DE PRAIRIE—The name given by Lewis and Clark to the *Aä'ninĕna* or Arapaho Grosventres. The *Aä'ninĕna* are known to the French Canadians as Gros Ventres des Prairies, while the Minitari are called by them Gros Ventres du Missouri, and the American explorers incorrectly compounded the two names.

Näa'wunani'nä—he takes pity on us. Compare *Hatäna'wunäni'na*.

Na'chichaba'n—they are still making it. *Nä'nĭstĭnä*, I make it; *Näsu'nistĭnä*, I still make it.

Naga'q—the morning star. See Arapaho songs 67 and 72. The word literally means "a cross."

Nahăbi'na—he saw me. Compare *Hätina'hawa'bä*.

Nä'hănĭ—here! look! Compare *Ächiqa'hăwă*.

Naha'ta—look at it! (imperative singular). Compare *Ächiqa'hăwă*.

Na'hawaŭ'—for *Na'hawŭ'*.

Na'hawŭŭ—I saw him. Compare *Hätina'hawä'bä*.

Nä'hibiwa'huna—then I begin to cry or lament. Compare *Bähibiwă'hĭna*.

Nä'hibi'wahuna'na—then I wept. Compare *Bähibiwă'hĭna*.

Nä'higu'tha—I throw it. *Nina'gu'tha*, I throw it where it can not be found.

Nä'hinä'n—stop!

Nä'inaha'tdäbä'naq—I then saw the multitude plainly.

Na'kash—sage; the wild sage (Artemisia); the name of a prominent northern Arapaho.

Na'kasinĕ'na—the name by which the northern Arapaho call themselves. It signifies "sagebrush men," from *na'kash*, "sagebrush," and *hinĕ'na* or *hinĕ'nina*, the plural of *hinĕ'n*, "man." They are called *Ba'achinĕ'na* by the other Arapaho, and *Tägyä'ko* by the Kiowa.

Nănä'—it is that, that is the thing.

Na'nagă'qănĕt—white-skinned (singular); from *na'guă*, white (organic) and *wană'q*, skin. *Nŭna'chă*, white (inorganic); either *na'guă* or *nŭna'chă* may be used in speaking of a house. *Na'nagă'qănĕt* is one of the Arapaho names for the whites, the ordinary term being *Nia'thn*, q. v. See also *Niha'nătaye'chet*.

Nanaha'thăhi—he showed me. *Nanaha'tha*, I show him.

Nänä'nina—it is I, I am he (emphatic).

Nana'thina'ni—he came to take me, he came for me. In the songs the adverb "when" or "where" is sometimes understood with the verb. See Arapaho song 38.

Näne'th—when I met him.

Nä'niahu'na—for *Näniĭ'ahu'na*.

Nänibä'tawă—I am singing it; *Näni'bina*, I sing; *nibä't*, a song.

Nänibä'tia—for *Nänibä'tawă*.

Nä'nihithätu'hăna—thus I shouted, or called. *Nä'ni* in composition signifies "thus."

Näni'ibä—it is spotted.

Nani'nibinä'sĭ—the wind makes them sing. *Näni'bina*, I sing. Compare *Nänibä'tawă*.

Nänisa'na—for *Näni'sanăŭ'*.

Näni'sanăŭ' or *Näni'sanăq*—my children. *Näni'sa*, my older child; *näni'sanĕ'ăĕ'*, my young child.

Nänisa'taqi—for *Ni'sataq*, seven.

Nänisa'tăquthi—for *Ni'sataq*, seven.

Nä'nitha'tuhŭ'na—for *Nä'nihithatu'hăna*.

Näniwu'hună—I carry it as I fly about in circles. Compare *Hi'bithini'na* with *Tahĕti'niahu'na*.

Nasu'siyakunawa—I am stripping it. I am unsheathing it. Compare *Să'niyagu'nawa'*.

Na'tănu'ya—what I am using. *Tanu'-năwa'*, I use it.

Na'tenehi'na—another form of *Natni* or *Na'tnihi'na*.

Na'tni or *Na'tnihi'na*—the Arapaho name for the Sioux. The etymology is unknown, but it may possibly be a form of *Na'dowe*, the generic Algonquian name for Indians of a different stock.

Natu'wani'sa—my top (a toy); from *uwani'sa*, a top. See Arapaho song 65.

Na'waa'tănû—I prayed to him; *ni'awăaa'-tanû*, I am praying (to him).

Na'wat—"Left Hand," present head chief of the southern Arapaho.

Na'wathinĕ'ha—the name by which the southern Arapaho are known to the rest of the tribe. It signifies "southerners," and is said to be an archaic form for *Nawunĕ'na*, the name by which the southern Arapaho call themselves.

Na'wunĕ'na—the proper name of the southern Arapaho. It signifies "southern men," from *na'wun*, "south," and *hinĕ'na*, "men." They are called *Nawa'-thinĕ'ha*, "southerners," by the northern Arapaho, which is said to be the archaic form.

Năya'qât—the whirlwind. The powers and phenomena of nature are generally personified in Indian thought and language.

Nä'yu—there it is. Compare *Iyu*.

Nea-i'qaha'ti—for *Ne'ia-i'qahat*.

Neä'thibiwa'na—the place where crying begins. Compare *Bähibiwä'hĭna*.

Nĕ'băku'thana—the "awl game" of the women of the prairie tribes. See Arapaho song 64.

Nĕ'chäi'hit—he gave me this grateful gift; he gave me this, for which I am thankful.

Nĕ'cha'wu'nani—have pity on me (imperative singular). Compare *Hatana'wunani'na*.

Nehawa'wunä'na—I have no sympathy with him. Compare *Ti'awawu'nănu*.

Nĕ'ia-i'qahat—now he is collecting them; now he begins to gather them.

Ne'na(-hu)—my mother. *Nesû'na*, my father.

Nesû'na—another form of *Nisû'na*.

Nĕtĭ'qtawa—my *tĭ'qtawa* or throwing-stick. The game is called *bătĭ'qtŭba*, abbreviated to *tĭ'qtûp*. The throwing-stick is called *bătĭ'qtawa* or *tĭ'qtawa*. See Arapaho song 68.

Nĕ'tita'wahu—for *Netĭ'qtawa*.

Ni'ănĕ'thăhi'nani'na—he did not recognize me. The negative idea is contained in *änĕ'th; ä'ninani'na*, he recognized me.

Ni'ănita'wathi—they push hard, i. e., they persevere. *Näni'äni'tawana*, I push hard; I do my best; I do right.

Nia'rhari's - kúrikiwa's - húski—proper Wichita name for the Arapaho.

Ni'äsa'kua'na—I am looking on, or watching. Compare *Hätina'hawa'bä* and *Ächiqa'hăwa*.

Nia'thu or *Nia'' thuă*—the white people; singular, *Nia'tha*. The word signifies literally expert, skillful, or wise, and is also the Arapaho name for the spider. The word for "white" is *nu'na'cha'ă*. Compare *Na'nagă'qănĕt* and *Niha'nă-tayc'chet*.

Niathu'a-u—for *Niathu'a*.

Niati'biku'thahu—for *Niati'biku'thathi*.

Niati'biku'thathi—they are rolling it.

Nibäi'naku'nithi—they all wear it on their heads. *Ninaku'na*, I wear it on my head.

Nibä't—song. Compare *Nänibä'tawă*.

Nibä'tia—for *Nibä't*.

Ni'binu—for *Niibi'na*.

Ni'bithi't—I have nothing to eat.

Ni'chiă—river.

Ni'chihinĕ'na—"river men," the Arapaho name for the Kiowa. From *ni'chiă*, river, and *hinĕ'na*, men, so called from the former residence of the Kiowa on upper Arkansas river, from which they were driven by the Arapaho and Sioux.

Niesa'na, or *Ni'ehisa'na*—the young birds. *Niĕ'hĕ*, bird; *niĕ'hisa*, a young bird.

Niha'nătaye'chet—yellow - hided (singular); from *niha'ne*, yellow, and *nata'-yech*, a hide; one of the Arapaho names for the whites. The ordinary term is *Nia'thu*, q. v.

Nĭ'higa'hu—he is running. *Näniga'na*, I run; *năni'higa*, he runs; *nĭhiga'huna*, I am running swiftly.

Nĭ'higa'huna—I am running swiftly. Compare *Nĭhiga'hu*.

Nihii'nä—forcibly, swiftly.

Niibi'na—I gave it to them. Compare *Bĕni'nina*.

Niitegu—for *Nii'tĕhăg*.

Nii'tĕhăg—it was he, he was the one.

Niitu'qawigú'niĕ'—where they were coming down; where they were descending toward us.

Ninaä'niahu'na—I fly in circles (habitual); I am constantly flying about in circles. Compare *Hi'bithini'na* and *Tahĕti'niahu'na*.

Ninaä'niahu'tawa—I am flying about it. Compare *Hi'bithini'na*.

Ninaä'qäwa'—I go around it.

Ni'naganawa'ni—we have danced until daylight. Compare *He'nagana'ʳwanĕn* and *Bäta'hina'ni*.

Ni'nahawa'na—we see them. Compare *Hätina'hawa'bä*.

Ninä'ninati'nakuni'na—It is I who have (wear) it on my head; I am the one who ties it on my head.

Ninĕʳn—tallow.

Niniha'niahu'na—I fly around yellow. *Niha'ne*, yellow. Compare *Hi'bithini'na* and *Nänii'ahu'na*.

Ni'nini'tubi'na—he has called me.

Nini'tänä'û—I heard him. Compare *Hatni'täni'na*.

Ninitu'sa—making a sound, resounding.

Ni'qa—father (vocative; no possessive pronoun implied). A more reverential or affectionate form than *nisúna*.

Niqaga'yätusa—the loudest sounding, the loudest of all. The idea of "loudest" is contained in *qaga'y*, and of "sounding" in *tusa*. See *N'initu'sa*.

Ni'qahu'hu'—for *Ni'qa*.

Ni'qana'ga—that one buffalo bull; there is a solitary bull. *Hänä'chä*, a buffalo bull, is changed in the song to *qana'ga*. *Ni* in composition denotes alone, single, from *nisi*, only one; *chäsaiy'*, one.

Nisa'na—the same as *nisú'na* or *nesúna*, my father.

Ni'sataq—seven. See *Yathún*.

Nisú'na—my father. Compare *Hesú'na*.

Ni'tabä'na—I hear it. Compare *Hatni'-tani'na*.

Nitabä'tani—we are dancing. Compare *Bäta'hina'ni*.

Nita-i'sa—my relative.

Ni'tawuna'na—I take pity on them. Compare *Hatäna'wunani'na*.

Nithi'na—he said it, he has said it (immediate past). Compare *Häthi'na*.

Nuha'wŭ—Fox dance; the dance of the *Nuhinĕʳna*. See Arapaho song 43.

Nuhinĕʳna--Fox men, from *nu*, fox and *hinĕʳna*, men; one of the degrees of the Arapaho military organization. See Arapaho song 43.

Nu'nagúna''-u'ät—he came with it, he brought it with him.

Núnaha'wŭ—one of the degrees of the Arapaho military organization; the meaning of the word is unknown. See Arapaho song 43.

Nú'nanú'naa'täni'na—he is circling above me. See Arapaho song 39.

Nú'nanú'naku'ti—I am circling it, I am waving it about in circles.

Nu'sa-icha'tha—the ceremonial crook or lance carried by the leader of the *Bita'hinĕna*. See Arapaho song 43.

Qa'qa-u'nútha—the "throwing sticks" used in the game of the *bä'qati*. See Arapaho song 49.

SANI'TIKA—Pawnee name for the Arapaho · from the Comanche name *Sä'rĕtĭka*, "dog eaters."

Sä'niyagu'nawa'—I have stripped it, I have unsheathed it. *Nasu'siyakunawa*, I am stripping it, I am unsheathing it.

SÄ'PANI—the Shoshoni name for the *Aä'ninĕna* or Arapaho Grosventres. It signifies "belly people," from *säp*, belly, and *ni*, the tribal suffix.

SÄ'RĔTĔKA—Comanche and Shoshoni name for the Arapaho. It signifies "dog-eaters," from *sä're*, dog, and *tĕka*, a form of the verb to eat, in allusion to their special fondness for dog flesh. The name is also sometimes used by the Wichita.

Säsa'bä-ithi—looking around, i. e., watchers or lookouts. One of the five bands of the southern Arapaho.

Se'hiwúq—"weasel bear," from *sea* weasel, and *wûq*, bear; also rendered as "gray bear," from *se*, gray, and *wûq*, bear. The name of the keeper of the *sĕʳicha* or sacred pipe of the Arapaho. See Arapaho song 2.

Sĕʳicha—"flat pipe," from *sĕĭ*, flat, and *hicha*, pipe. The sacred pipe and tribal "medicine" of the Arapaho. See Arapaho song 2.

Ta'äwŭn—strike it (imperative singular).

Tabini'na—he (she) gave it to me. Compare *Bĕni'nĕna*.

Taʳchawa'gŭna—while I am carrying a load of (buffalo) beef on a horse. *Ha'gŭ*, I carry a load of beef on a horse in motion; second person, *hagŭ'nĭ*; third person, *hagŭ'tĭ; ta'*, prefix in composition with the verb, implies "while."

Tahĕti'niahu'na— I make the deep, or loud, thunder as I fly about in circles (habitual). Compare *Ninaä'niahu'na* and *Tahuna'änä'niahu'na*. See Arapaho song 27.

Ta'huna'änä'niahu'na— I make the thunder (or loud resounding noise) as I fly about in circles (habitual). Compare *Ninaä'niahu'na* and *Tahĕti'niahu'na*.

Tahu'nahathihi'na— to make me see them. Compare *Hätina'hawa'bä*.

Ta'na-u'qahe'na— he put me there. *Nita'-uqa'*, I put him there (present).

Tani'bäthä— "pierced noses," the Arapaho name for the Caddo; *tani*, nose.

Ta'thiaku'tawa— I stood upon it (?). The regular form for "I was standing upon it" is *Nĭqtä'saku'na*.

Ta'-usĕta'na or *Ta'-usĕta'tina*— literally "striking," or "throwing against" something; the dice game of the women of the prairie tribes. See Arapaho song 64.

Ta'wŭnä— for *Ta'äwŭn*.

Tĕ'bĕ— at first, the first time, in the beginning.

Tĕ'bĕ' tana'-isĕt— when he first came; *tĕ'bĕ*, the first time.

Tha'kú'hinĕna— "whetstone men," or "knife-whetting men," the Arapaho name for the Kiowa Apache (Na-diisha-Dena), and for all other southern Athapascan tribes known to them, including the Lipan, Mescalero, Jicarilla, and Apache proper. The sign for Apache in the sign language of the plains also conveys the same idea, being made by briskly rubbing the left forefinger with the right, as though whetting a knife. *Gäta'ka*, the Pawnee name for the Kiowa Apache, seems to have a connection with this word.

Thĕni'ehi'nina— I am a bird, from *niĕ'hĕ*, bird.

Thi'aku— they are there.

Thi'äya— the sweat-house mound. The name is also applied to a stone heap or monument. See Arapaho song 34.

Thiäya'na— on the *thi'äya* or sweat-house mound.

Thiäya'nĕ— at the *thi'äya* or sweat-house mound.

Thigŭnäwa't— the Ghost dance, from *thig*, ghost or spirit of a dead person, and *bäta't*, a dance. Compare *Bäta'hina'ni*.

Ti'awawu'nänu— when I sympathized with them, when I liked them. I sympathize with him, *tiäwu'nänä*. *Ti* or *tihi* in composition with verbs usually conveys the idea of "when." *Nehawa'-wunäna*, I have no sympathy with him. Compare *Hatäna'wunäni'na*.

Ti'naha'thihu— I show it to them (habitual), or to show it to them. *Ni'naha'-thihu*, I show it to him.

Ti'qtŭp— the common abbreviated form of *Bätĭ'qtŭbä*, q. v.

Uhiyeyeheye!— an unmeaning exclamation used in the songs.

Ûtnitha'wuchä'wahänäni'na— we shall surely again be put (with something understood). The idea of "surely" is contained in *ûtni'thawĭ*; *chä* is from *chä'i'hĭi*, "again."

Wa'ku(-hu)— a feather to wear on the head.

Wa'ku'na— feathers worn on the head; a feather headdress. They are usually painted and beaded, and sometimes mounted on a small stick. A single feather thus worn is called *wa'ku*.

WAKIÑYAÑ-OI— Thunder's Track. The Sioux name of a locality in eastern South Dakota. See Arapaho song 14.

Waqui'si— Ugly Face Woman, an Arapaho man. *Hĭ'si*, woman, is frequently abbreviated to *si* in composition.

Wa'quithi— Bad faces, or Ugly faces; the principal of the five bands of the southern Arapaho. Their chief, Nawat, or Left Hand, is also the principal chief of the southern branch of the tribe.

Watäna'ni— a black mark or picture, from *watä'yä*, black. See Arapaho song 49.

Wa'tän-ga'a— Black Coyote, from *wa'tän*, black, and *ga'a*, coyote. A southern Arapaho, captain of the Indian police, and one of the principal leaders of the Ghost dance among the Arapaho.

Wa'wa— now; it also gives the idea of done, or completed.

Wa'wagathä'na— I have already put him aside, now I have put him aside. *Wawa* or *waw'*, "now," in composition, gives the idea of "already" or completed action.

Wa'wäna'danä'diä— I am about to hum (i. e., with the *Hätiku'tha*). See Arapaho song 25.

Wawäthäbichă῾chinĭnabänaguwa-u-inagathi —I have given you (plural) again, a headdress of magpie feathers; from *wa'-wäthä'bichă῾chinĭ'nabä'nak*, I have given it back again; *wa'-u-i*, magpie; *waga'thi*, a bird's tail feathers. In the verb the root is from *bĭni'na*, I give it to him; *waw*' denotes completion, as "already" done; *chä* implies repetition or return of action. See Arapaho song 56.

Wŭnayu'uhu—for *Wŭ'nayu'ŭ*, they are new. *Wŭ'nayă'*, it is new.

Ya'gaahi'na—for *Ya'hagaahi'na.*

Ya'hagaahi'na—the "coyote gun" or ceremonial club of the *Ga'ahinĕ'na* or "Coyote men." See Arapaho song 41.

Yahe'eye'!—an unmeaning exclamation used in the songs.

Ya῾na-u'si'ya—how bright the moonlight is! *Na'-u'si'ya*, the moonlight is bright.

Ya'thäyŭ'na—five places, in five places; from *ya'thŭn*, five, and *yŭna*, places.

Ya'thŭn—five. Other numerals are: 1, *chä'saiy*; 2, *hĕni'si*; 3, *hĕnä'si*; 4, *yen*; 5, *ya'thŭ* or *ya'thŭn*; 6, *ni'tataq*; 7, *ni'sataq*; 8, *näsataq*; 9, *thi'ataq*; 10, *wĕtätaq*; 20, *ni'sa*; 29, *ni'sa-thi'atăqu'n*; 30, *näsa*; 40, *ye'ya*; 50, *ya'thaiya*; 60, *nitatŭ'sa*; 70, *ni'satŭsa*; 80, *nä'satŭ'sa*; 90, *thi'-atŭ'sa*; 100, *wĕ'tätŭ'sa.*

Ye'nis—the wild rose. The rosebush is *ye'nis*; the seed berry is *ye'nun*, literally "louse child," from the resemblance of the seeds to nits or lice. See Arapaho song 29.

Ye'nisiti'na—with the wild rose; from *ye'nis*, the wild rose, and *ti'naq*, with.

Yĭ'hä'ä'ä'hi'hĭ'—an unmeaning word combination of syllables used in the gambling songs. See Arapaho song 69.

THE CHEYENNE

TRIBAL SYNONYMY

Ba'hakosĭn—Caddo name; "striped arrows," *bă*, arrow. The Caddo sometimes also call them Siä'näbo, from their Comanche name.

Cheyenne—popular name, a French spelling of their Sioux name. It has no connection with the French word *chien*, "dog."

Dzĭtsĭ'stäs—proper tribal name; nearly equivalent to "our people."

Gatsa'lghi—Kiowa Apache name.

Hĭtäsi'na (singular *Hĭ'täsi*)—Arapaho name, signifying "scarred people," from *hĭtäshi'ni*, "scarred or cut." According to the Arapaho statement the Cheyenne were so called because they were more addicted than the other tribes to the practice of gashing themselves in religious ceremonies. The name may have more special reference to the tribal custom of cutting off the fingers and hands of their slain enemies. (See tribal sign, page 1024.)

Ităsupuzi—Hidatsa name, "spotted arrow quills" (Matthews).

Ka'naheăwastsĭk—Cree name, "people with a language somewhat like Cree" (Grinnell).

Niere'rikwats-kŭni'ki—Wichita name.

Nanonĭ'ks-kare'nĭki—Kichai name.

Pägănävo—Shoshoni and Comanche name; "striped arrows," from *päga*, "arrow," and *nävo*, "striped."

Säk῾o'ta—Kiowa name; seems to refer to "biting."

Sa-sis-e-tas—proper tribal name according to Clark (Indian Sign Language, 99, 1885). The form should be *Dzĭtsĭ'stäs* as given above.

Shaiela or *Shaiena*—Sioux name; "red," or decorated with red paint. According to Riggs, as quoted by Clark, the Sioux call an alien language a "red" language, while they designate one of their own stock as "white," so that the name would be equivalent to "aliens." The Sioux apply the same name also to the Cree.

Shiä'navo—another Comanche name, probably a derivative from the word *Cheyenne*.

Shiĕ῾da—another Wichita name, derived from the word *Cheyenne*.

Staitan—unidentified tribal name, given by Lewis and Clark. Identical with the Cheyenne, from their own word *Hĭstä'itän*, "I am a Cheyenne."

TRIBAL SIGN

The Cheyenne tribal sign, made by drawing the right index finger several times across the left forefinger, is commonly interpreted "cut fingers" or "cut wrists," and is said to be derived from their custom of cutting off the fingers and hands of slain enemies. Although the same practice was found among other tribes, the Cheyenne were particularly distinguished in this regard. In Mackenzie's great fight with the Cheyenne in Wyoming, in 1876, two necklaces made of human fingers were found in the captured Indian camp, together with a small bag filled with hands cut from the bodies of children of the Shoshoni tribe, their enemies. One of these necklaces was afterward deposited in the National Museum at Washington. (See *Bourke* in *Ninth Annual Report of the Bureau of Ethnology.*) Some competent Indian authorities say, however, that the sign is intended to indicate "stripe people," or "striped-arrow people," referring to the fact that the Cheyenne usually feathered their arrows with the striped feathers of the wild turkey. This agrees with the interpretation of the name for the Cheyenne in several different languages.

SKETCH OF THE TRIBE

The Cheyenne are one of the westernmost tribes of the great Algonquian stock. In one of their ghost songs they sing of the "turtle river," on which they say they once lived. (*Cheyenne song 3.*) From several evidences this seems to be identical with the Saint Croix, which forms the boundary between Wisconsin and Minnesota. This statement agrees with the opinion of Clark (*Indian Sign Language*), who locates their earliest tradition in the neighborhood of Saint Anthony falls. They were driven out by the Sioux and forced toward the northwest, where they came in contact with the Asiniboin (called by them Hohe'), with whom they were never afterward at peace. At a later period, according to Lewis and Clark, they lived on the Cheyenne branch of Red river, in northern Minnesota, whence they were again driven by the Sioux into the prairie.

In 1805 they wandered about the head of Cheyenne river of Dakota and in the Black hills, and were at war with the Sioux, though at peace with most other tribes. Since then they have pushed on to the west and south, always in close confederation with the Arapaho. These two tribes say they have never known a time when they were not associated. About forty years ago, in Wyoming, the band since known as the northern Cheyenne separated from the others (Clark), and have since lived chiefly in Montana or with the Sioux, with whom the Cheyenne made peace about sixty years ago. The other and larger portion of the tribe continued to range chiefly on the lands of the Arkansas and Canadian in Colorado and the western part of

Kansas and Oklahoma. They and the Arapaho made peace with the Kiowa and Comanche in 1840, and raided in connection with these tribes into Texas and Mexico until assigned in 1869 to a reservation in what is now western Oklahoma. In 1874 they, as well as the Kiowa, Comanche, and Kiowa Apache, again went on the warpath in consequence of the depredations of the buffalo hunters, but the outbreak was speedily suppressed. In 1890 they sold their reservation and took allotments in severalty. The northern Cheyenne joined the Sioux in the "Custer war" of 1876–77. At the surrender of the hostiles they were removed to Oklahoma and placed with the southern Cheyenne, but were much dissatisfied with their location, the dissatisfaction culminating in the attempt of a large party, under Dull Knife, to escape to the north, in September, 1878. They were pursued, and a part of them captured and confined at Fort Robinson, Nebraska, whence they made a desperate attempt to escape on the night of January 9, 1879, resulting in the killing of nearly all of the prisoners. They were finally assigned a reservation in Montana, where they now are, with the exception of a few among the Sioux. According to the official report for 1892, the southern Cheyenne in Oklahoma numbered 2,119, the northern Cheyenne in Montana, 1,200, and those with the Sioux at Pine Ridge, South Dakota, 120, a total of 3,439.

The Cheyenne have eleven tribal divisions. They have at least two dialects, but probably more. The tribal divisions in their order in the camping circle are—

1. *Evĭ'sts-unĭ'pahĭs* (" smoky lodges"—Grinnell, *fide* Clark).

2. *Sŭta'ya* or *Sŭ'tasi'na*. This is one of the most important divisions and formerly constituted a distinct tribe, but was afterward incorporated with the Cheyenne. According to concurrent Cheyenne and Blackfoot tradition, as given by Grinnell, they seem originally to have been a part of the Blackfeet, who became separated from the main body of their tribe by the sudden breaking up of the ice while crossing a large river. They drifted to the southward and finally met and joined the Cheyenne in the Black hills. Their name, spelled *Suti* by Grinnell, is said to mean "strange talkers." They live now on the upper Washita in Oklahoma and speak a dialect differing considerably from that of the rest of the tribe.

3. *Ĭ'sium-itä'niuw'*, ("ridge-people;" singular, *Ĭ'siumi-tän*—Grinnell, *fide* Clark).

4. *Hĕwă-tä'niuw'*, "hairy men." The name is also sometimes used collectively to designate all of the southern Cheyenne as distinguished from the northern Cheyenne, called collectively *Hmĭ'sĭs*. The southern Cheyenne are also designated collectively as *So'wăniă*, "southerners."

5. *Ŏ'ivimă'na*, "scabby." This name is said to have been given them originally on account of an epidemic which once broke out among their horses and rendered them mangy.

6. *Wĭ'tapi'u* ("haters"—Grinnell, *fide* Clark).

7. *Hotă'mi-tä'niuw'*, "dog men," or *Mĭ'stăvĭĭ'nŭt*, "heavy eyebrows." This is also the name of one of the divisions of their warrior organization.

8. *O'tu'gŭnŭ*.

9. *Hmĭ'sĭs*, "eaters." This is the most important division of the northern Cheyenne, and the name is also used by those of the south to designate all the northern Cheyenne collectively.

10. *Anskowĭ'nĭs*.

11. *Pĭnŭ'tgŭ'*.

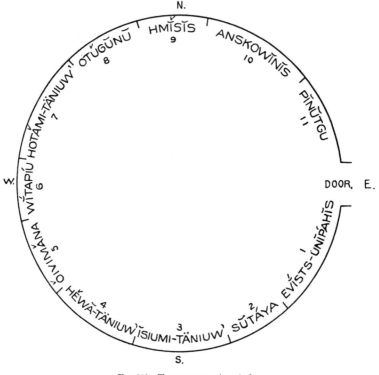

FIG. 100—Cheyenne camping circle.

These are the names given to the author by the Cheyenne themselves as the complete list of their tribal divisions. Grinnell, on the authority of the Clark manuscript, names six of these with two others, *Matsĭ'shkota*, "corpse from a scaffold," and *Miayŭma*, "red lodges," which may be identical with some of the others named above, or may perhaps be degrees of their military organization instead of tribal divisions.

In the great ceremony of the "medicine arrow," last enacted on the Washita in 1890, the camping circle opened to the south. At all other gatherings of the tribe the circle opened to the east, agreeable to the general Indian custom, the several divisions encamping in the order shown in figure 100.

The Cheyenne, like the prairie tribes generally, are, or were until within a few years past, a nation of nomads, living in skin tipis, and depending almost entirely on the buffalo for food. Yet they have a dim memory of a time when they lived in permanent villages and planted corn, and in their genesis tradition, which occupies four "smokes" or nights in the telling, they relate how they "lost" the corn a long time ago before they became wanderers on the plains. They deposit their dead on scaffolds in trees, unlike their confederates, the Arapaho, who bury in the ground. Their most sacred possession is the bundle of "medicine arrows," now in possession of the southern division of the tribe. They have a military organization similar to that existing among the Arapaho and other prairie tribes, as described under number 43 of the Arapaho songs. Above all the tribes of the plains they are distinguished for their desperate courage and pride of bearing, and are preeminently warriors among people whose trade is war. They are strongly conservative and have steadily resisted every advance of civilization, here again differing from the Arapaho, who have always shown a disposition to meet the white man half-way. In fact, no two peoples could well exhibit more marked differences of characteristics on almost every point than these two confederated tribes. The Cheyenne have quick and strong intelligence, but their fighting temper sometimes renders them rather unmanageable subjects with whom to deal. Their conservatism and tribal pride tend to restrain them from following after strange gods, so that in regard to the new messiah they assume a rather skeptical position, while they conform to all the requirements of the dance code in order to be on the safe side.

Clark, in his *Indian Sign Language*, thus sums up the characteristics of the Cheyenne:

As a tribe they have been broken and scattered, but in their wild and savage way they fought well for their country, and their history during the past few years has been written in blood. The men of the Cheyenne Indians rank as high in the scale of honesty, energy, and tenacity of purpose as those of any other tribe I have ever met, and in physique and intellect they are superior to those of most tribes and the equal of any. Under the most demoralizing and trying circumstances they have preserved in a remarkable degree that part of their moral code which relates to chastity, and public sentiment has been so strong in them in regard to this matter that they have been, and are still, noted among all the tribes which surround them for the virtue of their women.

The Cheyenne language lacks the liquids *l* and *r*. It is full of hissing sounds and difficult combinations of consonants, so that it does not lend itself readily to song composition, for which reason, among others, the Cheyenne in the south usually join the Arapaho in the Ghost dance and sing the Arapaho songs.

SONGS OF THE CHEYENNE

1. O'TÄ NÄ'NISĬ'NÄSISTS

O'tä nä'nisĭ'näsĭsts—Ehe'e'ye'!
O'tä nä'nisĭ'näsĭsts—Ehe'e'ye'!
Mä'tesemä'moestä'nowe't—Ähe'e'ye'!
Mä'tesemä'moestä'nowe't—Ähe'e'ye'!
Ho'ivitu'simo'moĭ'ts—E'ähe'e'ye'!
Ho'ivitu'simo'moĭ'ts—E'ähe'e'ye'!
Nu'ka'eshe'väo'e'tse'
Nitu'si'mitä'nun,
Nitu'si'mitä'nun.

Translation

Well, my children—*Ehe'e'ye'!*
Well, my children—*Ehe'e'ye'!*
When you meet your friends again—*Ä'he'e'ye'!*
When you meet your friends again—*Ä'he'e'ye'!*
The earth will tremble—*E'ähe'e'ye'!*
The earth will tremble—*E'ähe'e'ye'!*
The summer cloud (?)
It will give it to us,
It will give it to us.

The interpretation of this song is imperfect and the meaning is not clear. It evidently refers to the earthquake which it is supposed will occur at the moment of contact of the spirit world with the old earth. The literal meaning of the second line, rendered "when you meet your friends again," is "when you are living together again."

2. EHÄ'N ESHO'INI'

Ehä'n esho'ini',
Ehä'n esho'ini',
Hoi'v esho'ini',
Hoi'v esho'ini',
I'yohä'—Eye'ye'!
I'yohä'—Eye'ye'!
I'nisto'niwo'ni—Ahe'e'ye'!
I'nisto'niwo'ni—Ahe'e'ye'!

Translation

Our father has come,
Our father has come,
The earth has come,
The earth has come,
It is rising—*Eye'ye'!*
It is rising—*Eye'ye'!*
It is humming—*Ahe'e'ye'!*
It is humming—*Ahe'e'ye'!*

This is the song composed by Porcupine, the great leader of the Ghost dance among the northern Cheyenne. It refers to the coming of the new earth which is to come over this old world and which is represented as making a humming or rolling noise as it swiftly approaches.

3. NÄ′NISO′NÄSĬ′STSIHI′

Nä′niso′näsĭ′stsihi′,
Nä′niso′näsĭ′stsihi′,
Hi′tää′ni mä′noyu′hii′,
Hi′tää′ni mä′noyu′hii′,
Owa′ni tsi′nitai′-wosi′hi′,
Owa′ni tsi′nitai′-wosi′hi′,
Tsĭ′nitai′-womai′-wosihi′,
Tsĭ′nitai′-womai′-wosihi′.
I′häni′ i′hiwo′uhi′,
I′häni′ i′hiwo′uhi′.

Translation

My children, my children,
Here is the river of turtles,
Here is the river of turtles,
Where the various living things,
Where the various living things,
Are painted their different colors,
Are painted their different colors.
Our father says so,
Our father says so.

This song has a very pretty tune. The Cheyenne claim to have lived originally in the north on a stream known to them as the "River of Turtles." Reverend H. R. Voth, former missionary among the Cheyenne and Arapaho, states that the Indians say that along the banks of this stream were clays of different colors which they used for paint. In a letter of October 1, 1891, he says: " I have now in my possession some red and some gray or drab paint that Black Coyote brought with him from the north, which he claims came from that ancient Turtle river, and which the Indians are now using to paint themselves. They say there are more than two kinds of color at that river, or at least used to be." According to Clark (*Indian Sign Language*, page 99) the oldest traditions of the Cheyenne locate their former home on the headwaters of the Mississippi in Minnesota, about where Saint Paul now is. Other facts corroborate this testimony, and the traditional "Turtle river" would seem to be identical with the Saint Croix, which is thus described by Coxe in 1741:

A little higher up is the river Chabadeda, above which the Meschacebe makes a fine lake twenty miles long and eight or ten broad. Nine or ten miles above that lake, on the east side, is a large fair river, called the river of Tortoises, after you have entered a little way, which leads far into the country to the northeast, and is navigable by the greatest boats forty miles. About the same distance farther up, the Meschacebe is precipitated from the rocks about fifty feet, but is so far navigable by considerable ships, as also beyond, excepting another fall, eighty or ninety miles higher, by large vessels, unto its sources, which are in the country of the Sieux, not at a very great distance from Hudson's bay.   There are many other smaller rivers which fall into the Meschacebe, on both sides of it, but being of little note, and the description of them of small consequence, I have passed over them in silence. (Coxe, Carolana, 1741, in French's Hist. Coll. of La., part 2, 233, 1850.)

4. NÄ′SEE′NEHE′ EHE′YOWO′MI

Nä′see′nehe′ ehe′yowo′mi,
Nä′see′nehe′ ehe′yowo′mi,
E′nää′ne mä′noyo′h ehe′yowo′mi,
E′nää′ne mä′noyo′h ehe′yowo′mi.

Translation

I waded into the yellow river,
I waded into the yellow river,
This was the Turtle river into which I waded,
This was the Turtle river into which I waded.

This song is probably explained by the one immediately preceding.

5. WOSI′VÄ-Ä′Ä′

Wosi′vä-ä′ä′,
Wosi′vä-ä′ä′,
Nänima-iyä,
Nänima-iyä,
Ä′hiya′e′yee′heye′!
Ä′hiya′e′yee′heye′!

Translation

The mountain,
The mountain,
It is circling around,
It is circling around,
Ä′hiya′e′yee′heye′!
Ä′hiya′e′yee′heye′!

The interpretation of this song is not satisfactory.   It was explained that by the mountain was meant the new earth, which was represented as approaching rapidly with a circular motion.

6. NI′HA-I′HI′HI′

Ni′ha-i′hi′hi′,
Ni′ha-i′hi′hi′,
Na′eso′yutu′hi′,
Na′eso′yutu′hi′,
U′guchi′hi′hi′,
U′guchi′hi′hi′,
Na′nisto′hewu′hi′,
Na′nisto′hewu′hi′,
Ga′! Na′hewu′hi,
Ga′! Na′hewu′hi.

Translation

My father,
My father,
I come to him,
I come to him,
The crow,
The crow,
I cry like it,
I cry like it,
Caw! I say,
Caw! I say.

The connection of the crow with the doctrine of the Ghost dance has already been explained. See Arapaho song 36.

7. Hɪ'ᴀᴡᴜ'ʜɪ — ʜɪ'ʜɪ'ʜᴀɪ'-ʏᴀɪ'

Hi'awu'hi — Hi'hi'hai'-yai'!
Hi'awu'hi — Hi'hi'hai'-yai'!
Ni'äsï'tano'ni — Hi'hi'hai'-yai'!
Ni'äsï'tano'ni — Hi'hi'hai'-yai'!
Hi'äma' wihu'i — Hi'hi'hai'-yai'!
Hi'äma' wihu'i — Hi'hi'hai'-yai'!
Ni'hihi'no'ni — Hi'hi'hai'-yai'!
Ni'hihi'no'ni — Hi'hi'hai'-yai'!
Nï'shibä'tämo'ni — Hi'hi'hai'-yai'!
Nï'shibä'tämo'ni — Hi'hi'hai'-yai'!

Translation

The devil — *Hi'hi'hai'-yai'!*
The devil — *Hi'hi'hai'-yai'!*
We have put him aside — *Hi'hi'hai'-yai'!*
We have put him aside — *Hi'hi'hai'-yai'!*
The White Man Above — *Hi'hi'hai'-yai'!*
The White Man Above — *Hi'hi'hai'-yai'!*
He is our father — *Hi'hi'hai'-yai'!*
He is our father — *Hi'hi'hai'-yai'!*
He has blest us — *Hi'hi'hai'-yai'!*
He has blest us — *Hi'hi'hai'-yai'!*

It is hardly necessary to state that the idea of a devil is not aboriginal, although now embodied in the Indian mythology and language from contact with the whites. The "White Man Above" is understood to mean the ruler whose precursor the messiah is, equivalent to our idea of God.

8. Nɪ'ʜᴀ — E'ʏᴇʜᴇ'! E'ʜᴇ'ᴇʏᴇ

Ni'ha — E'yehe'! E'he'eye'!
Ni'ha — E'yehe'! E'he'eye'!
Tsï'stamo'nohyo't — Ehe'eye'!
Tsï'stamo'nohyo't — Ehe'eye'!
O'täta'wome'mäpe'wä — He'eye'!
O'täta'wome'mäpe'wä — He'eye'!
Ni'mistä'tuhä'mi — He'eye'!
Ni'mistä'tuhä'mi — He'eye'!
E'hiwou', E'hiwou' — He'!

Translation

My father—*E'yehe'! E'he'eye'!*
My father—*E'yehe'! E'he'eye'!*
When I first met him—*Ehe'eye'!*
When I first met him—*Ehe'eye'!*
"In the blue-green water—*He'eye'!*
"In the blue-green water—*He'eye'!*
You must take a bath"—*He'eye'!*
You must take a bath"—*He'eye'!*
Thus he told me, thus he told me—*He'!*

Quite a number of the Cheyenne ghost songs refer to rivers seen in the spirit world, these being frequently designated by colors, as yellow, blue, etc. It may be that certain rivers play a prominent part in their mythology, and as has been said they locate their earliest traditional home on the "Turtle river." The word here rendered "blue-green" might mean either blue or green, as in Cheyenne and in many other Indian languages the two colors are not differentiated. Compare Cheyenne song number 16.

9. Ä'MINÛ'QI

Ä'minû'qi—I'yahe'yahe'e'!
Ä'minû'qi—I'yahe'yahe'e'!
Nĭ'stsishi'hiyo'honi'mäni—Ahe'e'ye'!
Nĭ'stsishi'hiyo'honi'mäni—Ahe'e'ye'!
Nĭ'shka'nĭ nĭ'stsishĭ'nutsi'mani—Ahe'e'ye'!
Nĭ'shka'nĭ nĭ'stsishĭ'nutsi'mani—Ahe'e'ye'!
Ehä'ni ni'nĭni'etä'ni—Ahe'e'ye'!
Ehä'ni ni'nĭni'etä'ni—Ahe'e'ye'!

Translation

My comrade—*I'yahe'yahe'e'!*
My comrade—*I'yahe'yahe'e'!*
Let us go and play shinny—*Ahe'e'ye'!*
Let us go and play shinny—*Ahe'e'ye'!*
Let us look for our mother—*Ahe'e'ye'!*
Let us look for our mother—*Ahe'e'ye'!*
Our father tells us to do it—*Ahe'e'ye'!*
Our father tells us to do it—*Ahe'e'ye'!*

This song was composed by Mo ki, "Little Woman," the Cheyenne wife of Grant Left-hand. Although a young woman, she is regarded as a leader in the Cheyenne Ghost dance, having been in frequent trances and composed numerous songs. In this she relates her experience in one trance, during which she and her girl comrade played together the woman's game of shinny, already described, and then went to look for their mothers, who had gone to the spirit world years before.

10. HE'STUTU'AI

He'stutu'ai—Yä'hä'yä'!
He'sutu'äi—
[*Ad libitum*].

Translation

The buffalo head — *Yä'hä'yä'!*
The half buffalo —
[*Ad libitum*].

This song refers to the crazy dance, which the author of the song saw the former warriors of his tribe performing in the spirit world. The crazy dance, called *Psam* by the Cheyenne and *Ahaka'wŭ* by the Arapaho, belonged to one order of the military organization already described in treating of the Arapaho songs. (See Arapaho song 43.) The name in both languages is derived from the word for "crazy." Men, women, and children took part in the ceremony, dressed in skins or other costume to represent various animals, as buffalos, panthers, deer, and birds, with one bear, two foxes, and seven wolves, besides two "medicine wolves." Each strove to imitate the animal personated in action as well as in appearance. It was the business of the two foxes to be continually running and stumbling over the others in their efforts to escape from the crowd. The dance, whose essential feature was the doing of everything by contraries, had its parallel among many eastern tribes, particularly among the old Huron and Iroquois. It was considered the most picturesque and amusing dance among the prairie tribes. The "half buffalo" of the song refers to the robe worn by certain of the dancers, which consisted of the upper half of a buffalo skin, the head portion, with the horns attached, coming over the head of the dancers. The dance was an exhibition of deliberate craziness in which the performers strove to outdo one another in nonsensical and frenzied actions, particularly in constantly doing the exact opposite of what they were told to do. It was performed only in obedience to a vow made by some person for the recovery of a sick child, for a successful war expedition, or for some other Indian blessing. It lasted four days, the performers dancing naked the first three days and in full dance costume on the fourth. The leaders in the absurdities were two performers whose bodies and cheeks were painted with white clay, and whose ears were filled with hair shed by the buffalo, which was believed to confer strong "medicine" powers. They carried whistles, and shot at the spectators with blunt arrows. Almost every license was permitted to these two, who in consequence were really held in dread by the others. Among other things the crazy dancers were accustomed to dance through a fire until they extinguished it by their tramping. This was done in imitation of the fire-moth, called *aha'kăa'*, "crazy," by the Arapaho, which hovers about a flame or fire and finally flies into it. They also handled poisonous snakes, and sometimes, it is said, would even surround and kill a buffalo by their unaided physical strength. The Cheyenne dance differed somewhat from that of the Arapaho. It was last performed in the south about ten years ago.

11. NÄ'MIO'TS

Nä'mio'ts — Ehe'ee'ye'!
Nä'mio'ts — Ehe'ee'ye'!
Nä'tosĭ'noe'yotsĭ'nots he'wowi'täs — E'yahe'eye'!
Nä'tosĭ'noe'yotsĭ'nots he'wowi'täs — E'yahe'eye'!
NĬ'tsävĭ'siwo'mätsĭ'nowa' —
NĬ'tsävĭ'sĭwo'mätsĭ'nowa'.

Translation

I am coming in sight — *Ehe'ee'ye'!*
I am coming in sight — *Ehe'ee'ye'!*
I bring the whirlwind with me — *E'yahe'eye'!*
I bring the whirlwind with me — *E'yahe'eye'!*
That you may see each other —
That you may see each other.

The whirlwind is regarded with reverence by all the prairie tribes. In the mythology of the Ghost dance it seems to be an important factor in assisting the onward progress of the new world and the spirit army. It is mentioned also in several Arapaho ghost songs.

12. A'GACHI'HI

A'gachi'hi,
A'gachi'hi,
I'nimä'iha',
I'nimä'iha'.
Hi'tsina'yo,
Hi'tsina'yo —
Na'vishi'nima' yu'suwu'nutu',
Na'vishi'nima' yu'suwu'nutu'.

Translation

The crow, the crow,
He is circling around,
He is circling around,
His wing, his wing —
I am dancing with it,
I am dancing with it.

This song refers to the sacred crow feathers, which certain of the dancers wear upon their heads in the Ghost dance, as explained in the Arapaho songs.

13. NÄ'NISE'NÄSĔ'STSE

Nä'nise'näsĕ'stse nä'shi'nisto'ni'va — He'eye'!
Nä'nise'näsĕ'stse näˑshi'nisto'ni'va — He'eye'!
Nä'niso'niwo', nä'niso'niwo',
I'votä'omo'mĕstä'o — He'eye'!
I'votä'omo'mĕstä'o — He'eye'!
Nä'visi'vämä', nä'vi'sivämä'.

Translation

My children, I am now humming — *He'eye'!*
My children, I am now humming — *He'eye'!*
Your children, your children,
They are crying — *He'eye'!*
They are crying — *He'eye'!*
They are hurrying me along,
They are hurrying me along.

This song is supposed to be addressed by the father or messiah to his disciples. He tells them that their children in the spirit world are crying to be reunited with their friends here, and thus are hastening their coming. The expression, "I am humming," may possibly refer to his rapid approach.

14. Ogo'ch—Ehe'eye'

Ogo'ch — Ehe'eye'!
Ogo'ch — Ehe'eye'!
Tseä'nehä'sĭ nä'viho'm,
Tseä'nehä'sĭ nä'viho'm.
A'ae'vä, A'ae'vä,
Nĭ'stsistä'nä' e'wova'shimä'nĭsts,
Nĭ'stsistä'nä' e'wova'shimä'nĭsts.
Ni'shivä'tämä'ni,
Ni'shivä'tämä'ni.

Translation

The crow — *Ehe'eye'!*
The crow — *Ehe'eye'!*
I saw him when he flew down,
I saw him when he flew down.
To the earth, to the earth.
He has renewed our life,
He has renewed our life.
He has taken pity on us,
He has taken pity on us.

This song was composed by Grant Left-hand's wife. The Crow is here considered as the lord of the new spirit world.

15. Tsĭso'soyo'tsĭto'ho

Tsĭso'soyo'tsĭto'ho,
Tsĭso'soyo'tsĭto'ho,
He'stänowä'hehe',
He'stänowä'hehe',
Näviho'säni'hi,
Näviho'säni'hi,
Tse'novi'tätse'stovi,
Tse'novi'tätse'stovi,
Ä'koyoni'vähe',
Ä'koyoni'vähe'.

Translation

While I was going about,
While I was going about,
Among the people, at my home,
Among the people, at my home,
I saw them,
I saw them,
Where they gambled,
Where they gambled,
With the *ä′ko′yo* wheel,
With the *ä′ko′yo* wheel.

This song was also composed by Mo′ki, the wife of Grant Left-hand. The expression here rendered "my home" is literally "where I belonged," as, since the death of her children, she speaks of the spirit world as her own proper home. In this song she tells how she found her departed friends playing the game of the *ä′ko′yo* or *bä′qăti* wheel, as described in Arapaho song 49.

16. NI′HA—E′YEHE′E′YEYE′

Ni′ha—E′yehe′e′yeye′!
Ni′ha—E′yehe′e′yeye′!
Hi′niso′nihu′—Hi′yeye′!
Hi′niso′nihu′—Hi′yeye′!
O′tätä′womi′ mä′piva′—He′e′ye′!
O′tätä′womi′ mä′piva′—He′e′ye′!
E′tätu′hamo′tu—He′eye′!
E′tätu′hamo′tu—He′eye′!
Nä′hisi′maqa′niwo′m—Ähe′eye′!
Nä′hisi′maqa′niwo′m—Ähe′eye′!
E′ta′wu′hotä′nu—He′eye′!
E′tä′wu′hotä′nu—He′eye′!

Translation

My father—*E′yehe′e′yeye′!*
My father—*E′yehe′e′yeye′!*
His children—*Hi′yeye′!*
His children—*Hi′yeye′!*
In the greenish water—*He′e′ye′!*
In the greenish water—*He′e′ye′!*
He makes them swim—*He′eye′!*
He makes them swim—*He′eye′!*
We are all crying—*Ähe′eye′!*
We are all crying—*Ähe′eye′!*

This song conveys nearly the same idea as that of number 8. The expression "We are all crying" might be rendered "We are all pleading, or praying" to the father, to hasten his coming.

17. A′GA′CH—EHE′E′YE′

A′ga′ch—Ehe′e′ye′!
A′ga′ch—Ehe′e′ye′!
Ve′ta chi—He′e′ye′!
Ve′ta′chi—He′e′ye′!
E′hoi′otsĭ′stu,
E′hoi′otsĭ′stu.
Ma′e′tumu′nu′—He′e′ye′!
Ma′e′tumu′nu′—He′e′ye′!
E′ho′i′o′tso′,
E′ho′i′o′tso′.
Nä′vi′sivû′qewo′nĭt,
Nä′vi′sivû′qewo′nĭt.
Nĭstä′kona′oe′vo,
Nĭstä′kona′oe′vo.
E′he′vo′o′, E′he′vo′o′

Translation

The crow — *Ehe′e′ye′!*
The crow — *Ehe′e′ye′!*
The grease paint — *He′e′ye′!*
The grease paint — *He′e′ye′!*
He brings it to me,
He brings it to me.
The red paint — *He′e′ye′!*
The red paint — *He′e′ye′!*
He brings it,
He brings it.
I prepare myself with it,
I prepare myself with it.
It will make you strong,
It will make you strong.
He tells me, He tells me.

Red is a sacred color with all Indians, and is usually symbolic of strength and success, and for this reason is a favorite color in painting the face and body for the dance or warpath, and for painting the war pony, the lance, etc. On all important occasions, when painting the face or body, the skin is first anointed with grease to make the paint adhere better, so as not to obscure the sharp lines of the design.

18. NÄ′NISO′NÄSĬ′STSI—HE′E′YE′

Nä′niso′näsĭ′stsi—He′e′ye′!
Nä′niso′näsĭ′stsi—He′e′ye′!
Vi′nänä′tuu′wa o′gochi′—Ahe′e′ye′!
Vi′nänä′tuu′wa o′gochi′—Ahe′e′ye′!
Nĭ′stsivĭ′shiwo′mätsĭ′no,
Nĭ′stsivĭ′shiwo′mätsĭ′no.

Translation

My children — *He′e′ye′!*
My children — *He′e′ye′!*

Kill a buffalo (or beef) for the Crow — *Ahe'e'ye'!*
Kill a buffalo (or beef) for the Crow — *Ahe'e'ye'!*
By that means I shall see you,
By that means I shall see you.

This song refers to the feast which accompanies every dance. The implied meaning is that the people must get ready for a dance in order that they may see the Crow, their father.

19. A'GUGA'-IHI

A'guga'-ihi,
A'guga'-ihi.
Tsi'shistä'hi'sihi',
Tsi'shistä'hi'sihi'.
I'hoo'ʿtsihi',
I'hoo'ʿtsihi'.
Tsïtäwo'ʿtähi',
Tsïtäwo'ʿtähi'.
Hi'nisa'nûhi',
Hi'nisa'nûhi'.
Tsïtäwo'mohu',
Tsïtäwo'mohu'.

Translation

The crow woman —
The crow woman —
To her home,
To her home,
She is going,
She is going.
She will see it,
She will see it.
Her children,
Her children.
She will see them,
She will see them.

This song was also composed by Mo'ʿki, "Little Woman," the wife of Grant Left-hand. On account of her frequent trances and consequent leadership in the Cheyenne Ghost dance, she assumes the title of the Crow Woman, i. e., the woman messenger from the spirit world. The story of her own and her husband's connection with the Ghost dance is of interest for the light it throws on the working of the Indian mind, especially with regard to religion.

Mo'ʿki is a young Cheyenne woman married to a young Arapaho, Grant Left-hand, about 30 years of age, a former Carlisle student, and the son of Nawat, or Left-hand, the principal chief of the southern Arapaho. Notwithstanding several years of English education, Grant is a firm believer in the doctrine and the dance, and the principal organizer and leader of the auxiliary "crow dance" in his own tribe, while his wife is as prominent in the Ghost dance among the Cheyenne, and has composed a series of a dozen or more songs descriptive of her various trance experiences in the other world.

Her first child died soon after birth, and the young mother was keenly affected by the bereavement. Afterward a boy was born to them, and became the idol of his parents, especially of the father. He grew up into a bright and active little fellow, but when about 4 years of age was suddenly seized with a spasm in the night and died in a few minutes, almost before his father could reach his bed. This second loss brought deep sorrow to them both, and the mother brooded over it so that there was serious fear for her own life. Then came the Ghost dance and the new doctrine of a reunion with departed friends. The mother went to the dance, fell into a trance, met her children as in life, and played with her little boy. On awaking and returning home she told her husband. He could hardly believe it at first, but it required but little persuasion to induce him to attend the next Ghost dance with her, because, as he said, "I want to see my little boy." He himself fell into a trance, saw his children, and rode with his little boy on the horse behind him over the green prairies of the spirit land. From that time both became devoted adherents and leaders of the Ghost dance; their trances have been frequent, and every dance is welcomed as another opportunity of reunion with departed friends. The young man was deeply affected as he spoke of his love for his children, the sudden death of the little boy, and their second meeting in the other world, and as his wife sat by his side looking up into our faces and listening intently to every word, although she understood but little English, it could not be doubted that their faith in the reality of the vision was real and earnest. Every Indian parent who has lost a child, every child who has lost a parent, and every young man and woman who has lost a brother, sister, or friend affirms a similar reason for belief in the Ghost dance.

CHEYENNE GLOSSARY

A'ae'vä—for Hoi'vă.

A'gach —for O'go'chi.

A'gachi'hi—for O'go'chi.

A'guga'-ihi— for Ogo'ˈgač.

Ahe'eye' — an unmeaning exclamation used in the songs.

Ähiya'eyee'heye' —ibid.

Ä'ko'yo—the Cheyenne name for the bä'qăti gaming wheel. See Arapaho song 49.

Ä''koyoni'vă — with the ä'ko'yo wheel.

Äkwi'u — for ä'ko'yo, the Cheyenne name of the bä'qati wheel.

Ä'minăqi—my (female) comrade (vocative).

Anskowi'nis — a Cheyenne division. The meaning of the name is unknown.

Cheyenne — the popular name for the Cheyenne tribe. It is derived from their Sioux name Shaie'na or Shai'ela, "red," and figuratively "alien."

Dzitsi'stäs — "our people;" the name used by the Cheyenne for themselves.

Eähe'eye' — an unmeaning exclamation used in the songs.

Ehän or Ehäni — for Ïhänh.

Ehe'ee'ye'— an unmeaning exclamation used in the songs.

Ehe'eye' — ibid.

E'hevo — for I'hiwo.

E'heyowo'mi — yellowish.

Ehoi'otsist — he brings it. Another form is Ehoi'otso. Nä'hoiotsi'st, I bring it.

Ehoi'otso' — another form of Ehoi'otsist.

E'nää'ne — for Hïnä'änï.

E'shoin — he has come. Nä'hoin, I come.

Etätu'hamo'tu—for Ïtätu'hamo˝t.

E'täwu'hotä'nu—for Ïtäwohwitä'nu.

Evi′sts- Uni′ʳpahĭs — "s m o k y l o d g e s" (Clark) a Cheyenne division.

Ewo′ra′shimä′nĭsts — he has renewed it, he has changed it. *Näwova′shimä′nĭsts*, I have renewed it.

E′yahe′eye′ — an unmeaning exclamation used in the songs.

E′yehe′ — ibid.

E′yehe′e′yeye′ — ibid.

Eyeye — ibid.

Ga! — caw! an imitation of the cry of the crow.

GATSALGHI — the Kiowa Apache name for the Cheyenne.

He! — an unmeaning exclamation used in the songs.

He′eye′ — ibid.

Hestäno′wh — the people, among the people.

Hestutu′ai — for *Ĭ′hĭstutuai*.

Hesutu′äh — for *I′s-hotu′-ai*.

He′wä′-Tä′niuw′ — "hairy men;" the name of a principal division of the southern Cheyenne, and also used to designate all of the southern Cheyenne collectively.

He′wowĭtä′su — the whirlwind.

Hĭä′ama-Wihu′i — for *Hĭä′mh-Wĭhu*.

Hĭä′mh-Wĭhu — God; literally the "white man" (*wihu*) "above" (*hĭä′mh*). See Cheyenne song 7.

Hĭa′wŭhi — the devil. See Cheyenne song 7.

Hĭ′hĭ′hai′yai′ — an unmeaning exclamation used in the songs.

Hĭnä′änĭ — that is it; it is that one. Compare *Hĭtä′änĭ*.

Hĭnisa′nŭhi — for *Hĭnĭ′sonh*.

Hĭnĭ′sonh — her (his) children. Compare *Nänĭ′sonästs*.

Hĭtä′änĭ — here it is. Compare *Hĭnä′änĭ*.

Hĭtä′niwo′ĭv — "cloud men," the Cheyenne name for the Arapaho. From *hitän*, man, and *wo′ĭv*, cloud.

Hĭ′tsina′yo — for *Hĭ′tsino′n*.

Hĭ′tsino′n — his wing. There is no word for wing alone.

Hĭ′yeye′ — an unmeaning exclamation used in the songs.

Hmĭ′sĭs — "eaters," the name of one of the most important divisions of the northern Cheyenne, and also used collectively in the south to designate the whole of the northern band.

Hohe′ — the Cheyenne name for the Asiniboin. The name is originally from the Sioux language, and is said to mean "rebels."

Hoĭ′rä — the earth, the ground.

Hoo′isi′yonots — the Cheyenne name for the *qaqa-u′nútha*, or throwing sticks, used in the game of the *bä′qati*. See Arapaho song 49.

Ho′so′ewo′nät — dancing with it, dancing by means of it. *Nä′ho′so*, I dance.

Hotä′m-itä′niuw′ — "dog men;" the name of a division of the Cheyenne and also of one order of their military organization.

Ĭ′hänh — our father. Compare *Ni′häw′e*.

Ĭ′hĭstutuai — buffalo head; *hotu′-ai*, buffalo.

Ĭ′hiwo — he says, he says so. *Nä′hĭr*, I say, I say so.

Ihiwo′uhi — for *Ĭ′hiwo*.

Ihoo′ʳts — she (he) is going there.

Ĭnĭ′mäihä′ — he is circling around. *Nävĭ′shinĭ′maih*, I am circling (going) around; *nänĭ′ma-ia*, it is circling around.

Ĭ′nisto′niwon — he (she, it) is humming, or making a rolling noise. *Nänisto′nivä*, *näshĭnisto′niva*, I am humming, etc.

Ĭ′s-hotu′-ai — a half buffalo, i. e., the upper half of a buffalo hide, including the head and horns, worn in the Crazy dance. See Cheyenne song 10. From *ĭs*, half, and *hotu′-ai*, buffalo.

Ĭ′sium-itä′niuw′ — "r i d g e p e o p l e" (Clark), a Cheyenne division.

ITA′SUPUZI — "spotted arrow quills;" the Hidatsa name for the Cheyenne (Matthews).

Ĭtätu′hamoʳt — he causes them to swim. *Nä′tuham*, I swim; *nä′tätu′häm*, let me swim.

Ĭtäwohwĭtä′nu — he makes them better.

Itu′simo′moĭts — it will tremble, or shake. *Nä′momoĭts*, I tremble.

I′votäomo′mĕstä′o — they are crying. *Nä-qai′m*, I am crying; *nähĭ′simaqä′niwom*, we are all crying. Compare *Nänĭ′stohew′*.

I′yahe′yahe′e — an unmeaning exclamation used in the songs.

Iyo′häĭ — he (she, it) is rising. *Nä′ohä*, I rise.

Ma′etu′mŭn — red paint. *Ma′etämh*, paint.

Mä′ĭnoyo′hi — Turtle river; for *mä-ĭ′nh*, turtle (plural, *mäĭno′nh*), *o′′hĭ*, river. *Mäpĭ′vä*, water.

Mä′noyo′h — for *Mä′ĭnoyo′hi*.

Mänoyu′hii — for *Mä′ĭnoyo′hĭ*.

Mäpĭ′vä — water.

MARANSHOBISHGO — "cut-throats;" according to Long, the name applied by the Cheyenne to the Sioux. The form is incorrect, as there is no *r* in the Cheyenne language. According to Hayden, the Cheyenne call the Sioux *Oo'homoi'o.*

Mätä'sĭvamämowĭstä'nowĭt—w h e n y o u (plural) are living together again. *Nävĭstä'nowimonh,* I live with him; *nama'mowĭ'stä'nowĭn,* we are living together.

Mä'tesemä' moestä' nowet—for *Mätä' sĭvamämowĭstä'nowĭt.*

Matsĭ'shkota—"corpse from the scaffold;" an unidentified Cheyenne division, on the authority of Clark (Grinnell).

Miayŭma—"red lodges," an unidentified Cheyenne division, on the authority of Clark (Grinnell).

Mĭ'stävĭ'inût—"heavy eyebrows;" another name for the *Hotä'm-itä'niuw',* q. v.

Mo"ki—"little woman;" a Cheyenne woman prominent in the Ghost dance.

Mo'nshimonh—The Cheyenne name of the dice game, called *ta'-usĕta'na* by the Arapaho. See Arapaho song 64.

Na'eso'yutuhi—for *Na'suyut.*

Nä'hew'—I say.

Nä'hewu'hi—for *Nä'hew'.*

Nä'hĭsimaqä'niwom—we are all crying. Compare *Ivotä'omomĕstä'o.*

Nämi'io'ts—I am coming in sight.

Nä'miots—for *Nämi'io'ts.*

Nänĭ'ma-i'ă—it is circling around. Compare *Ĭmĭ'mäihă'.*

Nä'nise'näsĕ'stse—for *Nänĭ'sonästs.*

Nänisĭ'näsĭsts—for *Nänĭ'sonästs.*

Nä'niso'näsĭ'stsi—for *Nänĭ'sonästs.*

Nänĭ'sonästs—my children. Compare Arapaho *Nänĭ'sanaû. Nänĭ'soniwo,* your children; *hĭnĭ'sonh,* his, or her, children.

Nänĭ'soniwo—your children. Compare *Nänĭ'sonästs.*

Nänĭ'stohew'—I make the sound, I make a cry. Compare *I'votäomo'mestä'o.*

Näsee'nehe'—for *Näsĕĭn-hnă.*

Näsĕĭn-hnă—I waded in.

Nä'shĭnisto'niva—I am now humming. See *Ĭ'nisto'niwon.*

Nä'suyut—I come to him.

Nä'tosĭ'noeyots—I shall have it with me.

Nä'tänoeyo'tsĭ'nots, I have it.

Nä'vihomh—I looked at him, I saw him. The present tense has the same form: *Näviho't,* I look at it; *näviho'sänh,* I looked on. Compare *Tsĭtäwo'moh.*

Näviho'sänh—I looked on (present tense, same form). Compare *Nä'vihomh.*

Nävĭ'shinĭ'maih—I am going (circling) around. Compare *Ĭnĭ'mäihă'.*

Nävĭ'sevûqewo'nit—I prepare myself with it.

Nävĭ'sivämä—they are hurrying me along. *Nä'vĭsitä'n,* I hurry.

Niäsătä'nonh—we have put him away, or aside. *Nä'satonh,* I have put him aside.

NIERERIKWATS-KÛNI'KI—the W i c h i t a name for the Cheyenne. See also *Shiĕda.*

Ni'ha—for *Ni'hûw'e.*

Ni'ha-i'hihi'—for *Ni'hûw'e.*

Nihi'hininh—he is our father. Compare *Ni'hûw'e.*

Ni'hûw'e—my father. *Ni'hûw',* father; *Ni'hûw'e,* my father; *nihi'hinonh,* he is our father. Compare *I'hänh* and Arapaho *niqa,* father.

Nĭ'mĭ'stätu'häm—you should take a swim or bath. *Nätu'ham,* I swim or bathe.

Nĭ'nh-nitä'n—he asks, or tells, us to do it. *Nänh-itŭ',* I ask, or tell, him to do it.

Ninĭni'etäni—for *Nĭ'nh-nitä'n.*

Nĭshivä'tämä'ĭnh—he has taken pity on us, he has blest us, he has sympathy for us. *Näshivä'tämh,* I pity him.

Nĭ'shivä'tämoni—for *Nĭshivä'tämä'ĭnh.*

Nĭshkă'nh or *N'shkă'nh*—our mother. *Na"ku,* mother; *na"kui,* my mother.

Nĭstäko'naoe'vo—it will strengthen you. *Nä'hĭko'nähi,* I am strong; *nähĭko'nă-mäni'hu,* I strengthen him.

Nĭstsävĭ'siwomätsĭ'nowä—so that, in order that, you shall see each other; *Näwo'm,* I see him; *näwo't,* I see it.

Nĭ'stsishihi'yohoni'mäni—for *Nĭstsishi'yoho'nĭ'mänh.*

Nĭstsishĭ'nutsĭmä'nh—let us seek her, or ask for her. *Nähĭ'nutsĭnh,* I am looking for her.

Nĭstsishi'yoho'nĭ'mänh—let us go and play shinny. *Näho'qu,* I am playing shinny; *ohonĭ'stuts,* shinny. See Cheyenne song 9.

Nĭ'stsistä'nä—for *Nĭ'stsĭstä'nowän.*

Nĭ'stsĭstä'nowän—our life, or existence. *Näwŭ'stänĭ'hivĭ'stŭts,* my existence.

Nĭ'stsivĭ'shiwomä'tsĭnoh—by that means I shall see you (plural). Compare *Tsĭtäwo'moh.*

Nĭ'tusimĭ'tänun—he (she, it) will give it to us. *Nĭ'mĭtûts,* I give it to you; *nä'mĭt,* I give it to him.

Nuka'eshe'väoe'tse—This form occurs in Cheyenne song 1. The correct form and rendering are uncertain, but it is doubtfully rendered "the summer cloud." It seems to contain the word *ĭshi'r,* day.

O'go'ch or *O'go''chi* or *O'go'ki* — the crow. In the Ghost dance the crow is the messenger of the spirit world. The messiah and God are frequently spoken of as "The Crow." See Arapaho song 36.

Ogo''gač — "the crow woman;" from *o'go''chi*, crow.

Ohonĭ'stuts — the shinny game. See Cheyenne song 9 and Arapaho song 7.

O'ivima'na — "scabby;" a Cheyenne division.

Otä — now! well!

Otä'si-Tä'niuw' — "pierced-nose people:" the Cheyenne name for the Caddo.

O'tätawo'm — greenish.

O'täta'womemäpewä — for *Otä'tawo'm-mä̆p-ĭ'va*. In the greenish (bluish) water, or river. *O'tätawom*, greenish; *mä̆p*, water.

O'tu'gŭnŭ — a Cheyenne division. The meaning of the name is unknown.

Owa̤'ni — living things, creatures, animals (including quadrupeds, birds, insects, etc).

Pägänä'vo — "striped arrows," from *päga*, arrow, and *nävo*, striped; the Shoshoni and Comanche name for the Cheyenne. See also *Shiä'navo*.

Pĭnŭ'tgŭ — a Cheyenne division. The meaning of the name is unknown.

Psam — the "crazy dance" of the Cheyenne; *psa*, crazy. It is somewhat different from the Arapaho crazy dance. See Cheyenne song 10 and Arapaho song 43.

Sa-sis-e-tas — the name used by the Cheyenne to designate themselves, according to Clark. It should be *Dzĭtsĭ'stäs* q. v.

Shiä'navo — another Comanche name for the Cheyenne, probably a derivation from the word Cheyenne.

Shiĕda — another Wichita name for the Cheyenne, probably a derivation from the word Cheyenne. See also *Niererik-wats-kûni'ki*.

Shĭshino'wĭts-itä'niuw' — "snake people," the Cheyenne name for the Comanche.

So'wänia — "southerners;" Cheyenne name sometimes used to designate the southern portion of the tribe in Oklahoma.

Staitan — a name used by Lewis and Clark to designate a tribe identical with the Cheyenne. It is a corruption of the Cheyenne word *hĭstä'itän*, "I am a Cheyenne."

Sŭtasi'na or *Sŭta'ya* — "strange talkers" (Clark), one of the most important Cheyenne divisions and formerly a distinct tribe.

Tseä'nehä'sĭ — for *Tsi'änu'iäs*.

Tsenovi'tätse'stovi — for *Tsenowĭ'tätsĭ'stowĭ*.

Tsenowĭ'tatsĭ'stowĭ — where there was gambling. *Nä'now'shĭ*, I gamble.

Tsi'änu'iäs — (when) he flew down. *Nä'miha'-u*, I fly; *nä'nuiha'-u*, I fly down.

Tsĭnitai'womai'wosihi — for *Tsĭ'unĭtai'womai'w's*.

Tsinitai'wosi'hi — for *Tsĭunĭ'taiw's*.

Tsi'shistä'hisihi — for *Tsĭshĭ'stäs*.

Tsĭshĭ'stäs — where she belongs, i. e., her home. Compare *Dzĭtsĭ'stäs*, the name given by the Cheyenne to themselves.

Tsĭsoso'yotsĭ'to — while I was going about. *Näsoso'yots*, I go about, I ramble about.

Tsĭ'stamo'nohyot — when I first reached him, when I arrived where he was. *Näta'hyot*, I shall reach him.

Tsĭstäwo'moh — she (he) will see them. *Näwo'm*, I see him; *stawo'matsĭ'mh*, I see you; *tsĭtäwo''t*, he (she) will see it; *nĭ'stsivĭ'shiwomätsĭnoh*, by that means I shall see you (plural). Compare *Nä'vihomh*.

Tsĭtäwo''t — she (he) will see it. Compare *Tsĭstäwo'moh*.

Tsĭ'ŭnĭtai'womai'w's — where they are painted in different colors; *tsĭŭnĭ'taiw's* different; *mai'-tŭmh*, paint.

Tsĭŭnĭ'taiw's — different, various.

Tû''gani — the Cheyenne name for the Wichita; evidently a derivative from their Comanche name, *Do''kana*, tattooed people.

Ugu'chi'hihi — for *O'go''chi*.

Veta'chi — for *Vĭchk*.

Vĭchk — grease, used in painting or anointing the face and body.

Vĭ'nänätu'uwă — kill a beef or buffalo for him (imperative). *Nä'nätun*, I kill it; *nä'nätu'uh*, I kill it for him; *hoiwo'ĭts*, a beef.

Wităpä'hät or *Wităpä'tu* — the Cheyenne name for the Kiowa; from their Sioux name *Wi'tapähä'tu*, people of the island butte.

Wĭ'tapi'u — "haters" (Clark); a Cheyenne division.

Wosĭ'vă — a mountain.

Yä'häyä' — an unmeaning exclamation used in the songs.

Yu'suwu'nutu — for *Ho'so'ewo'năt*.

THE COMANCHE

TRIBAL SYNONYMY

Bo'dălk''iñago — common Kiowa name, signifying "reptile people" or "snake men," from *bo'dal*, reptile, insect, and *k'iñago*, people.

Cha'tha — (singular *Cha'*) Arapaho name, signifying "enemies."

Comanche — popular name; of Mexican-Spanish origin and unknown meaning. It occurs as early as 1757, and in the form *Cumanche* as early as 1720.

Gyai'-ko — the common name given by the Kiowa to the Comanche, signifying "enemies."

Iatan — the French spelling of the name applied by several of the plains tribes to the Ute Indians, and by extension to the cognate Comanche and Shoshoni. It is a derivative from the name Yuta or Ute, the final *n* representing a nasalized vowel sound. The nearest approximation is perhaps *Iätä-go*, the Kiowa (plural) name for the Ute. Variants are *L'Iatan, Aliatan, Halitane, Ayutan, Tetau* (for *Ietau* or *Ietan*), *Jetan, Yutan*, etc. The form *Läitanes* occurs as early as 1740 (Margry, VII, 457).

Idahi — Kiowa Apache name; meaning unknown.

Ietan — a name applied by some of the prairie tribes to several Shoshonean tribes, particularly the Shoshoni and the *Comanche*. It occurs in a number of forms and appears as *Läitanes* as early as 1740 (Margry, VII, 457).

La Playe — former French trader's name, perhaps a corruption of *Tête Pele'e.*

Na''lani — Navaho name, signifying "many aliens" or "many enemies," applied collectively to the southern plains tribes, but more especially to the Comanche.

Na'nita — Kichai name.

Na'tăa' — Wichita name, variously rendered "snakes," i. e., "enemies" or "dandies."

Nüma — proper tribal name used by themselves, and signifying "people." The Shoshoni and Paiute designate themselves by the same name.

Pa'douca — the name given to the Comanche by the Osage, Quapaw, Kansa, Oto, and other Siouan tribes. It has several dialectic forms and is used in this form by Pénicaut as early as 1719. It may perhaps be a contraction of *Pe'nä-tĕka*, the name of the principal eastern division of the Comanche.

Sänko — obsolete Kiowa name; it may signify "snakes," from *säne*, snake.

Sau'hto — Caddo name.

Shishino'wïts-Itäniuw' — Cheyenne name, signifying "snake people."

Tête Pele'e — a name said to have been applied to the Comanche by the French traders, signifying "bald heads." The identification seems doubtful, as the Comanche cut their hair only when mourning.

Yä'mpai-ni or *Yä'mpai-Rï'kani* — Shoshoni name, signifying "yampa people," or "yampa eaters." It is properly the name of only one division, but is used collectively for the whole tribe. The yampa plant is the *Carum gairdneri.*

TRIBAL SIGN

The tribal sign for the Comanche is "snakes," the same as that for the Shoshoni, but with the finger drawn toward the rear instead of thrust forward.

SKETCH OF THE TRIBE

The Comanche are one of the southern tribes of the great Shoshonean stock, and the only one of that group living entirely on the plains. Their language and traditions show that they are a comparatively recent offshoot from the Shoshoni of Wyoming, both tribes speaking practically the same dialect and until very recently keeping up constant and friendly communication.   Within the traditionary period the two tribes lived adjacent to each other in southern Wyoming, since which time the Shoshoni have been beaten back into the mountains by the Sioux and other prairie tribes, while the Comanche have been driven steadily southward by the same pressure.   In this southern migration the Pe′nätĕka seem to have preceded the rest of the tribe. The Kiowa say that when they themselves moved southward from the Black-hills region, the Arkansas was the northern boundary of the Comanche.

In 1719 the Comanche are mentioned under their Siouan name of Pa′douca as living in what now is western Kansas.   It must be remembered that from 500 to 800 miles was an ordinary range for a prairie tribe, and that the Comanche were equally at home on the Platte and in the Bolson de Mapimi of Chihuahua.   As late as 1805 the North Platte was still known as Padouca fork.   At that time they roamed over the country about the heads of the Arkansas, Red, Trinity, and Brazos rivers, in Colorado, Kansas, Oklahoma, and Texas.   For nearly two hundred years they were at war with the Spaniards of Mexico and extended their raids far down into Durango.   They were friendly to the Americans generally, but became bitter enemies of the Texans, by whom they were dispossessed of their best hunting grounds, and carried on a relentless war against them for nearly forty years.   They have been close confederates of the Kiowa for perhaps one hundred and fifty years.   In 1835 they made their first treaty with the government, and by the treaty of Medicine Lodge in 1867 agreed to go on their present reservation, situated between Washita and Red rivers, in the southwestern part of Oklahoma; but it was not until after the last outbreak of the southern prairie tribes in 1874–75 that they and their allies, the Kiowa and Apache, finally settled on it.   They were probably never a large tribe, although supposed to be populous on account of their wide range.   Within the last fifty years they have been terribly wasted by war and disease.   They numbered 1,512 in 1893.

The gentile system seems to be unknown among the Comanche. They have, or still remember, thirteen recognized divisions or bands, and may have had others in former times.   Of these all but five are practically extinct.   The Kwă′hări and Pe′nätĕka are the most important.   Following in alphabetic order is the complete list as given by their leading chiefs:

1. *Detsăna′yuka* or *No′koni*.   This band, to which the present head chief Quanah Parker belongs, was formerly called *No′koni*, "wanderers," but on the death of Quanah's father, whose name was also No′koni, the name was tabued, according to Comanche custom, and the division took the name of *Detsăna′yuka*, "bad campers," intended to convey the same idea of wandering.

2. *Ditsä′kăna*, *Wĭ′dyu*, *Yäpä*, or *Yä′mpäri′ka*.   This division was formerly known as *Wĭ′dyu*, "awl," but for a reason similar to that just

mentioned the name was changed to *Ditsä'kăna*, "sewers," which conveys the same idea, an awl being the substitute for a needle. They are equally well known as *Yäpä*, the Comanche name of the root of the *Carum gairdneri*, known to the Shoshoni and Bannock as *yampa*, or sometimes as *Yämpä-ri'ka*, a dialectic form signifying "yampa eaters." The whole Comanche tribe is known to the Shoshoni under the name of *Yä'mpaini* or *Yämpai-ri'kani*, "yampa people" or "yampa eaters." The Yäpä are sometimes known also as *Etsitü'biwat*, "northerners," or "people of the cold country," from having usually ranged along the northern frontier of the tribal territory; a fact which may account for the Shoshoni having designated the whole tribe by their name.

3. *Kewa'tsăna*. "No ribs;" extinct.

4. *Kotsa'i*. Extinct.

5. *Ko'tso-tĕ'ka*. "Buffalo eaters," from *ko'tso*, buffalo, and *tĕ'ka*, the root of the verb "to eat."

6. *Kwa'hări* or *Kwa'hădi*. "Antelopes." This division was one of the most important of the tribe, and was so called because its members frequented the prairie country and the staked plains, while the Pe'nätĕka and others ranged farther east on the edge of the timber region. They were the last to come in after the surrender in 1874. The Kwa'hări, Ditsä'kána, and Detsăna'yuka were sometimes designated together by the whites as northern Comanche as distinguished from the Pe'nätĕka, who were known as eastern or southern Comanche.

7. *Motsai'*. Perhaps from *pä-motsan*, "a loop in a stream." These and the Tĕna'wa were practically exterminated in a battle with the Mexicans about 1845.

8. *Pä'gatsû*. "Head of the stream" (*pä*, a stream); extinct.

9. *Pe'nätĕka*, or *Penä'nde*. "Honey eaters." These and the Kwa'hări were the two most important divisions in the tribe. They lived on the edge of the timber country in eastern Texas, and hence were frequently known to the whites as eastern or southern Comanche. They had but a loose alliance with their western kinsmen, and sometimes joined the Texans against them. Other Comanche names for them are *Te'yuwĭt*, "hospitable;" *Tĕʳkăpwai* "no meat," and *Ku'baratpat*, "steep climbers."

10. *Po'hoi*. "Wild-sage people," i. e., Shoshoni. This is not properly the name of a Comanche division, but of some immigrant Shoshoni from the north incorporated with the Comanche.

11. *Tänĭ'ma*. "Liver eaters," from *nĭm* or *nüm*, liver. This band is extinct, only one old man being known to survive.

12. *Tĕna'wa* or *Te'năhwĭt*. From *tĕʳnäw'*, "down stream." Extinct. See *Motsai'* above.

13. *Wa-ai'h*. "Maggot." Extinct.

The Comanche were nomad buffalo hunters, constantly on the move, cultivating nothing from the ground, and living in skin tipis. Excepting that they are now confined to a reservation and forced to depend on government rations, they are but little changed from their original condition. They are still for the most part living in tipis of canvas, and are dressed in buckskin. They were long noted as the finest horsemen of the plains, and bore a reputation for dash and courage. They have a high sense of honor, and hold themselves superior to the other tribes with which they are associated. In person they are well built and rather corpulent. Their language is the trade language of the region, and is more or less understood by all the neighboring tribes. It is sonorous and flowing, its chief characteristic being a rolling *r*. It has no *l*. The language has several dialects, and is practically the same as that of the Shoshoni in the north. Their present head chief is Quanah Parker, an able man, whose mother was an American captive. His name, *Kwäna* or *Kwai'na*, signifies a sweet smell.

Having taken but little part in the Ghost dance, the Comanche have but few songs in their own language, but these are particularly pleasing for their martial ring or soothing softness. They call the dance *A'p-Ane̊'ka'ra*, "the father's dance" (from *a'pă*, father; *ne̊'ka'ra*, a dance), or by another name which signifies the "dance with joined hands."

SONGS OF THE COMANCHE

1. Heyo'hänä Häe'yo

He'e'yo'!
Heyo'hänä' Häe'yo!
Heyo'hänä' Häe'yo!
Te'äyä' torä'bi ai"-gi'na—He'e'yo'!
Te'äyä' torä'bi ai"-gi'na—He'e'yo'!
Te'äyä' toa'hä tä'bi wo'n'gin—Ähi'ni'yo'!
Te'äyä' toa'hä tä'bi wo'n'gin—Ähi'ni'yo'!

Translation

He'e'yo'!
Heyo'hänä' Häe'yo!
Heyo'hänä' Häe'yo!
The sun's beams are running out—*He'e'yo'!*
The sun's beams are running out—*He'e'yo'!*
The sun's yellow rays are running out—*Ähi'ni'yo'!*
The sun's yellow rays are running out—*Ähi'ni'yo'!*

This song was probably sung at daylight, when the first rays of the sun shone in the east, after the dancers had been dancing all night. The introductory part is a suggestion from the songs of the mescal rite, to which the Comanche are so much attached. Although the words convey but little meaning, the tune is unique and one of the best of all the ghost songs on account of its sprightly measure.

Te'äyä refers to the sun's rays or beams; *torä'bi*, a possessive form of *tä'bi*, sun; (*mû'ä*, moon); *toa'hä*, from *a'häp*, yellow; *ai'ᶜ-gi'na* and *wo'n'gin* or *wa'n'gin*, running out, streaming out.

2. Ya'hi'yû'niva'hu

Ya'hi'yû'niva'hu
Hi'yû'niva'hi'yû'niva'hu
Ya'hi'yû'niva'hi'na'he'ne'na'
Hi'ya'hi'nahi'ni'na'
Hi'yû'niva'hu
Hi'yû'niva'hi'yû'niva'hu
Ya'hi'yû'niva'hi'ya'he'ne'na'.

This song has no meaning, but is of the lullaby order, with a sweet, soothing effect.

3. Yani'tsini'hawa'na

Yani'tsini'hawa'na!
Yani'tsini'hawa'na!
Hi'niswa'vita'ki'nĭ,
Hi'niswa'vita'ki'nĭ.

Translation

Yani'tsini'hawa'na!
Yani'tsini'hawa'na!
We shall live again,
We shall live again.

The term *hi'niswa'vita'ki'nĭ* signifies "we are coming to life again," or "we shall live again;" from *nŭswa'vitaki'nĭ*, "I am beginning to be alive again."

4. Nĭ'nini'tuwi'na

Ni'nini'tuwi'na hu'hu
Ni'nini'tuwi'na hu'hu
Wäta'tsina'na hu'hu
Wäta'tsina'na hu'hu
Ni'hima'tsi asi'si
Ni'hima'tsi asi'si.

This is the Arapaho closing song (Arapaho song 52), as adopted by the Comanche, to whom, of course, it has no real meaning. It is given here as an example of the change which comes to an Indian song when adopted by an alien tribe.

THE PAIUTE, WASHO, AND PIT RIVER TRIBES

PAIUTE TRIBAL SYNONYMY

Hogăpä'goni—Shoshoni name, "rush arrow people" (*hogăp*, a small water reed; *pägă*, "arrow").

Nüma—proper tribal name, signifying "people" or "Indians;" the same name is also used for themselves by the Shoshoni and Comanche.

Pai-yu'chimŭ—Hopi name.

Pai-yu'tsĭ—Navaho name.

Palŭ—Washo name.

Paiute or *Piute*—popular name, variously rendered "true (*pai*) Ute" or "water (*pä*) Ute"—pronounced among themselves *Paiuti*.

NOTE.—The northern bands of the Paiute are frequently included with Shoshoni and others under the name of Snakes, while the others are often included with various Californian tribes under the collective name of Diggers

SKETCH OF THE PAIUTE

CHARACTERISTICS

The Paiute belong to the great Shoshonean stock and occupy most of Nevada, together with adjacent portions of southwestern Utah, northwestern Arizona, and northwestern and southeastern California. The Pahvant and Gosiute on their eastern border are frequently, but improperly, classed as Paiute, while the Chemehuevi, associated with the Walapai in Arizona, are but a southern offshoot of the Paiute and speak the same language. With regard to the Indians of Walker River and Pyramid Lake reservations, who constitute the main body of those commonly known as Paiute, Powell claims that they are not Paiute at all, but another tribe which he calls Paviotso. He says: "The names by which the tribes are known to white men and the department give no clue to the relationship of the Indians. For example, the Indians in the vicinity of the reservation on the Muddy and the Indians on the Walker River and Pyramid Lake reservations are called Pai or Pah Utes, but the Indians know only those on the Muddy by that name, while those on the other two reservations are known as Paviotsoes, and speak a very different language, but closely allied to, if not identical with, that of the Bannocks." (*Comr.*, 45.) The Ghost dance originated among these Indians in the neighborhood of Walker river, from whom the songs here given were obtained, and for convenience of reference we shall speak of them under their popular title of Paiute, without asserting its correctness.

The different small bands have little political coherence and there is no recognized head chief. The most influential chiefs among them in modern times have been Winnemucca, who died a few years ago, and Natchez. Wovoka's leadership is spiritual, not political. The Indians of Walker river and Pyramid lake claim the Bannock as their cousins, and say that they speak the same language.   As a rule they have been peaceable and friendly toward the whites, although in the early sixties they several times came into collision with miners and emigrants, hostility being frequently provoked by the whites themselves.   The

Fig. 101—Paiute wikiup.

northern Paiute are more warlike than those of the south, and a con- siderable number of them took part with the Bannock in the war of 1878.   Owing to the fact that the great majority of the Paiute are not on reservations, many of them being attached to the ranches of white men, it is impossible to get any correct statement of their population, but they may be safely estimated at from 7,000 to 8,000 and are thought to be increasing. In 1893 those on reservations, all in Nevada, were reported to number, at Walker River, 563; at Pyramid Lake, 494; at Duck Valley (Western Shoshone agency, in connection with the Shoshoni), 209. Nevada Indians off reservation were estimated to number 6,815, nearly all of whom were Paiute.

As a people the Paiute are peaceable, moral, and industrious, and are highly commended for their good qualities by those who have had the best opportunities for judging. While apparently not as bright in intellect as the prairie tribes, they appear to possess more solidity of character. By their willingness and efficiency as workers, they have made themselves necessary to the white farmers and have been enabled to supply themselves with good clothing and many of the comforts of life, while on the other hand they have steadily resisted the vices of civilization, so that they are spoken of by one agent as presenting the "singular anomaly" of improvement by contact with the whites. Another authority says: "To these habits and excellence of character may be attributed the fact that they are annually increasing in numbers, and that they are strong, healthy, active people. Many of them are employed as laborers on the farms of white men in all seasons, but they are especially serviceable during the time of harvesting and haymaking." (Comr., 46.) They would be the last Indians in the world to preach a crusade of extermination against the whites, such as the messiah religion has been represented to be. Aside from their earnings among the whites, they derive their subsistence from the fish of the lakes, jack rabbits and small game of the sage plains and mountains, and from piñon nuts and other seeds which they grind into flour for bread. Their ordinary dwelling is the wikiup or small rounded hut of tulé rushes over a framework of poles, with the ground for a floor and the fire in the center and almost entirely open at the top. Strangely enough, although appreciating the advantages of civilization so far as relates to good clothing and such food as they can buy at the stores, they manifest no desire to live in permanent houses or to procure the furniture of civilization, and their wikiups are almost bare of everything excepting a few wicker or grass baskets of their own weaving.

The Paiute ghost songs have a monotonous, halting movement that renders them displeasing to the ear of a white man, and are inferior in expression to those of the Arapaho and the Sioux. A number of words consisting only of unmeaning syllables are inserted merely to fill in the meter. Like the cognate Shoshoni and Comanche, the language has a strong rolling r.

GENESIS MYTH

At first the world was all water, and remained so a long time. Then the water began to go down and at last Kura'ngwa (Mount Grant) emerged from the water, near the southwest end of Walker lake. There was fire on its top (it may have been a volcano), and when the wind blew hard the water dashed over the fire and would have extinguished it, but that the sage-hen (*hutsi—Centrocercus urophasianus*) nestled down over it and fanned away the water with her wings. The heat scorched the feathers on the breast of the sage-hen and they remain black to this day. Afterward the Paiute got their first fire from the mountain through the help of the rabbit, who is a great wonder-worker, "same as a god." As the water subsided other mountains appeared, until at last the earth was left as it is now.

Then the great ancestor of the Paiute, whom they call *Nümi'naǎ'*, "Our Father," came from the south in the direction of Mount Grant, upon which his footprints can still be seen, and journeyed across to the mountains east of Carson sink and made his home there. A woman, *Ibidsíi*, "Our Mother," followed him from the same direction, and they met and she became his wife. They dressed themselves in skins, and lived on the meat of deer and mountain sheep, for there was plenty of game in those days. They had children—two boys and two girls. Their father made bows and arrows for the boys, and the mother fashioned sticks for the girls with which to dig roots. When the children grew up, each boy married his sister, but the two families quarreled until their father told them to separate. So one family went to Walker lake and became *Aga'ih-tïka'ra*, "fish eaters" (the Paiute of Walker lake), while the other family went farther north into Idaho and became *Kotso'-tïkǎra*, "buffalo eaters" (the Bannock), but both are one people and have the same language. After their children had left them, the parents went on to the mountains farther east, and there *Nüminaǎ'* went up into the sky and his wife followed him.

THE WASHO

Associated with the Paiute are the Washo, or *Wâ'siu*, as they call themselves, a small tribe of about 400 souls, and having no affinity, so far as known, with any other Indians. They occupy the mountain region in the extreme western portion of Nevada, about Washo and Tahoe lakes and the towns of Carson and Virginia City. They formerly extended farther east and south, but have been driven back by the Paiute, who conquered them, reducing them to complete subjection and forbidding them the use of horses, a prohibition which was rigidly enforced until within a few years. Thus broken in spirit, they became mere hangers-on of the white settlements on the opening up of the mines, and are now terribly demoralized. They have been utterly neglected by the government, have never been included in any treaty, and have now no home that they can call their own. They are devoted adherents of the messiah, but usually join in the dance with the nearest camp of Paiute, whose songs they sing, and have probably no Ghost songs in their own language. We quote a gloomy account of their condition in 1866. The description will apply equally well today, excepting that their numbers have diminished:

This is a small tribe of about 500 Indians, living in the extreme western part of the state. They are usually a harmless people, with much less physical and mental development than the Piutes, and more degraded morally. They are indolent improvident, and much addicted to the vices and evil practices common in savage life. They manifest an almost uncontrollable appetite for intoxicating drinks. They are sensual and filthy, and are annually diminishing in numbers from the diseases contracted through their indulgences. A few have learned the English language and will do light work for a reasonable compensation. They spend the winter months about the villages and habitations of white men, from whom they obtain tolerable supplies of food and clothing. The spring, summer, and autumn months are spent in fishing about Washo and Tahoe lakes and the streams which flow through their country. They also gather grass seed and pine nuts, hunt rabbits, hares, and ducks. There is no suitable place for a reservation in the bounds of their territory, and, in view of their rapidly diminishing numbers and the diseases to which they are subjected, none is required. (*Comr., 47.*)

THE PIT RIVER INDIANS

Another group of Indians closely associated with the Paiute on the northwest consists of a number of small tribes, known collectively to the whites as Pit River or Hot Springs Indians, holding the basin of Pit river in northeastern California from Goose lake to the junction with the Sacramento. Among their tribes or bands are the Achoma'wi, Huma'whi, Estakéwach, Hantéwa, Chumâ'wa, Atua'mih or Hamefku'ttelli, Ilma'wi, and Pa'kamalli. (*Powers, Tribes of California.*) They are at present supposed to constitute a distinct linguistic group, but it is probable that better information will show their affinity with some of the neighboring Californian stocks. With the exception of a few at Round Valley reservation, California, none of them are on reservations or have any official recognition by the government. They probably number 1,000 to 1,500 souls. The northern bands have suffered much from Modoc slave raids in former days, and are much inferior in physique and intellect to those lower down the river, who were the terror of northern California thirty years ago, and who are described by recent observers as good workers, intelligent, brave, and warlike. (*A. G. O., 9.*)

SONGS OF THE PAIUTE

1. Nüvä′ ka ro′răni′

Nüvä′ ka ro′răni′!
Nüvä′ ka ro′răni′!
Nüvä′ ka ro′răni′!
Nüvä′ ka ro′răni′!
Gosi′pa′ hävi′gĭnû′,
Gosi′pa′ hävi′gĭnû′.

Translation

The snow lies there—*ro′răni′!*
The snow lies there—*ro′răni′!*
The snow lies there—*ro′răni′!*
The snow lies there—*ro′răni′!*
The Milky Way lies there,
The Milky Way lies there.

This is one of the favorite songs of the Paiute Ghost dance. The tune has a plaintive but rather pleasing effect, although inferior to the tunes of most of the ghost songs of the prairie tribes. The words as they stand are very simple, but convey a good deal of meaning to the Indian. It must be remembered that the dance is held in the open air at night, with the stars shining down on the wide-extending plain walled in by the giant sierras, fringed at the base with dark pines, and with their peaks white with eternal snows. Under such circumstances this song of the snow lying white upon the mountains, and the Milky Way stretching across the clear sky, brings up to the Paiute the same patriotic home love that comes from lyrics of singing birds and leafy trees and still waters to the people of more favored regions. In the mythology of the Paiute, as of many other tribes, the Milky Way is the road of the dead to the spirit world. *Ro'răni'* serves merely to fill in the meter.

2. Dĕna' gayo'n

Dĕna' gayo'n, Dĕ'na ga'yoni',
Dĕna' gayo'n, Dĕ'na ga'yoni',
Bawă' doro'n, Ba'wă do'roni',
Bawă' doro'n, Ba'wă do'roni'.

Translation

A slender antelope, a slender antelope,
A slender antelope, a slender antelope,
He is wallowing upon the ground,
He is wallowing upon the ground,
He is wallowing upon the ground,
He is wallowing upon the ground.

This song evidently refers to a trance vision in which the sleeper saw an antelope rolling in the dust, after the manner of horses, buffalo, and other animals.

3. Do'' tĭ'mbi

Do' tĭ'mbi, Do' tĭ'mbi-nä'n,
Do' tĭ'mbi, Do' tĭ'mbi-nä'n,
Tĭ'mbi bai'-yo, Tĭ'mbi ba'i-yo-ä'n,
Tĭ'mbi bai'-yo, Tĭ'mbi ba'i-yo-ä'n.

Translation

The black rock, the black rock,
The black rock, the black rock,
The rock is broken, the rock is broken,
The rock is broken, the rock is broken.

This song may refer to something in Paiute mythology. *Nä'n* and *ä'n* are unmeaning syllables added to fill out the measure.

4. Päsü' wĭ'noghän

Päsü' wĭ'noghän,
Päsü' wĭ'noghän,
Päsü' wĭ'noghän,

Wai'-va wĭ'noghän,
Wai'-va wĭ'noghän,
Wai'-va wĭ'noghän.

Translation

The wind stirs the willows,
The wind stirs the willows,
The wind stirs the willows,
The wind stirs the grasses,
The wind stirs the grasses,
The wind stirs the grasses.

Wai'-va (or *wai* in composition) is the sand grass or wild millet of Nevada (*Oryzopsis membranacea*), the seeds of which are ground by the Paiute and boiled into mush for food.

5. Pägü'nävä'

Pägü'nävä'! Pägü'nävä'!
Tûngwü'kwiji'! Tûngwü'kwiji'!
Wûmbe'doma'! Wûmbe'doma'!

Translation

Fog! Fog!
Lightning! Lightning!
Whirlwind! Whirlwind!

This song is an invocation of the elemental forces. It was composed by an old woman, who left the circle of dancers and stood in the center of the ring while singing it.

6. Wûmbĭ'ndomä'n

Wûmbĭ'ndomä'n, Wûmbĭ'ndomä'n,
Wûmbĭ'ndomä'n, Wûmbĭ'ndomä'n.
Nuvä'rĭ'p noyo'wană', Nuvä'rĭ'p noyo'wană',
Nuvä'rĭ'p noyo'wană', Nuvä'rĭ'p noyo'wană'.

Translation

The whirlwind! The whirlwind!
The whirlwind! The whirlwind!
The snowy earth comes gliding, the snowy earth comes gliding;
The snowy earth comes gliding, the snowy earth comes gliding.

This song may possibly refer to the doctrine of the new earth, here represented as white with snow, advancing swiftly, driven by a whirlwind. Such an idea occurs several times in the Arapaho songs.

7. Kosi' wûmbi'ndomä'

Kosi' wûmbi'ndomä',
Kosi' wûmbi'ndomä',
Kosi' wûmbi'ndomä'.

Kai'-va wûmbi'ndomä',
Kai'-va wûmbi'ndomä',
Kai'-va wûmbi'ndomä'.

Translation

There is dust from the whirlwind,
There is dust from the whirlwind,
There is dust from the whirlwind.
The whirlwind on the mountain,
The whirlwind on the mountain,
The whirlwind on the mountain.

8. DOMBI'NA SO'WINA'

Dombi'na so'wina',
Dombi'na so'wina',
Dombi'na so'wina'.
Kai'-va so'wina',
Kai'-va so'wina',
Kai'-va so'wina'

Translation

The rocks are ringing,
The rocks are ringing,
The rocks are ringing.
They are ringing in the mountains,
They are ringing in the mountains,
They are ringing in the mountains.

This song was explained to refer to the roaring of a storm among the rocks in the mountains.

9. SÛ'NG-Ä RO'YONJI'

Sû'ng-ä ro'yonji', Sû'ng-a ro'yon,
Sû'ng-ä ro'yonji', Sû'ng-a ro'yon,
Sû'ng-ä ro'yonji', Sû'ng-a ro'yon.
Pu'i do'yonji', Pu'i do'yon,
Pu'i do'yonji', Pu'i do'yon,
Pu'i do'yonji', Pu'i do'yon.

Translation

The cottonwoods are growing tall,
The cottonwoods are growing tall,
The cottonwoods are growing tall.
They are growing tall and verdant,
They are growing tall and verdant,
They are growing tall and verdant.

This song seems to refer to the return to spring. Throughout the arid region of the west the cottonwood skirting the borders of the streams is one of the most conspicuous features of the landscape. See Arapaho song 13.

PAIUTE GLOSSARY

Agai'h-tĭka'ra — "fish eaters;" the distinctive name of the Paiute of Walker lake, Nevada.

Bai'-yo — it is broken.

Ba'wă — going around in a circle

Dĕna — for *Tĭ'na.*

Do — black.

Dombi'na — for *Tĭ'mbi* or *Tŭbi.*

Do'roni — rolling on the ground, wallowing.

Do'yon or *Do'yonji* — it is growing tall.

Ga'yon or *Ga'yoni* — slender, tall and slender.

Gosi'pa — the Milky Way, the road of the dead. See Paiute song 1

Hävi'gĭnŭ — it lies there, it lies there asleep; *hävi'kwă*, sleep.

Hogăpä'goni — "rush-arrow people;" the Shoshoni name for the Paiute; from *hogăp*, a small water reed; *pägă*, arrow, and *ni*, the tribal suffix.

Hutsi — the sage-hen (*Centrocercus urophasianus*).

Ĭbidsi'ĭ — "our mother;" the mythic maternal ancestor of the Paiute.

JACK WILSON — see *Wovoka.*

Ka — the root of the verb *sit*; *yä'nakatü'*, I am sitting down.

Kai-va — mountain.

Kosi — for *Kosi'ba.*

Kosi'ba — dust.

Kotso'-tĭka'ra — "buffalo eaters;" the Paiute name for the Bannock. Compare *Ko'tso-tĕ'ka*, a Comanche division.

Kura'ngwa — "very high peak;" applied to Mount Grant, the sacred mountain of the Paiute, west of Hawthorne and near the southwestern end of Walker lake, Nevada.

Kwohi'tsauq or *K'wijau'h* — "big rumbling belly," one of the names assumed by Wovoka the messiah. It was originally the name of his paternal grandfather.

Nänigü'kwa — the Paiute name of the Ghost dance. The word signifies the "dance in a circle;" *nüka*, a dance.

Noyo'ä — to come gliding or creeping; the verb is applied to the movement of a snake or of an object which progresses without the aid of feet.

Noyo'wana — for *Noyo'ä.*

Nümä — "people," or "Indians," the name used to designate themselves by the Paiute, Shoshoni, and Comanche.

Nümi'-naă' — "our father;" the mythic ancestor of the Paiute.

Nüvä — for *Nüvä'bi.*

Nüvä'bi — snow.

Nüvä'-ri'pă — snowy earth, snow-covered earth (compound word); from *nüvä'bi*, snow, and *ri'pă* or *ti'pă*, earth.

Pägü'nävä — fog.

Paiute or *Piu'te* — (*Pai-yu't*) the name by which the *Nüma* of Nevada and the adjacent region are popularly and officially known. It has been rendered as "true (*pai*) Ute" or "water (*pä*) Ute." They themselves pronounce the word in three syllables, *Pai-u'-ti.*

PAI-YU'CHIMŬ — the Hopi name for the Paiute.

PAI-YU'TSĬ — the Navaho name for the Paiute.

PALŬ — the Washo name for the Paiute.

Päsü' — for *Päsü'bi.*

Päsü'bi — willow.

PAVIO'TSO — the proper tribal name of the Indians of Walker River and Pyramid Lake reservations in Nevada, according to Powell, who considers them distinct from the Paiute.

Pu'i — for *Pu'igai-yu.*

Pu'igai'-yu — verdant, green (applied to growing plants).

Ro'răni — an unmeaning word used to fill out the measure of the songs.

Ro'yon or *Ro'yonji* — other forms of *Do'yon.*

SNAKE INDIANS — a name loosely applied to various northern bands or tribes of Shoshonean stock, including Paiute, Bannock, Shoshoni, and sometimes even the Comanche.

Sowi'na — ringing like a bell, roaring.

Sû'ng-ä — for *Sû'ng-äbi.*

Sû'ng-äbi — cottonwood.

Taivo — the Paiute, Shoshoni, and Comanche name for a white man. See *Tä'vibo.*

Tăkwû'kwij — lightning.

Tä'vibo — "white man," the father of Wovoka the messiah. The word has a connection with *täbi* or *tävi*, the sun; *tävä'năgwăt*, the east or sunrise place, and *tai'-vo*, the Shoshoni and Comanche name for a white man.

Tĭ'mbi or *Tĭ'mbin*—a rock; another form is *tübi*.

Tĭ'na—antelope.

Túngwü'kwiji—for *Tăkwû'kwij*.

Wai'-va—the sand grass or wild millet of Nevada (*Oryzopsis membranacea*). In composition the word becomes *wai*. See Paiute song 4.

WA'SIU—the name by which the Washo call themselves.

WĬ'KIUP—the popular name of the Paiute dwelling, made in conical form, about 8 or 10 feet high, and open at the top, of tulé rushes woven over a framework of poles. The word is of uncertain origin.

Wĭ'noghän—shaken by the wind, waving in the wind.

Wo'voka or *Wü'voka*—"the cutter," the proper name of the Paiute messiah, known to the whites as Jack Wilson. A few years ago he assumed also the name of *Kwohi'tsauq*, "big rumbling belly," from his paternal grandfather. See chapter IX *ante*.

Wûbi'doma—whirlwind, hurricane. *Hi'gwă*, wind; *pitä'năgwă-higwă'*, the south wind.

Wûmbe'doma—for *Wûbi'doma*.

Wûmbĭ'ndomän—for *Wûbi'doma*.

THE SIOUX

TRIBAL SYNONYMY

Chahrarat—Pawnee name (Grinnell).

Dakota, Nakota, or *Lakota*—proper tribal name, according to dialect, "allies, friends;" sometimes also they speak of themselves as *Oceti Sakowin*, the "seven council fires," in allusion to their seven great divisions.

Itahatski—Hidatsa name, "long arrows" (Matthews).

K'odalpä-K'iñago—Kiowa name, "necklace people," perhaps a misconception of neck-cutting people, i. e., beheaders.

Maranshobishgo—Cheyenne name, "cut-throats" (Long). The name is plainly incorrect, as the Cheyenne language has no *r*.

Nadowesi or *Nadowesiu*—"little snakes" or "little enemies," *Nadowe*, "snake" and figuratively "enemy," being the common Algonquian term for all tribes of alien lineage. The Ojibwa and others designated the Iroquois, living east of them, as *Nadowe*, while the Sioux, living to the west, were distinguished as *Nadowesi* or *Nadowesiu*, whence come Nadouessioux and Sioux.

Natnihina or *Natni*—Arapaho name; Hayden gives the form as *Natenehina*, which he renders "cut-throats or beheaders," but it may be derived from *Nadowe*, as explained above.

Niake'tsikûtk—Kichai name.

Pambizimina—Shoshoni name, "beheaders."

Papitsinima—Comanche name, "beheaders," from *papitsi*, signifying to behead, and *nĭma* or *nüma*, people.

Shahañ—Osage, Kansa, Oto, etc, name (Dorsey).

Sioux—popular name, abbreviated from Nadouessioux, the French form of their Ojibwa name.

Tsaba'kosh—Caddo name, "cut-throats."

TRIBAL SIGN

A sweeping pass of the right hand in front of the neck, commonly rendered "cut-throats" or "beheaders," but claimed by the Kiowa to refer to a kind of shell necklace formerly peculiar to the Sioux.

SKETCH OF THE TRIBE

The Sioux constitute the largest tribe in the United States, and are too well known to need an extended description here. Although now thought of chiefly as a prairie tribe, their emergence upon the plains is comparatively recent, and within the historic period their range extended as far eastward as central Wisconsin, from which, and most of Minnesota, they have been driven out by the westward advance of the Ojibwa. There is ground for believing that the true home of the whole Siouan stock is not in the west, or even in the central region, but along the south Atlantic slope. (See the author's *Siouan Tribes of the East*.)

The Sioux language has three well-marked dialects — the eastern or Santee, the middle or Yankton (including the Asiniboin in the north), and the western or Teton. The tribe consists of seven great divisions, each of which again has or had subdivisions. Dorsey enumerates over one hundred in all. Each grand division had its own camping circle, and when two or more such divisions camped together they usually camped in concentric circles. (*Dorsey.*) The seven great divisions are: 1. *Mde-wakañ-toñwañ* (Medewacanton), "village of the Spirit lake;" 2. *Waqpekute* (Wahpacoota), "leaf shooters;" 3. *Waqpetoñwañ* (Wahpeton), "leaf village;" 4. *Sisitoñwañ* (Sisseton), variously rendered "slimy village" or "swamp village;" 5. *Ihanktoñwañ* (Yankton), "end village;" 6. *Ihanktoñwañna* (Yanktonais), "upper end village;" 7. *Titoñwañ* (Teton), "prairie village."

The first four divisions collectively are known as Isañati or Santee Sioux. The name is supposed to be derived from *isañ*, the dialectic word for "knife." They formerly held Mississippi, Minnesota, and upper Red rivers in Minnesota and were afterward gathered on reservations at Devils lake, North Dakota; Lake Traverse (Sisseton agency) and Flandreau, South Dakota; and Santee agency, Nebraska. Those at Lake Traverse and Flandreau have now taken allotments as citizens.

The Yankton and Yanktonais, together speaking the middle dialect, occupied chiefly the country of James river, east of the Missouri, in North Dakota and South Dakota and extending into Iowa. They are now on Yankton and Crow Creek reservations in South Dakota, and Fort Peck reservation, Montana.

The Teton constitute more than two-thirds of the whole Sioux tribe, and held nearly the whole country southwest of the Missouri from Cannonball river to the South Platte, extending westward beyond the Black hills. They are all now on reservations in South and North Dakota. They are again subdivided into seven principal divisions: 1. *Sichañgu*, "burnt thighs" (Brulés), now on Rosebud reservation; 2. *Ogalala*, referring to "scattering" of dust in the face (Clark), now on Pine Ridge reservation, under the celebrated chief Red Cloud (*Maqpe-Luta*); 3. *Hunkpapa*, "those who camp at the end (or opening) of the camping circle" (Clark), on Standing Rock reservation; 4. *Mini-kañzu*, "those who plant by the water," on Cheyenne River reservation; 5. *Itazipko*, "without bows" (Sans Arcs), on Cheyenne River reservation; 6. *Sihasapa*, "black feet" (not to be confounded with the Blackfoot tribe), on Cheyenne River and Standing Rock reservations; 7. *Ohenoñpa*, "two kettles," on Cheyenne River and Rosebud reservations. According to the official report for 1893, the Sioux within the United States number about 23,410, which, with 600 permanently settled in Manitoba, make the whole population about 24,000 souls.

The Sioux, under the name of Nadouessi, are mentioned by the Jesuit missionaries as early as 1632. They made their first treaties with our government in 1815. The most prominent events in their history since that date have been the treaty of Prairie du Chien in 1825, which defined their eastern boundary and stopped the westward advance of the Ojibwa; the Minnesota massacre of 1862, which resulted in the expulsion of the Sioux from Minnesota; the Sioux war of 1876–77, largely consequent on the unauthorized invasion of the Black hills by miners, and the chief incident of which was the defeat and massacre of an entire detachment under General Custer; the treaty by which the great reservation was broken up in 1889, and the outbreak of 1890, with the massacre of Wounded Knee.

By reason of their superior numbers the Sioux have always assumed, if not exercised, the lordship over all the neighboring tribes with the exception of the Ojibwa, who, having acquired firearms before the Sioux, were enabled to drive the latter from the headwaters of the Mississippi, and were steadily pressing them westward when stopped by the intervention of the United States government. The Sioux in turn drove the Cheyenne, Crow, Kiowa, and others before them and forced them into the mountains or down into the southern prairies. The eastern bands were sedentary and largely agricultural, but the Teton were solely and preeminently wandering buffalo hunters. All dwelt in *tipis*—the word is from the Sioux language—which were of bark in the timber country and of buffalo skins on the plains. In warlike character they are probably second only to the Cheyenne, and have an air of proud superiority rather unusual with Indians. Clark says of them, "In mental, moral, and physical qualities I consider the Sioux a little lower but still nearly equal to the Cheyenne, and the Teton are the superior branch of the family." (*Indian Sign Language*, 345.) The eastern Sioux are now far advanced toward civilization through the efforts of teachers and missionaries for over a generation, and the same is true in a less degree of the Yankton, while the majority of the Teton are still nearly in their original condition.

I found the Sioux very difficult to approach on the subject of the Ghost dance. This was natural, in view of the trouble that had resulted to them in consequence of it. When I was first at Pine Ridge, the troops still camped there served as a reminder of the conflict, while in the little cemetery at the agency were the fresh graves of the slain soldiers, and only a few miles away was the Wounded Knee battlefield and the trench where the bodies of nearly three hundred of their people had been thrown. To my questions the answer almost invariably was, "The dance was our religion, but the government sent soldiers to kill us on account of it. We will not talk any more about it." Another reason for their unwillingness was the fact that most of the interpreters were from the eastern or Santee portion of the tribe, and looked with contempt on the beliefs and customs of their more primitive western brethren, between whom and themselves there was in consequence but little friendly feeling. On one occasion, while endeavoring to break

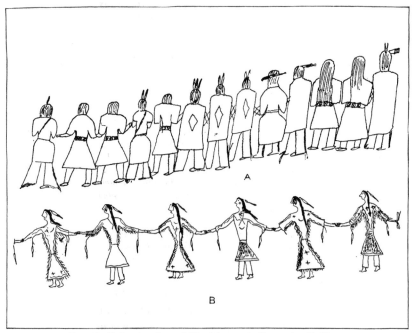

FIG. 102—Native drawings of Ghost dance—A, Comanche; B, Sioux

the ice with one of the initiates of the dance, I told him how willingly the Arapaho had given me information and even invited me to join in the dance. "Then," said he, " don't you find that the religion of the Ghost dance is better than the religion of the churches?" I could not well say yes, and hesitated a moment to frame an answer. He noticed it at once and said very deliberately, "Well, then, if you have not learned that you have not learned anything about it," and refused to continue the conversation.

The Sioux ghost songs are all in the dialect of the Teton, who took the most active interest in the dance, which was hardly known among the bands east of the Missouri. The vocalic character of the language, and the frequent liquid *l* of this dialect, renders these songs peculiarly musical, while for beauty of idea and expression they are second only to those of the Arapaho.

SONGS OF THE SIOUX

1. A′TE HE′YE E′YAYO

Opening song

A′te he′ye e′yayo!
A′te he′ye e′yayo!
A′te he′ye lo,
A′te he′ye lo.
Nitu′ñkañshi′la wa′ñyegala′ke—kta′ e′yayo′!
Nitu′ñkañshi′la wa′ñyegala′ke—kta′ e′yayo′!
A′te he′ye lo,
A′te he′ye lo.
Ni′takuye wañye′găla′ke—kta e′yayo′!
Ni′takuye wañye′găla′ke—kta e′yayo′!
A′te he′ye lo,
A′te he′ye lo.

Translation

The father says so — *E′yayo!*
The father says so — *E′yayo!*
The father says so,
The father says so.
You shall see your grandfather — *E′yayo′!*
You shall see your grandfather — *E′yayo′!*
The father says so,
The father says so.
You shall see your kindred — *E′yayo′!*
You shall see your kindred — *E′yayo′!*
The father says so,
The father says so.

This is the opening song of the dance. While singing it, all the dancers stand motionless with hands stretched out toward the west, the country of the messiah and the quarter whence the new spirit world is to come. When it is ended, all cry together, after which they join hands and begin to circle around to the left. "Grandfather," as well as "father," is a reverential term applied to the messiah.

2. MI′CHĬ′NKSHI NAÑPE

Michĭ′nkshi nañpe ma′yuzaye,
Michĭ′nkshi nañpe ma′yuzaye,
A′te he′ye lo,
A′te he′ye lo.
Ini′chaghe-kte,
Ini′chaghe-kte,
A′te he′ye lo,
A′te he′ye lo.
Chăno′ñpa wa′ñ chi′cha-u′pi,

Chăno′ñpa wa′ñ chi′cha-u′pi,
A′te he′ye lo′,
A′te he′he lo′.
Cha′-yani′pi-kta′,
Cha′-yani′pi-kta′,
A′te he′ye lo′,
A′te he′ye lo′.

Translation

My son, let me grasp your hand,
My son, let me grasp your hand,
Says the father,
Says the father.
You shall live,
You shall live,
Says the father,
Says the father.
I bring you a pipe,
I bring you a pipe,
Says the father,
Says the father.
By means of it you shall live,
By means of it you shall live,
Says the father,
Says the father.

This song refers to the sacred pipe which, according to the Sioux tradition, was brought to them by a mysterious young woman from the spirit world. The story, as outlined by Captain J. M. Lee, is as follows: In the old times the Sioux were always at war, not only with other tribes, but also among themselves. On one occasion two young men were out hunting when they saw a young woman approaching them with folded arms. Seeing that she was not of their own tribe, one proposed to the other that they kill her, but he refused and urged that they wait until they learned what she wanted. The first speaker, however, was about to kill her as she drew near, when she suddenly stooped down and took from around her ankle something resembling an anklet, which she waved about her head. The motion was so rapid that it seemed as though a cloud encircled her for a few moments, when she ceased, and the snake which she had taken from off her ankle glided away through the grass. But the young warrior who had thought to kill her had disappeared, swept from the face of the earth.

Turning now to his companion, she said, "To you I come as a friend and helper. Your people have been killing each other. I bring you a pipe, which is a token of peace," and she held out a pipe as she spoke. "When you smoke it your thoughts will be of peace, and no murderer (i. e., no one who kills a member of his own tribe) must be allowed to smoke it." She returned with him to his village, where the women prepared for her reception a large tipi, to which the chiefs of the tribe came to listen to her instructions. She taught them to be at peace with one another, if they would be happy, and when they listened to her words and accepted her teachings, she gave them the sacred medicine pipe to smoke thenceforth in their councils as a perpetual reminder of the peace covenant of the Lakota. Her mission now ended, she said she must leave them, and although they begged her earnestly to stay with them, she could not tarry longer, but disappeared as suddenly and mysteriously as she had come.

A variant of this legend is given by Colonel Mallery in his paper in the Tenth Annual Report of the Bureau of Ethnology, where it is illustrated by a colored plate from a picture by the Indian story teller. According to this version, the pipe maiden was the mysterious white Buffalo Cow, and brought, with the pipe, a package of four grains of maize of different colors. This corn sprang from the milk which dropped from her udder, and was thus, with the flesh of the buffalo itself, appointed from the beginning to be the food of all the red tribes. The seeming snakes about her waist and ankles were really blades of grass (corn?). She taught the people to call her "grandmother," a reverential title among Indians, and after leading them to her relatives, the buffalo, she faded from their sight as they stood gazing at her.

The pipe holds an important part in the mythology and ritual of almost all our tribes, east and west, and no great ceremony is complete and no treaty was ever ratified without it. It is generally symbolic of peace and truth. As a peace emblem, it was formerly carried by every bearer of a friendly message from one tribe to another and was smoked in solemn ratification of treaties, the act of smoking being itself in the nature of an oath. Among the prairie tribes an individual accused of crime is offered the sacred pipe, and if he accepts it and smokes he is declared innocent, as no Indian would dare to smoke it if guilty. The ordinary ceremonial pipe of the prairie tribes is made of the red stone, known as catlinite, from the famous pipestone quarry in Minnesota in the old country of the Sioux. The peace pipe of the Cherokee was made of a white stone, somewhat resembling talc, from a quarry near Knoxville, Tennessee. It is said to have had seven stem holes, emblematic of the seven clans of the Cherokee, and was smoked by seven counselors at the same time. In every case the tribe has a legend to account for the origin of the pipe. A flat pipe is the tribal "medicine" of the Arapaho, and is still preserved with the northern band in Wyoming. (See Arapaho songs 1 and 2.) Besides the stone pipe, there are also in use pipes of clay or bone, as well as cigarettes, but as a rule no ceremonial character attaches to these. In ceremonial smoking the pipe is passed around the circle of councilors, each of whom takes only a few whiffs and then hands it to his neighbor. Each one as he receives the pipe offers it first to the sun, holding the bowl up toward the sky and saying, "Grandfather, smoke;" then to the earth, the fire, and perhaps also to each of the four cardinal points and to one or another of their mythologic heroes. Among the Kiowa

I have seen a man hold up the pipe to the sky, saying, "Smoke, Sinti" (Sinti being their great mythologic trickster), and then in the same way, "Smoke, Jesus."

In the Ghost dance at Rosebud and Pine Ridge, as usually performed, a young woman stood in the center of the circle holding out a pipe toward the messiah in the west, and remained thus throughout the dance. Another young woman usually stood beside her holding out a *bäqati* wheel (see Arapaho song 49) in the same way. This feature of the dance is said to have been introduced by Short Bull.

3. HE TUWE'CHA HE

He tuwe'cha he u echa'ni hwo?
He tuwe'cha he u echa'ni hwo?
Huñku oki'le chaya he u hwo?
Huñku oki'le chaya he u hwo?
A'te-ye he'ye lo,
A'te-ye he'ye lo.

Translation

Who think you comes there?
Who think you comes there?
Is it someone looking for his mother?
Is it someone looking for his mother?
Says the father,
Says the father.

In this the singer tells how he was greeted by his former friend upon entering the spirit world, to which he had gone in search of his mother.

4. WANA'YAÑ MA'NIYE

Wana'yañ ma'niye,
Wana'yañ ma'niye.
Tata'ñka wañ ma'niye,
Tata'ñka wañ ma'niye,
A'te he'ye lo,
A'te he'ye lo.

Translation

Now he is walking,
Now he is walking.
There is a buffalo bull walking,
There is a buffalo bull walking,
Says the father,
Says the father.

The maker of this song, in her vision of the spirit world, evidently saw a herd of buffalo, with a bull walking about near them. The form of the verb shows that a woman is supposed to be talking.

5. Lechel miyo'qañ-kte

Lechel miyo'qañ-kte lo — Yo'yoyo'!
Lechel miyo'qañ-kte lo — Yo'yoyo'!
Taku maka' a-icha'gha hena mita'wa-ye lo — Yo'yoyo'!
Taku maka' a-icha'gha hena mita'wa-ye lo — Yo'yoyo'!
A'te he'ye lo — Yo'yoyo'!
A'te he'ye lo — Yo'yoyo'!
E'ya Yo'yoyo'!
E'ya Yo'yoyo'!

Translation

This is to be my work — *Yo'yoyo'!*
This is to be my work — *Yo'yoyo'!*
All that grows upon the earth is mine — *Yo'yoyo'!*
All that grows upon the earth is mine — *Yo'yoyo'!*
Says the father — *Yo'yoyo'!*
Says the father — *Yo'yoyo'!*
E'ya Yo'yoyo'!
E'ya Yo'yoyo'!

6. Michinkshi'yi tewa'qila che

Michinkshi'yi tewa'qila che — Ye'ye'!
Michinkshi'yi tewa'qila che — Ye'ye'!
Oya'te-ye i'nichagha'pi-kta che — Ye'ye'!
Oya'te-ye i'nichagha'pi-kta che — Ye'ye'!
A'teye he'ye lo,
A'teye he'ye lo.
Haye'ye' E'yayo'yo'!
Haye'ye' E'yayo'yo'!

Translation

I love my children — *Ye'ye'!*
I love my children — *Ye'ye'!*
You shall grow to be a nation — *Ye'ye'!*
You shall grow to be a nation — *Ye'ye'!*
Says the father, says the father.
Haye'ye' Eyayo'yo'! Haye'ye' E'yayo'yo'!

7. Mila kiñ hiyu'michi'chiyana

Mila kiñ hiyu'michi'chiyana,
Mila kiñ hiyu'michi'chiyana.
Wa'waka'bla-kte — Ye'ye'!
Wa'waka'bla-kte — Ye'ye'!
Oñchi he'ye lo — Yo'yo'!
Oñchi he'ye lo — Yo'yo'!
Puye chiñyi wa'sna wakaghiñyiñ-kte,
Puye chiñyi wa'sna wakaghiñyiñ-kte,
Oñchi heye lo — Yo'yo!
Oñchi heye lo — Yo'yo!

Translation

Give me my knife,
Give me my knife,
I shall hang up the meat to dry — *Ye'ye'* !
I shall hang up the meat to dry — *Ye'ye'* !
Says grandmother — *Yo'yo'* !
Says grandmother — *Yo'yo'* !
When it is dry I shall make pemmican,
When it is dry I shall make pemmican,
Says grandmother — *Yo'yo* !
Says grandmother — *Yo'yo* !

This song brings up a vivid picture of the old Indian life. In her trance vision the old grandmother whose experience it relates came upon her friends in the spirit world just as all the women of the camp were engaged in cutting up the meat for drying after a successful buffalo hunt. In her joy she calls for her knife to assist in the work, and says that as soon as the meat is dry she will make some pemmican.

Fig. 103—Jerking beef.

In the old days an Indian camp during the cutting up of the meat after a buffalo hunt was a scene of the most joyous activity, some faint recollection of which still lingers about ration day at the agency. Thirty years ago, when a grand hunt was contemplated, preparations were made for days and weeks ahead. Couriers were sent out to collect the neighboring bands at a common rendezvous, medicine-men began their prayers and ceremonies to attract the herd, the buffalo songs were sung, and finally when all was ready the confederated bands or sometimes the whole tribe—men, women, children, horses, dogs, and travois—moved out into the buffalo grounds. Here the immense camp of hundreds of tipis was set up, more ceremonies were performed, and the mounted warriors rode out in a body to surround and slaughter the herd. The women followed close after them to strip the hides from the fresh carcasses and cut out the choice portion of the meat and tallow and bring it into camp. Here the meat was cut into thin strips and hung upon frames of horizontal poles to dry, while the tallow was stripped off in flakes. In the dry prairie atmosphere one day is usually sufficient to cure the meat, without the aid of salt or smoke. When thus dried it is known as "jerked beef." While the meat is fresh, for the first day or two the camp is a scene of constant feasting, the juicy steaks or the sweet ribs being kept broiling over the coals in one tipi or another until far into the night. It is the harvest home of the prairie tribes. As soon as the meat is dry, the tipis are taken down and packed into the wagons along with the meat, and one family after another starts for home until in a short time the great camp is a thing of the past.

The jerked beef or venison is commonly prepared for eating by being boiled until reasonably tender. In eating, the Indian takes a strip thus cooked, dips one end into a soup made by dissolving some salt in warm water, takes the portion thus salted between his teeth, and saws off enough for a mouthful with a knife held in his other hand. Between mouthfuls he takes bites from a strip of dried tallow placed in the dish with the meat.

For pemmican the jerked beef or other meat is toasted over a fire until crisp and is then pounded into a hash with a stone hammer. In the old times a hole was dug in the ground and a buffalo hide was staked over so as to form a skin dish, into which the meat was thrown to be pounded. The hide was that from the neck of the buffalo, the toughest part of the skin, the same used for shields, and the only part which would stand the wear and tear of the hammers. In the meantime the marrow bones are split up and boiled in water until all the grease and oil come to the top, when it is skimmed off and poured over the pounded beef. As soon as the mixture cools, it is sewed up into skin bags (not the ordinary painted parfléche cases) and laid away until needed. It was sometimes buried or otherwise cached. Pemmican thus prepared will keep indefinitely. When prepared for immediate use, it is usually sweetened with sugar, mesquite pods, or some wild fruit mixed and beaten up with it in the pounding. It is extremely nourishing, and has a very agreeable taste to one accustomed to it. On the march it was to the prairie Indian what parched corn was to the hunter of the timber tribes, and has been found so valuable as a condensed nutriment that it is extensively used by arctic travelers and explorers. A similar preparation is in use upon the pampas of South America and in the desert region of South Africa, while the canned beef of commerce is an adaptation from the Indian idea. The name comes from the Cree language, and indicates something mixed with grease or fat. (*Lacombe.*)

8. LE HE′YAHE′

Le he′yahe′—Ye′ye!
Le he′yahe′—Ye′ye!
Kañghi-ye oya′te-ye cha-ya waoñ we lo,
Kañghi-ye oya′te-ye cha-ya waoñ we lo.

Translation

This one says—*Ye′ye!*
This one says—*Ye′ye!*
I belong indeed to the nation of Crows,
I belong indeed to the nation of Crows.

This song may better be rendered, "I am a Crow nation," i. e., I represent the nation of Crows, the Crow nation probably typifying the spirits of the dead in the other world, as explained in Arapaho song 36. In several of the ghost songs there occur such expressions as "I am a Crow," "the Crow woman is going home," etc. Compare Sioux song 18.

9. NIYA′TE-YE′ HE′UW′E

Niya′te-ye′ he′uw′e, niya′te-ye′ he′uw′e,
Wa′ñbăli gălĕ′shka wa′ñ-yañ nihi′youwe,
Wa′ñbăli gălĕ′shka wa′ñ-yañ nihi′youwe.

Translation

It is your father coming, it is your father coming,
A spotted eagle is coming for you,
A spotted eagle is coming for you.

This song probably refers to a transformation trance vision, such as is frequently referred to in the ghost songs, where the spirit friend suddenly assumes the form of a bird, a moose, or some other animal.

10. MIYO′QAÑ KIÑ WAÑLA′KI

Miyo′qañ kiñ wañla′ki—Ye′yeye′!
Miyo′qañ kiñ wañla′ki—Ye′yeye′!
Hena wa′ñlake,
Hena wa′ñlake,
Ha′eye′ya he′yeye′,
Ha′eye′ya he′yeye′.

Translation

You see what I can do—*Ye′yeye′!*
You see what I can do—*Ye′yeye′!*
You see them, you see them,
Ha′eye′ya he′yeye′! Ha′eye′ya he′yeye′!

In this song the Father is probably represented as calling his children to witness that he has shown them visions of the spirit world and their departed friends.

11. Michǐ′nkshi mita′waye

E′yaye′ye′! E′yaye′ye′!
Michǐ′nkshi mita′waye,
Michǐ′nkshi mita′waye.

Translation

E′yaye′ye′! E′yaye′ye′!
It is my own child,
It is my own child.

The form of the verb indicates that this song was composed by a woman, who had evidently met her dead child in the spirit world.

12. A′te he′ u-we

A′te he′ u-we, A′te he′ u-we,
A′te eya′ya he′ u-we′ lo,
A′te eya′ya he′ u-we′ lo,
Ya′nipi-kta′ e′ya u′-we lo,
Ya′nipi-kta′ e′ya u′-we lo.

Translation

There is the father coming,
There is the father coming.
The father says this as he comes,
The father says this as he comes,
" You shall live," he says as he comes,
" You shall live," he says as he comes.

This is a reiteration of the messiah's promise of eternal life in the new spirit world.

13. Wa′sna wa′tiñ-kta′

Wa′sna wa′tiñ-kta′ — E′yeye′yeye′!
Wa′sna wa′tiñ-kta — E′yeye′yeye′!
Le′chiya′-ya eya′pi-lo — E′yeye′yeye′!
Le′chiya′-ya eya′pi-lo — E′yeye′yeye′!
E′ya he′-ye lo, E′ya he′-ye lo,
A′te-ye he′ye lo, A′te-ye he′ye lo.

Translation

I shall eat pemmican — *E′yeye′yeye′!*
I shall eat pemmican — *E′yeye′yeye′!*
They say so, they say so,
The father says so, the father says so.

For the explanation of this song reference, see song number 7.

14. A′te lena ma′qu-we

A′te lena ma′qu-we — Ye′ye′ye′!
A′te lena ma′qu-we — Ye′ye′ye′!
Peta wañ — yañyañ ma′qu-we — Ye′ye′ye′!
Peta wañ — yañyañ ma′qu-we — Ye′ye′ye′!
A′te ma′qu-we — Ye′ye′ye′!
A′te ma′qu-we — Ye′ye′ye′!

Translation

It was the father who gave us these things — *Ye'ye'ye'!*
It was the father who gave us these things — *Ye'ye'ye'!*
It was the father who gave us fire — *Ye'ye'ye'!*
It was the father who gave us fire — *Ye'ye'ye'!*
The father gave it to us — *Ye'ye'ye'!*
The father gave it to us — *Ye'ye'ye'!*

This was frequently used as the opening song of the Sioux Ghost dance. Fire is held in reverence among all Indian tribes as one of the greatest gifts of the Author of Life, and every tribe has a myth telling how it originated and how it was obtained by the people. In most of these myths the fire is represented as being at first in the possession of some giant or malevolent monster, from whom it is finally stolen by a hero, after a series of trials and difficulties worthy of the heroes of the Golden Fleece.

15. INA' HE'KUWO'

Ina' he'kuwo'; ina' he'kuwo'.
Misu'nkala che'yaya oma'ni-ye,
Misu'nkala che'yaya oma'ni-ye.
I'na he'kuwo'; i'na he'kuwo'.

Translation

Mother, come home; mother, come home.
My little brother goes about always crying,
My little brother goes about always crying.
Mother, come home; mother, come home.

This touching song was a favorite among the Sioux. It was composed by a young woman who saw her dead mother in the other world, and on waking out of her trance vision implores the mother to come back to them again, as her little brother is forever crying after her.

16. WA'NA WANASA'PI-KTA

Wa'na wanasa'pi-kta,
Wa'na wanasa'pi-kta.
Ŭñchi' ita'zipa michu'-ye,
Ŭñchi' ita'zipa michu'-ye,
A'te he'ye lo, a'te he'ye lo.

Translation

Now they are about to chase the buffalo,
Now they are about to chase the buffalo,
Grandmother, give me back my bow,
Grandmother, give me back my bow,
The father says so, the father says so.

The author of this song, in his trance vision of the spirit world, sees his old-time friends about to start on a buffalo hunt, and calls to his grandmother to give him back his bow, so that he may join them. The form, "give it back to me," is intended to show how far remote is the old life of the Indians, before they used the guns and other things of the white man. The last line has no particular connection with the rest, except as a common refrain of the ghost songs.

17. He′! kii′ñyañka a′gali′-ye

He′! kii′ñyañka a′gali′-ye,
He′! kii′ñyañka a′gali′-ye,
Wañ! le′chiya wanasa′pi-kta′ keya′pi lo,
Wañ! le′chiya wanasa′pi-kta′ keya′pi lo,
Wañhi′nkpe ka′gha-yo!
Wañhi′nkpe ka′gha-yo!
A′te he′ye lo, A′te he′ye lo.

Translation

He! They have come back racing,
He! They have come back racing,
Why, they say there is to be a buffalo hunt over here,
Why, they say there is to be a buffalo hunt over here,
Make arrows! Make arrows!
Says the father, says the father.

This song may be considered supplementary to the last. In the old times, when going on a buffalo hunt, it was customary among the Sioux to send out a small advance party to locate the herd. On finding it, these men at once returned at full gallop to the main body of hunters, but instead of stopping on reaching them they dashed past and then turned and fell in behind. It is to this custom that the first line refers. The author of the song, on waking up in the spirit world, sees the scouting party just dashing in with the news of the presence of the buffalo. Everyone at once prepares to join the hunt and "the father" commands him to make (or get ready) his arrows and go with them.

18. Mi′ye wañma′yañka-yo

Mi′ye wañma′yañka-yo!
Mi′ye wañma′yañka-yo!
Ka′ñghi oya′te wañ chañku′ waka′ghe lo,
Ka′ñghi oya′te wañ chañku′ waka′ghe lo,
Yani′pi-kta′-cha, yani′pi-kta′-cha.
Kola he′ye lo, kola he′ye lo.

Translation

Look at me! Look at me!
I make a road for one of the Crow nation (?),
I make a road for one of the Crow nation (?).
You shall live indeed, you shall live indeed.
Our friend says so, our friend says so.

The idea of this song is somewhat similar to that of number 8. It has no reference to the Crow Indians. As has been already explained, the crow is symbolic of the spirit world, and when the "friend"—the father or messiah—declares that he makes a road for one of the Crow nation he means that he has prepared the way for the return of their friends who are gone before.

19. Maka′ sito′maniyañ

Maka′ sito′maniyañ ukiye,
Oya′te uki′ye, oya′te uki′ye,
Wa′ñbali oya′te wañ hoshi′hi-ye lo,
Ate heye lo, ate heye lo,
Maka o′wañcha′ya uki′ye.
Pte kiñ ukiye, pte kiñ ukiye,
Kañghi oya′te wañ hoshi′hi-ye lo,
A′te he′ye lo, a′te he′ye lo.

Translation

The whole world is coming,
A nation is coming, a nation is coming,
The Eagle has brought the message to the tribe.
The father says so, the father says so.
Over the whole earth they are coming.
The buffalo are coming, the buffalo are coming,
The Crow has brought the message to the tribe,
The father says so, the father says so.

This fine song summarizes the whole hope of the Ghost dance—the return of the buffalo and the departed dead, the message being brought to the people by the sacred birds, the Eagle and the Crow. The eagle known as *wañ′bali* is the war eagle, from which feathers are procured for war bonnets.

20. Le′na wa′kañ

Le′na wa′kañ waka′gha-che,
A′te he′ye lo, a′te he′ye lo,
O′găle kiñhañ wakañ waka′gha-che,
A′te he′ye lo, a′te he′ye lo,
Chănoñ′pa kiñ waka′gha-che,
A′te he′ye lo, a′te he′ye lo.

Translation

It is I who make these sacred things,
Says the father, says the father.
It is I who make the sacred shirt,
Says the father, says the father.
It is I who made the pipe,
Says the father, says the father.

This song refers to the sacred pipe (see Sioux song 2 and Arapaho song 2) and the ghost shirt.

21. Miyo′qañ kiñ chichu′-che

Miyo′qañ kiñ chichu′-che,
A′te he′ye lo′, a′te he′ye lo′,
O′găle kiñ ni′niye′-kta,
A′te he′ye lo′, a′te he′ye lo′.

Translation

Verily, I have given you my strength,
Says the father, says the father.
The shirt will cause you to live,
Says the father, says the father.

This song also refers to the ghost shirt, which was supposed to make the wearer invulnerable.

22. MICHĬ′NKSHI TAHE′NA

Michĭ′nkshi tahe′na ku′piye,
Michĭ′nkshi tahe′na ku′piye,
Mako′che wañ washte aya′găli′pi-kte,
A′te he′ye lo′, a′te he′ye lo′.

Translation

My child, come this way,
My child, come this way.
You will take home with you a good country,
Says the father, says the father.

This song may refer to the vision of the new earth, which the messiah showed to the Sioux delegates when they visited him. (See page 797.) The first line means literally "return in this direction," the imperative form used being between a command and an entreaty.

23. WANA WICHĔ′SHKA

Wana wichĕ′shka a′ti-ye,
Wana wichĕ′shka a′ti-ye.
Wihu′ta oho′măni, wihu′ta oho′măni,
Oka′tañna, oka′tañna,
Koyañ wowa′hiñ-kte,
Koyañ wowa′hiñ-kte.

Translation

Now set up the tipi,
Now set up the tipi.
Around the bottom,
Around the bottom,
Drive in the pegs,
Drive in the pegs.
In the meantime I shall cook,
In the meantime I shall cook.

The form of the verb *oka′tañna* shows that it is a woman speaking, even if we did not learn this from the context. To those who know the Indian life it brings up a vivid picture of a prairie band on the march, halting at noon or in the evening. As soon as the halt is called by some convenient stream, the women jump down and release the horses from the wagons (or the travois in the old times), and hobble them to

prevent them wandering away.   Then, while some of the women set up
the tipi poles, draw the canvas over them, and drive in the pegs around
the bottom and the wooden pins up the side, other women take axes
and buckets and go down to the creek for wood and water.   When they
return, they find the tipis set up and the blankets spread out upon the
grass, and in a few minutes fires are built and the meal is in preparation.   The woman who composed the song evidently in her vision
accompanied her former friends on such a march.

24. A′TE MI′CHUYE

A′te mi′chuye,
A′te mi′chuye,
Wañhi′nkpe mi′chuye,
Wañhi′nkpe mi′chuye,
A′hiye, a′hiye.
Wa′sna wa′tiñkte,
Wa′sna wa′tiñkte.

Translation

Father, give them to me,
Father, give them to me,
Give me my arrows,
Give me my arrows.
They have come, they have come.
I shall eat pemmican,
I shall eat pemmican.

The maker of this song, while in the spirit world, asks and receives
from the Father some of the old-time arrows with which to kill buffalo,
so that he may once more feast upon pemmican.

25. HAÑPA WECHA′GHE

Hañpa wecha′ghe,
Hañpa wecha′ghe,
Tewa′qila-la he,
Tewa′qila-la he.
Wa′ñbleni′chala he kaye lo,
Wa′ñbleni′chala he kaye lo,
Toke′cha wa′ñwegalaki′ñ-kte,
Toke′cha wa′ñwegalaki′ñ-kte,
Nihu′ñ koñ he he′ye lo,
Nihu′ñ koñ he he′ye lo.

Translation

I made moccasins for him,
I made moccasins for him,
For I love him,
For I love him.
To take to the orphan,
To take to the orphan.

Soon I shall see my child,
Soon I shall see my child,
Says your mother,
Says your mother.

This song evidently relates the trance vision of a mother who saw her child in the spirit world, and expresses the hope that she may soon be united with him. In accordance with the custom of the Ghost dance, it is probable that she made a pair of moccasins to give him when next they met, and that she carried them in the dance as she sang.

26. Waka'ñyañ iñya'ñkiñ-kte

Waka'ñyañ iñya'nkiñ-kte,
Waka'ñyañ iñya'nkiñ-kte,
Chañgăle'shka wañ luza'hañ iñya'ñkiñ-kte,
Chañgăle'shka wañ luza'hañ iñya'ñkiñ-kte,
Wañwa'yag upo, wañwa'yag upo,
A'te he'ye lo, a'te he'ye lo.

Translation

The holy (hoop) shall run,
The holy (hoop) shall run,
The swift hoop shall run,
The swift hoop shall run.
Come and see it,
Come and see it,
Says the father,
Says the father.

This song refers to the game wheel and sticks (*bä'qati*, Arapaho) already described in the Arapaho songs. It is said that the medicine-man of Big Foot's band carried such a hoop with him in their flight from the north, and displayed it in every dance held by the band until the fatal day of Wounded Knee. A similar hoop was carried and hung upon the center tree at the dance at No Water's camp near Pine Ridge. To the Indian it symbolizes the revival of the old-time games.

SIOUX GLOSSARY

A'găli (-ye)—they have returned; *waku*, I am returning or coming home; *wagali'*, I have returned.

Ahi' (-ye)—they have come; *wa-u'*, I come; *hi*, he has come.

A-icha'gha—growing upon; from *kagha*, to grow or spring up.

A'te or *Ate-ye*—father; *ate kiñ*, the father; *ate-mita*, my father; *ni'-ate*, your father; *at-kuku*, his or her father. *Ye* is a syllable sometimes added to fill in the meter.

Ati'-ye—set up the tipi; here *ye* is the imperative suffix.

Aya'găli'pi-kte—you (plural) will take home with you, you will bring back with you; from *awa'găle*, I take it home.

Chañgăle'shka—a hoop; the *bä'qati* hoop. See Sioux song 26, and Arapaho songs.

Chañku'—road, trail.

Chăno'ñpa—pipe; *o'ñpa*, to smoke; *cha'ñ-li*, tobacco.

Cha-yani'pi-kta—you (plural) will live; from *ni'wa-uñ*, I live, I go about alive; the regular form is *Yanipi-kta* q. v.

Cheya'ya—he is constantly crying. *Wa-che'yă*, I cry; the final *ya* implies repetition or habit.

Chi'cha-u'pi—I bring it to you (plural). *Chicha* implies I to thee, or I mean thee; *u* implies *come*, from *wa-u*, I come; *pi* is the plural participle, and with *chicha* implies I bring it to you, or I come with it to you.

Chichu'-chĕ—I give it to you, indeed; *waku'*, I give it to him; *chĕ* conveys the idea of verily or indeed. Compare *Maqu'-we*.

Chiñyi—for *Kiñhiñ*, when, when it is so.

Echani—you think so about it; *echa'mi*, I think; *echa'ni hwo*, who do you think?

Eya!—an unmeaning exclamation used in the songs.

Eya—he says; *epa*, I say. *Eya'ya*, he reiterates, he says again; *e'yahe, eya'pi*, they say.

E'yahe—another form of *eya*, he says, q. v.

Eya'pi—they say. Compare *Eya*.

Eya'ya—he reiterates, he says again. The final *ya* implies repetition. Compare *Eya*.

E'yaye'ye!—an unmeaning exclamation used in the songs.

E'yayo'!—an unmeaning exclamation used in the songs to fill in the measure.

E'yeye'yeye!—an unmeaning exclamation used in the songs.

Găle'shka—spotted.

Ha'eye'ya!—an unmeaning exclamation used in the songs.

Hañpa—moccasin.

Ha'yeye'!—an unmeaning exclamation used in the songs.

He—(1) an exclamation, look! look here! (2) an interrogative particle, after the sentence; (3) the demonstrative "that."

Hĕku'wo—come home now, return home at once; *wa-u*, I come; *he*, a prefix implying now, or directly.

He'na—those, plural of *he*, that.

He'uwĕ—that is he coming; from *he*, that; *u*, coming; and *wĕ*, the feminine particle.

Heyahe (-*ye*)—he says that, he says this; *ye* is usually the female suffix. Compare *He'ye*.

He'ye—he says.

He'yeye'!—an unmeaning exclamation used in the songs.

Hiyumichi'chiya'na—hand me my own; *na*, the female imperative particle.

Hoshi'hi (-*ye*)—he has arrived with a message; he has brought a message; from *hoshi'*, to tell news, to carry a message.

Húñku—his mother; *inú'ñ*, mother.

Hwo—an interrogative sign, used by a man; a woman says *wi*.

Ina'—mother; my mother.

Ini'chaghapi-kte—you (plural) will grow or live. Compare *Inichaghe-kte*.

Inichaghe-kte—you (singular) will grow, i. e., you will live; *icha'ghehe*, it is growing.

Iñyañkiñ-kte—it shall run; from *iñyañka*, to run.

Ita'zipa—a bow (to shoot with).

Ka'gha-yo—make them; *waka'ghe*, I make it; *yo*, an imperative particle.

Kañghi'—a crow.

Kaye—another form of *kaya*, to take to one.

Keya'pi—they say that, they say it; *epa*, to say.

Kii'ñyañka—racing; from *iñyañka*, to run; the prefix *ki* implies a contest or emulation.

Kiñ—the.

Kiñhañ—explained as another form of *kiñ*; the ordinary meaning is *when* or *if*.

Ko'la—friend.

Koñ—that (demonstrative); it sometimes conveys the idea of "aforesaid."

Ko'yañ—in the meantime.

Ku'pi-ye—you will return.

Lecheb—thus, in this way; from *le*, this.

Lechi'ya—over here in this place; from *le*, this.

Lena—these things; from *le*, this.

Lo—an emphatic or euphonic particle used at the end of a phrase or sentence; it may be described as an emphatic or euphonic period. *Lo* is used by men, *ye* by women.

Lu'zahañ—swift.

Maka'—earth, the earth.

Mako'che—a country.

Mani'ye—he walks (habitual); *mawani*, I walk; the suffix *ye* usually denotes a female speaker.

Maq'pe-Luta—Red Cloud, the noted chief of the Ogalala Teton Sioux at Pine Ridge; from *maqpi'ya*, a cloud, and *luta*, red.

Maqu'-we—he gave to me, indeed; from *waku'*, I give it; *we* is an emphatic particle. Compare *Chichu'-chĕ*.

Ma'yuza (-*ye*)—grasp it with me, let me grasp it.

Michĭ'nkshi (-*yi*)—my son, my offspring; *chĭnksh*, son.

Mi'chu (-*ye*)—give it back to me.

Mila—knife.

Misu'ñkala—my little brother. *Mi*, my; *la*, the diminutive.

Mita'wă or *Mita'waye*—it is mine, from *mi*, I, my, and *tawă*, it belongs.

Mi'ye—I, myself, me.

Miyo'qañ—my power, my work. Compare *Miyo'qañ-kte*.

Miyo'qañ-kte—it will be my work, my power, the way I shall do; from *mi*, my; *o'qañ*, action, work, strength, and *kte*, the future suffix.

Nañpe—hand; *mi-na'ñpe*, my hand.

Nihi'youwĕ—he is coming for you; from the root *u*, to come; *wĕ* is the feminine particle, which shows that a woman is speaking.

Nihu'ñ—your (singular) mother.

Niniye'-kta—it will cause you to live; *miye'*, to come to live; *ni*, in composition, you, your; *kta*, the future suffix.

Nita'kuye—your kindred; *mita'kuye*, my relative.

Nitu'ñkañshi'la—your grandfather; *mi-tu'ñkañshi'la*, my grandfather. The final *la* is a euphonic diminutive.

Niya'te—for *Ni-a'te*, your father.

O'găle—shirt, coat.

Oho'măni—around, round about.

Oka'tañna—drive it in, drive them in (as nails or tipi pegs); *na* is the female imperative particle.

Oki'le—looking for its own; *owa'le*, I look for it; *owa'kile*, I look for my own.

Oma'ni (-*ye*)—walking around, going about.

Oñchi—grandmother.

O'wañcha'ya—all over, everywhere.

Oya'te—tribe, nation.

Peta—fire.

Pte—buffalo (generic), buffalo cow.

Puze or *Puza*—dry.

Shaie'la or *Shaie'na*—"red," i.e., "alien;" the Sioux name for the Cheyenne. The root of the word is *sha*, red, with *la* or *na*, the diminutive, frequently used merely for euphony.

Sitomăni-yañ—everybody, all over, everywhere.

Tahe'na—on this side, this way, in this direction.

Ta'ku—something, whatever.

Tatañka—a buffalo bull; *pte*, a buffalo cow, or a buffalo (generic).

Tewa'qi'la or *Tewa'qila-la*—I love him; the final *la* is a diminutive or endearing particle, sometimes added to verbs as well as to nouns.

Tipi—a tent, a house; from *ti*, to dwell or abide.

Toke'cha—soon, before long.

Tuwe'-cha—who indeed? who can it be? *tu'we*, who?

U—coming; *wa-u*, I come.

Uki'ye—they are coming; *wa'-u*, I come.

Uñchi'—grandmother, my grandmother.

Upo—you come (plural imperative); from *wa'-u*, I come.

U-we—coming, as he comes; see *u*; *we* is another form of *ye*, an emphatic or euphonic particle.

Wa'chipi—a dance.

Wa'kañ—sacred, mysterious, sacred thing.

Waka'gha-chĕ—it is I who made it, I made it indeed. The particle *chĕ* conveys the idea of indeed, verily.

Waka'ghe—I make it.

Wakaghi'ñyiñ-kte—I shall make it; *wa-ka'ghe*, I make it.

Waka'ñyañ—sacredly, mysteriously; from *wa'kañ*, sacred, mysterious.

Wañ—a.

Wañ!—look! see! why!

Wana—now.

Wana'ghi—ghost, spirit of the dead.

Wana'ghi wa'chipi—Ghost dance, from *wana'ghi*, ghost, or spirit of the dead, and *wa'chipi*, a dance.

Wanasa'pi—see *Wanasa'pi-kta*.

Wanasa'pi-kta—they will chase buffalo, they are about to chase buffalo; from *wana'sa*, to hunt game by surrounding and shooting it. *Kta* or *kte* is the future sign.

Wañbale'nichala—a little orphan; from *wa'ñbăle'nicha*, an orphan.

Wa'ñbăli—eagle, the war eagle.

Wañhi'nkpe—arrow, arrows.

Wañ-la'ki—you see it; *wañbăla'ki*, I see it.

Wañma'yañka-yo—look at me! *wañbăla-a'ka*, I see it; *yo*, the imperative suffix.

Wa'oñ we—I am in that condition, I am it; *we* is the feminine suffix.

Wañwayag—to see it. Compare *Wañma'yañka-yo.*

Wañwe'gala'kiñ-kte—I shall see my own. Compare *Wañma'yañka-yo.*

Wañyañ—for *wañ*, a (the article).

Wañyegalake-kta—you (plural) shall see your own; from *wañbála'ki*, I see it. *Kte* or *kta* is the future suffix.

Washte'—good.

Wa'sna—pemmican. See Sioux song 7.

Wati'ñ-kte—I shall eat; *wawa'te*, I eat.

Wawa'kabla-kte—I shall spread out the meat to dry; *ka'bla*, to spread out meat for drying.

Wa'yana—now; another form of *wana*.

We—an emphatic suffix particle equivalent to verily or indeed.

Wecha'ghe—I made them for him.

Wichĕ'shka—a tipi; the word literally means only the opening at the top of the tipi.

Wihu'ta—the bottom of a tipi.

Wowa'hiñ-kte—I shall cook; *wowa'hañ*, I cook (generic).

Yanipi-kta—you (plural) will live; from *ni'wa-uñ*, I am alive.

Yañyañ—an unmeaning word used in the songs to fill up the measure.

Ye—an emphatic, imperative, or precatory particle or suffix, usually spoken by a woman. In the songs it seems frequently to be used merely for euphony.

Ye'ye!—an unmeaning exclamation used in the songs.

Yoyoyo—ibid.

THE KIOWA AND KIOWA APACHE

KIOWA TRIBAL SYNONYMY

Be'shĭltchă—Kiowa Apache name, meaning unknown.

Caygua—Spanish form, from their proper name, *Kaijwu.*

Gahe'wa—Wichita and Kichai name; another form of Kiowa.

Kâ'igwŭ—"real or principal people," proper tribal name.

Kai-wă—Comanche and Caddo name; from their proper name, *Kaigwu.*

Kiowa—popular name, a corruption of the name used by themselves.

Kwŭ'da—"going out;" old name formerly used by the Kiowa for themselves.

Ñĭ'chihinĕⁿna—"river men," Arapaho name; so called because they formerly lived on upper Arkansas river, from which the Arapaho claim to have driven them.

Tepda—"coming out," "issuing;" another old name formerly used by the Kiowa for themselves.

Witapä'hat or *Witapä'tu*—Cheyenne name, from their Sioux name, *Witapähä'tu.*

Wi'tapähä'tu—"island butte people" (?), Sioux name.

KIOWA TRIBAL SIGN

The Kiowa tribal sign indicates "hair cut off at right ear," in allusion to a former custom of the warriors. From a careless habit in making this sign it has sometimes been wrongly interpreted to mean "foolish," or "rattle-brain."

SKETCH OF THE KIOWA

So far as present knowledge goes, the Kiowa constitute a distinct linguistic stock; but it is probable that more material will enable us to prove their connection with some tribes farther north, from which direction they came. They are noticed in the Spanish records as early at least as 1732. Their oldest tradition, which agrees with the concurrent testimony of the Shoshoni and Arapaho, locates them about the junction of Jefferson, Madison, and Gallatin forks, at the extreme head of Missouri river, in the neighborhood of the present Virginia

City, Montana. They afterward moved down from the mountains and formed an alliance with the Crow, with whom they have since continued on friendly terms. From here they drifted southward along the base of the mountains, driven by the Cheyenne and Arapaho. About 1840 they made peace with the latter tribes, with which they have since commonly acted in concert. The Sioux claim to have driven them out of the Black hills, and in 1805 they were reported as living upon the North Platte. According to the Kiowa account, when they first reached Arkansas river they found their passage opposed by the Comanche, who claimed all the country to the south. A war followed, but peace was finally concluded, when the Kiowa crossed over to the south side of the Arkansas and formed a confederation with the Comanche, which continues to the present day. In connection with the Comanche they carried on a constant war upon the frontier settlements of Mexico and Texas, extending their incursions as far south at least as Durango. Among all the prairie tribes they were noted as the most predatory and bloodthirsty, and have probably killed more white men in proportion to their numbers than any of the others. They made their first treaty with the government in 1837, and were put upon their present reservation jointly with the Comanche and Apache in 1868. Their last outbreak was in 1874–75, in connection with the Comanche, Apache, and Cheyenne. While probably never very numerous, they have been greatly reduced by war and disease. Their last terrible blow came in the spring of 1892, when the measles destroyed over 300 of the three confederated tribes. Their present chief is *Gu'i-pä'go*, Lone Wolf. They occupy the same reservation with the Comanche and Apache, between Washita and Red rivers, in southwestern Oklahoma, and numbered 1,017 in 1893.

The Kiowa do not have the gentile system, and there is no restriction as to intermarriage among the divisions. They have six tribal divisions, including the Apache associated with them, who form a component part of the Kiowa camping circle. A seventh division, the *K uăto*, is now extinct. The tribal divisions in the order of the camping circle are:

1. *K̓a't̓a*—"biters," i. e., Arikara or Ree; so called, not because of Arikara origin, but because they were more intimate with that tribe in trade and otherwise when the Kiowa lived in the north.

2. *Ko'̓gu'i*—"elks."

3. *Kä'igwŭ*—"Kiowa proper." This is the oldest division, to which belongs the keeping of the medicine tipi, in which is the grand medicine of the tribe.

4. *Kiñep*—"big shields." This is the largest division in the tribe and of corresponding importance.

5. *Semät*—"thieves," the Apache.

.6. *Koñtä'lyui*—"black boys." Sometimes also called *Si'ndiyu'i*, "Sindi's children." Said to be of darker color than the rest of the tribe, which, if true, might indicate a foreign origin.   Sindi is the great mythic hero of the Kiowa.

7. *K'u'ato*—"pulling up from the ground or a hole."   An extinct division, speaking a slightly different dialect, and exterminated by the Sioux in one battle about the year 1780.   On this occasion, according to tradition, the Kiowa were attacked by an overwhelming force of Sioux and prepared to retreat, but the chief of the K'uato exhorted his people not to run, "because, if they did, their relatives in the other

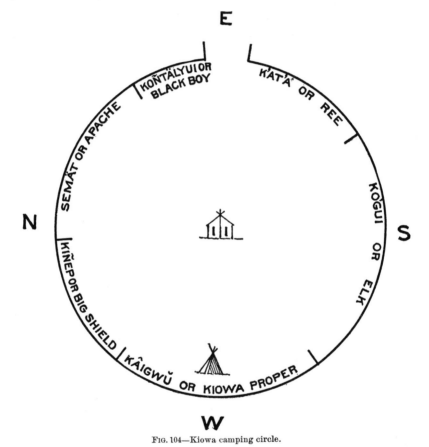

Fig. 104—Kiowa camping circle.

world would not receive them."   So they stood their ground and were killed, while the others escaped.   Their place in the tribal camp circle is not known.

In the annual sun dance and in other great tribal gatherings the several divisions camped in the order shown in figure 104.

Although brave and warlike, the Kiowa are considered inferior in most respects to the Comanche.   In person they are dark and heavily built, forming a marked contrast to the more slender and brighter-complexioned prairie tribes farther north.   Their language is full of choking and nasal sounds, and is not well adapted to rhythmic composition, for which reason they frequently used the Arapaho songs in the Ghost dance, without any clear idea of the meaning or correct pronunciation, although they have quite a number of songs of their own.

THE KIOWA APACHE

A small tribe of Athapascan stock, calling themselves *Na'-isha* or *Na-di'isha-de'na*, and popularly known as Apache or Kiowa Apache, has been associated with the Kiowa as far back as the traditions of either tribe go. While retaining their distinct language, they nearly all speak and understand Kiowa and form a component part of the Kiowa camping circle. In dress and general habits of life they are in no way distinguishable. They have come from the north with the Kiowa, and are mentioned under the name of Cataka as living in the Black-hills country in 1805. La Salle speaks of them under the name of Gattacka as early as 1681. There is no reason to suppose that they ever formed a part of the Apache proper of Arizona and New Mexico, but are probably, like the Sarsi, a distinct Athapascan people who have always lived east of the mountains, and who, having been obliged by weakness of numbers to unite themselves with a stronger tribe, have since shared their migratory fortunes southward along the plains. The Na-isha are called *Ga'taqka* by the Pawnee and sometimes by the Wichita; *Cataka* by Lewis and Clark, in 1805; *Kataka* in their first treaty with the government, made jointly with the Kiowa in 1837; *Ta'shĭn* by the Comanche; *Gĭnä'ĭs* by the Wichita; *Ka'ntsi*, "deceivers," by the Caddo; *Kĭri'nähĭs* by the Kichais; *Tha'kahinĕ'na*, "knife-whetting men (?)" by the Arapaho, and *Mûtsiănătä'niuw'*, "whetstone people," by the Cheyenne. They have several names among the Kiowa, but are commonly known by them as *Semät*, "thieves." Other Kiowa names for them are *Tagu'i*, of unknown meaning, and *Sa'dălso'mte-k'iñago*, "weasel people." The tribal sign for them, as for the Apache, Lipan, and Navaho, conveys the idea of "knife whetters." In 1891 they numbered 325. In 1893 they had been reduced, chiefly by an epidemic of measles, to 224.

More extended information in regard to the Kiowa and Kiowa Apache will be given in the author's memoir, "Calendar History of the Kiowa Indians," now in preparation for the Bureau of Ethnology.

SONGS OF THE KIOWA

1. DA'TA-I SO'DA'TE.

Da'ta i so'da'te,
Da'ta-i so'da'te.
Do'm ezä'nteda'te,
Do'm ezä'nteda'te.
De'ĭmhä'date,
De'ĭmhä'date.
Be'a'ma'nhäyi',
Be'a'ma'nhäyi'.

Translation

The father will descend,
The father will descend.
The earth will tremble,
The earth will tremble.
Everybody will arise,
Everybody will arise.
Stretch out your hands,
Stretch out your hands.

This is a summary of the Ghost-dance doctrine, closing with an invocation to all present to stretch out their hands toward the west and pray to the Father to hasten his coming.

2. Da′k′i′ñago (Ĭm) zä′nteähe′dal

Da′k′i′ñago (ĭm) zä′nteähe′dal,
Da′k′i′ñago (ĭm) zä′nteähe′dal,
De′dom ezä′nteähe′dal,
De′dom ezä′nteähe′dal.
De′ĭmgo (ä-)dä′tode′yo′,
De′ĭmgo (ä-)dä′tode′yo′.
De′beko′datsä′,
De′beko′datsä′.

Translation

The spirit army is approaching,
The spirit army is approaching,
The whole world is moving onward,
The whole world is moving onward.
See! Everybody is standing watching,
See! Everybody is standing watching.
Let us all pray,
Let us all pray.

In this song the verb *ĭmzä′nteähe′dal* implies that the spirits are coming on like an army or like a great herd of animals. The termination *he′dal* implies that it is a matter of report or common belief and not of personal knowledge.

3. Gu′ato Ädâ′ga

Gu′ato ädâ′ga nyä′ongu′m,
Gu′ato ädâ′ga nyä′ongu′m,
Go′mtäyä′ ätso′dalsâ′dal,
Go′mtäyä′ ätso′dalsâ′dal.
Ä′nyä′gâlo′nte,
Ä′nyä′gâlo′nte.
Tä′lyi ĭmhä′go,
Tä′lyi ĭmhä′go.

Translation

I scream because I am a bird,
I scream because I am a bird,
I bellow like a buffalo,
I bellow like a buffalo.
The boy will rise up,
The boy will rise up.

This song was composed by Pa-guadal, "Red Buffalo," at a Ghost dance held on Walnut creek in the summer of 1893, under the direction of the prophet Pa-iñgya (see page 907), for the purpose of resurrecting Red Buffalo's son, who had recently died. Pa-iñgya assured the people that if they held the dance as he directed, the dead boy would rise up alive from the ground before their eyes. In the dance Red Buffalo became "crazy" and composed this song. In his trance he evidently imagined himself a bird. His father was one of the "buffalo doctors," or surgeons of the tribe, who are under the special protection of the buffalo and whose war cry is an imitation of the bellowing of a buffalo bull. Red Buffalo claims to have inherited his father's knowledge; hence his assertion that he bellows like a bull. The boy was not resurrected.

4. DA′TA-I NYÄ′HOĂNGA′MO

Ä′häyä′ Ehä′eho′! Ä′häyä′ Ehä′eho′!
E′häyä′ Ehä′eho′! E′häyä′ Ehä′eho′!
Da′ta-i nyä′hoănga′mo,
Da′ta-i nyä′hoănga′mo.
Äde′tepo′nbä,
Äde′tepo′nbä,
Ä′guănpo′nbä,
Ä′guănpo′nbä.

Translation

Ä′häyä′ Ehä′eho′ ! Ä′häyä′ Ehä′eho′!
E′häyä′ Ehä′eho ! E′häyä′ Ehä′eho′!
The father shows me the road,
The father shows me the road.
I went to see my friends,
I went to see my friends,
I went to see the dances,
I went to see the dances.

The composer of this song went, in her trance, to the other world, led by the Father, who pointed out the way, and saw there her former friends and joined them in the dance.

5. DAK′IÑ′A BATE′YÄ

Dak′iñ′a bate′yä,
Dak′iñ′a bate′yä.
Guăto ton nyäâmo,

Guăto ton nyäâ′mo.
Ähiñ′äih nyäâ′mo,
Ähiñ′äih nyäâ′mo.

Translation

The spirit (God) is approaching,
The spirit (God) is approaching.
He is going to give me a bird tail,
He is going to give me a bird tail.
He will give it to me in the tops of the cottonwoods,
He will give it to me in the tops of the cottonwoods.

The "bird tail" refers to the feathers (*wakuna*, Arapaho) worn on the heads of the dancers (figure 91). The song is peculiar in implying that the recipient must climb up into the tree tops to obtain it.

6. NA′DA′G ÄKA′NA

Heyĕ′heyĕ′heyĕ′heye′ Äho′ho′!
Heyĕ′heyĕ′heyĕ′heye′ Äho′ho′!
Na′da′g äka′na,
Na′da′g äka′na,
De′gyägo′mga da′tsä′to,
De′gyägo′mga da′tsä′to.
Äo′ñyo, Äo′ñyo.

Translation

Heyĕ′heyĕ′heyĕ′heye′ Äho′ho′!
Heyĕ′heyĕ′heyĕ′heye′ Äho′ho′!
Because I am poor,
Because I am poor,
I pray for every living creature,
I pray for every living creature.
Äo′ñyo! Äo′ñyo!

Although the words of this song do not contain much meaning, the tune is one of the best among the Kiowa ghost songs. The introductory line gives somewhat the effect of Comanche song 1. The last line is supposed to be a prayer or entreaty to the messiah, and is an imitation of the Kiowa funeral wail.

7. ZE′BÄT-GÂ′GA IGU′ÄNPA′-IMA′

Ze′bät-gâ′ga igu′änpa′-ima′,
Ze′bät-gâ′ga igu′änpa′-ima′.
Bälä′gâ na′ta′dălgo′ma,
Bälä′gâ na′ta′dălgo′ma.
Tä′lyiă be′′pe′te,
Tä′lyiă be′′pe′te.

Translation

He makes me dance with arrows,
He makes me dance with arrows.
He calls the bow my father,

He calls the bow my father.
Grandmother, persevere,
Grandmother, persevere.

This song embodies the Ghost-dance idea of a return to the old Indian things. The expression, "He calls the bow my father," is worthy of an oriental poet. The last line is a general exhortation to the women to persevere or "push hard" in the dance.

8. BE′TA! TO′NGYÄ-GU′ADĂL

Be′ta! To′ngyä-gu′adăl äto′tl-e′dal,
Be′ta! To′ngyä-gu′adăl äto′tl-e′dal.
Bä′ate′ñyi, Bä′ate′ñyi.
Da′te gyäko′m ä′omhe′dăl,
Da′te gyäko′m ä′omhe′dăl.

Translation

Now I understand! Red Tail has been sent,
Now I understand! Red Tail has been sent.
We cry and hold fast to him,
We cry and hold fast to him.
He was made to live a long time,
He was made to live a long time.

This song was made by Mary Zoñtom, a woman who speaks very fair English, and refers to a young man named *To′ngyä-gu′adal*, Red Tail, who used to go into frequent trances. The expression "he was sent" implies that he is a recognized messenger to the spirit world, while "we hold fast to him" is equivalent to "we have faith in him."

9. DA′TA′-I ÄNKA′ÑGO′NA

Da′ta′-i änka′ñgo′na,
Da′ta′-i änka′ñgo′na.
Da′mânhä′go, Da′mânhä′go.
Ka′ante damânhä′go,
Ka′ante damânhä′go.

Translation

My father has much pity for us,
My father has much pity for us.
I hold out my hands toward him and cry,
I hold out my hands toward him and cry.
In my poverty I hold out my hands toward him and cry,
In my poverty I hold out my hands toward him and cry.

10. DA′TA-I IÑKA′ÑTÄHE′DAL

Ähä′yä Ehä′eho′,
Ähä′yä Ehä′eho′.
Da′ta-i iñka′ñtähe′dal.

A'da'ta'-i dä'sa,
Ä'da'ta'-i mâ'nsâ'dal,
Ä'da'ta'-i to'ñsâ'dal,
Ä'da'ta'-i o'mda.

Translation

Ähä'yä Ehä'eho',
Ähä'yä Ehä'eho'.
My father has had pity on me.
I have eyes like my father's,
I have hands like my father's,
I have legs like my father's,
I have a form like my father's.

" So God created man in his own image."

11. DAK'IÑ'AGO ÄHO'ÄHE'DAL

Dak'iñ'ago äho'ähe'dal,
Dak'iñ'ago äho'ähe'dal.
Gâ'dal-gâ'ga äho'ähe'dal,
Gâ'dal-gâ'ga äho'ähe'dal.
Do'm-gâ'ga äho'ähe'dal,
Do'm-gâ'ga äho'ähe'dal.

Translation

The spirit host is advancing, they say,
The spirit host is advancing, they say.
They are coming with the buffalo, they say,
They are coming with the buffalo, they say.
They are coming with the (new) earth, they say,
They are coming with the (new) earth, they say.

12. E'HYU'ÑI DEGI'ÄTA

E'hyuñ'i degi'äta,
E'hyuñ'i degi'äta.
Tsä'hop ä'ä'he'dal,
Tsä'hop ä'ä'he'dal.
Na de'gu'änta, de'gu'änta; Na de'gu'änta, de'gu'änta;
Gâ'dal-guñ t'añ'gya deo'ta,
Gâ'dal-guñ t'añ'gya deo'ta.
Go' dehi'äta, dehi'äta,
Go' dehi'äta, dehi'äta.

Translation

I am mashing the berries,
I am mashing the berries.
They say travelers are coming on the march,
They say travelers are coming on the march.
I stir (the berries) around, I stir them around;
I take them up with a spoon of buffalo horn,
I take them up with a spoon of buffalo horn.
And I carry them, I carry them (to the strangers),
And I carry them, I carry them (to the strangers).

This song gives a pretty picture of the old Indian home life and hospitality. In her dream the woman who composed it imagines herself cooking fruit, when the word comes that travelers are approaching, the verb implying that they are on the march with their children, dogs, and household property. She stirs the berries around a few times more, lifts them out with a spoon of buffalo horn, and goes to offer them to the strangers. The translation is an exact paraphrase of the rhythmic repetition of the original. The berry called *ehyuñ'i,* "principal or best fruit," is not found in the present country of the Kiowa, but is remembered among the pleasant things of their old home in the north. It is described as a species of cherry.

13. Go′mgyä-da′ga

Go′mgyä-da′ga,
Go′mgyä-da′ga,
Do′ nyä′zä′ngo,
Do′ nyä′zä′ngo,
Go′ da′gya iñhä′po,
Go′ da′gya iñhä′po.

Translation

That wind, that wind
Shakes my tipi, shakes my tipi,
And sings a song for me,
And sings a song for me.

To the familiar this little song brings up pleasant memories of the prairie camp when the wind is whistling through the tipi poles and blowing the flaps about, while inside the fire burns bright and the song and the game go round.

14. Dak'iñ′a daka′ñtähe′dal

Dak'iñ′a daka′ñtähe′dal,
Dak'iñ′a daka′ñtähe′dal.
Tsi′sûs-ä daka′ñtähe′dal,
Tsi′sûs-ä daka′ñtähe′dal.
Da′gya nyäpa′de,
Da′gya nyäpa′de.
Da′gya iñatä′gyi,
Da′gya iñatä′gyi.

Translation

God has had pity on us,
God has had pity on us.
Jesus has taken pity on us,
Jesus has taken pity on us.
He teaches me a song,
He teaches me a song.
My song is a good one,
My song is a good one.

In their confounding of aboriginal and Christian ideas the Kiowa frequently call the Indian messiah " Jesus," having learned the latter as a sacred name through the whites.

15. Anso′ gyä̆tä′to

An-so′ gyä-tä′-to, an-so′ gyä-tä′-to; â′-dal-te′m ga′-tä-dal-to′-o′,

â′-dal-te′m ga′-tä-dal-to′-o′; ä̆-nim-hä̆′-go, ä̆-nim-hä̆′-go.

Anso′ gyä̆tä′to,
Anso′ gyä̆tä′to;
Â′dalte′m ga′tä̆dalto′-o′,
Â′dalte′m ga′tä̆dalto′-o′;
Änĭmhä̆′go, Änĭmhä̆′go.

Translation

I shall cut off his feet,
I shall cut off his feet;
I shall cut off his head,
I shall cut off his head;
He gets up again, he gets up again.

This is one of the favorite Kiowa ghost songs and refers to the miraculous resurrection of the dismembered buffalo, according to the promise of the messiah, as related in Sword's narrative. See page 797.

KIOWA GLOSSARY

Äähe′dal—they are coming, it is said (*ää′*, I come); the suffix *hedal* implies a report.

Ädä′ga—because I am; the suffix *ga* gives the idea of because.

Â′daltem—head; literally hair bone, i. e., skull; from *â′dal*, hair, and *tem*, bone.

Ädalto′yui—"young mountain sheep," literally "herders" or "corralers," one of the degrees of the Kiowa military organization. Also called *Teñbeyu′i.* (See Arapaho song 43.)

Ä′¹data′i—like my father, resembling my father; from *data′-i*, father, my father.

Ädä′tode′yo′—he is standing watching it; *ädä′tode*, I stand watching it.

Äde′tepo′nbä—I went to see my friends; *äde′teponbäta*, I am going, etc; *de′te*, friend.

Äguănpo'nbä — I went to see dancing; *ägu'anponbä'ta*, I am going to see a dance; *guan*, a dance.

Ähäyä' — an unmeaning exclamation. used in the songs.

Ä'hiñ-aih — in the tops of the cottonwood; from *ä'hiñ*, cottonwood, and *aih*, in or on the tree tops.

Aho'ähe'dal — they are approaching, it is said (as a family on the move, or an army on the march, with household goods, etc); the suffix *hedal* implies a report or rumor. *Äho'ä*, I am coming on, with my family and possessions. Compare *Imzä'nteähe'dal*.

Äho'ho! — an unmeaning exclamation used in the songs.

Ähyä'to — the Kiowa name for the Arapaho, meaning unknown. The Kiowa call the wild plum by the same name.

Äka'na — for *Äka'on*, q. v.

Äka'on — I am poor. The words for "rich" and "poor" refer rather to reputation and mental and moral qualities than to temporal possessions. A man may own many horses, but if he has no war record he is accounted poor.

Änïmhä'go — he gets up again, he rises again. *Dehä'go*, I rise; *behä'*, get up; *ïmhä'go*, he will get up.

Ankañ'gona — he pities us much; *gyäkañ'ti*, it is a pity. Compare *Iñkañ'tähe'dal*.

Anso — feet; *anso'i*, foot.

Ä'nyä'gálo'nte — I bellow like a buffalo (habitual); *nyäo'nto*, I am bellowing like a buffalo.

Äomhe'dal — he was made so; *äo'mdatso'-ha*, I am made so, I am rendered thus.

Ä'piatañ — "wooden stabber, or lance;" the name of a Kiowa sent by his tribe as a delegate to the messiah in 1890.

Asa'tito'la — "he whom we send to work," i. e., "the messenger;" the name by which the Kiowa prophet, *Bi'äñk'i*, is now known.

Äto'tl-e'dal — he was sent; *gyäto'*, I send him.

Ätso'dalsä'dal — I have wings (attached); from *tsodal*, wing.

Bä'ateñ'yi — we cry and hold fast to him; *gyäteñ'ta*, I cry and hold fast to him.

Bate'yä — he is approaching; *äba'teyä*, I am approaching. Compare *Imzä'nteä-he'dal*.

Be'a'mä'nhäyi — stretch out your (plural) hands in entreaty. *Dea''mänhä'go*, I

stretch out, etc; *bea''mánhä*, stretch out your (singular vocative), etc.

Be'dälgu'at — another Kiowa name for the Wichita; signifying "painted or tattooed lips;" from *bedal*, lips or mouth, and *guat*, painted, tattooed, or written. See *Do'gu'at*.

Be'dälpago — "hairy mouths;" one of the Kiowa names for the whites; from *bedal*, lips or mouth, *pa*, downy hair or fuzz, and *go* or *gua*, the tribal terminal. Compare *Ta'ka'-i*.

Beta! — an exclamation about equivalent to I see, I understand.

Bi'äñk'i — "eating man," "eater," a Kiowa prophet and medicine-man; also known as *Asa'tito'la*, "the messenger."

Botk'iñ'ago — the Kiowa name for the *Aä'nine̅'na* or Arapaho Grosventres. The name signifies "belly people;" from *bot*, belly or stomach, and *k'iñago*, people, from *k'iñahi*, "man."

Dä-e'dal — "great star;" from *dä*, star, and *e'dal*, great; one of the Kiowa names for the morning star. It is more commonly called *T'aiñso*, "the cross." (See Arapaho song 72.)

Da'gya — a song.

Dakañ'äthe'dal — another form of *Iñkañ'tä-he'dal*, q. v.

Dak'iñ'a — spirit, God; plural *dak'iñ'ago*; from *da-i*, medicine, mystery, and *k'iña* or *k'iñahi*, man.

Dak'iñ'ago — spirits, the spirits; spirit, God, *dak'iñ'a*.

Da'mânhägo — for *Dea''mänhä'go*.

Däsa — I have eyes; *dä*, *t'ä*, eye.

Da'ta-i — father.

Da'te — a long time.

Da'tekañ — "keeps his name always," a Kiowa prophet about 1881, who undertook to bring back the buffalo.

Datsä'to — I pray for them; *nï'ndatsä'to*, I pray for him.

Dea''mänhä'go — I hold out my hands toward him in entreaty. Compare *Be'a'-mä'nhayi*.

De'beko'datsä — let us all pray or worship, we must all pray or worship; *deda'tsäto*, I pray.

De'dom — all the world; from *dom*, the earth, and *de*, all, complete.

Degi'äta — I am mashing or pounding it.

De'gu'änta — I stir it around.

De'gyägo'mga—every living creature; the prefix *de* conveys the idea of every or all.

Dehi'äta—I take it.

De'ĭmgo—look, everybody! See, everybody around! The prefix *de* gives the idea of everybody or all.

De'ĭmhä'date—everybody will arise; from *dehä*, I rose up from a reclining position. The prefix *de* gives the idea of everybody, all, or completeness, according to context.

Deo'ta—I lift it up, I raise it.

Do'—tipi.

Do'gu'at—the Kiowa name for the Wichita, signifying "painted or tattooed faces," from *dobä*, face, and *gu'at*, painted, engraved, or written.

Dom—the earth.

Dom-gäga—with the earth; *gâga*, with, in composition.

Ehä'eho'!—an unmeaning exclamation used in the songs.

E'häyä!—ibid.

E'hyuñi—"principal, real, or best fruit;" a berry, probably a dwarf cherry, described as a black grape-like fruit growing in clusters on bushes from 4 to 6 feet high, in the Sioux country. It was eaten raw or mixed with pemmican.

E'manki'na—"can't hold it," a Kiowa policeman, now dead, seen by Asatitola in a vision.

E''peya—"afraid of him," a Kiowa warrior who died while a prisoner at Fort Marion, Florida, about 1875.

Ezä'nteähe'dal—it is approaching, they say. Compare *Imzä'nteähe'dal*.

Ezä'nteda'te—it will shake, or tremble (impersonal).

Gâ'dal-gâ'ga—with the buffalo; *gâga*, with, in composition; *gâdal*, buffalo, generic; *pa*, a buffalo bull.

Gâ'dal-guñ—a buffalo horn; from *gâdal*, buffalo; and *gu'ñti*, horn.

Gatä'dalto—I shall cut it off, I am cutting it off (present and future alike).

Go—and.

Go'mgyä-da'ga—that wind; from *gomgyä*, wind, and *daga*, that, the, in composition.

Go'mtäyä—on (my) back; from *gomtä* or *gombă*, back.

Guadal—red.

Guăn—a dance.

Guan-â'dalka-i—"dance frenzy;" from *guan*, a dance, and *â'daika-i*, crazy or foolish; the Kiowa name for the Ghost-dance ecstasy.

Gu'ato—bird.

Gyäko'm—life, living; *hita' ägyä'komta'yä*, I am alive.

Gyätä'to—I shall cut them off; *gatä'dalto*, I cut it off.

Häoñ'yo, or *Äoñ'yo*—a cry of grief, especially at funerals.

Heyě'heyě'heyě'heye!—an unmeaning exclamation used in the songs.

Imhä'go—he would get up, he would arise. Compare *Änĭmhä'go*.

Imzä'nteähe'dal—they are approaching, it is said; from *dezä'nteä*, I move about; the termination *hedal* makes it a matter of report or common belief, equivalent to "they say." Compare *Ezä'nteähe'dal*. The verb implies coming on like a herd or company or like persons on a march. The simple verb for approaching is *äba'teä*. Compare *Bate'yä* and *Äho'ähe'dal*.

Iñatä'gyi—it is a good one; from *tägya* or *gyätä'gya*, good.

Iñhä'po or *Iñhäpa'de*—he sings for me (as if to teach me); *dagya gehäpo*, I sing a song for him.

Iñkañ'tähe'dal—he has had pity on me; from *gyäkañ'ti*, (it is a) pity. Compare *Ankañ'gona*.

Ka'ante—another form of *Ka'on*, poor. Compare *Äka'on*.

Kâitseñ'ko—"principal, or real dogs;" the highest degree of the Kiowa military organization. (See Arapaho song 43.)

Komse'ka-k'iñ'ahyup—the former Kiowa name for the Arapaho. It signifies "men of the worn-out leggings;" from *komse*, "smoky, soiled, or worn-out," *kati*, "leggings," and *k'iñ'ahyup*, "men."

Mânsâ'dal—I have hands or arms; *mânto*, hand, arm.

Ma'sep—the Kiowa name for the Caddo, signifying "pierced noses;" from *ma-k'on*, nose, and *sep*, the root of a verb signifying to pierce or sew with an awl.

Na—I, my; sometimes put before the verb to make it emphatic.

Na ädâ'ga—because I am (emphatic); from *na*, I, my, and *ädâ'ga* (q. v.), because I am.

Nada'g—for *Na ädá'ga*, q. v.

Nyää'mo—he will give it to me; *nyänä'mo*, I shall give it to him. There are a number of verbs for *give*, according to the nature of the thing given.

Nyä'hoănga'mo—he shows or tells me the road; *nyän'hoănga'mo*, I show him the road; *hoăn*, road.

Nyäo'ngum—I scream; from *äno'nde*, it screams, or makes utterance with the mouth.

Nyäpa'de—for *Iñhä'po* or *Iñhäpa'de*, q. v.

Nyäzä'ngo—it shakes mine; *änzä'ngo*, it shakes his.

O'mda—I have a shape or form (implying a likeness, as *ä'data'-i o'mda*, I have a form like my father's).

Pa-gu'adal—"red buffalo;" from *pa*, a buffalo bull, and *gu'adal*, red. A Kiowa man, the author of one of the Ghost-dance songs.

Pa'-iñgya—"standing in the middle;" a Kiowa prophet who, in 1887, preached the speedy destruction of the whites and the return of the buffalo.

Polän'yup—"rabbits;" the lowest degree of the Kiowa military organization. (See Arapaho song 43.)

Sa'he—green. (See Arapaho song 64.)

Säk'o'ta—the Kiowa name for the Cheyenne; the word seems to refer to "biting."

Set-t'aiñ'ti—"white bear," a noted Kiowa chief, about 1865–1875. The name comes from *set*, bear, *t'aiñ*, white, and *ti*, the personal suffix.

Soda'te—he will descend; *äso'ta*, I descend.

Tägyä'ko—the Kiowa name for the Na'-kasinĕ'na or northern Arapaho. The word has the same meaning, "sage-bush people," from *tägyi*, "sage brush," and *ko*, the tribal suffix.

T'aiñ'so—the morning star; literally "the cross;" it is sometimes also called *Dä-e'dal*, the "great star." (See Arapaho song 43.)

Ta'ka'-i—one of the Kiowa names for the whites; the word means literally "prominent ears, or ears sticking out," as compared with the ears of the Indian, which are partly concealed by his long hair. The same name is also applied to a mule or donkey. Compare *Be'dal-pa'go*.

Tälyi—a boy.

T'añgya—a spoon; under certain circumstances the suffix *gyä* is dropped and the word becomes *t'a*.

Tañ'peko—skunkberry (?) people; one of the degrees of the Kiowa military organization. (See Arapaho song 43.)

Teñ'beyui—"young mountain sheep," another name for the *Ädalto'yui*, q. v.

Ton—tail; *gu'ato-ton*, bird tail; frequently used to denote a fan or headdress made of the tail feathers of an eagle, hawk, or other bird.

Tongyä-gu'adal—"red tail;" the name of a Kiowa man; from *ton* or *tongyä*, tail, and *gu'adal*, red.

Toñkoñ'go—"black legs," one of the degrees of the Kiowa military organization. (See Arapaho song 43).

To'ñsädal—I have legs; from *toñti*, leg.

Tsä'hop—movers, emigrants (moving with household goods, etc). The word has no singular form.

Tsäñ'yui—"rabbits;" another name for the *Polän'yup* degree of the Kiowa military organization. (See Arapaho song 43.)

Tseñtän'mo—horse headdress people (?), one of the degrees of the Kiowa military organization. (See Arapaho song 43.)

Tsi'sûs (*Tsi'sûs-ä*)—Jesus.

Tsoñ—an awl.

Tsoñ'-ä—the awl game. (See Arapaho song 64.)

Yä''pähe—soldiers; the military organization of the Kiowa. (See Arapaho song 43.)

THE CADDO AND ASSOCIATED TRIBES

CADDO TRIBAL SYNONYMY

Asinais—an old French name, from *Hasinai*.

Caddo—popular name, from *Kä'dohadä'cho*.

Cadodaquio—Joutel (1687), another form of *Kä'dohadä'cho*.

Cenis—old French name used by Joutel in 1687; from *Hasinai*.

Dä'sha-i—Wichita name.

Dĕ'sa—another form of *Dä'sha-i*.

Hasi'nai or *Hasi'ni*—the proper generic term for at least the principal Caddo divisions, and perhaps for all of them. It is also used by them as synonymous with "Indians."

Kä'dohădä'cho—the name of the Caddo proper, as used by themselves.

Ma'se'p—Kiowa name; "pierced nose," from *mak'on*, nose, and *sep*, the root of a verb signifying to pierce or sew with an awl.

Na'shonĭt or *Na'shoni*—Comanche name, frequently used also by the neighboring tribes to designate the Caddo; the Nassonite of the early French writers on Texas.

Nez Percé—French traders' name; "pierced nose."

Ni'rĭs-hări's-kĭ'riki—another Wichita name.

Otä'ĕ-itä'niuw'—Cheyenne name; "pierced nose people."

Tani'bänĕn, Tani'bänĕnina, Tani'bätha—Arapaho name; "pierced nose people," *tani*, nose.

CADDO TRIBAL SIGN

"Pierced nose," in allusion to their former custom of boring the nose for the insertion of a ring.

SKETCH OF THE CADDO

The Caddo are the principal southern representatives of the Caddoan stock, which includes also the Wichita, Kichai, Pawnee, and Arikara. Their confederacy consisted of about a dozen tribes or divisions, claiming as their original territory the whole of lower Red river and adjacent country in Louisana, eastern Texas, and southern Arkansas. The names of these twelve divisions, including two of foreign origin, have been preserved as follows:

Kä'dohadä'cho (Caddo proper).

Nädä'ko (Anadarko).

Hai'-nai (Ioni).

Nä'bai-dä'cho (Nabedache).

Nä'kohodo'tsi (Nacogdoches).

Näshi'tosh (Natchitoches).

Nä'ka͞na'wan.

Hădai'-i (Adai, Adaize).

Hai'-ĭsh (Eyeish, Aliche, Aes).

Yä'tăsi.

I'măha—a band of Omaha, or perhaps more probably Kwâpâ, who lived with the Kä'dohadä'cho, but retained their own distinct language.

There are still a few living with the Caddo, but they retain only the name. It will be remembered that when the Caddo lived in eastern Louisiana the Arkansas or Kwâpâ were their nearest neighbors on the north, and these Imaha may have been a part of the Kwâpâ who lived "up stream" (*U'mañhañ*) on the Arkansas. The Caddo call the Omaha tribe by the same name.

Yowa'ni—originally a band of the Heyowani division of the Choctaw. They joined the Caddo a long time ago, probably about the time the Choctaw began to retire across the Mississippi before the whites. Some few are still living with the Caddo and retain their distinct language. There is evidence that some Koasati (Cooshatties) were mixed with them.

The Kä'dohadä'cho seem to be recognized as the principal Caddo division, and the generic term *Hasi'nai* by which the confederates designate themselves is sometimes regarded as belonging more properly to the three divisions first named. According to their own statements some of the dialects spoken by the several divisions were mutually unintelligible. At present the Kädohadächo and Nädäko are the ruling dialects, while the Näbaidächo, Näkohodotsi, Hădai'-i, and Hai'-ïsh are practically extinct. The Kichai, Bidai, and Akokisa, who formerly lived near the Caddo on the eastern border of Texas, did not belong to the confederacy, although at least one of these tribes, the Kichai, is of the same stock and is now on the same reservation.

The Caddo have ten gentes: *Na'wotsi*, Bear; *Tasha*, Wolf; *Ta'năhă*, Buffalo; *Ta'o*, Beaver; *Iwi*, Eagle; *Oăt*, Raccoon; *Ka'g̣aih*, Crow; *Ka'gă-hănïn*, Thunder; *Kĭshi*, Panther; *Sûko*, Sun. The Bear gens is the most numerous. The Buffalo gens is sometimes called also *Koho'* or Alligator, because both animals bellow in the same way. These of a particular gens will not kill the animal from which the gens takes its name, and no Caddo in the old times would kill either an eagle or a panther, although they were not afraid to kill the bear, as are so many of the western tribes. The eagle might be killed, however, for its feathers by a hunter regularly initiated and consecrated for that purpose.

The original home of the Caddo was on lower Red river in Louisiana. According to their own tradition, which has parallels among several other tribes, they came up from under the ground through the mouth of a cave in a hill which they call *Cha' kani'nă*, "The place of crying," on a lake close to the south bank of Red river, just at its junction with the Mississippi. In those days men and animals were all brothers and all lived together under the ground. But at last they discovered the entrance to the cave leading up to the surface of the earth, and so they decided to ascend and come out. First an old man climbed up, carrying in one hand fire and a pipe and in the other a drum. After him came his wife, with corn and pumpkin seeds. Then followed the rest of the people and the animals. All intended to come out, but as soon as the wolf had climbed up he closed the hole, and shut up the rest of the people and animals under the ground, where they still remain. Those who had come out sat down and cried a long time for their friends below, hence the name of the place. Because the Caddo came out of the ground they call it *inä′*, mother, and go back to it when they die. Because they have had the pipe and the drum and the corn and pumpkins since they have been a people, they hold fast to these things and have never thrown them away.

From this place they spread out toward the west, following up the course of Red river, along which they made their principal settlements. For a long time they lived on Caddo lake, on the boundary between Louisiana and Texas, their principal village on the lake being called Sha′chidï′ni, "Timber hill." Their acquaintance with the whites began at a very early period. One of their tribes, the Nädäko, is mentioned under the name of Nandacao in the narrative of De Soto's expedition as early as 1540. The Kädohadächo were known to the French as early as 1687. The relations of the Caddo with the French and Spaniards were intimate and friendly. Catholic missions were established among them about the year 1700 and continued to exist until 1812, when the missions were suppressed by the Spanish government and the Indians were scattered. In the meantime Louisiana had been purchased by the United States, and the Caddo soon began to be pushed away from their ancient villages into the western territory, where they were exposed to the constant inroads of the prairie tribes. From this time their decline was rapid, and the events of the Texan and Mexican wars aided still further in their demoralization. They made their first treaty with the United States in 1835, at which time they were chiefly in Louisiana, southwest of Red river and adjoining Texas. They afterward removed to Brazos river in Texas, and to Washita river in Indian Territory in 1859. When the rebellion broke out, the Caddo, not wishing to take up arms against the government, fled north into Kansas and remained there until the close of the war, when they returned to the Washita. Their present reservation, which they hold only by executive order and jointly with the Wichita, lies between Washita and Canadian rivers in western Oklahoma, having the Cheyenne and Arapaho on the north and west and the Kiowa, Comanche, and Apache on the south. In 1893 they numbered 507.

In person the Caddo are rather smaller and darker than the neighboring prairie tribes, and from their long residence in Louisiana, they have a considerable admixture of French blood. They are an agricultural tribe, raising large crops of corn, pumpkins, and melons, and still retaining industrious habits in spite of their many vicissitudes of fortune. They were never buffalo hunters until they came out on the plains. They formerly lived in conical grass houses like the Wichita, but are now in log houses and generally wear citizen's dress excepting in the dance. The old custom which gave rise to the name and tribal sign of "Pierced Nose" is now obsolete. In 1806 Sibley said of them, "They are brave, despise danger or death, and boast that they have never shed white man's blood." Their former enemies, the prairie tribes, bear witness to their bravery, and their friendship toward the whites is a part of their history, but has resulted in no great advantage to themselves, as they have been dispossessed from their own country and are recognized only as tenants at will in their present location.

They and the Wichita received the new doctrine from the Arapaho, and were soon among its most earnest adherents, notwithstanding the fact that they were regarded as the most advanced of all the tribes in that part of the country. It may be that their history had led them to feel a special need of a messiah. They have been hard and constant dancers, at one time even dancing in winter when there was nearly a foot of snow upon the ground. Their first songs were those which they had heard from the Arapaho, and sang in corrupted form, with only a general idea of their meaning, but they now have a number of songs in their own language, some of which are singularly pleasing in melody and sentiment.

THE WICHITA, KICHAI, AND DELAWARE

Closely associated with the Caddo on the same reservation are the Wichita, with their subtribes, the Tawakoni and Waco, numbering together 316 in 1893; the Delaware, numbering 94, and the Kichai (Keechies), numbering only 52. Of these, all but the Delaware, who are Algonquian, belong to the Caddoan stock. The Wichita and their subtribes, although retaining in indistinct form the common Caddoan tradition, claim as their proper home the Wichita mountains, near which they still remain. Sixty years ago their principal village was on the north side of the north fork of Red river, a short distance below the mouth of Elm creek, in Oklahoma. They live in conical grass houses and, like the other tribes of the stock, are agricultural. They call themselves *Kĭ'tikĭti'sh*—they are called *Tawe'hash* by the Caddo and Kichai—and are known to most of their other neighbors and in the sign language as the "Tattooed People" (*Do' kănă*, Comanche; *Do'gu'at*, Kiowa), from an old custom now nearly obsolete. For the same reason and from their resemblance to the Pawnee, with whose language their own has a close connection, the French called them *Pani Pique's*.

The Kichai or Keechie, or *Kĭ'tsäsh*, as they call themselves, are a small tribe of the same stock, and claim to have moved up Red river in company with the Caddo. Their language is different from that of any of their neighbors, but approaches the Pawnee.

The Delaware are a small band of the celebrated tribe of that name. They removed from the east and settled with the main body in Kansas, but drifted south into Texas while it was still Spanish territory. After a long series of conflicts with the American settlers of Texas, before and after the Mexican war, they were finally taken under the protection of the United States government and assigned to their present reservation along with other emigrant tribes from that state.

SONGS OF THE CADDO

1. HA′YO TĂ′IA′ Ă′Ă′

Nä′nisa′na, Nä′nisa′na,
Ha′yo tă′ia′ ă′ă′,
Ha′yo tă′ia′ ă′ă′,
Na′wi hă′iă′ i′nă′,
Na′wi hă′iă′ i′nă′.

Translation

Nä′nisa′na, Nä′nisa′na,
Our father dwells above,
Our father dwells above,
Our mother dwells below,
Our mother dwells below.

"Our mother" here refers to the earth.

2. WŮ′NTI HA′YANO′ DI′WITI′A

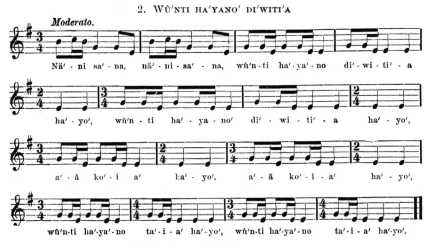

Nä′nisa′na, nä′nisa′na,
Wŭ′nti ha′yano′ di′witi′a ha′yo′,
Wŭ′nti ha′yano′ di′witi′a ha′yo′,
A′ă ko′ia′ ha′yo′,
A′ă ko′ia′ ha′yo′,
Wŭ′nti ha′ya′no ta′-ia′ ha′yo′,
Wŭ′nti ha′ya′no ta′-ia′ ha′yo′.

Translation

Nä′nisa′na, nä′nisa′na,
All our people are going up,
All our people are going up,
Above to where the father dwells,
Above to where the father dwells,
Above to where our people live,
Above to where our people live.

3. Nǔ′na Ɩ′tsiya′

He′yawe′ya! He′yawe′ya!
Nǔ′na Ɩ′tsiya′ si′bocha′ha′,
Nǔ′na Ɩ′tsiya′ si′bocha′ha′,
Wǔ′nti ha′yano′ ha′nĭn gǔ′kwǔ′ts-a′,
Wǔ′nti ha′yano′ ha′nĭn gǔ′kwǔ′ts-a′,
He′yahe′eye′! He′yahe′eye′!

Translation

He′yawe′ya! He′yawe′ya!
I have come because I want to see them,
I have come because I want to see them,
The people, all my children,
The people, all my children.
He′yahe′eye! He′yahe′eye!

This song was composed by a woman named Nyu′taa. According to her story, she saw in her trance a large company approaching, led by a man who told her he was the Father and that he was coming because he wished to see all his children.

4. Na′tsiwa′ya

Na′tsiwa′ya, na′tsiwa′ya,
Na′ ika′—Wi′ahe′e′ye′,
Na′ ika′—Wi′ahe′e′ye′,
Wi′ahe′e′ye′ye′yeahe′ye′,
Wi′ahe′e′ye′ye′yeahe′ye′.

Translation

I am coming, I am coming,
The grandmother from on high, *Wi′ahe′e′ye′*,
The grandmother from on high, *Wi′ahe′e′ye′*,
Wi′ahe′e′ye′ye′yeahe′ye′,
Wi′ahe′e′ye′ye′yeahe′ye′!

This song also was composed by the woman Nyu′taa. In her trance vision she fell asleep and seemed (still in the vision) to be awakened by the noise of a storm, when she looked and saw approaching her the Storm Spirit, who said to her, "I come, the grandmother from on high." The Caddo call thunder the "grandmother above" and the sun the "uncle above."

5. Na′-iye′ ino′ ga′nio′sĭt

Wa′hiya′ne, wa′hiya′ne,
Na′-iye′ ino′ ga′nio′sĭt,
Na′-iye′ ino′ ga′nio′sĭt.
Wa′hiya′ne, wa′hiya′ne.

Translation

Wa′hiya′ne, wa′hiya′ne,
My sister above, she is painted,
My sister above, she is painted.
Wa′hiya′ne, wa′hiya′ne.

This is another song composed by Nyu'taa, who herself explained it. In this trance vision she saw a spirit woman painted with blue stripes on her forehead and a crow on her chin, who told her that she was "her sister, the Evening Star." While singing this song Nyu'taa was sitting near me, when she suddenly cried out and went into a spasm of trembling and crying lasting some minutes, lifting up her right hand toward the west at the same time. Such attacks were so common among the women at song rehearsals as frequently to interfere with the work, although the bystanders regarded them as a matter of course and took only a passing notice of these incidents.

6. NA'A HA'YO HA'WANO

Nä'nisa'na, nä'nisa'na,
Na'a ha'yo ha'wano,
Na'a ha'yo ha'wano.

Translation

Nä'nisa'na, nä'nisa'na,
Our father above (has) paint,
Our father above (has) paint.

This refers to the sacred paint used by the participants in the Ghost dance, and which is believed to confer health and the power to see visions.

7. WÛ'NTI HA'YANO KA'KA'NA'

Nänisa'na, nänisa'na,
Wû'nti ha'yano ka'ka'na' ni"tsiho',
Wû'nti ha'yano ka'ka'na' ni"tsiho',
Aa' ko'ia' ta'-ia' ha'yo',
Aa' ko'ia' ta'-ia' ha'yo',

Translation

Nä'nisa'na, nänisa'na,
All the people cried when I returned,
All the people cried when I returned,
Where the father dwells above,
Where the father dwells above.

This song was composed by a girl who went up to the spirit world and saw there all her friends, who cried when she started to leave them again.

8. NA'WI I'NA

Nä'nisa'na, nä'nisa'na,
E'yahe'ya, e'yahe'ya, he'e'ye'!
E'yahe'ya, e'yahe'ya, he'e'ye'!
Na'wi i'na ha'yo ä'ä—He'yoi'ya, he'e'ye'!
Na'wi i'na ha'yo ä'ä—He'yoi'ya, he'e'ye'!

Translation

Nä'nisa'na, nä'nisa'na,
E'yahe'ya, e'yahe'ya, he'e'ye'!
E'yahe'ya, e'yahe'ya, he'e'ye'!
We have our mother below; we have our father above—*He'yoi'ya, he'e'ye'!*
We have our mother below; we have our father above—*He'yoi'ya, he'e'ye'!*

This song was composed by a woman named Niaha'no', who used to have frequent trances in which she would talk with departed Caddo and bring back messages from them to their friends. "Our mother below" is the earth. (See page 1096.)

9. Ni' ika' na'a

Ni' ika' na'a ha'na',
Ni' ika' na'a ha'na';
Na'a-a' ha'na',
Na'a-a' ha'na'.

Translation

There are our grandmother and our father above,
There are our grandmother and our father above;
There is our father above,
There is our father above.

By "grandmother" is meant the storm spirit or thunder. (See Caddo song 4.)

10. Hi'na ha'natobi'na

Hi'na ha'natobi'na i'wi-na',
Hi'na ha'natobi'na i'wi-na',
Na' iwi' i'wi-na',
Na' iwi' i'wi-na';
Na'nana' ha'taha',
Na'nana' ha'taha'.

Translation

The eagle feather headdress from above,
The eagle feather headdress from above,
From the eagle above, from the eagle above;
It is that feather we wear,
It is that feather we wear.

This refers to the eagle feather worn on the heads of the dancers. (See song number 12.) This song is in the Hai-nai dialect.

11. Na' ăă' o'wi'ta'

Na' ăă' o'wi'ta',
Na' ăă' o'wi'ta',
Na' kiwa't Hai'-nai',
Na' kiwa't Hai'-nai'.

Translation

The father comes from above,
The father comes from above,
From the home of the Hai-nai above,
From the home of the Hai-nai above.

This song, like the last, was composed by one of the Hai-nai tribe, and refers to the silent majority of the band in the spirit world.

12. Na′ iwi′ o′wi′ta′

Na′-i-wi′ o′-wi′-ta′, na′-i-wi′-o′-wi′-ta′; do′-hya di′-wa-bo′n na′ na′-i-wi′ o′-wi′-ta′,

do′-hya di′-wa-bo′n na′ na′-i-wi′ o′-wi′-ta′; na′-ha′ na′-da-ka′-a′, na′-ha′ na′-da-ka′-a′.

Na′ iwi′ o′wi′ta′,
Na′ iwi′ o′wi′ta′;
Do′hya di′wabo′n na′ na′ iwi′ o′wi′ta′,
Do′hya di′wabo′n na′ na′ iwi′ o′wi′ta′;
Na′ha′ na′daka′a′, Na′ha′ na′daka′a′.

Translation

See! the eagle comes,
See! the eagle comes;
Now at last we see him — look! look! the eagle comes,
Now at last we see him — look! look! the eagle comes;
Now we see him with the people,
Now we see him with the people.

This refers to what the Caddo call the "return of the eagle feathers" in the Ghost dance. With the Caddo, as with other tribes, the eagle is a sacred bird, and in the old times only the few medicine-men who knew the sacred formula would dare to kill one for the feathers. Should any-one else kill an eagle, his family would die or some other great misfor-tune would come upon him. The formula consisted of certain secret prayers and ritual performances. Among the Cherokee the eagle killer's prayer was a petition to the eagle not to be revenged upon the tribe, because it was not an Indian, but a Spaniard, who had killed him — an indication of the vivid remembrance in which the cruelty of the early Spaniards was held among the southern tribes. To further guard against the anger of the eagles, the Cherokee eagle killer, on his return to the village, announced that he had killed, not an eagle, but a snowbird, the latter being too small and insignificant to be dreaded. The eagle-killing ceremony among the northern prairie tribes has been already described under Arapaho song 47. The Caddo eagle killer always took with him a robe or some other valuable offering, and after shooting the eagle, making the prayer, and pulling out the tail and wing feathers he covered the body with the robe and left it there as a peace offering to the spirit of the eagle. The dead eagle was never brought home, as among the Cherokee. The last man of the Caddo who knew the eagle-killing ritual died some years ago, and since then they have had to go without eagle feathers or buy them from the Kiowa and other tribes. Since Sitting Bull came down and "gave the feather" to the leaders of the dance the prohibition is removed, and men and women alike are now at liberty to get and wear eagle feathers as they will.

13. A′NANA′ HANA′NITO′

A′nana′ hana′nito′ ni′ahu′na — *He′e′ye′!*
A′nana′ hana′nito′ ni′ahu′na — *He′e′ye′!*
A′nana′sa′na′? A′nana′sa′na′?
Ha′yo ha′nitu′ ni′ahu′na — *He′e′ye′!*
Ha′yo ha′nitu′ ni′ahu′na — *He′e′ye′!*
A′nana′sa′na′? A′ana′sa′na′?

Translation

The feather has come back from above — *He′e′ye′!*
The feather has come back from above — *He′e′ye′!*
Is he doing it? Is he doing it?
The feather has returned from on high — *He′e′ye′!*
The feather has returned from on high — *He′e′ye′!*
Is he doing it? Is he doing it?

This refers to the return of the eagle feathers, as noted in the preceding song. The question "Is he doing it?" is equivalent to asking, "Is this the work of the father?"—an affirmative answer being understood.

14. NA′ IWI′ HA′NAA′

Na′ iwi′ ha′naa′,
Na′ iwi′ ha′naa′;
Wû′nti ha′yano′ na′nia′sana′,
Wû′nti ha′yano′ na′nia′sana′.
Na′ha na′ni′asa′,
Na′ha na′ni′asa·.

Translation

There is an eagle above,
There is an eagle above;
All the people are using it,
All the people are using it.
See! They use it,
See! They use it.

This song also refers to the use of eagle feathers in the dance.

15. WI′TŬ′ HA′SINI′

E′-ye - he′! Nä′-ni-sa′ - na, E′-ye - he′! Nä′-ni-sa′ - na. Wi′ - tŭ′ Ha′ - si - ni′

di′ - wi - ti′ - a′ - a′, wi′ - tŭ′ Ha′ - si - ni′ di′ - wi - ti′ - a′ - a′ ki′-wat ha′- i - me′ He′-

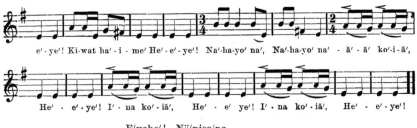

e'-ye'! Ki-wat ha'-i-me' He'-e'-ye'! Na'-ha-yo' na', Na'-ha-yo' na' - ă'- ă' ko-i-ă',
He' - e'-ye'! I'-na ko'-iă', He' - e' ye'! I'-na ko'-iă', He'- e'-ye'!

E'yehe'! Nä'nisa'na,
E'yehe'! Nä'nisa'na.
Wi'tü' Ha'sini' di'witi'a'a'.
Wi'tü' Ha'sini' di'witi'a'a'
Ki'wat ha'-ime' — He'e'ye'!
Ki'wat ha'-ime' — He'e'ye'!
Na'hayo' na',
Na'hayo' na'ă'ă' ko'iă' — He'e'ye'!
I'na ko'iă' — He'e'ye'!
I'na ko'iă — He'e'ye'!

Translation

E'yehe'! Nä'nisa'na,
E'yehe'! Nä'nisa'na.
Come on, Caddo, we are all going up,
Come on, Caddo, we are all going up
To the great village — *He'e'ye'!*
To the great village — *He'e'ye'!*
With our father above,
With our father above where he dwells on high — *He'e'ye'!*
Where our mother dwells — *He'e'ye'!*
Where our mother dwells — *He'e'ye'!*

The sentiment and swinging tune of this spirited song make it one of the favorites. It encourages the dancers in the hope of a speedy reunion of the whole Caddo nation, living and dead, in the "great village" of their father above, and needs no further explanation.

CADDO GLOSSARY

Ăă — father.

Ăă Kakĭ'mbawiŭt — "the prayer of all to the Father;" from *aa*, the Father, i. e., God, and *tsĭmba'dikŭ*, I pray; the Ghost dance, also called *Nä'nisa'na Gao'shăn*, Nä'nisa'na dance.

A'nana — for *Năñă*.

A'nanasa'na — for *Nana'sana*.

Ba'hakosĭn — "striped arrows," from *bah*, arrow; the Caddo name for the Cheyenne. They sometimes call them *Siä'näbo*, from their Comanche name.

Cha'kanĭ'na — "the place of crying;" the traditional first settlement of the Caddo tribes, where they came up out of the ground, at the mouth of Red river, on the south bank, in Louisiana.

Detse-ka'yăă — "dog eaters;" the Caddo name for the Arapaho.

Di'wabon — we see him; *tsibo'nă*, I see him.

Di'wĭti'ă — we are all going up, we shall all ascend; *tsidiŭ'*, I ascend.

Do'hya — now, at once.

E'yahe'ya! — an unmeaning exclamation used in the songs.

E'yehe'! — ibid.

Ganio'sĭt — he (she) is painted; *atsĭno'sĭt*, I paint myself.

Gao'shăn — a dance; *ga'tsioshăn*, I dance.

Gŭ'kwŭts—my (plural); *gŭkwŭ'nda,* my (singular); *ha'nĭn gŭ'kwŭts,* my children.

Hă'-iă—he (she) dwells there below. Compare *Ko'iă.*

Ha'-imi—large.

Hai'-nai—a tribe of the Caddo confederacy.

Hă'naă or *Hă'nă*—there he is! that is he!

Ha'nani'to—this feather, the feather; *ni'toh,* feather; *ha'taha,* feather (generic).

Ha'natobi'na—a feather headdress; feathers prepared to wear on the head.

Ha'nĭn—children.

Ha'nitu—for *Ni'toh.*

Hasi'ni or *Hasi'nai*—the Caddo; the generic name used by themselves.

Ha'taha—feather (generic); *nitoh,* feather (specific).

Ha'wano—paint.

Ha'yano—people.

Ha'yo—above, on high. Compare *Naha'yo.*

He'eye'!—an unmeaning exclamation used in the songs.

He'yahe'eye'!—ibid.

He'yawe'ya!—ibid.

He'yoi'ya!—ibid.

Hi'na—eagle feathers.

Ika—grandmother; a term sometimes applied to the thunder or storm spirit.

Ină'—mother; *na ină',* mother above.

I'tsiya—I have come; *hatsi'ûs,* I come.

I'wi—eagle; also the name of a Caddo gens.

Ka'găhănĭn—thunder; a Caddo gens.

Ka'g'aih—crow; a Caddo gens.

Kaka'na—they cried; *ha'tsikaka's,* I cry.

Ka'ntsi—"cheats;" the Caddo name for the Kiowa Apache, Lipan, and Mescalero.

Kĭ'shi—panther; a Caddo gens.

Kiwa't—village, town, settlement.

Koho'—alligator; another name for the Ta'năhă or Buffalo gens of the Caddo.

Ko'iă—where he dwells above; *tă'-iă,* he dwells above; *datsii'ă,* I dwell above.

Na—see! look! now!—also coming down from above, as *iwi-na,* the eagle coming down from above.

Năă'—father above, i. e., God; from *ăă',* father, and *na,* above, on high.

Na'daka—with the people.

Nahă'—that's all! now you see! there now!

Naha'yo—up, above, the plural of *Ha'yo. Hasi'ni diwĭti'a na'hayo,* all the Caddo are going up, everybody of the Caddo is going up.

Na-iye'—sister above; from *na,* above, in composition, and *iye',* sister.

Nănă' or *Nă'nănă'*—that one (demonstrative).

Nana'sana—is he making it?

Na'ni'asa—they are using it; *ha'tsĭna'sa,* I use it.

Na'nia'sana—for *Na'ni'asa.*

Nä'nisa'na—an Arapaho word, adopted by the Caddo in the Ghost-dance songs and meaning "my children."

Nä'nisa'na gao'shăn—"Nänisana dance," one of the Caddo names for the Ghost dance, from *gao'shăn,* a dance, and *nänisa'na* (q. v.), an Arapaho word which forms the burden of so many Arapaho Ghost-dance songs. It is also called *Ăă Kakĭ'mbawiût,* "the prayer of all to the Father."

Na'tsiwa'ya—I am coming.

Na'wi—below; *ha'yo,* above.

Nawotsi—bear; a Caddo gens.

Ni—a syllable prefixed merely to fill in the meter.

Niahu'na—for *Nĭ'tahŭ'nt.*

Nĭ'tahŭ'nt—it has returned. It has come back; *tsĭtsihŭ'nă,* I return; *Ni'tsiho,* when I returned.

Ni'toh—feather (specific); *ha'taha,* feather (generic).

Ni'tsiho—when I returned. Compare *Nĭ'tahŭ'nt.*

Nŭ'na—because.

O'ăt—raccoon; a Caddo gens.

O'wita—he comes; *a'tsiûs,* I come.

Sha''chadĭ'ni—"Timber hill," a former Caddo settlement on Caddo lake, Louisiana.

Si'bocha'ha—I want to see them; *hatsi'bos,* I see.

Sŭko—sun; a Caddo gens.

Tă'-iă—he dwells above. Compare *Ko'iă.*

Ta'năhă—buffalo; a Caddo gens.

Ta'o—beaver; a Caddo gens.

Tasha—wolf; a Caddo gens.

Tsaba'kosh—cut-throats; the Caddo name for the Sioux.

Wa'hiya'nc!—an unmeaning exclamation used in the songs.

Wi'ahe'eye'!—ibid.

Wi'tă!—come on! get ready.

Wŭ'nti—all of them.

AUTHORITIES CITED

Adjutant-General's Office [*A. G. O.*].—
(Documents on file in the office of the
Adjutant-General, in the War Department at Washington, where each is
officially designated by its number,
followed by the initials A. G. O. In
response to specific inquiries additional
information was received in letters from
the same office and incorporated into
the narrative.)

    1—Report of Captain J. M. Lee, on the aban-
donment of Fort Bidwell, California (1890),
Doc. 16633-1, 1890; 2—Documents relating to the
Apache outbreak, 1881; 3—Documents relating
to Sword-bearer and the Crow outbreak, 1887;
4—Captain J. M. Lee, abandonment of Fort
Bidwell, Doc. 16633-1, 1890; 5—Report on the
Ghost dance, by Lieutenant H. L. Scott, February 10, 1891, Doc. ——; 6—Report on the
abandonment of Fort Bidwell, by Captain J.
M. Lee, Doc. 16633-1, 1890; 7—Statement of
Judge H. L. Spargur in Lee's report on Fort
Bidwell, Doc. 16633-1, 1890; 8—Letters of As-
sistant Adjutant-General Corbin and Quarter-
master-General Batchelder; 9—Affidavits with
Lee's report on the abandonment of Fort Bidwell, Doc. 16633-1, 1890.

Albany Institute. *See* MacMurray.

Allis, *Rev.* Samuel. Forty Years Among
the Indians and on the Eastern Borders
of Nebraska. (Transactions and Reports of the Nebraska State Historical
Society, II. Lincoln, Nebraska, 1887.
8°. 133–166.)

    1—135.

American Anthropologist. *See* Phister.

American Ethnology and Archæology,
Journal of. *See* Bandelier.

Archæological Institute of America,
Report of. *See* Bandelier.

Bancroft, G. History of the United States
of America, from the discovery of the
continent. The author's last edition.
New York, 1884. 8°.

    1—II, 371; 2—II, 378; 3—II, 463.

Bandelier, A. F. Documentary history of
the Zuñi tribe. (Journal of American
Ethnology and Archæology, III. Boston
and New York, 1892. 4°.)

    1 a —103-115.

Bandelier, A. F.—Continued.
—— Final report of investigations among
the Indians of the southwestern United
States, Part II. (Papers of the
Archæological Institute of America,
American Series, IV. Cambridge, 1892.
8°.)

    1 b—62.

Barclay, Robert. The inner life of the
religious societies of the common-
wealth; considered principally with
reference to the influence of church
organization on the spread of Christianity. London, 1876. 8°.

Bartlett, C. H. Letter to the Bureau of
Ethnology, dated October 29, 1895.

Bible. The Holy Bible, containing the
Old and New Testaments; translated
out of the original tongues, etc. New
York (American Bible Society), 1870.
12°.

Bourke, *Capt.* J. G. The medicine-men
of the Apache. (Ninth Annual Report
of the Bureau of Ethnology. Washington, 1892. 4°. The description of
the dance of the medicine-man, Nakai-
doklini, is taken from the account in
this paper, supplemented by a personal
letter from the author.)

    1—505.

Brinton, *Dr* D. G. Myths of the New
World: A treatise on the symbolism
and mythology of the Red race of
America. New York, Leypoldt and
Holt, 1868. 12°.

    1—168, passim.

Brown, John P. The Dervishes; or oriental spiritualism. By John P. Brown,
secretary and dragoman of the legation
of the United States of America at
Constantinople, etc. London, 1868.
12°.

Bureau of Ethnology, Reports of. *See*
Bourke and Mallery.

Catlin, G. Letters and notes on the manners, customs, and condition of the
North American Indians. Written dur-

Catlin, G.—Continued.

ing eight years' travel (1832–1839) among the wildest tribes of Indians in North America, etc. Two volumes. 4th edition. London, 1844. 8°.

1—II, 117; 2—II, 118; 3—II, 98; 4—II, 99.

Century Magazine. *See* Roosevelt.

Clark, Benjamin. The Cheyenne Indians. (A manuscript history and ethnography of the Cheyenne Indians, written at the request of General Philip Sheridan by Benjamin Clark, interpreter at Fort Reno, Oklahoma.)

Now in possession of Dr George Bird Grinnell of New York city.

Clark, W. P. The Indian sign language, with brief explanatory notes, etc, and a description of some of the peculiar laws, customs, myths, superstitions, ways of living, code of peace and war signals of our aborigines. Philadelphia, 1885. 8°.

Colby, *Gen.* L. W. The Sioux Indian war of 1890–91. By Brigadier-General L. W. Colby, commanding the Nebraska National Guard. (Transactions and reports of the Nebraska State Historical Society, III, 144–190; Fremont, Nebraska, 1892. 8°.)

1—153; 2—150; 3—155; 4—157; 5—159–170; 6—159; 7—164; 8—165–170; 9—(McGillycuddy) 180; 10—165.

Commissioner [*Comr.*]. Annual report of the Commissioner of Indian Affairs to the Secretary of the Interior. (Sixtyfirst annual report, Washington, 1892. 8°.)

1—Report of Agent W. P. Richardson, 1852, 71, and report of Agent W. P. Badger, 1859, 144; 2—Agent Danilson, 1875, 258; 3—Agent Tiffany, 1881, 10; 4—Commissioner Price, 1881, viii–ix; Agent Tiffany, 1881, 10–11; 5—Agent Linn, 1884, 102; 6—Agent Patrick, 1885, 111; 7—Agent Scott, 1891, vol. I, 258; 8—Agent Smith, 1873, 319; 9—Agent Boyle, 1870, 58; 10—Superintendent Meacham, 1870, 50; 11—Agent Cornoyer, 1873, 317–18; 12—Commissioner Brunot, 1871, 98; 13—Umatilla council, 1891, 95–7; 14—Superintendent Colonel Ross, 1870, 30; 15—Superintendent Meacham, 1870, 50–54; 16—Report, 1871, 95; 17—Superintendent Odeneal, 1872, 362; 18—Subagent White, 1843, 451; 19—ibid, 453; 20—Commissioner Hayt, 1877, 10; 21—ibid, 10; 22—ibid, 12; 23—ibid, 11; 24—ibid, 12; 25—ibid, 12–13; 26—Commissioner Hayt, 1878, xxxiv; 27a—ibid, xxxv; 27b—Agent Rust, 1891, I, 223; 28—Commissioner Morgan, 1891, I, 132–3; 29—Agent Wright,

Commissioner—Continued.

ibid, 411–2; 30—Dorchester report, ibid, 529; 31—Commissioner Morgan, ibid, 124; 32—Agent Wright, ibid, 411–12; 33—ibid, 128, 130; 34—ibid, 130; 35—ibid, 130; 36—ibid, 130; 37—ibid, 130; 38—ibid, 131; 39—ibid, 132; 40—ibid, 132; 41—Commissioner Morgan, 1892, 128; 42—Dorchester, 1891, vol. I, 532; 43—Agent Wood, 1892, 396, 399; 44—Mrs Z. A. Parker, in report of Superintendent Dorchester, vol. I, 1891, 529–531; also published in the New York Evening Post of April 18, 1891, and in Journal of American Folk-lore, April–June, 1891; 45—Report on the Utes, Pai-Utes, etc, by J. W. Powell and G. W. Ingalls, 1873, 45; 46—Superintendent Parker, 1866, 115; 47—ibid, 115.

Dorsey, *Rev.* J. O. *See* Journal of American Folk-lore.

Drake, B. Life of Tecumseh and of his brother the Prophet; with a historical sketch of the Shawanoe Indians. Cincinnati, 1852. 12°.

1—87, passim; 2—88; 3—93; 4—130; 5—142; 6—151; 7—153; 8—158; 9—193.

Drake, S. G. The aboriginal races of North America, comprising biographical sketches of eminent individuals and an historical account of the different tribes, from the first discovery of the continent to the present period, etc, 15th edition, revised with valuable additions, by Professor H. L. Williams. New York, 1880 (?). 8°.

1—625.

Dutton, *Major* C. E. The submerged trees of the Columbia river. (Science, New York, February 18, 1887, page 156.)

Eells, *Rev.* Myron. (Letter in regard to the Shakers of Puget sound, quoted at length in the chapter on that subject. Works by the same author, referred to in the same chapter and in the tribal synopsis accompanying the chapter on the Nez Percé war, are "History of Indian Missions on the Pacific Coast," and "Ten Years of Missionary Work among the Indians at Skokomish, Washington Territory, 1874–1884."—Congregational House, Boston, 1886. 12°.)

Mr Eells was born in the state of Washington, has been for many years engaged in mission work in that section, and is the author o valuable works relating to the tribes and lan guages of the state.

Eells, Myron—Continued.

—— History of Indian missions on the Pacific coast—Oregon, Washington, and Idaho. By Reverend Myron Eells, missionary of the association. Philadelphia and New York, American Sunday School Union, 1882 (?). 12°.

Evans, F. W. Shakers: Compendium of the origin, history, principles, rules and regulations, government, and doctrines of the United Society of Believers in Christ's second appearing, with biographies of Ann Lee, etc. New York, 1859. 12°.

Fletcher, J. E. *See* Schoolcraft, Indian Tribes.

Ghost Dance [*G. D.*]. (Documents relating to the Ghost dance and the Sioux outbreak of 1890, on file in the Indian Office in special case 188, labeled "Ghost Dance and Sioux Trouble.")

1—Fisher, Document 37097-1890; 2—Campbell, Document 36274-1890; 3—Campbell, Document 26274-1890; 4—Report of Lieutenant H. L. Scott (copy from A. G. O.), Document 9234-1891; 5—Statement of Porcupine, the Cheyenne, Document 24075-1890; 6—Blakely, September 30, 1890, Document 32876-1890; 7—Agent McLaughlin, October 17, 1890, Document 32670-1890; 8—Document 17236-1891; 9—Statement of Porcupine, Document 24075-1890; 10—Agent Bartholomew, December 15, 1890, Document 39419-1890; 11—Clipping from Santa Fé (New Mexico) News, December 11, 1890, Document 39419-1890; 12—Agent Plumb, Document 35519-1890; 13—ibid, Document 38743-1890; 14—ibid, Document 2178-1891; 15—Agent Fisher, Document 37097-1890; 16—Clipping from Omaha (Nebraska) Bee, February 10, 1891, Document 6155-1891; 17—Blakely and Captain Bowman, Document 32876-1890; 18—Agent Simons, Document 37359-1890; 19—Agent Warner, Document 37260-1890; 20—Agent McChesney, Document 18807-1890; Document 17024-1890; 21—Gallagher, Document 18482-1890; McChesney, 18807-1890; Wright, 18823-1890; McLaughlin, 19200-1890; 22—Cook letter, September 11, Document 30628-1890; 23—Special Agent Reynolds, September 25, 30046-1890; 24—Wright, December 5, 38608-1890; 25—McLaughlin, October 17, 32607-1890; 26—Royer, October 12, 32120-1890; 27—Palmer, October 29 and November 4, 34061-1890, 34656-1890; 28—Letters and telegrams, October 30 to November 21, from Royer, Palmer, Dixon, Belt, et al., 34060-1890; 34807-1890; 34904-1890; 34906-1890; 34910-1890; 35104-1890; 35105-1890; 35349-1890; 35412-1890; 35413-1890; 35831-1890; 36021-1890; 29—McLaughlin, November 19, 36346-1890; 30—President Harrison, November 13, 35104-1890; 31—Secretary Noble, December 1, 37003-1890; 32—

Ghost Dance—Continued.

Palmer, 35956-1890; Reynolds, 36011-1890; McLaughlin, 36022-1890; Royer, 36560-1890; 33—Noble, 37003-1890; Wright, 37174-1890; Palmer, 38688-1890; 34—McLaughlin, 36868-1890; 37465-1890; Cody order, 37559-1890; Belt, 39602-1890; 35—McLaughlin, December 24, 1890-26; 36—McLaughlin, 38860-1890; 39602-1890; December 24, 1890-26; Miles, 39535-1890; 37—General Miles, December 11, 39216-1890; 38—Miles, December 28, 1890-415; 39—Miles, December 30, 1890-504; 40—Royer, December 29, 40115-1890; Miles, December 29, 1890-414; 41—Miles, December 29, 1890-414; 42—Cooper, 40415-1890; 43—Royer, December 31, 1890-529; 44—Royer, January 2, 1891-145; 45—Miles order, January 12, 6040-1891; 46—Corbin, 7724-1891; military letters, etc, 10937-1891; Welsh, etc, 12772-1891; Burns, 12561-1891; 47—Documents 3512-1891; 7720-1891; 7976-1891; 10937-1891; 11944-1891; including statements of Acting Agent Captain Pierce, of army officers, Dr McGillycuddy, Indian survivors, and Deadwood Pioneer; 48—Kingsbury, 8217-1891; 49—Viroqua, 38445-1890; 50—Texas Ben, 36087-1890; Johnson, November 27, 1890; 51—Herrick, 37440-1890; 52—Belt, 8699-1893; Hopkins, 9379-1893; 11305-1893; 13243-1893; Browne, 14459-1893; 53—Scott, February 10, 9234-1891; 54—ibid; 55—Commissioner Morgan, November 24, 36342-1890; 36467-1890.

Grinnell, *Dr* G. B. *See* Journal of American Folk-lore; also article on Early Blackfoot History (American Anthropologist, Washington, April, 1892), and personal letters.

Dr Grinnell, editor of Forest and Stream, in New York city, and author of Pawnee Hero Stories and Blackfoot Lodge Tales, is one of our best authorities on the prairie tribes.

Hamilton, *Rev.* William. Autobiography. (Transactions and Reports of the Nebraska State Historical Society, I, 60–73. Lincoln, Nebraska, 1885. 8°.) 1–72.

Hayden, F. V. Contributions to the ethnography and philology of the Indian tribes of the Missouri valley, etc. Prepared under the direction of Captain William F. Reynolds, T. E., U. S. A., and published by permission of the War Department. Philadelphia, 1862. 4°.

Heckewelder, J. History, manners, and customs of the Indian nations who once inhabited Pennsylvania and the neighboring states. New and revised edition, with introduction and notes by Reverend William C. Reichel. Philadelphia, 1876. 8°. Originally

Heckewelder, J.—Continued.
published in the Transactions of the American Philosophical Society, Vol. I.

1—291-293.

Howard, *Gen.* O. O. Nez Percé Joseph; an account of his ancestors, his lands, his confederates, his enemies, his murders, his war, his pursuit, and capture. By O. O. Howard, brigadier-general, U. S. A. New York, 1881. 12°.

1—52; 2—64-72; 3—83.

Huggins, E. L. Smohalla, the prophet of Priest rapids. (Overland Monthly, February, 1891; vol. XVII, No. 98; second series, pages 208-215.)

Captain Huggins, now of the staff of General Miles, visited Smohalla in an official capacity about the same time as Major MacMurray. Some additional details were furnished by him in personal conversation with the author.

1—209; 2—209-215.

Humboldt, A. Political essay on the kingdom of New Spain, etc. Translated from the original French by John Black. London, 1811; 4 volumes, 8°.

1—I, 200-203; IV, 262.

Indian Informants. (Among the Paiute in Nevada information and songs were obtained directly from Wovoka, the messiah, from his uncle, Charley Sheep, and others; among the Shoshoni and northern Arapaho in Wyoming, from Norcok, Shoshoni interpreter, Henry Reid, half-blood Cheyenne interpreter, Nakash, Sharp Nose, and others; at Pine Ridge, among the Sioux, from Fire-thunder, American Horse, Edgar Fire-thunder of Carlisle, Louis Menard and Philip Wells, mixed-blood interpreters, and others; among the Arapaho and Cheyenne in Oklahoma, from Black Coyote, Left-hand, Sitting Bull, Black Short Nose, and numerous others, and from the Carlisle students, Paul Boynton, Robert Burns, Clever Warden, Grant Left-hand, Jesse Bent, and others; among the Comanche, from Quanah, William Tivis (Carlisle) and his brother, Mo'tumi; among the Kiowa, from Biäñk'i, Gunaoi, Tama (a woman), Igiagyähona (a woman), Mary Zoñtam, and others, with the Carlisle or Hampton students, Paul Setk'opti, Belo Cozad, and Virginia Stumbling Bear,

Indian Informants—Continued.
and from Andres Martinez, a Mexican captive and interpreter; among the Caddo, from George Parton and his daughter Eliza, John Wilson, and Robert Dunlap, half-blood interpreter; among the Wichita, from the chief Towakoni Jim. Detailed information in regard to the Smohalla and Shaker beliefs and rituals among the Columbia river tribes was obtained in Washington from Charles Ike, half-blood Yakima interpreter, and chief Wolf Necklace of the Pälus.)

Indian Office [*Ind. Off.*]. (Documents on file in the Indian office, exclusive of those relating directly to the Ghost dance and Sioux outbreak of 1890, those being filed in separate cases labeled "Ghost Dance." *See* **Commissioner** and **Ghost Dance.**)

1—Letter of Agent Graham to General Clark, dated February 22, 1827; 2—Document indorsed "The Kickapoo Prophet's Speech," dated St Louis, February 10, 1827.

Jackson, Helen ("H. H."). A century of dishonor. A sketch of the United States government's dealings with some of the Indian tribes, etc. New edition, etc. Boston, 1885. 12°.

Janney, S. M. The life of George Fox; with dissertations on his views concerning the doctrine, testimonies, and discipline of the Christian church, etc. Philadelphia, 1853. 8°.

Journal of American Folk-lore [*J. F. L.*]. (An octavo quarterly magazine published at Boston.)

1—"The Ghost Dance in Arizona," an article originally published in the Mohave Miner, and reprinted from the Chicago Inter-Ocean of June 25, 1891, in V, No. 16, January-March, 1892, pages 65-67; 2—ibid; 3—ibid; 4—Mrs Z. A. Parker, "The Ghost Dance at Pine Ridge," from an article in the New York Evening Post of April 18, 1891, quoted in IV, No. 13, April-June, 1891, pages 160-162. The same number of the journal contains other notices of the messiah and the Ghost dance; 5—G. B. Grinnell, "Account of the Northern Cheyennes Concerning the Messiah Superstition," in IV, No. 12, January-March, 1891, pages 61-69; 6—"Messianic Excitements among the White Americans," from an article in the New York Times of November 30, 1890, in IV, No. 13, April-June, 1891; Rev. J. O. Dorsey, The Social Organization of the Siouan Tribes, in IV, No. 14, July-September, 1891.

Keam, Thomas V. Letters and oral information.

Mr Keam, of Keams Cañon, Arizona, has been for a number of years a trader among the Navaho and Hopi (Moki), speaks the Navaho language fluently, and takes an intelligent interest in everything relating to these tribes. He has furnished valuable information orally and by letter, together with much kind assistance while the author was in that country.

Kendall, E. A. Travels through the northern parts of the United States in the years 1807 and 1808. In three volumes. New York, 1809. 8°.

1—II, 290; 2—II, 292 and 296; 3—II, 287; 4—II, 292.

Lee, *Captain* J. M. *See* Adjutant-General's Office.

Additional information has been furnished by Captain Lee in personal letters and in conversation.

Letter Book [*L. B.*]. (The letter book of the Indian Office containing, among other things, letters bearing on the Ghost dance, supplementary to the documents in the "Ghost dance files.")

1—Belt, October 3 and October 20, 205–287; 206–211; 2—Belt, November 15, 207–237; 3—Noble, 208–245.

Lewis and Clark. Explorations. Washington, 1806. 12°.

The edition used is the earliest printed account, in the form of a message to Congress from the President, Thomas Jefferson, communicated February 19, 1806.

McCullough, J. *See* Pritts, J.

McKenney, T. L., and Hall, J. History of the Indian tribes of North America, with biographical sketches and anecdotes of the principal chiefs. Embelished with one hundred and twenty portraits from the Indian gallery in the Department of War at Washington. In three volumes. Philadelphia, 1858. 8°.

1—vol. I, 64, 65.

MacMurray, *Major* J. W. [*MacMurray MS.*]. The Dreamers of the Columbia River valley in Washington Territory. A revised manuscript copy, with notes and other additions of an article originally read before the Albany Institute January 19, 1886, and published in the

MacMurray, *Major* J. W.—Continued. Transactions of the Albany Institute, XI, Albany, 1887, pages 240–248.

Under instructions from General Miles, commanding the Department of the Columbia, Major MacMurray, in 1884, made an official investigation of the Smohalla religion, with special reference to the Indian land grievances in that section, and his report on the subject contains a large body of valuable information.

Mallery, *Colonel* Garrick. Picture writing of the American Indians. (Tenth Annual Report of the Bureau of Ethnology (1888–89), 1–822. Washington, 1893. 8°.)

1—290.

Matthews, *Dr* Washington. Ethnography and philology of the Hidatsa Indians. Washington, 1877. 8°. (Published as No. 7 of Miscellaneous publications of the United States Geological Survey.)

—— (Personal letters and oral information.)

Dr Matthews, surgeon in the United States Army, lately retired, formerly stationed on the upper Missouri and afterward for several years at Fort Wingate, New Mexico, is the authority on the Navaho and Hidatsa Indians.

1—Letter of October 23, 1891; 2—ibid.

Merrick, J. L. Life and religion of Mohammed, as contained in the Sheeah tradition of the Hyat-ul-Kuloob; translated from the Persian. Boston, 1850. 8°.

Minnesota Historical Collections. *See* Warren.

Mormons. The Mormons have stepped down and out of celestial government; the American Indians have stepped up and into celestial government. 8°. 4 pages. (n. d.)

An anonymous leaflet, published apparently at Salt Lake City, Utah, about July, 1892, advertising a series of lectures on the fulfillment of Mormon prophecies through the Indian messiah movement and the Sioux outbreak.

Nebraska Historical Society. *See* Allis; Colby; Hamilton.

Overland Monthly. *See* Huggins.

Parker, Z. A. *See* Commissioner and Journal of American Folk-lore.

Parkman, Francis. The conspiracy of Pontiac, and the Indian war after the conquest of Canada. Two volumes. Boston, 1886. 8°.

1—II, 328; 2—I, 207; 3—I, 183; 4—I, 187; 5—I, 255; 6—II, 311.

Parr, Harriet. The life and death of Jeanne d'Arc, called the Maid, etc. Two volumes, London, 1866. 12°.

Phister, *Lieut.* N. P. The Indian Messiah. (American Anthropologist, Washington, IV, No. 2, April, 1891.)

A statement by Lieutenant Phister is also appended to the report of Captain Lee on the abandonment of Fort Bidwell. *See* Adjutant-General's Office.

1—American Anthropologist, IV, No. 2, 105–7; 2—ibid; 3—ibid.

Powers, Stephen. Tribes of California. (Vol. III of Contributions to North American Ethnology; U. S. Geographical and Geological Survey of the Rocky Mountain Region.) Washington, 1877. 4°.

Prescott, W. H. History of the Conquest of Mexico. Edited by John Foster Kirk. Three volumes. (1873?) Philadelphia. 12°.

1—I, 61; 2—I, 346; 3—I, 309.

Pritts, J. Incidents of border life, illustrative of the times and condition of the first settlements in parts of the middle and western states, etc. Chambersburg, Pennsylvania, 1839. 8°.

1—98 (McCullough's narrative).

Remy, J., and Brenchley, J. A Journey to Great Salt Lake City, with a sketch of the history, religion, and customs of the Mormons, and an introduction on the religious movement in the United States. Two vols., London, 1861. 8°.

Roosevelt, T. In cowboy land. (Century Magazine, XLVI, No. 2, New York, June, 1893.)

1—283 (Century).

Schaff, Philip. A Religious Encyclopedia; or, dictionary of biblical, historical, doctrinal, and practical theology. Based on the Real-Encyklopädie of Herzog, Plitt, and Hauck. Edited by Philip Schaff, D. D., LL. D., professor in the Union Theological Seminary, New York, etc. Three volumes. Vol. I, New York, 1882. Large 8°.

Schoolcraft, H. R. Historical and statistical information respecting the history, condition, and prospects of the Indian tribes of the United States. Collected and prepared under the direction of the Bureau of Indian Affairs, etc. Published by authority of Congress. Six volumes, 4°. Philadelphia, 1851–1857.

1—IV, 240 (Fletcher); 2—IV, 259.

Science. *See* Dutton.

Scott, *Capt.* H. L. The Messiah dance in the Indian Territory. Essay for the Fort Sill lyceum, March, 1892 (manuscript).

Additional valuable information has been obtained from Captain Scott's official reports on the Ghost dance (*see* Ghost Dance and Adjutant-General's Office) and from personal letters and conversations.

Scribner's Magazine. *See* Welsh.

Shea, J. G. History of the Catholic missions among the Indian tribes of the United States, 1529–1854. New York, (1855?). 12°.

Contains references to the Columbia river missions.

Short Bull. Sermon delivered at the Red Leaf camp, October 31, 1890. Copy kindly furnished by George Bartlett, formerly of Pine Ridge agency, South Dakota. It appears also in the report of General Miles, in Report of the Secretary of War, Vol. I, 1891, 142.

Sickels, *Miss* E. C. (Notes and oral information in regard to the dance and songs at Pine Ridge.)

The author is also indebted to the kindness of Miss Sickels for the manuscript copy of Sword's account of the Ghost dance.

Snyder, *Colonel* Simon. (Personal letter concerning the Sword-bearer outbreak of 1887.)

Southey, Robert. The life of Wesley and rise and progress of Methodism. By Robert Southey. Second American edition with notes, etc, by the Reverend David Curry, A. M. Two volumes, New York, 1847. 12°.

Stenhouse, *Mrs* T. B. H. Tell it all: The story of a life's experience in Mormonism. Hartford, Connecticut, 1874.

Contains particular reference to the endowment robe.

Stephen, A. M. Letters and oral information.

The late Mr Stephen lived and studied for years among the Navaho, Hopi (Moki), Cohonino, and other Indians of northern New Mexico and Arizona, and was a competent authority on these tribes, particularly the Hopi, whose ethnology he was investigating in conjunction with Dr J. Walter Fewkes, for the Hemenway Archeological Expedition.

1—Letter of September 17, 1891; 2—Letter of November 22, 1891; 3—Oral information; 4—Letter of September 17, 1891.

Sutherland, T. A. Howard's campaign against the Nez Percé Indians. By Thomas A. Sutherland, volunteer aid-de-camp on General Howard's staff. Portland, Oregon, 1878. Pamphlet, 8°.

1—39.

Tanner, John. A narrative of the captivity and adventures of John Tanner. New York, 1830. 8°.

1—155-158.

Thompson, A. H. (Of the United States Geological Survey. Oral information concerning the religious ferment among the Paiute of Utah in 1875.)

Treaties. A compilation of all the treaties between the United States and the Indian tribes, now in force as laws. Prepared under the provisions of the act of Congress approved March 3, 1873, etc. Washington, 1873. 8°.

1—439.

Voth, *Rev.* **H. R.** (Correspondence and notes.)

Mr Voth, now stationed among the Hopi, at Oraibi, Arizona, was formerly superintendent of the Mennonite Arapaho Mission, at Darlington, Oklahoma. Being interested in the ethnology and language of the Arapaho, he gave close attention to the Ghost dance during the excitement, and has furnished much valuable information, orally and by letter, in regard to the songs and ritual of the dance.

War. Annual report of the Secretary of War. Washington. 8°. (Volumes quoted: 1877—I; 1881—I; 1888—I; 1891—I.)

1—Colonel Carr; Brevet Major-General Will-

War—Continued.

cox, department commander, and Major-General McDowell, division commander, in Report 1881—I, 140-154; 2—Report of Brigadier-General Ruger and of Special Agent Howard, with other papers in the same connection, 1888—I; 3a—General Howard in Report, 1877, I, 630; 3b—(Referred to) Report of scout Arthur Chapman, 1891—I, 191-194; 4—Short Bull's sermon, 1891—I, 142-143; 5—Report of General Brooke, ibid, 135-126; 6—Report of General Miles, ibid, 147-148; 7—Miles, ibid, 145; 8—Miles, ibid, 146-147; General Ruger, 182-183; Lieutenant-Colonel Drum, 194-197; Captain Fechét, 197-199; 9—Miles, ibid, 147; 10—Miles, ibid, 147 and 153; 11—Miles, ibid, 147; Ruger, 184; Lieutenant Hale, 200-201; Captain Hurst, 201-202; Lieutenant-Colonel Sumner, 224; 12—Miles, ibid, 147; Lieutenant-Colonel Sumner, etc, 209-238; 13—Miles, ibid, 150; 14—Miles, ibid, 150; 15—Ruger, ibid, 185; Maus, ibid, 214; 16—Miles, ib'd, 130; 17—Miles, ibid, 130; 18—Miles, ibid, 150; 19—Miles, ibid, 154; 20—Miles, ibid, 151; 21—Miles, ibid, 151; 22—Miles, ibid, 152; 23—Miles, ibid, 152-153; 24—Report of Lieutenant Getty, ibid, 250-251; 25—Reports of Colonel Merriam, Lieutenant Marshall, et al., ibid, 220-223; 26—Miles, ibid, 154; 27—Miles, ibid, 154.

Warren, W. W. History of the Ojibways, based upon traditions and oral statements. (In collections of the Minnesota Historical Society, V. St. Paul, 1885.) 8°.

1—321-324; 2—321-324.

Welsh, Herbert. The meaning of the Dakota outbreak. (Scribner's Magazine, IX, No. 4; New York, April, 1891, pages 429-452.)

Mr Welsh is president of the Indian Rights Association, and a close and competent observer of Indian affairs.

1—445; 2—450; 3—452.

Wickersham, James. Tschaddam or Shaker religion. (Manuscript published almost entire in chapter VIII herein, together with extracts from personal letters on the same subject.)

Judge James Wickersham is the historian of the state of Washington and the attorney for the Shaker Indian organization. He has devoted considerable attention to the Indians of the state, and is now engaged in preparing a monograph on the Nisqually tribe.

INDEX

Page

ẮĂ KAKI MBAWI'UT, Caddo name of ghost
dance 153
AĂ'NINĔNA, an Arapaho division......... 317
—, an Arapaho synonym.................. 375
AANŮ'HAWĂ, an Arapaho division....... 318
ACHOMA'WI, a Pit river band.............. 414
ADAI, a Caddo division.................... 454
ADAIZE, a Caddo division................. 454
Ắ'DAL-K'ATO'IGO, a Sahaptin synonym... 106
ÄDALTO'YUI, a Kiowa warrior order..... 351
ADAMS, AGENT, at Anadarko council.... 275
ADAMS, WM., killed at Wounded Knee.. 234
ADVENTISTS, account of the.............. 306
AES, a Caddo division.................... 454
AFRAID-OF-HIM, Biǎñk'i's vision of....... 272
AGA'IH-TĬKA'RA, see FISH-EATERS.
AGENTS, knowledge of, concerning in-
dians 129
—, inconsiderateness of.................. 199
—, placed under military orders......... 212
—, policy concerning...................... 190
—, replacement of.................... 207, 249
—, Sioux, ghost dance beyond control of. 212
—, Sioux, irresponsibility of............. 195
AGRICULTURE of the Caddo.............. 456
AHA'KÄNĔ'NA, an Arapaho warrior order. 350
ÄHYÄTO, Kiowa name of the Arapaho... 315
AIYAL, correction concerning............ 473
—, see YOWALUCH, LOUIS.
AKOKISA, status of the................... 455
ALIATAN, a synonym of Comanche....... 405
ALICHE, a Caddo division................. 454
ALLIS, SAMUEL, on Kickapoo prayer stick. 59
ALMOTU, a Pälus village................. 97
ALONE MAN, Catch-the-Bear killed by... 219
AMERICAN HORSE, acknowledgments to. 17
—, ghost-dance council held by......... 182
— on Wounded Knee massacre 231, 247
— on the Sioux outbreak 201, 205
—, emissary to Bad-lands refugees........ 229
—, Kicking Bear's surrender effected by.. 230
—, delegate to Washington............... 253
AMERICANS, indian belief of origin of..... 83
—, indian regard for.... 38
AMULET, Caddo, described................ 266
ANADARKO, a Caddo division............. 454
—, Kiowa council at...................... 275
ANGELL, HENRY, in Sioux outbreak....... 225
ANOINTMENT of body...................... 399
ANOS-ANYOTSKANO, Kichai name of the
Arapaho 315
ANSKOWI'NĬS, a Cheyenne division 388
APACHE, absence of ghost dance among.. 167

APACHE in ghost dance......... 15, 164, 167, 260
— and Kiowa early warfare 441
—, medicine-man of the 66
—, refusal of, to accept Äpiatañ's report.. 276
—, use of bull-roarer by.................. 337
A'P-ANĔKA'RA, Comanche name of ghost
dance 153
ÄPIATAÑ, journey of, to the Sioux 270
—, Kiowa delegate to Wovoka 265, 273, 275
—, portrait of............................. 274
—, result of interview of.................. 273
—, report of messiah visit of 275
—, report on messiah doctrine by......... 262
—, medal presented to..................... 276
AQA'THINĔ'NA, an Arapaho division...... 319
ARAPAHO, ceremonial smoking by the.... 280
—, cycles of the.......................... 63
—, delegation of, to Wovoka.............. 262
—, early knowledge of messiah by 159
—, etymology of.......................... 375
—, features of ghost dance among........ 164
—, ghost dance among the 15
148, 317, 496, 182, 257, 288, 289
—, ghost-dance doctrine spread by........ 264
—, glossary of the........................ 374
—, knowledge of messiah among 256
— name of the Caddo..................... 454
— name of the Cheyenne 385
— name of the Comanche................. 405
— name of ghost dance................... 153
— name of the Kiowa Apache............ 443
— name of the Sioux..................... 419
— police, acknowledgments to............ 17
—, population of the....................... 319
—, religion of the 137
—, sacred pipe of the..................... 425
—, sketch of the.......................... 316
—, songs of the........................... 320
—, symbolic representation of............. 142
— tribal signs 316
— tribal synonymy........................ 315
—, visit of Äpiatañ to..................... 273
—, visit of, to Wovoka.................. 136, 169, 263
—, visit to the............................ 140
ÄRÄPA'KATA, Crow name of the Arapaho. 315, 376
ARCS PLATS, a synonym of Kutenai...... 93
ARIKARA, ghost dance among the......... 179
ARIZONA visited by Smohalla............. 81
ARMSTRONG, JAMES, visit of Kickapoo delegation to................................ 61
ARMSTRONG, R. B., prayer stick in posses-
sion of.................................. 61
ARNOLD, MRS L. B., acknowledgments to . 17

Page

ARNOLD, MRS L. B., adoption of Sioux child
by... 242
ARROW, medicine, ceremony of........... 388
ARROW GAME of the Arapaho............. 324
ARROWS of the Cheyenne.................. 386
—, sacred, in Sioux ceremony............. 185
—, sacred, in Sioux ghost dance...... 150, 277, 278
—, symbolism of, in ghost dance.......... 151
ÄSATIIOLA, present name of Biäñk'i..... 271
ASAY, J. F., on mortality at Wounded
Knee..................................... 232
—, on Sioux ghost dance.................. 277
ASINAIS, a Caddo synonym............... 454
ASINIBOIN and Cheyenne hostility........ 386
—, ghost dance among the................ 179
—, Tenskwatawa religion among the..... 41
ATAHNAM, a Yakima mission............. 79
Ä'TÄNCM-'LĚMA, sketch of the.......... 100
ATSINA, Blackfoot name of Gros Ventres. 317
ATUA'MIH, a Pit river band.............. 414
AUTHORITIES CITED, list of.............. 466
AWL GAME of plains tribes........... 364–366
AYUTAN, a synonym of Comanche....... 405
AZTECS, culture of the.................. 20

BA'ACHINĚNA, name of northern Arap-
aho.................................. 316, 376
BÄÄKU'NI, Arapaho name of Paul Boyn-
ton..................................... 333
BAD FACES, an Arapaho division........ 319
BAD LANDS, flight of Sioux to....212, 213, 223, 246
—, Sioux in, surrounded by troops....... 228
—, return of Sioux from.................. 230
BAD PIPES, an Arapaho division......... 318
BAHAKOSÍN, Caddo name of the Chey-
enne.................................... 385
BAHWETEGOW-ĚNINNEWUG, Ojibwa name
of Gros Ventres........................ 317
BALL of the Arapaho.................... 326
BANCROFT, GEORGE, on French and Indian
war...................................... 25
—, on the Lenape....................... 24
BANNOCK and Paiute affinity........ : 410, 413
—, early knowledge of messiah by........ 164
—, ghost dance among.............. 147, 167, 169
—, messiah delegates among the......... 256
—, Mormon emissaries among the........ 66
—, Porcupine's visit to the.............. 155
—, present habitat of the............... 168
—, reception of, into Mormon church.... 152
—, Tävibo among the................... 63
—, visit of Äpiatañ among.............. 273
—, visit of, to Wovoka.................. 180
BANNOCK JIM, Wovoka confounded with. 127
BÄ'QATI GAME described................. 356
— in ghost song..................... 398, 437
BÄQATI WHEEL, use of, in ghost dance.... 426
BARK, Cheyenne delegate to Wovoka.... 257
BARK, cedar, headdress of, in Shaker cere-
mony.................................... 123
BARTLETT, C. H., acknowledgments to... 17
—, prayer stick presented by............ 60
BÄ'SAWUNĚ'NA, an Arapaho division..... 317
BASKET, mystic, in Columbia indian cos-
mology.................................. 84

Page

BASKET used in dice game................ 366
BATHING in ghost-dance ceremony....... 283
BÄTI'QTÚBA game of the Arapaho........ 369
BATTLEMULEEMAUCH, a Mitaui synonym. 96
—, an Okanagan division................. 96
BED of prairie tribes.................... 325
BE'DÄLPAGO, Kiowa name of the whites.. 340
BEEKMAN, DORA, founder of the Beek-
manites................................ 307
BEEKMANITES, account of................ 307
BELL, —, a wilderness worshiper........ 308
BELLS used in Shaker ceremony.......... 111, 117
— used in Smohalla worship............. 92
BÉNI'NĚNA, an Arapaho warrior society.. 348
BENOIT, FELIX, interpreter in Sioux out-
break.................................. 227
BENT, GEORGE, acknowledgments to..... 17
—, on absence of clans among Cheyenne.. 318
BENT, JESSE, acknowledgments to....... 17
BERLINER, EMILE, acknowledgments to.. 17
BERRY DANCE of northwestern indians... 90
BE'SHILTCHÄ, Kiowa synonym........... 440
BÉTIDEË, Kiowa Apache name of the
Arapaho................................ 315
BIÄÑK'I, account of................... 271–272
— compared with other prophets......... 292
—, influence of, in ghost dance.......... 276
BIBLE, Shaker regard for the........... 112, 117
BIDAI, status of the.................... 455
BIG FOOT, complaints by band of........ 198
—, excitement among band of........... 210
—, game-wheel carried by band of....... 437
—, ghost dance at camp of............ 209, 215
— joined by Sitting Bull's warriors...... 222
—, participation of, in Sioux outbreak... 223
—, arrest of band of.................... 238
—, surrender of........................ 229
—, second flight of..................... 227
—, military movement against........... 226
—, illness of........................... 230
— killed at Wounded Knee.............. 232
BIG ROAD as a peacemaker.............. 249
—, delegate to Washington.............. 253
—, emissary to Bad-lands refugees...... 229
BILLY JOHN, see SHA'AWĚ.
BIRD HEAD, use of, in battle............ 152
BIRDS, stuffed, used in ghost dance...... 278
BITAHI'NĚNA, an Arapaho warrior band.. 350
BITÄYE, another name of Sitting Bull.... 258
BLACK, BUFFALO, a ghost-dance leader... 264
BLACK COAL, an Arapaho chief.......... 318
—, opposition of, to ghost dance........ 170
BLACK COYOTE, an Arapaho ghost-dance
leader............................... 259, 260
—, acknowledgments to................. 17
—, sacred paint obtained by............. 391
—, song rehearsal in tipi of............. 181
—, visit of, to Wovoka....136, 137, 256, 262, 265
BLACKFEET, a Teton division............ 421
—, absence of ghost dance among........ 178, 179
—, dog soldiers of the.................. 348
—, eagle trapping by the................ 355
—, former union of, with Cheyenne....... 387
—, native name of the.................. 319
—, name of Gros Ventres by............. 317

Page

BLACKFEET, Tenskwatawa religion among the...................................... 42
BLACK FOX, firing at Wounded Knee begun by.. 231
BLACK HILLS formerly occupied by Kiowa. 441
— inhabited by Cheyenne 386
—, result of settlement of 187, 188, 421
BLACK-LEG PEOPLE, a Kiowa warrior order................................... 351
BLACK SHORT NOSE, acknowledgments to. 17
—, an Arapaho chief 318
—, Wovoka's message delivered by 142
BLOOD, use of, in Sioux arrow ceremony . 185
BLOWING in Shaker ceremonial........... 123
BLUE CLOUD PEOPLE, an Arapaho synonym 151
BLUE WHIRLWIND, portrait of............ 239
—, wounding of, at Wounded Knee 231
BOBBYDOKLINNY, see NAKAI-DOKLI'NI.
BODĂLK'IÑAGO, Kiowa name of the Comanche 405
BONE, arrowheads of, in Sioux ceremony. 185
BONE, ALBERT S., killed at Wounded Knee................................... 234
BOSTON MEN, application of name........ 83
BOT-K'IÑ'AGO, Kiowa name of Gros Ventres................................. 317
BOURKE, J. G., acknowledgments to..... 17
—, on Apache medicine-man.............. 66
—, on Apache use of bull-roarer 337
—, on necklaces of human fingers........ 386
BOW, SACRED, in Sioux ceremony......... 185
—, in Sioux ghost dance 150
BOYNTON, PAUL, acknowledgments to.... 17
—, ghost song composed by 333
—, experience of, while in trance......... 285
BRADDOCK, Pontiac at defeat of.......... 30
BRINTON, D. G., cited on white deliverer among indians 20
BROKEN ARM, delegate to Wovoka....... 182
BROOKE, GEN. J. R., troops under, in Sioux outbreak 212
—, operations of, in Sioux outbreak....... 237, 244
—, on reduction of Sioux rations......... 207
—, conference of, with Sioux chiefs...... 229
BROWN, A. J., mission of 308
BROWN, J. P., quoted on the Dervishes.. 310
BROWNE, H. G., acknowledgments to.... 17
BRULÉS, a Teton division................. 420
—, ghost dance among the............... 209
BRUNOT —, on Columbia river land reserve.................................... 71
BUFFALO, ceremony for restoration of.... 268
—, effect of extermination of..... 187, 191, 193, 195
— hair used in medicine................. 395
— hunting by the Sioux................. 186
— hunting, how conducted.............. 433
— in Biắnk'i's vision.................... 272
— in ghost-dance doctrine 183, 426
— in Sioux mythology 425
—, indian dependence on 342
—, Kiowa belief concerning............. 268
—, belief in restoration of........... 161, 269, 450
— skull, use of, in Sioux ceremony 184
—, vision of 159, 183

Page

BUFFALO BILL, see CODY, W. F.
BUFFALO BLACK, see BLACK.
BUFFALO-EATERS, name applied to the Bannock 413
BUFFALO GAP, appearance of troops at... 212
BULL HEAD, Sioux police under 217
— at arrest of Sitting Bull 219
—, Sitting Bull shot by.................. 219
— shot by Catch-the-Bear 219
— killed in Sitting Bull fight 220
BULL-ROARER of the Arapaho 336, 337
BURNS, ROBERT, acknowledgments to.... 17

CADDO, account of the................... 454
—, clan system of the 318
—, delegation of, to Wovoka.............. 263, 265
—, ghost-dance among the................ 15
148, 164, 170, 257, 264, 267, 288, 289
—, glossary of the....................... 464
— name of ghost dance 153
— name of the Arapaho 315
— name of the Cheyenne 385
— name of the Comanche 375
— name of the Kiowa Apache 443
— name of the Sioux 419
— name of the Wichita 457
—, refusal of, to accept Äpiatañ's report . 276
—, songs of the......................... 458
—, synonymy of the..................... 454
—, tribal sign of the.................... 454
CADDOAN STOCK, tribes composing the... 454
CADODAQUIO, a Caddo synonym.......... 454
CAILLOUX, a Cayuse synonym............ 105
CALENDAR, Kiowa, pictography of .. 268, 269, 271
CALISPEL, a synonym of Pend d'Oreille.. 93
CAMPBELL, FRANK, account of Tävibo by. 64
CAMPING by prairie tribes................ 435
CAMPING CIRCLE of the Arapaho 318
— of the Cheyenne...................... 388
— of the Kiowa 442
— of the Sioux......................... 420
CANDLES used in Shaker ceremony.. 117, 123, 124
CAN'T-HOLD-IT, Biắñk'i's vision of...... 272
CAPRON, CAPTAIN, troops under, at Pine Ridge 212
CAPTAIN DICK, account of ghost dance by 146
CAPTOR, another name of Sitting Bull... 258
CARDINAL POINTS, fires at, in ghost dance. 277
— in ghost dance 151
— in Sioux ceremony 185
—, smoke offering to.................... 280, 425
CARIGNAN, —, on movements of Sitting Bull...................................... 217
CARLISLE STUDENTS as messiah delegates. 262
— in ghost dance 285, 286, 333, 400
CARR, GEN. E. A., arrest of Nakai-dokli'ni by 67
—, operations of, in Sioux outbreak....... 244
—, troops under, in Sioux outbreak....... 212
CARROLL, MAJOR, Porcupine's account made to 155
CASCADE INDIANS, a Kwikwûlt synonym. 103
CASEY, LIEUT. E. W., killed in Sioux outbreak 234, 250
CASWELL, —, on the Kentucky revival.... 305

Page

CATAKA, a synonym of Kiowa Apache... 443
CATCH-THE-BEAR, an adherent of Sitting
Bull.................................... 219
— killed in Sitting Bull fight 219
CATLIN, GEORGE, on Känakŭk............ 54, 59
—, on meaning of Känakŭk.............. 55
—, on Shawano prophet 35
—, on Shawano religion among Blackfeet. 42
—, on Tecumtha........................ 53
—, visit of, to Känakŭk................ 58
CAUTANTOUWIT, an Algonquian god 344
CAYGUA, a Kiowa synonym.............. 440
CAYUSE and Klŭkatät hostility 100
— opinion of land assignments........... 72
—, present habitat of the................ 167
—, sketch of the....................... 105
CEDAR, sacred regard for.............. 171, 341
— used in ghost dance 273, 283
CEDAR TREE, hypnotism performed by... 286
CELILO, Smohalla performances at....... 87
CENIS, a Caddo synonym................. 454
CEREMONIAL, see RITUAL.
CEREMONIAL SMOKING by the Arapaho.... 280
CEREMONY of the ghost dance........... 277
CHAHRARAT, Pawnee name of the Sioux.. 419
CHA''KANĬ'NÄ, a Caddo mythic cave....... 455
CHÄMNÄ', location of 101
CHÄMNÄ'PŬM, sketch of the 101
CHAPMAN, ARTHUR, interview of, with
Wovoka 128
CHASING HAWK, vision of................ 159, 183
CHA'THA, Arapaho name of the Co-
manche 405
CHAUDIÈRE, a Colville synonym.......... 94
CHEESCHAPAHDISCH, see CHEEZ-TAH-PAEZH.
CHEEZ-TAH-PAEZH, account of 68
—, see SWORD-BEARER.
CHEHALIS membership in Shaker church. 121
—, Shaker religion among the 109
CHEKISSCHEE, a Lower Spokan synonym.. 94
CHEMEHUEVI, a Paiute offshoot........... 410
—, ghost dance among the................ 167, 176
CHEROKEE and Iroquois treaty........... 32
—, cedar in mythology of................. 171
— conception of the sun 333
— myth of the cedar 341
—, peace pipe of the..................... 425
—, power of Shawano prophet among.... 38
—, sacred regard of, for the crow 344
—, sacred regard of, for the eagle 462
CHESCHOPAH, see CHEEZ-TAH-PAEZH.
CHESE-CHA-PAHDISH, see CHEEZ-TAH-PAEZH.
CHESE-TOPAH, see CHEEZ-TAH-PAEZH.
CHEYENNE, absence of clans among 318
— and Kiowa early warfare.............. 441
— and Sioux early warfare.............. 421
—, Arapaho warrior order derived from.. 350
— delegates, visit of, to Wovoka........ 136
                                140, 179, 256, 262, 263
—, effect of Porcupine's visit on the...... 181
—, fires built by, in ghost dance.......... 283
—, former habitat of the 391
—, ghost dance among the................ 15
                                148, 164, 179, 257, 277, 288, 289
—, ghost-dance doctrine spread by........ 264

Page

CHEYENNE, glossary of the 401
—, knowledge of messiah among......... 256
— name of the Arapaho.................. 315
— name of the Comanche................. 405
— name of the Kiowa Apache 443
— name of the Sioux.................... 419
— notion concerning thunder............ 331
—, population of the..................... 387
—, religion of the....................... 137
—, reservation experience of the......... 195
— scouts in Sioux outbreak............. 229, 243
—, sketch of the........................ 386
—, songs of the........................ 390
—, Sword-bearer among the.............. 68
—, symbolic representation of............ 151
—, synonymy of the..................... 385
—, tribal divisions of the................. 387
CHEYENNE RIVER AGENCY, delegates from,
to Washington......................... 253
—, delegates from, to Wovoka............ 182
—, indians of, in Sioux outbreak 247
—, table of rations at.................... 201
—, waning of ghost dance at............. 208
CHILDREN killed at Wounded Knee.. 238, 239, 247
CHILLUCKITTEQUAW, a Chilŭ'ktkwa synonym 103
CHILŬ'KTKWA, sketch of the 103
CHIMNAHPUM, a Chämnä'pŭm synonym... 101
CHIMNAPOOS, a Chämnä'pŭm synonym ... 101
CHINACHICHIBAT, native name of Dog sol-
diers 348
CHĬ'NACHINĔ'NA, an Arapaho priestly or-
der.................................... 351
CHINESE, indian belief of origin of 83
CHINOOK, hypnotism among the.......... 124
CHIVINGTON and Wounded Knee massa-
cres compared......................... 243
CHOHOPTINS, a Sahaptin synonym........ 106
CHOPUNNISH, a Pä'lus synonym.......... 97
—, a Sahaptin synonym 106
CHRISTIANITY, effect of, on indian ceremonials 80
—, influence of, in indian religion........ 61
—, influence of, in Shaker religion...... 112, 123
—, influence of, on the Kiowa............ 450
—, see CIVILIZATION.
CHUALPAY, a Colville synonym........... 94
CHUMÁ'WA, a Pit river band............. 414
CIVILIZATION, effect of, on Arapaho and
Cheyenne 389
—, effect of, on indians.................. 37, 191
—, effect of, on savagery................ 31
—, effect of, on the Caddo............... 456
—, see CHRISTIANITY.
CLAMS, BILLY, a Shaker enthusiast...... 118
CLAN SYSTEM unknown to Arapaho...... 318
— unknown to Comanche................. 406
— unknown to Kiowa.................... 441
CLARK, GENERAL, visit to, by Känakŭk.. 55-56
CLARK, W. P., on Cheyenne characteristics 389
—, on Cheyenne divisions................ 387
—, on Cheyenne early habitat 386, 391
—, on meaning of Hunkpapa............. 421
—, on meaning of Ogalala 420
—, on Sioux characteristics 421

Page

CLARKE, BEN, on absence of clans among
Cheyenne................................. 318
CLAWS, animal, use of, in battle.......... 152
— attached to amulet...................... 266
— used in ghost dance..................... 278
CLICKAHUT, a Klŭ′kătät synonym........ 100
CLICKITAT, a Klŭ′kătät synonym......... 100
CLOUD HORSE, visit of, to Wovoka....... 159, 181
CLUB MEN, an Arapaho warrior order..... 349
CODY, W. F., ordered to arrest Sitting
Bull..................................... 216
CŒUR D′ALÊNE⁵, present habitat of...... 167
—, sketch of the........................... 95
COFFEY, DORA S., killed at Wounded Knee 234
COHONINO, ghost dance among the....... 147, 173
COLBY, GEN. L. W., acknowledgments to.. 17
—, in Sioux outbreak...................... 238
—. letter from McGillycuddy to.......... 193
—, on close of Sioux outbreak............ 250
—, on killing of Lieutenant Casey........ 251
—, on mortality at Wounded Knee........ 233
—, on second encounter at Wounded Knee 244
- , on Sioux outbreak..................... 223, 229
—, Sioux child adopted by................ 241
COLOR, differentiation of, by indians..... 394
—, sacred, red as a........................ 399
— symbolism in ghost dance.............. 281
— symbolism in Shaker ceremony........ 123
— symbolism in Smohalla ritual.......... 7 87, 91
COLUMBIA REGION, tribes of the......... 93
COLUMBIA RIVER INDIANS defined........ 78
—, a synonym of Wa′napŭm............... 97
— in Shaker church........................ 121
—, Smohalla doctrine among.............. 78
COLUMBIAS, an Isle de Pierre synonym... 96
COLVILLE, sketch of the................... 94
COMANCHE, absence of clans among...... 318
— and Kiowa early warfare............... 441
— drawings of the ghost dance........... 422
—, ghost dance among the........ 15, 263, 288-289
—, Kiowa inferior to the.................. 442
— myth concerning thunderbird......... 330
— name of the Arapaho................... 316
— name of the Caddo..................... 454
— name of the Cheyenne................. 385
— name of the ghost dance.............. 153
— name of the Kiowa Apache........... 443
— name of the Sioux..................... 419
— name of the whites.................... 65, 340
— name of the Wichita................... 457
—, sketch of the.......................... 405
—, songs of the........................... 408
—, synonymy of the...................... 405
—, tribal sign of the..................... 405
CONDORCANQUI, Peruvian insurrection
under................................... 22
CONRAD, CAPTAIN, orders Selwyn to visit
Kuwapi................................. 161
CONSECRATION of dance ground.......... 280
— of the earth............................ 286
— of feathers............................ 281
COOK, R. L., killed at Wounded Knee..... 234
COOKE, C. S., interpreter for Sioux dele-
gation.................................. 253
COOLIDGE, SHERMAN, acknowledgments to 17

Page

COOPER, A., acknowledgments to......... 17
COOSHATTI, see KOASATI.
COOSPELLAR, a synonym of Pend d′Oreille 93
COPUNNISH, a Sahaptin synonym........ 106
CORN, Arapaho mythic origin of.......... 321
— in Caddo mythology.................... 455
— in Cheyenne mythology................ 389
—, Sioux mythic origin of................ 425
— pollen used in Navaho ceremonies 67
CORONADO on indian dependence on
buffalo................................. 342
CORPSE-FROM-A-SCAFFOLD, a Cheyenne
division................................ 388
CORWINE, R. W., killed at Wounded Knee 234
COSĬ′SPÄ, see KASĬ′SPÄ.
COSMOLOGY explained by Smohalla....... 82
— of the Arapaho...................... 321, 345
— of the Caddo........................... 455
— of the Cherokee........................ 333
— of Columbia tribes..................... 84
— of the Paiute.......................... 412
COSTELLO, JOHN, killed at Wounded Knee 234
COSTUME of ghost dancers........... 150, 176, 278
-, see GHOST SHIRT.
CUTEEA′KUN, see KOTAI′AQAN.
COTONNÉ, a synonym of Kutenai......... 93
COTTONOI, a synonym of Kutenai 93
COTTONWOOD in Paiute ghost song....... 417
—, sacred character of.................... 330
—, use of, by indians..................... 329
COUTANIE, a synonym of Kutenai........ 93
COVILLE, F. V., acknowledgments to 17
COWEJO, name applied to Wovoka........ 127
COWLITZ membership in Shaker church.. 121
COXE, D., on Turtle river 391
COYOTE MEN, duties of.................... 347
COZAD, BELO, acknowledgments to....... 17
CRAFT, FATHER, regard of indians for.... 236
—, at battle of Wounded Knee........... 234
—, wounded at Wounded Knee........... 240
CRAZY DANCE of the Arapaho............ 350
—, description of the..................... 395
CRAZY MEN, an Arapaho warrior order... 350
CREE, absence of ghost dance among..... 179
— name of the Cheyenne................. 385
—, Tenskwatawa religion among the..... 41
CREEK INDIANS, power of Shawano proph-
et among............................... 38
—, Tecumtha among the 49
—, war of the 39
CREMATION practiced by the Shawano... 36
CROOK, GENERAL, Sioux commissioner... 201
—, Sioux regard for 188
CROSS, sign of, in Shaker religion 110, 123
—, symbolism of the...................... 373
CROW, personification of the. 363, 397, 400, 430
—, reference to, in ghost song 340
346, 356, 359, 393
—, sacred regard for the 281, 344, 434
—, symbolism of the 185, 434
CROW CREEK, control of indians at....... 211
CROW DANCE described 283
—, organization of 263
CROW DOG, ghost dance led by........... 209
—, removal of, advised 206

CROW DOG, flight of, to Bad lands 246
—, surrender of 230
CROW FEATHERS. indians defrauded with. 361
—, sacred regard for 396
CROW FOOT killed in Sitting Bull fight .. 220-221
CROW INDIANS, absence of ghost dance
    among 178
—, account of medicine-man of 68
— and Sioux early warfare 421
—, hostility of the 69
—, name of the Arapaho by 315, 375
— scouts in the Nez Percé war 76
— scouts in Sioux outbreak 212, 243
—, symbolic representation of 151
CROW WOMAN, name applied to Mo'ki... 400
CRUCIFIX used in Shaker ceremonies..... 117
CUIMNAPUM, a Chämnä'p̂um synonym.... 101
CULBERTSON BROTHERS, outlaws, account
    of 251
CUMANCHE, a synonym of Comanche,.... 405
CUMMINGS, PIERCE, killed at Wounded
    Knee................................... 234
CUSTER MASSACRE, references to.... 187, 222, 421
— and Wounded Knee affair compared ... 243
CUSTER WAR, Cheyenne in the........... 387
—, Sioux compensated for losses in 253
CUTSAHNIM, a Yä'k̄ĭmá synonym........ 99
CYCLES of time among indians 63

DAKOTA, a synonym of Sioux 419
—, geographic location of 188
—, nonagricultural character of 200
DALLES INDIANS, a Wasko synonym 103
DANCE, berry, of northwestern indians... 90
—, friendship, introduced by Pa'thĕskĕ... 62
—, mortuary, of northwestern indians ... 90
—, salmon, of norteastern indians 90
— of Arapaho warrior orders 349
— of the Dervishes 312
— of Saint John, account of 297
—, see CRAZY DANCE, CROW DANCE, GHOST
    DANCE, OMAHA DANCE.
DANCE WHEEL of the Apache 66
DÄ'SHA-I, a Caddo synonym 454
DATEKAÑ, mystic performances of 268
DAWES, SENATOR, telegram to, on Sioux
    trouble................................. 197
DELAWARE INDIANS, account of........... 457
—, delegation of, to Wovoka.............. 265
—, final defeat of 34
—, ghost-dance doctrine among 148, 264
—, opposition of the, to Tecumtha........ 46
DELAWARE PROPHET, account of the 24
DEOÑ, acknowledgments to 17
DERVISHES, hypnotism among the........ 310
DĔ'SA, a Caddo synonym................. 454
DES CHUTES (LOWER), a Waiäm synonym. 103
DE SOTO, Caddo encountered by 456
DETSÄNA'YUKA, a Comanche band 406
DETSEKAYAA, Caddo name of the Arap-
    aho 315
DEVIL, indian idea of the................ 393
DE VREEDE, JAN, killed at Wounded
    Knee................................... 234
DICE GAME of the Arapaho............. 366-367

DIGGERS, application of term 410
—, ghost dance among the................ 166
DISEASE cured by ghost dance........... 148
—, indian notion of origin of............. 83
DITSÄ'KÄNA, a Comanche band 406
DOCK SPUS, a Tûkspû'sh synonym....... 105
DOCTRINE of the ghost dance 139
DO'GU'AT, Kiowa name of the Wichita .. 457
DOG MEN, a Cheyenne division 388
—, an Arapaho warrior order............. 350
DOG RIVER INDIANS, a Kwikwûlît syn-
    onym 103
DOG SOLDIERS, insignia of the 349
—, sketch of the 348
DO''KÄNÄ, Comanche name for Wichita.. 457
DORSEY, J. O., on Omaha game 370
—, on Siouan camping circles 420
—, on Siouan names of the Sioux........ 419
DOW, LORENZO, on the Kentucky revival. 305
DRAKE, B., on losses at Prophet's town... 51
—, on Tecumtha.................... 34, 46, 48, 53
DREAMER RELIGION in the northwest..... 75, 81
DREAMS as part of Shaker religion 110
— confounded by indians................ 28
—, divination by 78, 85
— in ancient times....................... 291
—, indian belief in....................... 35
—, scarification as a result of............ 260
—, see HYPNOTISM, TRANCE, VISION.
DREXEL MISSION during Wounded Knee
    trouble................................. 236
DRUM in Caddo mythology............... 455
— in Crow dance 284
— in Smohalla ritual..................... 87
DRUM, COLONEL, indian police praised by. 222
—, ordered to arrest Sitting Bull......... 217
DUCK in Arapaho mythology 321
DULL KNIFE, a Cheyenne leader.......... 387
DUNBAR, J. B., on etymology of Arapaho. 375
DUNLAP, ROBERT, acknowledgments to... 17
DUNMOI, LAURA, Äpiatañ's letter read by. 273
DUNN, —, in Sioux outbreak 227
DUTTON, C. E., on submerged trees of Co-
    lumbia river 84
DYER, A. C., killed at Wounded Knee.... 234
DYER, D. B., acknowledgments to........ 17
—, guide on visit to Wovoka.............. 130
—, interpreter on visit to Wovoka........ 133
DZĬTSĬ'STÄS, a synonym of Cheyenne 385

EAGLE represented on ghost shirts....... 160, 185
—, sacred regard for the... 281, 344, 354, 434, 462
—, vision of, in ghost dance.............. 279
—, when killed by the Caddo 455, 462
EAGLE-BONE whistle used by medicine-
    man..................................... 230
EAGLE FEATHERS in Cohonino ceremony. 175
— on ghost shirts........................ 160
—, sacred use of 354
—, song pertaining to 462
—, use of, by Wovoka.................... 138
— used in ghost dance 278, 341, 461, 463
— used in hypnotism................... 285, 287
EAGLE PIPE, flight of, to Bad lands....... 246
EAGLES, how trapped by the Arapaho.... 354

	Page
EAGLES kept by pueblo tribes	354
EARTH, personification of the	1458, 461
—, regeneration of the	321, 416, 435
—, sacred regard for the	280
—, turtle as a symbol of	338
EARTHQUAKE, effect of, on the Creek	49
—, myth concerning	338
—, reference to, in Cheyenne song	390
EATER, see BIÄÑK'I.	
EATERS, a Cheyenne division	388
ECHEBOOL, a Tlaqluit synonym	102
ECHELOOT, a Tlaqluit synonym	102
ECLIPSE, how regarded by indians	36
—, Paiute notion of	135
— predicted by Smohalla	82
—, Wovoka entranced during	133
ECLIPSES, calendar of, in Nevada	136
EDSON, CASPER, Arapaho delegate to Wovoka	262
—, Wovoka's letter written by	142
EDUCATION, how regarded by the Sioux	199
—, see CHRISTIANITY, CIVILIZATION.	
EDWARDS, CAPTAIN, in Sword-bearer affair	69
EDWARDSVILLE, treaty of	54
EELLS, EDWIN, attitude of, toward Shaker religion	118
EELLS, MYRON, acknowledgments to	17
—, attitude of, toward Shaker religion	118
—, on Shaker religion	109
—, on Slocum's trance	108
ELLIOTT, GEORGE, killed at Wounded Knee	234
ELOOT, a Tlaqluit synonym	102
EMANKINA, Biäñk'i's vision of	272
ENDOWMENT ROBE of the Mormons	152
ENEESHUR, a Tapänäsh synonym	102
ENGLISH, indian belief of origin of	83
—, indian regard for the	38
ENTEATKEON, a tribe mentioned by Stevens	98
E'PEA, Biäñk'i's vision of	272
EPIDEMICS among the Sioux	192, 202
ESTAKÉWACH, a Pit river band	414
ETSITÜ'BIWAT, a Comanche band	407
EVANS on French prophets	301
— on the Kentucky revival	304
— on the Shakers	304
EVĬ'STS-UNĬ''PAHĬ-ᵻ, a Cheyenne division	387
EWERS, CAPT. E. P., ordered to arrest Hump	224
—, Sitting Bull's fugitives surrendered to	224
EYACKIMAH, a Yä'kĭma synonym	99
EYEISH, a Caddo division	454
FACIAL PAINTING by the Arapaho	333
—, ceremonial	399
— in Smohalla ceremony	91
—, see PAINTING.	
FALL INDIANS, a synonym of Gros Ventres	317
FAST THUNDER, conduct of, in Sioux outbreak	246
— on the Sioux outbreak	201

	Page
FASTING as a medium for trances	62
— during eagle trapping	355
— preliminary to ghost dance	184
FEAST, ghost dance accompanied by	400
— in Smohalla ceremony	91
—, sacred, in Sioux ceremony	186
FEATHER, ghost-dance ceremony of the	271
FEATHERS as medium of exchange	354
— as protecting "medicine"	152
— attached to amulet	266
—, ceremonial use of	361
—, crow, indians defrauded with	263
—, crow, sacred regard for	396
—, eagle, attached to ghost shirts	160
—, eagle, Caddo sacred use of	455
—, eagle, in Cohonino ceremony	175
—, eagle, sacred use of	354
—, eagle, song pertaining to	462
—, eagle, used in hypnotism	285, 287
—, eagle, used in ghost dance	278, 341, 461, 463
—, eagle, used in war bonnets	434
—, head, of the Arapaho	326, 327
— in Smohalla ceremony	91
—, Kiowa robe of	268
—, magpie, ceremonial use of	361
—, magpie, presented by Wovoka	263
—, magpie, prized by Paiute	137
—, sacred use of, by Wovoka	138
—, symbolism of, in ghost dance	151
—, turkey, on Cheyenne arrows	386
— used in Crow dance	284
—, use of, in ghost dance	148, 281, 446
FECHÉT, CAPT. E. G., at arrest of Sitting Bull	218, 219
—, pursuit of Sitting Bull's warriors by	220
FEWKES, J.W., on Hopi use of bull-roarer	337
FEW TAILS affair, account of	251, 252
FIFTH-MONARCHY MEN, account of	300
FINGERS, human, necklace of	386
FIRE, forest, how regarded by indians	170
— handling by crazy dancers	395
— in Caddo mythology	455
— in ghost-dance circle	277, 283
— in ghost-dance doctrine	148
— in Paiute dance circle	164
—, Paiute mythic origin of	413
—, sacred, method of making	30
—, sacred regard for	281, 432
— tabued in certain ghost dances	164
FIRE THUNDER, acknowledgments to	17
—, visit of, to Wovoka	256
FISHEATERS, a Paiute band	180, 413
FISKE, JOHN, on turtle in primitive mythology	338
FLAG, heraldic, of Smohalla	87, 88
—, use of, in ghost dance	185
FLAGELLANTS, account of the	297
FLAGS used in Smohalla ceremony	91
FLATBOW, a synonym of Kutenai	93
FLATHEAD INDIANS, land treaty with	93
—, present habitat of	167
FLETCHER, AGENT, on Winnebago cycles	63
FLOOD in ghost-dance doctrine	150
—predicted in ghost-dance doctrine	146
—, see COSMOLOGY.	

Page

Fog in Paiute ghost song 416
Food, berries used as 449
—, cottonwood pith used as 329
—, grass seed used as....:............... 416
— of Columbia river tribes 84
—, process of jerking beef for............. 428
—, rose seeds used as..................... 340
—, thunderberries used as................. 358
—, see Pemmican.
Forks-of-the-river men, an Arapaho division.................................. 318
Forrest, H. R., killed at Wounded Knee. 234
Forsyth, Colonel, at Wounded Knee massacre................................ 232
—, at surrender of Big Foot 229
—, operations of, in Sioux outbreak 237
—, troops under, at Pine Ridge........... 212
Fort Hall, ghost dance at 169
Fort Wayne, passage of indian delegations through 46
—, Tecumtha at 52
Foster, E. W., on Selwyn's interview with Kuwapi.......................... 160
Foster, Governor, Sioux commissioner . 201
Fox, George, claims of 299
Fox indians, ghost dance among the..... 264
Fox men, an Arapaho warrior order 349
Francischetti, Dominic, killed at Wounded Knee 234, 237
French and Indian war, reference to.... 25
Frenchmen, indian belief of origin of... 83
—, indian regard for 38
—, settlement of, among indians.......... 24
French prophets, account of the......... 300
Frey, Henry, killed at Wounded Knee.. 234
Friday, visit of, to Wovoka 179, 256
Friendship dance, introduced by Pa'-thĕskŏ 62
Furniture of the Arapaho 326
— of the Paiute 132

Gahe'wa, a Kiowa synonym.............. 440
Gaisberg, F. W. V., acknowledgments to...................................... 17
Gallagher, Agent, arrest of Sioux delegates by 182
—, ghost dance stopped by................ 209
—, on reduction of Sioux rations......... 207
—, resignation of.......................... 207
—, Selwyn's report to 160, 161
Gambling song of the Paiute............ 371
Game, awl, of plains tribes............. 364-366
—, băti'qtûba, of the Arapaho 356, 369
— of hunt-the-button................... 370-371
Game, restoration of, predicted by indians........................... 149, 150, 159
—, see Buffalo.
Games of the Arapaho.................... 324
Game-sticks, reference to, in ghost song. 369
Game wheel in ghost dance 278
— in Sioux ceremony 185
Gardiner, —, on causes of Sioux outbreak 202
Gardner cited on Mohammedanism 293
Garlands in Shaker ceremony 123

Page

Garlington, Lieut. E. A., wounded at Wounded Knee 233
Ga'taqka, Pawnee name of Kiowa Apache.................................. 443
Gatsalghi, Kiowa Apache name of the Cheyenne 385
Gatschet, A. S., on etymology of Tecumtha.................................. 44
—, on the name Tushipa.................. 93
Gattacka, name of Kiowa Apache...... 443
Ga'wunĕhäna, an Arapaho division..... 319
Gawunĕ'na, an Arapaho division........ 319
Genesis myth of the Paiute............. 412
—, see Cosmology.
Gentile system, see Clan.
Geologic phenomena, indian tradition concerning.............................. 84
Ghost dance among the Arapaho....... 257
— among the Caddo...................... 457
— among the Kiowa...................... 268
— among the Sioux...................... 158
— among southern tribes 249
— and Shaker ceremony compared 124
—, area covered by....................... 288
—, ceremony of the................... 277, 282
—, construction of circle for............. 164
— doctrine compared with other systems. 290
—, doctrine of the....................... 139
— doctrine, Sioux belief concerning...... 422
—, features of, among Sioux............. 184
—, first, at Walker lake 164
—, how performed........................ 158
—, inauguration of, among Sioux........ 183
— introduced the Arapaho 256
— introduced among Cheyenne 257
—, Kiowa, number of attendants at...... 276
—, native drawings of................... 422
—, native names of...................... 153
—, large number of indians in....... 257, 260
—, number of indians influenced by...... 288
— performed at Walker lake 180
—, preparations for the................... 280
—, present condition of the.............. 289
—, responsibility of, for Sioux outbreak.. 195
—, spread of the................... 166, 208, 264
—, time for performance of 373, 374
—, see Messiah, Wovoka.
Ghost shirts, description of.............. 151
—, first use of, by Sioux............... 208, 278
— gathered after Wounded Knee battle.. 240
—, invulnerability of........... 160, 193, 231, 435
—, reference to, in ghost song.......... 434, 435
—, responsibility for, disclaimed by Wovoka................................ 134, 153
—, symbolic decoration of.............. 160, 185
—, turtle pictured on...................... 338
—, use of, among Sioux............... 150, 277
—, use of, among various tribes.......... 153
Ghost song, see Song.
Gill, De Lancey W., acknowledgments to...................................... 17
Gïnä's, Wichita name of Kiowa Apache. 443
Glennan, Dr J. D., at Wounded Knee massacre................................ 232
Glossary of the Arapaho............... 374

GLOSSARY of the Caddo................... 464
— of the Cheyenne..................... 401
— of the Kiowa....................... 450
— of the Paiute...................... 418
— of the Sioux....................... 437
GOD, indian idea of 393
GODBE, W. S., acknowledgments to...... 17
GOODALE, ELAINE, on causes of Sioux outbreak 202
GOOD LANCE on the Sioux outbreak..... 201
GOOD THUNDER, visit of, to Wovoka. 159, 181, 182
—, vision of son of..................... 159, 183
GOOSE in Tlaqluit myth................. 102
GOSIUTE confounded with the Paiute.... 410
—, ghost dance among the.............. 167
GRACE at meals by Shakers............. 117
GRAHAM, —, quoted on Känakûk........ 6(55-56
GRASS, JOHN, conduct of, in Sioux outbreak 246
GRASS SEED used as food............... 416
GRAUBERG, HERMAN, killed at Wounded Knee.................................. 234
GRAY BEAR, another name of Weasel Bear 321
GREASY FACES, an Arapaho division.... 318
GREAT SPIRIT, Känakûk's ideas concerning 57
GREENVILLE, indian assemblage at....... 45
—, treaty of 33
GREETING, religious, described........... 267
GREGORY, J. O., cited concerning Wovoka. 135
GRINNELL, G. B., acknowledgments to.... 17
—, on absence of ghost dance among Blackfeet 179
—, on Blackfoot Dog soldiers.............. 348
—, on Blackfoot eagle trapping........... 355
—, on Cheyenne divisions................ 387, 388
—, on Cheyenne ghost dance............. 277
—, on etymology of Arapaho............. 376
—, on ghost dance among Cheyenne...... 181
—, on Pawnee name of the Sioux......... 419
—, on the name Arapaho................ 315
GROS VENTRES, an Arapaho subtribe..... 316
—, ghost dance among the.............. 179
GROS VENTRES OF THE MISSOURI, Hidatsa so called 317
GROS VENTRES OF THE PRAIRIE, an Arapaho division 317
GUERRIER, EDWARD, visit of, to Wovoka. 263
GU'I-PÄ'GO, native name of Lone Wolf... 441
GYAI·KO, Kiowa name of the Comanche.. 405

HĂDAI'I, a Caddo division.............. 454
HĂHAU', location of..................... 101
HĂHAU'PŬM, sketch of the.............. 101
HAI·AI'NĬMA, a Sanpoil synonym......... 95
HAI'·ĬSH, a Caddo division.............. 454
HAIL, symbolism of, in ghost dance...... 151
HAI'·NAI, a Caddo division.............. 454
—, ghost songs of the.................. 461
HAIR, buffalo, use of, in medicine.... 342, 343, 395
—, cutting of, as mortuary custom....... 144
HAIRY MEN, a Cheyenne division........ 387
HALE, LIEUT. H. E., in Sioux outbreak... 224
—, ordered to arrest Sitting Bull fugitives 224
—, Sitting Bull fugitives arrested by..... 225
HALITANE, a synonym of Comanche...... 405
HAMEFKU'TTELLI, a Pit river band....... 414

HAMILTON, WILLIAM, on prayer-stick symbolism 61
HĂNÄ'CHÄ·THI'ĂK, Arapaho name of Sitting Bull.............................. 256
HA'NAHAWUNĔNA, an Arapaho division... 318
HANFORD, JUDGE, decision of, in land severalty case.............................. 119
HANTÉWA, a Pit river band.............. 414
HA'QIHANA, an Arapaho division......... 319
HARE, BISHOP W. H., on causes of Sioux outbreak 202
—, on deficiency of Sioux rations......... 189
HARRISON, GEN. W. H., conference of Tecumtha with 47, 48
—, on Tecumtha 48
—, treaty pipe......................... 50
HARRY, JACK, Delaware delegate to Wovoka 265
HASI'NAI, a Caddo synonym............. 454
—, application of term.................. 455
HASI'NI, a Caddo synonym.............. 454
HATERS, a Cheyenne division........... 387
HĂ'THAHU'HA, an Arapaho warrior order . 349
HAVASUPAI, ghost dance among the...... 16
—, see COHONINO.
HAWK FEATHERS, ceremonial use of...... 354
HAWK MAN at arrest of Sitting Bull.... 218
HAWTHORNE, LIEUT. H. L., wounded at Wounded Knee 233
HAYDEN, F. V., on Arapaho name of Sioux. 419
—, on the Blackfeet.................... 319
HAYDEN, LIEUT. JOHN, operations of, at Wounded Knee 238
HAYWOOD, CHARLES, killed at Wounded Knee.................................. 234
HEAD FEATHERS of the Arapaho........ 326, 327
HEAD WASHING in Cohonino ceremony... 175
HEAVENLY MAP of Känakûk.............. 28, 56
HEAVENLY RECRUITS, account of......... 309
HEAVY EYEBROWS, a Cheyenne division.. 388
HEBREWS, supposed indian descent from. 65
HECKEWELDER on the Kickapoo prophet. 28
HE DOG, delegate to Washington........ 253
HELWITT, a Tlaqluit synonym........... 102
HENNISSEE, CAPTAIN, ordered to arrest Big Foot's band 227
HENRY, MAJOR, operations of, in Sioux outbreak............................... 237
—, troops under, at Pine Ridge........... 212
HERO GODS of indian tribes............ 20
HĔTHĔ'HINĔ'NA, an Arapaho warrior order...................................... 350
HĔWÄ·TÄ'NIUW, a Cheyenne division 387
HICHÄÄ'QUTHA, an Arapaho warrior order. 349
HIDATSA name of the Cheyenne.......... 385
— name of the Sioux 419
HIGH BACKBONE killed at Wounded Knee. 233, 234
HIGH HAWK, flight of, to Bad lands 246
HIGH WOLF, visit of, to southern tribes.. 270
HIHIGHENIMMO, a Sanpoil synonym 95
HILLERS, J. K., acknowledgments to..... 17
HINDU, turtle in mythology of........... 338
HITÄNIWOĬV, Cheyenne name of the Arapaho................................. 315
HĬTÄSINA, Arapaho name of the Cheyenne 385
HITU'NĔNA, an Arapaho division......... 317

Page

HMĬ′SĬS, a Cheyenne division........... 387, 388
HODDENTIN, *see* POLLEN.
HODGES, W. T., killed at Wounded Knee. 234
HOGĂPĂGONI, Shoshoni name of the Paiute 410
HOHE, Cheyenne name of Asiniboin 386
HOHILPO, a Kutenai band................. 93
HOPI, knowledge of ghost dance among.. 173
— name of the Paiute.................... 410
— name of the whites.................... 340
—, use of bull-roarer by.................. 337
HOPKINS, ALBERT, and the Sioux outbreak 255
HORNS used in ghost dance 278
HORSE HEADDRESS, a Kiowa warrior order................................... 351
HORSEMANSHIP of Sioux police........... 218
— of the Comanche 408
HORSES as medium of exchange.......... 354
—, indian belief as to origin of 86
—, possession of, by the Sioux............ 186
HOSA, native name of Little Raven...... 319
HOTĂ′MI-TĂ′NIUW′, a Cheyenne division.. 388
HOT SPRINGS INDIANS, Pit River indians so called............................... 414
HOUSES of the Caddo..................... 456
— of the Paiute 132
— of the Wichita 457
—, *see* LODGE, SWEAT-LODGE, WIKIUP.
HOWARD, HENRY, killed at Wounded Knee.................................... 234
HOWARD, GEN. O. O., appointed indian commissioner 73
—, on the Dreamer religion............... 75
HOWLING BULL, hypnotism produced by . 257
HUBBUB, game of 366
HUGGINS, CAPT. E. L., acknowledgments to 17
—, quoted on Smohalla.................... 79, 85
HUMA′WHI, a Pit river band.............. 414
HUMMER of the Arapaho.................336, 337
HUMP, ghost dance at camp of 209
— at surrender of Sitting Bull fugitives . 225
—, participation of, in Sioux outbreak.... 223
—, removal of, recommended 210
—, surrender of.......................... 222
—, arrest of 224
—, surrender of band of.................. 233
HUNKPAPA, a Teton division............. 420
HURST, CAPT. J. H., on causes of Sioux trouble................................. 198
—, on character of Sioux rations 189
—, arrest of Sitting Bull's band ordered by 224
—, at arrest of Sitting Bull's band........ 225
—, appointed indian agent................ 249
HURST, MAJOR, at battle of Prophet's town 50
HYDE, CHARLES L., notification by, of Sioux outbreak 205
HYPNOTISM among the Caddo............. 266
— among the Cohonino 175
— among the Dervishes 310
— in the Crow dance..................... 284
— in the ghost dance........ 161, 162, 257, 261, 278 279, 281, 284-288, 334, 401, 459, 460
— in indian ceremonies................... 284

Page

HYPNOTISM in Navaho ceremonies........ 173
— in Shaker ceremony 124
— practiced by Wovoka 117, 180, 263
—, *see* DREAM, TRANCE.

IĂTĂ-GO, Kiowa name of the Ute........ 405
IATAN, a synonym of Comanche.......... 405
ĬBIDSĬI, a Paiute goddess................. 413
IDAHI, Kiowa Apache name of the Comanche 405
IETAN, a synonym of Comanche.......... 405
IETAU, a synonym of Comanche.......... 405
IGIAGYĂHONA, acknowledgments to...... 17
IHANKTOŇWAŇ, a Sioux division.......... 420
IKE, CHARLES, on Shaker religion 122
—, on Smohalla ceremony 89
—, portrait of 90
ILMA′WI, a Pit river band................. 414
I′MĂHA, a Caddo division................. 454
IMMORTALITY in ghost-dance doctrine.... 148
IMOHALLA, a Smohalla synonym......... 79
INCENSE in Sioux ceremony.............. 185
INCOMECANE′TOOK, an Okanagan division 96
INDIAN OFFICE, acknowledgments to.... 17
INDIAN SAM on ghost-dance doctrine.... 146
INSPELLUM, a Nespelim synonym 95
—, an Okanagan division.................. 96
IN-THE-MIDDLE, *See* PA-IŇGYA.
INTIE′TOOK, an Okanagan division....... 96
INĈNA-INA, a synonym of Arapaho....... 315
IONI, a Caddo division 454
IOWA, absence of ghost-dance among the. 178
—, ghost dance among the................. 264
—, a Sanpoil synonym..................... 95
IROQUOIS and Cherokee treaty........... 32
ISAŇATI, a Santee synonym............... 420
ĬSIUM-ITĂ′NIUW′, a Cheyenne division.... 387
ISLE DE PIERRE, sketch of............... 96
ITAHATSKI, Hidatsa name of the Sioux .. 419
ITĂSUPUZI, Hidatsa name of the Cheyenne 385
ITAZIPKO, a Teton division............... 421

JACKSON, H. H., cited on Nez Percé war.. 76
JACKSON, RICHARD, appointed minister of Shaker church 120
JAMES, WILLIAM, elected elder of Shaker church................................. 120
—, land presented to Shaker church by .. 120
JANNEY, S. M., cited on the Quakers...... 299, 300
JERKED BEEF, how prepared.............. 428
JETAN, a synonym of Comanche.......... 405
JICARILLA, absence of ghost dance among 167
JOAN OF ARC and Smohalla compared.... 81
—, hallucination of, compared with ghost-dance doctrine.......................... 294
JOCKO RESERVE, indians on 167
JOHN DAY INDIANS, a Tûkspû′sh synonym 105
—, present habitat of...................... 167
JOHN DAY RIVERS, a Tûkspû′sh synonym. 105
JOHNSON, G. P., killed at Wounded Knee.. 234
JOHNSON, JOHN, name applied to Wovoka. 127
JOSEPH, CHIEF, and the Nez Percé war.... 73
—, of Cayuse blood....................... 106
—, refusal of, to recognize treaty 107
JOSEPHUS, description of Wovoka's inspiration by............................... 134

Page

JUMPERS, account of the 301
JUTZ, FATHER JOHN, interview with...... 236
—, at Wounded Knee...................... 234, 240
— Sioux conference effected by........... 229

KÄ'DOHÄDÄ'CHO, a Caddo synonym....... 391
—, account of the.......... 455
— early encountered by French........... 456
KAHLISPELM, a synonym of Pend d'Oreille. 93
KAHMILTPAH, a Qamïl-'lĕma synonym.... ' 98, 100
KÄ'IGWŬ, a Kiowa division................ 441
KÄ'ITSEÑ'KO, a Kiowa warrior order...... 351
KÄ'IGWŬ, proper name of the Kiowa..... 440
KAI-WÄ, a Kiowa synonym................ 440
KALISPELINES, a synonym of Pend d'Oreille 93
KALISPELUSSES, a synonym of Pend d'Oreille 93
KAMAI'ÄKAN, a Yakima war chief........ ' 84, 99
KANAHEÄWASTSĬK, Cree name of the Cheyenne 385
KÄNAKŬK, account of 28, 54
—, adherents to doctrine of............... 264
—, end of................................. 62
KANINAHOIC, Ojibwa name of the Arapaho 315
KANINÄVISH, Ojibwa name of the Arapaho. 315
KANSA, ghost dance among the........... 264
— name of the Comanche 405
— name of the Sioux..................... 419
KA'NTSI, Caddo name of Kiowa Apache.. 443
KASI'SPÄ, a Pälus village................. 97
KATAKA, name of Kiowa Apache......... 443
KAWINAHAN, an Arapaho division........ 319
KAYUSE, a Cayuse synonym............... 105
KEAM, T. V., acknowledgments to........ 17
—, on Cohonino ghost dance............. 175
KEECHIES, a synonym of Kichai.......... 457
KEEPS-HIS-NAME-ALWAYS, see DATETEKAÑ.
KEHTIPAQUONONK, proper form of Tippecanoe 46
KELLESPEM, a synonym of Pend d'Oreille. 93
KELLEY, JAMES E., killed at Wounded Knee..................................... 234
KELLNER, AUGUST, killed at Wounded Knee..................................... 234
KENDALL, E. A., cited on the Shawano... 35
—, quoted on Shawano prophet 37
KENDALL, FRANK, account of Tavibo by 65
KENTUCKY REVIVAL, account of the 304
KERR, CAPT., attacked by hostile Sioux.. 244
KETETAS, a K''tätäs synonym............. 98
KETTLE FALLS, a Colville synonym 94
KEWA'TSÄNA, a Comanche band.......... 407
KEWAUGHICHENUNAUGH, an Okanagan division 96
KICHAI, acknowledgments to.............. 17
KICHAI INDIANS, account of the.......... 457
—, ghost dance introduced among........ 264
— name of the Cheyenne 385
— name of the Comanche 405
— name of the Kiowa Apache 443
— name of the Sioux..................... 419
—, status of the 415
KICKAPOO, absence of ghost dance among. 178

Page

KICKAPOO, ghost dance among the....... 262, 264
—, land cession by the 54
—, present condition of the 62
—, Potawatomi prophet among the 67
—, southern migration of the............ 54
—, use of prayer stick by the 59
KICKAPOO PROPHET, see KÄNAKŬK.
KICKING BEAR, a ghost-dance leader...... 209
—, portrait of 215
—, delegate to Wovoka 182, 256
—, visit of, to the Arapaho 160, 182
—, ghost dance led by.................... 216
—, ghost-dance mission of................ 179
—, operations of, in Sioux outbreak....... 243
—, Cheyenne scouts attacked by......... 229
—, Pine Ridge agency attacked by....... 235
—, flight of, to Bad lands................. 212, 214
—, continued retreat of................... 229
—, surrender of, demanded............... 249
—, surrender of 230
KIGALTWALLA, a Kwikwûlit synonym... 103
KIMOOENIM, location of the............... 107
KIÑEP, a Kiowa division 441
KING GEORGE MEN, application of name.. 83
KIOWA, absence of clans among.......... 318
—, account of the........................ 440
— and Sioux early warfare 421
—, cedar used in ghost dance of.......... 171
—, confederation of Comanche with...... 406
—, ghost dance among the............... 148
164, 257, 260, 264, 268, 270
—, present condition of dance among..... 276, 289
—, glossary of the........................ 450
—, migration of the 406
— name of ghost dance................... 153
— name of the Arapaho.................. 315, 316
— name of Arapaho divisions............ 317
— name of the Caddo.................... 454
— name of the Cheyenne 385
— name of the Comanche................ 405
— name of the Kiowa Apache........... 443
— name of the Sioux 419
— name of the whites 340
— name of the Wichita.................. 457
—, sacred regard of, for cedar 341
—, synonymy of the...................... 440
—, tribal sign of the 440
—, warrior organization of the........... 351
KIOWA APACHE, account of the 443
— name of the Arapaho 315
— name of the Cheyenne 385
— name of the Comanche 405
KÏRI'NÄHĬS, Kichai name of Kiowa Apache 443
KI'TIKĬTI'SH, native name of the Wichita. 457
KI'TSÄSH, native name of the Kichai..... 457
KITUNAHA, a synonym of Kutenai....... 93
KITUNA'QA, see KUTENAI.
K'KA'SÄWI, sketch of the................. 101
K'KA'SÄWI-'LĔMA, a K'ka'säwi synonym . 101
KLAMATH, present habitat of the........ 167
KLAMATH RESERVE, indians on........... 167
KLIKATAT, a Klû'kätät synonym.......... 100
—, absence of Smohalla religion among.. 89
KLINQUIT, mention of the................. 100
KLÛ'KÄTÄT, sketch of the................. 100
KOASATI mixed with the Caddo.......... 455

Page

K'odalpä-K'iñago, Kiowa name of the
Sioux 419
Ko'gu'i, a Kiowa division................. 441
Koho', a Caddo gens...................... 455
Koit-tsow, name applied to Wovoka.... 127
Komseka-K'iñahyup, Kiowa name of the
Arapaho................................ 316
Koñtä'lyui, a Kiowa division............. 441
Kootenai, a synonym of Kutenai........ 93
Korn, Gustav, killed at Wounded Knee. 234
Kotai'aqan, a supporter of Smohalla.... 83
—, Smohalla ceremony conducted by..... 89
Kotsa'i, a Comanche band................ 407
Ko'tso-tě'ka, a Comanche band......... 407
Kotso'-tĭkăra, name applied to the Ban-
nock 413
Koutaine, a synonym of Kutenai........ 93
Ko-wee-jow, name applied to Wovoka.. 129
Kowwassayee, a K'ka'săwi synonym... 100, 101
K'tätäs, a Pĭskwaus band............... 98
K'tätäs-lě'ma, a K'tätäs synonym...... 98
K'u'ato, a Kiowa division.............. 441, 442
Kullas-Palus, a synonym of Pend
d'Oreille 93
Ku'shpělu, a synonym of Pend d'Oreille. 93
Kutenai, account of the................. 93
—, present habitat of the............... 167
Kutneha, a synonym of Kutenai........ 93
Kû'tsano't, a former Yakima chief...... 99
Kuwapi, account of messiah by......... 161
Kvit-Tsow, name applied to Wovoka.... 127
Kwa'hädi, a Comanche band............ 407
Kwana, see Parker, Quanah.
Kwikwû'lĭt, sketch of the............... 103
Kwohitsauq, name applied to Wovoka.. 127, 133
Kwü'da, a Kiowa synonym.............. 440

Laaptin, a Sahaptin synonym........... 106
Lacombe, A., on etymology of pemmican. 429
Lahannas, probable identification of..... 94
Läitanes, a synonym of Comanche...... 405
Lake indians, account of the........... 94
Lakota, a synonym of Sioux............ 419
Lakota-Kokipa-Koshkala, Sioux name
of Royer 210
Lance, flight of, to Bad lands........... 246
Lance, use of, by Arapaho warriors 350, 351
—, use of, by Kiowa warriors........... 352
Land treaty with Cheyenne and Arap-
aho.................................... 351
—, see Treaty.
Land severalty bill, effect of, on north-
western tribes........................ 119
Language, Arapaho, characteristics of.. 374
—, Cheyenne, characteristics of 389
—, Comanche, characteristics of........ 408
—, Kiowa, characteristics of 442, 443
—, Paiute, characteristics of 412
—, Sioux, characteristics of 422
—, Sioux, dialects of the 420
—, see Glossary.
La Playe, a synonym of Comanche...... 405
Lapwai, mission established at.......... 107
Lartielo, a Spokan synonym............ 94
La Salle, Kiowa Apache mentioned by.. 443

Page

Laulewasikaw, revelation of 34
Lea, Agent, Rosebud census by 192
Lee, Ann, founder of the Shakers........ 303
Lee, Capt. J. M., acknowledgments to.... 17
—, account of Tävibo by................. 63
—, appointed indian agent............... 249
—, on Paiute ghost dance 146
—, on Sioux story of sacred pipe......... 424
—, on Wovoka's father................. 127
—, respect of indians for............... 250
Left-hand, an Arapaho chief........... 141, 319
—, ghost song composed by............. 323
—, land treaty signed by............... 261
Left-hand, Grant, acknowledgments to. 17
—, crow dance organized by............. 263
—, delegate to Wovoka................. 262
—, in the ghost dance.................. 400, 401
—, song composed by wife of. 394, 397, 398, 400
Lepage, name applied to John Day river.. 105
Letter from Äpiatañ to the Kiowa...... 273
— from Wovoka 138, 142, 143
Lewis and Clark among Columbia river
tribes 104
—, mention of Wheelpoo by 94
— on Arapaho habitat.................. 318
— on Cheyenne early habitat........... 386
— on the Coospellar................... 94
— on the Kiowa Apache 443
— on the Kutenai..................... 93
— on the Sahaptin.................... 107
—, the Sokulk met by.................. 97
L'Iatan, a synonym of Comanche........ 405
Llaywas, mention of the............... 100
Light from coal oil, Shaker idea concerning.................................... 111
Lightning, indian notion concerning 330
— in Paiute ghost song 416
Linkinse, an Isle de Pierre synonym..... 96
Little, a Sioux prisoner................. 110
Little Bow, acknowledgments to....... 17
Little Chief, Cheyenne delegate to
Wovoka................................ 257
Little-no-heart, delegate to Washing-
ton.................................... 253
Little Raven, an Arapaho chief........ 319
—, delegate to Wovoka 262
—, song composed by 360
Little Woman, songs composed by...... 394
397, 398, 400
Little Wound, conduct of, in Sioux out-
break................................ 246
—, ghost-dance council held by.......... 182
— ignored in Sioux difficulty 194
—, Kicking Bear's surrender effected by.. 230
—, operations of, in Sioux outbreak...... 243
Lodge, Smohalla ceremonial........... 88
—, see House, Wikiup, Sweat-lodge.
Logan, James, killed at Wounded Knee. 234
Lohĭm, habitat of the.................. 104
—, sketch of the....................... 105
Lone Wolf, a Kiowa chief.............. 441
Long, —, on Cheyenne name of Sioux.... 419
Looking-glass, a Nez Percé chief....... 76
Looking-up, an Arapaho division........ 319
Lost Bird, see Zitkala-noni.

	Page
LOWER BRULÉ AGENCY, control of indians at	211
MACKINAW, meaning of	338
MACMURRAY, MAJ. J. W., acknowledgments to	17
—, on Columbia indian cosmology	84
—, on eclipses predicted by Smohalla	82
—, on indian troubles in the northwest	78
—, on Smohalla	79, 80
—, on Smohalla religion	81, 87
MAGPIE held sacred in ghost dance	185, 344
MAGPIE FEATHERS, ceremonial use of	361
— presented by Wovoka	263
— prized by Paiute	137
MALLERY, GARRICK, on Sioux pipe legend	425
MAMMALS, indian tradition concerning	84
MANDAN, ghost dance among the	179
MANN, LIEUT. JAMES D., killed at Wounded Knee	234, 237
MANN, M. G., Puget Sound missionary	122
MÂNPOSO'TIGUAN, Kiowa name of ghost dance	153
MAQPE-LUTA, native name of Red Cloud	420
MAQPIĂTO, Sioux name of the Arapaho	316
MARANSHOBISHGO, Cheyenne name of the Sioux	419
MARGRY, PIERRE, use of term Läitanes by	405
MARGUERITE, survivor of Wounded Knee	240, 241
MARICOPA, absence of ghost dance among	167
MARTIN, J. T., cited on Shaker ceremony	110
MARTIN, T. P., acknowledgments to	17
MARTINEZ, ANDRES, acknowledgments to	17
MA'SE'P, a Caddo synonym	454
MASON VALLEY, description of	127, 131
MATSĬ'SHKOTA, a Cheyenne division	388
MATTHEWS, WASHINGTON, acknowledgments to	17
—, on etymology of Nakai-dokli'ni	67
—, on ghost dance among the Navaho	171
—, on Hidatsa name of the Sioux	419
—, on Navaho hypnotism	173
—, on present condition of the Navaho	171
—, on significance of Navaho songs	371
MCCLINTOCK, W. F., killed at Wounded Knee	234
MCCUE, J. M., killed at Wounded Knee	234
MCCULLOUGH, JOHN, a Delaware captive	30
MCGILLYCUDDY, V. T., management of indians by	207, 214
—, on causes of Sioux outbreak	193, 202
—, on Sioux outbreak	250
—, relieved as indian agent	190
MCKENNEY AND HALL on Tecumtha among the Creek	49
MCLAIN, MISS L., acknowledgments to	17
MCLAUGHLIN, JAMES, advises against immediate arrest of Sitting Bull	214, 216
—, advises removal of Sitting Bull	210
—, effort of, to arrest Sitting Bull's band	222
—, effort of, to arrest Kicking Bear	209
—, indian police praised by	221
—, interview of, with Sitting Bull	211
—, on Sioux ghost dance	159
—, on the Sioux outbreak	205

	Page
MCLAUGHLIN, JAMES, Sitting Bull's arrest arranged by	217
—, Sitting Bull's removal advised by	216
MDE-WAKAŇ-TOŇWAŇ, a Sioux division	420
MEACHAM, A. D., on Smohalla religion	73
—, on character of Columbia river tribal lands	71
MEATWHO, a Mitaui synonym	96
MEDAL of Greenville treaty	33
— presented to Äpiatañ	276
MEDEWACANTON, a Sioux division	420
MEDICINE, practice of, by Shakers	123
—, rites of, before battle	51
—, see DISEASE.	
MEDICINE-ARROW ceremony	388
MEDICINE BAGS, destruction of, during Shawano craze	41
—, use of, condemned by Känakûk	56
MEDICINE LODGE, treaty of, in 1867	319
MEDICINE-MEN defined	342
—, position of, in ghost dance	278
MEIL, J. W., killed at Wounded Knee	234
MĔLI"LĔMA, a Tenino synonym	104
MENARD, L., acknowledgments to	17
MERRIAM, COLONEL, operation of, against Big Foot	227
—, troops under, in Sioux outbreak	212
MERRICK, J. L., cited on Mohammedanism	294
MESCALERO, absence of ghost dance among	167
MESCAL RITE introduced among the Caddo	266
MESHON, a Mitaui synonym	96
MESSENGER, another name of Biäñk'i	271
MESSIAH, idea of, among various peoples	20
— craze, responsibility of, for Sioux outbreak	190, 193
—, see WOVOKA.	
METAL, tabu of, in ghost dance	160
METEOWWEE, a Mitaui synonym	96
METHODISTS, account of	301
METHOW, a Mitaui synonym	96
MEZO, WM. S., killed at Wounded Knee	234
MIAMI, opposition of, to Tecumtha	46
MIAYUMA, a Cheyenne division	388
MICHIGAN HISTORICAL SOCIETY, Pontiac manuscript deposited with	25
MICKSUCKSEALTON, a Kutenai band	93
MILES, GEN. N. A., on aspect of Wounded Knee affairs	236
—, in Nez Percé war	76
—, on causes of ghost dance	178
—, on causes of Sioux outbreak	188, 195, 205
—, on dispatch of troops in Sioux outbreak	214
—, on mortality at Wounded Knee	232, 233
—, operations of, in Sioux outbreak	212, 244, 249, 250, 252
—, opinion of, on Sioux excitement	211
—, on Sitting Bull	223
—, on reduction of Sioux rations	189
MILKY WAY, indian conception of	415
MILLER, HENRY, killed at Wounded Knee	233, 243
MILLER, WILLIAM, an Adventist	306
MINIKAŇZU, a Teton division	421
MINITARI, ghost dance among the	179

Page

MINITARI, see HIDATSA.
MISSIONARIES at Wounded Knee.....236, 237, 240
MISSION FIGHT, description of the........ 237
MISSION INDIANS. ghost dance among the. 166
MISSIONS among the Caddo................ 456
MISSOURI INDIANS, ghost dance among... 264
MI'STÄVII'NŬT, a Cheyenne division...... 388
MITAUI, sketch of the 96
MITHAW, see MITAUI.
MITHOUIES, a Mitaui synonym 96
MNEMONIC symbols invented by Smohalla. 82
MODOC, Pit river tribes raided by 414
—, present habitat of the............... 167
MOHAMMED and Smohalla compared 81
MOHAMMEDANISM and ghost-dance doc-
    trine compared......................... 292
MOHAVE, attendance of, at ghost dance .. 167
—, knowledge of ghost dance by the..... 176
—, ghost-dance doctrine among the....... 147
MO'KI, account of 400
—, song composed by 394, 397, 398, 400
MOKI, see HOPI.
MONTCALM, consideration of, for Pontiac. 31
MOON, Arapaho myth concerning the.... 368
—, symbolism of the 267
MOON HEAD, a Caddo ghost-dance leader. 265, 266
—, account of............................. 266
MORGAN, T. J., acknowledgments to 17
—, on cause of Sioux outbreak 187,191
—, on flight of Sioux to Bad lands........ 213
—, on mortality at Wounded Knee 233
—, on reduction of Sioux rations 189
—, on Wounded Knee massacre 232
—, tour of inspection by 262
MORMONS, conversion of indians by...... 152
— and the ghost dance................... 154
—, belief of, regarding the indians........ 65
—, endowment robe of the................ 152
—, Smohalla among the 81
—, treatment of indians by............... 180
MORTUARY custom of the Cheyenne 389
— dance of northwestern indians........ 90
— sacrifice by prairie tribes 144
— use of sacred paint.................... 241
MOSES, chief of the Isle de Pierre........ 96
—, a Nez Percé priest 75
—, encounter of, with Smohalla........... 80
—, Smohalla's belief concerning.......... 83
MOTSAI', a Comanche band............... 407
MOUND, use of, with sweat-lodge......... 184, 343
MOUNT GRANT, Paiute name of........... 412
MURPHY, Jos., killed at Wounded Knee.. 234
MUSICAL INSTRUMENTS, lack of, in ghost
    dance 283
MŬTSIÄNÄTÄ'NIUW', Cheyenne name of
    Kiowa Apache 443
MYTH, regeneration of the Hopi.......... 173
—, see COSMOLOGY.

NÄ'BAI-DÄ'CHO, a Caddo division.......... 454
NABEDACHE, a Caddo division............ 454
NACOGDOCHES, a Caddo division......... 454
NÄDÄ'KO, a Caddo division............... 454
—, early mention of the........... 456
—, see ANADARKO.

Page

NADI'ISHA-DE'NA, native name of Kiowa
    Apache 443
NADOUESSI, a synonym of Sioux.......... 412
NADOWESI, a synonym of Sioux.......... 419
NADOWESIU, a synonym of Sioux......... 419
NA-ISHA, native name of Kiowa Apache.. 443
NAKAI-DOKLI'NI, account of 66
NÄ'KA'NA'WAN, a Caddo division 454
NAKASH, ghost song composed by........ 347
—, visit of, to Wovoka........... 165, 169, 179, 256
NA'KASINĚ'NA, name of northern Arapaho. 316
NAKAY-DOKLUNNI, see NAKAI-DOKLI'NI.
NÄ'KOHODO'TSI, a Caddo division......... 454
NAKOTA, a synonym of Sioux............ 419
NA'LANI, Navaho name of the Comanche. 405
NÄMI PIÄP, a Columbia indian god....... 92
NANDACAO, identified with Nadako....... 456
NÄNIGŮKWA, Paiute name of ghost dance. 153
NÄNISANA KA-AU'-SHAN, Caddo name of
    ghost dance........................... 151
NANITA, Kichai name of the Comanche.. 405
NANONÏ'KS-KARE'NÏKI, Kichai name of the
    Cheyenne 385
NARCELLE, NARCISSE, in Sioux outbreak. 224
NÄSHI'TOSH, a Caddo division............ 454
NA'SHONI, a Caddo synonym............. 454
NA'SHONĬT, a Caddo synonym............ 454
NASHTOWI, Wichita delegate to Wovoka. 265
NASSONITE, a Caddo synonym............ 454
NATÄA, Wichita name of the Comanche. 405
NATCHEZ, a Paiute chief................. 410
NATCHITOCHES, a Caddo division........ 454
NATENEHINA, Arapaho name of the Sioux. 419
NATNI, Arapaho name of the Sioux...... 419
NATNIHINA, Arapaho name of the Sioux.. 419
NATURAL PHENOMENA, indian idea con-
    cerning 83
—, sacred regard for..................... 281
—, symbolism of 267
NAVAHO, absence of ghost dance among. 172, 288
— and Arapaho warfare.................. 316
—, ghost-dance doctrine among........... 147
—, hypnotism in ceremony of............. 173
— name of the Comanche................ 405
— name of the Paiute 410
—, pollen used in ceremonies of.......... 67
—, significance of songs of............... 371
—, statistics concerning the.............. 171
NAWAT, native name of Left-hand....... 319
NAWATHI'NĚHA, name of southern Arap-
    aho 317
NA'WUNĚNA, name of southern Arapaho. 317
NEBRASKA troops in Sioux outbreak..... 238
NECKLACES of human fingers............ 386
NESPELIM and Sanpoil affinity 95
— and Spokan affinity.................... 95
—, sketch of the 95
NETTLES, R. H., killed at Wounded Knee. 234
NEVADA, geographic character of........ 127
NEWELL, C. H., killed at Wounded Knee. 234
NEZ PERCÉ, a Caddo synonym........... 454
—, a Sahaptin synonym.................. 106
—, affinity of the Pälus with............ 97
—, affinity of Wa'napûm with........... 97
— and Cayuse intermarriage............. 106

Page

Nez Percé, cause of war with............ 74
— habitat and population.............. 167
—, visit of, to Wovoka................. 167
—, see Sahaptin.
Niaha'no', song composed by............ 461
Niaketsikûtk, Kichai name of the Sioux. 419
Niärharïs-kûrikiwäs-hûski, Wichita
name of the Arapaho................ 316
Nia'thuä, Arapaho name for the whites. 324, 340
Ni'chiné'na, a Kiowa synonym........... 440
Niculuita, a Tlaqluit synonym......... 102
Niererikwats-kûniki, Wichita name of
the Cheyenne...................... 385
Ni'rïs-härï's-kï'riki, a Caddo synonym.. 454
Nïshk'ûntŭ, see Moon Head.
Nisqually in treaty of 1854............. 113
— membership in Shaker church........ 121
—, Shaker religion among the.......... 109
Nockay Delklinne, see Nakai-dokli'ni.
No Flesh, flight of, to Bad lands........ 246
No'koni, a Comanche band.............. 406
Norcok, acknowledgments to.......... 17
Nose-piercing by the Caddo............ 454
No Water's camp, game-wheel at....... 437
—, ghost dance at 185, 208, 277
N'pochle, a Sanpoil synonym........... 95
Nuhiné'na, an Arapaho warrior order ... 349
Nüma, a synonym of Comanche.......... 405
—, a synonym of Paiute................ 410
Number, sacred, in ghost dance........ 144, 281, 362
—, sacred, in Shaker religion.......... 113
Nümi'naä', a Paiute god 413
Nûnaha'wŭ, an Arapaho warrior order.. 351
Nyu'taa, song composed by 459

Oakinacken, an Okanagan division...... 96
—, a synonym of Okanagan............. 96
Oceti Sakowin, a synonym of Sioux..... 419
Ochechotes, a synonym of Uchi'chol.... 100, 102
Offering of sacred objects............. 278
— to the eagle 462
Offley, Colonel, troops under, in Sioux
outbreak.......................... 212
Ogalala, a Teton division 420
— in Sioux outbreak.................. 244, 247
— knowledge of the messiah.......... 181
Ohenoñpa, a Teton division............ 421
Ŏ'ivimä'na, a Cheyenne division 387
Ojibwa, absence of ghost dance among .. 178
—, early warfare by the.............. 421
—, effect of Shawano religion on the..... 42
— names of the Arapaho............. 315
— name of the Gros Ventres.......... 317
—, Potawatomi prophet among the...... 68
—, Tenskwatawa among the........... 39
Okanagan, sketch of the.............. 96
Okinakane, an Okanagan synonym...... 96
Okiwahkine, an Okanagan synonym..... 96
Omaha, absence of ghost dance among... 178
—, Caddo name of the................ 455
—, study of the 16
—, visit to the...................... 129
Omaha dance, crow dance a modification
of.............................. 263
One Feather in the Few-Tails affair.... 251, 252

Ootlashoot, a Kutenai band........... 93
Orientation of Arapaho tipi 318
— of camping circle 388
—, see Cardinal Points.
Osage, ghost dance among the.......... 264
— name of the Comanche.............. 405
— name of the Sioux................. 419
Otä's-itä'niuw', a Caddo synonym 454
Otermin, Antonio, flight of, to El Paso... 22
Oto, ghost dance among the........... 264
— name of the Comanche.............. 405
— name of the Sioux................. 419
—, condition of ghost dance among 289
O'tu'gŭnŭ, a Cheyenne division 388
Oualla-Oualla. a Wallawalla synonym . 106
Ouichram, a Tlaqluit synonym.......... 102
Owen, Col., at Battle of Prophet's town.. 50

Padouca, application of the name 405, 406
Pägänävo, Shoshoni and Comanche name
of the Cheyenne 385
Pä'gatsŭ, a Comanche band........... 407
Pa-guadal, native name of Red Buffalo. 445
Paha'na, Hopi name of the whites 340
Pah Utes, a synonym of Paiute......... 410
Pahvant confounded with the Paiute... 410
Pa-iñgya, a Kiowa prophet............ 445
—, reputed powers of................. 268, 269
Paint, how regarded by Cheyenne and
Arapaho......................... 141
—, mortuary use of.................. 241
— obtained from Wovoka............. 137, 140
— on ghost shirts................... 152
— on ghost dance................... 160
— presented by Wovoka............ 159, 262, 263
— used by the Arapaho.............. 333
— used by the Cheyenne............. 391
— used in ghost dance............... 160
                              176, 183, 185, 281, 282, 287, 460
Paiute, Cohonino knowledge of ghost
dance from....................... 174
—, gambling song of the 371
—, ghost dance among the............ 16
                              146, 164, 168, 288, 289
—, ghost dance introduced among Wala-
pai by.... 176
—, glossary of the.................. 418
— method of conversation 132
— mode of living................... 132
— name of ghost dance.............. 153
— name for the whites.............. 340
—, Navaho taught about messiah by...... 173
—, notion concerning eclipse.......... 135
— on Klamath reserve............... 167
— on Warmspring reserve............ 167
—, population of the 412
—, Porcupine among the 156
—, reception of, into Mormon church..... 152
—, sketch of the.................... 410
—, songs of the.................... 410
—, synonymy of the................. 414
—, Tavibo among the................ 410
—, see Wovoka.
Pai-yuchimŭ, Hopi name of the Paiute.. 410
Pai-yutsï, Navaho name of the Paiute... 410
Pa'kamalli, a Pit river band........... 414
Pa'kiut, Smohalla services at 89

	Page
Pa″kiut-′lĕ′ma, a Yä′kĭma synonym.....	99
Palmer, Agent, report of, on Sioux excitement.................................	210
Palouse, a Pä′lus synonym..............	97, 99
Palŭ, Washo name of the Paiute........	411
Pälus and Wa′napŭm affinity...........	97
—, incorporation of Chämnä′pŭm with...	101
—, sketch of the..........................	97
Pambzimina, Shoshoni name of the Sioux.	419
Pani Piqués, French name of the Wichita	457
Pansy Society and the Sioux outbreak..	255
Papago, absence of ghost dance among ..	167
Papitsinima, Comanche name of Sioux..	419
Papshpŭn-′lĕma, a synonym of Pend d' Oreille.................................	93
Parker, Quanah, a Comanche chief.....	409
—, opposition of, to ghost dance.........	264
Parker, Mrs Z. A., on the Sioux ghost dance..................................	278
Parkman, Francis, cited on Pontiac.....	27, 31
—, Pontiac manuscript referred to by....	25
Parr, Harriet, cited on Joan of Arc.....	297
Parton, Eliza, acknowledgments to.....	17
Parton, George, acknowledgments to...	17
Pa′tadal, influence of, in ghost dance ...	276
—, see Poor Buffalo.	
Pa′thĕskĕ, account of....................	62
Patrick, —, quoted on Potawatomi prophets' dance..............................	68
Patterson and Brown's mission........	308
Paviotso, application of term...........	410
Pawnee and Arapaho warfare...........	316
—, ghost dance among the................	264, 289
—, influence of ghost dance over the.....	288
— name of the Arapaho..................	316
— name of the Kiowa Apache...........	443
— name of the Sioux....................	419
Peace pipe of the Sioux.................	424
Pelloatpallah, a Pä′lus synonym......	97, 107
Peloose, a Pä′lus synonym..............	97
Pemmican, derivation of................	429
—, ghost song reference to...............	353
—, preparation of.......................	429
Pe′nä′nde, a Comanche band............	407
Pe′nätĕka, a Comanche band............	407
—, ghost dance among the................	263
—, migration of the....................	406
Pend d′Oreille, account of the.........	93
—, land treaty with the..................	93
—, present habitat of the................	167
Penney, Capt. C. G., appointed indian agent..................................	249
Perfume, grass used as.................	185
Personal names, Shawano, note on......	45
Peruvian belief in a messiah............	22
Phister, N. P., on ghost-dance doctrine..	146
—, on Wovoka's father...................	127
Photographs of the ghost dance........	16
Pictography of Kiowa calendar.268, 269, 271, 272	
ᴸ of the ghost dance....................	422
— on gaming wheel.....................	356
— on ghost-dance costume..............	344
— on ghost shirts.......................	152, 278
—, thunderbird in.......................	331
Pierce, F. E., appointed indian agent....	249
	Page
Pima, absence of ghost dance among.....	167
Pine Bird, flight of, to Bad lands........	246
Pine Ridge agency, arrival of troops at..	212
— attacked by Brulés.................	235, 237
—, changes in boundaries of............	192
—, delegates from, to Wovoka...........	182
—, delegation from, to Washington.......	253
—, destruction of property at...........	254
—, dissatisfaction of indians at..........	206
—, flight of indians of, to Bad lands......	212
—, ghost dance at......................	208
—, ghost-dance council held at..........	182
—, ghost-dance excitement at............	210
—, indians of, meet commissioners.......	203
—, missions on, abandoned...............	236
—, reduction of rations at..............	194, 207
—, report of Sioux delegates at..........	182
—, restlessness of indians at..............	207
—, return of Sioux hostiles to...........	223
—, visit of Äpiatañ to..................	273
Pinon nuts, how regarded by Cheyenne and Arapaho..........................	141
Pĭnûtgû′, a Cheyenne division..........	388
Pipe ceremony in ghost dance...........	277
— in Caddo mythology..................	455
—, peace, broken by Sitting Bull.........	216
—, peace, of the Cherokee...............	425
—, sacred, in charge of northern Arapaho.	317
—, sacred, of the Arapaho............	318, 425
—, sacred, of the Sioux...............	185, 424
—, sacred, referred to in ghost song.....	434
—, sacred regard for..................	321, 322, 323
—, symbolism of, in ghost dance..........	151
—, treaty, illustrated...................	50
—, use of, in ghost dance...............	426
Pishquitpah, sketch of the.............	101
Piskᵂaus and Isle de Pierre affinity.....	97
—, sketch of the........................	98
Pisquouse, a Pĭskwaus synonym........	99-101
Pisscow, an Okanagan division..........	96
Pit River indians, account of the.......	414
—, ghost dance among..................	147, 313
Piute, a synonym of Paiute..............	410
Pleasant men, an Arapaho division.....	319
Plenty Horses, Lieut. Casey killed by..	250
Plumb, Agent, account of ghost dance by.	168
P′nä, a village on Columbia river........	78, 79
—, meaning of..........................	97
—, Smohalla ceremonial at..............	89
—, see Priest Rapids.	
Po′hoi, a Comanche band................	407
Pointed Hearts, a Cœur d′Alène synonym.................................	95
Poland, Col., troops under, at Rosebud.	212
Polä̃yup, a Kiowa warrior order........	351
Pole, sacrifice, in Sioux ceremony........	185
—, see Tree.	
Police, Sioux, arrrest of Sitting Bull by.	218-220
—, Sioux, bravery of.....................	222
—, Sioux, moderation of.................	231
Pollen, use of, in Apache ceremony.....	67
Pollock, Oscar, killed at Wounded Knee.	233, 234
Poloi, Henry, acknowledgments to......	17
Polonches, a Pä′lus synonym............	97
Ponca, ghost dance among the..........	178, 264

Page

PONDERAS, see PEND D'OREILLE.
PONTIAC, character of 30
— manuscript, reference to 25
POOR BUFFALO, a ghost-dance leader..... 270
—, Kiowa messiah delegation under 269
—, portrait of 270
PORCUPINE, account of messiah by 155
—, effect of messiah visit of.............. 180
—, ghost song composed by 390
—, statement of, concerning messiah..... 181
—, visit of, to Wovoka....... 65, 146, 165, 179, 256
POTAWATOMI, absence of ghost dance
among 178
—, disciples of Känakûk.................. 58-59
—, ghost dance among the 264
— settlement at Tippecanoe.............. 46
POTAWATOMI PROPHET, account of....... 67
POTRERO, prophecy of indians of 166
POWDER, sacred. on dance ground........ 280
—, sacred, use of, in battle................ 152
—, see POLLEN.
POWELL, J. W., quoted on the Paiute..... 446
POWERS, JOHN, minister of Shaker church. 120
POWERS, STEPHEN, on Pit River indians.. 414
PRATHER, W. H., Sioux campaign song
by..244, 245
PRATT, ORSON, on the messiah belief 65
PRAYER, LORD'S, Arapaho equivalent of.. 328, 329
PRAYER STICK, used by Känakûk 59
PRESBYTERIANS, attitude of, toward Shak-
er religion............................... 122
PRESCOTT, W. H., on effect of civilization
in Peru.................................. 21
—, on golden age of Anahuac.............. 20
PRESTON, LIEUT. GUY, at battle of Wound-
ed Knee 235
PRETTY BACK on the Sioux outbreak 201
PRIEST RAPIDS, Smohalla performances at. 87
—, see P'NÄ.
PRIMEAU, LOUIS, guide in attack of Sitting
Bull.................................... 218
—, interpreter for Sioux delegation....... 253
PRINCIPAL DOGS, a Kiowa warrior order.. 351
PRITTS, J., cited on Delaware prophet.... 30
PROPHETS, various, compared 292
PROPHET'S TOWN, battle of 50-51
—, see TIPPECANOE.
PSHWA'NÄPÛM, a K''tätäs synonym....... 98
PUEBLOS, absence of ghost dance among. 167, 288
—, revolt of, in 1680...................... 21
—, see HOPI, TAOS.
PUMPKIN SEED in Caddo mythology...... 455
PÛTCI, information concerning Cohonino
from 175
PUYALLUP in treaty of 1854............... 113
PYRAMID LAKE, battle of, in 1860........ 133

QAMÍ'LH, a Pĭskwaus chief............... 98
QAMÍL-'LĔMA, a Pĭskwaus band 98
QA'PNĬSII-'LĔMA, sketch of the........... 101
Q'MA'SHPÄL, a Cœur d'Aléne synonym... 95
QUAKERS, account of the................. 298
QUANAH, former name of father of....... 406
—, see PARKER, QUANAH.
QUAPAW name of the Comanche.......... 410

Page

QUIARLPI, a Colville synonym............ 94
QUIRT of the Dog soldiers................. 349
QUOIT-TSOW, another name for Wovoka.. 64
QUOITZE OW, name applied to Wovoka... 127
QWÔ'LH-HWAI-PÛM, a Klû'kätät synonym. 100

RABBITS in Paiute myth................... 413
—, a Kiowa warrior order................ 351
RAIN invoked by the bull-roarer 337
— songs of Wovoka...................... 134
RANTERS, account of the................. 298
RAPID CITY, appearance of troops at..... 212
RAPID INDIANS, a synonym of Gros Ventres 317
RATIONS, Sioux, table of 201
—, see SIOUX OUTBREAK.
RATTLE of the Dog soldiers 349
— used by Arapaho warriors 350
RAVEN, sacred regard for the............ 344
REAL-DOGS, a Kiowa warrior order....... 351
RED as a sacred color 399
RED BUFFALO, song composed by 445
RED CLOUD, adherent of messiah doctrine. 210
—, an Ogalala chief...................... 207, 420
—, confidence in, by agent............... 194
—, declaration of, for ghost-dance doctrine. 183
—, ghost dance council held by........... 182
—, operations of, in Sioux outbreak 243
—, opposition of, to land cession.......... 207
—, portrait of............................. 208
—, responsibility of, for Sioux outbreak.. 214
—, surrender of band of.................. 244
— thwarted by McGillycuddy 207
RED CLOUD, JACK, conduct of, in Sioux
outbreak................................ 246
RED FEATHER, name of Paul Boynton... 333
RED-LODGES, a Cheyenne division........ 388
RED TAIL in the ghost dance............. 447
RED TOMAHAWK, a Sioux policeman..... 218
—, portrait of............................. 218
—, Sitting Bull shot by................... 219
RED WOLF, delegate to Wovoka.......... 262
REGAN, MICHAEL, killed at Wounded Knee 234
REGENERATION, idea of, ridiculed by south-
ern Ute 168
—, indian belief in 180
— in ghost-dance doctrine 147, 158
— of the earth 9,321, 392, 416, 435
—, power of, attributed to Wovoka....... 183
REID, HENRY, acknowledgments to...... 27
REINECKY, F. T., killed at Wounded Knee 234
REMY, J., on the Kentucky revival...... 305
RESURRECTION, see REGENERATION.
RETURN-FROM-SCOUT, vision of wife of.... 278
RICHARD, LOUIS, interpreter for Sioux
delegation.............................. 253
RIDGE PEOPLE, a Cheyenne division 387
RITUAL of Smohalla religion............. 87
RIVERS, reference to, in ghost song...... 394
ROBERTS, J., Arapaho sacred pipe seen by 323
ROBINSON, LIEUTENANT, scouts under, in
Sioux outbreak......................... 212
ROOSEVELT, THEODORE, quoted on the
Sword-bearer affair..................... 69
ROSE, wild, use of seeds of............... 340
ROSEBUD AGENCY, changes in land bound-
aries of.................................. 192

Page

ROSEBUD AGENCY, delegates from, to Washington 253

—, delegates from, to Wovoka 182

—, flight of indians of, to Bad lands 212

—, ghost dance at 209

—, number of Sioux at 207

—, outbreak of indians of, predicted 162

ROSS, —, on northwestern indian land troubles 72

ROYER, D. F., agent at Pine Ridge 190, 210

—, alarm of 211

—, consultation of, with General Miles ... 210

—, on mortality at Wounded Knee 233

—, removal of Sioux indians recommended by 214

—, statement to, on Sioux outbreak 201

RUGER, GENERAL, on Big Foot's movements 227

—, on causes of Sioux outbreak 196

—, on mortality at Wounded Knee 232

—, ordered to arrest Sword-bearer 69

SACRIFICE, mortuary, by prairie tribes 144

— pole of the Sioux 184

—, scarification as a 260

—, see OFFERING.

SA'DÄLSO'MTE-K'IÑAGO, Kiowa name of Kiowa Apache 443

SAGE, acknowledgments to 17

—, see NAKASH.

SAGEBRUSH, use of, in sweat-bath 184

SAGE-HEN held sacred in ghost dance 344

— in Paiute myth 413

— symbol on ghost shirts 185

SA'GHALEE TYEE, a Columbia indian god . 81, 84

SAHAPTIN, sketch of the 106

—, see NEZ PERCÉ.

SAINT JOHN, dance of, described 297

SAINT PAUL MISSION among the Colville .. 94

SAINT VITUS DANCE, origin of 297

SÄK'OTA, Kiowa name of the Cheyenne ... 385

SALISHAN TRIBES, absence of ghost dance among 167

SALMON dance of northwestern indians .. 90

— fishing among Columbia indians 79

SALTON SEA, indian belief concerning 166

SAMILKANUIGH, an Okanagan division ... 96

SANFORD, COLONEL, troops under, in Sioux outbreak 212

SANITIKA, Pawnee name of the Arapaho . 316

SÄNKO, Kiowa name of the Comanche.... 405

SANPOIL and Nespelim affinity 86

— and Spokan affinity 95

—, sketch of the 95

SANS ARCS, a Teton division 421

SANS PUELLES, a Sanpoil synonym 95

SANTEE, absence of ghost dance among .. 178

—, divisions of the 420

SÄ'PANI, Shoshone name of Gros Ventres. 317

SARAMINUKA, a Winnebago leader 62

SÄRÉTÏKA, Comanche and Shoshoni name of Arapaho 316

SÄRÉTÏKA, Wichita name of the Arapaho. 316

SARLILSO, a Spokan synonym 94

SARSI, absence of ghost dance among 179

Page

SÄSA'BÄ-ITHI, an Arapaho division 319

SA-SIS-E-TAS, a synonym of Cheyenne 385

SAUHTO, Caddo name of the Comanche... 405

SAUK, ghost dance among the 264

SAUK AND FOX, absence of ghost dance among 178

— allied with Tecumtha 47

—, influence of Potawatomi prophets among 68

SAWPAW, a Skïnpä synonym 102

SCABBY, a Cheyenne division 387

SCABBY BULL, name adopted by Sitting Bull 258

SCAFFOLD BURIAL by the Cheyenne 389

SCALPS in Cherokee myth 171

SCARIFICATION as a mortuary custom 144

—, sacrificial 260

SCHAFF, PHILIP, on dance of Saint John.. 297

—, on Fifth-monarchy men 300

—, on the Flagellants 298

SCHARTEL, T., killed at Wounded Knee.. 234

SCHOFIELD, GEN. J. M., telegram to, on Sioux trouble 198

SCHOOLCRAFT, H. R., on Pontiac 27

—, on Pontiac manuscript 25

—, on Tecumtha 53

—, on Winnebago prophecy 23

SCHOOLS, eastern, objection of Sioux to.. 199

—, see CARLISLE, CIVILIZATION, EDUCATION.

SCHROOYELPI, a Colville synonym 94

SCHWENKEY, P., killed at Wounded Knee. 234

SCHWOGELPI, a Colville synonym 94

SCHWOYELPI, a Colville synonym 94

SCOTT, CAPT. H. L., acknowledgments to. 17

—, on ghost-dance doctrine 147

—, on Moon Head 266

—, on Sitting Bull 257

—, on reputed power of Sitting Bull 258, 259

—, ordered to investigate ghost dance 262

SCOUTS, loyalty of, at Wounded Knee.... 243

SEAPCAT, a Si'äpkat synonym 99, 100

SË'HIWĈQ, native name of Weasel Bear.. 321

SÉICHA, the Arapaho sacred pipe 322

SELWYN, W. T., account of Sioux visit to Wovoka by 182

—, interview of, with Kuwapi 160

—, inauguration of Sioux ghost dance.... 181

—, warning by, of Sioux outbreak 183

SEMÄT, a Kiowa division 441

—, Kiowa name of Kiowa Apache 443

SEMINOLE allied with Tecumtha 49

SENIJEXTEE, see LAKE INDIANS.

SË'TÄS-LÈMA, habitat of the 100

SETKOPTI, PAUL, acknowledgments to.... 17

SETT'AIÑTI, tipi symbolism of 273

SEWATPALLA, a Pä'lus synonym 97

SHÄ'AWË, a Yakima chief 89

SHA''CHIDÏ'NI, a former Caddo village 456

SHAFTER, COL., on the Few-Tails affair... 252

—, troops under, in Sioux outbreak 212

SHAGAWAUMIKONG, location of 41

SHAHAÑ, Osage name of the Sioux 419

SHAHAPTIAN TRIBES, absence of ghost dance among 167

SHAIELA, Sioux name of the Cheyenne... 385

Page

SHAIENA, Sioux name of the Cheyenne... 385
SHAKERS, account of the.................. 108, 303
—, character of the........................ 122
—, growth of church of 121
—, organization of church of.............. 120
—, tenets of religion of.................... 121
—, Wickersham on religion of............ 113
SHALLATTOOS, a W'shä'nǎtu synonym.... 98
SHANGREAU, LOUIS, conduct of, in Sioux
   outbreak 246
—, interpreter for Sioux delegation....... 253
SHANWAPAPPOM, a K''tǎtäs synonym 98
SHÄPUPU-'LĔMA, native name of Yowa-
   luch's followers 122
SHARP NOSE, acknowledgments to....... 17
—, Cheyenne delegate to Wovoka........ 138, 262
SHAVE HEAD at arrest of Sitting Bull.... 219
— wounded in Sitting Bull fight 219
— killed in Sitting Bull fight............ 220
SHAWANO, final defeat of the............. 34
—, personal names of the 45
—, tribal range of the 45
SHAWANO PROPHET, see TENSKWATAWA.
SHAW-WAWA KOOTIACAN, see SHÄ'AWĔ.
SHEEP, CHARLEY, acknowledgments to... 17
—, uncle of Wovoka 129
SHELL, significance of the................. 363
SHERIDAN, GEN. P. H., promises of, to Nez
   Percés.................................... 76
SHIÄNAVO, Comanche name of the Chey-
   enne 385
SHIĔDA, Wichita name of the Cheyenne.. 385
SHINNY STICK of the Arapaho............. 326
SHIPAPU, a pueblo indian magic lagoon .. 21
SHIRT, see GHOST SHIRT.
SHĬSHINOWĬTS-ITÄNIUW', Cheyenne name
   of the Comanche........................ 405
SHIWANISH, a Cayuse synonym........... 105
SHI'WANĬSH, a Sahaptin synonym 106
SHMOQÛLA, see SMOHALLA.
SHORT BULL, arrest of band of............ 238
—, continued retreat of.................... 229
—, delegate to Wovoka.................... 182
—, flight of, to Bad lands.............. 212, 214, 246
—, ghost dance led by........... 150, 179, 209, 426
—, indians urged to dance by.............. 211
—, operations of, in Sioux outbreak...... 243
—, Pine Ridge agency attacked by........ 235
—, portrait of.............................. 213
—, surrender of, demanded................ 249
—, surrender of 230
—, visit of, to Wovoka........... 159, 181, 205, 256
SHOSHONI and Arapaho warfare.......... 316
— and Comanche affinity 405
—, ghost dance among... 167, 168, 169, 171, 179, 256
—, early knowledge of the messiah by ... 159
—, influence of ghost dance over the..... 288
—, messiah delegates among the.......... 180, 256
— name for ghost dance 153, 282
— name of the Arapaho 316
— name of the Cheyenne 385
— name of the Comanche................ 405
— name of the Gros Ventres............. 317
— name of the Paiute 410
— name of the Sioux 419

SHOSHONI name for the whites........... 65, 340
—, present habitat of the.................. 168
—, reception of, into Mormon church..... 152
—, study of the............................ 16
—, Tävibo among the...................... 63
—, visit of Äpiatañ to..................... 273
—, visit of, to Wovoka..................... 180, 256
SHYIKS, mention of the.................... 100
SI'XPKAT, a Pĭskwaus band 97
SIBLEY, —, quoted on the Caddo.......... 456
SICHAÑGU, a Teton division 420
SICKELS, MISS E. C., acknowledgments to. 17
—, Sword's account of ghost dance pre-
   sented by 159
SIDES, JOHNSON, visit of Captain Dick to. 146
—, Wovoka confounded with.............. 127
SIGN, TRIBAL, of Kiowa Apache.......... 443
—, of the Arapaho......................... 316
—, of the Caddo 454
—, of the Cheyenne 386
—, of the Comanche....................... 405
—, of the Kiowa........................... 440
—, of the Sioux............................ 419
SIGNAL, WAR, of the Sioux 231
SIGN LANGUAGE as medium of ghost-dance
   communication.......................... 170
SIHASAPA, a Teton division 421
SIMMONS, J. W., a delegate to the Yakima. 473
—, elected elder of Shaker church........ 120
SINAPOILS, a Sanpoil synonym............ 95
SINDI, a Kiowa hero god.................. 426, 442
SI'NDIYU'I, a Kiowa division.............. 441
SINEEGUOMENAH, an Upper Spokan syno-
   nym..................................... 94
SINHUMANISH, a Spokan synonym........ 94
SINIPOUALS, a Sanpoil synonym.......... 95
SINKOMAN, a Spokan synonym 94
SINPAIVELISH, a Sanpoil synonym........ 95
SINPOHELLECHACH, an Okanagan division. 96
—, a Sanpoil synonym..................... 95
SINPOILSCHNE, a Sanpoil synonym....... 95
SINSIUSE, an Isle de Pierre synonym..... 96
SINSPEELISH, a Nespelim synonym....... 95
SINTI, a Kiowa hero god................. 426, 442
SINTOOTOO, a Middle Spokan synonym... 94
SINWHOYELPPETOOK, an Okanagan division..................................... 96
SIOUX, absence of ghost dance among certain bands of........................... 178
—, account of the.......................... 419
— and Cheyenne hostility................. 386
— and Kiowa early warfare............... 442
—, delegation of, to Wovoka............. 205, 256
—, discontinuance of ghost dance among. 289
— drawings of the ghost dance.......... 422
—, failure of crops among................. 188
—, features of ghost dance among....... 164, 184
—, first knowledge of messiah among the. 181
—, ghost dance among the............... 16
                       149, 158, 178, 179, 181, 277
—, glossary of the......................... 437
—, how affected by the ghost dance 289
— habitat and population................. 186
— name of the Arapaho.................. 316
— name of the Cheyenne 385

Page

SIOUX, number of, in ghost dance........ 179
— name of ghost dance................... 153
— outbreak, account of the............... 205
— outbreak, causes of 186, 187, 191
— outbreak, cost of................... 205, 253, 254
— outbreak, effect of, on neighborhood... 254
— outbreak, end of the................... 250
— outbreak, number killed in 233, 253
— outbreak, warning of 183
— outbreak, see WOUNDED KNEE.
—, population of the 206
—, reduction of rations among 189
— reservation, division of 202
—, reservation experience of............. 195
—, songs of the 423
—, symbolic representation of............ 151
—, synonymy of the....................... 419
—, treatment of, by government.......... 189
— treaty of 1868 .... 186, 201
— treaty of 1876 187
— treaty of 1877 200
—, tree used by, in ghost dance 341
—, tribal sign of the..................... 419
—, visit to the........................... 129
SISITONWAÑ, a Sioux division............. 420
SISSETON, a Sioux division............... 420
SITANKA, see BIG FOOT.
SITTING BULL (Arapaho), acknowledg-
    ments to 17
—, belief of, regarding ghost dance....... 148
—, decline of interest of, in ghost dance.. 263
—, ghost song composed by............... 334
—, ghost song introduced by.............. 327
—, hypnotism performed by.......... 261, 285, 334
—, instruction in ghost-dance doctrine by. 257
—, portrait of............................ 258
—, prediction of 271
—, reputed power of...................... 258, 259
—, sacred feather conferred by........... 281
—, sketch of............................. 257
—, statement of, at Anadarko council 275
—, visit of, to Wovoka................. 179, 256, 263
SITTING BULL (Sioux), account of trouble
    with 205
—, arrest of 219
—, attempt to arrest...................... 216
—, death of............................. 219, 222
—, evil influence of...................... 206
—, flight of warriors of.................. 220
—, ghost dance at camp of................ 215
—, ghost dance continued by 209
—, ghost dance invited by................ 209
—, interview of McLaughlin with........ 211
—, map of fight at camp of 221
—, mischief plotted by................... 216
—, number killed in fight with 253
—, number of followers of................ 226
—, opposition of, to land cession.......... 207
—, order for arrest of.................... 217
—, peace pipe broken by 216
—, plan of, to evade arrest............... 217
—, portrait of........................... 220
—, removal of, advised 210, 216
—, responsibility of, for Sioux outbreak.. 194, 216
—, sketch of............................ 222

Page

SITTING BULL (Sioux), surrender of war-
    riors of............................. 222, 224, 233
SIUR POILS, a synonym of Sanpoil........ 95
SKADDAL, a synonym of Ska'utäl......... 98
SKALZI, a synonym of Kutenai 93
SKAMOYNUMACH, an Okanagan division .. 98
SKA'UTÁL, a Pïskwaus band.............. 96
SKEECHAWAY, a Cœur d'Alène synonym. 95
SKEETSOMISH, a Cœur d'Alène synonym. 95
SKIEN, a synonym of Skïnpä 102
SKIN, a synonym of Skïnpä.............. 102
SKÏNPÄ, sketch of the 102
SKINPAH, a synonym of Skïnpä 100, 102
SKITSÄMČQ, a synonym of Cœur d'Alène. 95
SKITSWISH, a synonym of Cœur d'Alène.. 95
SKOKOMISH, Shaker religion among the .. 109
SKULL, buffalo, figurative reference to.... 364
—, buffalo, use of, in ceremonials 342
SKUNKBERRY PEOPLE, a Kiowa warrior
    order................................. 351
SKU'TANI, Sioux name of Gros Ventres... 317
SKWA'NAÑX, a Pïskwaus band............ 98
SKYUSE, a Cayuse synonym 305
SLOCUM, JOHN, account of............. 108, 114
—, conversion of.......................... 113
—, elected elder of Shaker church........ 120
—, how regarded by the Shakers.......... 112
SMALLPOX, appearance of, in Columbia
    region................................ 305
SMAWHOLA, a Smohalla synonym......... 79
SMITH, JOHN, elected elder of Shaker
    church................................ 120
SMOHALLA, account of................... 70
— religion, account of the................ 70
— religion, doctrine of 78
— religion, tribes under influence of 93
SMOHALLER, a Smohalla synonym....... 79
SMOHALLOW, a Smohalla synonym........ 79
SMOHANLEE, a Smohalla synonym........ 79
SMOHOLLIE, a Smohalla synonym........ 79
SMOKEHOLER, a Smohalla synonym....... 79
SMOKELLER, a Smohalla synonym....... 73, 79
SMOKING, ceremonial, by Arapaho 280
SMOKY LODGES, a Cheyenne division...... 387
SMUXALE, a Smohalla synonym 79
SNAKES, handling of, by Crazy dancers... 395
— in Sioux mythology 395
SNOHOLLIE, a Smohalla synonym 79
SNOOHOLLER, a Smohalla synonym 79
SNOW-SNAKE and Arapaho game com-
    pared 369
SNYDER, SIMON, cited on Sword-bearer.... 69
SOKULK, a Wa'napûm synonym........... 97
SOMAHALLIE, a Smohalla synonym....... 79
SONG, closing, of the Arapaho............ 374
—, closing, significance of 280
—, gambling, of the Paiute............... 371
— of the Sioux campaign................. 245
SONGS, ghost-dance, rehearsal of.......... 280
— in Smohalla ceremony................. 92
— of the Arapaho........................ 320
— of the Caddo.......................... 458
— of the Cheyenne....................... 390
— of the Comanche....................... 408
— of the ghost dance................... 282, 315

Page

Songs of the Paiute........................ 414
— of the Shakers........................... 117
— of the Sioux......................... 279, 423
—, Paiute, character of.................... 412
—, rain, of Wovoka....................... 134
Sousa, J. P., acknowledgments to........ 17
Southey, R., cited on French prophets... 301
—, cited on Methodists.................... 303
So'wäniä, a Cheyenne synonym........... 387
Sowwani'u, the Algonquian spirit world. 344
Soyennom, mention of, by Lewis and
  Clark 107
Spaniards, indian regard for the......... 38
—, relations of, with the Caddo.......... 456
Spear men, an Arapaho warrior order... 350
Spirit world, location of................. 344, 345
Spofford, A. R., acknowledgments to.... 17
Spokan, present habitat of the........... 167
—, sketch of the........................... 94
Spokihnish, a Spokan synonym.......... 94
Spokomish, a Spokan synonym........... 94
Spotted Horse, an Arapaho chief........ 318
— on the Sioux outbreak.................. 201
— on the Wounded Knee massacre....... 247
Squannaroos, a Skwa'nänä synonym.... 98
Squaxin in treaty of 1854................. 113
— leaders in Shaker religion............. 108
— membership in Shaker church......... 121
Squirrel, Caddo delegate to Wovoka.... 265
Squ-sacht-un, see Slocum, John.
Staitan, a synonym of Cheyenne........ 385
Stalkoosum, a Piskwaus chief.......... 98
Standing Bear, Kicking Bear's surren-
  der effected by.......................... 230
Standing Bear, Ellis, acknowledgments
  to... 17
Standing Bull, Cheyenne delegate to
  Wovoka 262
Standing Rock agency, delegates from,
  to Washington........................... 253
—, disaffection of indians at............. 196
—, ghost dance at...................... 209, 210
Standing Soldier, scout at Wounded
  Knee..................................... 238
Star, evening, personification of the.... 460
—, morning, indian reverence for........ 373
Star men, an Arapaho warrior order.... 349
Stenhouse, T. B. H., cited on Mormonism 152
Stephen, A. M., acknowledgments to.... 17
—, on Cohonino ghost dance............. 174
—, on Hopi regeneration myth........... 173
—, on Navaho knowledge of ghost dance 172, 173
Steptoe, Col., fight of, with Chief Moses. 96
Stevens, I. I., on Cayuse and Klûkatät
  hostility 100
- , on the Cayuse 106
.., on the meaning of Yakima............ 99
—, on the Piskwaus....................... 98
—, treaty of 1854 by...................... 113
Stietshoi, a Cœur d'Alêne synonym..... 95
Stobshaddat, a Yä'kĭmâ synonym...... 99
Stone, H. B., killed at Wounded Knee... 234
Straight Head, a delegate to Washing-
  ton.. 253
Strings knotted as message bearer...... 21

Page

Sturgis, Colonel, in Nez Percé war..... 76
Sumner, Col. E. V., ordered to arrest Big
  Foot 226
—, troops under, in Sioux outbreak....... 212
Sun, indian myth concerning............. 333
—, Paiute notion concerning the......... 135
—, personification of the................. 459
—, prayer to the........................... 277
—, sacred regard for the.................. 281
—, symbolism of the...................... 267
—, see Eclipse.
Sun dance among the Cheyenne......... 68
— among the Kiowa 442
Sunday selected for the ghost dance..... 186
Sŭta'si'na, a Cheyenne division.......... 387
Sŭta'ya, a Cheyenne division 387
Sutherland, T. A., on Nez Percé war.... 76
Suti, a synonym of Sŭta'ya.............. 387
Sweat-bath, preliminary to ghost dance.. 149
                                     165, 184
—, use of, described....................... 184
Sweat-lodge, buffalo skull in front of.... 342
—, ceremonial, of the Arapaho........... 351
—, ghost-song reference to................ 343
— of the Arapaho.......................... 222
— of the Sioux described.................. 184
—, use of, in ghost dance 160
—, use of the.............................. 343
Swielpee, a Colville synonym............. 94
Sword, George, acknowledgments to.... 17
—, account of ghost dance by.............. 158
—, delegate to Washington................ 253
—, on advent of the messiah.............. 178
—, on Sioux knowledge of the messiah... 181
—, vision of............................... 183
—, on Wounded Knee massacre........... 247
Sword, Jennie, survivor of Wounded
  Knee.................................. 241, 242
Sword-bearer, account of 68
—, effect of affair of, on the Crow......... 178
—, origin of name......................... 68
Symbolism, ceremonial, in Shaker religion. 123
—, color, in ghost dance................... 281
—, color, in Smohalla ritual............... 87, 91
—, earth, turtle the representative of..... 338
—, mnemonic, invented by Smohalla...... 82
— of an amulet............................ 267
— of natural phenomena.................. 267
— of the buffalo.......................... 342
— of cedar............................. 171, 341
— of the cross 373
— of the crow 434
— of the ghost dance 282
— of the planets......................... 185
— on ghost shirts 185
Synonymy of the Caddo................... 454
— of the Cheyenne 385
— of the Comanche 405
— of the Kiowa 440
— of the Paiute 410
— of the Sioux 419

Täbinshi, visit of, to Wovoka............. 169
Tabu of certain articles in ghost dance.. 150
                                 .160, 278, 283

	Page
TABU of Comanche names	406
— of fire in certain ghost dances	164
TAGU'I, Kiowa name of Kiowa Apache	443
TÄGYÄ'KO, Kiowa name of northern Arapaho	317
TAI'-ĂQ, sketch of the	104
TAIGH, a Tai'-ăq synonym	104
TA-IH, a Tai'-ăq synonym	104
TAI-KIE-A-PAIN, a Taitinapam synonym	101
TAIRTLA, a Tai'-ăq synonym	104
TAITINAPAM and Klûkatät affinity	100
—, sketch of the	101
TAI'VO, Shoshonean name for the whites	340
TA'KA-I, Kiowa name of the whites	340
TALL BEAR, hummer used by	337
TALL BULL, Cheyenne delegate to Wovoka	137, 262
TAMA, acknowledgments to	17
TÄMANÄ'RAYÄRA, Shoshoni name of ghost dance	153
TÄNÄ'RÄYÜN, Shoshoni name of ghost dance	153
TANI'BÄNĔN, a Caddo synonym	454
TANI'BÄTHA, a Caddo synonym	454
TÄNÏ'MA, a Comanche band	407
TANNER, JOHN, on Ojibwa name of Gros Ventres	317
—, on the Shawano prophet	35
—, on Tenskwatawa among the Ojibwa	39
T'ÄSPE'KO, a Kiowa warrior order	351
TAOS, ghost dance at	167, 288
TAPÄNÄSH, sketch of the	102
TA'PTEAL, application of name	101
TA'SAWĬKS, a Pälus village	97
TA'SHĬN, Comanche name of Kiowa Apache	443
TATANKA IYOTANKE, native name of Sitting Bull	222
TATQUNMA, the proper form of Thatuna	107
TATTOOED PEOPLE, the Wichita so called	457
TATUM, LAWRIE, Wichita interpreter to Wovoka delegation	265
TÄ'VIBO, account of	63, 126
—, Wovoka's account of	133
TAWAKONI, a Wichita subtribe	457
TAWE'HASH, a synonym of Wichita	457
TAYLOR, LIEUT., at surrender of Big Foot	229
TAYLOR, MAJ., at battle of Prophet's town	50
TCHILOUIT, a Tlaqluit synonym	102
TECUMTHA, account of	43
—, address of, to Harrison	83
—, defeat of	51
—, end of	53
—, etymology of	43
— joins the British army	52
—, later career of	52
TELEGRAMS on Sioux trouble	197, 198
TE'NÄHWĬT, a Comanche band	407
TĔNA'WA, a Comanche band	407
TE'ÑBIYU'I, a Kiowa warrior order	351
TENINO, present habitat of	167
—, sketch of the	104
TENSKWATAWA, account of	32
—, etymology of	36
—, extent of influence of	289

	Page
TEPDA, a Kiowa synonym	449
TERRY, GEN., pursuit of Sitting Bull by	222
TETAU, a synonym of Comanche	405
TÉTE PELÉE, a synonym of Comanche	405
TETON, a Sioux division	420
—, account of the	420
—, number of, in ghost dance	179
TEXAS BEN, offer of services by	255
THA'KAHINĔ'NA, Arapaho name of Kiowa Apache	443
THATUNA, origin of name	107
THIGŪ'NAWAT, Arapaho name of ghost dance	153
THOMPSON, A. H., account of Tävibo by	65
—, acknowledgments to	17
—, on the Paiute prophet	64
THREE STARS, CLARENCE, interpreter for Sioux delegation	253
THUNDER, indian notion concerning	330
—, personification of the	459, 461
THUNDER BAY, origin of name	330
THUNDERBERRIES used as food	358
THUNDERBIRD, account of the	330
—, figure of the	331
—, reference to, in Arapaho song	340
—, song of the	338
THUNDER'S NEST, origin of name	330
TIANÄ'NI, death of	89
—, Smohalla service conducted by	89
TILFORD, COLONEL, troops under, in Sioux outbreak	212
TILHULHWIT, a Tlaqluit synonym	102
TI'LQÛNI, sketch of the	102
TIME reckoning among indians	136
TIPI, a Sioux word	421
— of the Arapaho	319
TIPPECANOE, account of	43
—, proper form of	46
TITOÑWAÑ, a Sioux division	420
—, see TETON	
TIVIS, WILLIAM, acknowledgments to	17
TLAQLUIT, sketch of the	102
TLINKIT, sacred regard of, for the crow	344
TOBACCO offering by the Sioux	184
TOBIN, JAMES, appointed minister of Shaker church	120
TO'NGYÄ-GU'ADAL, Kiowa name of Red Tail	447
TOÑKOÑ'KO, a Kiowa warrior order	351
TOOHULHULSOTE, a Dreamer priest	75
TOPINISH, a Qa'pnish-'lĕma synonym	101
— and Klûkatät affinity	100
TOPS used by Arapaho boys	368
TOTEM, significance of	58
TOWAHNAHIOOK, application of name	104
TOWAKONI JIM, acknowledgments to	17
TRANCES in ancient times	291
— in Shaker religion	108, 113, 114
— of the Shawano prophet	35
— of Smohalla	81
— of Wovoka	133
—, see DREAM, HYPNOTISM, VISION.	
TRANSFORMATION in ghost-dance doctrine	430
TREATY between Iroquois and Cherokee	32
—, Caddo, of 1835	456
—, Comanche, of 1835	406

Page

TREATY, effect of, on the Sioux........... 191
—, failure of government to fulfill....... 72-74
    189, 192, 193, 196, 197, 198, 202
—, Kiowa, of 1837......................... 443
— of Edwardsville........................ 54
— of Greenville.......................... 33
— of Medicine Lodge in 1867............. 319, 406
—, Sioux, of 1868....................... 186, 201
—, Sioux, of 1876....................... 187
—, Sioux, of 1877....................... 200
—, Yakima, of 1855...................... 99
TREATY PIPE illustrated.................. 50
TREE, sacred, in ghost-dance symbolism. 151
— used in Cohonino ceremony............. 175
— used in ghost dance...... 164, 185, 278, 341, 437
—, see CEDAR, COTTONWOOD, POLE.
TROOPS, appearance of, among the Sioux. 209, 212
—, conduct of, at Wounded Knee......... 238
—, effect of, on ghost dance............ 215
—, effect on Sioux of appearance of...... 214
— formed of indians..................... 253
— killed at Wounded Knee............... 233
—, necessity for, in Sioux outbreak...... 194
—, number of, in Sioux outbreak........ 212, 228
TSABAKOSH, Caddo name of the Sioux.... 419
TSÄÑ'YUI, a Kiowa warrior order......... 351
TSCHADDAM RELIGION, account of......... 113
TSEÑTÄ'NMO, a Kiowa warrior order...... 351
TSILLANE, an Okanagan division......... 96
TUKABACHI, visit of Tecumtha to........ 49
TŬKSPŬ'SH, sketch of the............... 105
TŬKSPŬSH-'LĔMA, a Tŭkspŭsh synonym.. 105
TULE POLLEN used in Navaho ceremony.. 67
TUMWATER, Smohalla performances at... 87
TUPAC AMARU, a Peruvian hero god..... 22
TUPPER, MAJOR, pursuit of Sioux by.... 223
TURKEY FEATHERS on Cheyenne arrows.. 386
TURNING BEAR, flight of, to Bad lands.... 246
TURNING HAWK, delegate to Washington...................................... 253
— on Wounded Knee massacre. 246, 247, 248
TURTLE in Arapaho mythology........... 321
— in primitive mythology................ 338
TURTLE RIVER, identification of......... 391
TUSHEPAW, a synonym of Kutenai...... 93
TU'SHIPA, application of the term........ 93
TWOHIG, DANIEL, killed at Wounded Knee 234
TWO KETTLES, a Teton division.... 421
TWO STRIKE at battle of Wounded Knee.. 235
—, flight of, to Bad lands................ 246
—, ghost dance led by..................... 209
—, operations of, in Sioux outbreak...... 243
—, surrender of.......................... 229, 230
—, Pine Ridge agency attacked by.... 235, 237
TYICH, a Tai'-äq synonym................ 104

UCHI'CHOL, sketch of the................. 102
UGLY-FACE-WOMAN, trance experience of. 324
U'MAÑHAÑ, meaning of word............. 455
UMATILLA opinion of land assignments... 72
—, present habitat of.................... 167
—, sketch of the........................ 106
—, Smohalla performances at............ 87
UMATILLA RESERVE, indians on.......... 167
—, visit of Sioux delegates to............ 182

Page

UPPER CHINOOK, a Kwikwŭlĭt synonym. 103
UTE and Arapaho warfare................. 316
—, attendance of, at ghost dance......... 164
—, ghost dance among the................ 167
—, present habitat of.................... 168
—, reception of, into Mormon church.... 152
—, southern, absence of ghost dance among.................................. 167, 168
UTENSILS of the Paiute................... 132
UTILLA, a Umatilla synonym............. 106

VIROQUA, account of..................... 255
VISION of Biäñk'i........................ 272
—, see DREAM, HYPNOTISM, TRANCE.
VOCABULARY, see GLOSSARY, LANGUAGE.
VOTH, H. R., acknowledgments to....... 17
—, on Cheyenne sacred paint............. 391
—, on figurative use of shell.............. 363

WA-AI'H, a Comanche band............... 407
WACO, a Wichita subtribe................ 457
WAFFORD, JAMES, on Shawano prophet among Cherokees....................... 38
WAHCLELLAH, a Kwikwŭlĭt synonym.... 103
WAHOWPUM, a Hähau'pûm synonym..... 101
WAHPACOOTA. a Sioux division........... 420
WAHPETON, a Sioux division............. 420
WAIÄM, sketch of the.................... 103
WAIÄM-'LĔMA, a Waiäm synonym........ 103
WĂI'LĔTMA, a Cayuse synonym.......... 105, 106
WAILĔ'TPU, a Cayuse synonym.......... 105
WAIP-SHWA, see SMOHALLA.
WALAPAI, ghost dance among the....... 147
    148, 167, 176, 283
WALAWALTZ, a Wallawalla synonym..... 106
WALKER, CHARLES, elected elder of Shaker church.................................. 120
WALKER. HENRY, cure of, by Shakers.... 116
WALKER, JAMES, elected elder of Shaker church.................................. 120
WALLACE, CAPT., killed at Wounded Knee 233
WALLAWALLA and Cayuse intermarriage. 106
— opinion of land assignments.......... 72
—, present habitat of.................... 167
—, sketch of the........................ 106
WALU'LA-PŬM, a Wallawalla band....... 106
WAMPUM BELT, significance of........... 24, 47
WANA'GHI WA'CHIPI, Sioux name of ghost dance.................................. 153
WA'NAPŬM and Pä'lus affinity........... 97
—, incorporation of Chämnä'pûm with... 101
—, note on the.......................... 78
—, sketch of the........................ 97
WAND, use of, in Sioux ceremony....... 185
WANWAUAI, application of name......... 104
WAPAKONETA, an indian settlement in Ohio................................... 34
WA'PAMĔTÄNT, a Sahaptin synonym..... 106
WAPTAI'LMĬM, a Yä'kĭmä synonym...... 99
WAQPEKUTE, a Sioux division........... 420
WAQPETOÑWAÑ, a Sioux division........ 420
WAQUI'SI, native name of Ugly-face-woman................................... 324
WA'QUITHI, an Arapaho division......... 319
WAR forbidden by ghost-dance doctrine.. 145, 158

Page

WAR bonnets, eagle feathers used in..... 434
— Department, acknowledgments to 17
— signal of the Sioux 231
WARDEN, CLEVER, acknowledgments to.. 17
WARMSPRING INDIANS, present habitat of. 167
—, see TENINO.
WARMSPRING RESERVE, indians on....... 167
WARNER, C. C., letter of, on Wovoka.... 129
WARNER, MAJOR, Sioux commissioner... 201
WARREN, W. W., on the Shawano prophet. 35
—, on Shawano religion among Ojibwa... 39
WARRIOR ORDER of the Kiowa........... 351
—, society of the Arapaho 348
WARRIORS, Cheyenne renowned as....... 389
—, Sioux, number of...................... 214
WASCO, present habitat of................ 167
—, sketch of the 103
WASCOPUM, a Wasko synonym........... 103
WASHEE, a delegate to Wovoka 256, 263
WASHINGTON, see COLUMBIA REGION.
WASHO, account of the.................... 413
—, ghost dance among the 147, 166
—, name of the Paiute 410
WĀ'SIU, a Washo synonym............... 413
WATĂN-GAA, see BLACK COYOTE.
WATER, sacred regard for................. 281
WATER-POURING MEN, an Arapaho priestly
order.................................... 351
WATLALA, a Kwikwûlĭt synonym 103
WATONGA, derivation of name........... 259
WAUGH-ZEE-WAUGH-BER among the Paiute 65
—, name applied to Tä'vibo.............. 127
WAYYAMPA, a Waiäm synonym.......... 103
WEAPONS of the Arapaho................. 349, 350
—— prohibited in ghost dance 150
WEASEL BEAR, portrait of................ 206
—, sacred pipe shown by................. 323
—, the sacred pipe keeper................ 317, 321
WELLS, PHILIP, interpreter at Wounded
Knee.................................... 243
—, acknowledgments to 17
WELLS, CAPTAIN, in Sioux outbreak..... 212, 223
WELLS, GEN., at battle of Prophet's town. 50
WELSH, HERBERT, on indian regard for
Crook 188
—, on Wounded Knee massacre.......... 231
WENATSHAPAM, a Pĭskwaus synonym... 100
WESLEY, CHARLES, on French prophets.. 301
—, on Methodists........................ 302
—, on the Jumpers 301
WEVOKAR, name applied to Wovoka 127
WEYEHHOO, a Klû'kätät synonym....... 100
WHEATON, COL., troops under, at Pine
Ridge 212
WHEEL-GAME of plains tribes........... 356, 357
WHEELPOO, a Colville synonym.......... 94
WHIRLWIND in Paiute ghost song...... 416, 417
—, indian reverence for 396
—, song of the 269
WHISTLE, eagle-bone, used by medicine-
man.................................... 230
—, use of, in the sun dance.............. 354
WHITE, FRANK, a Pawnee ghost-dance
leader 264
WHITE BEAR, see SETT'AIÑTI.

WHITE BIRD, delegate to Washington.... 253
— ignored in Sioux difficulty........... 194
WHITE BUFFALO, ghost shirt introduced
by...................................... 153
WHITE CLAY CREEK, destruction of prop-
erty on................................. 243
—, ghost dance on 208, 278
—, hostile Sioux on 235, 244
—, Sioux council on 183
WHITE HORSE, flight of, to Bad lands.... 246
WHITE SHIELD, Cheyenne delegate to Wo-
voka 257
WHITE-TAIL DEER PEOPLE, a synonym of
Kutenai................................ 93
WHITMAN, DR, accused of witchcraft..... 86
—, killed by indians..................... 105
WHITSIDE, MAJOR, Big Foot's band intercepted by 229
—, on mortality at Wounded Knee....... 232
WHULWHYPUM, a Klû'kätät synonym.... 100
WI'ALĔT-PŮM, a Cayuse synonym......... 106
WICHITA, account of the................. 457
—, delegation of, to Wovoka............. 263, 265
—, ghost dance among the. 15, 148, 257, 260, 264, 289
— name of the Arapaho.................. 316
— name of the Caddo.................... 454
— name of the Cheyenne 385
— name of the Comanche................ 405
— name of the Kiowa Apache 443
—, refusal of, to accept Ä'piatañ's report . 276
WICKERSHAM, JAS., acknowledgments to. 17
—, on Aiyal and Yowaluch............... 473
—, on the Shaker religion................ 112, 113
—, Shaker songs recorded by............. 117
WI'DYU, a Comanche band............... 406
WIKIUP, Paiute, description of......... 411, 412
WILDERNESS WORSHIPERS, account of.... 308
WILHAUER, GEORGE, killed at Wounded
Knee.................................... 233, 238
WILLEWAH, mention of, by Lewis and
Clark 107
WILLIAMS, ROGER, on indian regard for
crows 344
WILLOW CREEK INDIANS, a Lohĭm syn-
onym 105
WILSON, BILLY, Caddo delegate to Wovoka. 265
WILSON, DAVID, employer of Wovoka.... 127
WILSON, JACK, name applied to Wovoka. 127
WILSON, JACKSON, name applied to Wo-
voka 127
WILSON, JOHN, acknowledgments to...... 17
—, see MOON HEAD.
WINANS, —, on the Nespelim and Sanpoil. 95
WINĂ'TSHIPŬM, see PĬSKWAUS.
WINDBREAK of the Arapaho............. 319
WINNEBAGO, absence of ghost dance
among 178
—, Potawatomi prophet among the 68
—, prophecy of the...................... 23
—, prophet among the................... 62
—, study of the 16
—, visit to the.......................... 129
WINNEMUCCA, a Paiute chief 410
WINSON, JACK, name applied to Wovoka . 127
WISHAM, a Tlaqluit synonym 102

	Page
WISHHAM, a Tlaqluit synonym	102
—, a Wushqûm synonym	100
WISHRAM, a Tlaqluit synonym	102
WISSWHAM, a Tlaqluit synonym	102
WITAPÄ'HAT, a Kiowa synonym	440
WI'TAPÄHÄ'TU, a Kiowa synonym	440
WITAPÄ'TU, a Kiowa synonym	440
WĬTAPI'U, a Cheyenne division	387
WITCHCRAFT, indian crusade against	35
WOJAJI BAND, rebellion of, predicted	162
WOLF in Caddo mythology	455
WOLLAWOLLAH, a Wallawalla synonym	106
WOLLAW-WOLLAH, a Wallawalla synonym	106
WOLVES, an Arapaho division	319
WOMEN killed at Wounded Knee	238, 247
WOODEN LANCE, see Ä'PIATAÑ.	
WOODWORTH, MRS, a Heavenly Recruit	309
WOOLWORTH, ARNOLD, interpreter to messiah delegation	262
WOPOKAHTE, name applied to Wovoka	127
WORD-BUILDING by the Arapaho	360
WORLD'S COLUMBIAN EXPOSITION, collections for the	6{ 15, 16
WOUNDED KNEE, account of battle of	205, 231
—, native account of battle of	246
—, burial of dead at	238
—, graves of indians killed at	422
—, list of killed at	234
—, mortality at	232
—, result of battle of	235
—, second encounter of	244
—, survivors of	239-243
—, use of sacred paint at	141
—, see SIOUX OUTBREAK.	
WOVOKA, account of	126, 131, 133, 289
—, address of, to delegation	159
—, Arapaho and Cheyenne delegation to	262
—, Bannock and Shoshoni delegates to	180
—, Caddo delegation to	265
—, claims of, renounced	276
— compared with other prophets	292
—, derivation of	127
—, ghost dance led by	180
—, how regarded	128
—, hypnotism practiced by	180, 263
—, indian letter to	263
—, letter from	138, 142, 143
—, Porcupine's account of	165
—, photographing of	136
—, power of	410
—, reported to be a half-blood	256
—, reputed powers of	135, 183
—, responsibility of ghost shirt disclaimed by	153
—, Shaker contact with	125
—, Sioux knowledge concerning	162
—, speech of, communicated by Porcupine	146
—, vision of	135
—, visit of Ä'piatañ to	273, 275
—, visit of Arapaho to	256
—, visit of Cheyenne delegates to	
—, visit of Nakash to	165, 179
—, visit of Porcupine to	156, 165
—, visit of Shoshoni delegation to	169
—, visit of Sioux delegation to	181, 182

	Page
WOVOKA, visit of Ute delegates to	168
—, visits of various delegations to	159, 256, 263
WRIGHT, AGENT, advises removal of Crow Dog	206
—, ghost dance stopped by	209
—, messiah doctrine discouraged by	205
—. Rosebud census by	193
WRIGHT, COL., fight of, with Chief Moses.	96
WRITING, ideographic, of Biäñk'i	272
W'SHÄ'NÄTU, a Pĭskwaus band	98
WUSHKÛM, Smohalla ceremonial among	89
WŬSHQÛM, a Tlaqluit synonym	102
WŬVOKA, a synonym of Wovoka	127
WYAM, a Waiäm synonym	103
WYANDOT, final defeat of the	124
—, importance of the	47
—, Tecumtha among the	51
WYNIMA, account of	255
YACKAMANS, a Yä'kĭma synonym	99
YAKAMA, a Yä'kĭma synonym	99
— and Pĭskwaus intermarriage	98
— and Wa'napûm affinity	97
—, attempt of Shakers to influence	121
—, sketch of the	99
—, Smohalla ceremonial among the	89
—, war of the, in 1855–56	80
YAKIMA GAP, Smohalla performances at	87
YÄMPAI-NI, Shoshoni name of the Comanche	405
YÄMPAI-RĬKANI, Shoshoni name of the Comanche	405
YÄ'MPÄRI'KA, a Comanche band	406
YANKTON, a Sioux division	420
—, former habitat of the	420
—, interview with, concerning messiah	162
YANKTONAIS, a Sioux division	420
—, former habitat of the	420
—, ghost dance among the	179
YÄPÄ, a Comanche band	406
YÄ'PÄHE, a Kiowa warrior order	351
YÄ'TÄSI, a Caddo division	454
YAUMALOLAM, name applied to Umatilla river	105
YELETPO, a Cayuse synonym	107
YELETPO CHOPUNNISH, a Cayuse synonym	105
YELLOW BIRD, adoption of child of	242
—, responsibility of, for Wounded Knee fight	230
YELLOW BREAST, delegate to Wovoka	182
YELLOW EAGLE, delegation to Wovoka under	170
YELLOW KNIFE, visit of, to Wovoka	159, 181
YOOKOOMANS, a Yä'kĭma synonym	99
YOUNGER, COLE, Texas Ben indorsed by	255
YOUNG-MAN-AFRAID as a peacemaker	249
—, conduct of, in Sioux outbreak	246, 248
—, ghost-dance council held by	182
— ignored in Sioux difficulty	194
—, proper name of	249
—, speech of, to General Miles	252
YOUNG-MAN-AFRAID-OF-INDIANS, see ROYER, D. F.	
YOUNG MOUNTAIN SHEEP, a Kiowa warrior order	351

	Page			Page
YOWALUCH, LOUIS, account of	108, 116	ZEHNDER, BERNARD, killed at Wounded Knee		234
—, conversion of	122	ZEPHIER, DAVID, interpreter for Sioux delegation		253
—, correction concerning	473			
—, enters Presbyterian church	122	ZINGOMENES, a Spokan synonym		94
—, headman of Shaker church	120	ZITKALA–NONI, survivor of Wounded		
—, speech of	115, 116	Knee		240, 241
YOWA'NI, a Caddo division	455	ZITKALAZI, HERBERT, survivor of Wound-		
YUCHI myth of the cedar	341	ed Knee		242
YUMA, absence of ghost dance among	167	ZOÑTOM, MARY, ghost song composed by		447
YUTAN, a synonym of Comanche	405	—, acknowledgments to		17
YU'YUNIPI'TQANA, see SMOHALLA.				

O